Switching *to the* Mac *Lion Edition*
THE MISSING MANUAL

The book that
should have been
in the box®

Switching *to the* Mac *Lion Edition*

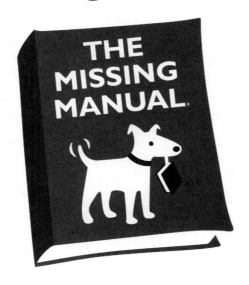

David Pogue

POGUE PRESS™
O'REILLY®

Beijing • Cambridge • Farnham • Köln • Sebastopol • Taipei • Tokyo

Switching to the Mac: The Missing Manual, Lion Edition
by David Pogue

Copyright © 2012 David Pogue. All rights reserved.
Printed in the United States of America.

Published by O'Reilly Media, Inc.,
1005 Gravenstein Highway North, Sebastopol, CA 95472.

O'Reilly Media books may be purchased for educational, business, or sales
promotional use. Online editions are also available for most titles: *safari@oreilly.
com.* For more information, contact our corporate/institutional sales department:
800-998-9938 or *corporate@oreilly.com.*

March 2012:   First Edition.

ISBN: 978-1449-39853-8   [03/12]

Table of Contents

Part Two: Making the Move

Part Three: Making Connections

Part Four: Putting Down Roots

Part Five: Appendixes

The Missing Credits

About the Author

 David Pogue (author) is the weekly tech columnist for *The New York Times*, an Emmy-winning correspondent for *CBS News Sunday Morning*, the host of "NOVA Science Now" on PBS, and the creator of the Missing Manual series. He's the author or coauthor of 60 books, including 25 in this series, six in the "For Dummies" line (including *Macs, Magic, Opera,* and *Classical Music*), two novels, and *The World According to Twitter*. In his other life, David is a former Broadway show conductor, a piano player, and a magician. He lives in Connecticut with his three awesome children.

Links to his columns and weekly videos await at *www.davidpogue.com*. He welcomes feedback about his books by email at *david@pogueman.com*.

About the Creative Team

Julie Van Keuren (copy editor) is a freelance editor, writer, and desktop publisher who runs her "little media empire" from her home in Billings, Montana. In her spare time she enjoys swimming, biking, running, and (hey, why not?) triathlons. She and her husband, M.H., have two sons, Dexter and Michael. Email: *little_media@yahoo.com*.

Kirill Voronin (technical editor) is the head of an IT consulting company, aptly called Shortcut, based in Moscow, Russia. He has worked with Macs since the '90s, and he's an Apple Certified System Administrator and Apple Certified Trainer for IT courses. He lives with his wife, Maria, and son, Nil. In his spare time, he enjoys backpacking. Email: *kirill.voronin@shortcut.ru*.

Phil Simpson (design and layout) runs his graphic design business from Southbury, Connecticut. His work includes corporate branding, publication design, communications support, and advertising. In his free time he is a homebrewer, ice cream maker, wannabe woodworker, and is on a few tasting panels. He lives with his wife and three great felines. Email: *phil.simpson@pmsgraphics.com*.

Acknowledgments

Over the years, over the various editions of this book, many friends and colleagues have contributed enthusiasm, expertise, and even prose to this book's editions. They include Zachary Brass, Dan Pourhadi, Rich Koster, J.D. Biersdorfer, Teresa Noelle Roberts, and Lesa Snider.

In addition to the dream team members identified above, I owe debts of thanks to O'Reilly's Missing Manuals editor-in-chief, Brian Sawyer; Apple's Monica Sarker for going beyond the call of duty to chase down tweaky tech answers; Kellee Katagi, my sharp-eyed proofreader; the NOVA crew, who gracefully accommodated my nutty book schedule during our shoots; and my spectacular screenshotter/index-marathoner, the lovely Emma Hollister.

I also wish I could send out an "I Made the Book Better!" T-shirt to every reader who ever took the time to write with corrections, suggestions, tips, and tricks. And thanks, as always, to David Rogelberg for believing in the idea.

Above all, this book owes its existence to the patience and affection of Kelly, Tia, and Jeffrey. They make these books—and everything else—possible.

—David Pogue

The Missing Manual Series

Missing Manuals are witty, superbly written guides to computer products that don't come with printed manuals (which is just about all of them). Each book features a handcrafted index; cross-references to specific page numbers (not just "see Chapter 14"); and an ironclad promise never to put an apostrophe in the possessive pronoun *its*.

Here's a list of current and upcoming titles:

For Macintosh

- *Mac OS X Lion: The Missing Manual* by David Pogue
- *Mac OS X Mountain Lion: The Missing Manual* by David Pogue
- *Photoshop Elements for Mac: The Missing Manual* by Barbara Brundage
- *iMovie '11 & iDVD: The Missing Manual* by David Pogue and Aaron Miller
- *iPhoto '11: The Missing Manual* by David Pogue and Lesa Snider
- *iWork '09: The Missing Manual* by Josh Clark
- *AppleScript: The Missing Manual* by Adam Goldstein
- *Office 2011 for Macintosh: The Missing Manual* by Chris Grover
- *FileMaker Pro 10: The Missing Manual* by Geoff Coffey and Susan Prosser

For Windows

- *Windows 7: The Missing Manual* by David Pogue
- *Windows Vista: The Missing Manual* by David Pogue
- *FrontPage 2003: The Missing Manual* by Jessica Mantaro
- *Office 2010: The Missing Manual* by Chris Grover, Matthew MacDonald, and E. A. Vander Veer
- *Word 2010: The Missing Manual* by Chris Grover
- *Excel 2010: The Missing Manual* by Matthew MacDonald
- *PowerPoint 2010: The Missing Manual* by Emily A. Vander Veer
- *Access 2010: The Missing Manual* by Matthew MacDonald

- *Microsoft Project 2010: The Missing Manual* by Bonnie Biafore
- *PCs: The Missing Manual* by Andy Rathbone
- *Photoshop Elements 10: The Missing Manual* by Barbara Brundage
- *Quicken 2009: The Missing Manual* by Bonnie Biafore
- *QuickBooks 2012: The Missing Manual* by Bonnie Biafore
- *QuickBase: The Missing Manual* by Nancy Conner
- *Windows XP Home Edition: The Missing Manual,* 2nd Edition by David Pogue
- *Windows XP Pro: The Missing Manual,* 2nd Edition by David Pogue, Craig Zacker, and L.J. Zacker
- *Windows XP Power Hound* by Preston Gralla

Web Sites
- *eBay: The Missing Manual* by Nancy Conner
- *Wikipedia: The Missing Manual* by John Broughton
- *Google: The Missing Manual* by Sarah Milstein and Rael Dornfest
- *Google Apps: The Missing Manual* by Nancy Conner
- *Google+: The Missing Manual* by Kevin Purdy
- *Google Sketchup: The Missing Manual* by Chris Grover
- *Facebook: The Missing Manual* by E.A. Vander Veer

Web and Graphic Design
- *Photoshop CS5: The Missing Manual* by Lesa Snider King
- *JavaScript & JQuery: The Missing Manual* by David Sawyer McFarland
- *CSS: The Missing Manual,* 2nd Edition, by David Sawyer McFarland
- *Creating a Web Site: The Missing Manual* by Matthew MacDonald
- *HTML5: The Missing Manual* by Matthew MacDonald
- *The Internet: The Missing Manual* by David Pogue and J.D. Biersdorfer
- *Dreamweaver CS5.5: The Missing Manual* by David Sawyer McFarland
- *Flash CS5.5: The Missing Manual* by Chris Grover
- *PHP & MySQL: The Missing Manual* by Brett McLaughlin

Phones, Tablets, and Gadgets
- *iPhone: The Missing Manual,* 5th Edition by David Pogue
- *iPhone App Design: The Missing Manual* by Craig Hockenberry

- *Nook Tablet: The Missing Manual* by Preston Gralla
- *Kindle Fire: The Missing Manual* by Peter Meyers
- *Droid X: The Missing Manual* by Preston Gralla
- *Droid X2: The Missing Manual* by Preston Gralla
- *Motorola Xoom: The Missing Manual* by Preston Gralla
- *Galaxy Tab: The Missing Manual* by Preston Gralla
- *Galaxy S II: The Missing Manual* by Preston Gralla
- *iPad 3: The Missing Manual* by J.D. Biersdorfer
- *iPod: The Missing Manual,* 10th Edition by J.D. Biersdorfer
- *David Pogue's Digital Photography: The Missing Manual* by David Pogue
- *Palm Pre: The Missing Manual* by Ed Baig
- *Netbooks: The Missing Manual* by J.D. Biersdorfer
- *Home Networking: The Missing Manual* by Scott Lowe

The Analog World
- *Your Brain: The Missing Manual* by Matthew MacDonald
- *Your Body: The Missing Manual* by Matthew MacDonald
- *Your Money: The Missing Manual* by J.D. Roth
- *Personal Investing: The Missing Manual* by Bonnie Biafore, Amy E. Buttell, and Carol Fabbri
- *Living Green: The Missing Manual* by Nancy Conner
- *Buying a Home: The Missing Manual* by Nancy Conner

Introduction

What's going on with the Mac these days?

Apple was the only computer company whose sales actually increased during the recession. The Mac's market share has quadrupled since 2005—it's now around 20 percent of computer sales in the U.S. And then there's the most significant statistic of all: you, sitting there reading this book—because, obviously, you intend to switch to (or add on) a Mac.

What's going on?

Maybe it's the "halo effect": the coolness of all those iPads and iPhones is rubbing off onto the rest of Apple's product line. Maybe people have grown weary of boring beige and black boxes. Maybe it's the convenience of the Apple Stores. Maybe potential switchers feel more confident to take the plunge, since more and more of life is moving online, where it makes no difference what kind of computer you have.

Or maybe people have just spent one Saturday too many dealing with viruses, worms, spyware, crapware, excessive startup processes, questionable firewalls, inefficient permissions, and all the other land mines strewn across the Windows world.

In any case, there's never been a better time to make the switch. Mac OS X version 10.7 (code-named Lion) is gorgeous, easy to understand, and virus-free. Apple's computers are in top form, too, complete with features like built-in video cameras, built-in Ethernet, DVD burners, illuminated keyboards, and two different kinds of wireless connections. If you're talking laptops, the story is even better: Apple's laptops generally cost less than similarly outfitted Windows laptops, and weigh less, too. Plus, they look a lot cooler.

And then there's that Intel processor that sizzles away inside today's Macs. Yes, it lets you *run Windows*—and Windows programs—at blazing speed, right there on your Macintosh. (Hell really has frozen over.) Chapter 8 has the details.

That's not to say, however, that switching to the Mac is all sunshine and bunnies. The Macintosh is a different machine, running a different operating system, and built by a company with a different philosophy—a fanatical control freak/perfectionist zeal. When it comes to their missions and ideals, Apple and Microsoft have about as much in common as a melon and a shoehorn.

In any case, you have three challenges before you. First, you'll probably want to copy your Windows stuff over to the new Mac. Some of that is easy to transfer (photos, music, Microsoft Office documents), and some is trickier (email messages, address books, buddy lists).

Second, you have to assemble a suite of Macintosh programs that do what you're used to doing in Windows. Most programs from Microsoft, Adobe, and other major players are available in nearly identical Mac and Windows formats. But occasionally, it's more difficult: Many programs are available only for Windows, and it takes some research (or Chapter 7 of this book) to help you find Macintosh replacements.

Finally, you have to learn Mac OS X itself; after all, it came preinstalled on your new Mac. In some respects, it resembles the latest versions of Windows: There's a taskbar-like thing, a Control Panel–like thing, and, of course, a Trash can. At the same time, hundreds of features you thought you knew have been removed, replaced, or relocated. (If you ever find yourself groping for an old favorite feature, see Appendix C, The "Where'd It Go?" Dictionary.)

Note: In Mac OS X, the X is meant to be a Roman numeral, pronounced "ten." Unfortunately, many people see "Mac OS X" and say "Mac Oh Ess Sex." That's a sure way to get funny looks in public.

FREQUENTLY ASKED QUESTION

All About "Lion"

What's this business about big cats?

Most software companies develop their wares in secret, using code names for new products to throw outsiders off the scent. Apple's code names for Mac OS X and its descendants have been named after big cats: Mac OS X was Cheetah, 10.1 was Puma, 10.2 was Jaguar, 10.3 was Panther, 10.4 was Tiger, 10.5 was Leopard, 10.6 was Snow Leopard. You have 10.7 Lion; the next version (summer 2012) will be called 10.8 Mountain Lion.

(A mountain lion is actually the same thing as a cougar, which is the same thing as a puma. But let's not quibble.)

Usually, the code name is dropped as soon as the product is complete, whereupon the marketing department gives it a new name. In Mac OS X's case, though, Apple thinks its cat names are cool enough to retain for the finished product.

You do have to wonder what Apple plans to call future versions. Apple says that it has no problem using double-digit decimal points for future versions of Mac OS X. There'll be 10.9, 10.10, 10.11, and so on.

But what about the code names?

Let's see: Bobcat, Cougar…um…Ocelot?

What Mac OS X Gives You

These days, a key attraction of the Mac—at least as far as switchers are concerned—is security. There isn't yet a single widespread Mac OS X virus. (Even Microsoft Word macro viruses don't run in Mac OS X.) For many people, that's a good enough reason to move to Mac OS X right there.

Along the same lines, there have been no reported sightings of *spyware* (malicious software that tracks your computer use and reports it back to a shady company) for Mac OS X. Mail, Mac OS X's built-in email program, deals surprisingly well with spam, the unsolicited junk email that's become the scourge of the Internet.

If you ask average people why the Mac isn't overrun by viruses and spyware, as Windows is, they'll probably tell you, "Because the Mac's market share is too small for the bad guys to write for."

That may be true (although 65 million machines isn't too shabby, as targets go). But there's another reason, too: Mac OS X is a very young operating system. It was created only in 2001, and with security in mind. (Contrast that with Windows, whose original versions were written before the Internet even existed.) Mac OS X is simply designed better. Its built-in firewall makes it virtually impossible for hackers to break into your Mac, and the system insists on getting your permission before *anything* gets installed on your Mac. Nothing can get installed behind your back.

But freedom from gunkware and viruses is only one big-ticket item. Here are a few other joys of becoming a Mac fan:

- **Stability.** Underneath the shimmering, translucent desktop of Mac OS X is Unix, the industrial strength, rock-solid OS that drives many a Web site and university. It's not new by any means; in fact, it's decades old, and has been polished by generations of programmers. That's precisely why Apple CEO Steve Jobs and his team chose it as the basis for the NeXT operating system, which Jobs worked on during his 12 years away from Apple and which Apple bought in 1997 to turn into Mac OS X.

- **No nagging.** Mac OS X isn't copy-protected. You can install the same copy on your desktop and laptop Macs, if you have a permissive conscience. When you buy a new Mac, you're never, ever asked to type in a code off a sticker. Nor must you "register," "activate," sign up for ".NET Passport," or endure any other friendly suggestions unrelated to your work. And you won't find any cheesy software demos from other companies clogging up your desktop when you buy a new Mac, either. In short, Mac OS X leaves you alone.

- **Great software.** Mac OS X comes with several dozen useful programs, from Mail (for email) to a 3-D, voice-activated Chess program. The most famous programs, though, are the famous Apple "iApps": iTunes for working with audio files, iMovie for editing video, iPhoto for managing your digital photos, GarageBand for creating and editing digital music, and so on. You also get iChat (a Yahoo-, AOL-,

Jabber-, and Google Talk-compatible instant messaging program that also offers videoconferencing) and iCal, a calendar program.

• **Simpler everything.** Most applications in Mac OS X show up as a single icon. All the support files are hidden away inside, where you don't have to look at them. There's no Add/Remove Programs program on the Macintosh; in general, you can remove a program from your Mac simply by dragging that one application icon to the Trash, without having to worry that you're leaving scraps behind.

• **Desktop features.** Mac OS X offers a long list of useful desktop features that will be new to you, the Windows refugee.

For example, *spring-loaded* folders let you drag an icon into a folder within a folder within a folder with a single drag, without leaving a wake of open windows. An optional second line under an icon's name tells you how many items are in a folder, what the dimensions of a graphic are, and so on. And there's a useful column view, which lets you view the contents of many nested folders at a glance. (You can think of it as a horizontal version of Windows Explorer's folder tree.)

When your screen gets cluttered with windows, you can temporarily hide all of them with a single keystroke. If you want to see *all* the windows on your screen without any of them overlapping, Mac OS X's Mission Control feature is your best friend (page 141).

A speedy, system-wide Find command called Spotlight is accessible from any program. It searches not only the names of your files and folders, but also the words *inside* your documents, and can even search your email, calendar, address book, Web bookmarks, and about 100 other kinds of data, all at once.

Finally, Mac OS X offers the Dashboard (which inspired the widgets in Windows Vista and Windows 7). It lets you summon dozens of miniprograms—a calculator, weather forecaster, dictionary, and so on—with a single keystroke, and dismiss them just as easily. You can download thousands more of these so-called widgets from the Internet, making it even easier to find TV listings, Google search results, local movie showtimes, and more, no matter what program you're using at the moment.

• **Advanced graphics.** Mac programmers get excited about the set of advanced graphics technologies called *Quartz* (for two-dimensional graphics) and *OpenGL* (for three-dimensional graphics). For the rest of us, these technologies translate into a beautiful, translucent look for the desktop, smooth-looking (*antialiased*) onscreen lettering, and the ability to turn any document on the screen into an Adobe Acrobat (PDF) file. And then there are the slick animations that permeate every aspect of Mac OS X: the rotating-cube effect when you switch from one logged-in person to another, the "genie" effect when you minimize a window to the Dock, and so on.

• **Advanced networking.** When it comes to hooking up your computer to others, including those on the Internet, few operating systems can touch Mac OS X. It offers advanced features like *multihoming,* which lets your laptop switch automatically from its cable modem settings to its wireless or dial-up modem settings when you take it on the road.

If you're not so much a switcher as an *adder* (you're getting a Mac but keeping the PC around), you'll be happy to hear that Macs and Windows PCs can "see" each other on a network automatically, too. As a result, you can open, copy, and work on files on both types of machines as though the religious war between Macs and PCs had never even existed.

- **Voice control, keyboard control.** You can operate almost every aspect of every program entirely from the keyboard—or even by voice. These are terrific timesavers for efficiency freaks. In fact, the Mac can also read aloud *any text in any program,* including Web pages, email, your novel, you name it.

- **Full buzzword compliance.** You can't read an article about Mac OS X without hearing certain technical buzzwords that were once exclusively the domain of computer engineers: *preemptive multitasking, multithreading, symmetrical multiprocessing, dynamic memory allocation,* and *memory protection,* for example.

What it all adds up to is that Mac OS X is very stable, that a crashing program can't crash the whole machine, that the Macintosh can exploit multiple processors, and that the Mac can easily do more than one thing at once—downloading files, playing music, and opening a program, for example—all simultaneously.

- **A command-line interface.** In general, Apple has completely hidden from you every trace of the Unix operating system that lurks beneath Mac OS X's beautiful skin. For the benefit of programmers and other technically oriented fans, however, Apple left uncovered a tiny passageway into that far more complex realm: Terminal, a program in your Applications→Utilities folder.

If the idea of an all-text operating system gets you going, you can capitalize on the *command-line interface* of Mac OS X by typing out commands in the Terminal window, which the Mac executes instantly and efficiently. Think DOS prompt, just faster and more useful. (Curious? There's a free online PDF appendix to this book—called "Terminal Crash Course"—waiting for you. It's on this book's "Missing CD" at *www.missingmanuals.com.*)

What Mac OS X Takes Away

Besides quirks like viruses, spyware, and the Start menu, there are some substantial things on a PC that you lose when you switch to the Mac:

- **Programs.** As mentioned above, there are certain programs that are stubbornly Windows-only. You can always search for replacements—using Chapter 7 of this book as a guide, for example—but you may end up having to pay for them. And, of course, there are *certain* programs—like some proprietary accounting and laboratory software, and lots of games—where the Windows versions are simply irreplaceable. For those, you have to keep a PC around or run Windows on your Mac (Chapter 8).

- **Peripherals.** Most add-on devices nowadays work equally well on both Windows PCs and Macs. That includes printers, scanners, digital cameras (still- and video-varieties), and "multifunction" devices that incorporate several of those attributes into one machine.

Unfortunately, sometimes the Mac software for a gadget isn't as full-featured as the Windows version. Sometimes some of the features on a multifunction printer/scanner aren't available on the Mac. If you have a device made by an obscure manufacturer—especially if the device is more than a few years old—it may not work with your Mac at all.

Still, all hope is not lost. Chapter 9 can get you out of most hardware ruts you may find yourself in while making the Big Switch.

About This Book

Switching to the Mac: The Missing Manual is divided into five parts, each containing several chapters:

- Part 1, **Welcome to Macintosh,** covers the essentials of the Macintosh. It's a crash course in everything you see onscreen when you turn on the machine: the Dock, Sidebar, icons, windows, menus, scroll bars, Trash, aliases, menu, and so on.

- Part 2, **Making the Move,** is dedicated to the actual process of hauling your software, settings, and even peripherals (like printers and monitors) across the chasm from the PC to the Mac. It covers both the easy parts (copying over your documents, pictures, and music files) and the harder ones (transferring your email, address books, buddy lists, and so on). It also covers the steps for running Windows on your Mac, which is an extremely attractive option.

- Part 3, **Making Connections,** walks you through the process of setting up an Internet connection on your Mac. It also covers Apple's Internet software suite: Mail, Address Book, Safari, and iChat.

Note: Much of Parts 2 and 3 is adapted from *Mac OS X Lion: The Missing Manual.* That book is a fatter, more in-depth guide to Mac OS X.

- Part 4, **Putting Down Roots,** deals with more advanced topics—and aims to turn you into a Macintosh power user. It teaches you how to set up private accounts for people who share a Mac, create a network for file sharing and screen sharing, navigate the System Preferences program (the Mac equivalent of the Windows Control Panel), and operate the 50 freebie bonus programs that come with Mac OS X.

- Part 5, **Appendixes.** At the end of the book, you'll find four appendixes. The first two cover installation and troubleshooting. The third is the "Where'd It Go?" Dictionary—an essential reference for anyone who occasionally (or frequently) flounders to find some familiar control in the new, alien Macintosh environment. The last is a master keyboard-shortcut list for the entire Mac OS X universe.

About→These→Arrows

Throughout this book—and throughout the Missing Manual series—you'll find sentences like this one: "Open the System→Libraries→Fonts folder." That's shorthand for a much longer instruction that directs you to open three nested folders in sequence, like this: "On your hard drive, you'll find a folder called System. Open that. Inside the System folder window is a folder called Libraries; double-click it to open it. Inside *that* folder is yet another one called Fonts. Double-click to open it, too."

Similarly, this kind of arrow shorthand helps to simplify the business of choosing commands in menus, as shown in Figure I-1.

Figure I-1:
In this book, arrow notations help to simplify folder and menu instructions. For example, "Choose ⌘→Dock→Position on Left" is a more compact way of saying, "From the ⌘ menu, choose Dock; from the submenu that then appears, choose Position on Left," as shown here.

About MissingManuals.com

If you visit *www.missingmanuals.com*, click the "Missing CD-ROM" link, and then click the title of this book, you'll find a neat, organized, chapter-by-chapter list of the shareware and freeware mentioned in this book. (As noted on the inside back cover, having the software online instead of on a CD-ROM saved you $5 on the cost of the book.)

The Web site also offers corrections and updates to the book (to see them, click the book's title, and then click Errata). In fact, you're encouraged to submit such corrections and updates yourself. In an effort to keep the book as up-to-date and accurate as possible, each time we print more copies of this book, we'll make any confirmed corrections you've suggested. We'll also note such changes on the Web site, so that you can mark important corrections into your own copy of the book, if you like.

The Very Basics

To use this book, and indeed to use a Macintosh, you need to know a few basics. This book assumes you're familiar with a few terms and concepts:

- **Clicking.** This book gives you three kinds of instructions that require you to use the Mac's mouse. To *click* means to point the arrow cursor at something on the screen and then—without moving the cursor—press and release the clicker button on the mouse (or your laptop trackpad). To *double-click,* of course, means to click twice in rapid succession, again without moving the cursor at all. And to *drag* means to move the cursor while holding down the button.

  When you're told to ⌘-*click* something, you click while pressing the ⌘ key (which is next to the space bar). *Shift-clicking, Option-clicking,* and *Control-clicking* work the same way—just click while pressing the corresponding key.

- **Menus.** The *menus* are the words at the top of your screen: , File, Edit, and so on. Click one to make a list of commands appear.

  Some people click and release to open a menu and then, after reading the choices, click again on the one they want. Other people like to press the mouse button continuously after the initial click on the menu title, drag down the list to the desired command, and only then release the mouse button. Either method works fine.

- **Dialog boxes.** See Figure I-2 for a tour of the onscreen elements you'll frequently be asked to use, like checkboxes, radio buttons, tabs, and so on.

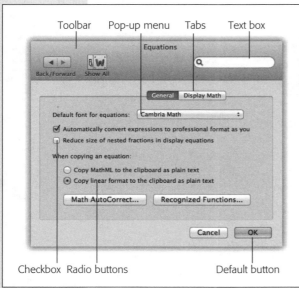

Figure I-2:
Knowing what you're doing on the Mac often requires knowing that things are called. Here are some of the most common onscreen elements. They include checkboxes (turn on as many as you like) and radio buttons (only one can be turned on in each grouping).

Pressing Return is usually the same as clicking the default button–the lower-right button that almost always means "OK, I'm done here."

A few more tips on mastering the Mac keyboard appear in Chapter 1. Otherwise, if you've mastered this much information, you have all the technical background you need to enjoy *Mac OS X Lion: The Missing Manual.*

- **Keyboard shortcuts.** If you're typing along in a burst of creative energy, it's disruptive to have to grab the mouse to use a menu. That's why many computer fans prefer to trigger menu commands by pressing certain combinations on the keyboard. For example, in word processors, you can press ⌘-B to produce a **boldface** word. When you read an instruction like "press ⌘-B," start by pressing the ⌘ key, then, while it's down, type the letter B, and finally release both keys.

Tip: You know what's really nice? The keystroke to open the Preferences dialog box in every Apple program—Mail, Safari, iMovie, iPhoto, TextEdit, Preview, and on and on—is always the same: ⌘-comma. Better yet, that standard is catching on with other software companies, too; Word, Excel, Entourage, and PowerPoint use the same keystroke, for example.

- **Icons.** The colorful inch-tall pictures that appear in your various desktop folders are the graphic symbols that represent each program, disk, and document on your computer. If you click an icon one time, it darkens, indicating that you've just *highlighted* or *selected* it. Now you're ready to manipulate it by using, for example, a menu command.

The Lion Difference: iPad Techniques

If you could choose only one word to describe Apple's overarching design goal in Mac OS X Lion, there's no doubt about what it would be: *iPad.* That's right. In Lion, Apple has gone about as far as it could go in trying to turn the Mac into an iPad.

Two things have made the iPad the fastest-selling electronic gadget in history. First, it's so simple. No overlapping windows; every app runs full screen. No Save command; everything's autosaved. No files or folders. No menus. All your apps are in one place, the Home screen. To beginners, technophobes, and even old-timers, the iPad's software represents a refreshing decluttering of the modern computer.

The second huge iPad sales point is that multitouch screen. You operate the whole thing by touching or dragging your fingers on the glass. For example, you cycle through screens by swiping. You zoom out on a map, photo, or Web page by pinching two fingers. You rotate a photo by twisting two fingers, and so on.

So Apple thought: If simplicity and touch gestures made the iPad a megahit, why can't we do the same for the Mac?

And it set out to bring as many of the iPad's features and as much of its personality to your Mac as possible. Lion features like Full Screen mode, Auto Save, and Launchpad are total iPad rip-offs; if Apple hadn't stolen these features from itself, it would surely be suing for copyright infringement.

Apple even brought over the whole multitouch thing to the Mac. No, you don't touch the screen; you'd get screaming arm pain if you had to spend the day with your arm outstretched, manipulating tiny controls on a vertical surface 3 feet away. (The resulting ache actually has a name in the computer biz: gorilla arm.)

Instead, you use all those same iPad gestures and more, right on the surface of your laptop trackpad or (if you have Apple's Magic Mouse) the top surface of the mouse.

It's a new way to work, for sure. And it's optional. If it doesn't float your boat, you can ignore all of it (full-screen, gestures, Launchpad, Auto Save).

But you should at least make an informed decision—and that's the purpose of the next few pages. They're a tutorial. They walk you through a typical Lionized working session the way Apple intended you to work. If you follow along, you'll wind up with a good sense of how much you like (or don't like) the iPaddified Mac.

Note: In this book, you'll see touch gestures provided separately for *trackpads* (either the one on your laptop, or Apple's external Magic Trackpad) and the *Magic Mouse* (Apple's latest mouse, whose surface is touch sensitive).

Why aren't the gestures identical? Because the Magic Mouse requires at least two fingers to *hold,* so some of the more multi-fingered gestures aren't practical. And remember, on the trackpad you need a finger just to move the cursor—and on the Magic Mouse, *moving the mouse* moves the cursor.

Launchpad

All right. It's Monday morning. You want to start with a quick Web check. And for that, you'll need Safari, the Mac's Web browser.

Figure I-3:
Launchpad is a new app that displays all your programs' icons at once, neatly spaced and ready to open with a single click. To see more pages full of icons, swipe left or right with two fingers on your trackpad.

1. **Put four fingers on the trackpad (thumb and three fingers), and pinch them inward toward the center.**

   If you have a Magic Mouse, just click Launchpad on the Dock.

   Your screen goes dark and fills up with what looks like the Home screen on the iPhone or iPad. You've just opened the new Launchpad. Here are the icons of all your Mac's programs, evenly spaced, arrayed (if there are lots of them) on multiple "pages." Figure I-3 shows the idea.

Note: The four-finger pinch gesture opens Launchpad only on trackpads. If you don't have one, click the Launchpad icon on the Dock instead. It looks like a rocket ship (⌖).

   Suppose, for the sake of this exercise, that you can't find the Safari icon. It's on a different page.

2. **With two fingers on the trackpad, swipe left or right to change "pages." Stop when you spot Safari.**

   If you have a Magic Mouse, swipe left or right with *one* finger.

Tip: This same gesture—swiping left or right—also works as Back or Forward in Safari.

   You could, if you liked, customize Launchpad just as you would on an iPhone or iPad. You can drag the icons around, put them on different pages, combine them into folders, or delete them. (See page 135.) For now, you just want to open the Web browser.

3. **Click the Safari icon once.**

   That's one difference between opening a program in Launchpad (one click) and in your Applications folder (two clicks).

Full Screen Mode, Safari

Once Safari opens, you're ready for your first full-screen experience.

1. **Click the ⤢ icon in the upper-right corner of the Safari window.**

   With a smooth animation, your Mac hides the menu bar and the bookmarks bar. The only thing remaining is the address bar. The window's edges expand all the way to the edges of the screen (Figure I-4).

Tip: You may as well learn the keyboard shortcut for the Enter Full Screen mode: Control-⌘-F. The same keystroke *leaves* Full Screen mode, but you can also tap the Esc key for that purpose.

   You don't have to panic, though. The menu bar is still available: Move the mouse to the top of the screen to make the menus reappear.

For the next demonstration, call up an actual Web page, preferably one with a lot of text on it—*www.nytimes.com,* for example. Now suppose you want to scroll down the page.

Figure I-4:
This, ladies and gentlemen, is Full Screen mode, one of the flagship features of Lion. The idea is to fight back against the forces of window clutter that have been encroaching on your document windows for years now. Your actual work, your photo or Web page, fills every pixel of that giant screen you paid so much money for.

2. **With two fingers on the trackpad, drag upward.**

   If you have a Magic Mouse, drag up with *one* finger.

   If you just tried this, you're no doubt frowning right now. You just scrolled *down* the page by moving your fingers *up.* That's backward, isn't it?

   For your entire computing career so far, you've always dragged the scroll bar *down* to move the contents of the page *up*—and now, in Lion, Apple swapped the directions. Why would Apple throw such a monkey wrench into your life?

   Well, the first reason is to make the Mac match the iPad/iPhone, where you drag your finger up to move the page up. The second reason, frankly, is that the old system never really made sense in the first place. Look, if you want to scroll left, you drag the scroll bar *left;* if you want to move right, you drag it *right.* Why have the vertical directions been reversed for all these years?

   Anyway, you have two choices: You can spend a couple of days getting used to the new arrangement—or you can put things back the way they've always been. (To do that, open System Preferences, click Trackpad, click Scroll & Zoom, and then turn off "Scroll direction: natural.")

3. **Find a photo or block of text. With two fingers, double-tap the trackpad.**

   These are *touches,* not full clicks. On the Magic Mouse, double-tap with *one* finger.

Safari neatly magnifies the photo or text block to fill the screen, just as on an iPhone or iPad. Neat, huh?

4. **Repeat the double-tap to restore the original size. Click a link to visit a different page.**

For this demonstration, it doesn't make any difference what other Web page you visit. The point is for you to see how cool it is when you swipe your trackpad instead of clicking the Back button.

5. **Go back to the first page by swiping leftward with two fingers on the trackpad.**

On a Magic Mouse, use *one* finger.

The previous page slides back into view as though it's a tile sliding back into place. You can swipe the other way, too—to the right—to go forward a page.

Once you've accumulated several full-screen apps, and you've full-screened them, you can use a similar swipe—with *three* fingers on the trackpad—to flip among full-screen apps. (On the Magic Mouse, swipe with *one* finger.)

Full-Screen Apps, Mission Control

You're still in Safari, right? And it's still full screen, right?

But if Safari is full screen, how are you supposed to get to other open programs? That's what you'll find out in this exercise. You'll get to see what it's like to run multiple full-screen apps.

1. **Pinch your trackpad with your thumb and three fingers.**

Launchpad appears, at your service. (If you're trackpadless, just click Launchpad on the Dock.)

2. **Find iCal and click it to open it.**

You may have to change Launchpad "pages" to find it. Swipe horizontally with two fingers (trackpad) or one finger (Magic Mouse) to change pages.

Now iCal opens.

3. **Make the new window full screen by clicking the ⬈ in the upper-right corner.**

In theory, you now have *two* apps running at full screen: Safari and iCal. Now comes the fun part.

4. **With three fingers on the trackpad, swipe left or right.**

(On the Magic Mouse, use *two* fingers.)

The full-screen apps slide into or out of view. If you keep three-finger swiping to the right, you'll see that Dashboard is all the way at the left end of the "channels" that you're changing. (If it doesn't work, somebody might have changed the setting to require *four* fingers in System Preferences.)

You'll also discover that any *other* programs—the ones that aren't full screen—are gathered onto a *single* screen, as they have been for years. Each full-screen app is one "screen," and the Finder and all your other apps huddle on another one. But it doesn't have to be that way.

5. **With three fingers on the trackpad, swipe upward.**

   If you have a Magic Mouse, tap (don't fully click) with two fingers.

   You now enter Mission Control, a special screen full of miniatures of all your *other* screens; see Figure I-5. (Again, if three fingers doesn't work, someone might have changed your trackpad preferences to require four fingers.)

Figure I-5:
Here in Mission Control, each full-screen app gets its own "screen," as indicated by the map at top. But every running program appears here in the main screen area, in miniature. You can click one to jump there, or point and then press the space bar to get a full-size Quick Look.

Mission Control has all kinds of cool features. It lets you jump to one window in a haystack. It lets you set up multiple virtual screens. It lets you reorganize the full-screen app screens you already have. For the full rundown, jump to page 141.

In this miniature Lion crash course, you've had a glimpse at the future that awaits you: a future of trackpad (or Magic Mouse) finger gestures, full-screen apps, and the new centralized organizing features like Launchpad and Mission Control.

If any of this seems intimidating (or unnecessary), remember: *It's all optional.* If you think the Mac works just fine without them, all the techniques you already know still work just fine. But if you think you could get efficiency and pleasure out of adopting a couple of these features, then Lion is ready for you. Full speed ahead!

Part One:
Welcome to Macintosh

1

How the Mac Is Different

When you get right down to it, the job description of every operating system is pretty much the same. Whether it's Mac OS X, Windows 7, or Billy Bob's System-Software Special, any OS must serve as the ambassador between the computer and you, its human operator. It must somehow represent your files and programs on the screen so you can open them; offer some method of organizing your files; present onscreen controls that affect your speaker volume, mouse speed, and so on; and communicate with your external gadgets, like disks, printers, and digital cameras.

In other words, Mac OS X offers roughly the same features as Windows. That's the good news.

The bad news is that these features are called different things and parked in different spots. As you could have predicted, this rearrangement of features can mean a good deal of confusion for you, the Macintosh foreigner. For the first few days or weeks, you may instinctively reach for certain familiar features that simply aren't where you expect to find them, the way your tongue keeps sticking itself into the socket of a newly extracted tooth.

To minimize the frustration, therefore, read this chapter first. It makes plain the most important and dramatic differences between the Windows method and the Macintosh way.

Power On, Dude

As a critic might say, Apple is always consistent with its placement of the power button: It's different on every model.

On iMacs and Mac Minis, the power button is on the back panel. On the Mac Pro, it's on the front panel. And on laptop Macs, the button is near the upper-right corner of the keyboard. (Then again, if you have a laptop, you should get into the habit of just closing the lid when you're done working and opening it to resume; the power button rarely plays a role in your life.)

In every case, though, the power button looks the same (Figure 1-1): It bears the ⏻ logo.

Figure 1-1:
Every Mac's power button looks like this, although it might be hard to find. The good news: Once you find it, it'll pretty much stay in the same place.

That One-Button Mouse

You can get terrific mileage out of *shortcut menus* on the Mac, just as in Windows (Figure 1-2).

Figure 1-2:
A shortcut menu is one that pops out of something you're clicking—an icon, a button, a folder. The beauty of a shortcut menu is that its commands are contextual. They bring up useful commands in exactly the spots where they're most useful, in menus that are relevant to what you're clicking.

Shortcut menus are so important, in fact, that it's worth this ink and this paper to explain the different ways you can trigger a right-click (or a *secondary click*, as Apple calls it, because not all these methods actually involve a second mouse button, and it doesn't *have* to be the right-side one):

- **Control-click.** You can open the shortcut menu of something on the Mac screen by Control-clicking it. That is, while pressing the Control key (bottom row), click the mouse on your target.

- **Right-click.** Windows veterans have always used the one-handed method: right-clicking. That is, clicking something by pressing the *right* mouse button on a two-button mouse.

"Ah, but that's what's always driven me nuts about Apple," goes the common refrain. "Their refusal to get rid of their stupid one-button mouse!"

Well, not so fast.

First of all, you can attach any old $6 USB two-button mouse to the Mac, and it'll work flawlessly. Use the one from your old PC, if you like.

Furthermore, if you've bought a desktop Mac since late 2005, you probably already *have* a two-button mouse—but you might not realize it. Is your mouse a white, shiny plastic capsule with tiny gray scrolling track-pea on the far end? That would be what Apple calls the Mighty Mouse. Or is it a sculpted, winglike, wireless mouse with a wide top surface? That would be the newer Magic Mouse.

Both of them have a secret: an invisible right mouse button. It doesn't work until you ask for it.

To do that, choose →System Preferences. Click Mouse. There, in all its splendor, is a diagram of the mouse. (There's a picture on page 524.)

Your job is to choose Secondary Button from the pop-up menu that identifies the right side of the mouse. (The reason it's not called a "right button" is because left-handers might prefer to reverse the right and left functions.)

From now on, even though there aren't two visible mouse buttons, your mouse does, in fact, register either a left-click or a right-click, depending on which side of the button you push down. It actually works a lot more easily than it sounds like it would.

- **Use the trackpad.** If you have a trackpad (a laptop, for example), then you have all kinds of ways to trigger a right-click.

Out of the box, you do it by clicking the trackpad with *two* fingers. The shortcut menu pops right up.

Or you can point to whatever you want to click. Rest two fingers on the trackpad—and then click with your thumb.

But those aren't the end of your options. In System Preferences→Trackpad, you can also turn on even more right-click methods (and watch little videos on how to do them; see Figure 1-3). For example, you can "right-click" by clicking either the lower-right or lower-left corner of the trackpad—one finger only.

Figure 1-3:
The Trackpad pane of System Preferences looks different depending on your laptop model. But this one shows the three ways to get a "right-click."

On, Off, and Sleep

If you're the only person who uses your Mac, finishing up a work session is simple. You can either turn off the machine or simply let it go to sleep, in any of several ways.

Sleep Mode

Apple expects its customers *not* to shut down their machines between sessions, and that's fine. Instead, you're encouraged to use *sleep mode* (formerly called Standby on the PC). Sleep mode consumes very little power, keeps everything you were doing open and in memory, and wakes the Mac almost immediately when you press a key or click the mouse. To make your machine sleep, use any of these techniques:

• **Close the lid.** (Hint: This tip works only on laptops.)

• **Choose** **→Sleep.** Or press Option-⌘-⏏.

- **Press Control-⏏** (or Control-F12, if you don't have a ⏏ key). In the dialog box shown in Figure 1-4, click Sleep (or type *S*).

- **Press the power button (⏻) on your machine.** On desktop models, doing so makes it sleep immediately; on laptops, you get the dialog box shown in Figure 1-4.

Figure 1-4:
Once the Shut Down dialog box appears, you can press the S key instead of clicking Sleep, R for Restart, Esc for Cancel, or Return for Shut Down.

Are you sure you want to shut down your computer now?

☑ Reopen windows when logging back in

[Restart]   [Sleep]   [Cancel]   [**Shut Down**]

- **Just walk away,** confident that the Energy Saver setting described on page 516 will send the machine off to dreamland automatically at the specified time.

Restart

You shouldn't have to restart the Mac very often—only in times of severe trouble-shooting mystification, in fact. Here are a few ways to do it:

- **Choose ⬤→Restart.** A confirmation dialog box appears; click Restart (or press Return).

Tip: If you press Option as you release the mouse on the ⬤→Restart command, then you won't be bothered by an "Are you sure?" confirmation box.

- **Press Control-⌘-⏏.** (If you don't have that key, substitute F12.)
- **Press Control-⏏** to summon the dialog box shown in Figure 1-4; click Restart (or type *R*).

Shut Down

To shut down your machine completely (when you don't plan to use it for more than a couple of days, when you plan to transport it, and so on), do one of the following:

- **Choose ⬤→Shut Down.** A simple confirmation dialog box appears; click Shut Down (or press Return).

Tip: Once again, if you press Option as you release the mouse, no confirmation box appears.

- **Press Control-Option-⌘-⏏.** (It's not as complex as it looks—the first three keys are all in a tidy row to the left of the space bar.)

- **Press Control-⏏ (or Control-F12)** to summon the dialog box shown in Figure 1-4. Click Shut Down (or press Return).

- **Wait.** If you've set up the Energy Saver preferences (page 516) to shut down the Mac automatically at a specified time, then you don't have to do anything.

The "Reopen windows" Option

In the Shut Down dialog box illustrated in Figure 1-4, you'll notice one of Lion's most-hyped new features: a checkbox called "Reopen windows when logging back in." That simple box does something very useful: The next time you start up your Mac, every running program, and every open window, will reopen exactly as it was at the moment you used the Restart or Shut Down command. The new option gives the Mac something like the old Hibernate feature in Windows—and saves you a lot of reopening the next time you sit down to work.

If you turn off that checkbox when you click Restart or Shut Down, then your next startup will take you to the desktop, with no programs running, as though this were still some year between 1984 and 2010. And if you want the Mac to stop asking—if you never want your programs and windows to reopen—then open →System Preferences→General and turn off "Restore windows when quitting and re-opening apps."

Log Out

If you share your Mac with other people, then you should *log out* when you're done. Doing so ensures that your stuff is safe from the evil and the clueless when you're out of the room. To do it, choose →Log Out (or press Shift-⌘-Q). When the confirmation dialog box appears, click Log Out, press Return, or just wait for 2 minutes. The Mac hides your world from view and displays the login dialog box, ready for its next victim.

Another option is to use *fast user switching*—a feature that lets you switch from one user to another without actually logging out, just as in Windows. With fast user switching turned on, your Mac can have several people logged in at once, although only one person at a time actually sees his own desktop.

In either case, this whole accounts system is described in much more detail in Chapter 14.

Tip: If you press the Option key as you release the mouse when choosing the Restart, Shut Down, or Log Out commands, you eliminate the "Are you sure?" confirmation dialog box. The saved mouse clicks can really add up.

The Menu Bar

On the Mac, there's only one menu bar. It's always at the top of the screen. The names of these menus, and the commands inside them, change to suit the window you're currently using. That's different from Windows, where a separate menu bar appears at the top of *every* window.

Mac and Windows devotees can argue the relative merits of these two approaches until they're blue in the face. All that matters, though, is that you know where to look when you want to reach for a menu command. On the Mac, you always look upward.

Finder = Windows Explorer

In Mac OS X, the "home base" program—the one that appears when you first turn on the machine and shows you the icons of all your folders and files—is called the Finder. This is where you manage your folders and files, throw things away, manipulate disks, and so on. (You may also hear it called the *desktop,* since the items you find there mirror the files and folders you might find on a real-life desktop.)

Getting used to the term "Finder" is worthwhile, though, because it comes up so often. For example, the first icon on your Dock is labeled Finder, and clicking it always takes you back to your desktop.

Dock = Taskbar

At the bottom of almost every Mac OS X screen sits a tiny row of photorealistic icons. This is the Dock, a close parallel to the Windows taskbar. (As in Windows, it may be hidden or placed on the left or the right edge of the screen instead—options that appeal primarily to power users and eccentrics.)

The Dock displays the icons of all your open windows and programs, which are denoted by small, glowing dots beneath their icons. Clicking these icons opens the corresponding files, folders, disks, documents, and programs. If you click and hold (or right-click) an open program's icon, you'll see a pop-up list of the open windows in that program, along with Quit and a few other commands.

When you close a program, its icon disappears from the Dock (unless you've secured it there for easy access, as described on page 79).

Tip: You can cycle through the various open programs on your Mac by holding down the ⌘ key and pressing Tab repeatedly. (Sound familiar? It's just like Alt-Tabbing in Windows.) And if you just *tap* ⌘-Tab, you bounce back and forth between the two programs you've used most recently.

What you may find confusing at first, though, is that the Dock also performs one function of the Windows Start menu: It provides a "short list" of programs and files that you use often, for easy access. To add a new icon to the Dock, just drag it there (put programs to the left of the divider line; everything else goes on the right). To remove an icon from the Dock, just drag it away. As long as that item isn't actually open at the moment, it disappears from the Dock with a little animated puff of smoke when you release the mouse button.

The bottom line: On the Mac, a single interface element—the Dock—exhibits characteristics of *both* the Start menu (it lists frequently used programs) and the taskbar (it lists currently open programs and files). (The Windows 7 taskbar does the same thing.)

If you're still confused, Chapter 2 should help clear things up.

Menulets = Tray

Most Windows fans refer to the row of tiny status icons at the lower-right corner of the screen as the *tray,* even though Microsoft's official term is the *notification area.* (Why use one syllable when eight will do?)

Macintosh fans wage a similar battle of terminology when it comes to the little menu-bar icons shown in Figure 1-5. Apple calls them Menu Extras, but Mac fans prefer to call them *menulets.*

Figure 1-5:
These little guys are the cousins of the controls found in the Windows system tray.

In any case, these menu-bar icons are cousins of the Windows tray—each is both an indicator and a menu that provides direct access to certain settings. One menulet lets you adjust your Mac's speaker volume, another lets you change the screen resolution, another shows you the remaining power in your laptop battery, and so on.

Making a menulet appear usually involves turning on a certain checkbox. These checkboxes lurk on the various panes of *System Preferences* (Chapter 16), which is the Mac equivalent of the Control Panel. (To open System Preferences, choose its name from the menu or click the gears icon on the Dock.)

Here's a rundown of the most useful Apple menulets, complete with instructions on where to find the magic on/off checkbox for each.

- **Wi-Fi** lets you turn your WiFi (wireless networking) circuitry on or off, join existing wireless networks, and create your own private ones. *To find the Show checkbox:* Open System Preferences→Network. Click Wi-Fi.

Tip: Once you've installed this menulet, you can *Option-click* it to produce a secret menu full of details about the wireless network you're on right now. You see its channel number, password-security method (WEP, WPA, None, whatever), speed, and such geeky details as the MCS Index and RSSI.

- **Battery** shows how much power remains in your laptop's battery, how much time is left to charge it, whether it's plugged in, and more. Using the Show submenu, you can control whether the menulet appears as an hours-and-minutes-remaining display (2:13), a percentage-remaining readout (43%), or a simple battery-icon gauge that hollows out as the charge runs down. *To find the Show checkbox:* Open System Preferences→Energy Saver.

- **Bluetooth** connects to Bluetooth devices, "pairs" your Mac with a cellphone, lets you send or receive files wirelessly (without the hassle of setting up a wireless network), and so on. *To find the Show checkbox:* Open System Preferences→Bluetooth.

- **Clock** is the menu-bar clock that's been sitting at the upper-right corner of your screen from Day One. Click it to open a menu where you can check today's date, convert the menu-bar display to a tiny analog clock, and so on. *To find the Show checkbox:* Open System Preferences→Date & Time. On the Clock tab, turn on "Show date and time in menu bar."

- **Displays** adjusts screen resolution. On Macs with a projector or second monitor attached, it lets you turn *screen mirroring* on or off—a tremendous convenience to anyone who gives PowerPoint or Keynote presentations. *To find the Show checkbox:* Open System Preferences→Displays→Display tab.

- **iChat** is a quick way to let the world know, via iChat and the Internet (Chapter 13), that you're away from your keyboard, or that you're available and ready to chat. Via the Buddy List command, it's also a quick way to open iChat itself. *To find the Show checkbox:* Open iChat, which is in your Applications folder. Choose iChat→Preferences→General.

- **Script Menu** lists a variety of useful, ready-to-run AppleScript programs. *To find the Show checkbox:* Open the AppleScript Editor program (in your Applications Utilities folder). Choose AppleScript Editor→Preferences→General.

- **Text Input** switches among different text input modes. For example, if your language uses a non-Latin alphabet, like Russian, or thousands of characters, like Chinese, this menulet summons and dismisses the alternative keyboards and input methods you need. Details are on page 188. *To find the Show checkbox:* Open System Preferences→Language & Text→Input Sources.

- **Time Machine** lets you start and stop Time Machine backups (page 201). *To find the Show checkbox:* Open System Preferences→Time Machine.

- **Universal Access** offers simple on/off status indicators for features that are designed to help with visual, hearing, and muscle impairments. Chapter 15 has a rundown of what they do. *To find the Show checkbox:* Open System Preferences→Universal Access.

- **User** identifies the account holder (Chapter 14) who's logged in at the moment. To make this menulet appear (in bold, at the far-right end of the menu bar), turn on *fast user switching,* which is described on page 448.

- **Volume** adjusts your Mac's speaker or headphone volume (surprise!). *To find the Show checkbox:* Open System Preferences→Sound.

- **VPN** stands for virtual private networking, which allows you to tap into a corporation's network so you can, for example, check your work email from home. You can use the menulet to connect and disconnect, for example. *To find the Show checkbox:* Open System Preferences→Network. Click the name of your VPN.

- **WWAN** is useful only if you've equipped your Mac with one of those glorious *cellular modems,* sold by Verizon, Sprint, AT&T, or T-Mobile. These little USB sticks get you onto the Internet wirelessly at near-cable-modem speeds (in big cities, anyway)—no WiFi required—for $60 a month. And this menulet lets you start and stop that connection. *To find the Show checkbox:* Open System Preferences→Network. Click the name of your cellular modem.

To remove a menulet, ⌘-drag it off the menu bar, or turn off the corresponding checkbox in System Preferences. You can also rearrange menulets by ⌘-dragging them horizontally.

These little guys are useful, good-looking, and respectful of your screen space. The world could use more inventions like menulets.

Keyboard Differences

Mac and PC keyboards are subtly different. Making the switch involves two big adjustments: Figuring out where the special Windows keys went (like Alt and Ctrl)—and figuring out what to do with the special Macintosh keys (like ⌘ and Option).

Where the Windows Keys Went

Here's how to find the Macintosh equivalents of familiar PC keyboard keys:

- **Ctrl key.** The Macintosh offers a key labeled Control (or, on laptops, "ctrl"), but it isn't the equivalent of the PC's Ctrl key. The Mac's Control key is primarily for helping you "right-click" things, as described earlier.

  Instead, the Macintosh equivalent of the Windows Ctrl key is the ⌘ key. It's right next to the space bar. It's pronounced "command," although novices can often be heard calling it the "pretzel key," "Apple key," or "clover key."

  Most Windows Ctrl-key combos correspond perfectly to ⌘ key sequences on the Mac. The Save command is now ⌘-S instead of Ctrl+S, Open is ⌘-O instead of Ctrl+O, and so on.

Note: Mac keyboard shortcuts are listed at the right side of each open menu, just as in Windows. Unfortunately, they're represented in the menu with goofy symbols instead of their true key names. Here's your cheat sheet to the menu keyboard symbols: ⇧ represents the Shift key, ⌥ means the Option key, and ^ refers to the Control key.

- **Alt key.** On North American Mac keyboards, a key on the bottom row is labeled both Alt and Option. This is the closest thing the Mac offers to the Windows Alt key.

  In many situations, keyboard shortcuts that involve the Alt key in Windows use the Option key on the Mac. For example, in Microsoft Word, the keyboard short-cut for the Split Document Window command is Alt+Ctrl+S in Windows, but *Option-⌘-T* on the Macintosh.

  Still, these two keys aren't exactly the same. Whereas the Alt key's most popular function is to control the menus in Windows programs, the Option key on the Mac is a "miscellaneous" key that triggers secret functions and special characters.

  For example, when you hold down the Option key as you click the Close or Minimize button on a Macintosh window, you close or minimize *all* open desktop windows. And if you press the Option key while you type *R, G,* or *2,* you get the ®, ©, and ™ symbols in your document, respectively. (See page 189 to find out how you can see which letters turn into which symbols when pressed with Option.)

- **⊞ key.** As you probably could have guessed, there is no Windows-logo key on the Macintosh. Then again, there's no Start menu to open by pressing it, either.

Tip: Just about any USB keyboard works on the Mac, even if the keyboard was originally designed to work with a PC. Depending on the manufacturer of the keyboard, the Windows-logo key may work just like the Mac's ⌘ key.

- **Backspace and Delete.** On the Mac, the backspace key is labeled Delete, although it's in exactly the same place as the Windows Backspace key.

  The Delete key in Windows (technically, the *forward delete* key, because it deletes the character to the right of the insertion point) is a different story. On a desktop Macintosh with a full-size keyboard, it's labeled with *Del* and the ⌦ symbol.

  On small Mac keyboards (like laptop and wireless keyboards), this key is missing. You can still perform a forward delete, however, by pressing the regular Delete key while pressing the Fn key in the corner of the keyboard.

- **Enter.** Most full-size Windows keyboards have *two* Enter keys: one at the right side of the alphabet keyboard and one in the lower-right corner of the number pad. They're identical in function; pressing either one serves to "click" the OK button in a dialog box, for example.

  On the Mac, the big key on the number pad still says Enter, but the key on the alphabet keyboard is labeled Return. Most of the time, their function is identical—either can "click" the OK button of a dialog box. Every now and then, though, you'll run across a Mac program where Return and Enter do different things. In Microsoft Word for Mac OS X, for example, Shift-*Return* inserts a line break, but Shift-*Enter* creates a page break.

What the Special Mac Keys Do

So much for finding the Windows keys you're used to. There's another category of keys worth discussing: those on the modern Macintosh keyboard you've never seen before.

To make any attempt at an explanation even more complicated, Apple's keyboards keep changing. The one you're using right now is probably one of these models:

- **The current keyboards,** where the keys are flat little jobbers that poke up through square holes in the aluminum (Figure 1-6). That's what you get on current laptops, wired keyboards, and Bluetooth wireless keyboards.

- **The older, plastic desktop keyboards,** or the white or black plastic laptop ones.

Tip: To see closeups of Apple's current wired and wireless keyboards, visit www.apple.com/keyboard.

Figure 1-6:
On the top row of aluminum Mac keyboards, the F-keys have dual functions. Ordinarily, F1 through F4 keys correspond to Screen Dimmer, Screen Brighter, Exposé, and Dashboard. Pressing the Fn key in the corner changes their personalities, though.

Here, then, is a guided tour of the non-typewriter keys on the modern Mac keyboard:

- **Fn.** How are you supposed to pronounce Fn? Not "function," certainly; after all, the F-keys on the top row are already known as function keys. And not "fun"; goodness knows, the Fn key isn't particularly hilarious to press.

  What it *does*, though, is quite clear: It changes the purpose of certain keys. That's a big deal on laptops, which don't have nearly as many keys as desktop keyboards. So for some of the less commonly used functions, you're supposed to press Fn and a regular key. (For example, Fn turns the ↑ key into a Page Up key, which scrolls upward by one screenful.)

Note: On most Mac keyboards, the Fn key is in the lower-left corner. The exception is the full-size Apple desktop keyboard (the one with a numeric keypad); there, the Fn key is in the little block of keys between the letter keys and the number pad.

You'll find many more Fn examples in the following paragraphs.

- **Numeric keypad.** The number-pad keys do exactly the same thing as the numbers at the top of the keyboard. But with practice, typing things like phone numbers and prices is much faster with the number pad, since you don't have to look down at what you're doing.

  Apple has been quietly eliminating the numeric keypad from most of its keyboards, but you can still find it on some models.

- ☀, ☀ (**F1, F2**). These keys control the brightness of your screen. Usually, you can tone it down a bit when you're in a dark room or when you want to save laptop battery power; you'll want to crank it up in the sun.

- ▦ (**F3**). This one fires up Mission Control, the handy window-management feature described in Chapter 4.

- ☼ or ⊞ (**F4**). If your Mac came with Lion already installed, then the F4 key bears a ⊞ logo. Tapping it opens Launchpad, which is described on page 135.

  If you see a ☼ logo instead, then the key opens Dashboard, the archipelago of tiny, single-purpose widgets like Weather, Stocks, and Movies. Chapter 4 describes Dashboard in detail.

- ☼, ☼ (**F5, F6**). Most Mac laptops have light-up *keys,* which is very handy when you're typing in the dark. The key lights are supposed to come on automatically when it's dark, but you can also control the illumination yourself by tapping these keys. (On most other Macs, the F5 and F6 keys aren't assigned to anything. They're free for you to use as you see fit.)

- ◄◄, ►▮▮, and ►► (**F7, F8, F9**). These keys work in the programs where it's handy to have Rewind, Play/Pause, and Fast Forward buttons, like iTunes, QuickTime Player, and DVD Player.

Tip: Tap either ◄◄ or ►► to skip to the previous or next track or chapter. Hold the key down to rewind or fast-forward.

- ◄, ◄◦, ◄)) (**F10, F11, F12**). These three keys control your speaker volume. The ◄ key means Mute; tap it once to cut off the sound completely, and again to restore its previous level. Tap the ◄◦ repeatedly to make the sound level lower and the ◄)) key to make it louder.

  With each tap, you see a big white version of each key's symbol on your screen, your Mac's little nod to let you know it understands your efforts.

- ⏏. This is the Eject key. When there's a CD or DVD in your Mac, tap this key to make the computer spit it out. If your Mac has a DVD *tray* (rather than just a slot), then hold down this button for about a second to make the tray slide open.

- **Home, End.** The Home key jumps to the top of a window, the End key to the bottom. If you're looking at a list of files, the Home and End keys jump to the top or bottom of the list. In iPhoto, they jump to the first or last photo in your collection. In iMovie, the Home key rewinds your movie to the very beginning. In Safari, they send you to the top or bottom of the Web page.

  (In Word, they jump to the beginning or end of the line. But then again, Microsoft has always had its own ways of doing things.)

  On keyboards without a dedicated block of number keys, you get these functions by holding down Fn as you tap the ← and → keys.

- **Pg Up, Pg Down.** These keys scroll up or down by one screenful. The idea is to let you scroll through word-processing documents, Web pages, and lists without having to use the mouse.

  On keyboards without a numeric keypad, you get these functions by pressing Fn plus the ↑ and ↓ keys.

- **Esc.** Esc stands for Escape, and it means "cancel." It's fantastically useful. It closes dialog boxes, closes menus, and exits special modes like Quick Look, slideshows, screen savers, and so on. Get to know it.

- **Delete.** The backspace key.

- **⌘.** This key triggers keyboard shortcuts for menu items.

- **Control.** The Control key triggers shortcut menus, described earlier.

- **Option.** The Option key (labeled Alt on keyboards in some countries) is sort of a "miscellaneous" key. It's the equivalent of the Alt key in Windows.

  It lets you access secret features—you'll find them described all through this book—and type special symbols. For example, you press Option-4 to get the ¢ symbol, and Option-y to get the ¥ (yen) symbol.

- **Help.** In the Finder, Microsoft programs, and a few other places, this key opens up the electronic help screens. But you guessed that.

The Complicated Story of the Function Keys

As the previous section makes clear, the F-keys at the top of modern Mac keyboards come with predefined functions. They control screen brightness, keyboard brightness, speaker volume, music playback, and so on.

But they didn't always. Before Apple gave F9, F10, and F11 to the fast-forward and speaker-volume functions, those keys controlled the Exposé window-management function described in Chapter 4.

So the question is: What if you don't *want* to trigger the hardware features of these keys? What if you want pressing F1 to mean "F1" (which opens the Help window in some programs)? What if you want F9, F10, and F11 to control Exposé's three modes?

For that purpose, you're supposed to press the Fn key. The Fn key (lower left on small keyboards, center block of keys on the big one) switches the function of the function keys. In other words, pressing Fn *and* F10 triggers an Exposé feature, even though the key has a Mute symbol (◄) painted on it.

But here's the thing: What if you use those F-keys for software features (like Cut, Copy, Paste, and Exposé) *more often* than the hardware features (like brightness and volume)?

In that case, you can reverse the logic, so that pressing the F-keys *alone* triggers software functions, and governs brightness and audio only when you're pressing Fn. To do that, choose →System Preferences→Keyboard. Turn on the cryptically worded checkbox "Use F1, F2, etc. as standard function keys."

And that's it. From now on, you press the Fn key to get the functions painted on the keys (◄◄, ►II, ►►, ◄, ◄), ◄))), ☼, ☼, and so on).

Disk Differences

Working with disks is very different on the Mac. Whereas Windows is designed to show the names (letters) and icons for your disk *drives,* the Mac shows you the names and icons of your *disks.* You'll never, ever see an icon for an empty drive, as you do in Windows.

As soon as you insert, say, a flash drive, you see its name and icon appear on the screen. In fact, *every* disk inside, or attached to, a Macintosh is represented on the desktop by an icon (see Figure 1-7). (Your main hard drive's icon may or may not appear in the upper-right corner, depending on your settings in Finder→Preferences.)

Figure 1-7:
You may see all kinds of disks on the Mac OS X desktop (shown here: hard drive, CD, iPod, flash drive)–or none at all, if you've chosen to hide them using the Finder→Preferences command. But chances are pretty good you won't be seeing many floppy disk icons.

If you do decide to hide your disk icons, you can always get to them as you do in Windows: by opening the Computer window (Go→Computer).

If you prefer the Windows look, in which no disk icons appear on the desktop, it's easy enough to recreate it on the Mac; choose Finder→Preferences and turn off the four checkboxes you see there ("Hard disks," "External disks," "CDs, DVDs, and iPods," and "Connected servers.")

Ejecting a disk from the Mac is a little bit different, too, whether it's a CD, DVD, USB flash drive, shared network disk, iDisk, iPod, or external hard drive. You can go about it in any of these ways:

- Hold down the ⏏ key on your keyboard (CDs and DVDs only).
- Right-click the disk's desktop icon. From the shortcut menu that appears, choose "Eject [whatever the disk's name is]."
- Click the disk's icon and then choose File→"Eject [disk's name]" (or press ⌘-E).
- Drag the icon of the disk onto the Trash icon at the end of the Dock. (You'll see its icon turn into a giant ⏏ symbol, the Mac's little acknowledgment that it knows what you're trying to do.)

Where Your Stuff Is

If you open the icon for your main hard drive (Macintosh HD) from the Go→ Computer window, for example, all you'll find in the Macintosh HD window is a set of folders called Applications, Library, and Users.

Most of these folders aren't very useful to you, the Mac's human companion. They're there for Mac OS X's own use (which is why Apple no longer puts the Macintosh HD icon on the desktop of new Macs, as it did for 25 years). Think of your main hard drive window as storage for the operating system itself, which you'll access only for occasional administrative purposes.

In fact, the folders you really do care about boil down to these:

Applications Folder

Applications is Apple's word for programs.

When it comes to managing your programs, the Applications folder (which you can open by choosing Go→Applications) is something like the Program Files folder in Windows—but without the worry. You should feel free to open this folder and double-click things. In fact, that's exactly what you're supposed to do. This is your complete list of programs. (What's on your Dock is more like a Greatest Hits subset.)

Better yet, on the Mac, programs bear their real, plain-English names, like *Microsoft Word,* rather than eight-letter abbreviations, like *WINWORD.EXE.* Most are self-contained in a single icon, too (rather than being composed of hundreds of little support files), which makes copying or deleting them extremely easy.

Home Folder

Your documents, files, and preferences, meanwhile, sit in an important folder called your *Home folder*. Inside (Figure 1-8) are folders that closely resemble the My Documents, My Pictures, and My Music folders on the Windows versions of old. (The "My" prefix disappeared in Windows Vista, but you get the point.)

Mac OS X is rife with shortcuts for opening this all-important folder:

- Choose Go→Home.

- Press Shift-⌘-H.

- Click the ⌂ icon in the Sidebar (page 39). (If you don't see it there, choose Finder→Preferences→Sidebar and turn on the ⌂ checkbox in the list of Places.)

- Click the ⌂ icon on the Dock.

Within your Home folder, you'll find another set of standard Mac folders. (You can tell the Mac considers them holy because they have special logos on their folder icons.) Except as noted, you're free to rename or delete them; Mac OS X creates the following folders solely as a convenience:

- **Desktop.** When you drag an icon out of a folder or disk window and onto your Mac OS X desktop, it may appear to show up on the desktop. But that's just an optical illusion, a visual convenience. In truth, nothing in Mac OS X is really on the desktop. It's actually in this Desktop folder, and mirrored on the desktop area.

  You can entertain yourself for hours by proving this point to yourself. If you drag something out of your Desktop folder, it also disappears from the actual desktop. And vice versa. (You're not allowed to delete or rename this folder.)

- **Documents.** Apple suggests that you keep your actual work files in this folder. Sure enough, whenever you save a new document (when you're working in Keynote or Word, for example), the Save As box proposes storing the new file in this folder.

  Your programs may also create folders of their own here. For example, you may find a Microsoft User Data folder for your Outlook email, a Windows folder for use with Parallels or VMWare Fusion (Chapter 9), and so on.

- **Library.** The main Library folder (the one in your main hard drive window) contains folders for your Mac's system-wide fonts, preferences, help files, and so on.

  You have your *own* Library folder, too. It stores the same kinds of things—but they're *your* fonts, your preferences, and so on. It's generally hidden, although you can get to it by pressing Option as you choose Go→Library.

- **Movies, Music, Pictures.** These folders, of course, are designed to store multimedia files. The various Mac OS X programs that deal with movies, music, and pictures will propose these specialized folders as storage locations. For example, when you plug a digital camera into a Mac, the iPhoto program automatically begins to download the photos on it—and stores them in the Pictures folder. Similarly, iMovie is programmed to look for the Movies folder when saving its files, and iTunes stores its MP3 files in the Music folder.

- **Public.** If you're on a network, or if others use the same Mac when you're not around, this folder can be handy: It's the "Any of you guys can look at these files" folder. Other people on your network, as well as other people who sit down at this machine, are allowed to see whatever you've put in here, even if they don't have your password. (If your Mac isn't on an office network and isn't shared, you can throw this folder away.) More details on sharing and networking on the Mac are in Chapter 15.

- **Sites.** Mac OS X has a built-in Web server: software that turns your Mac into a Web site that people on your network—or, via the Internet, all over the world—can connect to. This Mac OS X feature relies on a program called the Apache Web server, which is so highly regarded in the Unix community that programmers lower their voices when they mention it. This is the folder where you'll put the actual Web pages you want to make available to the Internet at large.

Forcing you to keep all your stuff in a single folder has some major advantages. Most notably, by keeping such tight control over which files go where, Mac OS X keeps itself pure—and very, very stable.

Figure 1-8:
When Steve Jobs unveiled Mac OS X at Macworld Expo in 2000, he said his goal was to oversee the creation of an interface so attractive, "you just want to lick it." Desktop windows, with their juicy, fruit-flavored controls, are a good starting point.

System Folder

This folder is the same idea as the Windows or WINNT folder on a PC, in that it contains hundreds of files that are critical to the functioning of the operating system. These files are so important that moving or renaming them could render the computer useless, as it would in Windows. And although there are thousands of files within, many are hidden for your protection.

For maximum safety and stability, you should ignore Mac OS X's System folder just as thoroughly as you ignored the old Windows folder.

Window Controls

As in Windows, a window on the Mac is framed by an assortment of doodads and gizmos (Figure 1-8). You'll need these to move a window, to close it, to resize it, to scroll it, and so on. But once you get to know the ones on a Macintosh, you're likely to be pleased by the amount of thought those fussy perfectionists at Apple have put into their design.

Here's an overview of the various Mac OS X window-edge gizmos and what they do.

Title Bar

When several windows are open, the darkened window name and colorful upper-left controls tell you which window is *active* (in front). Windows in the background have gray, dimmed lettering and gray upper-left control buttons. As in Windows, the title bar also acts as a *handle* that lets you move the entire window around on the screen.

Figure 1-9:
Right-click, or ⌘-click, a Finder window's title bar to summon the hidden folder hierarchy menu. This trick also works in most other Mac OS X programs. For example, you can ⌘-click a document window's title to find out where the document is actually saved on your hard drive.

Tip: Here's a nifty keyboard shortcut with no Windows equivalent: You can cycle through the different open windows in one program without using the mouse. Just press ⌘-` (that's the tilde key, to the left of the number 1 key). With each press, you bring a different window forward within the current program. It works both in the Finder and in your programs.

After you've opened one folder inside another, the title bar's secret *folder hierarchy menu* is an efficient way to backtrack—to return to the enclosing window. Figure 1-9 reveals everything about the process after this key move: pressing the ⌘ key as you click the name of the window. (You can release the ⌘ key immediately after clicking.)

One more title bar trick: By double-clicking the title bar, you *minimize* the window (see page 37).

The Folder Proxy Icon

Virtually every Macintosh title bar features a small icon next to the window's name (Figure 1-10), representing the open window's actual folder or disk icon. In the Finder, dragging this tiny icon (technically called the *folder proxy icon*) lets you move or copy the folder to a different folder or disk, to the Trash, or into the Dock, without having to close the window first. (When clicking this proxy icon, hold down the mouse button for half a second, or until the icon darkens. Only then are you allowed to drag it.) It's a handy little function with no Windows equivalent.

Figure 1-10:
When you find yourself confronting a Finder window that contains useful stuff, consider dragging its proxy icon to the Dock. That will install its folder or disk icon there for future use. It's not the same as minimizing the window, which puts the window icon into the Dock only temporarily. (Note: Most document windows also offer a proxy-icon feature, but it usually produces only an alias when you drag the proxy to a different folder or disk.)

Tip: In some programs, including Microsoft Word, dragging this proxy icon lets you move the *actual file* to a different disk or folder—without even leaving the program. It's a great way to make a backup of the document you're working on without interrupting your work.

Close Button

As the tip of your cursor crosses the three buttons at the upper-left corner of a window, tiny symbols appear inside them: **✕**, **—**, and **+**. The most important one is the Close button, the red, droplet-like button in the upper-left corner (see Figure 1-8). It closes the window, exactly like the **✕** button at the upper-*right* corner in Windows. Learning to reach for the upper-left corner instead of the upper right will probably confound your muscle memory for the first week of using the Mac.

If you can't break the habit, learn the keyboard shortcut: ⌘-W (for *window*)—an easier keystroke to type than the Windows version (Alt+F4), which for most people is a two-handed operation. If you get into the habit of dismissing windows with that deft flex of your left hand, you'll find it far easier to close several windows in a row, because you won't have to aim for successive Close buttons.

Tip: If, while working on a document, you see a tiny dot in the center of the Close button, Mac OS X is trying to tell you that you haven't yet saved your work. The dot goes away when you save the document.

Minimize Button

Click this yellow drop of gel to minimize any Mac window, sending it shrinking, with a genie-like animated effect, into the right end of the Dock, where it now appears as

Figure 1-11:
Clicking the Mini-mize button sends a window scurrying down to the Dock, collapsing in on itself as though being forced through a tiny, invisible funnel. A little icon appears on the lower-right corner of its minimized image to identify the program it's running in.

an icon. It's exactly like minimizing a window in Windows, except that the window is now represented by a Dock icon rather than a taskbar button (Figure 1-11). To bring the window back to full size, click the newly created Dock icon. See Chapter 2 for more on the Dock.

Tip: You actually have a bigger target than the tiny minimize button. The entire title bar is a giant Minimize button when you double-click anywhere on it. Or just press ⌘-M for Minimize.

Zoom Button

A click on this green geltab (Figure 1-8) makes a desktop window just large enough to show you all the icons inside it. If your monitor isn't big enough to show all the icons in a window, then the zoom box resizes the window to show as many as possible. In

All My Files

There it is, staring you in the face at the top of the Sidebar in every window: an icon called All My Files. What is this, some kind of geeked-out soap opera?

Nope. It's a feature that Apple thought you might find handy: a massive, searchable, sortable list, all in a single window, of every human-useful file on the computer. That is, pictures, movies, music, and documents—no system files, preference files, or other detritus. No matter what folders they're actually in, they appear here in a single window. You can summon it whenever you want, just by clicking the All My Files icon in the Sidebar.

When you first open All My Files, it has your files grouped by type: Contacts, Events & To Dos, Images, PDF Documents, Music, Movies, Presentations, Spreadsheets, Developer (which lists HTML Web-site files and Xcode programming files), and Documents (meaning, "everything else"). In icon view—the factory setting—each class of icons appears in a single scrolling row. Use a two-finger scroll (trackpad) or one-finger slide (Magic Mouse) to move through the horizontal

list. (If you'd rather not have to scroll, click the tiny Show All button that appears at the right end of each row. Now you're seeing *all* the icons of this type; click Show Less to return to the single-row effect.)

You can see how this sorting method might be useful. Suppose, for example, that you're looking for a certain PowerPoint or Keynote presentation, but you can't remember what you called it or where you filed it. Open All My Files, make sure it's arranged by Kind, and presto: You're looking at a list of every presentation file on your Mac. Using Quick Look (page 37), you can breeze through them, inspecting them one at a time, until you find the one you want.

Apple thinks you'll like All My Files as a starting point for standard file-fussing operations so much that All My Files is the window that appears automatically when you choose File→New Finder Window (or press ⌘-N). (Of course, you can change that in Finder→Preferences.)

either case, a second click on the zoom button restores the window to its original size. (The Window→Zoom Window command does the same thing.)

This should sound familiar: It's a lot like the Maximize button at the top right of a Windows window. On the Mac, however, the window rarely springs so big that it fills the *entire* screen, leaving a lot of empty space around the window contents; it grows only enough to show you as much of the contents as possible.

The Finder Sidebar

The Sidebar (Figure 1-12) is the pane at the left side of every Finder window, unless you've hidden it. (It's also at the left side of every Open dialog box and every full-size Save dialog box.) It has as many as three sections, each preceded by a collapsible heading.

Tip: If you point to a heading without clicking, a tiny Hide or Show button appears. Click it to collapse or expand that heading's contents.

Figure 1-12:
The Sidebar makes navigation very quick, because you can jump back and forth between distant corners of your Mac with a single click. In column view, the Sidebar is especially handy because it eliminates all the columns to the left of the one you want, all the way back to the hard-drive level. You've just folded up your desktop! Good things to put here: favorite programs, disks on a network you often connect to, a document you're working on every day, and so on. Folder and disk icons here work just like normal ones. You can drag a document onto a folder icon to file it there, drag a document onto a program's icon to open it with the "wrong" program, and so on.

Here are the headings you'll soon know and love:

- **Favorites.** This primary section of the Sidebar is the place to stash things for easy access. You can stock this list with the icons of disks, files, programs, and folders.

  Each icon is a shortcut. For example, click the Applications icon to view the contents of your Applications folder in the main part of the window. And if you click the icon of a file or a program, it opens.

  Here, too, you'll find the icons for two of Lion's new features: All My Files (see the box on the previous page) and AirDrop, the instant-file-sharing feature described on page 470.

- **Shared.** It took 20 years for an operating system to list all the other computers on the home or small-office network, right there in every window, without any digging, connecting, button clicking, or window opening. But here it is: a complete list of the other computers on your network whose owners have turned on File Sharing, ready for access (see Chapter 14 for details).

- **Devices.** This section lists every storage device connected to, or installed inside, your Mac: hard drives, iPhones, iPads, iPods, CDs, DVDs, memory cards, USB flash drives, and so on. (Your main hard drive doesn't usually appear here, but you can drag it here.) The removable ones—like CDs, DVDs, flash drives, i-gadgets—bear a little gray ⏏ logo, which you can click to eject that disk.

Fine-tuning the Sidebar

The beauty of this parking lot for containers is that it's so easy to set up with your favorite places. For example:

- **Remove an icon** by ⌘-dragging it out of the Sidebar entirely. It vanishes with a puff of smoke (and even a little whoof sound effect). You haven't actually removed anything from your Mac; you've just unhitched its alias from the Sidebar.

Tip: You can't drag items out of the Shared list. Also, if you drag a Devices item out of the list, you'll have to choose Finder→Preferences→Sidebar and then turn on the appropriate checkbox to put it back in.

- **Rearrange** the icons by dragging them up or down in the list. (You're not allowed to rearrange the computers listed in the Shared section, though.)

- **Install a new icon** by dragging it off your desktop (or out of a window) into any spot in the Favorites list of the Sidebar. You can't drag icons into any section of the Sidebar—just Favorites.

Tip: You can also highlight an icon wherever it happens to be and then choose File→Add to Sidebar, or just press ⌘-T.

- **Adjust the width** of the Sidebar by dragging its right edge—either the skinny divider line or the extreme right edge of the vertical scroll bar, if there is one. You "feel" a snap at the point when the line covers up about half of each icon's name.

Any covered-up names sprout ellipses (…) to let you know there's more (as in "Secret Salaries Spreadsh…").

- **Hide the Sidebar** by pressing ⌘-Option-S, which is the shortcut for the View→Hide Sidebar command. Bring it back into view by pressing the same key combination (or by using the Show Sidebar command).

Then again, why would you ever want to hide the Sidebar? It's one of the handiest navigation aids since the invention of the steering wheel. For example:

- **It takes a lot of pressure off the Dock.** Instead of filling up your Dock with folder icons (all of which are frustratingly alike and unlabeled anyway), use the Sidebar to store them. You leave the Dock that much more room for programs and documents.

- **It's better than the Dock.** In some ways, the Sidebar is a lot like the Dock, in that you can stash favorite icons of any sort there. But the Sidebar reveals the names of these icons, and the Dock doesn't until you use the mouse to point there.

- **It makes ejecting easy.** Just click the ⏏ button next to any removable disk to make it pop out. After 25 years, Mac has finally beaten the "It's illogical to eject a disk by dragging it to the Trash!" problem.

- **It makes burning easy.** When you've inserted a blank CD or DVD and loaded it up with stuff you want to copy, click the radioactive-looking Burn button next to its name to begin burning that disc. (Details on burning discs are in Chapter 6.)

- **You can drag onto its folders and disks.** That is, you can drag icons onto Sidebar icons, exactly as though they were the real disks, folders, and programs they represent.

- **It simplifies connecting to networked disks.** Park your other computers' shared folder and disk icons here, as described in Chapter 15, to shave several steps off the usual connecting-via-network ritual.

Window Management

Mac OS X prefers to keep only one Finder window open at a time. That is, if a window called United States is filled with folders for the individual states, double-clicking the New York folder doesn't open a second window. Instead, the New York window replaces the United States window, just as in Windows.

So what if you've now opened the New York folder, and you want to backtrack to the United States folder? In that case, just click the tiny ◄ (Back) button or use one of these alternatives:

- Choose Go→Back.

- Press ⌘-[(left bracket).

- Press ⌘-↑.

None of that helps you, however, if you want to copy a file from one folder into another, or to compare the contents of the two windows. In such cases, you'll probably want to see both windows open at the same time.

You can open a second window using any of these techniques:

- Choose File→New Finder Window (⌘-N).

Tip: The window that appears when you do this is the All My Files window (page 38), but you can change that setting in Finder→Preferences→General.

- ⌘-double-click a disk or folder icon.

- Choose Finder→Preferences→General, and turn on "Always open folders in a new window." Now when you double-click a folder, it always opens into a new window.

Scroll Bars

A scroll bar, of course, is the traditional window-edge slider that lets you move through a document that's too big for the window. Without scroll bars in word processors, for example, you'd never be able to write a letter that's taller than your screen.

In Lion, Apple expects that you'll do most of your scrolling on your trackpad, Magic Mouse top surface, or scroll ball/scroll wheel. You almost never use the antiquated method of dragging the scroll bar's handle manually, with the mouse.

Tip: More reasons nobody uses the mouse to scroll: You can scroll using the keyboard. Your Page Up and Page Down keys let you scroll up and down, one screen at a time, without having to take your hands off the keyboard. The Home and End keys are generally useful for jumping directly to the top or bottom of your document (or Finder window). And if you've bought a mouse that has a scroll wheel on the top, you can use it to scroll windows, without pressing any keys at all.

That's a long-winded way of explaining why, in most Lion programs, the scroll bars are hidden. See Figure 1-13 for details.

NOSTALGIA CORNER

How the Scroll Bar Used to Work

If you are that rare, special individual who still operates the scroll bar by clicking it with the mouse, the old-style controls are still around.

For example: Ordinarily, when you click in the scroll bar track above or below the dark gray handle bar, the window scrolls by one screenful. But another option awaits when you choose →System Preferences→Appearance and turn on "t° that's clicked." Now when you click the scroll-bar track, the Mac considers the entire scroll bar a proportional map

of the document and jumps precisely to the spot you clicked. That is, if you click at the very bottom of the scroll-bar track, you see the very last page.

No matter which scrolling option you choose in the Appearance panel, you can always override your decision on a case-by-case basis by *Option*-clicking the scroll-bar track. In other words, if you've selected the "Jump to the spot that's clicked" option, you can produce a "Jump to the next page" scroll by Option-clicking in the scroll-bar track.

Note: If the missing scroll bars leave you jittery and disoriented, you can bring them back. Open System Preferences→General and then turn on "Show scroll bars: Always."

Figure 1-13:
In Lion, scroll bars don't appear at all while you're working (lower right); you have that much more screen area dedicated to your work. If you begin to scroll by sliding your fingers across the trackpad or Magic Mouse, only the scroll-bar handle appears, so you know where you are (middle). The actual scroll bar—the track itself—doesn't appear until you move your cursor onto it (top left).

Resizable Edges

For the first 28 years of its existence, the Mac offered only one way to make a window bigger or smaller: Drag the ribbed-looking lower-right corner. You couldn't change the shape of a Macintosh window by dragging its *edges,* as you can in Windows.

Now you can. Just move the mouse carefully to the exact top, bottom, left, or right edge; once its shape changes to a double-headed arrow, you can drag to move that window's edge in or out.

Tip: If you press the Option key while dragging, you resize the *opposite edge* simultaneously. For example, if you Option-drag the bottom edge upward, the top edge simultaneously collapses downward.

If you press Shift as you drag, you resize the *entire* window, retaining its proportions.

And if you Shift-Option drag, you resize the window around its center, rather than from its edges.

Path Bar

This little item appears when you choose View→Show Path Bar. It's a tiny map at the bottom of the window that shows where you are in the folder hierarchy. If it says Casey→Pictures→Picnic, well, then, you're looking at the contents of the Picnic folder, which is inside Pictures, which is inside your Home folder (assuming your name is Casey).

Tip: Each tiny folder icon in this display is fully operational. You can double-click it to open it, Control-click (right-click) it to open a shortcut menu, or even drag things into it.

Status Bar

Out of the box, Lion hides yet another information strip at the bottom of a window—the status bar, which tells you how many icons are in the window ("14 items," for example) and the amount of free space remaining on the disk. To make it appear, choose View→Show Status Bar.

Terminology Differences

There are enough other differences between Mac and Windows to fill 15 pages. Indeed, that's what you'll find the end of this book: an alphabetical listing of every familiar Windows feature and where to find its equivalent on the Mac.

As you read both that section of the book and the chapters that precede it, however, you'll discover that some functions are almost identical in Mac OS X and Windows, but have different names. Here's a quick-reference summary:

Windows term	Macintosh term
Control Panel	System Preferences
Gadget	Widget
Drop-down menu	Pop-up menu
Program	Application
Properties	Get Info
Recycle Bin	Trash
Search command	Spotlight
Shortcuts	Aliases
Sidebar	Dashboard
Taskbar	Dock
Tray (notification area)	Menulets
Windows Explorer	Finder
Windows folder	System folder

With that much under your belt, you're well on your way to learning the ways of Mac OS X.

Folders, Dock & Windows

Getting into Mac OS X

When you first turn on the Mac, an Apple logo greets you, soon followed by an animated, rotating "Please wait" gear cursor—and then you're in. No progress bar, no red tape.

Figure 2-1:
Top: On Macs used by multiple people, this is one of the first things you see upon turning on the computer. Click your name. (If the list is long, you may have to swipe the trackpad to find your name—or just type its first few letters.)

Inset: At this point, you're asked to type in your password. Type it, and then click Log In (or press Return). If you type the wrong password, the box vibrates, in effect shaking its little dialog-box head, suggesting that you guess again.

Logging In

What happens next depends on whether you're the Mac's sole proprietor or have to share it with other people in an office, school, or household.

- **If it's your own Mac,** and you've already been through the Mac OS X setup process described in Appendix A, no big deal. You arrive at the Mac OS X desktop.

- **If it's a shared Mac,** you may encounter the login screen shown in Figure 2-1. It's like a portrait gallery, set against a handsome piece of dark gray linen. Click your icon.

  If the Mac asks for your password, type it and then click Log In (or press Return). You arrive at the desktop.

Note: The *very* first time you run Lion, you get a huge "Scrolling in Lion" warning window. It's Apple's attempt to draw your attention to the new, drag-up-to-scroll-up behavior of a fresh Lion installation; clearly, the company correctly anticipated that this reversal of scrolling direction would freak out an awful lot of baffled customers. For details on this whole reversed-scrolling business (and how to turn it off), see page 12.

Chapter 13 offers much more on this business of user accounts and logging in.

The Elements of the Mac OS X Desktop

The desktop is the shimmering, three-dimensional Mac OS X landscape shown in Figure 2-2. On a new Mac, it's covered by a photo of a spectacular spiral galaxy; if you lean forward and squint, you might just be able to make out Apple's headquarters.

Most of the objects on your screen are nothing more than updated versions of elements you already know from Windows. Here's a quick tour.

Disk icons

In Windows, disk icons remain safely caged in the My Computer window; they don't appear on the desktop automatically. The Mac starts out the same way; to find the icons of disks you've inserted, you have to look in the Sidebar (page 39) or the Computer window (Go→Computer).

If you'd like to save yourself that burrowing, though, you can choose Finder→Preferences, click General, and turn on the checkboxes of the disks whose icons you want on the desktop: hard disks, external disks, iPods, and so on.

The Dock

This row of translucent, almost photographic icons is a launcher for the programs, files, folders, and disks you use often—and an indicator to let you know which programs are already open. They rest on what appears to be a polished, highly reflective shelf.

Because the Dock is such a critical component of Mac OS X, Apple has decked it out with enough customization controls to keep you busy experimenting for months. You can change its size, move it to the sides of your screen, hide it entirely, and so on. Page 71 begins a complete discussion of using and understanding the Dock.

The menu

The menu at the top left of the screen houses important Mac-wide commands like Sleep, Restart, and Shut Down. In a sense, it's like the Start menu on a diet: It lists recent programs, system-wide functions, and includes a quick way to jump to System Preferences.

Figure 2-2:
The Mac OS X landscape looks like a more futuristic version of the operating systems you know and love. This is just a starting point, however. You can dress it up with a different background picture, adjust your windows in a million ways, and, of course, fill the Dock with only the programs, disks, folders, and files you need.

Apple menu   Menu bar   Desktop   Menulets

Dock   Trash

The menu bar

The first menu in every program, in boldface, tells you at a glance what program you're in. The commands in this Application menu include About (which tells you what version of the program you're using), Preferences, Quit, and others like Hide Others and Show All (which help you control window clutter, as described on page 161).

The File and Edit menus come next, exactly as in Windows. The last menu is almost always Help. It opens a miniature Web browser that lets you search the online Mac help files for explanatory text.

The Four Window Views

You can view the files and folders in a desktop window in any of four ways: as icons; as a single, tidy list; in a series of neat columns; or as giant document icons that you flip through like they're CDs in a record-store bin (called Cover Flow view). Some of these are sort of like the corresponding views in Windows; others, not so much. Figure 2-3 shows the four different views.

Every window remembers its view settings independently. You might prefer to look over your Applications folder in list view (because it's crammed with files and folders), but you may prefer to view the Pictures folder in icon or Cover Flow view, where the larger icons serve as previews of the photos.

To switch a window from one view to another, just click one of the four corresponding icons in the window's toolbar, as shown in Figure 2-3.

Figure 2-3:
From the top: the same window in icon view, list view, column view, and Cover Flow view. Very full folders are best navigated in list or column views, but you may prefer to view emptier folders in icon or Cover Flow views, because larger icons are easier to preview and click. Remember that in any view (icon, list, column, or Cover Flow), you can highlight an icon by typing the first few letters of its name. In icon, list, or Cover Flow views, you can also press Tab to highlight the next icon (in alphabetical order), or Shift-Tab to highlight the previous one.

You can also switch views by choosing View→as Icons (or View→as Columns, or View→as List, or View→as Cover Flow), which can be handy if you've hidden the toolbar. Or, for less mousing and more hardbodied efficiency, press ⌘-1, ⌘-2, ⌘-3, or ⌘-4 for icon, list, column, or Cover Flow views, respectively.

The following pages cover each of these views in greater detail.

Note: One common thread in the following discussions is the availability of the View Options palette, which lets you set up the sorting, text size, icon size, and other features of each view, either one window at a time or for *all* windows.

Apple gives you a million different ways to open View Options. You can choose View→Show View Options, or press ⌘-J, or choose Show View Options from the ✿ menu at the top of the window.

Icon View

In icon view, every file, folder, and disk is represented by a small picture—an *icon*. This humble image, a visual representation of electronic bits and bytes, is the cornerstone of the entire Macintosh religion. (Maybe that's why it's called an icon.)

Icon Size

You can scale your icons to almost any size without losing any quality or clarity. Just use the size slider at the bottom of any icon-view window, shown in Figure 2-4. (If you don't see it, choose View→Show Status Bar.) Drag it to the right or left to make

Figure 2-4:
Once you make the status bar appear, you can choose an icon size to suit your personality. For picture folders, it can often be very handy to pick a jumbo size, in effect creating a slide-sorter "light table" effect. Icons can be an almost ridiculously large 512 pixels square.

---

that window's icons larger or smaller. (For added fun, make little cartoon sounds with your mouth.)

Tip: Got a laptop? Then you can also make the icons larger or smaller by pinching or spreading two fingers on the trackpad, which may be quicker than fussing with the slider. Details on this feature (and the location of the on/off switch for it) are revealed on page 537.

Icon Previews

The Mac expands the notion of "an icon is a representation of its contents" to an impressive extreme. As you can see in Figure 2-5, each icon actually looks like a miniature of the first page of the *real document*.

THE HALF STEP.pdf   *Kelly Balloons.mov*

Figure 2-5:
You can actually page through PDF and presentation icons, or play movies and sounds, right on their icons. During movie playback, you even get a circular progress bar around the Play/Pause button to let you know where you are in the movie.

Because you can make icons so enormous, you can actually watch movies, or read PDF and text documents, *right on their icons.*

To check out this feature, make the icons at least about an inch tall (64 pixels square). A Play button (▶) appears on any movie or sound file, as shown in Figure 2-5; ❶ and ❷ page buttons appear on a multipage document (like PDF, Pages, or even presentation documents like PowerPoint and Keynote). You can actually page through one of these documents right there on its icon, without having to open the program!

Tip: If you Option-click the little ❶ and ❷ buttons on a PDF, PowerPoint, or Keynote icon preview, you jump to the first or last page or slide in the document.

Icon View Options

Mac OS X offers a number of useful icon-view options, all of which are worth exploring. Start by opening any icon view window, and then choose View→Show View Options (⌘-J).

Always open in icon view

It's easy to set up your preferred look for *all folder windows* on your entire system. With one click on the Use as Defaults button (described below), you can change the window view of 20,000 folders at once—to icon view, list view, or whatever you like.

The "Always open in icon view" option lets you *override* that master setting, just for *this* window.

For example, you might generally prefer a neat list view with large text. But for your Pictures folder, it probably makes more sense to set up icon view, so you can see a thumbnail of each photo without having to open it.

That's the idea here. Open Pictures, change it to icon view, and then turn on "Always open in icon view." Now every folder on your Mac is in list view *except* Pictures.

Note: The wording of this item in the View Options dialog box changes according to the view you're in at the moment. In a list-view window, for example, it says "Always open in list view." In a Cover Flow–view window, it says "Always open in Cover Flow." And so on. But the function is the same: to override the *default* (master) setting.

Figure 2-6:
Drag the "Grid spacing" slider to specify how tightly packed you want your icons to be. At the minimum setting (top), they're so crammed it's almost ridiculous; you can't even see the full names if they're longer than a few characters. At more a spacious setting (bottom), you get a lot more white space.

Browse in icon view

This option makes sure that any folders inside the current window open up into icon view, too, even if you'd previously set them to open into some other view. So if you're looking at your Pictures folder in icon view and you open the Grand Canyon Jaw-Droppers folder inside it, then that folder also will be in icon view.

Arrange By, Sort By

For a discussion of these pop-up menus, see "Arrange By and Sort By" on page 55.

Icon size

It's super easy to make all your icons bigger or smaller; just drag the Icon Size slider in the lower-right corner of the window.

But for the benefit of longtime Mac users who expect to find that slider here, in the View Options window, well, there's an identical slider here.

Grid spacing

You can control how closely spaced icons are in a window. If you want to see a lot of them without making the window bigger, you can pack 'em in like sardines. Figure 2-6 shows all.

Text size

Using this slider, you can adjust the type *size* for your icons. And for people with especially big or small screens—or people with aging retinas—this feature is handy indeed.

Label position

Click either Bottom or Right to indicate where you want an icon's *name* to appear, relative to its *icon.* As shown in Figure 2-7, it lets you create, in effect, a multiple-column list view in a single window.

Show item info

While you've got the View Options palette open, try turning on "Show item info." Suddenly you get a new line of information (in tiny blue type) for certain icons, saving you the effort of opening up the folder or file to find out what's in it. For example:

- **Folders.** The info line lets you know how many icons are inside each without having to open it up. Now you can spot empties at a glance.

- **Graphics files.** Certain other kinds of files may show a helpful info line, too. For example, graphics files display their dimensions in pixels.

- **Sounds and QuickTime movies.** The light-blue bonus line tells you how long the sound or movie takes to play. For example, an MP3 file might say "03' 08"," which means 3 minutes, 8 seconds.

- **.zip files.** On compressed archives like .zip files, you get to see the archive's total size on disk (like "48.9 MB").

You can see some of these effects illustrated in Figure 2-6.

Show icon preview

This option is what makes icons display their contents, as shown in Figure 2-5. If you turn it off, then icons no longer look like miniature versions of themselves. Photos no longer look like tiny photos, PDF and Word documents no longer display their contents, and so on. Everything takes on identical, generic icons (one for all text documents, one for all JPEG photos).

You might prefer this arrangement when, for example, you want to be able to pick out all the PDF files in a window full of mixed document types. The matching icons make it easy.

Arrange by

For a discussion of this pop-up menu, see page 55.

Background

Here's another Mac OS X luxury that other operating systems can only dream about: You can fill the background of any icon view window on your Mac with a certain color—or even a photo.

Figure 2-7:
The View Options dialog box for an icon view window offers the chance to create colored backgrounds for certain windows or even to use photos as window wallpaper (bottom). Using a photo may have a soothing, annoying, or comic effect—like making the icon names completely unreadable. (Note, by the way, how the icons' names have been set to appear beside the icons, rather than underneath, in the lower illustration. You now have all the handy, freely draggable convenience of an icon view, along with the more compact spacing of a list view.)

Color-coordinating or "wallpapering" certain windows is more than just a gimmick. In fact, it can serve as a timesaving psychological cue. Once you've gotten used to the fact that your main Documents folder has a sky-blue background, you can pick it out like a sharpshooter from a screen filled with open windows. Color-coded Finder windows are also especially easy to distinguish at a glance when you've minimized them to the Dock.

Note: Background colors and pictures disappear in list, column, and Cover Flow views.

Once a window is open, choose View→View Options (⌘-J). The bottom of the resulting dialog box offers three choices, whose results are shown in Figure 2-7.

- **White.** This is the standard option (not shown).

- **Color.** When you click this button, you see a small, rectangular button beside the word "Color." Click it to open the Color Picker, which you can use to choose a new background color for the window. (Unless it's April Fool's Day, pick a light color. If you choose a dark one—like black—you won't be able to make out the lettering of the icons' names.)

- **Picture.** If you choose this option, a Select button appears. Click it to open the Select a Picture dialog box, already open to your Library→Desktop Pictures folder. Now choose a graphics file—one of Apple's in the Desktop Pictures folder, or one of your own. When you click Select, you see that Mac OS X has superimposed the window's icons on the photo. As you can see in Figure 2-7, low-contrast or light-background photos work best for legibility.

  Incidentally, the Mac has no idea what sizes and shapes your window may assume in its lifetime. Therefore, Mac OS X makes no attempt to scale down a selected photo to fit neatly into the window. If you have a high-res digital camera, therefore, you see only the upper-left corner of a photo in the window. For better results, use a graphics program to scale the picture down to something smaller than your screen resolution.

Use as Defaults

This harmless-looking button can actually wreak havoc on—or restore order to—your kingdom with a single click. It applies the changes you've just made in the View Options dialog box to *all* windows on your Mac (instead of only the *frontmost* window).

If you set up the frontmost window with a colored background, big icons, small text, and a tight grid, and then you click Use as Defaults, you'll see that look in *every* disk or folder window you open.

You've been warned.

Fortunately, there are two auxiliary controls that can give you a break from all the sameness.

First, you can set up individual windows to be weirdo exceptions to the rule; see "Always open in icon view," page 51.

Second, you can *remove* any departures from the default window view—after a round of disappointing experimentation on a particular window, for example—by using a secret button. To do so, choose View→Show View Options to open the View Options dialog box. Now hold down the Option key. The Use as Defaults button magically changes to say "Restore to Defaults," which means "Abandon all the changes I've foolishly made to the look of this window."

Arrange By and Sort By

You can wield two different kinds of control over the files in a Finder window: arranging and sorting. You can perform all these obsessive reorganizations in any view: icon view, list view, column view, or Cover Flow view.

Figure 2-8:
You can view your Finder-window files in neat little groups, separated by headings.

Top left: the Applications window, in icon view, arranged by Application Category.

Middle: the Documents folder, in list view, arranged by Application (meaning "which program opens this document").

Bottom: the Desktop folder, in column view, arranged by Date Added.

Arranging

In Lion, arranging means, "Putting my files into related clumps, separated by headings that identify them." There are some incredibly useful options here.

For example, you can arrange your documents into Application groups (meaning, which program opens each one); now you can see at a glance which files will open in, say, iTunes when you double-click them. Or you can organize your Pictures folder into Date Added groups, with headings like "Today," "Last 7 Days," and "Earlier."

Figure 2-8 shows a few examples.

Tip: In icon view, the icons under each heading appear in a *single row*, scrolling off endlessly to the right. Use the usual sideways-scrolling gesture to flip through a row. (That is, swipe to the left on a trackpad with two fingers, or with one finger on a Magic Mouse.)

If you're not into gestures, or if you don't have a swipeable input device, click the tiny Show All button at the right end of a row. Now you've turned off that one-row-per-heading thing, and all the icons under that heading appear in the usual rows and columns; scroll down to see them all.

Apple wants to make extra, extra sure you're aware of the Arrange commands. It gives you four different ways to find them:

- **Choose View→Arrange By.** Choose one of the criteria from the submenu. Your options are Name (alphabetically); Kind (type of file, like Images, Movies, and Documents); Application (which program opens which documents); Date (Last Opened, Added [to the window], Modified, or Created); Size; or Label (Finder label colors, described on page 98). Marvel as the Finder puts your files into tidy categorized groups.

Note: When you're looking at the Applications folder, you get a special choice: Application Category. It clumps your programs by what they do: Productivity, Social Networking, Music, Video, Board Games, Entertainment, Utilities, Reference, Photography, and so on. Pretty cool, actually.

- **Choose from the** ⊞▾ **icon.** This icon appears in the toolbar of every Finder window. It contains the same options listed in the previous paragraph.

- **Right-click an empty spot in an icon-view window; choose from the Arrange By shortcut menu.** Yep, it's those same commands yet again.

- **In the View Options palette (seen in Figure 2-6), use the Arrange By pop-up menu.** Yes, it's a fourth place to find the same six options.

Note: In each case, you can choose None to turn off the grouping altogether.

Remember, arranging (clumping) is not sorting. You can, in fact, sort the icons differently within each arranged group; read on.

Sorting

Sorting means just what it says: You can sort your files alphabetically (by Name), chronologically (by Date), in order of hugeness (by Size), and so on.

You can sort a window whether or not you've also arranged (grouped) it. You can even sort by different criteria. For example, you might have the programs in your Applications folder arranged by Application Category, but sorted alphabetically within each category.

Once again, Apple gives you four ways to sort:

- **While pressing the Option key, choose View→Sort By.** (Pressing Option turns the Arrange By submenu into the Sort By submenu.) Choose one of the criteria: Name, Size, and so on.

- **While pressing the Option key, click the ✿ icon.** Once again, the Option key turns the Arrange By options into Sort By options.

- **Right-click an empty spot in an icon-view window. Press the Option key.** And again, Option turns the Arrange By options into Sort By options.

- **In the View Options palette, use the Sort By pop-up menu.** Hey, guess what? You didn't have to press the Option key this time.

Tip: In icon view, you get an additional option: Snap to Grid. It means, "Let me drag these icons into any sequence I want, using the trackpad or mouse." When you release each drag, the icon jumps into the nearest position on the underlying spacing grid (unless you press the ⌘ key, which gives you full manual control of the icon's position).

This option appears only if Arrange By is set to None. After all: If you've asked the Mac to arrange your icons into groups, then you've relinquished control of their grid spacing.

Free dragging—and grid spacing

Whenever you've applied an Arrange or a Sort to an icon view, the icons remain rooted to an invisible underlying grid. You can't budge them.

Tip: You can, however, control how tight or loose that grid is, using the "Grid spacing" slider described above.

But there are two situations when you're allowed to drag icons freely into any order you want:

- **Icons never snap to the grid.** If both Arrange By and Sort By are set to None, then you can go nuts, freely dragging icons into sloppy, off-the-grid positions.

  If, later, you become overwhelmed by shame at your untidiness, you can choose View→Clean Up (if nothing is selected) or View→Clean Up Selection (if some icons are highlighted). Now all icons in the window, or those you've selected, jump to the closest positions on the invisible underlying grid.

(There's even a Clean Up By submenu in the View menu and the shortcut menu. These commands don't just put icons back onto the closest grid positions; they put the icons into their proper sorted positions among the other icons—by name, size, date, and so on.)

Tip: If you press Option, then the Mac swaps the wording of the command. Clean Up changes to Clean Up Selection, and vice versa.

• **Icons always snap to the grid.** If Arrange By is set to None but Sort By is set to Snap to Grid, then you can drag icons into any order you like (that is, not in any particular sorted order)—but they'll snap to the grid when you let go of the mouse button.

Tip: If you press the ⌘ key as you release the drag, you can reverse the snapping logic. That is, the icons *will* snap to the grid if Sort By is set to None, but you can drag them freely if it's set to Snap to Grid. (Don't press the key until after you've begun to drag.)

List View

In windows that contain a lot of icons, list view is a powerful weapon in the battle against chaos. It shows you a tidy table of your files' names, dates, sizes, and so on. Very faint alternating blue and white background stripes help you read across the columns.

You get to decide how wide your columns should be, which of them should appear, and in what order (except that Name is always the first column). Here's how to master these columns.

Sorting the List

Most of the world's list-view fans like their files listed alphabetically. It's occasionally useful, however, to view the newest files first, largest first, or whatever.

When a desktop window displays its icons in a list view, a convenient new strip of column headings appears (Figure 2-9). These column headings aren't just signposts; they're buttons, too. Click Name for alphabetical order, Date Modified to view newest first, Size to view largest files at the top, and so on.

It's especially important to note the tiny ▼ or ▲ that appears in the column you've most recently clicked. It shows you which way the list is being sorted. When it's ▲, then the oldest files, smallest files, or files beginning with numbers (or the letter A) appear at the top of the list, depending on which sorting criterion you have selected.

Tip: It may help you to remember that when the smallest portion of the triangle is at the top (▲), the smallest files are listed first when viewed in size order.

To reverse the sorting order, click the column heading a second time. Now the ▼ shows you that the newest files, largest files, or files beginning with the letter Z appear at the top of the list.

Figure 2-9:
You control the sorting order of a list view by clicking the column headings (top). Click a second time to reverse the sorting order (bottom). You'll find the ▲ or ▼ triangles—indicating the identical information—in email programs, iTunes, and anywhere else where reversing the sorting order of a list can be useful.

Name	Size ▼	Date Modified
Final Cut Pro	2.1 GB	6/21/11
Microsoft Office 2011	1.3 GB	9/20/11
iWork '09	766.1 MB	3/31/11
Adobe Photoshop CS5	742.4 MB	9/2/10
Adobe Illustrator CS4	682.7 MB	11/30/09
Adobe InDesign CS4	506 MB	8/23/11
FileMaker Pro 10	484.2 MB	11/20/09
iMovie	416.7 MB	7/22/11
Utilities	376.5 MB	9/12/11
iWeb	304.6 MB	7/22/11

95 items, 389.06 GB available

Name	Size ▲	Date Modified
Dashboard	168 KB	6/20/11
Logorrhea	293 KB	3/4/06
Time Machine	375 KB	6/20/11
Mission Control	398 KB	6/20/11
MoviesHunt Pro	687 KB	6/28/11
Launchpad	1.1 MB	6/20/11
Flip4Mac	1.2 MB	8/14/11
System Preferences	1.6 MB	6/23/11
Adobe Download Assistant	1.9 MB	6/8/11

95 items, 389.06 GB available

Arranging the List

You can arrange your list view into groups by name, date, kind, and so on, with tidy headings that help you make sense of it all. See "Arranging" on page 55.

Flippy Triangles

One of the Mac's most attractive features is the tiny triangle that appears to the left of a folder's name in a list view. In its official documents, Apple calls these buttons *disclosure triangles;* internally, the programmers call them *flippy triangles.*

Either way, these triangles are very useful: When you click one, the list view turns into an outline, which displays the contents of the folder in an indented list, as shown in Figure 2-10. Click the triangle again to collapse the folder listing. You're saved the trouble and clutter of opening a new window just to view the folder's contents.

By selectively clicking flippy triangles, you can, in effect, peer inside two or more folders simultaneously, all within a single list view window. You can move files around by dragging them onto the tiny folder icons.

Figure 2-10:
Click a "flippy triangle" (left) to see the list of the folders and files inside that folder (right). Or press the equivalent keystrokes: → (to open) and ← (to close).

Your Choice of Columns

Choose View→Show View Options. In the dialog box that appears, you're offered on/off checkboxes for the different columns of information Mac OS X can show you: Date Modified, Size, Kind, Comments, and so on.

- **Date Modified.** This date-and-time stamp indicates when a document was last saved. Its accuracy, of course, depends on the accuracy of your Mac's built-in clock.

Note: Many an up-to-date file has been lost because someone spotted a very old date on a folder and assumed that the files inside were equally old. That's because the modification date shown for a folder doesn't reflect the age of its contents. Instead, the date on a folder indicates only when items were last *moved into or out of* that folder. The actual files inside may be much older, or much more recent.

- **Date Created.** This date-and-time stamp shows when a document was *first* saved.

- **Date Added.** This option shows when a file was added to this folder or window.

- **Size.** With a glance, you can tell from this column how much disk space each of your files and folders is taking up in kilobytes, megabytes, gigabytes, or terabytes— whichever the Mac thinks you'll find most helpful.

Tip: For disks and folders, you see only a dash—at first. You can, however, instruct the Mac to reveal their sizes, as described on the facing page.

- **Kind.** In this column, you can read what kind of file each icon represents. You may see, for example, Folder, JPEG Image, Application, and so on.

- **Version.** This column displays the version numbers of your programs. For folders and documents, you just see a dash.

- **Comments.** This rarely seen column can actually be among the most useful. Suppose you're a person who uses the Comments feature (select an icon, choose File→Get Info, and type notes about that item into the Spotlight Comments box). This column displays the first line of those comments about each icon, which comes in handy when tracking multiple versions of your documents.

- **Label.** Labels are colors and identifying phrases that you can slap onto icons, wherever they appear, to help you categorize and group them. For details, see page 98.

Even with this column turned off, you can still see an icon's color, of course. But only by turning on this column do you get to see the text phrase you've associated with each label.

FREQUENTLY ASKED QUESTION

Calculate All Sizes

When I sort my list view by size, I see only dashes for folder sizes. What am I doing wrong?

Nothing at all; that's normal. When viewing a Finder window, you see a Size statistic for each file. For folders and disks, however, you're shown only an uninformative dash.

Most Mac fans study this anomaly only momentarily, scratch their chins, and then get back to their work. Former Windows users don't even scratch their chins; Windows PCs *never* show folder-size or disk-size information in list views.

Here's what's going on: It can take a computer a long time to add up the sizes of all the files inside a folder. Your System→ Library folder alone, for example, contains over 1,500 files. Instead of making you wait while the Mac does all this addition, Mac OS X simply shows you a dash in the Size column for a folder.

On occasion, however, you really do want to see how big your folders are. In such cases, choose View→Show View Options and turn on "Calculate all sizes." You see the folder sizes slowly begin to pop onto the screen, from the top of the window down, as the Mac crunches the numbers of the files within.

In fact, you can even turn on the "Calculate all sizes" option *globally*—that is, for all windows. In the Mac operating systems of days gone by, this act would have caused a massive slowdown of the entire computer. But the Mac OS X is multithreaded—that is, it has the opposite of a one-track mind. It's perfectly capable of devoting all its attention to calculating your folder sizes *and* all its attention to whatever work you're doing in the foreground.

Now consider this anomaly: Suppose you've opted to sort a particular window by folder size—in other words, you've clicked the word "Size" at the top of the column. Turning on "Calculate all sizes" bewilders the unprepared, as folders begin leaping out of order, forcing the list to rearrange itself a couple of times per second.

What's happening, of course, is that all folders begin at the bottom of the list, showing only dashes in the Size column. Then, as the Mac computes the size of your folders' contents, they jump into their correct sorted order at what may seem to be random intervals.

Other View Options

The View Options for a list view include several other useful settings; choose View→Show View Options or press ⌘-J.

- **Always open in list view.** Turn on this option to override your system-wide preference setting for all windows. See "Always open in icon view" on page 51 for details.

- **Browse in list view.** Ensures that any folder inside this one will also open up in list view, even if its regularly scheduled view is something else.

- **Icon size.** These two buttons offer you a choice of icon sizes for the current window: either standard or tiny. Unlike icon view, list view doesn't give you a size slider. Fortunately, even the tiny icons aren't so small that they show up blank. You still get a general idea of what they're supposed to look like.

- **Text size.** You can change the type size for your icon labels, either globally or one window at a time.

- **Show columns.** Turn on the columns you'd like to appear in the current window's list view, as described in the previous section.

- **Use relative dates.** In a list view, the Date Modified, Date Added, and Date Created columns generally display information in a format like this: "Tuesday, March 6, 2012." (The Mac uses shorter date formats as the column gets narrower.) But when the "Use relative dates" option is turned on, the Mac substitutes the words "Yesterday" or "Today" where appropriate, making recent files easier to spot.

- **Calculate all sizes.** See the box on the previous page.

- **Show icon preview.** Exactly as in icon view, this option turns the icons of graphics files into miniatures of the photos or images within.

- **Use as Defaults.** Click to make your changes in the View Options box apply to all windows on your Mac. (Option-click this button to restore a wayward window back to your defaults.)

Rearranging Columns

You're stuck with the Name column at the far left of a window. However, you can rearrange the other columns just by dragging their gray column headers horizontally. If the Mac thinks you intend to drop a column to, say, the left of the column it overlaps, you'll actually see an animated movement—indicating a column reshuffling—even before you release the mouse button.

Adjusting Column Widths

If you place your cursor carefully on the dividing line between two column headings, you'll find that you can drag the divider line horizontally. Doing so makes the column to the left of your cursor wider or narrower.

What's delightful about this activity is watching Mac OS X scramble to rewrite its information to fit the space you give it. For example, as you make the Date Modified (or Created) column narrower, "Friday, March 9, 2012, 2:22 PM" shrinks first to "Fri, Mar 9, 2012, 2:22 PM," then to "3/9/12, 2:22 PM," and finally to a terse "3/9/12."

If you make a column too narrow, Mac OS X shortens the file names by removing text from the middle. An ellipsis (…) appears to show you where the missing text would have appeared. (Apple reasoned that truncating the ends of file names, as certain other operating systems do, would hide useful information, like the numbers at the end of "Letter to Marge 1," "Letter to Marge 2," and so on. It would also hide the three-letter extensions, such as Thesis.doc, that may appear on file names in Mac OS X.)

For example, suppose you've named a Word document "Justin Bieber—A Major Force for Humanization and Cure for Depression, Acne, and Migraine Headache." (Yes, file names can really be that long.) If the Name column is too narrow, you might see only "Justin Bieber—A Major…Migraine Headache."

Tip: You don't have to make the column mega-wide just to read the full text of a file whose name has been shortened. Just point to the icon's name without clicking. After a moment, a yellow, floating balloon appears—something like a tooltip in Microsoft programs—to provide the full name.

In fact, now you can move your mouse up or down a list over truncated file names and their tooltip balloons appear instantaneously. (This trick works in list, column, or Cover Flow views—and in Save and Open dialog boxes, for that matter.)

Column View

The goal of column view is simple: to let you burrow down through nested folders without leaving a trail of messy, overlapping windows in your wake.

Figure 2-11:
If the rightmost folder contains pictures, sounds, Office documents, or movies, you can look at them or play them, right there in the Finder. You can drag this jumbo preview icon anywhere—into another folder or to the Trash, for example.

The solution is shown in Figure 2-11. It's a list view that's divided into several vertical panes. The first pane (not counting the Sidebar) shows whatever disk or folder you first opened.

When you click a disk or folder in this list (once), the second pane shows a list of everything in it. Each time you click a folder in one pane, the pane to its right shows what's inside. The other panes slide to the left, sometimes out of view. (Use the horizontal scroll bar to bring them back.) You can keep clicking until you're actually looking at the file icons inside the most deeply nested folder.

If you discover that your hunt for a particular file has taken you down a blind alley, it's not a big deal to backtrack, since the trail of folders you've followed to get here is still sitting before you on the screen. As soon as you click a different folder in one of the earlier panes, the panes to its right suddenly change, so that you can burrow down a different rabbit hole.

Furthermore, the Sidebar is always at the ready to help you jump to a new track; just click any disk or folder icon there to select a new first-column listing for column view.

The beauty of column view is, first of all, that it keeps your screen tidy. It effectively shows you several simultaneous folder levels, but contains them within a single window. With a quick ⌘-W, you can close the entire window, panes and all. Second, column view provides an excellent sense of where you are. Because your trail is visible at all times, it's much harder to get lost—wondering what folder you're in and how you got there—than in any other window view.

Note: You can change how column view is sorted; it doesn't have to be alphabetical. Press ⌘-J to open the View Options dialog box, and then choose the sorting criterion you want from the "Arrange by" pop-up menu (like Size, Date Created, or Label).

Manipulating the Columns

The number of columns you can see without scrolling depends on the width of the window. That's not to say, however, that you're limited to four columns (or whatever fits on your monitor). You can make the columns wider or narrower—either individually or all at once—to suit the situation, according to this scheme:

- **To make a single column wider or narrower,** drag the fine vertical line that separates it from the column to its right.

- **To make *all* the columns wider or narrower simultaneously,** hold down the Option key as you drag one of the divider lines.

- **To make a column precisely as wide as necessary** to reveal all the names of its contents, double-click the divider line on its right side.

- **To make *all* columns as wide as required**—when you absolutely, positively don't want any names truncated—Option-double-click a column's right-side divider line.

Tip: If you're having trouble remembering all of those key and click combinations, you're not alone. Fortunately, if you right-click the divider line at the right side of a column, you get a shortcut menu that offers these commands: Right Size This Column (make it exactly as wide as necessary), Right Size All Columns Individually (make *every* column exactly as wide as necessary), and Right Size All Columns Equally (make all columns *the same width,* based on whatever width is necessary to see all the names in the *narrowest* one).

Grouping the Column Contents

Yes, the Arrange commands are available in column view, too; you can add those gray category headings to the clumps of files in each window. And, once again, you can also use the Sort By commands to change the sequence of files within each grouping. It all works exactly as described starting on page 55.

View Options

Just as in icon and list views, you can choose View→Show View Options to open a dialog box—a spartan one, in this case—offering additional control over your column views.

- **Always open in column view.** Once again, this option lets you override your system-wide preference setting for all windows. See "Always open in icon view" on page 51 for details.

- **Browse in column view.** Ensures that any folder inside this one will open up in column view when double-clicked.

- **Arrange By, Sort By.** You can put column-view icons into arranged groups—and sort them within those groups—just as described starting on page 55.

- **Text size.** Whatever point size you choose here affects the type used for icons in all column views.

- **Show icons.** For maximum speed, turn off this option. Now you see only file names—not the tiny icons next to them—in all column views. Weird!

- **Show icon preview.** Turn off this option if you don't want the tiny icons in column view to display their actual contents—photos showing their images, Word and PDF documents showing their first pages, and so on. You get generic, identical icons for each file type (text, photo, or whatever).

- **Show preview column.** The far-right Preview column can be handy when you're browsing graphics, sounds, or movie files. Feel free to enlarge this final column when you want a better view of the picture or movie; you can make it really big.

  The rest of the time, though, the Preview column can get in the way, slightly slowing down the works and pushing other, more useful columns off to the left side of the window. If you turn off this checkbox, the Preview column doesn't appear.

Tip: No matter what view you're in, remember this: If you ever start dragging an icon and then change your mind, just press the Esc key or ⌘-period, even while the mouse button is still down. The icon flies back to its precise starting place. Or, if you've already dragged something to a new window and now you regret it, press ⌘-Z (for Undo). Too bad real life doesn't have a similar feature.

Cover Flow View

As you can sort of see from Figure 2-13, Cover Flow is a visual display that Apple stole from its own iTunes software, where Cover Flow simulates the flipping "pages" of a jukebox, or the CDs in a record-store bin. There, you can flip through your music collection, marveling as the CD covers flip over in 3-D space while you browse.

Figure 2-13:
The top half of a Cover Flow window is an interactive, scrolling "record bin" full of your own stuff. It's especially useful for photos, PDF files, Office documents, and text documents. When a PDF or presentation document comes up in this virtual data jukebox, you can click the arrow buttons to page through it; for a movie, click the little ▶ button to play the video, right in place.

The idea is the same in Mac OS X, except that now it's not CD covers you're flipping—it's gigantic file and folder icons.

To fire up Cover Flow, open a window. Then click the ▐■▌ button highlighted in Figure 2-13, or choose View→as Cover Flow, or press ⌘-4.

Now the window splits. On the bottom: a traditional list view, complete with sortable columns, exactly as described above.

On the top: the gleaming, reflective, black Cover Flow display. Your primary interest here is the scroll bar. As you drag it left or right, you see your own files and folders float by and flip in 3-D space. Fun for the whole family!

The effect is spectacular, sure. It's probably not something you'd want to set up for every folder, though, because browsing is a pretty inefficient way to find something. But in folders containing photos or movies (that aren't filled with hundreds of files), Cover Flow can be a handy and satisfying way to browse.

And now, notes on Cover Flow:

- **You can adjust the size of Cover Flow display** (relative to the list-view half) by dragging up or down on the grip strip area just beneath the Cover Flow scroll bar.

- **Multipage PDF documents are special.** When you point to one, circled arrow buttons appear on the jumbo icon. You can click them to page through the document—without even opening it for real (Figure 2-13).

- **QuickTime movies are special, too.** When you point to one's jumbo display, a ▶ button appears. Click it to play the movie, right there in the Cover Flow window.

- **You can navigate with the keyboard, too.** Any icon that's highlighted in the list view (bottom half of the window) is also front and center in the Cover Flow view. Therefore, you can use all the usual list-view shortcuts to navigate both at once. Use the up or down arrow keys, type the first few letters of an icon's name, press Tab or Shift-Tab to highlight the next or previous icon alphabetically, and so on.

- **Cover Flow shows whatever the list view shows.** If you expand a flippy triangle to reveal an indented list of what's in a folder, the contents of that folder now become part of the Cover Flow.

- **The previews are actual icons.** When you're looking at a Cover Flow minidocument, you can drag it with your mouse—you've got the world's biggest target—anywhere you'd like to drag it: another folder, the Trash, whatever.

Quick Look

As the preceding several thousand pages make clear, there are lots of ways to view and manage the seething mass of files and folders on a typical hard drive. Some of them actually let you see what's in a document without having to open it—the Preview column in column view, the giant icons in Cover Flow, and so on.

Quick Look, a star feature of Mac OS X, takes this idea to another level. It lets you open and browse a document nearly at full size—without switching window views or opening any new programs. You highlight an icon (or several), and then press the space bar (or click the ◉ button at the top of the window, or choose File→Quick Look).

The Quick Look window now opens, showing a nearly full-size preview of the document (Figure 2-14). Rather nice, eh?

The idea here is that you can check out a document without having to wait for it to open in the traditional way. For example, you can find out what's in a Word, Excel, or PowerPoint document without actually having to *open* Word, Excel, or PowerPoint, which saves you about 45 minutes.

Figure 2-14:
Once the Quick Look window is open, you can play a file (movies and sounds), study it in more detail (most kinds of graphics files), or even read it (PDF, Word, and Excel documents). You can also click another icon, and another, and another, without ever closing the preview; the contents of the window simply change to reflect whatever you've just clicked. Supertip: Quick Look even works on icons in the Trash, so you can figure out what something is before you nuke it forever.

What Quick Look Knows

You might wonder: How, exactly, is Quick Look able to display the contents of a document without opening it? Wouldn't it have to somehow understand the internal file format of that document type?

Exactly. And that's why Quick Look doesn't recognize *all* documents. If you try to preview, for example, a Final Cut Pro video project, a sheet-music file, a .zip archive, or a database file, all you'll see is a 6-inch-tall version of its generic icon. You won't see what's inside.

Over time, people will write plug-ins for those nonrecognized programs. Already, plug-ins that let you see what's inside folders and .zip files await at *www.qlplugins.com.* In the meantime, here's what Quick Look recognizes right out of the box:

- **Graphics files and photos.** This is where Quick Look can really shine, because it's often useful to get a quick look at a photo without having to haul iPhoto or Photoshop out of bed. Quick Look recognizes all common graphics formats, including TIFF, JPEG, GIF, PNG, Raw, and Photoshop documents (except really huge Photoshop files).

- **PDF and text files.** Using the scroll bar, you can page through multipage documents, right there in the Quick Look window.

- **Audio and movie files.** These begin to play instantly when you open them into the Quick Look window. Most popular formats are recognized (MP3, AIFF, AAC, MPEG-4, H.264, and so on). A scroll bar appears so that you can jump around in the movie or song.

- **Pages, Numbers, Keynote, and TextEdit documents.** Naturally, since these are Apple programs, Quick Look understands the document formats.

- **Microsoft Word, Excel, and PowerPoint documents.** Because these formats are so common, Mac OS X comes with a Quick Look plug-in to recognize them. Move through the pages using the vertical scroll bar; switch to a different Excel spreadsheet page using the Sheet tabs at the bottom.

- **Fonts.** Totally cool. When you open a font file in Quick Look, you get a crystal-clear, huge sampler that shows every letter of the alphabet in that typeface.

- **vCards.** A *vCard* is an address-book entry that people can send one another by email to save time in updating their Rolodexes. When you drag a name out of Apple's or Microsoft's address books and onto the desktop, for example, it turns into a vCard document. In Quick Look, the vCard opens up as a handsomely formatted index card that displays all the person's contact information.

- **HTML (Web pages).** If you've saved some Web pages to your hard drive, here's a great way to inspect them without firing up your Web browser.

In Lion, Quick Look has started seeping into other programs—not just the Finder. For example, you can view a preview of any of the following:

- **A link in a Mail message.** In Mail, there's a tiny ▾ next to each Web link. Click it to view the actual Web page it leads to, right there in a pop-up bubble!

- **An address in Mail or Safari.** If you ever see a street address in an email message or on a Web page, click the tiny ▾ next to it. You're offered the chance to add this person to your Address Book, or to see a map of that address in Safari, courtesy of Google Maps.

- **An address in Address Book.** In the Address Book program, click the label for an address (like "Work" or "Home"); from the shortcut menu, choose Map This Address. You get to see an aerial photo of that spot in Safari, thanks to Google.

- **Anything in the Spotlight menu.** When you use the Spotlight search feature described in Chapter 3, point to anything in the results menu without clicking. In a moment, a big Quick Look bubble pops out to the left, showing what's actually in that document or file.

- **Anything in Mission Control, or a Dock menu.** You can also tap the space bar to get a Quick Look preview of anything in the Mission Control view (page 141) or the stack, list, or grid of a Dock folder (page 73).

To exit the Quick Look display, press the space bar again.

Fun with Quick Look

Here are some stunts that make Quick Look even more interesting:

- **Full screen.** When you click the Full Screen button (⊡), the Quick Look window expands to fill your screen. Keep this trick in mind when you're trying to read Word, Excel, or PDF documents, since the text is usually too small to read otherwise. (When you're finished with the closeup, click the Full Screen button again to restore the original Quick Look window, or the ⊗ button to exit Quick Look altogether.)

Tip: How's this for an undocumented shortcut?

If you press Option-space bar, or Option-click the 👁 icon in any Finder window, you go straight into Full Screen mode without having to open the smaller Quick Look window first. Kewl.

(OK, this is actually part of the slideshow feature described on the next page, but it's also good for super-enlarging a single icon.)

- **Open with [Program Name].** This button shows up at the top-right corner of your Quick Look window. It might say, for example, "Open with Preview."

  Handy, really. It says: "Oh, so you've been Quick-Looking to find a particular document, and this is the one you wanted? Click me to jump directly into the program that opens it, so you can get to work reading or editing. I've just saved you having to close the window and double-click the icon."

Tip: Actually, you have a much bigger target than the "Open with" button in the corner. You can double-click *anywhere in the Quick Look window* to open the document (in whatever program is named on the "Open with" button).

  Better yet: If you click and hold your cursor on that "Open with" button, you get a secret pop-up menu of other programs that could open the file you're looking at.

- **Keep it going.** Once you've opened Quick Look for one icon, you don't have to close it before inspecting another icon. Just keep clicking different icons (or pressing the arrow keys to walk through them); the Quick Look window changes instantly with each click to reflect the new document.

The Quick Look Slideshow

Mac OS X is supposed to be all about graphics and other visual delights. No wonder, then, that it offers a built-in, full-screen slideshow feature.

It works like this: Highlight a bunch of icons, and then open Quick Look. Click the ⬓ (Full Screen) button in the top-right corner. The screen goes black, and the documents begin their slideshow. Each image appears on the screen for about 3 seconds before the next one appears. (Press the Esc key or ⌘-period to end the show.) It plays all documents it recognizes, not just graphics.

It's a useful feature when you've just downloaded or imported a bunch of photos or Office documents and want a quick look through them. Use the control bar shown at the bottom to manage the playback.

Note: This same slideshow mechanism is available for graphics in Preview and Mail; Preview even offers crossfades between pictures.

The Dock

For years, most operating systems maintained two different lists of programs. One listed *unopened* programs until you needed them, like the Start menu in Windows. The other kept track of which programs were *open* at the moment for easy switching, like the Windows taskbar.

In Mac OS X, Apple combined both functions into a single strip of icons called the *Dock*. (And soon thereafter, Microsoft adopted the idea for Windows 7. But that's another book.)

Setting Up the Dock

Apple starts the Dock off with a few icons it thinks you'll enjoy: Launchpad, iTunes, the Safari Web browser, and so on. But using your Mac without putting your own favorite icons in the Dock is like buying an expensive suit and turning down the free alteration service. At the first opportunity, you should make the Dock your own.

The concept of the Dock is simple: Any icon you drag onto it (Figure 2-15) is installed there as a button.

A single click, not a double-click, opens the corresponding icon. In other words, the Dock is an ideal parking lot for the icons of disks, folders, documents, programs, and Internet bookmarks that you access frequently.

Here are a few aspects of the Dock that may throw you at first:

- **It has two sides.** See the whitish dotted line running down the Dock? That's the divider (Figure 2-15). Everything on the left side is an application—a program. Everything else goes on the right side: files, documents, folders, disks, and minimized windows.

It's important to understand this division. If you try to drag an application to the right of the line, for example, Mac OS X teasingly refuses to accept it. (Even aliases observe that distinction. Aliases of applications can go only on the left side, and vice versa.)

- **Its icon names are hidden.** To see the name of a Dock icon, point to it without clicking. You'll see the name appear above the icon.

Divider

← Programs side ┆ Everything else →

Open programs

Minimized document windows

Figure 2-15:
To add an icon to the Dock, simply drag it there. You haven't moved the original file; when you release the mouse, it remains where it was. You've just installed a pointer—like a Macintosh alias or a Windows shortcut.

When you're trying to find a certain icon in the Dock, run your cursor slowly across the icons without clicking; the icon labels appear as you go. You can often identify a document just by looking at its icon.

- **Folders and disks sprout lists of their contents.** If you click a folder or disk icon in the Dock, a list of its contents sprouts from the icon. It's like X-ray vision without the awkward moral consequences. See the facing page for details.

- **Programs appear there unsolicited.** Nobody but you (and Apple) can put icons on the right side of the Dock. But program icons appear on the left side of the Dock automatically whenever you open a program, even one that's not listed in the Dock. Its icon remains there for as long as it's running.

Organizing and Removing Dock Icons

You can move the tiles of the Dock around by dragging them horizontally. As you drag an icon, the other icons scoot aside to make room. When you're satisfied with its new position, drop the icon you've just dragged.

To remove a Dock icon, just drag it away. (You can't remove the icons of the Finder, the Trash, the Dock icon of an open program, or any minimized document window.) Once your cursor has cleared the Dock, release the mouse button. The icon disappears, and the other Dock icons slide together to close the gap.

Pop-up Dock Folders ("Stacks")

When you click a disk or folder icon on the Dock, you'll witness the effect shown in Figure 2-16. In essence, Mac OS X is fanning out the folder's contents so you can see all of them. If it could talk, it would be saying, "Pick a card, any card."

Tip: You can change how the icons in a particular stack are sorted: alphabetically, chronologically, or whatever. Use the "Sort by" section of the shortcut menu (Figure 2-16, top left).

Pop-up folders are a great idea, because they save you time and clicking. Click a folder to see what's in it; click the icon you want inside; and you're off and running, without having had to open, manage, and close a window.

Fan vs. grid vs. list

When you click a disk or folder icon on the Dock, you see its contents, arrayed in your choice of three displays:

- **Fan.** The fan is a single, gently curved column of icons that pops out of the disk or folder icon. It's ideal for folders that contain very few icons, because there's room for only a handful of items in a fan (the exact number depends on your screen size). After the first few, you see only a "31 more in Finder" button, which you can click to see everything in that folder—but now you've *wasted* time, not saved it.

Note: When your Dock is positioned on a side of the screen instead of the bottom, the fan option isn't available.

- **Grid.** If you've set a folder to open as a grid, you get to see the icons in a big rectangular window. File names often get abbreviated because there's not enough horizontal room, but you get to see many more icons this way. Actually, thanks to the scroll bar (or the type-selecting trick described on page 91), you get to see *all* the icons this way.

- **List.** If you don't care about seeing the actual icons, you can also opt for a simple list of the folder's contents, like a pop-up menu. After all, if the folder contains nothing but a bunch of identical-looking audio or database icons, then seeing their icons isn't going to help you much—and a list appears much faster than a fan or a grid does.

  There's no scroll bar in a list balloon, but you can scroll the list nonetheless just by pointing to the top or bottom of it with your mouse. And, again, you can type-select as described on page 91.

Tip: The list view also displays a little ▸ to the right of each folder within the Dock folder. That is, it's a hierarchical list, meaning that you can burrow into folders within folders, all from the original Dock icon, all without opening a single new window. You can stick your entire Home folder, or even your whole hard drive icon, onto the Dock; now you have complete menu access to everything inside, right from the Dock.

• **Automatic.** There's a fourth option in the shortcut menu for a Dock folder, too: automatic. If you turn this on, then Mac OS X chooses either fan or grid view, depending on how many icons are in the folder.

List view

Fan view

Grid view

Figure 2-16:
What happens when you click a folder in the Dock? You see its contents in one of three views. Here's how you choose the file you're looking for in each:

Top left: In List view, the folder contents appear as a menu; you can "drill down" into subfolders, and you open something by choosing its name.

Top right: In Fan view, click an icon to open it.

Bottom: In Grid view, many more icons appear than can fit in Fan view.

In any of the views, you can get a quick look at a document's contents by using Quick Look. That is, highlight the icon (point without clicking, or use the keyboard to type-select), and then press the space bar. A window sprouts, showing the actual document contents.

So how do you choose which display you want? Right-click the Dock folder's icon, and make a selection from the shortcut menu. Each disk or folder icon remembers its own fan/grid/list setting.

The Finer Points of Pop-up Dock Folders

Those were the basics of pop-up Dock folders. Here's the advanced course:

• **Ever-Changing Folder-Icon Syndrome (ECFIS).** When you add a folder or disk icon to the Dock, you might notice something wildly disorienting: Its icon keeps *changing* to resemble whatever you most recently put into it. For example, your Downloads folder might look like an Excel spreadsheet icon today, a PDF icon tonight, or a photo tomorrow—but never a folder. The annoying part is that you can't get to know a folder by its icon.

Fortunately, this problem is easy to fix. Right-click the Dock folder. From the shortcut menu, in the "Display as" section, you can choose either Folder (which looks like a folder forever) or Stack (which changes to reflect its contents).

- **Ready-made pop-up folders.** When you first start out, you get a couple of starter Dock folders, just to get you psyched. One is Downloads; the other is Documents. (Both of these folders are physically inside your Home folder. But you may well do most of your interacting with them on the Dock.)

The Downloads folder collects three kinds of Internet arrivals: files you download from the Web using Safari, files you receive in an iChat file-transfer session, and file attachments you get via email using Mail. Unless you intervene, they're sorted by the date you downloaded them.

It's handy to know where to find your downloads, and nice not to have them all cluttering your desktop.

Tip: Once you've opened a stack's fan or grid, you can drag any of the icons right out of it. Just drag your chosen icon onto the desktop or into any visible disk or folder. In other words, what lands in the Downloads folder doesn't have to stay there. (You can't drag out of a list, however.)

- **Hierarchical folders.** The fans and grids are hierarchical—that is, you can drill down from their folders into *their* folders. Figure 2-17 makes this concept clearer.

Figure 2-17:
If you spot a folder inside a list or a grid (left), click it once. You're now looking at a fan or grid of its contents (right). You can go on burrowing like this as deeply as your folders go. You can also "back out" again by clicking the Back button in the upper-left corner.

- **Type selecting.** Once a list, fan, or grid is on the screen, you can highlight any icon in it by typing the first few letters of its name. For example, once you've popped open your Applications folder, you can highlight Safari by typing *sa*. (Press Return to open the highlighted icon.)

Tip: Alternatively, you can "walk" through the fan, grid, or list by pressing the arrow keys. A highlighting effect makes it crystal clear which icon you're selecting. Once an icon is selected, press Return to open it.

- **Two ways to bypass the pop-up.** If you just want to see what's in a folder, without all the graphic overkill of the fan or the grid, then right-click the Dock folder's icon and choose "Open 'Applications' " (or whatever the folder's name is) from the shortcut menu. You go straight to the corresponding window.

  Actually, if you *really* value your time, you'll learn the shortcut: Option-⌘-click the Dock folder's icon. That accomplishes the same thing.

  (You jump immediately to the window that *contains* that folder's icon. That's not exactly the same thing as opening the Dock folder, but it's sometimes even more useful.)

Tip: Alternatively, you can ⌘-click a folder on the Dock—or, indeed, any icon on the Dock—to jump to the window that contains that folder's icon. (Bonus: This same ⌘-clicking trick also works in the menu of Spotlight search results.)

Three Ways to Get the Dock Out of Your Hair

The bottom of the screen isn't necessarily the ideal location for the Dock. All Mac screens are wider than they are tall, so the Dock eats into your limited vertical screen space. You have three ways out: Hide the Dock, shrink it, or rotate it 90 degrees.

Many Mac fans prefer to hide and show the Dock at will by pressing the hide/show keystroke, Option-⌘-D. This method makes the Dock pop on and off the screen without requiring you to move the cursor.

Shrinking and enlarging the Dock

Depending on your screen's size, you may prefer smaller or larger Dock buttons. The official way to resize them goes like this: Choose →Dock→Dock Preferences. In the resulting dialog box, drag the Dock Size slider, as shown in Figure 2-18.

There's a much faster way to resize the Dock, however: Just position your cursor carefully in the Dock's divider line, so that it turns into a double-headed arrow. Now drag up or down to shrink or enlarge the Dock.

You may not be able to *enlarge* the Dock, especially if it contains a lot of icons. But you can make it almost infinitely *smaller*. This may make you wonder: How can you distinguish between icons if they're the size of molecules?

The answer lies in the →Dock→Turn Magnification On command. What you've just done is trigger the swelling effect shown in Figure 2-19. Now your Dock icons balloon to a much larger size as your cursor passes over them. It's a weird, magnetic, rippling, animated effect that takes some getting used to. But it can come in handy when you find your icons shrinking away to nothing.

Auto-hiding the Dock

To turn on the Dock's auto-hiding feature, choose →Dock→Turn Hiding On (or press Option-⌘-D).

Figure 2-18:
To make your Dock icons bigger or smaller, choose →Dock→Dock Preferences. Leave the Dock Preferences window open on the screen, as shown here. After each adjustment of the Dock size slider, try out the Dock (which still works when the Dock Preferences window is open) to test your new settings.

When the Dock is hidden, it doesn't slide into view until you move the cursor to the Dock's edge of the screen. When you move the cursor back to the middle of the screen, the Dock slithers out of view once again. (Individual Dock icons may occasionally shoot upward into Desktop territory when a program needs your attention—cute, very cute—but otherwise, the Dock lies low until you call for it.)

On paper, an auto-hiding Dock is ideal; it's there only when you summon it. In practice, however, you may find that the extra half-second the Dock takes to appear and disappear makes this feature slightly less appealing.

Moving the Dock to the sides of the screen

Yet another approach to getting the Dock out of your way is to rotate it, so that it sits vertically against a side of your screen. You can rotate it in either of two ways:

- **The menu way.** From the →Dock submenu, choose Position on Left, Position on Right, or Position on Bottom, as you see fit.

- **The mouse way.** While pressing Shift, drag the Dock's divider line, like a handle, to the side of the screen you want.

You'll probably find that the right side of your screen works better than the left. Most Mac OS X programs put their document windows against the left edge of the screen, where the Dock and its labels might get in the way.

Note: When you position your Dock vertically, the "right" side of the Dock becomes the bottom of the vertical Dock. In other words, the Trash now appears at the bottom of the vertical Dock. So as you read references to the Dock in this book, mentally substitute the phrase "bottom part of the Dock" when you read references to the "right side of the Dock."

Using the Dock

Most of the time, you'll use the Dock as either a launcher (you click an icon once to open it) or as a status indicator (the tiny, shiny reflective spot, identified in Figure 2-15, indicates which programs are running).

But the Dock has more tricks than that up its sleeve. Observe:

Switch applications

The Dock isn't just a launcher; it's also a switcher. For example, it lets you perform the following tricks:

- Jump among your open programs by clicking their icons.

- Drag a document (such as a text file) onto a Dock application (such as the Microsoft Word icon) to open the former with the latter. (If the program balks at opening the document, yet you're sure the program *should* be able to open the document, then add the ⌘ and Option keys as you drag.)

- Hide all windows of the program you're in by Option-clicking another Dock icon.

- Hide all *other* programs' windows by Option-⌘-clicking the Dock icon of the program you *do* want (even if it's already in front).

Secret menus

If you right-click a Dock icon, or click-and-hold on it, you see its very useful shortcut menu (Figure 2-19).

If you've clicked a minimized window icon, this shortcut menu says only Open (unless it's a minimized Finder window, in which case it also says Close).

But if you've clicked any other kind of icon, you get some very useful hidden commands. For example:

- **[Window names].** The secret Dock menu of a running program usually lists one or more tiny, neatly labeled window icons, like those shown in Figure 2-19. This useful feature means you can jump directly not only to a certain program, but also to a certain open window in that program.

For example, suppose you've been using Word to edit three different chapters. You can use Word's Dock icon as a window menu to pull forward one particular chapter, or (if it's been minimized) to pull it up—even if a different program is in front of Word. (The checkmark indicates the *frontmost* window, even if the entire program is in the background. A diamond symbol means that the window is minimized and therefore not visible on the screen at the moment.)

In Lion-aware applications like TextEdit and the iWork programs, there are actually two lists of documents, separated by a horizontal line. (You can see the effect in Figure 2-19.) The top group lists files you've recently opened in that program; the next batch lists currently open documents.

Figure 2-19:
Left: Control-click a Dock icon to open the secret menu. In Lion-aware programs, the top half of the menu lists recently opened documents, followed by currently open ones.

Right: Control-click the divider bar to open a different hidden menu. This one lists a bunch of useful Dock commands, including the ones listed in the ⬢→Dock submenu.

- **Show All Windows/Show Recents.** When a program on the Dock is open, this command says Show All Windows; when it's not running, it says Show Recents. Either way, it takes you to the screen shown in Figure 2-19, where the icons of recently opened documents appear for easy clicking and reopening. (OK, they *may* appear. Apple programs like TextEdit and Pages show these recent icons, but non-Apple programs have to be Lion-updated before they'll show you the recent-document icons.)

  To exit the Recents screen, press Esc or ⌘-period.

- **Options.** This submenu contains a bunch of miscellaneous commands:

  Options→Keep In Dock. Whenever you open a program, Mac OS X puts its icon in the Dock—marked with a shiny, white spot—even if you don't normally keep its icon there. As soon as you quit the program, its icon disappears again from the Dock.

Tip: You can get rid of that shiny white "running program" indicator dot, if you like. Open System Preferences→Dock and turn off "Show indicator lights for open applications."

If you understand that much, then the Keep In Dock command makes a lot of sense. It means, "Hello, I'm this program's icon. I know you don't normally keep me in your Dock, but I *could* stay here even after you quit my program. Just say the word." If you find you've been using, for example, Terminal a lot more often than you thought you would, this command may be the ticket.

If you don't want a program's icon to appear on the Dock when it's not running, then choose this command again so that the checkmark disappears.

Note: If the program is already running, turning off Keep In Dock doesn't *immediately* remove its icon from the Dock. That's because a program always appears in the Dock when it's open. What you're doing here is saying, "Disappear from the Dock when you're *not* running"—and you'll see the proof as soon as you quit that program.

Options→Open at Login. This command lets you specify that you want this icon to open itself automatically each time you log into your account. It's a great way to make sure your email inbox, your calendar, or the Microsoft Word thesis you've been working on is fired up and waiting on the screen when you sit down to work.

To make this item *stop* auto-opening, choose this command again so that the checkmark no longer appears.

Options→Show in Finder. This command highlights the actual icon (in whatever folder window it happens to sit) of the application, alias, folder, or document you've clicked. You might want to do this when, for example, you're using a program that you can't quite figure out, and you want to jump to its desktop folder in hopes of finding a Read Me file there.

Tip: Once again, there's a much faster way to reveal a Dock icon in its enclosing window: ⌘-click its Dock icon.

• **Hide/Show.** You can hide all traces of the program you're using by choosing Hide from its Dock icon.

What's cool here is that (a) you can even hide the Finder and all *its* windows, and (b) if you press Option, the command changes to say Hide Others. This, in its way, is a much more powerful command. It tells all the programs you're *not* using—the ones in the background—to get out of your face. They hide themselves instantly.

Note: Once you've hidden a program's windows, this command changes to say Show, which is how you make them reappear.

• **Quit.** You can quit any program directly from its Dock shortcut menu. (Finder, Launchpad, and Mission Control are exceptions.) The beauty of this feature is that you don't have to switch into a program to get to its Quit command.

Tip: If you hold down the Option key—even after you've opened the pop-up menu—the Quit command changes to say Force Quit. That's your emergency hatch for jettisoning a locked-up program.

- **Miscellaneous.** You might find other commands in Dock shortcut menus; software companies are free to add specialty options to their own programs.

Drag and Drop

Dock icons are spring-loaded. That is, if you drag any icon onto a Dock icon and pause—or, if you're in a hurry, tap the space bar—then the Dock icon *opens* to receive the dragged file.

> **Note:** It opens, that is, *if* the spring-loaded folder feature is turned on in Finder→Preferences.

This technique is most useful in these situations:

- **Dragging a document icon onto a Dock folder icon.** The folder's Finder window pops open so you can continue the drag into a subfolder.

- **Dragging a document into an application.** The classic example is dragging a photo onto the iPhoto icon. When you tap the space bar, iPhoto opens automatically. Since your mouse button is still down, and you're technically still in mid-drag, you can now drop the photo directly into the appropriate iPhoto album or Event. You can drag an MP3 file into iTunes or an attachment into Mail or Entourage the same way.

Do Your Filing

Once you've tried stashing a few important folders on the right side of your Dock, there's no going back. The folders you care about are always there, ready for opening with a single click.

Better yet, they're easily accessible for *putting away* files; you can drag files directly into the Dock's folder icons as though they were regular folders.

In fact, you can even drag a file into a *subfolder* in a Dock folder. That's because the Dock's folders are spring-loaded. When you drag an icon onto a Dock folder and pause, the folder's window appears around your cursor, so you can continue the drag into an inner folder (and even an *inner* inner folder, and so on). Page 94 has the details on spring-loaded folders.

> **Tip:** When you try to drag something into a Dock folder icon, the Dock icons scoot out of the way; the Dock assumes you're trying to put that something *onto* the Dock. But if you press the ⌘ key as you drag an icon to the Dock, the existing Dock icons freeze in place. Without the ⌘ key, you wind up playing a frustrating game of chase-the-folder.

The Finder Toolbar

At the top of every Finder window is a small set of function icons, all in a gradient-gray row (Figure 2-20). The first time you run Mac OS X, you'll find only these icons on the toolbar:

- **Back (◄), Forward (►).** The Finder works something like a Web browser. Only a single window remains open as you navigate the various folders on your hard drive.

  The Back button (◄) returns you to whichever folder you were just looking at. (Instead of clicking ◄, you can also press ⌘-[, or choose Go→Back—particularly handy if the toolbar is *hidden*, as described below.)

  The Forward button (►) springs to life only after you've used the Back button. Clicking it (or pressing ⌘-]) returns you to the window you just backed out of.

- **View controls.** The four tiny buttons next to the ◄ button switch the current window into icon, list, column, or Cover Flow view, respectively. And remember, if the toolbar is hidden, you can get by with the equivalent commands in the View menu at the top of the screen—or by pressing ⌘-1 for icon view, ⌘-2 for list view, ⌘-3 for column view, or ⌘-4 for Cover Flow view.

- **Quick Look.** The 👁 icon opens the Quick Look preview for a highlighted icon (or group of them).

- **Action (✿).** This little pop-up menu contains the same commands you'd see if you right-clicked something.

- **Search bar.** This little round-ended text box is yet another entry point for the Spotlight feature described in Chapter 3.

Figure 2-20:
If you Control-click (or right-click) a blank spot on the toolbar, you get a pop-up menu that offers you a choice of looks for the buttons here: Icons Only, Text Only, or Icons and Text. In Text Only mode (bottom), the four View buttons are replaced by a little pop-up menu called View. Furthermore, the search box turns into a one-word button called Search. Clicking it brings up the Searching window.

Hiding or Shrinking the Toolbar

With the toolbar, the Dock, the Sidebar, and the large icons of Mac OS X, it almost seems like there's an Apple conspiracy to sell big screens.

Fortunately, the toolbar doesn't have to contribute to that impression. You can hide it by choosing View→Hide Toolbar or by pressing Option-⌘-T. (The same keystroke, or choosing View→Show Toolbar, brings it back.)

Of course, you can also just make it smaller by hiding the labels (or the icons), as shown in Figure 2-20.

Rearranging, Customizing, or Removing Toolbar Icons

You can drag toolbar icons around, rearranging them horizontally, by pressing ⌘ as you drag. Taking an icon off the toolbar is equally easy. While pressing the ⌘ key, just drag the icon clear away from the toolbar. You can also get rid of a toolbar icon by right-clicking it and choosing Remove Item from the shortcut menu.

You can also drag a different set of icons onto the toolbar. That's the purpose of the View→Customize Toolbar command.

Getting Help in Mac OS X

It's a good thing you've got a book about Mac OS X in your hands, because the only user manual you get with it is the Help menu, a browser-like program that reads a set of help files that reside in your System→Library folder.

Tip: The general-information help page about each topic is on your Mac, but thousands of the more technical pages actually reside online and require an Internet connection to read.

You're expected to find the topic you want in one of these three ways:

- **Use the search box.** When you click the Help menu, a tiny search box appears just beneath your cursor. You can type a few words here to specify what you want help with: "setting up printer," "disk space," whatever.

  After a moment (sometimes several moments), the menu becomes a list of Apple help topics pertaining to your search. Click one to open the Help browser described next; you've just saved some time and a couple of steps.

Tip: The results menu does not, however, show all of Help's results—only the ones Apple thinks are most relevant. If you choose Show All Help Topics at the bottom of the menu, the Help browser opens (described below). It shows a more complete list of Help search results.

- **Drill down.** Alternatively, you can begin your quest for assistance the old-fashioned way: by opening the Help browser first. To do that, choose Help→Help Center. (That's the wording in the Finder. In other programs, it might say, for example, "Mail Help." Either way, this command appears only when nothing is typed in the search box. To empty the search box, click the ⊗ button at the right end.)

After a moment, you arrive at the Help browser program shown at top in Figure 2-21. The starting screen offers several "quick click" topics that may interest you—presumably the ones that trigger the most help-hotline calls to Apple. If so, keep clicking text headings until you find a topic you want to read.

You can backtrack by clicking the ◄ button at the top of the window. And you can always return to the starting screen by clicking the little ⌂ icon at the top.

Figure 2-21:
The Help Center likes to help with big-ticket computer tasks like joining a network, setting up your email program, or browsing the Web. Once you click a top-tier topic (top), you get a details page (bottom) that offers a list of more finely grained step-by-steps.

Tip: Annoyingly, the help window still insists on floating in front of all other windows; you can't send it to the back like any normal program. Therefore, consider making the window tall and skinny, so you can put it beside the program you're working in. Drag any edge of the box to change the window's shape.

- **Use the "Search Help" blank.** Type the phrase you want, like *printing* or *switching applications,* into the search box at the top of the window, and then press Return. As you type, a list of proposed matches drops down from the search box. When you click the closest match, you're shown a list of help-screen topics that may pertain to what you need; see Figure 2-22 for details.

Note: Actually, there's one more place where Help crops up: in System Preferences dialog boxes. Click the circled question-mark button (⑦) in the lower-right corner of most System Preferences panels to open a help page that identifies each control.

GEM IN THE ROUGH

Menu Help in the Help Menu

Mac OS X contains a weird, wonderful little enhancement to its online help system. It helps you find menu commands you can't find.

Say you're floundering in some program. You're *sure* there's a page numbering command in those menus somewhere. But there are 11 menus, and 143 submenus hiding in those menus, and you haven't got time for the pain.

That's when you should think of using the Help menu. When you type *page number* (or whatever) into its search box, the results menu lists, at the top, the names of any menu commands in that program that contain the words you typed. Better still, it actually *opens that menu* for you, and displays a big, blue, animated, floating arrow pointing to the command you wanted. You'd have to have your eyes closed to miss it.

Simply slide your cursor over, click the menu command

you wanted, and get on with your life.

Supertip: This feature is especially helpful in Web browsers like Safari and Firefox, because it can even find entries in your Bookmarks and History menus!

In Safari, for example, you can pluck a recently visited site out of the hundreds in the daily History submenus, like the "Wednesday, January 4" submenu. You've just saved yourself a *lot* of poking around menus, trying to find the name of a site you know you've seen recently.

Ultratip: If you think about it, this feature also means that you have complete keyboard power over every menu in every program in the world. Hit ⌘-Shift-/ (that is, ⌘-?) to open the Help search box, type a bit of the command's name, and then use the arrow keys to walk down the results. Hit Return to trigger the command you want.

Along the way, keep in mind that you can always bookmark useful Help pages for quick reference later, saving you the trouble of searching or burrowing the next time (Figure 2-22).

Figure 2-22:
Click the new Add Bookmark icon (📕) to flag a page for quick finding later (left). When that later time comes, click the Bookmarks icon (📖) to see a list of all your saved bookmarks; double-click one to jump to its page.

Files, Icons & Spotlight

E very document, program, folder, and disk on your Mac is represented by an *icon:* a colorful little picture that you can move, copy, or double-click to open. In Mac OS X, icons look more like photos than cartoons, and you can scale them to practically any size.

This chapter is all about manipulating those icons—that is, your files, folders, and disks. It's all about naming them, copying them, deleting them, labeling them—and then, maybe most important of all, finding them, using the Mac's famous Spotlight instant-search feature.

Renaming Icons

A Mac OS X icon's name can have up to 255 letters and spaces. If you're accustomed to the 31-character or even eight-character limits of older computers, that's quite a luxurious ceiling.

As a Windows veteran, furthermore, you may be delighted to discover that in Mac OS X, you can name your files using letters, numbers, punctuation—in fact, any symbol except for the colon (:), which the Mac uses behind the scenes for its own folder-hierarchy designation purposes. And you can't use a period to *begin* a file's name.

To rename a file, click its name or icon (to highlight it) and then press Return. (Or, if you have time to kill, click once on the name, wait a moment, and then click a second time.)

In any case, a rectangle now appears around the name (Figure 3-1). At this point, the existing name is highlighted; just begin typing to replace it. If you type a very long name, the rectangle grows vertically to accommodate new lines of text.

Tip: If you simply want to add letters to the beginning or end of the file's existing name, press the left or right arrow key immediately after pressing Return. The insertion point jumps to the corresponding end of the file name.

Figure 3-1:
Click an icon's name (top left) to produce the renaming rectangle (top right), in which you can edit the file's name. The Mac is kind enough to highlight only the existing name, and not the suffix (like .jpg or .doc).

Now just begin typing to replace the existing name (bottom left). When you're finished typing, press Return, Enter, or Tab to seal the deal, or just click somewhere else.

When you're finished typing, press Return, Enter, or Tab—or just click somewhere else—to make the renaming rectangle disappear.

As you edit a file's name, remember that you can use the Cut, Copy, and Paste commands in the Edit menu to move selected bits of text around, just as though you were word processing. The Paste command can be useful when, for instance, you're renaming many icons in sequence (*Quarterly Estimate 1, Quarterly Estimate 2,* and so on).

And now, a few tips about renaming icons:

• When the Finder sorts files, a space is considered alphabetically *before* the letter A. To force a particular folder to appear at the top of a list view window, insert a space before its name.

• Older operating systems sort files so that 10 and 100 come before 2, the numbers 30 and 300 come before 4, and so on. You wind up with alphabetically sorted files like this: "1. Big Day," "10. Long Song," "2. Floppy Hat," "20. Dog Bone," "3. Weird Sort," and so on. Generations of computer users have learned to put zeros in front of their single-digit numbers just to make the sorting look right.

In Mac OS X, though, you get exactly the numerical list you'd hope for: "1. Big Day," "2. Floppy Hat," "3. Weird Sort," "10. Long Song," and "20. Dog Bone." At long last, you can get out of the habit of putting zeros in front of file names to make them sort properly.

Selecting Icons

To highlight a single icon in preparation for printing, opening, duplicating, or deleting, click the icon once. Both the icon and the name darken in a uniquely Lionish way.

Tip: You can change the color of the oval highlighting that appears around the name of a selected icon. Choose →System Preferences, click Appearance, and use the Highlight Color pop-up menu.

That much may seem obvious. But lots of people have no idea how to manipulate *more* than one icon at a time—an essential survival skill. These techniques are essentially the same as in Windows, except that the keys you hold down are different.

Selecting by Clicking

To highlight multiple files in preparation for moving or copying, use one of these techniques:

- **To highlight all the icons.** To select all the icons in a window, press ⌘-A (the equivalent of the Edit→Select All command).

- **To highlight several icons by dragging.** You can drag diagonally to highlight a group of nearby icons, as shown in Figure 3-2. In a list view, in fact, you don't even have to drag over the icons themselves—your cursor can touch any part of any file's row, like its modification date or file size.

Figure 3-2:
You can highlight several icons simultaneously by dragging a box around them. To do so, drag from outside the target icons diagonally across them, creating a translucent gray rectangle as you go. Any icons or icon names touched by this rectangle are selected when you release the mouse. If you press the Shift or ⌘ key as you do this, then any previously highlighted icons remain selected.

Tip: If you include a particular icon in your diagonally dragged group by mistake, just ⌘-click it to remove it from the selected cluster.

- **To highlight consecutive icons in a list.** If you're looking at the contents of a window in list view or column view, you can drag vertically over the file and folder names to highlight a group of consecutive icons, as described above. (Begin the drag in a blank spot.)

  There's a faster way to do the same thing: Click the first icon you want to highlight, and then Shift-click the last file, just as in Windows. All the files in between are automatically selected, along with the two icons you clicked.

- **To highlight any icons.** If you want to highlight only the first, third, and seventh icons in a window, for example, start by clicking icon No. 1. Then ⌘-click each of the others (or ⌘-drag new rectangles around them). Each icon darkens to show that you've selected it.

  If you're highlighting a long string of icons and click one by mistake, you don't have to start over. Instead, just ⌘-click it again, so that the dark highlighting disappears. (If you do want to start over, you can deselect all selected icons by clicking any empty part of the window—or by pressing the Esc key.)

  The ⌘ key trick is especially handy if you want to select *almost* all the icons in a window. Press ⌘-A to select everything in the folder, then ⌘-click any unwanted icons to deselect them.

Once you've highlighted multiple icons, you can manipulate them all at once. For example, you can drag them en masse to another folder or disk by dragging any *one* of the highlighted icons. All other highlighted icons go along for the ride. This technique is especially useful when you want to back up a bunch of files by dragging them onto a different disk, to delete them all by dragging them to the Trash, and so on.

When multiple icons are selected, the commands in the File and Edit menus—such as Duplicate, Open, and Make Alias—apply to all of them simultaneously.

UP TO SPEED

The Wacky Keystrokes of Mac OS X

Mac OS X offers a glorious assortment of predefined keystrokes for jumping to the most important locations on your Mac: your Home folder, the Applications folder, the Utilities folder, the Computer window, your iDisk, the Network window, and so on.

Better yet, the keystrokes are incredibly simple to memorize: Just press Shift-⌘ and the first letter of the location you want. Shift-⌘-H opens your Home folder, Shift-⌘-A opens

the Applications folder, and so on. You learn one, you've learned 'em all. The point here is that Shift-⌘ means *places*.

The other system-wide key combo, Option-⌘, means *functions*. For example, Option-⌘-D hides or shows the Dock, Option-⌘-H is the Hide Others command, Option-⌘-+ magnifies the screen (if you've turned on this feature), Option-⌘-Esc brings up the Force Quit dialog box, and so on. Consistency is always nice.

Selecting Icons from the Keyboard

For the speed fanatic, using the mouse to click an icon is a hopeless waste of time. Fortunately, you can also select an icon by typing the first few letters of its name.

When looking at your Home window, for example, you can type *M* to highlight the Movies folder. And if you actually intended to highlight the Music folder instead, then press the Tab key to highlight the next icon in the window alphabetically. Shift-Tab highlights the previous icon alphabetically. Or use the arrow keys to highlight a neighboring icon.

(The Tab-key trick works in icon, list, and Cover Flow views—but not in column view, alas. You can always use the ← and → keys to highlight adjacent columns, however.)

After highlighting an icon this way, you can manipulate it using the commands in the File menu or their keyboard equivalents: Open (⌘-O), put it into the Trash (⌘-Delete), Get Info (⌘-I), Duplicate (⌘-D), or make an alias (⌘-L), as described later in this chapter. By turning on the special disability features described on page 539, you can even *move* the highlighted icon using only the keyboard.

Moving and Copying Icons

In Mac OS X, there are two ways to move or copy icons from one place to another: by dragging them or by using the Copy and Paste commands.

Copying by Dragging

You can drag icons from one folder to another, from one drive to another, from a drive to a folder on another drive, and so on. (When you've selected several icons, drag any *one* of them; the others tag along.) While the Mac is copying, you can tell that the process is still under way even if the progress bar is hidden behind a window, because the icon of the copied material shows up *dimmed* in its new home, darkening only when the copying process is over. You can cancel the process by pressing either ⌘-period or the Esc key.

Understanding when the Mac *copies* a dragged icon and when it *moves* it bewilders many a beginner. However, the scheme is fairly simple when you consider the following:

- Dragging from one folder to another on the same disk *moves* the icon.

- Dragging from one disk (or disk partition) to another *copies* the folder or file. (You can drag icons either into an open window or directly onto a disk or folder icon.)

- If you press the Option key as you release an icon you've dragged, you *copy* the icon instead of moving it. Doing so within a single folder produces a duplicate of the file called "[Whatever its name was] copy."

- If you press the ⌘ key as you release an icon you've dragged from one disk to another, you *move* the file or folder, in the process deleting it from the original disk.

Tip: This business of pressing Option or ⌘ *after* you begin dragging is a tad awkward, but it has its charms. For example, it means you can change your mind about the purpose of your drag in mid-movement, without having to drag back and start over.

And if it turns out you just dragged something into the wrong window or folder, a quick ⌘-Z (the shortcut for Edit→Undo) puts it right back where it came from.

Copying by Using Copy and Paste

Dragging icons to copy or move them probably feels good because it's so direct: You actually see your arrow cursor pushing the icons into the new location.

But you pay a price for this satisfying illusion. You may have to spend a moment or two fiddling with your windows to create a clear "line of drag" between the icon to be moved and the destination folder.

There's a better way. Use the Copy and Paste commands to move icons from one window into another, just as you can in Windows. You can even *move* files this way, not just copy them, although the steps are slightly different on the Mac. Anyway, here's the routine:

GEM IN THE ROUGH

Two Lion Goodies: Smart Handling of Identically Named Icons

What if you're dragging a file or folder into some window—and there's already a file or folder there with the same name?

In operating systems in days of yore, a warning message appeared. It let you Stop (the whole operation) or Replace (the existing items with the ones you were moving).

Lion is just a little bit smarter. It offers a third option: Keep Both.

For example, if you drag or paste *files* of the same name, you're offered a button called Keep Both Files. If you click it, Lion adds the number 2 (or 3, or 4…) to the end of the incoming file's name, so you can tell it apart from the existing one in the destination.

Tip: If you're dragging *several* files whose names match existing files in the destination folder, then Mac OS X asks you individually about each one (Stop, Replace, Keep Both Files?). If you intend to answer the same way for every single file, save yourself the insanity by turning on the "Apply to all" checkbox before answering the question.

There's another, related feature that comes into play when you paste a *folder* into a spot where there's another folder with the same name. In this case, Lion offers to *merge the contents* of the two folders.

It might say, for example: "An item named 'Notes' already exists in this location. Do you want to replace it with the one you're moving? Each folder has unique items such as 'Salary Projections' and 'Stealth Projects.doc.' " And your choices are Stop, Keep Both, or Replace All. (These options appear only when you're *pasting* a folder into a new window—not dragging it. They also appear when you Option-drag a folder into a new window to copy it there, or when you drag it to a different disk.)

If you click Keep Both, the Finder *combines the contents* of the two folders. The folder you're pasting disappears, but its contents join the contents of the other folder (the one in the destination window) in blissful harmony.

---

1. **Highlight the icon or icons you want to move.**

   Use any of the techniques described on page 89.

2. **Choose Edit→Copy.**

   Or press the keyboard shortcut: ⌘-C.

Tip: You can combine steps 1 and 2 by right-clicking an icon and choosing the Copy command from the shortcut menu that appears—or by using the ✿ menu. If you've selected several icons, say five, then the command will say, "Copy 5 items."

---

3. **Open the window where you want to put the icons. Choose Edit→Paste.**

   Once again, you may prefer to use the keyboard equivalent: ⌘-V. And once again, you can also Control-click (right-click) inside the window and then choose Paste from the shortcut menu that appears, or you can use the ✿ menu.

   If you add the Option key—press Option-⌘-V—you *move* the icons to the new window instead of copying them. That is, the originals disappear after they appear in the new location. (This might make more sense if you use the menu way: If you open the Edit menu and press Option, you'll see the Paste Items command change to say Move Items Here.)

A progress bar may appear as Mac OS X copies the files or folders; press Esc or ⌘-period to interrupt the process. When the progress bar goes away, it means you've successfully transferred the icons, which now appear in the new window.

Tip: If you paste a folder into a spot where there's another folder with the same name, Lion does something awfully thoughtful: It offers to *merge the contents* of the two folders. For details, see the box on page 92.

FREQUENTLY ASKED QUESTION

Printing a Window—or a List of Files

I'd like to get a neat list of the files in a folder that I can use as a label for a CD I was going to burn. How do I print out a Finder window in Mac OS X? (The File→Print command prints a selected document, not the list of files in a window.)

It's easy enough to make a list of files for printing. Once the window is open on your screen, choose Edit→Select All. Choose Edit→Copy. Now switch to a word processor and paste. (If you're using TextEdit, use Edit→Paste and Match Style instead.) You get a tidy list of all the files in that window, ready to format and print.

This simple file name list isn't the same as printing a window, that's true; you don't get the status bar showing how many items are on the disk and how full the disk is. For that purpose, you can always make a screenshot of the window (page 242), and print that. Of course, that technique's no good if the list of files is taller than the window itself.

Really, what you want is Print Window, a handy shareware program dedicated to printing out your Finder windows, without any of these workarounds or limitations. You can download it from this book's "Missing CD" page at *www.missingmanuals.com.*

Spring-Loaded Folders: Dragging Icons into Closed Folders

Here's a common dilemma: You want to drag an icon not just into a folder, but into a folder nested *inside* that folder. This awkward challenge would ordinarily require you to open the folder, open the inner folder, drag the icon in, and then close both the windows you opened. As you can imagine, the process is even messier if you want to drag an icon into a sub-subfolder or even a *sub*-sub-subfolder.

Fortunately, there's a better way: Use the *spring-loaded folders* feature (Figure 3-3).

With a single drag, drag the icon onto the first folder—but keep your mouse button pressed. After a second, the window opens automatically, centered on your cursor.

Still keeping the button down, drag onto the inner folder; its window opens, too. Now drag onto the *inner* inner folder—and so on. (If the inner folder you intend to open isn't visible in the window, you can scroll by dragging your cursor close to any edge of the window.)

Tip: You can even drag icons onto disks or folders whose icons appear in the Sidebar (Chapter 1). When you do so, the main part of the window flashes to reveal the contents of the disk or folder you've dragged onto. When you let go of the mouse, the main window changes back to reveal the contents of the disk or folder where you *started* dragging.

In short, Sidebar combined with spring-loaded folders make a terrific drag-and-drop way to file a desktop icon from anywhere to anywhere—without having to open or close any windows at all.

Designing Your Own Icons

You don't have to be content with the icons provided by Microsoft, Apple, or whoever wrote your software. You can paste new icons onto your file, disk, and folder icons to help you pick them out at a glance.

The easiest way to replace an icon is to copy it from another icon. To do so, highlight the icon, hold down the Option key and choose File→Show Inspector. In the resulting window, click the existing icon, and then choose Edit→Copy.

Next, click the icon to which you want to transfer the copied picture. Its icon now appears in the Info dialog box that's still open on the screen. Click the icon in the dialog box, and this time choose Edit→Paste.

If you'd rather introduce all-new icons, you're welcome to steal some of the beautifully designed ones waiting at *www.iconfactory.com* and the icon sites linked to it. Once you've

downloaded these special icon files, you can copy their images from the Get Info window as you would any icon.

To design an icon from scratch, use a graphics program like Photoshop or the shareware favorite GraphicConverter.

Once you've saved your icon file, select it, and then copy and paste its icon using the Show Inspector method described above.

Note that you can't change certain folder icons that Mac OS X considers important, such as Applications or System. You're also not allowed to change icons that belong to other people who share your Mac and sign in under a different name (Chapter 14).

You can, however, change the special Mac OS X folder icons in your Home folder—Pictures, Documents, and so on, and your hard drive icon.

When you finally release the mouse, you're left facing the final window. All the previous windows closed on the way. You've neatly placed the icon into the core of the nested folders.

Making Spring-Loaded Folders Work

That spring-loaded folder technique sounds good in theory, but it can be disconcerting in practice. For most people, the long wait before the first folder opens is almost enough wasted time to negate the value of the feature altogether. Furthermore, when the first window finally does open, you're often caught by surprise. Suddenly your cursor—mouse button still down—is inside a window, sometimes directly on top of another folder you never intended to open. But before you can react, its window, too, has opened, and you find yourself out of control.

Fortunately, you can regain control of spring-loaded folders using these tricks:

- Choose Finder→Preferences. On the General pane, adjust the "Spring-loaded folders and windows" delay slider to a setting that drives you less crazy. For ex-

Figure 3-3:
Top: To make spring-loaded folders work, start by dragging an icon onto a folder or disk icon. Don't release the mouse button. Wait for the window to open automatically around your cursor.

Bottom: Now you can either let go of the mouse button to release the file in its new window or drag it onto yet another, inner folder. It, too, will open. As long as you don't release the mouse button, you can continue until you've reached your folder-within-a-folder destination.

ample, if you find yourself waiting too long before the first folder opens, drag the
slider toward the Short setting.

- You can turn off this feature entirely by choosing Finder→Preferences and turning
off the "Spring-loaded folders and windows" checkbox.

- Tap the space bar to make the folder spring open at your command. That is, even
with the Finder→Preferences slider set to the Long delay setting, you can force
each folder to spring open when *you* are ready by tapping the space bar as you
hold down the mouse button. True, you need two hands to master this one, but
the control you regain is immeasurable.

Tip: The space bar trick works even when the "Spring-loaded folders and windows" checkbox (in Find-
er→Preferences) is turned off. That's a handy arrangement, because it means folder windows never pop
open accidentally.

- Whenever a folder springs open into a window, twitch your mouse up to the newly
opened window's title bar or down to its information strip. Doing so ensures that
your cursor won't wind up hovering on, and accidentally opening up, an inner
folder. With the cursor parked on the gradient gray, you can take your time to
survey the newly opened window's contents, and plunge into an inner folder only
after gaining your bearings.

Tip: Email programs like Entourage and Mail have spring-loaded folders, too. You can drag a message out
of the list and into one of your filing folders, wait for the folder to spring open and reveal its subfolders, and
then drag it directly into one of them.

Aliases: Icons in Two Places at Once

Highlighting an icon and then choosing File→Make Alias (or pressing ⌘-L), generates an *alias,* a specially branded duplicate of the original icon (Figure 3-4). It's not
a duplicate of the *file*—just of the *icon;* therefore it requires negligible storage space.
When you double-click the alias, the original file opens. A Macintosh alias, in other
words, is essentially the same as a Windows *shortcut.*

Because you can create as many aliases as you want of a single file, aliases let you, in
effect, stash that file in many different folder locations simultaneously. Double-click
any one of them, and you open the original icon, wherever it may be on your system.

Tip: You can also create an alias of an icon by Option-⌘-dragging it out of its window. (Aliases you create
this way lack the word *alias* on the file name—a distinct delight to those who find the suffix redundant and
annoying.) You can also create an alias by right-clicking a normal icon and choosing Make Alias from the
shortcut menu that appears, or by highlighting an icon and then choosing Make Alias from the ✿ menu.

What's Good about Aliases

An alias takes up almost no disk space, even if the original file is enormous. Aliases are smart, too: Even if you rename the alias, rename the original file, move the alias, and move the original around on the disk, double-clicking the alias still opens the original icon.

Figure 3-4:
Top: You can identify an alias by the tiny arrow badge on the lower-left corner.

Bottom: If the alias can't find the original file, you're offered the chance to hook it up to a different file.

Elbow Grease

Elbow Grease alias

The alias "Elbow Grease alias" could not be opened, because the original item cannot be found.

Delete Alias   Fix Alias...   OK

Here are a few ways you can put aliases to work:

- You may want to file a document you're working on in several different folders, or place a particular folder in several different locations.

- You can use the alias feature to save you some of the steps required to access another hard drive on the network. (Details on this trick in Chapter 14.)

Tip: Mac OS X makes it easy to find the file to which an alias "points" without actually having to open it. Just highlight the alias and then choose File→Show Original (⌘-R), or choose Show Original from the ✿ menu. Mac OS X immediately displays the actual, original file, sitting patiently in its folder, wherever that may be.

Broken Aliases

An alias doesn't contain any of the information you've typed or composed in the original. Don't email an alias to the Tokyo office and then depart for the airport, hoping to give the presentation upon your arrival in Japan. When you double-click the alias, now separated from its original, you'll be shown the dialog box at bottom in Figure 3-4.

If you're on a plane 3,000 miles away from the hard drive on which the original file resides, click Delete Alias (to delete the orphan alias you just double-clicked) or OK (to do nothing, leaving the orphaned alias where it is).

In certain circumstances, however, the third button—Fix Alias—is the most useful. Click it to summon the Fix Alias dialog box, which you can use to navigate your entire Mac. When you click a new icon and then click Choose, you associate the orphaned alias with a different original icon.

Such techniques become handy when, for example, you click your book manuscript's alias on the desktop, forgetting that you recently saved it under a new name and deleted the older draft. Instead of simply showing you an error message that says " 'Enron Corporate Ethics Handbook' can't be found," the Mac displays the box that contains the Fix Alias button. By clicking it, thus reassociating it with the new document, you can save yourself the trouble of creating a new alias. From now on, double-clicking your manuscript's alias on the desktop opens the new draft.

Color Labels

This feature lets you tag selected icons with one of seven different labels, each of which has both a text label and a color associated with it. There's nothing exactly like it in Windows, but it can be very handy.

To do so, highlight the icons. Open the File menu (or the ✿ menu, or the shortcut menu that appears when you right-click the icons). There, under the heading Color Label, you'll see seven colored dots, which represent the seven different labels you can use. Figure 3-5 shows the routine.

What Labels Are Good For

After you've applied labels to icons, you can perform some unique file-management tasks—in some cases on all of them simultaneously, even if they're scattered across multiple hard drives. For example:

- **Round up files with Find.** Using the Find command, you can round up all icons with a particular label. Thereafter, moving these icons at once is a piece of cake—choose Edit→Select All, and then drag any one of the highlighted icons out of the results window and into the target folder or disk.

UP TO SPEED

Compressing, Zipping, and Archiving

Mac OS X comes with a built-in command that compresses a file or folder down to a single, smaller icon—an archive—suitable for storing or emailing.

Mac OS X creates .zip files, the same compression format used in Windows. That means you can send .zip files back and forth to PC owners without worrying that they won't be able to open them.

The software that does the compressing is built right in. Right-click a file or folder, and choose "Compress [the icon's name]" from the shortcut menu. (Of course, you can use the File menu or the ✿ menu instead.) Mac OS X thoughtfully creates a .zip archive, but it leaves the original behind so you can continue working with it.

Opening a .zip file somebody sends you is equally easy: Just double-click it. Zip!—it opens.

Using labels in conjunction with Find this way is one of the most useful and inexpensive backup schemes ever devised—whenever you finish working on a document that you'd like to back up, right-click it and apply a label called, for example, Backup. At the end of each day, use the Find command to round up all files with the Backup label—and then drag them as a group onto your backup disk.

Figure 3-5:
Use the File menu, the ✿ menu, or the shortcut menu to apply label tags to highlighted icons. You can even apply a label within an icon's Get Info dialog box.

Instantly, the icon's name takes on the selected shade. In a list or column view, the entire row takes on that shade, as shown in Figure 3-6. (If you choose the little X, you remove any labels you may have applied.)

- **Sort a list view by label.** No other Mac sorting method lets you create an arbitrary order for the icons in a window. When you sort by label, the Mac creates alphabetical clusters *within* each label grouping, as shown in Figure 3-6.

This technique might be useful when, for example, your job is to process several different folders of documents; for each folder, you're supposed to convert graphics files, throw out old files, or whatever. As soon as you finish working your way through one folder, flag it with a label called Done. The folder jumps to the top (or bottom) of the window, safely marked for your reference pleasure, leaving the next unprocessed folder at your fingertips, ready to go.

- **Track progress.** Use different color labels to track the status of files in a certain project. The first drafts have no labels at all. Once they've been edited and approved, make them blue. Once they've been sent to the home office, they turn purple. (Heck, you could have all kinds of fun with this: Money-losing projects get red tints; profitable ones get green; things that make you sad are blue. Or maybe not.)

Changing Labels

In Mac OS X's factory settings, the seven labels in the File menu are named for the colors they show: Red, Orange, Yellow, and so on. Clearly, the label feature would be much more useful if you could rewrite these labels, tailoring them to your purposes.

Doing so is easy. Choose Finder→Preferences. Click the Labels button. Now you see the dialog box shown in Figure 3-6, where you can edit the text of each label.

Figure 3-6:
Top left: In the Labels tab of the Preferences dialog box, you can change the predefined label text. Each label can be as long as you could possibly want it.

Bottom right: Now your list and column views reveal meaningful text tags instead of color names.

The Trash

No single element of the Macintosh interface is as recognizable or as famous as the Trash can, which appears at the end of the Dock. It is, of course, the inspiration for the Windows Recycle Bin.

You can discard almost any icon by dragging it onto the Trash icon (actually a wastebasket, not a trash can, but let's not quibble). When the tip of your arrow cursor touches the Trash icon, the little wastebasket turns black. When you release the mouse, you're well on your way to discarding whatever it was you dragged. As a convenience, Mac OS X even replaces the empty-wastebasket icon with a wastebasket-filled-with-crumpled-up-papers icon, to let you know there's something in there.

Tip: Learn the keyboard alternative to dragging something to the Trash: Highlight the icon, and then press ⌘-Delete. This technique is not only far faster than dragging, but it also requires far less precision, especially if you have a large screen. Mac OS X does all the Trash-targeting for you.

Rescuing Files and Folders from the Trash

File and folder icons sit in the Trash forever—or until you choose Finder→Empty Trash, whichever comes first.

If you haven't yet emptied the Trash, you can open its window by clicking the wastebasket icon once. Now you can review its contents: icons that you've placed on the waiting list for extinction. If you change your mind, proceed thusly:

- **Use the Put Back command.** This feature flings the trashed item back into whatever folder it came from, even if that was weeks ago—just as it does in Windows.

  You'll find the Put Back command wherever fine shortcut menus are sold. For example, it appears when you right-click the icon or click the icon and then open the ✿ menu.

Tip: The same keystroke you use to hurl something *into* the trash—⌘-Delete—also works to hurl it back out again. That is, you can highlight something in the Trash and press ⌘-Delete to put it back where it once belonged.

- **Hit Undo.** If dragging something to the Trash was the most recent thing you've done, you can press ⌘-Z—the keyboard shortcut for the Edit→Undo command. That keystroke not only removes it from the Trash, but also returns it to the folder from which it came. This trick works even if the Trash window isn't open.

- **Drag it manually.** Of course, you can also drag any icon out of the Trash with the mouse, which gives you the option of putting it somewhere new (as opposed to back in the folder it started from).

GEM IN THE ROUGH

Opening Things in the Trash

Now and then, it's very useful to see what some document in the Trash *is* before committing it to oblivion—and the only way to do that is to open it.

Trouble is, you can't open it by double-clicking; you'll get nothing but an error message.

Or at least that's what Apple *wants* you to think. There is, of course, a workaround or two. First of all, you can use Quick Look (page 67) to inspect something in the Trash.

Or, if Quick Look can't open the file—or if you want to *edit* it instead of just reading it—drag the document onto the icon of a program that can open it.

That is, if a file called Don't Read Me.txt is in the Trash, you can drag it onto, say, the Word or TextEdit icon in your Dock.

The document dutifully pops open on the screen. Inspect, close, and *then* empty the Trash (or rescue the document).

Emptying the Trash I: Quick and Easy

If you're confident that the items in the Trash window are worth deleting, use any of these three options:

- **Choose Finder→Empty Trash.**

- **Press Shift-⌘-Delete.** Or, if you'd just as soon not bother with the "Are you sure?" message, then throw the Option key in there, too.

- **Right-click the wastebasket icon,** or just click it and hold the mouse button down for a moment; choose Empty Trash from the shortcut menu.

The Mac asks you to confirm your decision. (Figure 3-7 shows this message.) When you click Empty Trash (or press Return), Mac OS X deletes those files from your hard drive.

Tip: If you'd rather not be interrupted for confirmation every time you empty the Trash, you can suppress this message permanently. To do that, choose Finder→Preferences, click Advanced, and then turn off "Show warning before emptying the Trash."

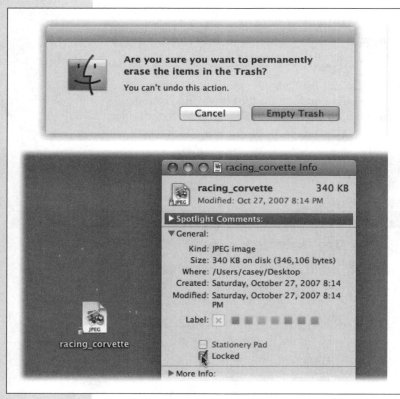

Figure 3-7:
Top: Your last warning. Mac OS X doesn't tell you how many items are in the Trash or how much disk space they take up.

Bottom: The Get Info window for a locked file. Locking a file in this way isn't military-level security by any stretch—any passing evildoer can unlock the file in the same way. But it does trigger a warning when you try to put it into the Trash, providing at least one layer of protection against losing or deleting it.

Emptying the Trash II: Secure and Forever

When you empty the Trash as described above, each trashed icon sure looks like it's disappeared. The truth is, though, the data *in* each file is still on the hard drive. Yes, the space occupied by the dearly departed is now marked with an internal "This space available" message, and in time, new files may overwrite that spot. But in the meantime, some future eBay buyer of your Mac—or, more imminently, a savvy family member or office mate—could use a program like Data Rescue or FileSalvage to resurrect those deleted files. (In more dire cases, when you're desperate to get something back, companies like DriveSavers.com can use sophisticated clean-room techniques to recover crucial information—for several hundred dollars, of course.)

That notion doesn't sit well with certain groups, like government agencies, international spies, and the paranoid. As far as they're concerned, deleting a file should *really, really* delete it, irrevocably, irretrievably, and forever.

Mac OS X has a command, therefore, called *Secure* Empty Trash. When you choose this command from the Finder menu, the Mac doesn't just obliterate the parking spaces around the dead file. It actually records *new* information over the old—random 0's and 1's. Pure static gibberish.

The process takes longer than the normal Empty Trash command, of course. But when it absolutely, positively has to be gone from this earth for good (and you're absolutely, positively sure you'll never need that file again), Secure Empty Trash is secure indeed.

Locked Files: The Next Generation

By highlighting a file or folder, choosing File→Get Info, and turning on the Locked checkbox, you protect that file or folder from accidental deletion (see Figure 3-7 at bottom). A little 🔒 icon appears on the corner of the full-size icon, also shown in Figure 3-7.

Locked files behave like this:

- Dragging the file into another folder makes a copy; the original stays put.

- Putting the icon into the Trash produces a warning message: "Item 'Shopping List' is locked. Do you want to move it to the Trash anyway?" If so, click Continue.

- Once a locked file is in the Trash, you don't get any more warnings. When you empty the Trash, that item gets erased right along with everything else.

You can unlock files easily enough. Press Option as you choose File→Show Inspector. Turn off the Locked checkbox in the resulting Info window. (Yes, you can lock or unlock a mass of files at once; read on.)

Get Info

By clicking an icon and then choosing File→Get Info, you open an important window like the one shown in Figure 3-8. It's a collapsible, multipanel screen that provides a wealth of information about a highlighted icon. In essence, this is the Properties window for the icon. For example:

- **For a document icon,** you see when it was created and modified, and what programs it "belongs" to.

- **For an alias,** you learn the location of the actual icon it refers to.

- **For a disk icon,** you get statistics about its capacity and how much of it is full.

- **If you open** the Get Info window when *nothing* is selected, you get information about the desktop itself (or the open window), including the amount of disk space consumed by everything sitting on or in it.

- **If you highlight** so many icons simultaneously that their Get Info windows would overwhelm your screen, Mac OS X thoughtfully tallies up their information into a single summary window. It shows you how many icons you highlighted, breaks

Figure 3-8:
Top: The Get Info window can be as small as this, with all its information panes collapsed.

Bottom: Or, if you click each flippy triangle to open its corresponding panel of information, it can be as huge as this—shown here split in two because this box isn't enough to show the whole thing. The resulting dialog box can easily grow taller than your screen, which is a good argument for either (a) closing the panels you don't need at any given moment or (b) running out to buy a really gigantic monitor.

There's a secret command called Get Summary Info. Highlight a group of icons, press Control-⌘-I, and marvel at the special Get Info box that tallies up their sizes and other characteristics.

them down by type ("23 documents, 3 folders," for example), and adds up the total of their file sizes. That's a great opportunity to change certain file characteristics on numerous files simultaneously, such as locking or unlocking them, hiding or showing their file name suffixes, changing their ownership or permissions (page 475), and so on.

Tip: You can force the Multiple Item Info dialog box to appear even if you've highlighted only a couple of icons. Just press Control-⌘-I. (The Option-⌘-I trick described next works for this purpose, too.)

The Get Info Panels

- **Spotlight Comments.** Here you can type in comments for your own reference. Later, you can view these remarks in any list view if you display the Comments column (page 61)—and you can find them when you conduct Spotlight searches.

- **General.** Here's where you can view the name of the icon and also see its size, creation date, most recent change date, locked status, and so on.

  If you click a disk, this info window shows you its capacity and how full it is. If you click the Trash, you see how much stuff is in it. If you click an alias, this panel shows you a Select New Original button and reveals where the original file is. The General panel always opens the first time you summon the Get Info window.

- **More Info.** Just as the name implies, here you'll find more info, most often the dimensions and color format (graphics only) and when the icon was last opened. These morsels are also easily Spotlight-searchable.

- **Name & Extension.** On this panel, you can read and edit the name of the icon in question. The "Hide extension" checkbox refers to the suffix on Mac OS X file names (the last three letters of Letter to Congress.doc, for example).

  Most Mac OS X documents, behind the scenes, have file name extensions of this kind—but Mac OS X comes factory-set to hide them. By turning off this checkbox, you can make the suffix reappear for an individual file. (Conversely, if you've elected to have Mac OS X *show* all file name suffixes, then this checkbox lets you hide the extensions on individual icons.)

- **Open with.** This section is available for documents only. Use the controls on this screen to specify which program will open when you double-click this document, or any document of its type.

- **Preview.** When you're examining pictures, text files, PDF files, Microsoft Office files, sounds, clippings, and movies, you see a magnified thumbnail version of what's actually *in* that document. This preview is like a tiny version of Quick Look (Chapter 2). A controller lets you play sounds and movies where appropriate.

- **Sharing & Permissions.** This panel is available for all kinds of icons. If other people have access to your Mac (either from across the network or when logging in, in person), this panel lets you specify who is allowed to open or change this particular icon. See Chapter 14 for a complete discussion of this hairy topic.

The Spotlight Menu

Every computer offers a way to find files. And every system offers several different ways to open them. But Spotlight, a star feature of Mac OS X, combines these two functions in a fast, efficient way.

See the little magnifying-glass icon (🔍) in your menu bar? That's the mouse-driven way to open the Spotlight search box.

The other way is to press ⌘-space bar. If you can memorize only one keystroke on your Mac, that's the one to learn. It works both at the desktop and when you're in other programs. In any case, the Spotlight text box appears just below your menu bar (Figure 3-9).

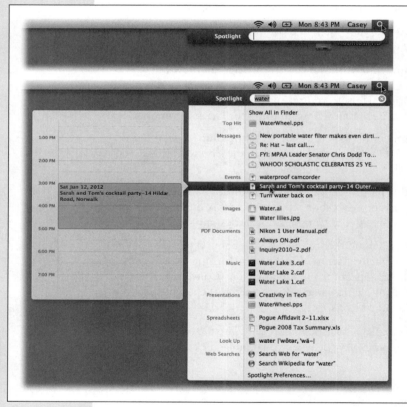

Figure 3-9:
Top: Press ⌘-space bar, or click the magnifying-glass icon, to make the search box appear.

Bottom: As you type, Spotlight builds the list of every match it can find, neatly organized by type: programs, documents, folders, images, PDF documents, and so on. But don't miss what may be one of the most useful tweaks in all of Liondom: If you're not sure what something is, point to it without clicking—or pause on it as you walk down the list with the arrow keys. A Quick Look preview pops out to the left. It shows exactly what's in that movie, picture, document, or whatever. If your search has found an appointment from your calendar, you actually see a slice of that day's calendar, showing the appointment in context!

Begin typing to identify what you want to find and open. For example, if you're trying to find a file called *Pokémon Fantasy League.doc,* typing just *pok* or *leag* would probably suffice. (Spotlight doesn't find text in the *middles* of words, though; it searches from the beginnings of words.)

A menu immediately appears below the search box, listing everything Spotlight can find containing what you've typed so far. (This is a live, interactive search; that is, Spotlight modifies the menu of search results *as you type.)* The menu lists every file, folder, program, email message, address book entry, calendar appointment, picture, movie, PDF document, music file, Web bookmark, Microsoft Office document (Word, PowerPoint, Excel, Entourage) , System Preferences panel, To Do item, chat transcript, Web site in your History list, photo, iChat buddy name, and even font that contains what you typed, regardless of its name or folder location.

Tip: Spotlight can even find photos according to *who is in them* (using iPhoto's Faces feature) or where they were taken (using iPhoto's Places feature). If you use iChat (Chapter 13), Spotlight also finds the lucky members of your Buddy lists. It can also find things according to their file types (type *.doc* to find Word files), download source (type *cnet.com* to find programs you downloaded from that site), sender (a name or email address), and Finder label.

If you see the icon you were hoping to dig up, just click it to open it. Or use the arrow keys to "walk down" the menu, and then press Return to open the one you want.

You can use the Quick Look preview to see what something is before you take the time to open it, as described in Chapter 2. Or check out Figure 3-10 to see how to find out *where something is.*

Figure 3-10:
If you press ⌘-Option as you point to one of the results, you get a line of text beneath the image that identifies the file's location.

If you click an application, it pops onto the screen. If you select a System Preferences panel, System Preferences opens and presents that panel. If you choose an appointment, the iCal program opens, already set to the appropriate day and time. Selecting an email message opens that message in Mail or Outlook. And so on.

Spotlight is so fast, it eliminates a lot of the folders-in-folders business that's a side effect of modern computing. Why burrow around in folders when you can open any file or program with a couple of keystrokes?

Tip: You can drag icons right out of the results list. For example, you can drag one onto the Desktop to park it there, into a window or a folder to move it, into the Trash to delete it, onto the AirDrop icon (in the Sidebar) to hand it over to a colleague, to another disk icon to back it up, and so on.

Spotlight-Menu Tips

It should be no surprise that a feature as important as Spotlight comes loaded with options, tips, and tricks. Here it is—the official, unexpurgated Spotlight Tip-O-Rama:

- If the very first item—labeled Top Hit—is the icon you were looking for, just press Return to open it. This is a huge deal, because it means that in most cases, you can perform the entire operation without ever taking your hands off the keyboard.

GEM IN THE ROUGH

Sweet Spotlight Serendipity: Equations and Definitions

Spotlight has two secret features that turn it into a different beast altogether.

First, it's a tiny pocket calculator, always at the ready. Click in the search box (or press ⌘-space bar), type or paste *38*48.2-7+55,* and marvel at the first result in the Spotlight menu: *1879.6.* There's your answer—and you didn't even have to fire up the Calculator.

(For shorter equations—only a few characters long—the first result in the Spotlight menu shows the *entire* equation, like *.15*234=35.1.*)

And it's not just a four-function calculator, either. It works with square roots: Type *sqrt(25),* and you'll get the answer 5. It also works with powers: Type *pow(6,6)*—that is, 6 to the power of 6—and you'll get 46656. You can even type *pi* to represent, you know, pi.

You can copy the result to the Clipboard, or even drag it out of the Spotlight bar into another program.

For a complete list of math functions in Spotlight, open Terminal (in your Mac's Applications→Utilities folder), type *man math,* and press Return.

Second, the Spotlight menu is now a full-blown English dictionary. Or, more specifically, it's wired directly into Mac OS X's *own* dictionary, which sits in your Applications folder.

So if you type a word—say, *myrmecophile*—into the search box, you'll see the Dictionary definition near the bottom of the results. Point to it without clicking to read the full-blown entry, thanks to the pop-out Quick Look preview. (In this example, that would be: "n: an invertebrate or plant that has a symbiotic relationship with ants.")

To open Safari in a hurry, for example, press ⌘-space bar (to open the Spotlight bar), type *safa,* and hit Return, all in rapid-fire sequence, without even looking. Presto: Safari is before you.

And what, exactly, is the Top Hit? Mac OS X chooses it based on its *relevance* (the importance of your search term inside that item) and timeliness (when you last opened it).

Tip: Spotlight makes a spectacular application launcher. That's because Job One for Spotlight is to display the names of matching *programs* in the results menu. Their names appear in the list nearly instantly—long before Spotlight has built the rest of the menu of search results.

If some program on your hard drive doesn't have a Dock icon, for example—or even if it does—there's no faster way to open it than to use Spotlight.

- To jump to a search result's Finder icon instead of opening it, ⌘-click its name.

- Spotlight's menu shows you only 20 of the most likely suspects, evenly divided among the categories (Documents, Applications, and so on). The downside: To see the complete list, you have to open the Spotlight *window* (page 112).

  The upside: It's fairly easy to open something in this menu from the keyboard. Just press ⌘-↓ (or ⌘-↑) to jump from category to category. Once you've highlighted the first result in a category, you can walk through the remaining four by pressing the arrow key by itself. Then, once you've highlighted what you want, press Return to open it.

  In other words, you can get to anything in the Spotlight menu with only a few keystrokes.

- The Esc key (top-left corner of your keyboard) offers a two-stage "back out of this" method. Tap it once to close the Spotlight menu and erase what you've typed, so that you're all ready to type in something different. Tap Esc a *second* time to close the Spotlight text box entirely, having given up on the whole idea of searching.

  (If you just want to cancel the whole thing in *one* step, press ⌘-space bar again, or ⌘-period, or ⌘-Esc.)

- Think of Spotlight as your little black book. When you need to look up a number in Address Book, don't bother opening Address Book; it's faster to use Spotlight. You can type somebody's name or even part of someone's phone number.

- If you're searching for just one word, you'll see a "Look Up" category near the bottom of the results menu. See the box on the previous page for details.

- The bottom of Spotlight always lists commands for "Search Web for [your phrase]" and "Search Wikipedia for [your phrase]." They take you straight to the Google search or the Wikipedia (online encyclopedia) results for whatever you typed.

- Among a million other things, Spotlight tracks the keywords, descriptions, faces, and places you've applied to your pictures in iPhoto. As a result, you can find, open, or insert any iPhoto photo at any time, no matter what program you're using, just by using the Spotlight box at the top of every Open File dialog box (page 175)! This is a great way to insert a photo into an outgoing email message, a presentation, or a Web page you're designing. iPhoto doesn't even have to be running.

- Spotlight is also a quick way to adjust one of your Mac's preference settings. Instead of opening the System Preferences program, type the first few letters of, say, *volume* or *network* or *clock* into Spotlight. The Spotlight menu lists the appropriate System Preferences panel, so you can jump directly to it.

- As shown in Figure 3-10, you get a preview of what's inside a file listed in the Spotlight menu when you point to it without clicking. But if you add the ⌘ key, you see a tiny line of text below the preview. It tells you the item's actual name—which is useful if Spotlight listed something because of text that appears *inside* the file, not its name—and if you wait a moment, you also see its folder path (that is, where it is on your hard drive).

Tip: If you're in a hurry, just press ⌘-Option as you point. That makes the folder path appear immediately.

- While you're pointing to something in the results list, you can press ⌘-I to open the Get Info window for it.

- Spotlight shows you only the matches from *your account* and the public areas of the Mac (like the System, Application, and Developer folders)—but not what's in anyone else's Home folder. If you were hoping to search your spouse's email for phrases like "meet you at midnight," forget it.

- If Spotlight finds a different version of something on each of two hard drives, it lets you know by displaying a faint gray hard drive name after each such item in the menu.

- Spotlight works by storing an *index,* a private, multimegabyte Dewey Decimal System, on each hard drive, disk partition, or USB flash (memory) drive. If you have some oddball type of disk, like a hard drive that's been formatted for Windows, Spotlight doesn't ordinarily index it—but you can turn on indexing by using the File→Get Info command on that drive's icon.

Tip: Spotlight can even find words inside files on other computers on your network—as long as they're also Macs running Leopard, Snow Leopard, or Lion. If not, Spotlight can search only for the names of files on other networked computers.

Advanced Menu Searches

Most people just type the words they're looking for into the Spotlight box. But if that's all you type, you're missing a lot of the fun.

Use quotes

If you type more than one word, Spotlight works just the way Google does. That is, it finds things that contain both words *somewhere* inside.

But if you're searching for a phrase where the words really belong together, put quotes around them. You'll save yourself from having to wade through hundreds of results where the words appear *separately*.

For example, searching for *military intelligence* rounds up documents that contain those two words, but not necessarily side by side. Searching for *"military intelligence"* finds documents that contain that exact phrase. (Insert your own political joke here.)

Limit by kind

You can confine your search to certain categories using a simple code. For example, to find all photos, type *kind:image*. If you're looking for a presentation document, but you're not sure whether you used Keynote, iWork, or PowerPoint to create it, type *kind:presentation* into the box. And so on.

Here's the complete list of kinds. Remember to precede each keyword type with *kind* and a colon.

To find this:	Use one of these keywords:
a program	app, application, applications
someone in your Address Book	contact, contacts
a folder	folder, folders
a message in Mail	email, emails, mail message, mail messages
an iCal appointment	event, events
an iCal task	to do, to dos, todo, todos
a graphic	image, images
a movie	movie, movies
a music file	music
an audio file	audio
a PDF file	pdf, pdfs
a System Preferences control	preferences, system preferences
a Safari bookmark	bookmark, bookmarks
a font	font, fonts
a presentation (PowerPoint, say)	presentation, presentations

You can combine these codes with the text you're seeking, too. For example, if you're pretty sure you had a photo called "Naked Mole-Rat," you could cut directly to it by typing *mole kind:images* or *kind:images mole*. (The order doesn't matter.)

Limit by recent date

You can use a similar code to restrict the search by chronology. If you type *date: yesterday,* then Spotlight limits its hunt to items you last opened yesterday.

Here's the complete list of date keywords you can use: *this week, this month, this year; today, yesterday, tomorrow; next week, next month, next year.* (The last four items are useful only for finding upcoming iCal appointments. Even Spotlight can't show you files you haven't created yet.)

Limit by metadata

These days, you can limit Spotlight searches by *any* of the 125 different info-morsels that may be stored as part of the files on your Mac: author, audio bit rate, city, composer, camera model, pixel width, and so on—so-called *metadata*. (Metadata means "data about the data"—that is, descriptive info-bites about the files themselves.) Here are a few examples:

- *author:casey.* Finds all documents with "casey" in the Author field. (This presumes that you've actually *entered* the name Casey into the document's Author box. Microsoft Word, for example, has a place to store this information.)

- *width:800.* Finds all graphics that are 800 pixels wide.

- *flash:1.* Finds all photos that were taken with the camera's flash on. (To find photos with the flash *off,* you'd type *flash:0.* A number of the yes/no criteria work this way: Use 1 for yes, 0 for no.)

- *modified:3/7/12-3/10/12.* Finds all documents modified between March 7 and March 10, 2012. You can also type *created:6/1/12* to find all the files you created on June 1, 2012. Type *modified:<=3/9/12* to find all documents you edited *on or before* March 9, 2012.

  As you can see, three range-finding symbols are available for your queries: <, >, and - (hyphen). The < means "before" or "less than"; the > means "after" or "greater than"; and the hyphen indicates a range (of dates, sizes, or whatever you're looking for).

Tip: Here again, you can string words together. To find all PDFs you opened today, use date:today kind:PDF. And if you're looking for a PDF document that you created on July 4, 2012, containing the word "wombat," you can type created:7/4/12 kind:pdf wombat—although at this point, you're not saving all that much time.

The Spotlight Window

As you may have noticed, the Spotlight menu doesn't list *every* match on your hard drive. Unless you own one of those extremely rare 60-inch Apple Skyscraper Displays, there just isn't room.

Instead, Spotlight uses some fancy behind-the-scenes analysis to calculate and display the *20 most likely* matches for what you typed. But at the top of the menu, it usually says something like "Show All," meaning that there are other candidates.

There is, however, a second, more powerful way into the Spotlight labyrinth. And that's the Spotlight *window,* shown in Figure 3-11.

From the Spotlight Menu

If the Spotlight menu—its Most Likely to Succeed list—doesn't include what you're looking for, then click Show All in Finder. You've just opened the Spotlight window.

Now you have access to the *complete* list of matches, neatly listed in what appears to be a standard Finder window.

Figure 3-11:
The Spotlight window either lists nothing *(top)*—or everything *on your hard drive (bottom), depending on how you open it. Either way, it's ready to search your entire hard drive (except other people's Home folders). But Spotlight has many tricks up its software sleeve.*

From the Finder

When you're in the Finder, you can also open the Spotlight window *directly,* without using the Spotlight menu as a trigger. Actually, there are three ways to get there:

• ⌘-F (for *Find,* get it?). When you choose File→Find (⌘-F), you get an *empty* Spotlight window, ready to fill in for your search (Figure 3-11, top).

Tip: When the Find window opens, what folder does it intend to search?

That's up to you. Choose Finder→Preferences→Advanced. From the "When performing a search" pop-up menu, you can choose Search This Mac, Search the Current Folder (usually what you want), or Use the Previous Search Scope (that is, either "the whole Mac" or "the current folder," whichever you set up last time).

• **Option-⌘-space bar.** This keystroke opens the same window. But it always comes set to search everything on your Mac (except other people's Home folders, of course), regardless of the setting you made in Preferences (as described in the tip above).

• **Open any desktop window, and type something into the search box.** Presto—the mild-mannered folder window turns into the Spotlight window, complete with search results.

The Basic Search

When the Spotlight window opens, you can start typing whatever you're looking for into the search box at the top.

As you type, the window fills with a list of the files and folders whose names contain what you typed. It's just like the Spotlight menu, but without the 20-item limit (Figure 3-12, middle).

Figure 3-12:

Top: The Spotlight window stands ready to search the currently open window.

Middle: When you begin to type your search term, Lion presents a pop-up menu of suggestions. For example, when you type apple, it's asking: "Would you like me to limit the search results to files with the word 'apple' in their names?" If you ignore the suggestions, the window shows you all matches—including files with the word "apple" inside them.

Bottom: But if you click one of those suggestions—"Filename contains apple," in this case—the results window changes. Now you're seeing only icons that contain the word "apple."

Where to look

The three phrases at the top of the window—This Mac, [Folder Name], and Shared—
are buttons. Click one to tell Spotlight where to search:

- **This Mac** means your *entire* computer, including secondary disks attached to it
  (or installed inside)—minus other people's files.

- **"Letters to Congress"** (or whatever the current window is) limits the search to
  whatever window was open. So if you want to search your Pictures folder, open
  it first and *then* hit ⌘-F. You'll see the "Pictures" button at the top of the window,
  and you can click it to restrict the search to that folder.

- **Shared.** Click this button to expand the search to your *entire network* and all the
  computers on it. (This assumes, of course, that you've brought their icons to your
  screen as described in Chapter 14.)

  If the other computers are Macs running Mac OS X Leopard, Snow Leopard, or
  Lion, Spotlight can search their files just the way it does on your own Mac—finding
  words inside the files, for example. If they're any other kind of computer, Spotlight
  can search for files only by name.

Tip: If the object of your quest doesn't show up, you can adjust the scope of the search with one quick
click on another button at the top of the window, like This Mac or Shared. Spotlight updates the results list.

Then again, if you always prefer one of those options, don't forget that you can save yourself a click by
choosing it to be the new factory setting. Specify your favorite "where to look" option by visiting Finder→Pref-
erences→Advanced and using the "When performing a search" pop-up menu. Your choices are Search This
Mac, Search the Current Folder, or Use the Previous Search Scope (that is, "whatever I chose last time").

The suggestions list

Mac OS X tries to figure out what you're looking for—file names or words inside files.
It may show you both in the same results list.

But more important, it offers a suggestions pop-up menu, shown in Figure 3-13. Its
purpose is to help you narrow down the results list with one quick click. Whatever
you click here is instantly immortalized as a search token, described below.

You may see any of these headings in the suggestions list:

- **Filenames.** The top option is always "Filenames"; click it to search by the files' names
  only. If you type *chris* into the box, you want files whose *names* contain that word.

- **Sent by.** If you type *chris,* the Mac wants to know if, by chance, you're looking for
  email messages and other documents from somebody *named* Chris (or Christina,
  or Christopher…).

- **Kinds.** If you type *image,* the Kinds option here offers you choices like *image* (any
  kind), *JPEG image, Disk image,* or *Portable Network Graphics Image.* If you type
  document, you get options like *Word document* and *PDF document.* If you search

for *photo,* the menu lets you pinpoint files whose *file type* contains "photo"—like iPhoto Libraries or Adobe Photoshop files. And so on.

Figure 3-13:
If you find these suggestions helpful, click one (or press the ↓ key to walk down the list, and then press Return to select the one you want). If you're fine with the search results as they've already popped up—no further refining necessary—tap the Esc key to close the drop-down list.

- **Downloaded From.** You see this option when what you type is a Web address. If you type *Macworld* into the search box, then "Downloaded From Macworld.com" appears in the results list—a handy way to round up all the files you've downloaded from a specific site.

- **Dates.** If you type a month (*august, aug,* or *august 2012*) or a year into the search box, the suggestions pop-up menu says, "Dates: August 2012" (or whatever). Clicking it lets you do a quick roundup of all files you created, modified, last opened, or added during that period.

- **Labels.** Here's yet another way to use the file labels described on page 98. When you type a search term that matches one of your labels (for example, *green*), the suggestions menu includes "Labels: green."

In each case, the suggestions in this menu reflect only files that actually *exist* on your Mac. If you search for "green," but green isn't one of your Finder labels, then the Labels suggestion doesn't appear. If you haven't downloaded anything from Macworld.com, then that option doesn't appear. And so on.

Once you learn to actually start *using* these suggestions—once you get a hang of the kinds of things they offer—you can get a lot of mileage out of them.

If, on the other hand, you just find them confusing, no big deal. Tap the Esc key to close the suggestions list and reveal the existing Spotlight window.

Power Searches with Tokens

The real beauty of the Spotlight window is that it can hunt down icons via more specific searches than you could do using the Spotlight menu. For example, a feature called *tokens* let you combine criteria, so you find only *music* files sent to you by *Casey*. (A token, in Apple's usage, means "a visual representation of a search criterion.")

Here, for example, is how you might search for pictures of Chris that were last opened in December 2010.

1. **In the Finder, press ⌘-F.**

   The Spotlight window opens.

2. **In the search box, type *image*.**

   Sure enough: The window now shows everything on your Mac that *is* an image or *contains* the word "image" in its name, or even contains the word "*image*" within the file. But the list of suggestions (Figure 3-14) wants to know: Which do you really want? Files that are images? Or files with the word "image" in their names?

Figure 3-14:
Each time you add a criterion by clicking the drop-down list shown in Figure 3-13, Lion adds a new token (criterion bubble) to the search box.

---

3. **In the suggestions menu, under Kinds, click *Image*.**

   You've just pared down the list of results. Now it shows only the files that *are* photos.

   Note, too, that the first *token* has appeared. Each time you click a refinement criterion, as you did in this step, Mac OS X enshrines it in the search box as a shaded bubble. In this case, it created a token that says, "Kind: Image." (You can see it in Figure 3-14.)

   Now you need to narrow the quest to files containing the word Chris.

4. **Continue typing in the search box. This time, type *chris*.**

   The suggestions appear again, offering options for file names and, probably, a Sent By list that lists everyone named Chris who's ever sent you messages or files. What you want is images whose names contain the *word* "Chris."

5. **Click *Filenames*.**

The list of files is much smaller now. It shows only image files with "Chris" in their names.

For your final stunt, you'll screen out all but the December images.

6. **Continue typing in the search box. This time, type** *dec.*

This time, the suggestions list offers dates like *December 2010* and *December 2011*. You can see the result so far in Figure 3-14.

7. **Click the month you want.**

And voilà: The results list shows you only the December photos of Chris.

To delete a token, click it and then press the Delete key, or backspace over it. You can also edit one: Double-click the right side of the token bubble; now you can retype the search term.

Note: This same feature is also in Mail, where it's even more useful; you have search options like Subject, From, To, and so on.

Power Searching the Old Way

Lion's search tokens are supposed to make multi-criteria searches easier than they used to be. But they're not as powerful as the Old Way, which is still around.

Using the Old Way of power searching, you can set up a search that finds a document whose name begins with the letters *Cro,* is over a megabyte in size, was created after 10/1/12 but before the end of the year, was changed within the past week, has the file name suffix *.doc,* and contains the phrase "attitude adjustment." (Of course, if you knew *that* much about a file, you'd probably know where it is, too. But you get the picture.)

In all, the Old Way lets you specify over 125 different search criteria: date modified, file size, the "last opened" date, color label, copyright holder's name, shutter speed (of a digital photo), tempo (of a music file), and so on. Figure 3-15 illustrates how detailed this kind of search can be.

Figure 3-15:
*By repeatedly clicking the **+** button, you can turn on as many criteria as you'd like; each additional row further narrows the search. To delete a row, click the **—** button at its right end.*

To set up a complex search like this, use the second row of controls at the top of the window.

And the third, and the fourth, and the fifth. Each time you click one of the **+** buttons at the right end of the window, a new criterion row appears; use its pop-up menus to specify *what* date, *what* file size, and so on.

Tip: If you press Option, the **+** button changes into a "..." button. When you click it, you get sub-rows of parameters for a single criterion. A pop-up menu lets you choose Any, All, or None, so that you can build what are called exclusionary searches.

The idea here is that you can set up a search for documents created between November 1 and 7 or documents created between November 10 and 14. Or files named Complaint that are also either Word or InDesign files.

The mind boggles.

Here's a rundown of the ways you can restrict your search, according to the options in the first pop-up menu of a row. Note that after you choose from that first pop-up menu (Last Opened, for example), you're supposed to use the additional pop-up menus to narrow the choice ("within last," "2," and "weeks," for example), as you'll read below.

Kind

When the first pop-up menu says Kind, you can use the second pop-up menu to indicate what kind of file you're looking for: Applications, Documents, Executables (programs and Dashboard widgets), Folders, Images, Movies, Music, PDF files, Presentations, Text files, or Other.

For example, when you're trying to free up some space on your drive, you could round up all your movie files, which tend to be huge. Choosing one of these file types makes the window begin to fill with matches automatically and instantly.

And what if the item you're looking for isn't among those 10 canned choices? What if it's an alias, or a Photoshop plug-in, or some other type?

That's what the Other option is all about. Here you can type in almost anything that specifies a kind of file: *Word, Excel, TIFF, JPEG, AAC, final cut, imovie, alias, zip, html,* or whatever.

Last opened date/Last modified date/Created date

When you choose one of these options from the first pop-up menu, the second pop-up menu lets you isolate files, programs, and folders according to the last time you opened them, the last time you changed them, or when they were created.

- **Today, yesterday, this week, this month, this year.** This second pop-up menu offers quick, canned time-limiting options.

- **Within last, exactly, before, after.** These let you be more precise. If you choose "before," "after," or "exactly," then your criterion row sprouts a month/day/year control that lets you round up items that you last opened or changed before, after, or on a specific day, like 5/27/12. If you choose "within last," then you can limit the search to things you've opened or changed within a specified number of days, weeks, months, or years.

These are awesomely useful controls, because they let you specify a chronological window for whatever you're looking for.

Tip: You're allowed to add two Date rows—a great trick that lets you round up files that you created or edited between two dates. Set up the first Date row to say "is after" and the second one to say "is before."

In fact, if it doesn't hurt your brain to think about it, how about this? You can even have more than two Date rows. Use one pair to specify a range of dates for the file's creation date and two other rows to limit when it was modified.

Name

Spotlight likes to find text *anywhere* inside your files, no matter what their *names* are. But when you want to search for an icon by the text that's in only its *name,* this is your ticket. (Capitalization doesn't matter.)

Wouldn't it be faster just to click Filenames in the suggestions pop-up menu (Figure 3-13)? Yes—but using the search window offers you far more control, thanks to the second pop-up menu that offers you options like "Matches" (you'll see files whose names contain entire words you're looking for), "Contains" (the position of the words you type doesn't matter), "Starts with," "Ends with," and "Is."

Contents

You can think of this option as the opposite of Name. It finds *only* the text that's inside your files and completely ignores their icon names.

That's a handy function when, for example, a document's name doesn't match its contents. Maybe a marauding toddler playing Kid Pix renamed your doctoral thesis "xggrjpO#$5%////." Or maybe you just can't remember what you called something.

Other

If this were a math equation, it might look like this: *options × options = overwhelming.*

Choosing Other from the first pop-up menu opens a special dialog box containing at least 125 *other* criteria. Not just the big kahunas like Name, Size, and Kind, but far more targeted (and obscure) criteria like "Bits per sample" (so you can round up MP3 music files of a certain quality), "Device make" (so you can round up all digital photos taken with, say, a Canon Rebel camera), "Key signature" (so you can find all the GarageBand songs you wrote in the key of F sharp), "Pages" (so you can find all Word documents that are really long), and so on. Each one comes with a short description.

You may think Spotlight is offering you a staggering array of file-type criteria. In fact, though, big bunches of information categories (technically called *metadata)* are all hooks for a relatively small number of document types. For example:

- **Digital photos and other graphics files** account for the metadata types alpha channel, aperture, color space, device make, device model, EXIF version, exposure mode, exposure program, exposure time, flash, f-number, focal length, ISO speed, max aperture, metering mode, orientation, pixel height, pixel width, red eye, resolution height, resolution width, and white balance.

- **Digital music files** have searchable metadata categories like album, audio bit rate, bits per sample, channel count, composer, duration, General MIDI sequence, key signature, lyricist, musical genre, recording date, sample rate, tempo, time signature, track number, and year recorded. There's even a special set of parameters for GarageBand and Soundtrack documents, including instrument category, instrument name, loop descriptors, loop file type, loop original key, and loop scale type.

- **Microsoft Office documents** can contain info bits like authors, contributors, fonts, languages, pages, publishers, and contact information (name, phone number, and so on).

This massive list also harbors a few criteria you may use more often, like Size, File Label, and Visibility (which lets you see all the invisible files on your hard drive).

Tip: Don't miss the search box in this dialog box. It makes it super-easy to pluck one useful criterion needle—Size, say—out of the haystack. Also don't forget about the In Menu checkbox in the right column. It lets you add one of these criteria to the main pop-up menu, so you don't have to go burrowing into Other again the next time.

What to Do with Search Results

The results window is a regular old Finder window, with all the familiar views and controls (Figure 3-16).

You can work with anything in the results window exactly as though it were in a regular Finder window: Drag something to the Trash, rename something, press the space bar for a Quick Look at it, drag something to the desktop to move it there, drag something onto a Dock icon to open it with a certain program, Option-⌘-drag it to the desktop to create an alias, and so on.

You can move up or down the list by pressing the arrow keys, scroll a "page" at a time with the Page Up and Page Down keys, and so on. You can also highlight multiple icons simultaneously, the same way you would in a Finder list view: Highlight all of them by choosing Edit→Select All, highlight individual items by ⌘-clicking them, drag diagonally to enclose a cluster of items, and so on. Or you can do the following:

- **Get more information** about a result by selecting it and then choosing File→Get Info (⌘-I). The normal Get Info window appears, complete with date, size, and location information.

- **Find out where it is.** It's nice to see all the search results in one list, but you're not actually seeing them in their native habitats: the Finder folder windows where they physically reside.

    If you click once on an icon in the results, then the bottom edge of the window becomes a folder map that shows you where that item is.

For example, in Figure 3-16, the notation in the Path strip means: "The Kids at Russian Academy.JPG icon you found is in the St. Pete Photos folder, which is in the Pictures folder, which is in d's Home folder."

To get your hands on the actual icon, choose File→Open Enclosing Folder (⌘-R). Mac OS X highlights the icon in question, sitting there in its window, wherever it happens to be on your hard drive.

- **Open the file (or open one of the folders it's in).** If one of the found files is the one you were looking for, double-click it to open it (or highlight it and press either ⌘-O or ⌘-↓). In many cases, you don't know or care where the file was—you just want to get into it.

Tip: You can also double-click to open any of the folders in the folder map at the bottom of the window. For example, in Figure 3-16, you could double-click the selected JPEG icon to open it, or the St Pete Photos folder to open it, and so on.

Figure 3-16:
Click a result once to see where it sits on your hard drive (bottom). If the window is too narrow to reveal the full folder path, run your cursor over the folders without clicking. As your mouse moves from one folder to another, the Mac briefly reveals its name, compressing other folders as necessary to make room. (Sub-Tip: You can drag icons into these folders, too.)

- **Move or delete the file.** You can drag an item directly out of the found-files list and into a different folder, window, or disk—or straight to the Dock or the Trash. If you click something else and then reclick the dragged item in the results list, the folder map at the bottom of the window updates itself to reflect the file's new location.

- **Start over.** If you'd like to repeat the search using a different search phrase, just edit the text in the search box. (Press ⌘-F to empty the search box and the Spotlight window.)

- **Give up.** If none of these avenues suits your fancy, you can close the window as you would any other (⌘-W).

Customizing Spotlight

You've just read about how Spotlight works fresh out of the box. But you can tailor its behavior, both for security reasons and to fit it to the kinds of work you do.

Here are three ways to open the Spotlight preferences center:

- **Choose Spotlight Preferences** at the bottom of the Spotlight menu just after you've performed a search.

- **Use Spotlight itself.** Hit ⌘-space bar, type *spotl,* and press Return.

- **Choose** ⌘→**System Preferences. Click Spotlight.**

In any case, you wind up face to face with the dialog box shown in Figure 3-17.

Figure 3-17:
Here's where you can specify what categories of icons you want Spotlight to search, which order you want them listed in the Spotlight menu, and what keystroke you want to use for highlighting the Spotlight search box.

You can tweak Spotlight in three ways here, all very useful:

- **Turn off categories.** The list of checkboxes identifies what Spotlight tracks. If you find that Spotlight uses up valuable menu space listing, say, Web bookmarks or fonts—stuff you don't need to find very often—then turn off their checkboxes. Now the Spotlight menu's 20 precious slots are allotted to icon types you care more about.

- **Prioritize the categories.** This dialog box also lets you change the *order* of the category results; just drag a list item up or down to change where it appears in the Spotlight menu. If you're a party planner who spends all day on the phone, and the most important Spotlight function for you is its ability to look up someone in your Address Book, then drag Contacts to the top of the list. You'll need fewer arrow-key presses once the results menu appears.

- **Change the keystroke.** Ordinarily, pressing ⌘-space bar highlights the Spotlight search box in your menu bar, and Option-⌘-space bar opens the Searching window. If these keystrokes clash with some other key assignment in your software, though, you can reassign them to almost any other keystroke you like.

Most people notice only the pop-up menu that lets you select one of your F-keys (the function keys at the top of your keyboard). But you can also click inside the white box that lists the keystroke and then press *any* key combination—Control-S, for example—to choose something different.

Apple assumes no responsibility for your choosing a keystroke that messes up some other function on your Mac. ⌘-S, for example, would not be a good choice.

On the other hand, if you choose a Spotlight keystroke that Mac OS X uses for some other function, a little yellow alert icon appears in the Spotlight pane. This icon is actually a button; clicking it brings you to the Keyboard & Mouse pane, where you can see exactly which keystroke is in dispute and change it.

Privacy Settings

Ordinarily, Spotlight looks for matches wherever it can, except in other people's Home folders. (That is, you can't search through other people's stuff).

But even within your account, you can hide certain folders from Spotlight searches. Maybe you have privacy concerns—for example, you don't want your spouse Spotlighting your stuff while you're away from your desk. Maybe you just want to create more focused Spotlight searches, removing a lot of old, extraneous junk from its database.

Either way, the steps are simple. Open the Spotlight panel of System Preferences, as described previously. Click the Privacy tab. Figure 3-18 explains the remaining steps.

Tip: When you mark a disk or folder as non-searchable, Spotlight deletes its entire *index* (its invisible card-catalog filing system) from that disk. If Spotlight ever seems to be acting wackily, you can use this function to make it rebuild its own index file on the problem disk. Just drag the disk into the Privacy list and then remove it again. Spotlight deletes, and then rebuilds, the index for that disk.

(Don't forget the part about "remove it again," though. If you add a disk to the Privacy list, Spotlight is no longer able to find *anything* on it, even if you can see it right in front of you.)

Once you've built up the list of private disks and folders, close System Preferences. Spotlight now pretends the private items don't even exist.

Figure 3-18:
You can add disks, partitions, or folders to the list of non-searchable items just by dragging them from the desktop into this window. Or, if the private items aren't visible at the moment, you can click the + button, navigate to your hard drive, select the item, and then click Choose. To remove something from this list, click it and then press the Delete key or click the − button.

Smart Folders

A *smart folder* is a self-updating folder that, in essence, performs a continual, 24/7 search for the criteria you specify. (Smart folders are a lot like smart albums in iPhoto and iTunes, smart mailboxes in Mail, and so on.)

Note: In truth, the smart folder performs a search for the specified criteria *at the moment you open it.* But because it's so fast, it feels as though it's been quietly searching all along.

The key to creating one, as it turns out, is the little Save button in the upper-right corner of the Spotlight window when you've built a search request (using either tokens or individual criteria rows).

Here's a common example—one that you can't replicate in any other operating system. You choose File→Find. You set up the pop-up menus to say "last opened date" and "this week." You click Save. You name the smart folder something like Current Crises, and you turn on Add to Sidebar (Figure 3-19).

Tip: Behind the scenes, smart folders you create are actually special files that are stored in your Home→Library→Saved Searches folder.

From now on, whenever you click that smart folder, it reveals all the files you've worked on in the past week. The great part is that these items' *real* locations may be all over the map, scattered around your Mac and your network. But through the magic of the smart folder, they appear as though they're all in one neat folder.

Tip: If you decide your original search criteria need a little fine-tuning, click the smart folder. From the ✿ menu, choose Show Search Criteria. You're back on the original setting-up-the-search window. Use the pop-up menus and other controls to tweak your search setup, and then click the Save button once again.

To delete a smart folder, just ⌘-drag its icon out of the Sidebar. (Or if it's anywhere else, like on your desktop, drag it to the Trash like any other folder.)

Figure 3-19:
Mac OS X can preserve your search as a smart folder listed in the Sidebar—at least, it can as long as Add to Sidebar is turned on. You can stash a smart folder in your Dock, too, although it doesn't display a stack of its contents, as normal folders do.

Documents, Programs & Mission Control

Тhe beauty of life in the Era of Switchers is that most of the big-boy programs are available in nearly identical versions for both the Mac and Windows. Word, Excel, and PowerPoint; Photoshop, Illustrator, and InDesign; FileMaker Pro; Dreamweaver; and many other programs are available for both systems. Sometimes you have to buy the Mac version separately; sometimes it comes in the same package.

The best part: The documents you create with the Mac versions are generally *identical in format* to the ones created in Windows. A Microsoft Word document, for example, requires no conversion when transferred from a Mac to a PC or vice versa. It is what it is—a .doc or .docx file.

Same thing with Excel spreadsheets (.xls), PowerPoint slideshows (.ppt), Photoshop documents (.psd), and on and on. You may occasionally encounter a tiny formatting difference—a line thickness change, a movie file that requires a plug-in—but most documents open flawlessly when moved between Macs and PCs. (Chapter 8 offers more detail on finding Mac versions of your favorite PC programs.)

But even if switching to the Mac OS X versions of your programs is relatively easy, learning how Mac OS X programs *in general* operate may require some study. As this chapter will make clear, the relationship between programs and their documents differs in several substantial ways from the way things work in Windows.

A Word About Lion Apps

The whole point of owning a computer, of course, is to run *programs*—or, as Apple likes to call them these days, apps. And here's where Apple has made the biggest changes of all in Mac OS X Lion. Hope you're sitting down.

In Lion, Apple wants programs to look and work like they do on the iPad: simply. As full-screen, autosaving worlds. You're supposed to open them from a simple Home screen arrayed with app icons, and you're supposed to switch among them once they're open by swiping with your fingers on your trackpad or mouse.

This radical new vision of running programs is actually possible in Lion—sort of. The hitch is that a lot of the iPaddy features, including full-screen mode and autosaving, don't work in pre-Lion programs. Software companies have to update their apps to add these features.

Most of them will do that, but in the meantime, you'll go through a weird period of mixed metaphors, where some programs can do those tricks and others can't.

In any case, this chapter covers Apple's New Way of Running Programs, and all of its Capitalized Elements: the Mac App Store, Launchpad, Mission Control, Full Screen, Auto Save, Versions, and more.

The Mac App Store

For years, people installed software onto their computers by buying disks: floppies, CDs, and, later, DVDs.

But starting with the iPhone, people installed software onto their *phones* by downloading it directly from the Internet. Once everybody saw how convenient (and profitable) that system was, it didn't take Apple long to realize it could bring the same convenience to the Mac.

So now there's the Mac App Store—or, as the program is called in your Applications folder, just App Store. It's an online catalog of offerings from huge software companies, tiny one-person software companies, and everything in between. You can read about the programs, check out customer reviews, and, finally, download them directly to your Mac. (As you may know, Lion itself is an App Store purchase if it didn't come preinstalled on your Mac.)

There are some huge advantages to this system. Since there's no box, no disc, no registration card, no shipping, no stocking, the software can cost a lot less; Apple's own programs certainly reflect this price advantage. Plenty of programs in the App Store are actually free.

Furthermore, Apple controls the transaction on both ends—it knows who you are—so there are no serial numbers to type in. The installation no longer interrupts you with warnings like "Please enter your password to install this software" or "This software appears to have been downloaded from the Internet"; once you click Buy, the software downloads and installs itself *automatically,* without any interaction from you at all.

And there are no discs to store and hunt down later. If you ever need to reinstall a program you bought from the App Store, or if you ever get a new Mac, you just redownload it; the App Store remembers that you're a legitimate owner. Better yet, you'll be downloading the latest version of that program; you won't have to install all the ".01" patches that have come along since.

Speaking of updates: Since Apple knows what programs you have, it can let you know when new versions are available. The Software Update program has always let you know when new *Apple* software versions are available—but now it can notify you about new versions of *any* programs you own.

One final advantage: If you decide to use Launchpad, described in the following pages, anything you've bought from the App Store is super easy to delete with a single click.

The only people bemoaning the App Store Era are people with slow Internet connections (or whose Internet services are limited to a certain amount of data each month). Apple cheerfully invites them to take their Macs to an Apple Store, where there's a free, high-speed, in-store WiFi network.

Figure 4-1:
Top: Mastering the App Store won't take you much time; just about everything you need is in the toolbar at the top, including a search box and buttons like Featured, Top Charts, and Categories, which are meant to help you dive into the enormous catalog of Mac software. The remaining tab, Purchases, shows everything you've ever bought using your Apple account. If you visit this page using a different Mac, you can re-download anything you've bought—no charge.

Bottom: As with the iPhone/iPad App Store, you can read reviews of each piece of software, written by other people who've tried it.

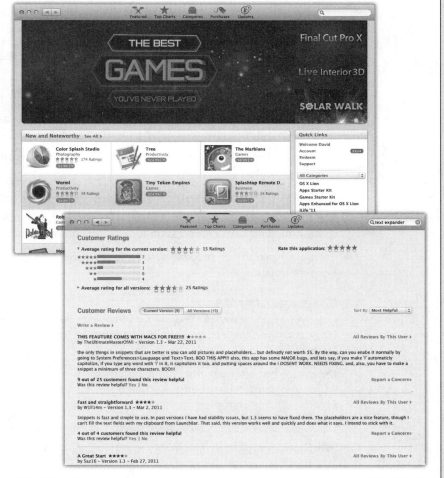

To use the Mac App Store, open the App Store program in your Applications folder (or on your Launchpad). See Figure 4-1 for details.

In general, the App Store here works exactly like the iPhone/iPad App Store. Click a program's icon to open its details page. Here you'll find reviews and ratings from other people, a description, pictures (screenshots) of the program, and much more information to help you make a good buying decision.

When you buy an app, Launchpad opens automatically, so you can see where it went.

Other Ways to Get Mac Software

In general, new programs arrive on your Mac via one of two avenues: as an Internet download (whether from the App Store or not), or on a CD or DVD.

Downloading Compressed Files

Programs you download from the Web (not the App Store) generally arrive in a specially encoded, compressed form. And unless you've changed the settings, they arrive in the Downloads folder on your Dock.

The downloaded file's name usually has one of these file name extensions:

- **.zip** is the standard compression file format for Windows and Mac files. In fact, Mac OS X has a built-in Compress command right in the File menu.

- **.sit** indicates a *StuffIt* file, the standard Macintosh file-compression format of years gone by.

- **.dmg** is a disk image, described below.

You may occasionally run into .tar files (*tape archive,* an ancient Unix utility), .gz (*gzip,* a standard Unix compression format), or combo formats like .tar.gz or .tgz.

Fortunately, your Web browser automatically unzips and unstuffs downloads of all types automatically.

Disk images (.dmg files)

Once you've downloaded a program, it often takes the form of a *disk image* file, whose name ends with the letters *.dmg* (second from the top in Figure 4-2).

Disk images are extremely common in Mac OS X. All you have to do is double-click the .dmg icon. After a moment, it magically turns into a disk icon on your desktop, which you can work with just as though it were a real disk (third from the top in Figure 4-2). For example:

- Double-click it to open it. The software you downloaded is inside.

- Remove it from your desktop by dragging it to the Trash (whose icon turns into a big silver ⏏ key as you drag), highlighting it and pressing ⌘-E (the shortcut for File→Eject), clicking its ⏏ button in the Sidebar, or Control-clicking (right-clicking) it and then choosing Eject from the shortcut menu.

You've still got the original .dmg file you downloaded, so you're not really saying goodbye to the disk image forever.

When you've finished unzipping or unstuffing a downloaded file, you may have several icons on your desktop or in the Downloads folder. Some are useful; some you're free to trash:

Figure 4-2:
Downloading a new program may strew your desktop or Downloads folder with icons. A: These are the downloaded files. Delete them after they're decompressed. B: The compressed file turns into this .dmg file. Double-click it to "mount" the disk image (if it didn't appear automatically). C: And now, the disk image itself. Double-click it to open the software installer window. (Dismiss the warning that the software came from the Internet.) "Eject" it after the installation is complete. D: Here's the actual software installer window. After the installation, you can delete all this stuff (except maybe the .dmg file, if you think you might want to install the software again later).

- **The original compressed file.** It's safe to throw away the .sit, .tar, .gz, or .tgz file you originally downloaded (after it's decompressed, of course).

- **The .dmg file.** Once you've turned it into an actual disk-drive icon, installed the software from it, and "ejected" the disk-drive icon, you can delete the .dmg file. Keep it only if you think you might need to reinstall the software someday.

Note: If you try to trash the .dmg file before removing the disk-drive icon from the screen, you'll get a "file in use" error message when you try to empty the Trash.

- **The disk image itself.** This final icon, the one that contains the actual software or its installer (third from the top in Figure 4-2), doesn't exist as a file on your hard drive. It's a phantom drive, held in memory, that will go away by itself when you log out. So after installing its software, feel free to drag it to the Trash (or highlight it and press ⌘-E to "eject" it).

Performing the installation

Once you've got a disk icon on your desktop—either a pseudo-disk from a disk image or a CD or DVD you've inserted—you're ready to install the software. You can install many Mac OS X programs just by dragging their icons or folders to your hard drive (usually the Applications folder). Others offer a traditional installer program that requires you to double-click, read and accept a license agreement, and so on.

Uninstalling Software

If you got a program from the App Store, it's easy to delete from the Launchpad (page 134).

If you got it from some other source, well, there's generally no Uninstall program. To uninstall a program, you just drag it (or its folder) to the Trash.

FREQUENTLY ASKED QUESTION

Submit to Apple

What the—I was working along in Safari, and all of a sudden it just vanished! Poof! And all I got was this lousy dialog box about "submitting to Apple." What's going on?

Apple is trying to assimilate you.

Or, more accurately, it's trying to enlist your help in ferreting out all the little glitches that make modern computing so much fun. If you're willing to click the Submit Report button and type a few comments ("I was running Word, minding my own business, and when I clicked the Print button, the whole thing just crashed"), then Apple will add your report to the thousands flowing in from everyone else.

The idea is that when its programmers get a moment, they'll study these reports, track down the patterns ("Hmm, we've received 50,000 reports about that Print button in Word"), and then chase down the software company responsible—and, presumably, get a fix under way.

The report you submit is full of technical info that helps the programmers figure out what was happening at the time of the crash, but no personal information goes along for the ride. So if you feel like doing some good for your fellow Mac fans, by all means submit the report (via the Internet) whenever you're offered the chance.

Some programs leave harmless scraps of themselves behind; to check for them, look for preference files or folders bearing the dearly departed program's name in your Library folders (especially in Application Support) and in your Home→Library→Preferences folder.

Opening Mac OS X Programs

You can launch (open) an application in any of several ways:

- Single-click an icon on the Launchpad, described on the following pages.

- Single-click a program's icon on the Dock, the Sidebar, or the Finder toolbar.

- Use Spotlight. Hit ⌘-space bar, type the first letters of the program's name, and then press Return.

- Double-click an app's icon in the Finder.

- If you've added the Applications folder to your Dock, click the Dock icon to open the pop-up fan, grid, or list of icons. Then click the program you want (or even type the first few letters of its name and then press Return).

- Highlight an application icon and then press ⌘-O (short for File→Open) or ⌘-down arrow.

- Use the submenus of the menu's Recent Items→Applications command.

- Open a *document* icon in any of these ways, or drag a document onto the icon of a program that can open it (whether in the Dock, the Finder toolbar, the Sidebar, or a folder window).

FREQUENTLY ASKED QUESTION

What's with the Big "Duh"?

So I've just installed Lion, I'm all excited, and I double-click an Excel document. And now the Mac asks me: "You are opening Microsoft Excel for the first time. Do you want to continue?" Well, HELLO! I double-clicked the icon, didn't I? Does Apple think I'm some kind of idiot?

It's not you Apple is worried about. It's the silent parade of evil hackers, lurking out there in Internet Land, waiting for the right moment to bring down the Mac.

See, spyware authors have to be sneaky about how they install their stuff on your computer. You wouldn't be so stupid as to double-click an application called Spyware Installer™, of course. So the spyware tricks you into running its installer.

In the Windows world, it commandeers a certain document type (like MP3 or JPEG), reassigning it to its installer. You innocently double-click some document, but an unanticipated program opens—and you've just opened Pandora's box.

In Mac OS X, that can't happen. When double-clicking some document opens a program for the first time, this dialog box appears, just to let you know what's about to happen. If the program that's about to open isn't the one you were expecting, well, you've got a chance to back out of it.

And if it *is* the program you were expecting, click Continue. You won't be asked again about this version of this particular program.

Tip: If you press Option as you open an application (or anything else) in the Finder, you automatically close the window that contains its icon. Later, when you return to the Finder, you find a neat, clean desktop—no loitering windows.

Launchpad

Launchpad is a dark background with evenly spaced icons that represent all your programs (Figure 4-3). You can open one with a single click.

Figure 4-3:
You can open Launchpad by clicking its Dock icon (it's the very next one after the Finder icon), or by using a four-finger pinching gesture on your trackpad. Launchpad covers your entire main monitor, hiding everything else.

Why did Apple feel the need to create yet *another* way to open programs?

First, because Launchpad fits right into the general theme of Lion: making the Mac look and work more like the iPad. Launchpad is a dead ringer for the Home screen of an iPad, iPhone, or iPod Touch.

Second, it's a much less intimidating place for technophobes to learn to love than, say, the Applications folder.

And third, it's a lot quicker to get to than the Applications folder. You can summon it instantly, using any of these methods:

- **Put four fingers on your trackpad and pinch them together.** The Launchpad appears instantly, no matter what program you were in; you don't have to duck back into the Finder, navigate to the Applications folder, and so on.

- **Press the Launchapd key.** If your Mac came with Lion preinstalled, it has a special Launchpad icon painted right on the F4 key (⊞).

- **Click its icon on the Dock.** It's the second one, resembling a rocket (◉).

- **Press a keyboard shortcut of your choice.** To set that up, choose →System Preferences→Keyboard. Click the Keyboard Shortcuts tab, and then click Launchpad & Dock in the left-side list. On the right, make sure Show Launchpad is turned on—and then double-click in the blank space to the right of it and press the key combination you want.

- **Move the cursor into one of the screen's four corners.** To set up these options, open →System Preferences→Mission Control. Click Hot Corners to choose a corner of the screen for Launchpad.

- **Open it as you would any other program.** It's in your Applications folder.

One thing's for sure: Sooner or later, you'll wind up in Launchpad.

Only two visual elements appear there:

- **Icons.** Each icon represents one of your programs. Apple's programs are listed first, in alphabetical order: Address Book, App Store, Automator, and so on. Then come all your other programs, again in A-to-Z order. Click one to open that program.

Note: The only program icon that *doesn't* appear in Launchpad…is Launchpad's. That's a good thing. You wouldn't want to wind up in an infinite loop, would you?

- **Home-page dots.** As you install more and more programs, you'll need more and more room for their icons. The standard Launchpad screen can't hold more than, say, 40 icons. As you add more apps, Launchpad makes room for them by creating additional screens. You can spread your new programs' icons across an unlimited number of launch screens.

  The little white dots are your map. Each represents one Launchpad screen. If the third one is "lit up," then you're on the third screen.

  To move among the screens, swipe horizontally with two fingers on the trackpad. (Magic Mouse: one finger.) Or press the ← or → arrow keys. Or tap directly on one of the little dots to jump to the corresponding screen.

Tip: To exit Launchpad without opening anything, click a blank spot, tap the Esc key, or—most fun of all—*spread* the same four fingers on the trackpad.

Redesigning the Launchpad Screens

If you use Launchpad a lot, it's worth taking a moment to arrange its icons into logical categories or a sensible sequence. As it turns out, you can freely drag them into new spots; the other icons scoot aside to make room.

You can create additional screens, too. To do that, drag an icon to the right edge of the screen; keep your mouse button down. The first screen slides off to the left, leaving you on a new, blank one, where you can deposit the icon.

You can organize your icons on these Home pages by category, frequency of use, color, or whatever tickles your fancy.

Tip: Launchpad's backdrop is a softly blurred version of your current Desktop picture. If the icons are still hard to read against it, press ⌘-B. With each press, you cycle through another version of that wallpaper: your original Desktop picture, the blurry version, a black-and-white version, and a blurry black-and-white version. One of those should do the trick.

When Programs Are Actually Folders

Mac OS X programs don't seem to have 50,000 support files strewn across your hard drive. Most programs just sit there, naked and shivering, in your Applications folder—seemingly unaccompanied by libraries, dictionaries, foreign language components, and other support files and folders.

The question is: Where did all those support files go?

Mac OS X features *packages* or *bundles*, which are folders that behave like single files. Every properly written Mac OS X program looks like a single, double-clickable application icon. Yet to the Mac, it's actually a folder that contains both the actual application icon and all its hidden support files. (Even documents can be packages, including iDVD project files, Keynote files, and some TextEdit documents.)

If you'd like to prove this to yourself, try this experiment. Choose Go→Applications. See the Calculator program? Right-click it. From the shortcut menu, choose Show Package Contents. You're asking Mac OS X to show you what's inside the Calculator's "application icon" folder.

The Calculator package window opens, revealing a Contents folder you've never seen before. If you open this folder, you'll find a handful of strange-looking, Unix-named folders and files that are, behind the scenes, pieces of the Calculator program itself.

The application-as-folder trick is convenient for you, of course, because it means you're generally free to move the application to a different window—or uninstall the program by dragging this single icon to the Trash—without worrying that you're leaving behind its entourage of support files. It's also convenient for programmers, because they can update certain aspects of their applications just by replacing one of these component files, without having to rewrite the entire program.

You can even try out this programmery benefit for yourself. In the case of the Calculator and many other Mac OS X programs, the Resources folder contains individual graphics file—PDF or TIFF files—that serve as the graphic elements you see when using the program. For example, the file lcd.tiff in the Calculator's Resources folder contains the image of the calculator's screen (where the numbers appear as you punch the calculator buttons).

Using a graphics program, you can change the background of this light-yellow calculator screen to, say, light blue. The next time you double-click Calculator—which you now realize is actually a folder behind the scenes—you'll see your modified calculator design.

(P.S. There are still hundreds or thousands of support files that aren't embedded within their programs' icons. They're sitting in your Library→Application Support folder, organized by software company.)

Folders

The Launchpad just wouldn't be like the iPad if it didn't also let you organize your apps into *folders*. Folders let you organize your apps, de-emphasize the ones you don't use often, and restore order to that horribly flat, multipage display of icons.

To create a folder, drag one app's icon *on top of another*. Lion puts both of them into a single new folder (Figure 4-4). If they're the same kind of app, it even tries to figure out what category they both belong to—and names the new folder accordingly ("Music," "Photos," "Games," or whatever). This new name is only a proposal; an editing window also appears so that you can type a custom name you prefer.

Figure 4-4:
Once you've got a folder, you can open it just by clicking once. A special black panel sprouts from the folder icon, revealing its contents; the rest of the screen goes dim. Now you can drag the icons around inside it. You can also edit the folder's name (click it first).

Take an app out of a folder by dragging its icon anywhere else on the screen. The other icons scoot aside to make room. If you remove all but one app from a folder, the folder disappears.

Move a folder around by dragging, as you would any other icon.

Deleting Mac Store Apps

If you've downloaded some apps from the App Store, you'll find a bonus feature here in Launchpad: They're especially fun to delete.

Start by holding the mouse down on any icon until, after about a second, all the icons begin to—what's the correct term?—*wiggle*. (If you have an iPhone, iPad, or iPod Touch, this should be familiar territory.)

Tip: You can also just press the Option key to trigger the wiggling. Sometimes, every second counts.

At this point, you may notice that some of them have sprouted little red X's. Those are the ones you downloaded from the App Store.

To delete an App Store program you don't need anymore, click that X to make it say bye-bye—instantly and for good. It doesn't even have a layover in the Trash.

Note: You can't delete non–App Store apps this way, so no X appears on those icons. Why not? Because this deletion method is fast and permanent. It's not much of a risk for App Store apps, because you can always download them again—but that would not be true of other apps.

Windows that Auto-Reopen

When you open a program, the Mac reads its computer code, which lies on your hard drive's surface, and feeds it quickly into RAM (memory). During this brief interval, the icon of the opening program jumps up and down eagerly in your Dock.

For decades, opening a program on the Mac presented exactly the same thing every time: a blank screen, or maybe a welcome screen. It was up to you to specify what *document* you then wanted to work on.

In Lion, though, whatever documents were open when you last quit that program magically *re*open, ready for you to get back to work. Everything is *exactly* as it was, including your window and palette positions. Incredibly, any text that was highlighted when you last quit the program is still highlighted, and the insertion point is just where you left it.

This is all extremely handy if you tend to work on the same documents day after day; the auto-reopened document serves as a nice refresher on what you were in the middle of doing. You can skip fussing with the Open command, remembering what you were doing, rearranging the windows the way you like them, and so on.

Then again, maybe you can't stand this feature.

Fortunately, it's easy to turn it off, either globally, on a per-program basis, or on a per-Quit basis.

- **Turn off auto-reopen for good.** Open System Preferences→General, and turn off "Restore windows when quitting and re-opening apps."

- **Prevent your current setup from being memorized.** You can also prevent just *one particular* program from reopening its documents the next time—at the time you're quitting it. To do that, press Option while you quit the program (for example, when you choose Safari→Quit or press ⌘-Q). The Quit command magically changes to say, "Quit and Discard Windows." The next time you open the program, it will have forgotten all about your window setup.

  (On the other hand, if you've turned *off* the "Restore windows" feature in System Preferences, pressing the Option key makes the Quit command say, "Quit and *Keep* Windows.")

- **Make a program forget its window setup as you reopen it.** If it's too late for the tip in the previous paragraph, you can force a program to start up in its empty, virginal state by pressing the Shift key as it opens. That forces the program to forget the previous window setup.

The Application Menu

In every app, the very first menu (to the right of the menu) appears with bold lettering and identifies the program you're using. It might say iTunes, or Microsoft Word, or Stickies.

This Application menu (Figure 4-5) offers a number of commands pertaining to the entire program and its windows, including About, Quit, and Hide.

Figure 4-5:
The first menu in every program lets you know, at a glance, which program you're actually in. It also offers overall program commands like Quit and Hide.

Quitting Programs

In Macintosh lingo, you don't "exit" a program when you're finished with it, you "quit" it. And the command to do so isn't in the File menu—it's at the bottom of the Application menu. But Mac OS X offers two much more fun ways to quit a program:

- Right-click a program's Dock icon to make its shortcut menu appear. Then choose Quit. (Or, if you do the *click-and-hold* thing on a program's Dock icon, a Quit button appears just above your cursor.)

- When you've pressed ⌘-Tab to summon the "heads-up display" of open programs, type the letter Q without releasing the ⌘ key. The highlighted program quits without further ado.

Force Quitting Programs

Mac OS X is a rock-solid operating system, but that doesn't mean that *programs* never screw up. Individual programs are as likely as ever to freeze—or, rather, to *hang* (to lock up and display the "spinning beach ball of death" cursor). In such cases, you have no choice but to *force quit* the program—the computer equivalent of terminating it with a blunt instrument.

Doing so doesn't destabilize your Mac; you don't have to restart it. In fact, you can usually reopen the very same program and get on with your life.

You can force quit a stuck program in any of several ways:

- Click-and-hold on the program's Dock icon, or Control-click it, or right-click it. A Quit button appears just above your cursor. Press the Option key to make the button say Force Quit (Figure 4-6, left). Click it. Bingo—that program is outta here.

- Press Option-⌘-Esc, the traditional Mac force-quit keystroke, or choose ⌘→Force Quit. Either way, proceed as shown in Figure 4-6 at bottom.

Figure 4-6:
Top: You can force quit a program from the Dock—by pressing Option as you click-and-hold (or after you've Control-clicked). Or, if the Mac knows that the program has frozen, this command says Force Quit without your needing the Option key.

Bottom: When you press Option-⌘-Esc or choose Force Quit from the ⌘ menu, a tidy box listing all open programs appears. Just click the one you want to abort, click Force Quit, and click Force Quit again in the confirmation box. (Using more technical tools, like the Unix kill command, there are other ways to jettison programs. But this is often the most convenient.)

Again, force quitting is not bad for your Mac. The only downside to force quitting a program is that you lose any unsaved changes to your open documents, along with any preference settings you may have changed while the program was open.

The "Heads-Up" Program Switcher

Just as in Windows, there's a handy keystroke for switching from one open program to another; it's the ⌘-Tab keystroke (see Figure 4-7).

You can use this feature in three different ways, which are well worth learning:

- If you keep the ⌘ key pressed, each press of the Tab key highlights the Dock icon of another program, in left-to-right Dock order. Release both keys when you reach the one you want. Mac OS X brings the corresponding program to the front. (To move *backward* through the open programs, press *Shift*-⌘-Tab.)

Figure 4-7:
Apple calls this row of open program icons a "heads-up display," named after the projected data screen on a Navy jet windshield that lets pilots avoid having to look down at their instruments.

- If you leave the ⌘ key pressed, you can choose a program by clicking its icon with your mouse, or by pressing the ← or → keys.

- A single press of ⌘-Tab takes you to the program you used most recently, and another, separate ⌘-Tab bounces back to the program you started in.

    Imagine, for example, that you're doing a lot of switching between two programs, like your Web browser and your email program. If you have five other programs open, you don't want to waste your time ⌘-Tabbing your way through all the open programs just to get back to your Web browser.

Tip: Here's a related keystroke, equally awesome. If you press ⌘-tilde (the ~ key next to the number 1), you switch to the next window in the same program.

Mission Control: Death to Window Clutter

In its day, the concept of overlapping windows on the screen was brilliant, innovative, and extremely effective. (Apple borrowed this idea—well, bought it in a stock swap—from a research lab called Xerox PARC.) In that era before digital cameras, MP3 files, and the Web, managing windows was easy this way; after all, you had only about three of them.

These days, however, managing all the open windows in all the open programs can be like herding cats. Off you go, burrowing through the microscopic pop-up menus of your Dock, trying to find the window you want. And heaven help you if you need to duck back to the desktop—to find a newly downloaded file, for example, or to eject a disk. You'll have to fight your way through 50,000 other windows on your way to the bottom of the "deck."

Mission Control, one of Lion's marquee features, tackles this problem in a fresh way. The concept: With one mouse click, keystroke, or finger gesture, Mac OS X shrinks all windows in all programs to a size that fits on the screen (Figure 4-8), like index cards on a bulletin board, clumped by open program. Now you feel like an air-traffic controller, with all your screens arrayed before you. You click the window or program you want, and you're there. It's fast, efficient, animated, and a lot of fun.

Figure 4-8:
Top: Quick! Where's System Preferences in all this mess?

Bottom: With a three-finger upward swipe on the trackpad, you can spot that window, shrunken but not overlapped. Each program's thumbnail cluster offers an icon and a label to help you identify it. These aren't static snapshots of the windows at the moment you Mission Controlled them. They're live, still-updating windows, as you'll discover if one of them contains a playing QuickTime movie or a Web page that's still loading.

Starting and Stopping Mission Control

Mission Control is a program, just like any other. So you can open it with a click on its Dock icon, from Launchpad, from the Applications folder, and so on.

But it's really meant to be opened quickly, fluidly, naturally, whenever the mood seizes you—with a *gesture*. On the trackpad, that's a swipe upward with three fingers. (On the Magic Mouse, it's a double-tap with *two* fingers—taps, not clicks.)

Note: You can change this gesture so that it requires an additional finger, if you like, in System Preferences→Trackpad (or Mouse)→More Gestures→Mission Control. Use the pop-up menu.

Or you can press the dedicated ⌗ key, if you have one, on the top row of your keyboard. Substitute the F9 key if you don't.

And even that's just the beginning of the ways you can open Mission Control; read on.

Note: To *exit* Mission Control without clicking any of your windows or virtual screens, swipe *down* with three fingers. Or tap the Esc key.

Mission Control keystrokes

You can reassign the Mission Control trigger to a huge range of other keys, with or without modifiers like Shift, Control, and Option. To view your options, choose ★→System Preferences and then click the Mission Control icon (Figure 4-9).

Here you'll find four pop-up menus. The first one, Mission Control, lets you specify how you want to open Mission Control. The other three—"Application windows," "Show Desktop," and "Show Dashboard"—correspond to the three functions of the older Exposé and Dashboard features, described later in this chapter.

Within each pop-up menu, for example, you'll discover that all your F-keys—F1, F2, F3, and so on—are available as triggers. If, while the pop-up menu is open, you press one or more of your modifier keys (Shift, Option, Control, or ⌘), all these F-key choices *change* to reflect the key you're pressing; now the pop-up menu says Shift-F1, Shift-F2, Shift-F3, and so on. That's how you can make *Shift*-F1 trigger Mission Control, for example.

These pop-up menus also contain choices like Left Shift, which refers to the Shift key on the left side of your keyboard. That is, instead of pressing F9 to open Mission Control, you could simply tap the Shift key.

Note: This is only an example. Repeat: This is only an example. *Actually* using the Shift key to open Mission Control is a terrible, terrible idea, as you'll quickly discover the next time you try to type a capital letter. This feature is intended exclusively for hunt-and-peck typists who never use the Shift key on one side.

If you have a laptop, you'll also find out that you can tap the Fn key alone for Mission Control—and this time, it's a great choice, because Fn otherwise has very little direction in life.

If your mouse has more than one button, you see a second column of pop-up menus in System Preferences. Each pop-up menu offers choices like Right Mouse Button, Middle Mouse Button, and so on. Use these pop-up menus to assign Mission Control (or Exposé, or Dashboard) to the various clickers on your mouse: right-click to hide all windows, left-side click to reveal the desktop, and so on.

Figure 4-9:
You can trigger Mission Control in any of five ways: by clicking its icon, with a finger gesture, by twitching your cursor into a certain corner of the screen, by pressing a key, or by clicking the extra buttons on a multibutton mouse, including Apple's Mighty Mouse. Of course, there's nothing to stop you from setting up all of these ways, so you can press or swipe in some situations and twitch or click in others.

Note, by the way, that on a laptop, for example, the wording isn't "right mouse button"—it's "secondary mouse button." Which means "right-click." Which means that on a laptop, you can set it up so that a "right-click" *trackpad gesture* triggers one of these functions.

Screen corners

If you click Hot Corners, you see a little map of your screen, including all four corners. Using the little pop-up menus, you can assign a Lion window-management feature to each corner; for example, if you choose Mission Control from the first pop-up menu, then when your pointer hits the upper-left corner of the screen, you'll open Mission Control. (Launchpad is an option here, too.)

Depending on the size of your screen, this option can feel awkward at first. But if you've run out of keystrokes that aren't assigned to other functions, be glad that Apple offers you this alternative.

Managing Windows in Mission Control

Once you open Mission Control, you see two major elements: your *Spaces* (virtual screens, described in a moment) at the top, and the actual window thumbnails below that.

You can click anything here to jump to it: Jump to a different Space (desktop) by clicking its thumbnail, switch to a different program by clicking its *icon,* or click one of the window miniatures.

Tip: Try holding down the Shift key as you do it. You'll enjoy watching all your windows shift around with slow-motion animation, which can be quite a sight.

Or, if you decide to abandon ship and return to whatever you were doing, swipe *down* with three fingers on the trackpad (two on the Magic Mouse), or press the Esc key.

The trouble with miniaturized windows is that, well, they're miniaturized. The more windows you have open, the smaller they are, and the harder it is to see what's in them.

If you need a little help identifying a window miniature, you have three options:

- Point to the cluster of windows in one app, and do a two-finger swipe up on the trackpad. Lion helpfully spreads the window thumbnails out and enlarges them a little bit, so it's easier to tell them apart and click the one you want.

- Point to a window thumbnail without clicking. Mac OS X puts a colored border on it to show that it's highlighted; now press the space bar. That, of course, is the Quick Look keystroke, and it works here, too. It magnifies the window you're point-ing to, making it full size—big enough for you to read its contents and identify it.

- Press ⌘-~. That keystroke takes you into Application Exposé, described later in this chapter.

Spaces in Mission Control

Mission Control's other star feature, Spaces, gives you up to 16 *full-size monitors.* Ordinarily, of course, attaching so many screens to a single computer would be a massively expensive proposition, not to mention the number it would do on your living space and personal relationships.

Fortunately, Spaces monitors are *virtual.* They exist only in the Mac's little head. You see only one at a time, and you switch using Mission Control or a gesture.

But just because the Spaces screens are simulated doesn't mean they're not useful. You can dedicate each one to a different program or *kind* of program. Screen 1 might contain your email and chat windows, arranged just the way you like them. Screen 2 can hold Photoshop, with an open document and the palettes carefully arrayed. On Screen 3: your Web browser in full-screen mode.

You can also have the *same* program running on multiple screens—but with different documents or projects open on each one.

These desktops are also essential to Lion's new *full-screen apps* feature, because each full-screen app gets its own Spaces desktop.

Now, virtual screens aren't a new idea—this sort of software has been available for years. But until the Mac came along, it had never been a standard feature of a consumer operating system, and rarely has it been executed with such finesse.

Creating a Desktop

Mission Control starts you off with two Spaces (or desktops, as they're labeled). One of them shows the Dashboard, described later in this chapter; the other shows your regular Mac world. If you've clicked the ⊡ button in an app to make it full screen, it fills an additional desktop unto itself.

To create another desktop, enter Mission Control. You can now proceed in either of two ways:

- **The long way.** Point to the upper-right corner of the screen; a big **+** button slides into view (Figure 4-10). Click it to create a new mini desktop in the top row.

    Now it's time to park some windows onto the new desktop. Either drag a window thumbnail onto the blank desktop—or, to move *all* of one program's windows there, drag the application icon. All the windows go along for the ride.

- **The short way.** Drag one window thumbnail into a blank spot at the upper-right corner of the screen—or, to move *all* of one program's windows there, drag the application icon. Again, all the windows go along for the ride.

Figure 4-10:
Create a new blank Space by clicking the big + button. Or save time and energy by dragging a window, or a whole program's icon, into the empty space at the right end of the Spaces thumbnails. You've just created a Space and loaded it up with windows in one fell swoop.

Tip: There are two ways to move a window to a different Space *without* opening Mission Control first. First, you can drag a window (using its title bar as a handle) all the way to the edge of the screen. Stay there with the mouse button still down. After about a second, you'll see the adjacent screen slide into view; you've just moved the window.

Second, switch to the new Space. Hold your mouse down on the app's icon; from the shortcut menu, choose Options→Assign To→This Desktop. Lion whisks that app's windows from whatever *other* screen they're on to *this* screen.

Switching Spaces

Once you've got Spaces set up and turned on, the fun begins. Start by moving to the virtual screen you want; it's like changing the channel. Here are some ways to do that:

- Swipe horizontally on your trackpad with three fingers. (On the Magic Mouse, it's two fingers.) If you have a trackpad or a Magic Mouse, this is definitely the method to learn; it's fast, fluid, and happy.

  (You can change this gesture so that it requires an additional finger, if you like, in System Preferences→Trackpad [or Mouse]→More Gestures→"Swipe between full-screen apps." Use the pop-up menu.)

Tip: If you perform this swipe *slowly,* you can drag the next Space only *partway* onto the screen. That's sometimes handy when you want to get your bearings, or to just *peek* into the next screen.

- Enter Mission Control. Click the desktop you want.
- Press Control-← or Control-→ to rotate to the previous or next desktop.

GEM IN THE ROUGH

Pinning One App to One Space—or to All Spaces

Usually, you slap each app (or each window) onto only one Spaces desktop. Your Web browser on Space 1. Email on Space 2. iTunes on Space 3. And so on.

Sometimes, though, you might find it useful to keep an app's windows on *all* your desktops—perhaps because you use it so often, you want it always with you. The Finder and System Preferences are great examples. Or maybe your calendar app, your browser, or your email program.

To do that, make sure the program's icon is in your Dock (either because you've put it there or because the program is running). Hold the mouse button down on the program's icon until the shortcut menu appears. From this menu, choose Options.

You'll see two useful options. One, Assign To→All Desktops, puts this program's windows on all your desktops. Wherever you go, there you are.

The other one, Assign To→This Desktop, gives you yet another quick way to *move* an app's windows—from whatever desktop they're on now to the one you're using at the moment. You've just "pinned" that app to that Space, and that's where it will stay. That's a convenience for neat freaks who like to know exactly where each app will live.

- While pressing the Control key, type the number of the desktop you want. For example, hit Control-3 to jump to your third screen. (You have to turn on this feature first, though. See Figure 4-11.)

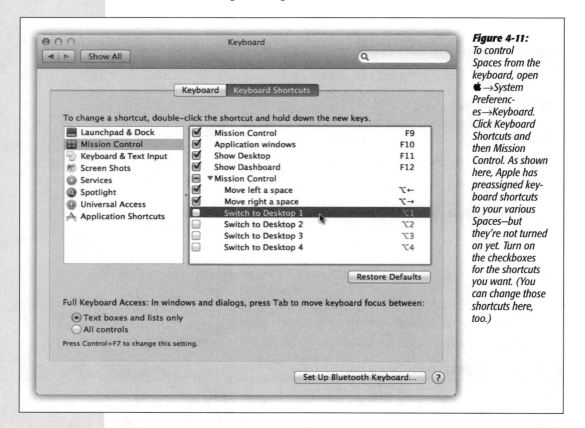

Figure 4-11:
To control Spaces from the keyboard, open ❖→*System Preferences→Keyboard. Click Keyboard Shortcuts and then Mission Control. As shown here, Apple has preassigned keyboard shortcuts to your various Spaces—but they're not turned on yet. Turn on the checkboxes for the shortcuts you want. (You can change those shortcuts here, too.)*

As you'll quickly discover, Lion thinks your desktops are arranged *horizontally*. You can't rearrange them.

When you make a switch, you see a flash of animation as one screen flies away and another appears. Now that you're "on" the screen you want, open programs and arrange windows onto it as usual.

Tip: What if you're using Spaces and you want to drag something from one screen (like a photo in iPhoto) into a window that's on a different screen (like an outgoing email message)?

Start dragging. With the mouse button still down, press ⌘-Tab to open the application switcher. Continue the drag onto the *icon* of the receiving program, and still keep the mouse button down. Mac OS X switches to the appropriate virtual screen automatically.

Deleting a Desktop

To delete a desktop, enter Mission Control. Point to one of the screen thumbnails without clicking until a **—** appears in its corner; click it. The desktop disappears, and whatever windows were on it get shoved onto Desktop #1, your main desktop.

Tip: If you don't have the 1½ seconds to wait for the **—** to appear, then press Option as you point. The Close button appears instantly.

By the way, this trick doesn't work for apps running in full-screen mode. You can't get rid of their desktops unless you first switch to them and get out of full-screen mode.

Dashboard

As you know, the essence of using Mac OS X is running *programs*, which often produce *documents*. In Mac OS X, however, there's a third category: a set of weird, hybrid entities that Apple calls *widgets*. They appear, all at once, on a virtual desktop—the leftmost of the ones in Mission Control.

Here, for example, is how you can find them:

• If your F4 key bears the Dashboard logo (⊙), press it.

Note: On the very newest Macs, F4 bears a Launchpad icon (⌸) instead. On the very oldest Lion-capable Macs, the Dashboard keystroke is usually F12. Or, on laptops where F12 is the ⊙ key, you have to hold down the Fn key (lower-left corner) to get Dashboard.

In all of these cases, you can change the Dashboard keystroke to whatever you like, as described below.

Figure 4-12:
When you summon the Dashboard, you get a fleet of miniprograms that convey or convert all kinds of useful information, on a Spaces screen all their own. You get rid of Dashboard either by pressing the same key again (F4 or whatever), by swiping three fingers to the right on your trackpad, or by clicking anywhere except on a widget.

- Swipe with three fingers on your trackpad, repeatedly if necessary, until you reach the far left "desktop." (On the Magic Mouse, swipe with two fingers.)

- Open Mission Control; click the Dashboard thumbnail at the top left of the screen.

- Dashboard is an actual program, with an icon of its own in your Applications folder. You can open it with a double-click, or by using any of the usual program-opening tricks.

In any case, you wind up at the display shown in Figure 4-12. Welcome to the Dashboard.

What are these weird, hybrid entities, anyway? They're not really programs, because they don't create documents or have Dock icons (although Dashboard itself has a Dock icon). They're certainly not documents, because you can't name or save them. What they most resemble, actually, is little Web pages. They're meant to display information, much of it from the Internet, and they're written using Web programming languages like HTML and JavaScript.

They're things like a calculator, a flight tracker, a dictionary, a quick Address Book lookup, a weather module, world clocks, and so on. If you're familiar with widgets in Windows Vista and Windows 7, then you already understand the Mac's gadgets.

Mastering the basics of Dashboard won't take you long at all:

- **To move a widget,** drag it around the screen. (Click anywhere except on a button or a control.)

- **To close a widget,** press the Option key as you move the mouse across the widget's face. You'll see the ⊗ button appear at the widget's top-left corner; click it.

Figure 4-13:
You'll probably have to scroll the Widget bar, by clicking the arrows at either end, to see all the widgets. When you're finished opening new widgets, close the Widget bar by clicking the ⊗ button at the left side of your screen.

Tip: If the Widget bar is open (as described below), every widget displays its ⊗ button. You don't need the Option key.

- **To open a closed widget,** click the big ⊕ button at the bottom of the screen. Now the entire screen image slides upward by about an inch to make room for the Widget bar: a "perforated metal" tray containing the full array of widgets, even the ones that aren't currently on the screen (Figure 4-13). Open one by clicking its icon.

- **To hide one of Apple's widgets,** or to delete one you've installed yourself, use the Widgets widget described below.

- **To rearrange your widgets as they appear in the Widget bar,** open your hard drive→Library→Widgets folder. Here you'll find the icons for the standard Apple Dashboard widgets. To rearrange them, you have to rename them; they appear on the Widget bar in alphabetical order. (You can also remove a widget for good, if you must, by deleting it from this folder.)

Dashboard Tips

Dashboard is crawling with cool tips and tricks. Here are a few of the biggies:

- If you just *click* an icon on the Widget bar, the widget appears right in the middle of your screen. But if you *drag* the widget's icon off the bar, you can deposit it anywhere you like.

- There's a great keystroke that opens and closes the Widget bar: ⌘-equal sign (=). (This keystroke may be different on non-U.S. keyboard layouts.)

- To refresh a certain widget—for example, to update its information from the Internet—click it and press ⌘-R. The widget instantly *twist-scrambles* itself into a sort of ice-cream swirl (you've got to see it to believe it) and then untwists to reveal the new data.

- You can open more than one copy of the same widget. Just click its icon more than once in the Widget bar. You wind up with multiple copies of it on your screen: three World Clocks, two Stock Trackers, or whatever. That's a useful trick when, for example, you want to track the time or weather in more than one city, or when you maintain two different stock portfolios.

- If you keep the Shift key pressed when you click the big ⊕ button, the Widget bar opens in gorgeous *slow motion*. Aren't you just glad to be alive?

Dashboard Preferences

To change the Dashboard keystroke to something other than F4 or F12, choose →System Preferences, and then click Mission Control.

Here you'll discover that you can choose almost any other keyboard combination to summon and dismiss the Dashboard, or even choose a screen corner that, when your mouse lands there, acts as the Dashboard trigger.

Note: Yes, yes, you can also change the Dashboard keystroke on the Keyboard→Keyboard Shortcuts pane of System Preferences. But if you use the Mission Control pane instead, then you can set up a screen corner or a mouse button to trigger Dashboard—not just a keyboard combo.

More Widgets

The best part of the Dashboard is that it's expandable. *Thousands* of new widgets, written by other people, are available on the Web: games, chat and email notifiers, gas-price reporters, calculators and translators, news and sports updaters, finance and health trackers, and on and on.

To see Apple's current list of goodies, use one of these tactics:

- **The short way.** Right-click the Dashboard icon in the Dock. From the shortcut menu, choose More Widgets.

- **The long way.** Open the Widgets widget; when it opens, click More Widgets.

Either way, you go to the Apple Dashboard downloads page. (Alternatively, check a Mac-downloads Web site like *www.macupdate.com* for an even more complete selection.)

Some of the most intriguing widget offerings include the Yahoo Local Traffic widget (gives you the traffic conditions in your area), Air Traffic Control (identifies wireless AirPort base stations within range of your laptop), and TV Tracker (shows you could be watching on TV right now instead of working). There are also FedEx package trackers, joke-of-the-day widgets, comic-strip-of-the-day widgets, and many other varieties. (See Figure 4-14.)

Figure 4-14:
Not all good things come from Apple. Here's a representative sample of widgets written by other people. Clockwise from top left: Facebook Alert, Dashboard Aquarium, Scenario Poker, and Dancing Gingerbread Man.

Installing a widget

When you download a widget, Mac OS X is smart enough to install it automatically. First, though, it offers you a trial run. It's a way to play with new widgets before you actually commit to adding them to your system.

Play with the widget, and then click Keep to install it (or Delete, if you think it's evil).

If you click Keep, then Mac OS X copies it into your Home→Library→Widgets folder. Only you will see that Dashboard widget, because it's been copied into the Widgets folder of *your account.* Anyone else who has an account on this Mac won't see it.

Web Clips: Make Your Own Widgets

You don't have to be satisfied with Apple's 17 widgets *or* the several thousand that other people have written. You can make a Dashboard widget of your own—in about three clicks.

Web Clips exploit an inescapable characteristic of widgets: An awful lot of them exist to deliver real-time information from the Web. That's the point of the Ski Report widget, Weather, Stocks, Flight Tracker, ESPN, and so on.

But what if your interest isn't skiing, stocks, or sports? What if it's *The New York Times* front page? Or the bestselling children's books on Amazon? Or the most-viewed video on YouTube? Or some cool Flash game you wish you could summon with the touch of a key?

That's the beauty of Web Clips, a joint venture of Dashboard and the Safari Web browser. They let you turn *any section of any Web page* into a Dashboard widget that

Figure 4-15:
Drag the little round handles to make the white box just big enough to surround the part of the page you want to enshrine. Or drag inside the box to move the whole thing.

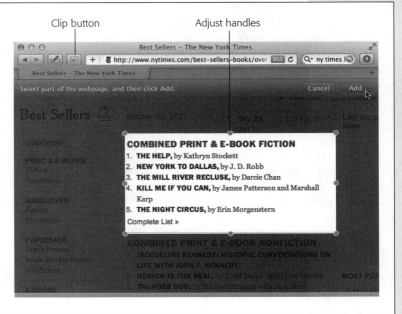

Clip button

Adjust handles

updates itself every time you open it. It's like having a real-time keyhole peek at all your favorite Web sites at once.

Creating a Web Clips Widget

Here's how you go about creating a do-it-yourself widget:

1. **Open Safari.**

   Safari is the Mac's Web browser. It's in your Applications folder.

2. **Go to the Web page that contains the information you want to snip. Choose File→Open in Dashboard.**

   The screen goes dark, with only a small window of white. As you move your cursor around the page, the white rectangle conveniently snaps to fit the various rectangular sections of the page.

   As shown in Figure 4-15, your job is to make a frame around the part of the page that usually shows the information you want. If the Web site ever redesigns its pages, it'll wreck your widget—but what the heck. It takes only 5 seconds to make it again.

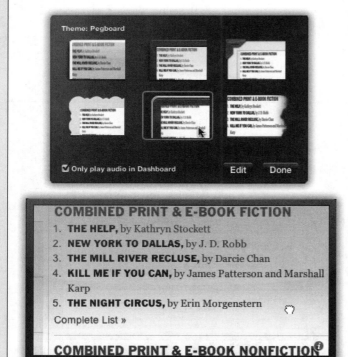

Figure 4-16:
Top: Click a frame style to give your widget better-looking edges. If the widget plays sound, it keeps playing sound when you close the Dashboard unless you turn on "Only play audio in Dashboard."

Bottom: Click Edit to return to the front of the widget, where you can adjust its position on the underlying Web page.

3. **Adjust the corner or side handles to enclose the piece of page you want. When you're finished, click Add or press Return.**

Now Dashboard opens automatically. But wait—what's this? There's a new widget here that wasn't here before.

At this point, you can dress up your widget, adding a little polish to this raw clipping you've ripped out of a Web page. Click the ❶ button that appears when you move your mouse to the lower-right corner. The widget flips around to reveal the controls shown in Figure 4-16.

Here you can click one of the frame styles to give your widget a better-looking border.

If you click Edit, the widget flips around to face you again, and here's where it gets weird: You can reposition your widget's contents as though they were a window on a Web page that's visible behind it. Drag the widget contents in any direction within the frame, or resize the frame using the lower-right resize handle. Click Done.

You can make as many Web Clips as you want.

But here's a big screaming caution: If you close one of these homemade widgets, it's gone forever (or at least until you recreate it). Web Clips are never represented as icons on the Widget bar, as ordinary widgets are.

Ah, well—easy come, easy go, right?

Exposé

Before Mission Control, there was Exposé. It was flexible, it was novel, it was a little confusing. In Lion, Apple incorporated the main functions of Exposé into Mission Control—but Apple didn't want to break all those Exposé fans' hearts. So in Lion, Exposé is still there, for the benefit of old-timers who don't like change.

Well, it's *mostly* there. There used to be three different Exposé modes. One showed you miniatures of *all* windows in *all* programs; one showed you miniatures of all windows in *just one program;* and one hid *all windows in all programs* so you could see the desktop.

In Lion, only the second and third Exposé functions still exist. (The first one—showing *all* windows in *all* programs—is what Mission Control is for.)

Both of these modes can be triggered using different combinations of the mouse and keyboard. The following pages will cover all of them, but of course you're not expected to learn all that. Just find the *one* trigger that seems most convenient, and stick with it.

One-App Exposé

When you trigger Mission Control, you see the thumbnails of *all* windows in *all* apps.

But sometimes it's useful to see only the windows of *one* app arrayed before you—the app you're *using.*

That's great when you're Web browsing or word processing. This Exposé function makes the program's windows spread out, and shrink if necessary, so you can click the one you want (Figure 4-17, top).

Here's how Apple intends most people to trigger this option:

Figure 4-17:
Top: When you trigger one-app Exposé, you get a clear shot at any window in the current program (TextEdit, in this example). In the meantime, the rest of your screen attractively dims. Often (especially with Apple programs, like TextEdit and Preview), you even get a little row of icons at the bottom. They represent recently opened files, ready for clicking.

Bottom: Trigger desktop Exposé when you need to duck back to the desktop for a quick administrative chore. Here's your chance to find a file, throw something away, eject a disk, or whatever, without having to disturb your application windows.

In either case, tap the same function key again to turn off Exposé. Or click one of the window edges, which you can see peeking out from all four edges of the screen.

- **Swipe down on your trackpad with three fingers.** (There's no equivalent on the Magic Mouse—although if you install the free BetterTouchTool, you can dream up a gesture of your own.)

- **Press Control-F3 ( ).** That's the keystroke on aluminum keyboards. (If you have a plastic keyboard, press F10 or Fn-F10, whichever works.)

Tip: As noted in the box below, you can also press Fn-F10 or, with some tweaking, F10 alone. Or you can change the keystroke altogether, as described on page 168.

- **Enter Exposé from the heads-up display.** The heads-up display is the Mac OS X application switcher—the row of "these are your open programs" icons—which appears when you press ⌘-Tab.

  The cool thing is that once you've got that heads-up display open, you can press ↑ or ↓ to enter Exposé for whatever program's icon is highlighted! From there, release the keys and hit Tab to cycle through your open apps.

- **Use Dock Exposé.** Click the program's Dock icon and hold the button down for half a second. (Or, for faster service, Control-click or right-click the program's Dock icon.)

  This feature has one chief advantage over the keystroke method: You can Exposé-ize *any* program's windows, not just the one you're using at the moment.

TROUBLESHOOTING MOMENT

A , Side Note about the Aluminum Apple Keyboards

In the beginning, you could trigger the three Exposé modes described on these pages with three simple keystrokes: F9, F10, and F11.

Then Apple's aluminum keyboards and laptops came along. On these, Apple devoted the F3 key to Exposé functions—and reassigned the F9, F10, and F11 keys to speaker-volume control!

You *can* make them operate as in the days of yore—by adding the Fn key. That is: Fn-F9 for Mission Control, Fn-F10 for one-app Exposé, and Fn-F11 for desktop Exposé. (Details on the Fn key appear on page 28.)

So here's the point: On modern Macs, you have a choice

of two Exposé keystroke suites: the F3 key (by itself, with Control, and with ⌘)—or the Fn key plus F9, F10, and F11.

Actually, it's even more complicated than that. If you find yourself using *Exposé* more than you use the volume keys, you can get rid of the requirement to press Fn. Open System Preferences→Keyboard→Keyboard. Here you'll find a checkbox that reverses this logic. It's called "Use all F1, F2, etc. keys as standard function keys."

If that checkbox is *on,* then you can use F9, F10, and F11 to trigger Mission Control and Exposé. Now you need the Fn key only when you want those keys to adjust the *volume.*

- **Shove your mouse into whatever corner of the screen you've chosen.** See page 144 for instructions.

Once you've triggered Exposé, you're not quite finished yet. As shown in Figure 4-17, beneath the window thumbnails, you get to see the icons of documents you've worked on recently in this app.

Furthermore, here's the Lion Exposé tip of the year: *Press the Tab key.* With each tap, you cycle through the open apps, each getting the Exposé treatment in turn. It's an informative way to inspect what's happening in each open program without losing your way. (Pressing ⌘-~ does the same thing.)

Desktop Exposé

The other flavor of Exposé is surprisingly handy. It sends *all* windows in *all* programs cowering to the edges of your screen, revealing the desktop beneath in all its uncluttered splendor (Figure 4-17, bottom).

Here's the keystroke scheme:

- **Current keyboards: Press ⌘-F3 (▦).** That's the trigger for current aluminum keyboards and laptops.

Note: Once again, you can also press Fn-11, or (if you set it up) F11 by itself. See the box on page 157.

- **Plastic keyboards: Press F11.**

The windows fly off to the edges of the screen, where they remain—forever, or until you tap the keystroke again, click a visible window edge, double-click an icon, or take some other window-selection step.

This is a spectacular opportunity to save headache and hassle in situations like these:

- You're writing an email message, and you want to attach a file. Tap the desktop Exposé keystroke, and then root around in the Finder until you locate the file you want. Begin to drag it, and then, without releasing the mouse button, tap the desktop Exposé keystroke again to bring back your email window. (Or drag the attachment directly onto your email program's icon on the Dock and pause until its window thumbnails appear.)

  Move your cursor, with the file in mid-drag, directly over the outgoing message window; release the cursor to create the attachment. You've just added an attachment from the desktop in one smooth motion.

Tip: You can apply the same life-changing shortcut to dragging a graphic into a page-layout program, a folder of photos into iPhoto, a sound or graphic into iMovie, and so on.

- You want to open a different document. For many people, having access to the entire Finder beats the pants off having to use the Open dialog box. Double-clicking the icon you want automatically opens it and turns off Exposé.

- You're on the Web, and you want to see if some file has finished downloading. Trigger desktop Exposé to survey the situation on your desktop.

If the layer of open programs is the atmosphere, the Finder is the earth below—and the ability to teleport back and forth is a huge timesaver.

Exposé Tip-O-Rama

Just having your world o' windows spread out like index cards is magic enough. But these windows are *live.* You can work with them. Let us count the ways.

- **Tab through Exposé'd apps.** Once you've started one-app Exposé and a program's windows are arrayed before you, tap the Tab key to switch to the *next* running program. All *its* windows spring to the fore. Tab, Tab, Tab through all your open programs. (Shift-Tab, as usual, cycles through the programs in the opposite direction.)

Tip: You can also switch to another app's micro-windows by clicking its Dock icon.

- **Change Exposé'd apps using the heads-up display.** Here's another way to change programs once you're in one-app Exposé: Press ⌘-Tab to bring up the heads-up display (yes, even while your windows are shrunken). Tab your way through the program icons (Figure 4-17) until the one you want is selected, and then release the keys. That program's windows spring to the front, still miniaturized and arrayed for your selection pleasure.

- **Hold down instead of two presses.** Most of the time, you'll probably use Exposé in two steps. You'll tap the keystroke once to get the windows out of the way, and tap it again to bring them back (if, indeed, you haven't *clicked* a window to bring them back).

  In some cases, though, you may find it easier to *hold down* the relevant key. For example, hold down ⌘-F3 (Show Desktop) to see if a file is finished copying to the desktop, and then release the keys to bring back all the windows. (Actually, you can let go of the ⌘ key as soon as you've entered Exposé.) For quick window-clearing situations, that method saves you the step of having to press the keystroke a second time to turn off Exposé.

- **Use the spring-loaded Dock.** This trick is great when you want to drop a file from one program into a particular window belonging to another.

  The most common example: You want to add an attachment to an outgoing email message. In the Finder, locate the file's icon. Drag it directly onto your email program's Dock icon—and *pause* with your finger still on the button. After a half second, Exposé happens, showing all your email program's open windows. Now continue your drag onto the miniaturized window of the outgoing message so it's highlighted, tap the space bar to open it, and then release. Presto! The file is attached.

This trick also works great when you want to drop a photo into a newsletter, for example, or a text clipping into a word-processing document.

- **Dip into Quick Look.** Once you've got shrunken windows on the screen, tap your arrow keys to highlight a window (or point with your mouse at them without clicking). A bright-blue border moves from window to window.

At any point, you can press the space bar to make that one window return to life size. You haven't really activated it—you can't edit it—but at least you can see it at full size.

And here's the very cool part: Once you've triggered Quick Look like this, you can press the arrow keys to zap *other* mini windows back to full size, without having to exit Quick Look. Or, again, point to other windows without clicking. Each zooms in to 100 percent size. (All of this is much easier to do than to imagine.)

You can keep examining your windows at full size until you spot the one you're after; now tap Return (or click the mouse in the window) to exit Quick Look *and* Exposé. You've just opened that window, and you're ready to roll.

Tip: Keep in mind that you can change all of these Exposé triggers—keyboard shortcuts, hot corners, and so on. See page 168.

Hiding Programs the Old-Fashioned Way

When it comes to getting windows out of your way, nothing can touch Mission Control and Exposé for speed and entertainment value. Once you've mastered those features, the traditional rituals of hiding windows will seem charmingly quaint. "When I was your age," you'll tell your grandchildren, "we used to have to *hold down the Option key* to hide windows!"

But you know the drill at software companies: They giveth, but they never taketh away. All the old techniques are still around for the benefit of Mac fans who use them by force of habit.

Hiding the Program You're Using

If your aim is to hide only the frontmost program's windows and palettes, Mac OS X offers a whole raft of approaches. Many of them involve the Option key, as listed here:

- **Option-click any visible portion of the desktop.** The program you were in vanishes, along with all its windows.

- **Option-click any other program's icon on the Dock.** You open that program (or bring all its windows to the front) *and* hide all the windows of the one you were using.

- **Option-click any visible portion of another program's windows.** Once again, you switch programs, hiding the one you were using at the time.

- **From the Application menu, choose Hide iPhoto (or whatever the program is).** The Application menu is the boldfaced menu that bears the program's name.

- **From the program's Dock icon shortcut menu, choose Hide.** You open the shortcut menu, of course, by right-clicking. You also get a Hide button if you click-and-hold on the Dock icon for half a second.

- **When you've highlighted a program's icon by pressing ⌘-Tab to rotate through the running programs, press the letter H key.** The program hides itself instantly. Leave the ⌘ key down the whole time, and after pressing the H, press Tab again to move on to the next program. If you release the keys while "stopped" on the program instead, you'll bring it forward rather than hiding it.

- **Press ⌘-H.** This may be the easiest and most useful trick of all (although it doesn't work in a few oddball programs). Doing so hides the program you're in; you then "fall down" into the next running program.

Tip: Consider this radical timesaving proposal: Never quit the programs you use frequently. Instead, simply hit ⌘-H whenever you're finished working in a program. That way, the next time you need it, the program launches with zero wait time.

There's a limit to this principle; if you have only 2 gigabytes of memory and you keep 20 programs open, and one of them is Photoshop, you'll incur a speed penalty. In more moderate situations, though, Mac OS X's virtual-memory scheme is so good that there's almost no downside to leaving your programs open all the time.

To unhide a program and its windows, click its Dock icon again, choose the Show All command in the Application menu, or press ⌘-Tab to summon the heads-up application display.

Hiding All Other Programs

Choosing Hide Others from your program's Application menu means, of course, "Hide the windows of every program but this one." It even hides your Finder (desktop) windows, although desktop icons remain visible.

Better yet, there's a keystroke for this command: Option-⌘-H. That's one small step for keystrokes, one giant leap for productivity geeks.

If this trick interests you, you might also enjoy its corollary, described next.

The Bring-Forward, Hide-All-Others Trick

Here's a terrific technique that lets you bring one program to the front (along with all its open windows), and hide all other windows of all *other* open programs—all with one click.

You might think of it as Hero mode, or Front-and-Center mode, or Clear My Calendar mode.

In any case, the trick is to Option-⌘-click the lucky program's icon on the Dock. As it jumps to the fore, all other windows on your Mac are instantly hidden. (You can bring them back, of course, by clicking the appropriate Dock icons.)

Hiding (Minimizing) Individual Windows

You can also hide or show *individual windows* of a single program. In fact, Apple must believe that hiding a window will become one of your favorite activities, because it offers at least three ways to do so:

• Choose Window→Minimize Window, if your program offers such a command, or press ⌘-M.

• Click the Minimize button on the window's title bar.

• Double-click the window's title bar. (If this doesn't work, choose ⌘→System Preferences→Appearance. Make sure "Double-click a window's title bar to minimize" is turned on.)

In any case, the affected window shrinks down until it becomes a new icon on the right side of the Dock. Click that icon to bring the window back.

How Documents Know Their Parents

Every operating system needs a mechanism to associate documents with the applications that created them. When you double-click a Microsoft Word document icon, for example, it's clear that you want Microsoft Word to launch and open the document.

So how does Mac OS X know how to find a document's mommy?

It actually has two different mechanisms.

• **File name extensions.** A *file name extension* is a suffix following a period in the file's name, as in *Letter to Mom.doc.* (It's usually three letters long, but it doesn't have to be.) These play a role in determining which documents open into which programs.

That's how Windows identifies its documents, too. If you double-click something called *memo.doc,* it opens in Microsoft Word. If you double-click *memo.wri,* it opens in Microsoft Write, and so on.

Note: Mac OS X comes set to hide most file name extensions, on the premise that they make the operating system look more technical and threatening. If you'd like to see them, however, choose Finder→Preferences, click the Advanced button, and then turn on "Show all filename extensions." Now examine a few of your documents; you'll see that their names display the previously hidden suffixes.

You can hide or show these suffixes on an icon-at-a-time basis, too (or a clump-at-a-time basis). Just highlight the icon or icons you want to affect, and then choose File→Get Info. In the resulting Info window, proceed as shown in Figure 4-18.

• **Your preferences.** If you've used the "Always Open with" command to *specify* which program opens your document (described next), that's the one that opens; this preference overrides the file name extension system. Mac OS X memorizes that new pairing.

It's possible to live a long and happy life without knowing anything about these suffixes and relationships. Indeed, the vast majority of Mac fans may never even encounter them. But if you're prepared for a little bit of technical bushwhacking, you may discover that understanding document-program relationships can be useful in troubleshooting, keeping your files private, and appreciating how Mac OS X works.

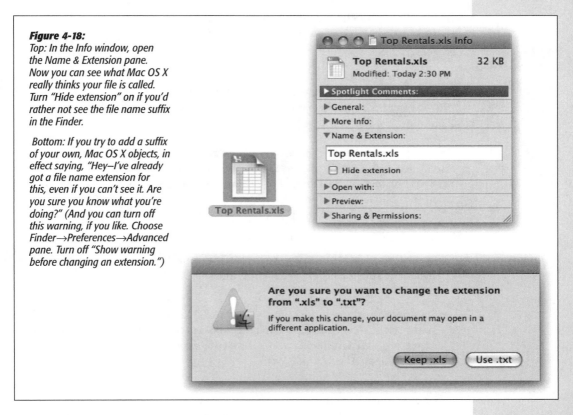

Figure 4-18:
Top: In the Info window, open the Name & Extension pane. Now you can see what Mac OS X really thinks your file is called. Turn "Hide extension" on if you'd rather not see the file name suffix in the Finder.

Bottom: If you try to add a suffix of your own, Mac OS X objects, in effect saying, "Hey—I've already got a file name extension for this, even if you can't see it. Are you sure you know what you're doing?" (And you can turn off this warning, if you like. Choose Finder→Preferences→Advanced pane. Turn off "Show warning before changing an extension.")

Reassigning Documents to Programs

Unfortunately, file name extensions aren't always especially specific. Suppose you've downloaded a graphic called Sunset.jpg. Well, almost any program these days can open a JPEG graphic—Photoshop, Pages, Word, Preview, Safari, and so on. How does Mac OS X know which of these programs to open when you double-click the file?

Fortunately, *you* can decide. You can *reassign* a document (or all documents of its kind) to a specific program. Here's the rundown.

Reassigning a certain document—just once

Double-clicking a graphics file generally opens it in Preview, the graphics viewer included with Mac OS X. Most of the time, that's a perfectly good arrangement. But Preview has only limited editing powers. What if you decide to edit a graphics file more substantially? You'd want it to open, just this once, into a different program—Photoshop Elements, for example.

To do so, you must access the Open With command. You can find it in three places:

- Highlight the icon, and then choose File→Open With.

- Highlight the icon and then open the ✿ menu. In the menu, choose Open With.

- Control-click (or right-click) the file's icon. From the shortcut menu, choose Open With.

Study the submenu for a moment (Figure 4-19, top). The program whose name says "(default)" indicates which program *usually* opens this kind of document. From this pop-up menu, choose the name of the program you'd *rather* open this particular file, right now, just this once.

Reassigning a certain document—permanently

After opening a TIFF file in, say, Photoshop Elements for editing, you haven't really made any changes in the fabric of your Mac universe. The next time you double-click that file, it opens once again in Preview.

If you wish this particular file would *always* open in Photoshop Elements, the steps are slightly different. In fact, there are three different ways:

- In the Choose an Application dialog box (the one that appears when you double-click a document whose "parent" program isn't clear), turn on "Always Open With" (shown at bottom in Figure 4-19).

- Start out with one of the previously described techniques (for example, File→Open With, or right-click the file's icon and choose Open With)—but after you see the menu, press the Option key, too. Before your very eyes, the Open With command changes to say *Always* Open With.

- Highlight the icon, and then choose File→Get Info. Open the "Open with" panel. Choose a new "parent" program's name from the pop-up menu. You'll see that the word "(default)" changes position, now tacking itself onto the name of the program you've chosen.

Tip: You can use a similar trick to reassign the parenthood of a whole *flock* of selected icons at once. Once you've selected them, keep the Option key pressed as you choose File→Show Inspector. In the Open With section of this specialized Get Info window, choose a new program from the pop-up menu. The message at the top of the window—"22 items," for example—reminds you that you're changing the whole batch at once.

Reassigning all documents of one type

So much for reassigning one document (or a group of documents) at a time. What if you're, say, writing a book about Mac OS X, and you've been taking a lot of screenshots? Mac OS X saves each captured screen illustration as a graphics file in something called PNG format. That's all fine, except that every time you double-click one of these, it opens into Preview, where you can't paint out unwanted details.

You could reassign all these files, one at a time, to a different program, but your grandchildren would have grandchildren by the time you finished. In this case, you want to tell Mac OS X, "For heaven's sake, make *all* PNG files open in Photoshop from now on!"

Figure 4-19:
Top: The shortcut menu offers a list of programs capable of opening an icon. If you were to press the Option key right now, the words Open With would suddenly change to say Always Open With.

Bottom: If you choose Other, you're prompted to choose a different program. Turn on Always Open With if you'll always want this document to open in the new parent program. Otherwise, this is a one-time reassignment.

To make it happen, start by highlighting *any* PNG file. Choose File→Get Info. (The shortcut menus won't help you in this case.) Open the "Open with" panel.

From its pop-up menu, choose the program you want to open this kind of document from now on.

Tip: If the one you prefer isn't listed, use the Other option, which opens the Choose an Application dialog box so you can navigate to the one you want, as shown in Figure 4-19 at bottom . Find and double-click the program.

Or, instead of choosing Other, you can also choose App Store. It's Apple's way of saying, "Hey—if you don't have a program that can open this document, maybe you should just *go buy one right now!"*

This time, follow up by clicking Change All beneath the pop-up menu. (This button is dimmed until you've actually selected a different program from the pop-up menu.) Mac OS X asks you to confirm by clicking Continue or pressing Return.

From now on, double-clicking any similar kind of document opens it in the newly selected program.

Keyboard Control

In Windows, of course, you can operate every menu in every program from the keyboard—and every control in every dialog box—thanks to the power of the Alt key.

Mac OS X offers full keyboard control, too. You can operate every control in every dialog box from the keyboard, including pop-up menus and checkboxes. And you can *redefine* many of the keyboard shortcuts in Mac OS X and even your programs. In short, if you were a keyboard power-user in Windows, you'll feel right at home in Mac OS X.

Here are some of the ways you can control your Mac mouselessly. In the following descriptions, you'll encounter the factory settings for the keystrokes that do the magic—but as you'll see in a moment, you can change these key combos to anything you like. (The System Preferences→Keyboard→Keyboard Shortcuts tab contains the on/off switches for these features.)

Note: On modern-day aluminum keyboards, the keystrokes described below may not work unless you also press the Fn key simultaneously.

If that seems just a tad clumsy, you can eliminate the Fn-key requirement either by using the "Use all F1, F2, etc. keys as standard function keys" option described in the box on page 157—or by choosing a different keystroke altogether (page 168).

Control the Menus

When you press Control-F2, the menu is highlighted. At this point, you can "walk" to another menu by pressing the ← or → keys (or Tab and Shift-Tab). When you reach the menu you want, open it by pressing ↓, space, Return, or Enter.

Walk down the commands in the menu by pressing ↑ or ↓, or jump directly to a command in the menu by typing the first couple of letters of its name. Finally, "click" a menu command by pressing Return, Enter, or the space bar.

You can also close the menu without making a selection by pressing Esc or ⌘-period.

Control the Dock

Once you've pressed Control-F3, you can highlight *any* icon on the Dock by pressing the appropriate arrow keys (or, once again, Tab and Shift-Tab).

Then, once you've highlighted a Dock icon, you "click" it by pressing Return or the space bar. Again, if you change your mind, press Esc or ⌘-period.

Tip: Once you've highlighted a disk or folder icon, you can press the ↑ or ↓ keys to make its shortcut menu appear. (If you've positioned the Dock vertically, use ← or → instead.)

Cycle Through Your Windows

Every time you press Control-F4, you bring the next window forward, eventually cycling through *every window in every open program*. Add the Shift key to cycle through them in the opposite order.

You may remember that Mac OS X offers a different keystroke for cycling through the different windows in your *current* program (it's ⌘-~, the tilde symbol at the upper left on your keyboard). Control-F4, on the other hand, tours all windows in *all* programs. Both keystrokes are useful in different situations.

Control the Toolbar

This one is on the unpredictable side, but it more or less works in most programs that display a Mac OS X–style toolbar: the Finder, System Preferences, and so on.

When you press Control-F5, you highlight the first button on that toolbar. Move the "focus" by pressing the arrow keys or Tab and Shift-Tab. Then tap Return or the space bar to "click" the highlighted button.

Control Tool Palettes

In a few programs that feature floating tool palettes, you can highlight the frontmost palette by pressing Control-F6. At this point, use the arrow keys to highlight the various buttons on the palette. You can see the effect when, for example, you're editing text in TextEdit and you've also opened the Font palette. Pressing Control-F6 highlights the Font palette, taking the "focus" off your document.

Control Menulets

Here's a gem you may not have heard about: You can now operate *menulets*—those menu-bar status indicators for your speaker volume, wireless networks, and so on—from the keyboard, too.

This time, the trick is to hit Control-F8. That highlights the leftmost Apple menulet. Now you can use your ← and → arrow keys to move around the menu bar; when you've highlighted the one you want, press Return or the space bar to "click" that menu and open it.

Control Dialog Boxes

You can also navigate and manipulate any *dialog box* from the keyboard.

See the dialog box shown in Figure 4-20? If you turn on "All controls" at the bottom, then pressing the Tab key highlights the next control of any type, whatever it may be—radio button, pop-up menu, and so on. Press the space bar to "click" a button or to open a pop-up menu. Once a menu is open, use the arrow keys (or type letter keys) to highlight commands on it, and use the space bar to "click" your choice.

Figure 4-20:
If you choose All Applications from the top pop-up menu, you can change the keyboard combo for a certain command wherever it appears. You could, for example, change the keystroke for Page Setup in every program at once. (Beware the tiny yellow triangles; they let you know if a chosen keystroke conflicts with another Mac OS X keystroke.)

Changing a Menu Keyboard Shortcut

Suppose you love iPhoto (and who doesn't?). But one thing drives you crazy: The Revert to Original command, which discards all the changes you've ever made since taking the photo, has no keyboard shortcut. You must trek up to the menu bar every time you need that command.

This is why Mac OS X lets you add keyboard shortcuts to menu commands that lack them—or change the commands in programs whose key assignments break with tradition. (It works in any program that uses the standard Mac OS X menu software, which rules out older versions of Microsoft Office.) Here's the routine:

1. **Choose ⌘→System Preferences→Keyboard. Click the Keyboard Shortcuts tab, and then click Application Shortcuts in the left-side list.**

   You're shown a list of any keyboard assignments you've created so far.

2. **Click the + button just beneath the list.**

   The dialog box shown in Figure 4-20 appears.

3. **Indicate which program needs behavior modification.**

   In this example, you'd choose iPhoto from the Application pop-up menu. (If the program's name doesn't appear in the pop-up menu, then choose Other; navigate to, and double-click, the program you want.)

4. **Carefully type in the name of the menu command whose keyboard shortcut you want to change or add.**

   Type it *exactly* as it appears in the menu, complete with capitalization and the little ellipsis (…) that may follow it. (You make the ellipsis character by pressing Option-semicolon.)

5. **Click in the Keyboard Shortcut box. Press the new or revised key combo you want.**

   For example, press Control-R for iPhoto's Revert to Original command. You'll see the Mac's notation of your keystroke appear in the Keyboard Shortcut box—unless, of course, the combo you selected is already in use within that program. In that case, you hear only an error sound that means, "Try again."

6. **Click Add.**

   The dialog box closes. By scrolling down in your Keyboard Shortcuts list, you see that the keystroke you selected has now been written down for posterity under the appropriate program's flippy triangle. (To get rid of it, click its name and then click the − button beneath the list.)

   The next time you open the program you edited, you'll see that the new keystroke is in place.

Tip: To delete or change one of your custom menu shortcuts, open System Preferences→Keyboard→Keyboard Shortcuts. Click Application Shortcuts in the list at left. Click the command you'd like to edit. Press Delete to get rid of it; or, to try a different key combo, click where the existing keyboard shortcut appears and then press a new one.

Redefining a Keystroke

As you've no doubt become painfully aware, there are *hundreds* of keyboard combinations for the various Mac OS X functions and settings. That's good, because keyboard shortcuts are efficient and quicker than using the mouse. But that's also bad, because there's no *way* you'll be able to remember all of them—and some of the most useful shortcuts are ridiculous, multikey affairs that you'll never remember at all.

In Lion's keyboard-shortcut center, shown in Figure 4-21, you can look over all the common Mac OS X hidden keyboard functions—for Mission Control, Exposé, Spotlight, Dashboard, the Dock, and many others—and *change them.*

Here's how it goes:

1. **Choose →System Preferences. Click Keyboard. Click the Keyboard Shortcuts tab.**

   You arrive at the dialog box shown in Figure 4-21.

Figure 4-21:
The keyboard-shortcut center lets you redefine the keystrokes that trigger many basic Mac OS X features, menu commands in your programs, and software you've built yourself using Automator (which is described in the free online Appendix to this chapter; see this book's "Missing CD" at www.missing-manuals.com.).

2. **In the left-side list, click the category or function you want.**

   Your choices include Launchpad & Dock, Mission Control, Keyboard & Text Input, and so on. When you click a category name, you see the available keyboard shortcuts.

Tip: You don't have to be content with *changing* one of these keyboard shortcuts. You can also *turn it off* by clicking the corresponding checkbox. That's great if one of Apple's predefined keystrokes—for a function you don't even use—is interfering with one in a program you like.

---

3. **Click the command you want to change. Then click the current keyboard combination.**

   Suppose, for example, that you wish the Show Desktop Exposé keystroke were something easier to remember, like Control-D. So in step 2, you'd click Mission Control. In this step, you'd click Show Desktop. Then you'd click where it currently says "F11."

4. Press a new key combination.

In this example, you'd press Control-D.

Be careful, though. Mac OS X keystrokes take precedence over *all others*. So if you choose a keystroke like ⌘-P for something, well, by golly, you'll no longer be able to use ⌘-P to print anything in any of your programs. Think before you assign. Run a couple of tests afterward.

The Save and Open Dialog Boxes

When you choose File→Save, you're asked where you want the new document stored on your hard drive. The resulting dialog box is a miniature Finder. All the skills you've picked up working at the desktop come into play here.

To give it a try, launch any program that has a Save or Export command—TextEdit, for example. Type a couple of words, and then choose File→Save. The Save sheet appears (Figure 4-22).

Tip: In most Mac OS X programs, a quick glance at the Close button in the upper-left corner of a document window tells you whether it's been saved. When a small dot appears in the red button, it means you've made changes to the document that you haven't saved yet. (Time to press ⌘-S!) The dot disappears as soon as you save your work.

In programs that offer the Auto Save and Versions features described later in this chapter, like TextEdit, the red-dot convention has been retired. Instead, when you've made changes to a document since saving it, you see the light-gray word "Edited" in the title bar.

Sheets

In the days of operating systems gone by, the Save dialog box appeared dead center on the screen, where it commandeered your entire operation. Moreover, because it seemed stuck to your *screen* rather than to a particular *document,* you couldn't actually tell which document you were saving—a real problem when you quit out of a program that had three unsaved documents open.

In most Mac OS X programs, there's no mystery regarding which document you're saving, because a little Save dialog box called a *sheet* slides directly out of the document's title bar.

Better still, this little Save box is a sticky note attached *to the document*. It stays there, neatly attached and waiting, even if you switch to another program, another document, the desktop, or wherever. When you finally return to the document, the Save sheet is still there, waiting for you to type a file name and save the document.

Tip: In most programs, you can enlarge the Save or Open dialog box by dragging one of its edges. You can also adjust the width of the Sidebar by dragging its right edge.

The Mini Finder

Of course *you*, O savvy reader, have probably never saved a document into some deeply nested folder by accident, never to see it again. But millions of novices (and even a few experts) have fallen into this trap.

When the Save sheet appears, a pop-up menu shows you precisely where Mac OS X proposes to put your newly created document: usually in the Documents folder of your own Home folder. For many people, this is an excellent suggestion. If you keep everything in your Documents folder, it will be extremely easy to find, and you'll be able to back up your work just by dragging that single folder to a backup disk.

As shown at top in Figure 4-22, the Where pop-up menu gives you direct access to some other places you might want to save a newly created file. (The keystrokes for the most important folders work here, too—Shift-⌘-H for your Home folder, for example.)

Compact Save sheet

Expanded Save sheet

Figure 4-22:
Top: The Save dialog box, or sheet, often appears in its compact form.

Right (inset): If you open the Where pop-up menu, you'll find that Mac OS X lists all the places it thinks you might want to save your new document: on the hard drive, in a folder you've put into your Sidebar, or into a folder you've recently opened.

Bottom: If you want to choose a different folder or create a new folder, click the ▼ button indicated by the cursor above to expand the dialog box. Here, you see the equivalent of the Finder—with a choice of icon, list, or column view. Even the Sidebar is here, complete with access to other disks on the network.

In any case, when you save a file, the options in the Where pop-up menu have you covered 90 percent of the time. Most people work with a limited set of folders for active documents.

But when you want to save a new document into a new folder, or when you want to navigate to a folder that isn't listed in the Where pop-up menu, all is not lost. Click the ▾ button identified in Figure 4-22. The Save sheet expands into a very familiar sight: a miniature version of the Finder.

There's your Sidebar, complete with access to the other computers on your network. There are the ◀/▶ buttons. There are your little buttons for icon, list, column, and (in most programs) even Cover Flow views.

Tip: In column view, your first instinct should be to widen this window, making more columns available. Do so by carefully dragging either edge of the dialog box. Mac OS X remembers the size of this Save sheet independently in each program.

And in list view, how's this for a tip? If you Control-click (or right-click) one of the column headings, like Name or Date Modified, you get a secret pop-up menu of column names: Last Opened, Size, Kind, Label, and so on. That's right: You can customize the list view within an Open or Save dialog box. You can sort, too, by clicking one of the column headings, just as at the desktop.

Most of the familiar Finder navigation shortcuts work here, too. For example, press the ← and → keys to navigate the columns, or the ↑ and ↓ keys to highlight the disk and folder names *within* a column. Once you've highlighted a column, you can also type to select the first letters of disk or folder names.

In fact, you can use Quick Look (page 67) in the Open and Save dialog box, too. Highlight any file or folder in the list and tap the space bar to view it in a full-size window.

When you're finished playing around, open the folder where you want to save your newly created document, and then click Save to store it there.

Alternatively, click New Folder (or press the usual New Folder keystroke, Shift-⌘-N) to create a new folder *inside* the folder you're looking at. (If you're in column view, then the new folder appears inside whichever folder is highlighted.)

You'll be asked to type the new name for the folder. After you've done so, click Create (or press Return). The new folder appears and opens before you, empty. You can now proceed with saving your new document into it, if you like.

The next time you save a new document, the Save sheet reappears in whatever condition you left it. That is, if you used column view the last time, it's still in column view. At any time, you can collapse it into simplified view, shown at top in Figure 4-22, by clicking the ▲ button to the right of the Where pop-up menu.

Insta-Jumping to a Folder Location

Whether you're using the mini-sheet or the expanded view, you can save yourself some folder-burrowing time by following the tip shown in Figure 4-23. This feature is totally undocumented—but well worth learning.

Spotlight

The search box at the top of the Open and Save dialog box is a clone of the Finder's search box (Chapter 3). Press ⌘-F to make your insertion point jump there. Type a few letters of the name of the file or folder you're looking for, and up it pops, regardless of its actual hard-disk location.

Your savings: 5 minutes of burrowing through folders to find it, and several pages of reading about how to navigate the Save and Open boxes.

Figure 4-23:
The quickest way to specify a folder location is to drag the icon of any folder or disk from your desktop directly into the Save or Open sheet. Mac OS X instantly displays the contents of that folder or disk.

The File Format Pop-up Menu

The Save dialog box in many programs offers a pop-up menu of file formats below the Save As box. Use this menu when preparing a document for use by somebody else—somebody whose computer doesn't have the same software. For example, if you've used a graphics program to prepare a photograph for use on the Web, this menu is where you specify JPEG format (the standard Web format for photos).

The Open File Dialog Box

The dialog box that appears when you choose File→Open is almost identical to the expanded Save File sheet. Because you encounter it only when you're opening an existing file, this dialog box lacks a Save button, file name field, and so on.

Note: Furthermore, the Open dialog box gives you access only to disks, folders, and documents that you can actually open at this moment. For example, when you're using GarageBand, picture files show up dimmed.

But the Open box adds a new Sidebar category called Media, which gives you direct access to all your photos, music, and movies. Apple figures you might want to import these items *into* a document you're working on.

Most of the other Save File dialog box controls are equally useful here. That handy Spotlight search bar is still there, only a ⌘-F away. Once again, you can begin your navigation by seeing what's on the desktop (press ⌘-D) or in your Home folder (Shift-⌘-H). Once again, you can find a folder or a disk by beginning your quest with the Sidebar, and then navigate using icon, list, or column view. And once again, you can drag a folder, disk, or file icon off your desktop directly into the dialog box to specify where you want to look. (If you drag a *file* icon, you're shown the folder that contains it.)

When you've finally located the file you want to open, do so by double-clicking it or highlighting it (which you can do from the keyboard), and then pressing Return, Enter, or ⌘-O.

In general, most people don't encounter the Open File dialog box nearly as often as the Save File dialog box. That's because the Mac offers many more convenient ways to *open* a file—double-clicking its icon in the Finder, choosing its name from →Recent Items, and so on—but only a single way to *save* a new file.

GEM IN THE ROUGH

Using the Dock or Sidebar for Drag-and-Drop

The Mac is smart about the relationship between documents and applications. If you double-click a TextEdit document icon, for example, TextEdit opens automatically and shows you the document.

But it's occasionally useful to open a document using a program other than the one that created it. Perhaps, as is often the case with downloaded Internet graphics, you don't *have* the program that created it, or you don't know which one was used. This technique is also useful if you want to open a Read Me file into your word processor, such as Word, instead of the usual TextEdit program.

In such cases, the Dock is handy: Just drag the mystery document onto one of the Dock's tiles, as shown here. Do-

ing so forces the program to open the document—if it can. (Dragging onto a program's icon in the Sidebar or even the Finder toolbar works just as well.)

Incidentally, in general only the Dock icons of programs that can, in fact, open the file you're dragging become highlighted. The others just shrug indifferently or even scoot aside, thinking you're trying to drag the file *into* the Dock.

Pressing Option-⌘ as you drag forces Dock icons to be more tolerant. Now all of them "light up" as your document touches them, indicating that they'll *try* to open your file. Even so, a "could not be opened" error message may result. As they say in Cupertino, sometimes what a can really needs is a can opener.

Auto Save and Versions

In the beginning, Jobs created the Save command—because computers were really slow. Every time you saved, your work was interrupted for a few seconds (or a lot of seconds) as the very slow program on your very slow computer saved your work onto a very slow floppy disk.

And *that,* ladies and gentlemen, is why most programs still don't autosave: because the interruptions were just too annoying.

But computers now have plenty of horsepower. They could be saving your work every few seconds, and you'd never even know it. Why shouldn't *all* programs save your work as you go, automatically and invisibly? As long as you also have the option to rewind and take your document in a different direction, what could possibly be the harm?

And so it is that, in Lion, Auto Save is one of the key new features.

Unfortunately, it's available in only a few programs, at least at the outset. You'll find it in Pages, Keynote, Numbers, Preview, and TextEdit. In these programs, your document is saved every time there's even the tiniest pause in your typing or working—in the background. No progress bar, no interruption. And if you're on a tear, typing nonstop, your work is saved every 5 minutes, even while you type.

In these programs, you'll never even *see* the Save command in the File menu—except in that short time before you've saved and named a new document for the first time. After that, the command says Save a Version, which is a different beast altogether (read on).

Versions

In those enlightened programs that work with Lion's Auto Save feature, there's a more complicated but more powerful feature at work: Versions. It's an invisible paper trail of every in-progress condition of your document—and you can return to any earlier version at any time. You can even return to an earlier version and copy just a *chunk* of it into the current version, which is great when one paragraph of your previous draft was gold, but the rest was junk.

It's all much more sensible, elegant, and useful than the old Save As command.

The Versions world of document management is quite a bit different from the old setup. Here's what you need to know:

- **All the version information is stored in the same original document file.** (It's not like there's a rat's nest of icons for each thing you're working on.) But when you send the document to somebody else (by email or network, for example), Lion is smart enough to send only the current version, stripping out all the history. Nobody will ever know how much you labored over your work (or how little).

Note: Behind the scenes, the various versions of each document are saved in an invisible folder on your hard drive called *.DocumentRevisions-V100.*

- **Lion creates a new snapshot of your document once an hour.** You can also create new snapshots manually at even shorter intervals—by using the File→Save a Version command (which is why your reflex of periodically hitting ⌘-S isn't wasted).

  These snapshots, or *versions,* represent rewind points that you can return to later, even months or years after you first created the document. Thoughtfully enough, Lion records, invisibly, only what's *changed* between versions, so your files don't get all big and bloated.

Note: All right, you don't have *total* time-rewinding control. Lion stores hourly versions for a day, daily versions for a month, and weekly versions for all previous months.

- **There's no Save As command anymore in these programs.** Instead, when you want to spin off a different version of a document—because you want to experiment with taking it into a radical new direction, for example—choose File→Duplicate. (Or choose Duplicate from the title-bar menu shown in Figure 4-24.)

  Before your very eyes, a duplicate version of the open window springs into existence. If the original was called "Kumquat Tarts," the new one is called "Kumquat Tarts copy."

  At least that's what it says in the title bar. Don't be fooled, however. In fact, you still have to save this new document (File→Save) to give it a folder location and new title, if you like.

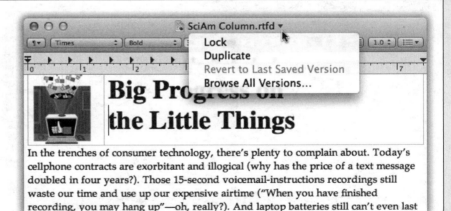

Figure 4-24:
Point to the title of your document to see this secret menu. It contains the full list of commands that pertain to Versions.

- **There's a secret Versions menu in the title bar.** Point to the name of your document. In Auto Save–compatible files, a little ▾ appears in the title bar (Figure 4-24).

Rewinding to an earlier version

The point of all of this, of course, is to make it easy to go back in time—to undo the mediocre work you've done, or to resurrect some genius work that you later deleted.

The quick way is to choose File→Revert to Saved. (You can also choose Revert to Last Saved Version from the menu shown in Figure 4-24.) That command restores the document to the last snapshot version (or to the way it was when you most recently opened it, if no new versions have been created). That, of course, is nothing new; lots of programs have Revert to Saved commands that work similarly.

What's new in Lion is that you can revert your document to *any* snapshot, even an ancient one from weeks or months ago.

To do that, open the Versions menu (shown in Figure 4-24). From the pop-up menu, choose Browse All Versions.

After a moment, you see the stunning display shown in Figure 4-25. On the left, you see your document in its current condition. On the right, you see a stack of windows that represent all the different snapshots of your document, going back in time. (And behind it all, you see another sort of version: Apple's animated, starry version of the galaxy.)

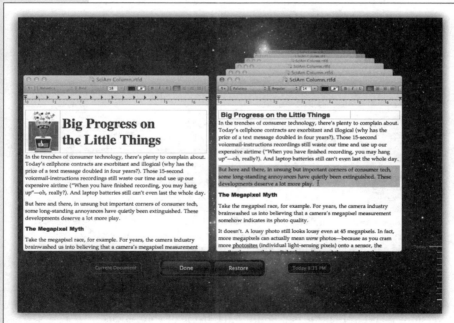

Figure 4-25:
If you've ever used Mac OS X's Time Machine feature, this display should look familiar. It's your chance to go back in time to recover an earlier, better version of your document (or just a part of it).

You can have all kinds of productive fun in this version browser:

- **Compare the current version (on the left) with the next-most-recent one (on the right).** These are live documents, so you can scroll through them as necessary. If you decide to stick with the latest edition on the left, just click Done. You leave the starry version-history world and go back to editing.

- **Zoom back in time to inspect older versions (snapshots) of your document.** On the right side of the screen, you see earlier versions of the document—maybe even dozens of them, stretching back in time.

  You can click individual windows' title bars to see what's in them. You can also click or drag your cursor through the notches at the right side. It's like a time ruler that flies through the windows into the past. (As you go, the time/date stamp below the right-side window identifies where you are in time—that is, which version you're examining.)

- **Restore an earlier version.** If you finally find the incarnation of the document you consider superior to your current one, click Restore. You leave Starry Versionland and return to your document, which has now been rewound to its earlier condition.

  If you later decide you should not have gone back to that earlier version, no problem. Your later version—the one you started out with—is still in the version browser, too. So you can go back to it, if necessary.

Tip: If you press Option, the Restore button changes to say Restore a Copy. In other words, you'll create a previous-version duplicate of the document, without disturbing the current condition of the one you've just been working on.

- **Restore *part* of an earlier version.** Often, the current version of your work is *generally* good, but you really wish you could recover *one* magical sentence or paragraph or section—something you've since edited or deleted.

  You can do that in Starry Versionland, too, because Copy and Paste work here!

  Use the time ruler to find the earlier edition of your document, the one containing the good stuff. Then drag through the desired text or graphics in the window on the right, as shown in Figure 4-25. Now copy the highlighted material (either press ⌘-C, or move your mouse to the top of the screen so that the menu bar appears, and choose Edit→Copy). Click in the *current* version of the document, the one at left, and now paste (⌘-V, or use the menu bar). Click Done to complete this astonishing act of salvation.

- **Delete a version.** There are all kinds of reasons why you might want to delete one of your older snapshots. Maybe you wrote it in a fit of pique (or exhaustion), and you want to make sure nobody ever, ever reads that awful prose. Maybe you know there's nothing valuable in it, and you'd rather not dedicate hard drive space to it.

  In any case, deleting a version is easy to do. Once you're in Starry Versionland, point to the ▾ in the title bar of the version (on the right side). You'll discover that the menu now contains only one command: Delete This Version. Click Delete in the confirmation box. Any questions?

Tip: If you press Option, the command says Delete *Old* Versions. Once you confirm your decision, you'll be left with only the most recent edition, without any way to rewind.

Locking documents

If all this version recording is making you dizzy, you can call a halt. You can freeze a document in its current condition so that nobody can make any further changes to it. You might lock a contract document before you send it to someone, for example, or just freeze your novel into what you hope is its final form.

To do that, click the ▼ in the title bar; from the shortcut menu, choose Lock. Now the title bar says "Locked." If you try to edit the document, you're offered the dialog box shown in Figure 4-26.

It's also worth noting that Mac OS X itself locks every document two weeks after you last made changes to it—what Apple considers a useful safety net.

Tip: You can turn off this auto-locking thing, or just change the interval. To find these controls, open → System Preferences. Click Time Machine. Click Options.

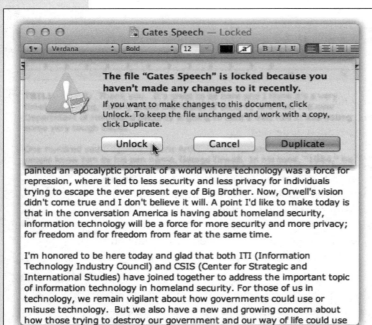

Figure 4-26:
If you try to make changes to a document, Lion gives you two choices. You can unlock the document or click Duplicate, which spins off an unlocked perfect copy.

Entering, Moving & Backing Up Data

The original 1984 Mac didn't make jaws drop because of its speed, price, or sleek looks. What amazed people was the simplicity and elegance of the user interface. At some point in every Apple demo, the presenter copied a graphic drawn in a painting program (MacPaint) and pasted it directly into a word processor (MacWrite), where it appeared neatly nestled between typed paragraphs of text.

We take these examples of data input and data exchange for granted today. But in those days, that little stunt struck people like a thunderbolt. After all, if this little computer let you copy and paste between different programs, it could probably do anything.

Today, the Mac is even more adept at helping you enter, move, and share your hard-won data. Mac OS X offers several ways to move information within a single document, between documents, between programs, and even between Mac and Windows computers. This chapter leads you through this broad cycle of data: from entering it with the mouse and keyboard, to moving it around, to backing it up.

Power Typing

Something strange has been quietly taking place at Apple: *Typing* has been getting a lot of attention.

It began when Apple created *system-wide* spelling and grammar checkers. For the first time in computer history, the *operating system* took over typos and grammos. You didn't have to maintain a separate spelling checker for each program you used. Now there's just one, and it works in most programs: TextEdit, Stickies, iChat, Mail, iCal, Safari, Pages, iPhoto, iMovie, and so on. Add a word to the dictionary in one program, and it's available to all the others.

Today, there's much more. There's text substitution, where you type *addr* and the system types out "Irwina P. McGillicuddy, 1293 Eastport Lane, Harborvilletown, MA, 02552." (The same system autocorrects common typos like *teh* instead of *the.*) There's also a case-flipping feature that can change selected text to ALL CAPS, all lowercase, or First Letter Capped. Both of these new features are available in most Apple programs and in any other programs that tap into Mac OS X's built-in text-processing circuitry (although not, alas, Microsoft programs).

The Mac OS X Spelling and Grammar Checker

Mac OS X can give you live, interactive spelling and grammar checking, just as in Microsoft Word and other word processors. That is, misspelled words or badly written sentences or fragments get flagged—spelling with a dashed red underline, grammar problems with a dashed green underline—the moment you type them. Here's the crash course:

- **Check the spelling of one word:** Highlight the word. Choose Edit→Spelling and Grammar→Show Spelling and Grammar. The spell-check dialog box opens, with the proposed corrections visible.

- **Check spelling as you type.** Choose Edit→Spelling and Grammar→Check Spelling While Typing. (If Check Grammar With Spelling is turned on in the same submenu, you'll get a grammar check, too.)

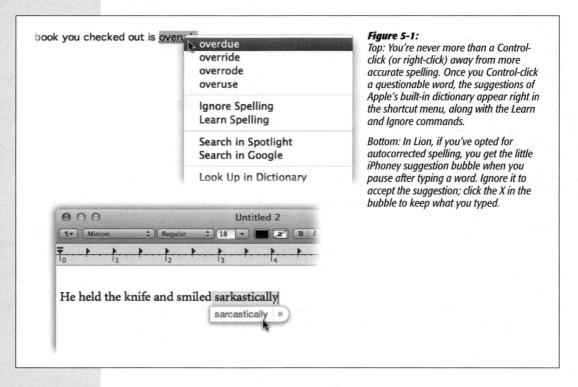

Figure 5-1:
Top: You're never more than a Control-click (or right-click) away from more accurate spelling. Once you Control-click a questionable word, the suggestions of Apple's built-in dictionary appear right in the shortcut menu, along with the Learn and Ignore commands.

Bottom: In Lion, if you've opted for autocorrected spelling, you get the little iPhoney suggestion bubble when you pause after typing a word. Ignore it to accept the suggestion; click the X in the bubble to keep what you typed.

Now, as you type, you'll see those red and green underlines on words the Mac thinks represent spelling or grammar mistakes. To fix one, Control-click (right-click) the underlined word, and proceed as shown in Figure 5-1.

Tip: In TextEdit, the factory setting for error-underlining is On. To turn it off, for all new documents, choose TextEdit→Preferences, click New Document, and then turn off "Check spelling as you type."

- **Check spelling after the document is finished.** Choose Edit→Spelling and Grammar→Show Spelling and Grammar (or press ⌘-:). The Spelling dialog box appears. The first error it spots appears in the top box, with the proposed corrections in the bottom one.

  If you like one of Apple's proposals, click it and then click Change. If the word was correct already (for example, the guy's last name really is Teh), then click Find Next ("Leave the word as I typed it"), Ignore ("It's OK everywhere in this document"), or Learn ("Never flag this word again").

  Handily enough, you can also click Define to look up a highlighted word (one of the spelling suggestions, for example) in the Mac's built-in Dictionary app. Also handily enough, the spelling checker is smart enough to maintain different spelling checkers (dictionaries) for different languages—and to recognize, within a single document, which language you're using!

- **Fix spelling as you type.** Note the difference. *Checking* your spelling just means "finding the misspelled words." *Fixing* means autocorrecting the errors as they occur, as you type. You might not even notice that it's happening!

  This most tantalizing option is found in Edit→Spelling and Grammar→Correct Spelling Automatically. And sure enough, when this option is turned on, common typos like *teh* and *frmo* and *dont* get fixed as you type; you don't have to do anything to make it happen.

Tip: If you're typing slowly enough, you might see the suggestion bubble illustrated in Figure 5-1. That, of course, is a feature Apple brought to the Mac from the iPhone/iPad. It's saying, "Here's the word I *think* you meant—and if you just keep on typing, I'll go ahead and make the change I'm proposing. If you disagree, click *on the X in the word bubble* to make me shut up and leave what you typed, just as you typed it."

It's not perfect. It doesn't correct all errors (or even most of them). It occasionally even corrects a word you didn't mean to have corrected. (When it makes a mistake, hit ⌘-Z, the Undo command, to restore what you typed.) And sometimes it doesn't make the change until you're halfway through the sentence.

Still, though. Kind of a good idea to have a single, system-wide spell checker.

Text Substitution (Abbreviation Expansion)

This useful feature autoreplaces *one* thing you type with something else. Why? Because it can do any of these things.

Insert the proper typographical symbols

For example, Mac OS X can insert attractive "curly quotes" automatically as you type "straight ones," or em dashes—like this—when you type two hyphens (--like that). It can also insert properly typeset fractions (like ½) when you type "1/2."

You can see the list of built-in substitutions—and create your own—in the System Preferences→Language & Text→Text tab, as shown in Figure 5-2.

Figure 5-2:
This is where you can manage Mac OS X's typographic substitutions. You can see that it can turn common fractions into typographically fancy ones as you type them. But you can add all kinds of auto-typo corrections and even boilerplate text paragraphs.

Apple doesn't want to drive you nuts, though, so it makes sure *you're* sure you really want these swappings to take place. So you have to turn on each of these features manually, in each program. (These commands are available anywhere you do a *lot* of typing, like TextEdit, Mail, and Stickies.)

• **Auto-quotes.** To make the quotes curlify themselves, choose Edit→Substitutions→ Smart Quotes, so that a checkmark appears.

Note: In the System Preferences→Language & Text→Text tab, you can specify which kind of fancy quotation mark you prefer: «this kind,» „this kind," or whatever. You international thing, you!

- **Auto-dashes.** To turn double hyphens into these (—) long dashes, choose Edit→ Substitutions→Smart Dashes, so that a checkmark appears.

- **Smart links.** There's also an option to create smart links, where any Web address you type turns into a blue, underlined, *clickable* link to a Web page. Turn on Edit→Substitutions→Smart Links.

Tip: You can also choose Edit→Substitutions→Show Substitutions to make a floating panel appear, complete with on/off checkboxes for all these features.

Replace abbreviations with much longer phrases

That is, you can program *addr* to type your entire return address. Create two-letter abbreviations for big legal or technical words you have to type a lot. Set up *goaway* to type out a polite rejection letter for use in email. And so on.

This feature has been in Microsoft Office forever (called AutoCorrect), and it's always been available as a shareware add-on (TypeIt4Me and TextExpander, for example). But now it's built right into most Apple programs, plus any others that use Apple's text-input plumbing.

You build your list of abbreviations in the System Preferences→Language & Text→Text tab, shown in Figure 5-2. See the list at left? Click the **+** button to create a new row in the scrolling table of substitutions.

Click in the left column and type the abbreviation you want (for example, *addr*). Click in the right column and type, or paste, the text you want Mac OS X to type instead.

Tip: Don't be shy—you're not limited to short snippets. The replacement text can be pages long, which is handy if you're a lawyer and you build your contracts out of boilerplate chunks of canned text.

You can even create multiple paragraphs—but not by hitting Return when you want a new line; no, hitting Return means, "I'm finished entering this text" and closes up the box. Instead, press Option-Return when you want a paragraph break.

Here again, you have to explicitly *turn on* the text-replacement feature in each program (TextEdit, Mail, Stickies, and so on). To do that, choose Edit→Substitutions→Text Replacement, so that a checkmark appears.

That's it! Now, whenever you type one of the abbreviations you've set up, the Mac instantly replaces it with your substituted text.

Case Swapping

The final chunk in Mac OS X's text-massaging tool chest is case swapping—that is, changing text you've already typed (or pasted) from ALL CAPS to lowercase or Just First Letters Capitalized.

This one's simple: Select the text you want to change, and then choose from the Edit→ Transformations submenu. Your options are Make Upper Case (all caps), Make Lower Case (no caps), and Capitalize (first letters, like a movie title).

Keep that in mind the next some raving lunatic SENDS YOU AN EMAIL THAT WAS TYPED ENTIRELY WITH THE CAPS LOCK KEY DOWN.

Tip: Here's a sneaky one in Lion: You can double-tap a word with three fingers on your trackpad to get a pop-up dictionary and thesaurus definition. (That's a light double-*tap,* not a full double-*click.*) This trick doesn't work in all programs, and it requires you to turn it on in System Preferences→Trackpad→Point & Click. And it's a tad bit finicky.

But once you have it working, check it out: It also works in text documents you're examining in Quick Look!

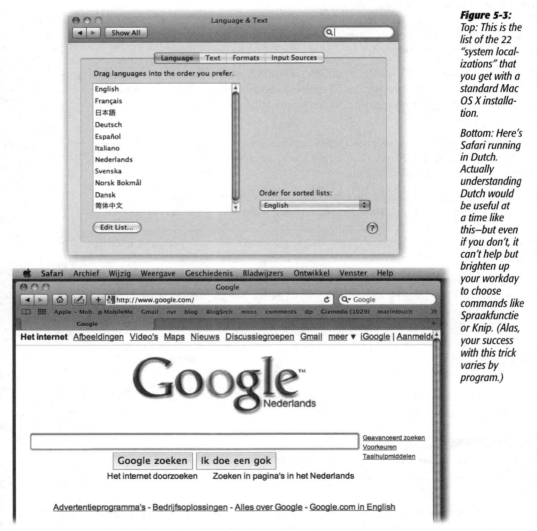

Figure 5-3:
Top: This is the list of the 22 "system localizations" that you get with a standard Mac OS X installation.

Bottom: Here's Safari running in Dutch. Actually understanding Dutch would be useful at a time like this—but even if you don't, it can't help but brighten up your workday to choose commands like Spraakfunctie or Knip. (Alas, your success with this trick varies by program.)

The Many Languages of Mac OS X Text

On the Mac, you can shift from language to language on the fly, as you type, even in midsentence—without reinstalling the operating system or even restarting the computer.

First, tell your Mac which languages you'd like to have available. Open System Preferences→Language & Text. On the Language tab, you see a listing of the languages the Mac can switch into, in the corresponding languages—Français, Español, and so on. Just drag one of the languages to the top of the list to select it as the target language, as shown in Figure 5-3.

Note: You can mix English with right-to-left languages like Hebrew and Arabic. There's even a split-cursor option that makes the pointer flip directions at the boundary between right-to-left and left-to-right text.

GEM IN THE ROUGH

Instant Accented Characters, Courtesy of the iPhone

It's been a problem since the dawn of computing: How do you produce accented characters–lĭké thêsë–on a keyboard with only 26 letter keys?

For most of computing history, the answer has been: You bring up some special palette on the screen, or you memorize key combinations. And yes, those options are still available in Mac OS X.

But in Lion, there's a new option, which Apple stole from its own iPhone software: Hold down the letter you want accented—e, for example. After a moment, you get a pop-up panel of possible accented versions. You can click the one you want, or, if you'd rather not lift your hands off the keyboard, you can type the corresponding number that appears in light gray beneath each letter.

This feature works in almost all programs, although there may be some where it doesn't…pop up.

Now, if you're the kind of person who needs accents from time to time, you're probably delighted with this new, clever way to get them. But if holding down a key produces an accented character, then that means holding down a key no longer *repeats* the key, right? It means you can no longer type, "You go, grrrrrrrrrrl!" or "rated XXXXXXXX" or "I love you SOOOOOOOOOOO much!" Right?

Right. A few characters that people routinely type lines of, like ***** and ……. and ____, still repeat when you hold them down. But none of the 26 letter keys repeat anymore.

There are, fortunately, a couple of quick and easy ways to restore the old key-repeating behavior, if you're a "SOOOOO much" kind of person.

The easiest way is to download the free program Lion Tweaks. It's available on this book's "Missing CD" page at *www.missingmanuals.com*. Open it up, and where it says, "Enable repeating keys," click Yes. Ta-da!

You've just flipped off the switch for the Lion accent picker. Now every key repeats, just as it always used to.

Now launch Safari, TextEdit, Mail, or Stickies. Every menu, button, and dialog box is now in the new language you selected! If you log out and back in (or restart) at this point, the entire Finder will be in the new language, too.

Note: Programs differ widely in their "language awareness." If you use a language beyond the 22 in the list, adding it (with the Edit List button) ensures that its relevant features will be available in all programs. (You may still have to add additional language software to make your menus and dialog boxes change.)

Formats Tab

Of course, if you're *really* French (for example), you'll also want to make these changes:

- On the Formats tab, choose your French-speaking country from the Region pop-up menu, so that time and date formats, number punctuation, and currency symbols also conform to your local customs. (Turn on "Show all regions" if necessary.)

  For example, the decimal and thousands separator characters for displaying large numbers differ from country to country. (The number 25,600.99, for example, would be written as "25 600,99" in France and as "25.600,99" in Spain.) And what appears to an American to be July 4 (the notation "7/4"), to a European indicates April 7.

  If, for some reason, Apple's preprogrammed settings aren't right for your region, you'll see Customize buttons that let you override them.

- Choose the French *keyboard layout* from the Input Sources tab, as explained next.

Input Sources Tab

While the Mac can display many different languages, *typing* in those languages is another matter. The symbols you use when you're typing in Swedish aren't the same as when you're typing in English. Apple solved this problem by creating different *keyboard layouts* for each language. Each rearranges the letters that appear when you press the keys. For example, when you use the Swedish layout and press the semicolon key, you don't get a semicolon (;)—you get an ö.

Apple even includes the famous Dvorak layout and the not-very-famous Colemak layout. Both are scientific rearrangements of the standard layout that put the most common letters directly under your fingertips on the home row. Fans of the Dvorak layout, and the more modern Colemak layout, claim greater accuracy, better speed, and less fatigue.

Use the list in the Input Sources pane to indicate which keyboard layout you want. If you select anything in the list, then "Show input menu in menu bar" turns on automatically. That option puts a tiny flag icon in your menu bar—a keyboard *menulet* that lets you switch from one layout to another just by choosing its name. (To preview a certain keyboard arrangement, launch the Keyboard Viewer program described next.)

Tip: The icon of the Input menulet changes. It becomes a colorful flag to show the currently selected language.

The Character Viewer

There you are, two-thirds of the way through your local matchmaker newsletter, when it hits you that you need a heart symbol. In Windows, you had the Character Map program. On the Mac, you have Character Viewer. To make it appear, choose Edit→Special Characters.

Most programs have this command. If yours doesn't, here's the long way: Open System Preferences, click Language & Text, click the Input Sources tab, and then turn on the Keyboard & Character Viewer checkbox. You've just installed the Keyboard menulet.

Then, next time you're word processing or doing page layout, choose Show Character Viewer from this menu. The resulting window (Figure 5-4, top) rounds up all symbols from all your fonts at once. To find a particular symbol, click the "by Category" tab, and then click the various category headings: Arrows, Math Symbols, and so on.

Figure 5-4:
Top: You can preview variations of the same symbol in the Font Variation panel. You can also use the search box to find a symbol by name: "heart" or "yen" or "asterisk," for example. And if you click the ⌘ menu in the top left, you can choose Customize List—and you'll have access to a staggering array of even more symbol categories, including wacky symbols from other alphabets.

Bottom: How do you make a π symbol? Keyboard Viewer reveals the answer. When you press the Option key, the Keyboard Viewer keyboard shows that the pi character (π) is mapped to the P key. To insert the symbol into an open document, just click it in the Keyboard Viewer window.

When you find the symbol you want, double-click it. The correct symbol pops into your document. (If not, you may have gotten the correct character in the wrong font. In that case, change the font of the inserted character manually. To find out what font it came from, click the symbol in the Font Variation panel to see the font name.)

Keyboard Viewer

Keyboard Viewer consists of a single window containing a tiny onscreen keyboard (Figure 5-4, bottom). When you hold down any of the modifier keys on your keyboard (like ⌘, Option, Shift, or Control), you can see exactly which keys produce which characters. The point, of course, is to help you learn which keys to press when you need special symbols or non-English characters, such as © or ñ, in each font.

Note: Keyboard Viewer shows only the symbols you can produce by typing keystrokes. A font may contain thousands of other characters that can't actually be typed; the Character Viewer is the only way to access these other symbols.

It's a great tool—if you can find it.

Here's how. Open System Preferences→Language & Text, click Input Sources, and then turn on Keyboard & Character Viewer at the top of the list. The Input menu-let—usually a tiny flag—appears at the top of the screen. You can open the Keyboard Viewer by choosing its name from this menulet.

To see the effect of pressing the modifier keys, either click the onscreen keys or press them on your actual keyboard. The corresponding keys on the onscreen keyboard light up as they're pressed.

Tip: You're not stuck viewing the characters in a 12-point font size—a good thing, because some of them are hard to read when displayed that small. You can make the Keyboard Viewer window nearly fill the screen by clicking its Zoom button. That will magnify the Keyboard Viewer window and its font size.

Data Detectors

Here's a cool step-saver, something no other operating system offers—a little something Apple likes to call *data detectors.*

In short, Mac OS X programs like Mail and TextEdit can recognize commonly used bits of information that may appear in your text: a physical address, a phone number, a date and time, and so on. With one quick click, you can send that information into the appropriate Mac OS X program, like iCal, Address Book, or your Web browser (for looking up an address on a map).

Here's how it works: When you spot a name, address, date, or time, point to it without clicking. A dotted rectangle appears around it. Control-click inside the rectangle, or right-click, or click the ▾ at the right side. As shown in Figure 5-5, a shortcut menu appears. Its contents vary depending on what you're pointing to:

- **A mailing address.** You can choose Show Address in Google Maps from the shortcut menu; your Web browser opens and shows you that address on a Google map.

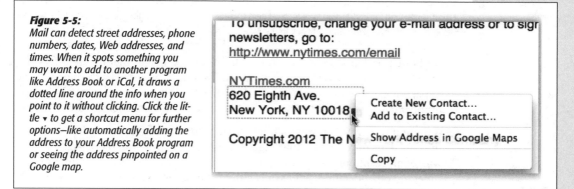

Figure 5-5:
Mail can detect street addresses, phone numbers, dates, Web addresses, and times. When it spots something you may want to add to another program like Address Book or iCal, it draws a dotted line around the info when you point to it without clicking. Click the little ▾ to get a shortcut menu for further options—like automatically adding the address to your Address Book program or seeing the address pinpointed on a Google map.

Alternatively, you can choose Create New Contact (to add an Address Book entry for this address) or Add to Existing Contact (if the *person* is in your Address Book—just not the *address*). Like magic, a little box sprouts out of the data-detected rectangle, prefilled with the information from the message, so that you can approve it.

- **A date and time.** When you click the ▾, you get the pop-up shown in Figure 5-6. It shows you the actual iCal day view where Lion wants to add the appointment.

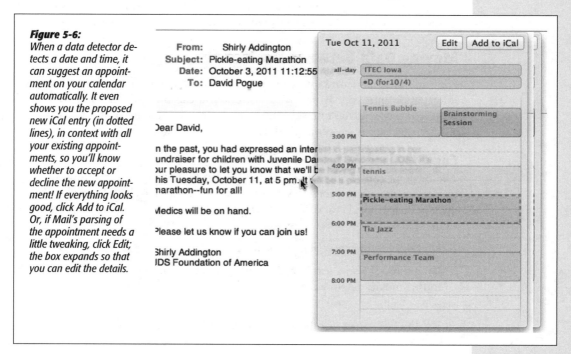

Figure 5-6:
When a data detector detects a date and time, it can suggest an appointment on your calendar automatically. It even shows you the proposed new iCal entry (in dotted lines), in context with all your existing appointments, so you'll know whether to accept or decline the new appointment! If everything looks good, click Add to iCal. Or, if Mail's parsing of the appointment needs a little tweaking, click Edit; the box expands so that you can edit the details.

The logic of this feature is overwhelming; after all, when someone emails you to ask if you're free for drinks next Thursday at 10, what's the first thing you usually want to do? Check your calendar, of course.

Tip: If, while working in iCal, you ever forget where this event came from, double-click it. In the Info balloon, you'll see a link that takes you right back to the Mail message that started it all.

- **A phone number.** As with mailing addresses, the shortcut menu here offers you things like Create New Contact and Add to Existing Contact. The third one, Large Type, is great when you want to call this person right now—it displays the phone number in *huge* type, filling your screen, so you can see it from across your mansion.

- **A flight number.** When you highlight flight information (for example, "AA 152"), the data detector offers a Show Flight Information command. It opens the Flights widget of Dashboard (page 149), so you can see the flight's departure time, arrival time, and other details. It works only if the airline is represented as a two-letter code.

- **A Web address.** When you click the ▾ next to a URL (like *www.nytimes.com)*, you get a pop-up balloon that contains the *actual Web page!* You get a quick look, without even having to leave your email message.

- **A package tracking number.** When you send a package using a service like FedEx, UPS, or the U.S. Postal Service, you usually get a confirmation email. A new Lion data detector can recognize such numbers and, when you click the ▾, offer you a Track Shipment command. Choosing it displays a pop-up window right there at your cursor, showing the courier company's tracking page for that package, and thereby letting you know exactly where your package is right now.

Moving Data Between Documents

You can't paste a picture into your Web browser, and you can't paste MIDI music information into your word processor. But you can put graphics into your word processor, paste movies into your database, insert text into Photoshop, and combine a surprising variety of seemingly dissimilar kinds of data.

Cut, Copy, and Paste

The original copy-and-paste procedure of 1984—putting a graphic into a word processor—has come a long way. Most experienced Mac fans have learned to trigger the Cut, Copy, and Paste commands from the keyboard, quickly and without even thinking. Here's how the process works:

1. **Highlight some material in a document.**

   Drag through some text in a word processor, for example, or highlight graphics, music, movie, database, or spreadsheet information, depending on the program you're using.

2. **Use the Edit→Cut or Edit→Copy command.**

Or press the keyboard shortcuts ⌘-X (for Cut—think of the X as a pair of scissors) or ⌘-C (for Copy). The Macintosh memorizes the highlighted material, socking it away on an invisible storage pad called the Clipboard. If you chose Copy, nothing visible happens. If you chose Cut, the highlighted material disappears from the original document.

At this point, most Mac fans take it on faith that the Cut or Copy command actually worked. But if you're in doubt, switch to the Finder (by clicking its Dock icon, for example), and then choose Edit→Show Clipboard. The Clipboard window appears, showing whatever you've copied.

3. **Click to indicate where you want the material to reappear.**

This may entail switching to a different program, a different document, or simply a different place in the same document.

4. **Choose the Edit→Paste command (⌘-V).**

The copy of the material you had originally highlighted now appears at your insertion point—*if* you're pasting into a program that can accept that kind of information. (You won't have much luck pasting, say, a block of spreadsheet numbers into World of Warcraft.)

The most recently cut or copied material remains on your Clipboard even after you paste, making it possible to paste the same blob repeatedly. Such a trick can be useful when, for example, you've designed a business card in your drawing program and want to duplicate it enough times to fill a letter-sized printout. On the other hand, whenever you next copy or cut something, whatever was already on the Clipboard is lost forever.

Drag-and-Drop

As useful and popular as it is, the Copy/Paste routine doesn't win any awards for speed. After all, it requires four steps. In many cases, you can replace that routine with the far more direct (and enjoyable) drag-and-drop method. Figure 5-7 illustrates how this works.

FREQUENTLY ASKED QUESTION

Smart Copy and Paste

Hey, I saw one more auto-fix feature in the Edit→Substitutions submenu: "Smart Copy/Paste." What's that about?

It's about spaces.

Ordinarily, when you cut or copy a word out of a sentence and then paste it into a new one, you have some cleanup to do. You leave an extra space behind, and you have to add a

space after the word when you paste.

Smart Copy/Paste simply cleans up these spaces for you. If you cut a word out of a sentence, only *one* space gets left between the words where it used to be. And when you paste text, a space is added on either side automatically—but only one.

Virtually every Mac OS X program works with the drag-and-drop technique, including TextEdit, Stickies, Mail, QuickTime Player, Preview, iMovie, iPhoto, and Apple System Profiler, not to mention other popular programs like Microsoft applications, Web browsers, and so on.

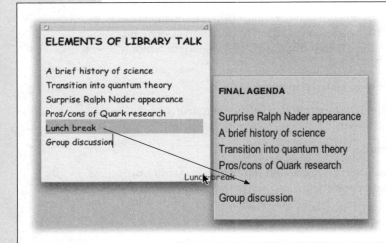

Figure 5-7:
To use drag-and-drop, highlight some material. Click anywhere in the highlighted area and press the mouse button for about half a second. Now, with the button still pressed, drag to another place in the document, into a different window, or into a different application. As your cursor enters the target window, a shaded outline appears inside the window's boundaries—the Mac's way of letting you know it understands your intention. When you release the mouse, the highlighted material appears instantly in its new location.

When to use drag-and-drop

As shown in Figure 5-7, drag-and-drop is ideal for transferring material between windows or between programs—from a Web page into Photoshop, for example. It's especially useful when you've already copied something valuable to your Clipboard, since drag-and-drop doesn't involve (and doesn't erase) the Clipboard.

Its most popular use, however, is rearranging text within a single document. In Word or Pages, for example, you can rearrange entire sections, paragraphs, sentences, or even individual letters, just by dragging them—a wonderfully efficient editing technique.

Tip: When you use drag-and-drop to move text within a document, the Mac moves the highlighted text, deleting it from its original location. If you press Option as you drag, however, you make a copy of the highlighted text.

Drag-and-drop to the desktop

You can also use drag-and-drop in the one program you use every single day: the Finder itself. As shown in Figure 5-8, you can drag text, graphics, sounds, and even movie clips out of your document windows and directly onto the desktop. Graphics and movies generally turn into ordinary graphics or movie files; text becomes an icon called a *clipping file*.

Later, you can examine a clipping's contents using Quick Look—just select its icon and then tap the space bar. Or you can double-click a clipping file and then select a portion of the text to copy.

When you drag a clipping from your desktop *back* into an application window, the material in that clipping reappears. Drag-and-drop, in other words, lets you treat your desktop itself as a giant, computer-wide pasteboard—an area where you can temporarily stash pieces of text or graphics as you work.

Tip: When the material you drag to the desktop contains nothing but an Internet address, such as an email address or Web page URL, Mac OS X gives it a special icon and a special function: an Internet location file. Double-click it to open your browser to that page.

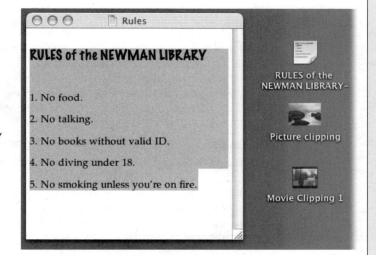

Figure 5-8:
When you drag material out of the document window and onto the desktop, you get a clipping file. Its icon depends on the kind of material contained within: (from top) text clipping, picture clipping, or movie clipping. (For easy identification, Mac OS X conveniently titles text clippings by the first line of the text contained inside.) You can view a clipping just by double-clicking it, so that it opens into its own window (left).

Export/Import

When it comes to transferring large chunks of information—especially address books, spreadsheet cells, and database records—from one program to another, none of the data-transfer methods described so far in this chapter does the trick. For these purposes, use the Export and Import commands found in the File menu of almost every database, spreadsheet, email, and address-book program. (In some programs, the Save As command serves this function.)

These Export/Import commands aren't part of Mac OS X, so the manuals (if any) of the applications in question should be your source for instructions. For now, however, the power and convenience of this feature are worth noting—it means that your four years' worth of collected addresses in, say, some old email program can find their way into a newer program, like Address Book, in a matter of minutes.

Exchanging Data with Other Macs

Considering how many ways there are to move files back and forth between Macs, it seems almost comical that anybody complained when Apple discontinued built-in floppy disk drives. Here's a catalog of the different ways you can move your files from one computer to another, including some that might not have occurred to you.

By Network

You can shoot a file to another Lion Mac with a single drag-and-drop operation, thanks to AirDrop (page 470) or another file-sharing method. You can open files from the other drives, copy stuff back and forth—anything you would do with your own disk. Step-by-step instructions are in Chapter 15.

Best for files of any size, when the computers are in the same building.

Tip: And for $0, you can create an ad hoc network, meaning a tiny wireless network between just two computers (or a handful). Great when you're in the car somewhere, or in the airport waiting lounge, or a hotel lobby, and someone says, "Hey, can I have a copy of that?" Details are on page 468.

By Email

Best for small files. High on convenience; computers can be in different countries.

Tip: Of course, the problem with email is that it generally can't handle file attachments larger than 5 or 10 megabytes. You can easily get around that limitation using a free Web site like Sendthisfile.com, which can handle enormous files by sending the recipient a link to them by email.

Using Dropbox

Dropbox is a free service, almost universally adored, that lets you create synchronized folders on multiple computers. Add a file to, say, your New Projects folder on your home Mac, and it appears instantly in the matching folder on your Windows folder at work.

You can use Dropbox to share folders with other people, too. Just drag a new file into a shared folder, and marvel as your associates get an auto-generated email message letting them know that you've posted a new document. They open the shared folder on their *own* desktops, and there are your files, waiting. (Details are at *www.dropbox.com/help/19.*)

The great thing about services like Dropbox is that you don't have to worry about the file-size limits imposed by email. (There's a 2-gigabyte storage limit on Dropbox's free accounts, but you can upgrade to larger storage capacities for a fee.)

By CD or DVD

You can always burn your files onto a blank CD or DVD and then carry or mail it to the recipient. Awfully slow and clumsy, but does result in a safety copy of whatever you're transferring.

FireWire Disk Mode/Thunderbolt Disk Mode (Target Disk Mode)

FireWire Disk Mode/Thunderbolt Disk Mode is a brilliant but little-known Macintosh-only feature that lets you turn one Mac into an external hard drive for another. This is by far the fastest method yet for transferring a lot of data—even faster than copying files over a network. It's extremely useful in any of these situations:

- **You're traveling with a laptop.** You want to copy your life onto it from your main Mac, including your entire 2 GB email folder and project files, before taking it on a trip, and then unload it when you return.

- **You have a new Mac.** You want to copy everything off the old one, without having to wait all night.

- **One Mac won't start up.** You want to repair it, using another Mac as a "front end."

Unfortunately, not all Macs have a FireWire or Thunderbolt jack. If you're among the lucky, though, you can use the following trick. (In the following steps, suppose your main Mac is an iMac and you want to use a MacBook as an external hard drive for it.)

1. **Connect the FireWire (Thunderbolt) jacks of both computers with a cable.**

   If you have an older Mac with a FireWire 400 jack, you need a *6-pin* FireWire cable—*not* the one that connects a camcorder to a Mac. The one you need has the same, large connector on both ends.

   Modern Macs have Apple's FireWire 800 jacks, which require a 9-pin FireWire cable (and give you much greater speed). If only one Mac has a FireWire 800 jack, then use that computer's traditional FireWire 400 connector instead. Otherwise, you need either a special FireWire 800–to–FireWire 400 cable, or the 400-to-800 adapter that came with your Mac.

2. **On the MacBook, choose ⬛→System Preferences. Click Startup Disk.**

   The Startup Disk panel opens.

3. **Click Target Disk Mode. In the confirmation box, click Restart.**

   The MacBook turns off, then on again. A giant gray FireWire icon (⛎) or Thunderbolt icon (⚡) bounces around the laptop screen.

   Now take a look at the iMac's screen: Sure enough, there's the MacBook's hard drive icon on the desktop. You're ready to copy files onto or off of it, at extremely high speeds, and go on with your life.

4. **When you're finished working with the MacBook, eject it from the iMac's screen as you would any disk. Then turn off the laptop by pressing the power button.**

The next time you turn on the MacBook, it'll start up from its own copy of Mac OS X, even if the cable is still attached. (You can disconnect the cable whenever you please.)

Note: The steps above describe the Lion method of setting up Target Disk Mode. But the old way still works, too. Leave the iMac turned on, but shut down the MacBook. (Make sure it's plugged in. You wouldn't want the battery to die in the middle of this process.) Now turn the MacBook on again, but hold down the T key immediately after the chime. After a moment, you see the big Y-shaped FireWire icon (ᛘ) on the laptop screen, and the laptop's hard drive shows up on the iMac's desktop. Continue from step 4 above.

This method is arguably quicker, because you don't have to open up System Preferences—and this method works when the Mac is too sick even to start up.

Via the iPod

An iPod is an extremely fine music player with enormous capacity. That's because it contains an actual hard drive (or a bunch of memory) that stores the songs.

But because the modern iPod has a USB connector, most models make dandy portable hard drives for everyday files, too—not just music.

To set the iPod up for data transfer, proceed like this:

1. **Connect the iPod to your Mac with its white USB cable. Open iTunes. Click the iPod icon in the left-side Source list.**

   The iPod Summary screen appears.

2. **Turn on "Enable disk use."**

   A dialog box warns you that even when you're just syncing up your music collection (and not using the iPod as a hard drive for files), you have to manually eject the iPod after each use.

3. **Click OK, and then OK again.**

   After a moment, you see the iPod's icon appear on your desktop.

Now you've got yourself a multigigabyte external hard drive. Just drag your files onto or off the iPod icon, exactly as though it's a disk (which it is). The iPod automatically keeps your data files separate from your music files; your other files won't be touched when you update your music collection from iTunes.

Whenever you're finished using the iPod as a hard drive, eject it in any of the usual ways. For example, in the Finder, drag its icon to the Trash, or Control-click it and choose Eject from the shortcut menu.

Via Flash Drive

A flash drive, also called a thumb drive, is one of those keychain-like doodads that plug into your USB jack. Inside is a big chunk of memory that acts like a miniature hard drive. When the flash drive is plugged into your Mac, its icon shows up on the desktop as a disk. Use it as a tiny, 8-gigabyte hard drive (or whatever size you've bought).

The beauty of a flash drive is that it works instantly and automatically with any Mac *or* any Windows machine, without any software installation or configuration. It's small and light enough to carry around on your keychain…and it's *so darned cool*. If you regularly transfer documents between Macs or between Macs and PCs, a flash drive will change your life.

Via Bluetooth

Bluetooth is a long-delayed, but promising, cable-elimination technology. It's designed to let Bluetooth-equipped gadgets communicate within about 30 feet, using radio signals.

Bluetooth comes built into most computers and cellphones, plus the occasional printer, pocket organizer, even camera or camcorder.

Bluetooth is built into all recent Macs. It's ready, therefore, to connect with Apple's wireless keyboard and mouse; to get on the Internet using a Bluetooth cellphone as a cordless modem; and to transfer files through the air to similarly equipped gear.

Bluetooth isn't especially fast—in fact, it's pretty slow. (You get transfer speeds of 30 to 150 K per second, depending on the distance.) But when you consider the time you'd have taken for wiring, passwords, and configuration using any other connection method, you may find that Bluetooth wins, at least in casual, spur-of-the-moment, airport-seat situations.

And when you consider that Bluetooth works no matter what the gadget—Mac, Windows, cellphone—you can see it has tremendous potential as a universal file-exchange translator, too.

Note: For more detail on configuring your Mac for Bluetooth connections, see page 505.

Sending a file

To shoot a file or two across the airwaves to a fellow Bluetooth-equipped Mac fan, first *pair* your Mac with the other Bluetooth machine, as described on page 505. In System Preferences→Bluetooth, make sure your Mac is Discoverable. *Discoverable* means, "Other Bluetooth gadgets can see me." (Check the receiving gadget, too, to make sure *it's* in Discoverable mode.) Then you're ready to send:

1. **From the Bluetooth ✳ menulet (Figure 5-9, top), choose Send File.**

   If you don't *have* the Bluetooth menulet on your menu bar, then open System Preferences. Click Bluetooth, and turn on "Show Bluetooth status in the menu bar."

   After a moment, the Select File to Send dialog box appears. (You've actually succeeded in opening a program called Bluetooth File Exchange, which sits in your Applications→Utilities folder.)

2. **Navigate to, and select, the files you want to send.**

   If you're trying to send a bunch of them, you may find it easier to drag their icons onto the Bluetooth File Exchange icon in your Applications→Utilities folder.

Either way, a new Send File dialog box appears, showing the list of Bluetooth machines within range (Figure 5-9, middle).

3. **In the list of found machines, click the name of the one you want to send your files to, and then click Send.**

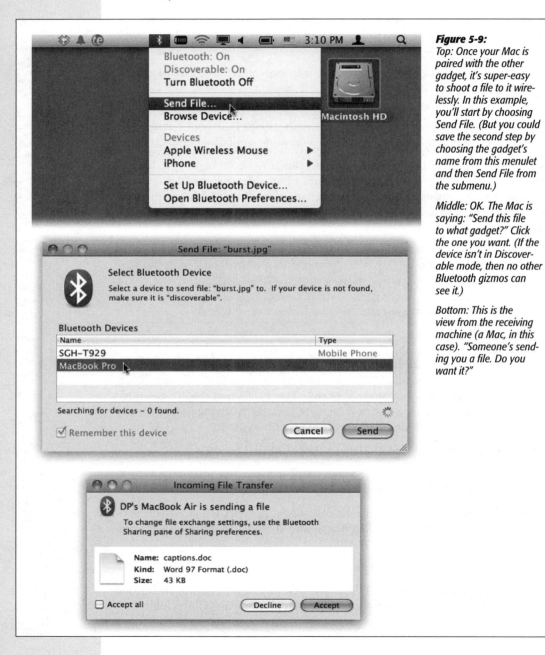

Figure 5-9:
Top: Once your Mac is paired with the other gadget, it's super-easy to shoot a file to it wirelessly. In this example, you'll start by choosing Send File. (But you could save the second step by choosing the gadget's name from this menulet and then Send File from the submenu.)

Middle: OK. The Mac is saying: "Send this file to what gadget?" Click the one you want. (If the device isn't in Discoverable mode, then no other Bluetooth gizmos can see it.)

Bottom: This is the view from the receiving machine (a Mac, in this case). "Someone's sending you a file. Do you want it?"

What happens now depends on how the receiving machine has been set up. In most cases, a dialog box tells the receiver that files are arriving (Figure 5-9, bottom); if he clicks Accept, the download proceeds. He's then offered the chance to either (a) open each transferred file or (b) reveal its highlighted icon in the Finder.

Tip: In System Preferences→Sharing→Bluetooth Sharing, you can control what happens when someone sends you files via Bluetooth. Usually, you'll want your Mac to ask whether or not to accept these files. (That's what the option Ask What to Do means.) You can also specify where you want received files to wind up—for example, in your Downloads folder.

Fetching a file

You can also perform this entire procedure in reverse. That is, you can go fishing through your buddy's files without her explicitly having to send anything.

To make a Mac invadable, the person to be invaded must open System Preferences→ Sharing and turn on Bluetooth Sharing. Here's also where she can specify what folder is available to you for examination (the Mac proposes her Home→Public folder), and what kind of security she wants to set up.

Then all you have to do is choose Browse Device from your own menulet (you can see it in Figure 5-9)—and let the rummaging begin!

Exchanging Data with Windows PCs

Documents can take one of several roads between your Mac and a Windows machine: via disk (such as a CD), flash drive, network, email, Bluetooth, iPod, Web page, FTP download, and so on.

But since transferring your life's work from your existing PC to your new Mac is such an important first hurdle, the PC-to-Mac transition gets a whole chapter unto itself—Chapter 6.

Time Machine

There are two kinds of people in the world: those who have a regular backup system—and those who *will.*

You'll get that grisly joke immediately if you've ever known the pain that comes with deleting the wrong folder by accident, or making changes that you regret, or worst of all, having your hard drive die. All those photos, all that music you've bought online, all your email—gone.

Yet the odds are overwhelming that at this moment, you do not have a complete, current, automated backup of your Mac. Despite about a thousand warnings, articles, and cautionary tales a year, guess how many do? About *four percent.* Everybody else is flying without a net.

If you don't have much to back up—you don't have much in the way of photos, music, or movies—you can get by with burning copies of stuff onto blank CDs or DVDs or using a free online backup system like Dropbox, CrashPlan, or IDrive. But those methods leave most of your Mac unprotected: all your programs and settings, not to mention Mac OS X itself.

What you really want, of course, is a backup that's rock-solid, complete, and *automatic*. You don't want to have to remember to do a backup, to insert a disc, and so on. You just want to know you're safe.

That's the idea behind Time Machine, a marquee feature of Mac OS X. It's a silent, set-it-and-forget-it piece of peace of mind. You sleep easy, knowing there's a safety copy of your *entire* system: your system files, programs, settings, music, pictures, videos, document files—*everything*. If your luck runs out, you'll be *so* happy you set up Time Machine.

Setting up Time Machine

Here's the bad news: Time Machine requires a second hard drive. That's the only way to create a completely safe, automatic backup of your *entire* main hard drive.

That second hard drive can take any of these forms:

- An external USB or FireWire hard drive.

- An Apple Time Capsule. That's an AirPort wireless base station/network backup hard drive in one; it's available in gigantic capacities.

- Another internal hard drive.

- A partition of any one of those drives.

- An iPod, if you've turned on "Enable disk use" (in iTunes) or if it's a flash-memory one like the Nano.

- The hard drive of another Mac on the network (Mac OS X 10.5 or later). You must first mount its drive on your screen (Chapter 14).

Tip: It's perfectly OK to back up several Macs onto the same external hard drive, as long as it's got enough room. You can also back up onto a hard drive that has other stuff on it, although of course that means you'll have less room for Time Machine backups.

In all cases, the backup disk must be bigger than the drive you're backing up (preferably *much* bigger).

Here's what you *can't* use as the backup disk: a CD or your startup drive.

Note: The backup drive must be a standard Mac-formatted hard drive—yet many new drives bought by Mac fans come preformatted as Windows disks. Fortunately, Time Machine automatically reformats them to the Mac OS Extended (Journaled) scheme, which it requires. Thoughtful, really.

Sure, it sounds like an Apple plot to sell more hard drives. But you'd be surprised at how cheap hard drives are. At this writing, you can buy a 1-*terabyte* hard drive (1,000 gigabytes) for $60, for goodness' sake—and hard drive prices-per-gigabyte go only down.

The first time the Mac sees your second hard drive, it invites you to use it as Time Machine's backup drive (Figure 5-10). That could be the moment you connect an external drive, or the first time you turn on the Mac after installing an internal drive.

Figure 5-10:
The Mac has just encountered a second hard drive. Time Machine still works if there's other stuff on the drive, but life is simpler if you don't use that drive for anything but Time Machine.

If you click Use as Backup Disk, you're taken immediately to the Time Machine pane of System Preferences (Figure 5-11). It shows that Time Machine is now on, your backup disk has been selected, and the copying process has begun. The Mac starts copying *everything* on your hard drive, including Mac OS X itself, all your programs, and everyone's Home folders. You know that because you see both a progress message and the ↻ symbol that appears next to the backup drive's name in your Sidebar.

Figure 5-11:
Use the big On/Off switch to shut off all Time Machine activity, although it would be hard to imagine why you'd want to risk it. You can click Select Disk to choose a different hard drive to represent the mirror of your main drive (after the first one is full, for example).

Your total involvement has been *one click*. And that, ladies and gentlemen, is the easiest setup for a backup program in history.

> **Note:** Unless you turn on encryption (in the System Preferences pane for Time Machine, click Select Disk, then "Encrypt backup disk"), Time Machine doesn't use any compression or encoding; it's copying your files exactly as they sit on your hard drive, for maximum safety and recoverability. On the other hand, it does save some space on the backup drive, because it doesn't bother copying cache files, temporary files, and other files you'll never need to restore.

Now go away and let the Mac do its thing. The first backup can take hours as the Mac duplicates your entire internal hard drive onto the second drive. The Mac may feel drugged during this time.

POWER USERS' CLINIC

Declaring Stuff Off-Limits to Time Machine

The whole point of Time Machine is to have a backup of your entire hard drive. That's how most people use it.

It's conceivable, though, that you might want to exclude some files or folders from the Time Machine treatment. There are two reasons.

First, you might not want certain, ahem, private materials to be part of your incriminating data trail.

Second, you might want to save space on the backup drive, either because it's not as big as your main drive or because you'd rather dedicate its space to more backups of the essential stuff. For example, you might decide not to back up your collection of downloaded TV shows, since video files are enormous. Or maybe you use an online photo-sharing Web site as a backup for all your photos, so you don't think it's necessary to include those in the Time Machine backup.

To eliminate certain icons from the backup, open the Time Machine pane of System Preferences. Click Options.

In the resulting list, click the **+** button; navigate to your hard drive, and then select the files or folders you don't want backed up. Or just find their actual icons in the Finder and drag them into the list here. (Use the **—** button to remove items from the list, thereby excluding them from the excluded list.)

If you're strapped for disk space, one logical candidate to exclude is the System folder on your main hard drive—that is, Mac OS X itself. After all, if you lose your hard drive, you already have a copy of Mac OS X: the original App Store installer.

When you add the System folder to the exclusion list, Time Machine makes another space-saving offer: "Would you like to also exclude other files installed with Mac OS X, such as system applications and UNIX tools?"

Agreeing (by clicking Exclude All System Files) saves you another several gigabytes of backup space.

How the Backups Work

From now on, Time Machine quietly and automatically checks your Mac once per hour. If any file, folder, or setting has changed, it gets backed up at the end of the hour. These follow-up backups, of course, take very little time, since Time Machine backs up only what's changed.

So, should disaster strike, the only files you can lose are those you've changed within the past 59 minutes.

Tip: And even then, you can force more frequent backups if you want to. Just choose Back Up Now from the Time Machine menulet. Or choose Back Up Now from the shortcut menu of the Dock's Time Machine icon.

You can pause the backup the same way—if you need to use the backup drive for another quick task, for example. Open System Preferences→Time Machine and turn the big switch Off. Don't forget to turn the backing-up on again when you're finished.

By the end of the day, you'll have 24 hourly backups on that second disk, all taking up space. So at day's end, Time Machine replaces that huge stash with a single *daily* backup. You can no longer rewind your system to 3:00 p.m. last Monday, but you can rewind to the way it was at the *end* of that day.

Similarly, after a month, Time Machine replaces all those 30 dailies (for example) with four weekly backups. Now you may not be able to rewind to October 14, but you can rewind to November 1. (Apple assumes it won't take you a whole week to notice that your hard drive has crashed.)

Tip: You can see these backups, if you want. Open your backup drive, open the *Backups.backupdb* folder, and then open the folder named for your computer. Inside, you'll find a huge list of backup folders, bearing names like 2012-03-22-155831. That's the backup from March 22, 2012, at 15:58 (that is, 3:58 p.m.) and 31 seconds.

FREQUENTLY ASKED QUESTION

The End of Time

What happens when my backup drive gets full?

Good question. The whole idea of Time Machine is that it preserves multiple backups, so that you can rewind a window or a drive not just to *a* backup, but to *any* date in the past. The bigger the hard drive, the farther back those monthly backups are preserved.

Eventually, of course, your backup drive runs out of space. At that point, Time Machine notifies you and offers you a choice: "Your backup disk is now full. The oldest remaining backup disk is..." (and then the date.)

You can keep using that drive; Time Machine will begin deleting the oldest backups to make room for newer ones.

Or you can install a new Time Machine backup drive. New backups will go on that one; your older backups will still be available on the original drive.

If you ever need to retrieve files or folders from the older disk, Control-click (right-click) the Time Machine icon in the Dock; from the shortcut menu, choose Browse Other Time Machine Disks. In the list of disks, choose the older one. Then click the Time Machine icon on the Dock to enter the Restore mode.

The point is that Time Machine doesn't just keep *one* copy of your stuff. It keeps *multiple* backups. It remembers how things were in every folder—not just yesterday, but last week, last month, and so on. It keeps on making new snapshots of your hard drive until the backup drive is full.

At that point, the oldest ones get deleted to make room for new ones.

Tip: Ordinarily, Time Machine alerts you when it has to start deleting old backups. If you'd rather have it just do it without bothering you, open System Preferences, click Time Machine, click Options, and then turn off "Notify after old backups are deleted."

By the way, if a backup is interrupted—if you shut down the Mac, put it to sleep, or take your laptop on the road—no big deal. Time Machine resumes automatically the next time you're home and connected.

Local Snapshots

If you're among the 75 percent of Mac fans with a laptop, Time Machine used to be something of a bust in one regard: Whenever you were away from your backup disk (at home or the office, for example), you lost the benefits of Time Machine.

In Lion, crazy as this may sound, Time Machine keeps on working even on a laptop that's far from home. Thanks to a new feature called local snapshots, Time Machine works as usual by making its backups right on the laptop's own hard drive.

Of course, this system won't help you if your hard drive dies; your backup is on the same drive, so you'll lose the originals and the backups simultaneously. But what local snapshots do provide is a safety net—a way to recover a file that you deleted or changed during this time away. Better yet, once you're home again, when your laptop rejoins the network, the local snapshots are intelligently merged with the master Time Machine backups, as though you'd never been away.

If Time Machine is turned on on your laptop, it makes local snapshots automatically—once an hour, as usual. As time goes on, Time Machine condenses those backups to daily or weekly snapshots to save disk space.

Note: If your laptop gets really low on disk space, Time Machine stops making new snapshots, and may even delete old ones so that you can keep using your Mac. When you make more space, snapshots resume automatically.

If you need to recover a file, enter Time Machine as usual. Your local snapshots show up on the same timeline as backups made on your regular, external backup disk, but they're color-coded: pink tick marks for external backups, gray for local ones. If the pink bars are dimmed, it's because you're not hooked up to your external Time Machine backup drive.

Tip: To see how much disk space your local snapshots are eating up, choose →About This Mac. Click More Info. Click the Storage tab. The color-coded graph clearly indicates the space being used for Backups.

Changing Time Machine Settings

Time Machine has four faces. There's the application itself, which sits in your Applications folder; open it only when you want to enter Restore mode. There's its Dock icon, which also enters Restore mode, but which has a shortcut menu containing useful commands like Back Up Now (and Stop Backing Up).

There's the Time Machine menulet, which may be the handiest of all. It identifies the time and date of the most recent backup; offers Back Up Now/Stop Backing Up commands; and has direct access to Time Machine's restore mode and preferences pane.

Tip: If you Option-click the Time Machine menulet, you get two secret new commands: Verify Backups (just in case you're a little nervous about your backups' integrity) and Browse Other Backup Disks. Yes, it's perfectly possible to back up onto multiple hard drives—to keep one offsite so you won't be hosed in case of fire, flood, or burglary, for example—and this is how. (Control-clicking the Time Machine icon on the Dock is another way to get this command.)

Finally, then there's its System Preferences pane, where you adjust its settings (Figure 5-11). To see it, choose →System Preferences→Time Machine. Or choose Time Machine Preferences from Time Machine's Dock icon or menulet.

Recovering Lost or Changed Files

All right, you've got Time Machine on the job. You sleep easy at night, confident that your life is in order—and your stuff is backed up.

Then, one day, it happens: Your hard drive crashes. Or you can't find a file or folder you know you had. Or you save a document in some non–Auto Save program and then wish you could go back to an earlier draft. Some kind of disaster—sunspots, clueless spouse, overtired self—has befallen your files. This is Time Machine's big moment.

Start by pinpointing what you're looking for, in one of these two ways:

- Open the disk or folder window where the missing or changed item was.

- Type what you're looking for into the search box at the top of any Finder window. Click the location button that makes the most sense: "This Mac" or the name of the window you're in.

   In the case of deleted files or folders, the search will probably come up empty; that's totally OK.

Now click the Time Machine icon on the Dock, or choose Enter Time Machine from the menulet (Figure 5-12, top). Don't look away; you'll miss the show.

Your desktop *slides down the screen* like a curtain that's been dropped from above. And it reveals…outer space. This is it, the ultimate Apple eye candy: an animated starry universe, with bits of stardust and meteors occasionally flying outward from the massive nebula at the center.

Front and center is your Finder window—or, rather, dozens of them, stretching back in time (Figure 5-12). Each is a snapshot of that window at the time of a Time Machine backup.

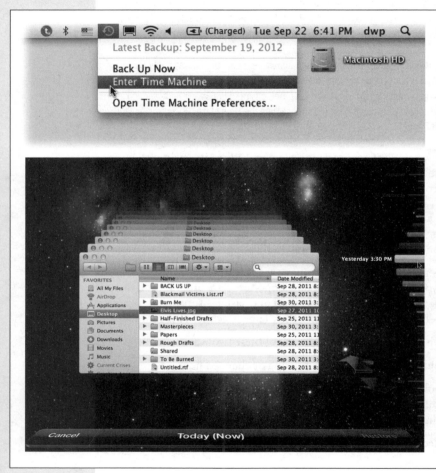

Figure 5-12:
Top: Choose Enter Time Machine from the menulet. (If you don't see this menulet, then turn on "Show Time Machine status in the menu bar," shown in Figure 5-11.)

Bottom: This is the big payoff for all your efforts. The familiar desktop slides down, dropping away like a curtain. For the first time, you get to see what's been behind the desktop all this time. Turns out it's outer space. Time Machine shows you dozens of copies of the Finder window, representing its condition at each backup, stretching back to the past. If the "ruler tick marks" are both pink and gray, you're seeing backups on both your laptop's own hard drive and the usual external drive, as described earlier in this chapter.

You have four ways to peruse your backup universe:

- **Click individual windows to see what's in them.**

- **Drag your cursor through the timeline at the right side.** It's like a master dial that flies through the windows into the past.

- **Click one of the two big, flat perspective arrows.** The one pointing into the past means, "Jump directly to the most recent window version that's *different* from the way it is right now."

In other words, it's often a waste of time to go flipping through the windows one at a time, because your missing or changed file might have been missing or changed for the last 25 backups (or whatever). What you want to know is the last time the contents of this window *changed*. And that's what the big flat arrows do. They jump from one *changed* version of this window to another. (Or, if you began with a search, the arrow takes you to the most recent version backup with a matching result.)

• **Use the search box in the corner of the window.** You can search for whatever you're missing in the current backup.

As you go, the very bottom of the screen identifies where you are in time—that is, which backup you're examining.

Tip: OK, it's all very dazzling and all. But if you're technically inclined, you don't have to sit still for the big show. Just open the backup disk itself, whose icon appears on your desktop. Inside, you'll find nested folders, neatly representing every computer, every backup, every day, and every hour—which you can rummage through by hand.

In many ways, the recovery mode is just like the Finder. You can't actually open, edit, rename, or reorganize anything here. But you can use Quick Look to inspect the documents, to make sure you've got the right version. And you can use icon, list, column, or Cover Flow views to sort through the files you're seeing.

If you're trying to recover an older *version* of a file or folder, highlight it and then click the flat arrow button that's pointing away from you; Time Machine skips back to the most recent version that's *different* from the current one.

If you're trying to restore a deleted file or folder that you've now located, highlight it and then click Restore (lower right). The Mac OS X desktop rises again from the bottom of the screen, there's a moment of copying, and then presto: The lost file or folder is back in the window where it belonged.

Note: Time Machine prides itself on not just on recovering files and folders, but also on putting them back where they belong.

If you recover a different version of something that's still there, Mac OS X asks if you want to replace it with the recovered version—or to keep both versions.

And if you're recovering a document whose original folder no longer exists, Time Machine automatically recreates the folder so that the recovered item feels at home.

Recovering from Address Book and Mail

The Finder isn't the only program that's hooked into Time Machine's magic. Address Book and Mail work with Time Machine, too. Other software companies can also revise their own applications to work with it. In other words, if you want to recover certain addresses or email messages that have been deleted, you don't start in the Finder; you start in Address Book or Mail.

Then click the Time Machine icon on the Dock. Once again, you enter the starry recovery mode—but this time, you're facing a strange, disembodied, stripped-down copy of Address Book or Mail.

You're ready to find your missing data. Click the Jump Back arrow to open the most recent version of your address book file or email stash that's different from what you've got now. (You can also use the timeline on the right if you remember the date when things went wrong.)

Tip: If you're looking for something particular, specify that before you start clicking. For example, type a name into the Address Book search box first.

At this point, you can select individual Address Book entries or email messages to restore; just click the Restore button.

Often, though, you'd rather reinstate the *entire* Address Book file or email collection from the backup. That's what the Restore All button is for.

If you click it, the experience is slightly different. Address Book may discover a lot of duplicate name-and-address entries and invite you to step through them, deciding which ones "win" (the old or the new).

Note: When you finish restoring in Mail, you'll find the restored messages in the On My Mac→Time Machine→Recovered folder at the left side of the window.

Recovering the entire hard drive

Every hard drive will die at some point. You just hope it won't happen while *you* own the computer.

But if it does, you, as a Time Machine aficionado, won't care. You'll just repair or replace the hard drive, and then proceed as follows.

1. **Connect the Time Machine backup disk to the Mac. Start the recovery mode.**

   There are actually three different ways to recover a dead Mac or a dead hard drive, none of which require an actual DVD, as in the days of yore. If the hard drive is fine, but it just can't start up your Mac, hold down ⌘-R during startup. If the hard drive is empty, you can restart from the Internet itself (if it's a Mac released since Lion came out). And if all else fails, you can always use the Recovery Disk Assistant that you wisely made long in advance of your horror-story dead-disk day.

   Appendix B covers all three of these recovery modes in more detail.

   The point is, however, that all three of them present "Restore from a Time Machine backup" as one of the options.

2. **Choose "Restore from a Time Machine backup." Click Continue.**

   Now you're shown a list of Time Machine backup disks. You probably have only one.

3. **Click your Time Machine backup disk. In the list of backups, click the most recent one.**

   The installer goes about copying *everything* from the backup disk onto your new, empty hard drive. When it's all over, you'll have a perfect working system, just the way it was before your series of unfortunate events.

Beware, however: Restoring your earlier version also *erases any files* you've created or changed since you installed the update. Back them up manually before you proceed!

Then follow the steps above; when you're asked to choose a backup to restore, choose the most recent one. When it's all over, copy the latest files (the ones that you manually backed up) back onto the hard drive.

Recovering to another Mac

Weirdly enough, you can also use Time Machine as a glorified data bucket that carries your world from one computer to another. You can bring over some or part of any Time Machine backup to a totally different Mac.

On the new machine, connect your backup disk. In the Applications→Utilities folder, open the program called Migration Assistant. On the first screen, click "From another Mac, PC, Time Machine backup, or other disk." The subsequent screens invite you to choose which backup, which Home folder, and which elements (applications, settings, files) you want to bring over.

Frequently Asked Questions

Time Machine is a very different kind of backup program, and a real departure for some. A few questions, therefore, are bound to come up—like these:

- **Can I back up more than one Mac onto the same disk?** Yes. Each Mac's backup is stored in a separate folder on that disk.

- **Does the backup disk have to be dedicated to Time Machine?** No. It can have other files and folders on it. Keep in mind, though, that the more space that's available, the farther back your backup trail can go.

- **Can I use more than one backup disk—like one at the office and one at home?** Yes. Just use the Time Machine panel of System Preferences (or the Time Machine Dock icon's shortcut menu) to select the new backup drive each time you switch.

- **Can I delete something for good, from all the backups at once?** Yes. Click the Time Machine icon on the Dock to enter the Restore (outer-space) mode. Find and select the file or folder you want to obliterate. From the ✿ menu, choose Delete All Backups of [the Thing's Name]. (Sneaky, huh? That command is never in the ✿ menu *except* when you're in Time Machine restoring mode.)

- **Can Time Machine back up other hard drives besides the main internal one?** Yes. Open System Preferences→Time Machine. Click Options. Your secondary drives are listed here on the excluded-items list. If you want them backed up too, *remove* them from the list (click the drive name and then click the **−** button.)

Part Two:
Making the Move

2

Transferring Your Files to the Mac

A huge percentage of "switchers" do not, in fact, *switch*. Often, they just *add*. They may get a Macintosh (and get *into* the Macintosh), but they keep the old Windows PC around, at least for a while. If you're in that category, get psyched. It turns out that communicating with a Windows PC is one of the Mac's most polished talents.

That's especially good news in the early days of your Mac experience. You probably have a good deal of stuff on the Windows machine that you'd like to bring over to the Mac. Somewhere along the line, somebody probably told you how easy this is to do. In fact, the Mac's reputation for simplicity may even have played a part in your decision to switch.

In any case, this chapter describes the process of building a bridge from the PC to the Mac, so that you can bring all your files and settings into their new home. It also tells you where to *put* them all.

As it turns out, files can take one of several roads from your old PC to your new Mac. For example, you can transfer them on a disk (such as a CD or iPod), by a network, or as an attachment to an email message.

Tip: The first part of this chapter covers the mechanical aspects of moving files and folders from your Windows PC to the Mac. On page 222, you'll find a more pointed discussion of where to put each kind of data (mail, photos, music, and so on) once it's on the Mac.

Transfers by Apple Genius

By far the easiest way to transfer all the stuff from your PC to your new Mac is to let Apple do it for you. Yes, that's right: Those busy Geniuses who work at the 360 Apple Stores around the world are prepared to bring your music, pictures, documents, address book, email, bookmarks, and other stuff to its new home on your Mac.

This service is included in the $100 One on One program, which is worth a look. (You're supposed to buy One on One at the time you buy the Mac.)

One on One gives you a year's worth of weekly *one-hour private lessons* at an Apple Store from an Apple rep. They'll teach you the Mac, help you organize your photos, teach you the software, whatever you need. That's gotta be the best private-lessons price ever offered for anything.

Once you're signed up, the Apple Genius will take your old PC and your new Mac and do the transferring for you. For example, all your Windows pictures (even if they're in Picasa or special photo-editing programs from HP or Kodak) get brought over to the Mac and imported into iPhoto. All your music is imported into iTunes on the Mac. Your documents and movies get copied to the Documents and Movies folders on the Mac. Your Web bookmarks from Internet Explorer or Firefox get transferred to Safari on the Mac. Even your email, address book, and calendar get transferred from Outlook or Outlook Express on the PC and brought into Mail and iCal on the Mac.

The rest of this chapter covers do-it-yourself ways to transfer your stuff. But man, there's nothing like having a professional do it for you.

The Windows Migration Assistant

If you don't really need the year's worth of private Mac lessons, then here's another low-effort option: Let the Lion Migration Assistant do the transferring for you.

Now, the 1.0 version has a reputation for bugginess. But if it works on your system, it's a nearly effortless automatic tool that copies all your important data from a Windows PC (running Windows XP SP3 or later) to your Mac. (And if it doesn't work, page 220 offers manual techniques that can do the same job.)

You'll find the Migration Assistant program in your Applications→Utilities folder. Before you open it, make sure your Mac and your PC are connected to the same network (WiFi or wired), as described in Chapter 14.

Now open Migration Assistant. Choose the first option: "From another Mac, PC, Time Machine backup, or other disk." Click Continue. (Enter your password if you're asked for it.)

When all is said and done, here's what it accomplishes:

- **Transfers your email** into Mail from Outlook, Outlook Express, Windows Mail, or Windows Live accounts (POP or IMAP). Your messages even show up correctly flagged as having been read, replied to, and flagged (except if they originated in Windows Live).

- **Transfers your address book** into Address Book from Outlook and Outlook Express contacts, and from Windows contacts in the Contacts folder on your PC.

- **Transfers your calendar** into iCal from Outlook's calendar.

- **Transfers your iTunes** collection from iTunes on Windows into iTunes for the Mac. Everything comes over, including music, photos, videos (but not rentals), and apps and games for iPhone/iPad/iPod Touch.

- **Transfers everything in your Windows Home folder** into the corresponding Mac Home folder folders: Music, Pictures, Desktop, Documents, and Downloads.

- **Transfers your browser bookmarks and preferred home page** into Safari from Explorer, Firefox, and Safari for Windows.

- **Transfers your account settings** like language and even your desktop wallpaper.

All of this winds up in a new user account on your Mac. The migration program doesn't make any attempt to merge your Windows world into your *existing* account on the Mac.

Now, the Migration Assistant app (in your Utilities folder) represents only the *Mac* end of this transaction. You also need the Windows end.

For that, download the free Windows Migration Assistant program. It's waiting at *www.apple.com/migrate-to-mac*. Install it on your PC, which is a matter of clicking through three screens. In your Control Panel, turn off Window Updates.

Now you're ready to begin.

1. **Make sure the PC and the Mac are on the same network.**

   It can be a WiFi network, but you'll get a much faster transfer, with much less risk of interference, if you connect them to a wired network. For example, connect each with an Ethernet cable to your router.

2. **On the PC, open the Windows Migration Assistant program that you downloaded. Click Continue.**

   The PC is now ready for action.

3. **On the Mac, quit all programs. In your Applications→Utilities folder, open the Migration Assistant program.**

   You're offered two choices: "From another Mac, PC, Time Machine backup, or other disk," and "To another Mac" (see Figure 6-1).

4. **On the Mac, click "From another Mac, PC, Time Machine backup, or other disk." Click Continue. Provide your name and password, and click Continue again. Click "From another Mac or PC," and click Continue.**

At this point, your Mac should "see" the PC on the network. You'll know, because you'll see the PC's name and icon in the dialog box shown in Figure 6-1, middle.

5. **Click Continue.**

On the Mac, you see something like Figure 6-1, bottom: a big passcode. On the PC, you're supposed to see a matching passcode.

If you don't see the passcode on the PC, then something—your firewall, your antivirus program, Migration Assistant flakiness—is getting in the way. You may have to opt for the manual procedures described below.

Figure 6-1:
Here's the Mac's view of the Windows Migration Assistant procedure.

Top: Tell it you're transferring data from a PC.

Middle: The Mac sees the PC on the network and displays its name and icon.

Bottom: Here's the passcode that, if you're lucky, also shows up on the PC's screen. (You don't have to type it in anywhere, so it's really not a passcode.)

6. **If you see the passcode on the PC's screen, then click Continue.**

After a few minutes of whirring and thinking, the Mac displays a list of files that it can transfer from the PC (Figure 6-2).

Figure 6-2:
The Mac shows the stuff on your PC.

These include check-boxes for the other user accounts, but you can't transfer them right now—it's a one-account-at-a-time thing. To transfer someone else's stuff, you'll have to log into your PC as that person and repeat this whole procedure. The copying process can take a very long time—hours. The "time remaining" indicator may not be especially accurate.

7. **On the Mac, turn on the checkboxes of the items you want copied. Click Continue to begin the transfer.**

If all goes well, after a few hours, the Mac says, "Your information has been transferred successfully."

8. **On the Mac, click Quit.**

If you choose →Log Out, you'll see that there's a new account on your Mac, named after the account you transferred from the PC. If you try to sign into it, you're asked to provide a password for this new Mac account. (If you didn't *want* your Windows stuff to wind up in a new Mac account, you can always copy it back into your main account using the Users→Shared folder as a tunnel between accounts.)

Tip: The Migration Assistant puts all your mail into Apple's Mail program, the one described in Chapter 11. If you'd prefer to use Microsoft Outlook for the Mac as your email program, here are the steps for transferring the mail stash from Mail to Outlook: http://j.mp/xtsGwi.

Manual Network Transfers

As you may have guessed from the paragraphs above, Mac and PCs can "see" each other on a network (wired or wireless). Seated at the Mac, you can open or copy files from any folders you've shared on a PC. In fact, you can go in the other direction, too: Your old PC can see shared folders on your Mac.

Chapter 14 offers a crash course in setting up a network. When it's all over, you'll be seated at the Mac, looking at the contents of your Windows PC in a separate window. At that point, you can drag whatever files and folders you want directly to the proper places on the Mac, as described on page 222.

Transfers by Disk

Another way to transfer Windows files to the Mac is to put them onto a disk that you then pop into the Mac. (Although Windows can't read all Mac disks without special software, the Mac can read Windows disks.)

This disk can take any of these forms:

- **An external hard drive or iPod.** If you have an external hard drive (USB or IEEE 1394, what Apple calls *FireWire*), you're in great shape. While it's connected to the PC, drag files and folders onto it. Then unhook the drive from the PC, attach it to the Mac, and marvel as its icon pops up on your desktop, its contents ready for dragging to your Mac's built-in hard drive. (The Mac can read Windows disks and flash drives, which use unappetizingly named formatting schemes like FAT32 and NTFS, but Windows can't read Mac hard drives or flash drives.)

  Most iPods work great for this process, too; they can operate as external hard drives—even the iPod Nano. For details, see page 198.

- **A Time Capsule.** An Apple Time Capsule is a sleek white box that contains a huge hard drive plus a wireless base station. The idea, of course, is to create a WiFi network for your house or office and include a built-in disk for backing up all your computers, automatically and wirelessly.

  That also means the Time Capsule makes a great transfer station between a PC and a Mac, since its icon shows up on the desktops of both.

- **A USB flash drive.** These small keychainy sticks are cheap and capacious, and they work beautifully on both Macs and PCs. Like a mini-external hard drive, a flash drive plugs directly into your USB port, at which point it shows up on your desktop just like a normal disk. You copy files to it from your PC, plug it into your Mac, and copy the files off, just like you would for any other disk. And you're left with a backup copy of the data on the drive itself.

- **A CD or DVD.** If your Windows PC has a CD or DVD burner, here's another convenient method. Burn a disc in Windows, eject it, and then pop it into the Mac (see Figure 6-3). As a bonus, you wind up with a backup of your data on the disc itself. CDs and DVDs use the same format on both kinds of computers, so you should have very little problem moving these between machines.

Note: If you're given a choice of file format when you burn the disc in Windows, choose ISO9660. That's the standard format that the Macintosh can read.

- **Move the hard drive itself.** This is a grisly, technical maneuver best undertaken by serious wireheads—but it can work. You can install your PC's hard drive directly into a Power Mac or Mac Pro, as long as it was prepared using the older FAT or FAT32 formatting scheme. (The Mac can handle FAT hard drives just fine, but it chokes with NTFS hard drives.)

When you insert a Windows-formatted disk, whatever the type, its icon appears in the Mac's Computer window (or on the desktop, if you've turned on the relevant checkbox in the Finder→Preferences→General tab.)

Figure 6-3:
Burned CDs generally show up with equal aplomb on both Mac and Windows, regardless of which machine you used to burn it. Here's a CD burned on a Windows XP machine (bottom), and what it looks like on the Mac (top)—same stuff, just a different look and a different sorting order. Either way, you can drag files to and from it, rename files, delete files, and so on.

Transfers by File-Sending Web Site

Free Web sites like *yousendit.com* and *sendthisfile.com* are specifically designed for sending huge files from one computer to another, without worrying about email file attachments or size limits.

On the Windows PC, zip up your files into a great big .zip file. Upload it to one of these free sites, and provide your Mac's email address.

On the Mac, click the link that arrives by email—and presto, that huge zip file gets downloaded onto your Mac. It's free, there's no file-size limit, and you can download the big file(s) at any time within three days of sending them. The only price you pay is a little bit of waiting while the stuff gets uploaded and then downloaded.

Tip: If you have your own Web site—a *.com* of your own, for example, or a free site through a university—you can also use *that* Web space as a transfer tool. Follow the uploading instructions you were given when you signed up for the space. (Hint: It usually involves a so-called *FTP* program.) Then, once all your files are on the site, download them onto your Mac.

Transfers by Email

Although sending files as email attachments might seem to be a logical plan, it's very slow. Furthermore, remember that many email providers limit your attachment size to 5 or 10 megabytes. Trying to send more than that at once will clog your system. If you've got a lot of stuff to bring over from your PC, use one of the disk- or network-based transfer systems described earlier in this chapter.

But for smaller transfer jobs or individual files, sending files as plain old email attachments works just fine.

Where to Put Your Copied Files

Getting your PC files onto the Mac is only half the battle. Now you have to figure out where they *go* on the Mac.

Here's the short answer: Everything goes into your Mac's Home folder. (Choose Go→Home, or click the ⌂ icon in your Sidebar.)

Some of the more specific "where to put it" answers are pretty obvious:

- **My Documents.** Put the files and folders from the PC's My Documents folder into your Home→Documents folder. Here's where you should keep all your Microsoft Office files, PDF files, and other day-to-day masterpieces.

- **My Music.** Your Windows My Music folder was designed to hold all your MP3 files, AIFF files, WAV files, and other music. As you could probably guess, you should copy these files into your Mac's Home→Music folder.

  After that, you can import the music directly into iTunes. If you used iTunes on your old PC, for example, see the steps on page 225 for specific transfer instructions.

  If you used some *other* music program on your PC (like Windows Media Player or MusicMatch), things are a little different. On your Mac, choose iTunes→Import, and navigate to the folder that contains all your music. (In either case, click Choose in the resulting dialog box.)

- **My Pictures.** Windows also offers a My Pictures folder, which is where your digital camera photos probably wound up. Mac OS X has a similar folder: the Home→Pictures folder.

  Here again, after copying your photos and other graphics faves over to the Mac, you're only halfway home. If you fire up iPhoto (in your Applications folder), choose File→Import, and choose the Pictures folder, you'll *then* be able to find, organize, and present your photos in spectacular ways.

- **My Videos.** The My Videos folder of Windows XP and later versions contains the video clips you've downloaded from your camcorder (presumably so that you can edit them with, for example, Microsoft's Movie Maker software). Once you've moved them to your Home→Movies folder, though, you're in for a real treat: You can now edit your footage (if it's *digital* footage) with iMovie, which, to put it kindly, runs rings around Movie Maker.

Other elements of your Windows world, though, are trickier to bring over. For example:

Desktop Pictures (Wallpaper)

Especially in recent versions of Windows, the desktop pictures, better known in the Windows world as *wallpaper,* are pretty cool. Fortunately, you're welcome to bring them over to your Mac and use them on your new desktop.

To find the graphics files that make up the wallpaper choices in Windows (version Me or later), proceed like this:

1. **Open My Computer, double-click your hard drive's icon, and open the Windows or WINNT folder.**

   If you see a huge "These files are hidden" message at this point, or if the window appears empty, click "Show the contents of this folder" or "View the entire contents of this folder" at the left side of the window.

2. **In the Windows or WINNT window, open the Web folder.**

   You're looking for a folder inside it called Wallpaper.

3. **Open the Wallpaper folder.**

   It's filled with .bmp or .jpg files ready for you to recycle for use on the Mac. See page 510 for instructions on choosing wallpaper for your Mac.

Note: In Windows 95 or 98, the wallpaper files are in your Program Files→Plus!→Themes folder instead.

Sound Effects

The Mac doesn't let you associate your own sound effects to individual system events (Low Battery Alarm, Maximize, Minimize, and so on) as Windows does. It lets you choose *one* sound effect for all attention-getting purposes (page 527).

Still, there's nothing to stop you from harvesting all the fun little sounds from your Windows machine for use as the Mac's error beep.

To find them on the PC, repeat step 1 of the preceding instructions. But in the Windows or WINNT folder, open the Media folder to find the WAV files (standard Windows sound files).

Once you've copied them to your Mac, you can double-click one to listen to it. (It opens up in something called QuickTime Player, which is the rough equivalent of Windows Media Player. Press the space bar to listen to the sound.)

To use these sounds as error beeps, you'll have to convert them from the PC's WAV format into the Mac's preferred AIFF format. You'll find step-by-step instructions in the free downloadable appendix for this chapter, "Converting WAV Sounds to Mac Error Beeps." You can find it on this book's "Missing CD" page at *www.missingmanuals.com*.

Bookmarks (Favorites)

Moving your Favorites (browser bookmarks) to a Mac is easy. The hardest part is exporting them as a file, and that depends on which browser you've been using on the PC.

WORKAROUND WORKSHOP

Transferring Your Mail and Address Book

If you're lucky, you can use Lion's Windows Migration Assistant to bring your PC's files over to the Mac—including your email stash and your contacts. Those are very difficult to transfer manually—the files themselves require conversion—so if the Migration Assistant doesn't work, you might wonder where to turn next.

Four solutions await you. None is free, fast, and easy—but each is either free, fast, *or* easy.

The Thunderbird method. Thunderbird is the free, open-source email companion to the Firefox Web browser. Among other virtues, it can easily open Outlook or Outlook Express email collections on the PC—and convert them into formats that Mac email programs can use. You can find step-by-step instructions in this chapter's free online PDF Appendix, "Transferring email with Thunderbird." It's on this book's "Missing CD" at *www.missingmanuals.com.*

The O2Mac solution. For several years, the easiest and most flexible method of transferring your email and contacts was a shareware program called O2M (short for Outlook2Mac). Unfortunately, the company who wrote it has disappeared without a trace. You might still be able to find a copy of O2Mac floating around online, though.

The 8Convert solution. For $14, you can buy 8Convert, a shareware program especially for extracting your data from Outlook (not Outlook Express). It handles your email (complete with attachments and date ranges that you choose), address book, and calendar; the online instructions (*www. eighthoof.com*) show you how to bring these three items into Mail, Address Book, and iCal on the Mac. (Similar shareware: MessageSave, *www.techhit.com*.)

The Gmail trick. You can use an online (IMAP) email account as an intermediary between Outlook and the Mac.

Sign up for a free Gmail account. Then, in Windows, open Outlook and add your Gmail account. Now copy the mail folders from your Outlook list into the Gmail account. (Don't drag-and-drop; that moves the messages instead of copying.) This process can take a very long time.

Then, in Mail on the Mac, add the same Gmail account, and after a while, presto: All your mail now shows up on the Mac.

- **Internet Explorer.** Fire up Internet Explorer; choose File→Import and Export. (In Internet Explorer 7, click the double-star icon in the upper-left corner of the window. From the pop-up menu, choose Import and Export.)

  When the Import/Export Wizard appears, click Next; on the second screen, click Export Favorites, and then click Next again. On the third screen, leave the Favorites folder selected, and click Next. Click Browse to choose a location for the exported bookmarks file. For now, save it to your desktop. Click Next, Finish, and then OK.

- **Firefox.** In Firefox, choose Bookmarks→Organize Bookmarks. In the Bookmarks Manager window, choose File→Export. Save the Bookmarks file to your desktop.

Now you've got an exported Bookmarks file on your desktop. Transfer it to your Mac using any of the techniques described earlier in this chapter (network, email, whatever).

Now open the Mac's Web browser, Safari (it's in your Applications folder). Choose File→Import Bookmarks. Navigate to, and double-click, the exported Favorites file to pull in the bookmarks.

Tip: Firefox is available for the Mac, too (*www.getfirefox.com*). If your Firefox bookmarks are already in Safari, you can import them to Firefox by choosing File→Import. If not, you can import them from your exported Windows bookmarks file by choosing Bookmarks→Manage Bookmarks; then, in the Bookmarks Manager window, choose File→Import. Find and select the exported bookmarks file.

---

iTunes Music

If you've kept your Windows music collection in iTunes, you can transfer it to the Mac with everything intact: play counts, ratings, playlists, and so on.

Before you begin, though, you have to do some Windows housekeeping. On the Mac, open iTunes and choose Edit→Preferences→Advanced. Turn on "Keep iTunes media folder organized" and "Copy files to iTunes media folder when adding to library." Then choose File→Library→Organize Library, turn on Consolidate Files, and click OK. If the option called "Upgrade to iTunes Media organization" is available, turn that on, too. (All these steps put all of your music and video files in the main iTunes Media folder, which you'll copy to the Mac.)

You may have to wait for iTunes to complete these steps. Once they're finished, copy the iTunes folder from your PC to the Mac. Here's where to find it on the PC:

- **Windows XP.** Documents and Settings→[your user name]→My Documents→My Music→iTunes

- **Windows Vista, Windows 7.** [your user name]→Music→iTunes

Copy that entire iTunes folder to your Mac using one of the method described in this chapter. It goes into your Home→Music folder.

If there is already an iTunes folder, it's OK to replace it. (Unless, of course, you've imported music into the Mac version of iTunes; in that case, you'll have to copy the Music files from it into the incoming PC's iTunes folder.)

Now, when you open iTunes on the Mac, you'll see your iTunes collection, safely transferred. All of it: music, videos, ratings, playlists, and all.

Tip: If you plan to abandon or sell your PC, don't forget to "deauthorize" its iTunes account so that it's not counting as one of the five machines that are allowed to play your copy-protected iTunes songs. Do that by opening iTunes. From the Store menu, choose Deauthorize This Computer.

Document Conversion Issues

Most big-name programs are sold in both Mac and Windows flavors, and the documents they create are freely interchangeable.

Files in standard exchange formats don't need conversion, either. These formats include JPEG (the photo format used on Web pages), GIF (the cartoon/logo format used on Web pages), PNG (a newer image format used on Web pages), HTML (raw Web-page documents), Rich Text Format (a word-processor exchange format), plain text (no formatting), QIF (Quicken Interchange Format), MIDI files (for music), and so on.

One reason: both Windows and Mac OS X use filename extensions to identify documents. ("Letter to the Editor.doc", for example, is a Microsoft Word document on *either* operating system.) Common suffixes include:

Kind of document	Suffix	Example
Microsoft Word	.doc, .docx	Letter to Mom.doc
text	.txt	Database Export.txt
Rich Text Format	.rtf	Senior Thesis.rtf
Excel	.xls, .xlsx	Profit Projection.xls
PowerPoint	.ppt, .pptx	Slide Show.ppt
FileMaker Pro	.fp5, fp6, fp7…	Recipe file.fp7
JPEG photo	.jpg, .jpeg	Baby Portrait.jpg
GIF graphic	.gif	Logo.gif
PNG graphic	.png	Dried fish.png
Web page	.htm, .html	Index.htm

Note: Recent versions of Microsoft Office for Mac and Windows offer a more compact file format ending with the letter x. For example, Word files are .docx, Excel files are .xlsx, and so on. The older, more widely compatible format doesn't have the x (.doc, .xls, and so on).

The beauty of Mac OS X is that most Mac programs add these file name suffixes automatically and invisibly—and recognize such suffixes from Windows with equal ease. You and your Windows comrades can freely exchange documents without ever worrying about this former snag in the Macintosh/Windows relationship. (You may, however, encounter snags in the form of documents made by Windows programs that don't exist on the Mac, such as Microsoft Access. Chapter 8 tackles these special cases one by one.

Special Software, Special Problems

Be glad you waited so long to get a Mac. By now, all the big-name programs look and work almost exactly the same on the Mac as they do on the PC. Once you've mastered the basic differences between the Mac and Windows (keyboard shortcuts, the menu bar, and so on), you'll find that programs from Microsoft, Adobe, and other major software companies feel distinctly familiar in their Mac incarnations. In fact, the documents that they create are in the same format and generally need no conversion.

Still, there are more software programs available for Windows than for the Mac. Sooner or later, you'll probably run into a familiar Windows program for which there's no equivalent on the Mac.

One solution is simply to run those Windows programs *on* the Mac, as described in Chapter 8. For thousands of people, that's the screamingly obvious, and extremely convenient, approach. Each time you read, "There's no Mac equivalent of this program" in this chapter, add, in your head, "but you can always run the Windows version."

Still, in other cases, you may not want to fool around with Windows anymore. You may prefer to identify Mac replacements for your favorite Windows programs. That's the purpose of this chapter: to guide you in finding Mac equivalents for the most popular Windows programs (listed here alphabetically), and to guide you in bringing your data and settings over from Windows to the Mac whenever possible.

ACDSee

As digital photography becomes more popular, so do programs like ACDSee, a popular Windows program that serves as a digital shoebox and basic retouching program for digital photos. Your Mac, of course, stands ready to run a far more elegant equivalent: iPhoto. It's one of the world's most pleasant photo-organizing programs—and it's free.

In its most recent incarnation, iPhoto has a pretty complete set of image-retouching features. Still, if you need more editing power, consider Photoshop Elements, a program that's available for both Mac and Windows and has won rave reviews on both platforms.

In any case, ACDSee doesn't have any documents of its own—it does all its work on your existing digital photos, wherever you keep them on your hard drive. All you have to do, then, is move the photos themselves to the Mac, using any of the techniques described in Chapter 6. From there, drag them into the iPhoto window to import them.

Acrobat Reader

Acrobat Reader, which lets you read Acrobat (PDF) files, works precisely the same on the Mac as it does in Windows. If you like, you can download Acrobat Reader from *www.adobe.com*.

However, you have a much nicer PDF-reading program right there in your Applications folder, called Preview.

Preview can display PDFs with the best of them—but it's got Acrobat Reader beat on several other counts. Preview can annotate PDFs with virtual yellow sticky-notes—a great tool for marking up book layouts before they go to press, for example. Also, Preview's search feature is so fast and convenient, it blows Acrobat Reader out of the water. And finally, Preview opens in a matter of seconds, while Acrobat Reader can take a minute or so to launch. (For more on Preview, see page 577.)

ACT

No Mac version of this address book/calendar program is available, but don't let that stop you. Export and Import commands are the bread and butter of address and calendar programs. Your ACT life can find a happy home in any of several Mac address books:

• Mac OS X's free, built-in Address Book.

Tip: Address Book syncs with Google Calendar on the Web, which opens up a fascinating possibility: All of your computers (Macs, Windows, iPhone) can maintain synchronized calendars, with Google Calendar serving as the mother ship.

• Outlook for Mac (part of Microsoft Office for Mac).

• BusyCal *(www.busycal.com)*, which is networkable. That is, if you have more than one computer in the house, you can check your Rolodex from any machine on the network.

In any case, here are the instructions for transferring your addresses from ACT (version 5 or later) to the Mac:

1. **In ACT for Windows, start by choosing File→Data Exchange→Export.**

   The Export Wizard dialog box appears.

2. **From the "File type" drop-down list, choose Text-Delimited. Specify a folder location and name for your exported file (call it Exported Contacts, for example). Click Next, and click Next on the next screen, too.**

   Now you're asked, "Which contact or group records do you want to export?"

3. **Click "All records," and then click Next.**

   Now you see a list of the *fields* (information tidbits like City, State, and Zip) that ACT is prepared to export. You can save yourself time later if you take a moment now to remove the ones you don't need (click a name and then click Remove Field).

4. **Click Finish.**

   If you plan to import your addresses into a commercial program like BusyCal, transfer the Exported Contacts file to the Mac (see Chapter 6), and then import them into BusyCal.

   If your aim is to import the addresses into Microsoft Entourage on the Mac, or Mac OS X's own Address Book program, though, read on.

5. **Open Outlook Express.**

   Yes, Outlook Express for Windows, the free program that comes on every PC. (The Windows Vista/Windows 7 version is called Windows Mail.) You'll use it as a glorified converter program.

6. **Follow the instructions on page 224 for exporting the contacts into a format suitable for your Mac.**

   That page outlines several ways to get your contacts from Outlook Express into Mac OS X's Address Book—your ACT info's final resting place.

Ad Subtract (Pop-up Stopper)

Nothing quite spoils the fun of the Web like pop-ups—those annoying miniature advertising windows that sprout in front of the Web page you're trying to read.

Safari, Mac OS X's Web browser, has a simple menu command for blocking pop-ups: Safari→Block Pop-Up Windows. Nowadays, so does just about every other Web browser made for the Mac—Firefox, Netscape, Camino, and so on. In other words, you don't even *need* Ad Subtract.

If you're interested in some of Ad Subtract's other features, like blocking animated ads or zapping all ads on Web pages, consider SafariBlock (for Safari) or Adblock (for Firefox). Or, for Safari, the awesome Click2Flash, which simply neutralizes all of those annoying *blinking* ads. All three are free and available for download from this book's "Missing CD" at *www.missingmanuals.com*.

Adobe [your favorite program here]

Most of Adobe's bestsellers are available in Mac OS X versions, including Photoshop, Photoshop Elements, After Effects, Illustrator, InDesign, GoLive, Acrobat, Acrobat Reader, Premiere, and so on.

You don't have to do any document conversion. A Windows Photoshop document is exactly the same thing as a Macintosh Photoshop document, for example.

America Online

Truth is, you don't actually need an AOL *program* on your Mac. You can access all your AOL mail, as well as all of AOL's features, on the Web at *www.aol.com*.

AIM (AOL Instant Messenger)

If you're an online chat junkie, switching to the Mac involves very little disruption to your routine. AIM is available for the Mac, too, and it awaits your download at *www.aim.com*. Better yet, the minute you fire it up, you'll discover that your entire Windows-version Buddies list is intact and ready to use. (That's because it actually lives on the America Online network, not on your Windows PC.)

Tip: Actually, you might have a lot more fun—and save a lot of effort—by just using iChat. It's a free Mac OS X chat program that's compatible with the whole AIM network, as described in Chapter 12.

Children's Software

Thanks to the vast number of Macs in schools, a huge percentage of educational software programs are available in both Mac and Windows versions—often on the same CD. That includes most programs from The Learning Company (including the Arthur, Carmen Sandiego, Little Bear, and Reader Rabbit series), Broderbund (Kid Pix, Mavis Beacon, Print Shop, and so on), Humongous Entertainment (series like Blue's Clues, Dora the Explorer, Putt-Putt, Backyard Sports), and other major educational publishers.

Easy CD Creator

You don't need any add-on software at all to burn CDs in Mac OS X. You can just drag files and folders onto the icon of a blank CD, as described on page 281.

If you want fancier features—recording less common disc formats, for example—what you need is Toast for the Macintosh. It comes from the same company that makes Easy CD Creator.

Its main rival is Discribe *(www.charismac.com).* Both programs can create audio CDs, video CDs, data DVDs, and so on. Both come with a program that helps you turn old vinyl records and tapes into digital CDs, too.

The only disappointment: Neither program can treat a CD as a glorified floppy disk, as Easy CD Creator for Windows can, so that you can add and delete files freely (rather than burning the CD all at once).

There's a workaround, though: Copy the contents of a rewriteable CD (a CD-RW disc) to a folder on your desktop; make whatever changes you like to the contents of this folder; and then burn the CD-RW again. (Use the Disk Utility program in your Applications→Utilities folder to erase the disc first.)

Tip: Ordinarily, the CD-burning feature of Mac OS X burns the entire CD each time, even if you've only filled a small portion of it. But if you download the handy $17 shareware program called CD Session Burner, you can perform additional "mini-burns" of new data to the CD until all the space is used up. Each such *session* shows up on your desktop with its own icon, as though it's a separate disc. You can download this program from *www.sentman.com/CD_Session_Burner.html.*

Encarta

Microsoft's best-selling encyclopedia program isn't available for the Macintosh. The World Book Encyclopedia is, however. (Details at *www.worldbook.com.*)

Of course, you can also use the Web-based versions of either encyclopedia (or Wikipedia, of course).

Eudora

The ancient Mac version of Eudora no longer runs in Mac OS X Lion. Your only option is to import your mail into a more modern Mac mail program, like Mail or Outlook for Mac.

Excel

See "Microsoft Office" in this chapter.

Firefox

On Windows, Firefox is a faster, more secure, better-featured Web-browsing alternative to Internet Explorer. If you'd like, you can download the identical Mac version from *www.getfirefox.com,* and then follow the instructions on page 224 for transferring your bookmarks.

Alternatively, you can switch to Mac OS X's built-in, super-fast Safari browser. Chapter 12 houses the coverage of the Safari adventure.

Games

Nobody switches to the Mac to play games; of the top 250 computer games for Windows, only about 150 are available for the Macintosh.

Still, that number includes the majority of the big-name titles and series, including Guitar Hero, Spore, Civilization, Madden NFL, Tiger Woods PGA, the various Sims games, Civilization, Quake, Harry Potter, Spider-Man, Tomb Raider, Warcraft, Jedi Knight, Soldier of Fortune, Max Payne, Links Championship Edition, Age of Empires, Medal of Honor, Return to Castle Wolfenstein, and hordes of others.

And once you do get these programs going on the Mac, you're likely to be impressed. Recent Macs generally come equipped with pleasantly high-horsepower graphics cards—the kind that serious computer games crave.

If you're a game nut, you can stay in touch with what's new and upcoming by reading the articles (and watching the game "trailers") at *www.apple.com/games,* not to mention *www.insidemacgames.com, www.macgamer.com,* and *www.macgamefiles.com.*

Google Desktop Search

Mac OS X's Spotlight feature does everything that Google Desktop does—searching inside files, finding favorite Web sites, and so on. Spotlight just does it better.

Google Earth

Google's wicked-cool searchable, navigable digital version of the planet Earth is available for the Mac, too. Download it at *earth.google.com.*

Google Chrome

Google's fast, popular Web browser is available for the Mac, just as it is in Windows. You can download it from *www.google.com/chrome.*

ICQ

If you're a fan of this Internet-wide chat program, look no further than ICQ for Mac or one of its many shareware rivals. To grab them, visit *www.versiontracker.com* and perform a search, on the Mac OS X tab, for *ICQ.*

Internet Explorer

Microsoft once wrote an Internet Explorer version for the Mac, but abandoned it years ago. Safari (Apple's built-in Web browser) blocks pop-up windows, loads pages faster, and doubles as an RSS reader for news sites. See Chapter 12.

If some Web site (like a banking site) refuses to work with Safari, then download Chrome or Firefox for the Mac instead; they work with almost everything.

iTunes

If you grew used to iTunes on Windows, you'll be glad to know that the Mac version is already sitting in your Applications folder. It works identically to the PC version.

Just move your iTunes Library folder from the Music folder of your old PC into the Music folder on your Mac. That's all there is to it!

LimeWire

LimeWire, of course, is the "new Napster." People use it to swap music and video files online, hard drive to hard drive—illegally, in many cases. You know who you are.

Or, rather, you know who you *were*. LimeWire has been shut down by the courts.

McAfee VirusScan

There's a Mac version of VirusScan, all right—but don't buy it. You don't even need a virus program for Mac OS X. (If you run Windows on your Mac, as described in the next chapter, then you can install your antivirus program onto that side of the computer, by all means.)

Microsoft Access

Microsoft has never been interested in creating a Macintosh equivalent of its flagship database program (which comes with the higher-priced versions of Microsoft Office for Windows). FileMaker, a much easier-to-use database program, towers over the Macintosh database market like the Jolly Green Giant (and has a decent following on the Windows side, too). Resistance, Microsoft apparently assumes, is futile.

UP TO SPEED

Viruses in Mac OS X (Not!)

One of the greatest perks of moving to Macintosh is that viruses are practically nonexistent. At this writing, in fact, not a *single virus* for Mac OS X has been reported in the wild.

The only viruses that manage to sneak into Mac OS X are Microsoft Word macro viruses that hide in ordinary Word files sent to you by your Windows friends.

Fortunately, on the Mac version of Word, most of these don't run at all. Also, whenever you try to open a document that contains macros that you didn't create yourself, you see the message shown here. All you have to do is click Disable Macros. The file opens normally, 100 percent virus free.

Warning

The document you are opening contains macros or customizations. Some macros may contain viruses that could harm your computer.

If you are sure this document is from a trusted source, click Enable Macros. If you are not sure and want to prevent any macros from running, click Disable Macros.

[Enable Macros]   [Tell Me More]   [Do Not Open]   [Disable Macros]

Tip: FileMaker's little brother, Bento (for the Mac), is even easier to use still.

It's easy enough to get your data out of Microsoft Access; just choose File→Export. In the resulting dialog box, you can choose from a number of common export formats that can serve as intermediaries between the Windows and Mac worlds (see Figure 7-1).

Figure 7-1:
When you export your data from Access, you can choose from any of several formats. The idea is that you'll transfer the resulting exported file onto your Mac and then import it into a proper database program there.

Among them is Microsoft Excel—that is, you can turn your database into a spreadsheet. The beauty here is that FileMaker on the Macintosh can turn Excel documents into FileMaker databases without even batting an eye. You just drag the exported Excel document onto the FileMaker icon, and FileMaker does the rest.

Unfortunately, there's more to an Access database than just its data. Your database may well have fancy forms (layouts), complete with letterhead and other graphic elements, not to mention relational links between database files. In these cases, the situation isn't quite so hopeful—there's no way to export layouts and relational links to the Macintosh.

Your best bet might be to run Microsoft Access itself on the Macintosh, as described in Chapter 8.

Microsoft Money

Microsoft has abandoned its Money personal-finance program, so you would have had to export your Money data to Quicken whether you switched to the Mac or not.

It's easy enough to export your Money data into Quicken for the Mac, although not every scrap of information comes through alive. You'll lose your Money abbreviations, comments, and Lifetime Planner information. Fortunately, the important stuff—your accounts and the transactions in them, including categories, classes, and stocks that you've set up—come through in one piece.

Unfortunately, you have to export one account at a time. Furthermore, you'll be creating something called a QIF (Quicken Interchange Format) file as an intermediary between Windows and the Mac—and this file format can't handle category names longer than 15 characters. Before you begin, then, you might want to take a moment either to shorten them or to make a note of which ones might get truncated in the transfer.

Ready? Fire up Money on your Windows PC and then proceed like this:

1. **Choose File→Export.**

   The Export dialog box appears. It wants to know if you are exporting your information to another version of Money ("Loose QIF") or to some other, rival financial program that shall, as far as Microsoft is concerned, remain nameless.

2. **In the resulting dialog box (Figure 7-2), choose Strict QIF, and then click OK.**

   Now you're supposed to name and save the exported file. Make sure you give each account a descriptive name (like Citibank Savings).

3. **Specify a name and a folder on your PC for the exported file, and then click OK.**

   Repeat these three steps for each of your Money accounts.

4. **Specify the kind of account (usually you'll want Regular, not Investment), and which one of your accounts to export.**

   Click OK when the exporting is done.

5. **Transfer the exported files to the Mac.**

   You can do it via network, email, or any of the other techniques described in Chapter 6. Then move to the Macintosh, open Quicken, and create a new file (see

Figure 7-2:
Use the Strict QIF option. It lops off category names longer than 15 characters.

the Quicken instructions). Then, once you've got an empty "check register" before you, continue like this:

6. **Choose File→Import QIF. In the "Select a QIF file" dialog box, navigate to, and open, the first exported account file.**

When the dust settles, you'll see your Money transactions safely ensconced in Quicken. (If you see a message that some transactions couldn't be completed, don't worry; it's usually just telling you that some of your category names were longer than 15 characters and have been marked with asterisks to help you spot them.)

If you have more than one account, choose File→New Account to set it up, and then repeat from step 4 to bring in your other Money accounts.

Microsoft Office

Microsoft Office is available for the Mac in what some critics have declared to be a more attractive, less frustrating version than the Windows incarnation. At this writing, the current version is called Office 2011 for Macintosh.

The beauty of Microsoft Word, Excel, and PowerPoint documents is that their format is the same on Mac and Windows. You can freely exchange files without having to go through any kind of conversion. (The big exception, as noted earlier, is Access; Microsoft doesn't make a database program for the Mac.)

In heavily formatted documents, you may occasionally see some strange differences: Windows documents containing many numbered paragraphs sometimes become confused on the Mac, for example. And if the Mac and the originating PC don't have the same fonts installed, you'll see different fonts, too. Otherwise, documents look identical despite having been shuttled to a different kind of computer.

___

Tip: With Office 2007 for Windows, Microsoft introduced a set of new file formats (.docx for Word, .pptx for PowerPoint, and so on) that are more compact than the previous set (.doc, .ppt, and so on). When you save a document, you can choose which format you want to use: the old one, which 400 million other people can open on their Macs and PCs, or the new one, which only recent upgraders can open.

Exactly the same conundrum presents itself on the Mac. Office 2008 and 2011 can open and create those same newfangled files, but the previous versions (like Office 2004 for the Mac) can open only the older formats.

___

Microsoft Publisher

Microsoft Publisher is a comprehensive page-layout program, complete with canned designs, clip art, and so on.

There's no Mac version of it, but you can perform most of the same tasks using Pages. (Pages is part of Apple's $80 iWork software suite; you can download a 30-day trial from *www.apple.com/iwork*.) Like Publisher, Pages offers dozens of attractive, ready-to-use page-design templates that you can adapt as you see fit.

There are also plenty of standalone page-design programs—this is the Mac, after all—including professional powerhouses like Adobe InDesign and QuarkXPress.

Microsoft Publisher

Microsoft Visio

If flowcharts, org charts, network diagrams, family trees, project processes, office layouts and similar diagrams are part of your own personal workflow, you're in luck—at least some luck. Microsoft Visio isn't available in a Macintosh version, but you'll probably find that OmniGraffle for Mac OS X is a satisfactory, even delightful, replacement (see Figure 7-3). The Pro version even lets you import and export Visio documents.

Figure 7-3:
OmniGraffle comes preinstalled in the Applications folders of many new Mac models, or you can download the latest version from www. omnigroup.com.

Minesweeper

Time wasters, rejoice! There are a number of free Minesweeper programs for Mac OS X, including CocoaMines and Aqua Mines. You can download them from the Mac App Store, or a site like *www.versiontracker.com* (search for *minesweeper*).

MSN Messenger

Online chat-aholics have nothing to worry about on the Mac. MSN Messenger, the instant-messaging program, is alive and well in a Mac OS X version that you can download from *www.microsoft.com/mac*. Like AOL Instant Messenger, described earlier in this chapter, you don't even have to worry about your carefully assembled buddy list. From the instant you start up MSN Messenger for Mac OS X, you'll see your buddy list in place (because the list is actually stored on the Internet, not on your computer).

NaturallySpeaking

Speech-recognition programs have traditionally been far more advanced on Windows than on the Macintosh. Windows programs like Dragon NaturallySpeaking transcribe your dictated text with almost *Star Trek*–like accuracy, and even let you make corrections and manipulate the computer itself using all voice commands.

Fortunately, the Mac program called MacSpeech Dictate (*www.macspeech.com*) uses precisely the same "recognition engine" as NaturallySpeaking. If you just can't use the keyboard, or don't want to, you'll be amazed at its speed and accuracy, although it's much younger (and therefore less fully featured) than NaturallySpeaking.

Netscape

Netscape, on both Mac and Windows, has grown up into the beloved Web browser called Firefox. It comes in a Mac OS X version—free, of course—from *http://getfirefox. com*.

Newsgroup Readers

If you're a fan of the online bulletin boards known as *newsgroups,* you've come to the right place. The Mac is crawling with newsgroup-reading programs. Microsoft Entourage, for instance, has one built in. In the shareware world (try searching the Mac App Store or *www.versiontracker.com)*, you can take your pick of MT-NewsWatcher X, NewsHunter, and Halime, to name a few.

Norton AntiVirus

You can buy Norton Antivirus for the Macintosh, no problem (*www.symantec.com*). The question is, why? See the box on page 233.

Norton Utilities

On Windows, this program defragments your hard drive, helps recover files in case of disaster, and repairs disk problems. There's no Mac version, but very similar Mac programs are available; for example, Mac veterans swear by DiskWarrior (*www.alsoft.com*).

Notepad

If you're an aficionado of this beloved note-taking tool in the standard Windows Start menu, you're in luck. Mac OS X's Stickies program is even more powerful, because it offers formatting and even graphics. Or, for more of a word-processor effect, check out TextEdit.

Outlook/Outlook Express/Windows Mail

Mac OS X's built-in Mail program is similar to Outlook Express for Windows (or Windows Mail in Vista and Windows 7), just more powerful and a lot better-looking. Chapter 6 describes the process of switching, and Chapter 11 covers the rest of the Mail experience.

If you want all the features from *Outlook,* though, you'd probably be better off using Microsoft Outlook for Mac, which is available as part of Microsoft Office for Mac.

Paint Shop Pro

If your goal is to retouch and edit digital photos, the closest you can come to Paint Shop on the Mac is probably Photoshop Elements, a terrific Mac OS X program (about $100) that belongs on the hard drive of any serious digital camera owner. (Any digital camera owner who doesn't own the full-blown Photoshop program, that is.)

If your goal is to organize and *use* your photos, rather than paint on them, remember that iPhoto is already on your hard drive.

Finally, if opening and converting graphics to other formats is your main concern, try Preview (page 577), whose exporting feature is surprisingly powerful. You may also want to investigate the beloved shareware program GraphicConverter (find and download it at *www.versiontracker.com*), which may be the last graphics editing/converting program you'll ever need.

Palm Desktop

If you're still tracking your calendar and address book on an ancient PalmPilot—which you store lovingly next to your gramophone and kerosene lamp—you should have no problem. You can sync your palmtop with the Mac version of Palm Desktop that still lurks at *www.palm.com*. (Getting your data from there to something more modern is another challenge, but not insurmountable. Google can help you.)

If your concern is syncing a non-Apple smartphone with your Mac (Treo, BlackBerry, whatever), you can buy a utility program called The Missing Sync at *www.markspace. com* that does precisely that.

Picasa

Google's Picasa, one of several Windows photo organizers, is also available for the Mac. Now, therefore, you have a choice; you can edit, organize, and order prints of your images with either Picasa or iPhoto.

PowerPoint

PowerPoint is available on the Mac; see "Microsoft Office" in this chapter. Remember, too, that Apple's own Keynote presentation program (available as part of iWork for $80) is the same idea as PowerPoint, but with more spectacular graphic effects.

QuickBooks

If you've been happily using QuickBooks for Windows to manage your small business—to prepare estimates and invoices, track bills, maintain lists of inventory and customers, and so on—there's good news and bad news. The good news is that QuickBooks is available on the Mac, and the steps for transferring your company files aren't difficult.

The bad news is that the transfer isn't perfect. Along the way, you might lose your memorized transactions, custom report designs, and reconciliations. Note, too, that you may not be able to send an older Windows file (like QuickBooks 2007) to an older version on the Mac (like QuickBooks 2006).

It's not especially hard; heck, there's a File→Utilities→Copy Company File for Quick-Books Mac command right in QuickBooks for Windows. You can find the rest of the step-by-step instructions in two places:

- Open the electronic Help for QuickBooks for Mac, and search for this topic: "Converting a QuickBooks file from Windows to Mac."

- Follow the do-it-yourself procedure described on Intuit's Support Web page (here's a short link to it: *http://j.mp/xS9PuS).*

Quicken

If you've been keeping track of your personal finances in Quicken on your PC, you'll feel right at home when you move to the Mac. Quicken 2007 is available for Mac OS X. (Be sure to get the Lion-compatible version, which wasn't available until March 2012.)

In general, switching over is quick and painless. You can import into the Mac version of Quicken all of the actual transaction information, including accounts, the categories and classes you've used to group them, and stock holdings. Certain kinds of Windows Quicken information—like schedule transactions, QuickFill transactions, online account information, stock histories, and loan information—don't make it, however.

For the official manual on transferring your Quicken data from Windows to the Mac, download the free "Transferring Quicken" PDF appendix from this book's "Missing CD" at *www.missingmanuals.com.*

If the technology gods are smiling, the Mac version of Quicken should take only a moment to import all of your Windows data, which now appears neatly in your Register windows, ready to use. Make sure the final balances match the final balances in Quicken for Windows. (If they don't, scan your Mac registers for duplicate or missing transactions.)

RealPlayer

Want to listen to Internet music and watch Internet video in Real format, just as you did on your PC? No sweat. Visit *www.real.com* and download RealPlayer for Mac OS X, either in the free basic edition or the fancy paid version.

If you just want to listen to music on your *hard drive,* though, you'd be better off using iTunes (page 284).

RssReader

RSS is a technology for reading quick Web site summaries, and it's taking the Net by storm. RSS returns the Internet to real utility, free from pop-up ads and the other annoyances of Web life.

To take advantage of RSS, however, you need a program to *subscribe* to Web sites that support RSS—and then to display the resulting summaries. On Windows, you might use a program like RssReader, or a Web site like *www.pluck.com.*

On Mac OS X, however, Apple's way ahead of you. Both Safari (Chapter 12), and Mail (Chapter 11) provide fantastic built-in RSS readers; both can subscribe to RSS sites with ease.

Skype

For making Internet-based phone calls, it's hard to beat Skype. If you call from one computer to another, you pay absolutely nothing—no matter how far away your recipient is.

Luckily, you can download a Mac version from *www.skype.com.* From there, you can audio-chat with all your Mac- and PC-using Skype buddies until you lose your voice.

Tip: iChat, Apple's own instant-messaging program, also offers free audio chats. If you and your buddy both have Web cams or video cameras, in fact, you can make free, Internet *video* calls. See Chapter 12 for the details.

SnagIt

If you prepare instructions for using any kind of computer or software—computer books, magazine articles, or how-to materials of any kind—you may already be familiar with this amazing screen-capture program. It captures any window, menu, or area of the Windows screen and saves it as a graphics file that you can print or pop into a layout program.

In Mac OS X, this feature is built right in. Here's how to capture:

- **The whole screen.** Press Shift-⌘-3 to create a picture file on your desktop, in PNG format, that depicts the entire screen image. A satisfying camera-shutter sound tells you that you were successful.

  The file is called *Picture 1*. Each time you press Shift-⌘-3, you get another file, called Picture 2, Picture 3, and so on. You can open these files in Preview, Photoshop, or another graphics program, in readiness for editing or printing.

- **One section of the screen.** You can capture only a rectangular *region* of the screen by pressing Shift-⌘-4. When you drag and release the mouse, you hear the camera-click sound, and the Picture file appears on your desktop as usual.

- **One menu, window, icon (with its name), or dialog box.** Once you've got your menu or window open onscreen, or the icon visible (even if it's on the Dock), press Shift-⌘-4. But instead of dragging diagonally, press the space bar.

  Now your cursor turns into a tiny camera. Move it so that the misty highlighting fills the window or menu you want to capture—and then click. The resulting Picture file snips the window or menu neatly from its background. (Press the space bar a second time to exit "snip one screen element" mode and return to "drag across an area" mode.)

Tip: If you hold down the Control key as you release your fingers from the click or drag (using any of the techniques described above), you copy the screenshot to your *Clipboard,* ready for pasting, rather than saving it as a new graphics file on your desktop.

Mac OS X also offers another way to create screenshots: a program called Grab, which offers a timer option that lets you set up the screen before it takes the shot. It's in your Applications→Utilities folder.

But if you're really serious about capturing screenshots, you should opt instead for Snapz Pro X (*www.ambrosiasw.com*), which can capture virtually anything on the screen—even movies of onscreen procedures, along with your narration—and save it in your choice of format.

Solitaire

Ah yes, Solitaire: possibly the most overused Windows software in the world.

The Mac doesn't come with a preinstalled copy of Solitaire, but the world is crawling with free and shareware solitaire games for the Mac. Open the Mac App Store app on your hard drive; in the search box, type *solitaire.*

When you click Go or press Return, you'll see a substantial list of solitaire games, ready to download: FreeCell, MacSolitaire, Klondike, and so on.

Street Atlas USA

Mapping software is, alas, a weak spot in the Mac software catalog. Street Atlas USA and Route 66, for example, are no longer available for the Mac.

Until these programs re-emerge in a Mac edition, your best bet is to run the Windows versions in Windows mode on your Mac, as described in Chapter 8.

Tip: If you're looking for driving directions and maps, don't forget about Google Maps (*http://maps.google. com*). It's fast, it's convenient, it works the same on both Mac and Windows, and it's free.

Also, don't forget about the Yellow Pages feature of the Dashboard (page 149). It's ready to print directions and draw maps.

TaxCut, TurboTax

Both TaxCut and TurboTax are available for the Mac. You can even buy state versions of TurboTax for the states that require income tax returns. You can buy them wherever fine Mac programs are sold: *www.macmall.com, www.macwarehouse.com, www.macconnection.com,* and so on.

WinAmp, MusicMatch

When it comes to playing MP3 files, creating MP3 files, burning music CDs, and otherwise organizing your music library, you'd be hard-pressed to beat iTunes, the free Mac OS X program that's already on your Mac (and a free download from *www. apple.com/itunes*).

Windows Media Player

The Macintosh equivalent for Windows Media Player is, of course, QuickTime Player. It handily plays and shows almost any kind of movie, picture, or sound (although you'll want to use iTunes for most music playback).

There are a few entertainment sources that come in the Windows Media format, however, notably Windows Media Video (.wmv) movies that play on Web sites. By itself, QuickTime Player can't play them.

Microsoft actually went to the trouble of creating a Macintosh version of Windows Media Player (never mind the irony of its name). You can download it from *www. microsoft.com/mac,* but it's officially been abandoned.

The more modern, equally free solution is to download and install Flip4Mac. It's technically a plug-in for QuickTime Player, but you don't need to know that. All you need to know is that once you've installed it, you can suddenly play all those Web videos that you couldn't play before. You can download it from this book's "Missing CD" at *www.missingmanuals.com.*

WinZip

In Mac OS X, you create a .zip file by right-clicking any Finder icon and choosing "Compress [the icon's name]" from the shortcut menu. You decompress a .zip file by simply double-clicking its icon in the Finder.

Word

See "Microsoft Office" in this chapter.

WordPerfect

Unfortunately, WordPerfect lost the battle with Microsoft Word on the Mac side pretty much the same way it did on the Windows side. If you're a die-hard WordPerfect fan, your best bet might be to invest in Microsoft Word and capitalize on its keystroke-customizing features to turn it into a living simulation of WordPerfect.

Or, if you'd rather not spend a significant portion of your life's savings on a word processor, use the free Word-importing and -exporting features of TextEdit (page 599).

Yahoo Messenger

The equivalent chat program on the Mac is, of course, Yahoo Messenger for Mac OS X. It's a free download from *http://messenger.yahoo.com.* (But iChat, described in Chapter 12, can also handle Yahoo.)

CHAPTER
8

Windows on Macintosh

T he very moment Apple announced in 2006 that all new Mac models would come with Intel chips inside, the geeks and the bloggers started going nuts. "Let's see," they thought. "Macs and PCs now use exactly the same memory, hard drives, monitors, mice, keyboards, networking protocols, *and processors.* By our calculations, it ought to be possible make a Mac run Windows!"

Now, some in the Cult of Macintosh were baffled by the very idea. Who on earth, they asked, wants to pollute the magnificence of the Mac with a headache like Windows?

Lots of people, as it turns out. Think of all the potential switchers who are tempted by the Mac's sleek looks, yet worry about leaving Windows behind entirely. Or the people who love Apple's iLife programs, but have jobs that rely on Microsoft Access, Outlook, or some other piece of Windows corporateware. Even true-blue Mac fans occasionally look longingly at some of the Windows-only games, Web sites, or movie download services they thought they'd never be able to use.

So hackers set about trying to make Windows run on Intel Macs almost immediately. But they were wasting their time; within weeks, Apple did the job for them—by inventing Boot Camp.

Actually, today, there are two ways to run Windows on a Mac:

- **Restart it in Boot Camp.** Boot Camp is a little Apple program that lets you *restart* your Mac into Windows.

Note: The new Boot Camp requires you to use Windows 7—nothing older. On the other hand, if you're *already* using Boot Camp with an older Windows version, you can keep using it.

CHAPTER 8: WINDOWS ON MACINTOSH 245

At that point, it's a full-blown Windows PC, with no trace of the Mac on the screen. It runs at 100 percent of the speed of a real PC, because it is one. Compatibility with Windows software is excellent. The only downsides: Your laptop battery life isn't as good, and you have to restart the Mac *again* to return to the world of Mac OS X.

Tip: *What's cool, though, is that even when you're running Windows, you can still access your Mac files and folders, as described below.*

- **Run Windows in a window.** For $80 or so, you can eliminate the Boot Camp Bummer—the business of having to restart the Mac every time you want to switch its operating-system personality. You can buy a program like Parallels or VMware Fusion, which let you run Windows *in a window*.

  You're still running Mac OS X, and all your Mac files and programs are still available. But you've got a parallel universe—Microsoft Windows—running in a window simultaneously.

  Compared with Boot Camp, this *virtualization software* offers only 90 percent of the speed and 90 percent of the software compatibility. But for thousands of people, the convenience of eliminating all those restarts—and gaining the freedom to copy and paste documents between Mac OS X and Windows programs—makes the Windows-in-a-window solution nearly irresistible.

Tip: *There's nothing wrong with using* both *on the same Mac, by the way. In fact, both Parallels and Fusion can use the* same copy of Windows *as Boot Camp, so you save disk space and don't have to manage two different Windows worlds.*

Both techniques require you to provide your own copy of Windows. And both are described on the following pages.

FREQUENTLY ASKED QUESTION

The Virus Question

Doesn't running Windows on my Mac mean that I'll be exposed to the nightmare of viruses and spyware, just like the rest of the Windows world?

Yep!

If you install Windows on your Mac, you should also install Windows antivirus and antispyware software to protect that half of the computer. The world is crawling with commercial programs that do the job. There are also lots of free programs, like Microsoft Security Essentials, which protects you against both viruses and spyware.

The good news is that even if your Windows installation gets infected, the Mac side of your computer is unaffected. Just as Mac OS X can't run Windows-only software like, say, Microsoft Access, it also can't run Windows virus software.

Some people, therefore, run Windows naked—without virus protection (especially when using Windows-in-a-window programs like Parallels and VMware Fusion). If a virus does strike, no big deal; they just drag the infected copy of Windows to the Trash and install a fresh one!

Boot Camp

To set up Boot Camp, you need the proper ingredients (plus an Intel-based Mac, which, since you have Lion, you obviously have):

- **A copy of Windows 7.** That's right: The Lion version of Boot Camp no longer works with Windows XP or Windows Vista—only the Home Premium, Business, or Ultimate editions of Windows 7.

Note: If you really want to install one of those older Windows versions, you can still do it. One way is to use the Snow Leopard version of Boot Camp. You should be able to find the (unauthorized) instructions with a quick Google search.

Another way: Partition the disk as you'd like with the Boot Camp Utility, as directed in Phase 2 below, and then skip the rest of the Lion Boot Camp instructions. Put in your Windows XP Install CD. Restart your Mac while pressing the Option key until you see the "boot menu" screen. Start up into the Windows XP Install CD, and install Windows XP as usual. When it's over, insert your old Snow Leopard DVD to install the necessary Mac drivers.

You need a full-installation copy of Windows—not just an upgrade version. (You can install either the 32-bit version of Windows or the 64-bit version.)

POWER USERS' CLINIC

Upgrading an Existing Boot Camp Installation

If your Mac already has Boot Camp (because you upgraded your Mac from Snow Leopard), you don't have to go through the procedure described on these pages. You can upgrade either your Boot Camp software or your Windows version without disturbing what you've got there.

Upgrading Boot Camp. Open Boot Camp Assistant. Obey the instructions, which guide you through copying the Windows drivers to a blank CD, DVD, or external drive that's been formatted in the MS-DOS (FAT) format, as described in "Phase 1." Restart the Mac into Windows.

Now insert your drivers disc, or connect the external disk. The drivers installer is supposed to start automatically. (If it doesn't, browse the disc or disk; double-click the *setup.exe* file in the Boot Camp folder.)

Now the installer runs; follow the instructions in "Phase 4" on these pages.

Upgrading Windows. If you have Windows XP or Windows Vista on your existing Boot Camp partition, you can upgrade

it to Windows 7 (Home Premium, Professional, or Ultimate) without having to start over with Boot Camp.

To upgrade from Windows Vista to Windows 7, start up your Mac in Windows. Run Apple Software Update to make sure you have all the latest versions of your Windows drivers. Then visit *www.apple.com/support/bootcamp*, and download the special "upgrade my copy of Windows" app that Apple has cheerfully called *Apple_Win7_Upgrade_Utility.exe*. It guides you through the upgrade process (including inserting your Windows 7 installation disc).

If you have Windows XP, though, things are a little more complicated; you can't upgrade directly to Windows 7. That involves erasing your Boot Camp partition and installing Windows 7 fresh. (Back up your Windows stuff first!)

To proceed, start up your Mac in Windows XP. Insert the Windows 7 DVD, and install it as usual. It will guide you through the process of wiping out your old Windows XP copy and replacing it with Windows 7. When that's over, install the Mac drivers as described in this chapter.

Tip: If you have a recent Mac model, you might be able to install a disk-image (downloadable) copy of Windows 7, which Microsoft sells. That's useful if you have a MacBook Air, which has no DVD drive.

To see if your Mac is one of the blessed ones, open Boot Camp Assistant and click Continue. If you see an option called "Create a Windows 7 install disk," you're in luck. If you click that button, Boot Camp Assistant will copy the Windows 7 disk image to a USB flash drive that you insert (you'll need one with 4 gigs of memory or more).

From now on, you'll be able to install Windows *and* Boot Camp from that one flash drive.

- **At least 10 gigs of free hard drive space** on your built-in hard drive, or a second internal drive. (You can't install Windows on an external drive using Boot Camp.)

- **A wired keyboard and mouse** for the installation process. You can use a Bluetooth keyboard and mouse once the installation is complete.

Then you're ready to proceed.

Installing Boot Camp

Open your Applications→Utilities folder. Inside, open the program called Boot Camp Assistant.

Phase 1: Prepare the drivers disk

On the Introduction screen, you can print the instruction booklet, if you like (although the following pages contain the essential info). There's a lot of good, conservative legalese in that booklet: the importance of backing up your whole Mac before you begin, for example.

One of Boot Camp's primary jobs is to teach Windows to recognize and operate all your Mac's hardware components: keyboard, trackpad, camera, WiFi, and so on. And as you may know, Windows does that by requiring an installed *driver* (software nugget) for each one of these components. Well, guess what? Out of the box, Windows does not know about any Apple hardware elements. Surprise, surprise.

So your first job is to create an installation disk that contains these drivers. It can be a blank CD or DVD, or some kind of external disk (a flash drive or hard drive) that's been formatted in a way that Windows understands. (The USB flash drive option is especially handy if you have a MacBook Air, which doesn't have a DVD drive.)

Note: The required format for the external drive is called MS-DOS (FAT). If you decide to use a flash drive or a hard drive as your drivers-installation disk, first use Disk Utility (page 610) to format it in MS-DOS (FAT) format. Otherwise, this driver-installation business won't work.

All right, then. Open the Boot Camp Assistant program (in your Applications→Utilities folder). Click Continue.

Next, on the Download Windows Support Software page, click "Download the Windows support software for this Mac," and then click Continue. (Enter an administrator's password when you're asked.)

Note: Select the other option, "I have already downloaded the Windows support software," only if you've already been through this procedure, keeping in mind that you can use an existing drivers disc only on an *identical Mac model.*

Once the drivers have been downloaded—it's a big chunk; it'll take awhile—your Mac asks how you're going to create an installer disk. Your choices are "Burn a copy to CD or DVD," or "Save a copy to an external drive." (This is the disk you prepared in FAT format earlier.) Click the option you want, and then click Continue.

When that's all over, you get the dialog box shown in Figure 8-1—the most interesting part of the whole process.

Phase 2: Partition your drive

You're being asked to *partition*—subdivide—your hard drive, setting aside a certain amount of space that will hold your copy of Windows and all the PC software you decide to install. This partitioning process doesn't involve erasing your whole hard drive; all your stuff is perfectly safe. (You can't install Boot Camp if your hard drive is already partitioned—except for Lion's own Recovery partition, of course.)

The dialog box offers a Divide Equally button, but it also lets you drag a space-divider handle to divide up your drive space between the Mac and Windows sides (Figure 8-1). Use your experience using Windows on a real PC to decide how big your Windows "hard drive" should be.

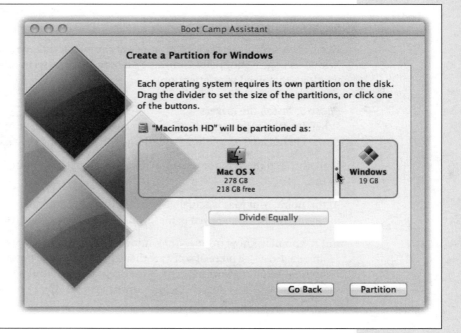

Figure 8-1:
How much hard drive space do you want to dedicate to your "PC"? It's not an idle question; whatever you give Windows is no longer available for your Mac. Drag the vertical handle between the Mac and Windows sides of this diagram.

Boot Camp Assistant

Create a Partition for Windows

Each operating system requires its own partition on the disk. Drag the divider to set the size of the partitions, or click one of the buttons.

"Macintosh HD" will be partitioned as:

Mac OS X
278 GB
218 GB free

Windows
19 GB

Divide Equally

Go Back   Partition

Most people choose to dedicate a swath of the main internal hard drive to the Windows partition. But if you have a second internal hard drive, you can also choose one of these options:

- **Create a Second Partition.** The Boot Camp Assistant carves out a Windows partition from *that* drive.

- **Erase Disk and Create a Single Partition for Windows.** Just what it says.

Phase 3: Install Windows

On the Start Windows Installation screen, you're supposed to—hey!—start the Windows installation. Grab your Windows 7 DVD and slip it into the Mac. Its installer goes to work immediately.

Following the "I agree to whatever Microsoft's lawyers say" screen, Microsoft's installer asks which partition you want to put Windows on. It's *really* important to pick the right one. Play your cards wrong, and you could erase your whole *Mac* partition.

Choose the one called "Disk 0 Partition 3 BOOTCAMP." (The number may be different, but it will say "BOOTCAMP.")

Then click "Drive options (advanced)," click Format, click OK, and finally click Next. Your Windows partition is now formatted (it uses the NTFS formatting scheme, if anybody asks).

Now your Mac looks just like a PC that's having Windows installed. Be patient; sit around for half an hour as the Windows installer flits about, restarts, does what it has to do.

Don't click any Cancel buttons. If you get a complaint that the software hasn't passed Windows Logo testing, click Continue Anyway. If things seem to stall, look for hidden windows that need your attention.

Phase 4: Install the drivers

When it's all over, a crazy, disorienting sight presents itself: your Mac, running Windows. There's no trace of the Mac desktop, Dock, or menu; it's Windows now, baby.

Walk through the Windows setup screens, creating an account, setting the time, and so on.

At this point, your Mac is actually a true Windows PC. You can install and run Windows programs, utilities, and even games; you'll discover that they run *really* fast and well.

But as you may know from your Windows days, every hardware feature of Windows requires a *driver*—a piece of software that tells the machine how to communicate with its own monitor, networking card, speakers, and so on. And it probably goes without saying that Windows doesn't include any drivers for *Apple's* hardware components.

That's why, at this point, you need the disc or flash drive you created in Phase 1. It contains all the drivers for the Mac's graphics card, Ethernet and WiFi networking, audio input and output, built-in camera, brightness and volume keys, eject key, multi-touch trackpad gestures, and Bluetooth transmitter. (It also installs a new Control Panel icon and system-tray pop-up menu, as described later in this chapter.)

When you insert this disc or flash drive, the driver installer opens and begins work automatically. (If it doesn't, double-click the *setup.exe* file in the WindowsSupport or Boot Camp folder.)

Click past the Welcome and License Agreement screens, and then click Install. You'll see a lot of dialog boxes come and go; just leave it alone (and don't click Cancel).

Tip: If the installation seems to stall, Windows may be waiting for you to click OK or Next in a window that's hidden behind other windows. Inspect the taskbar and look behind open windows.

When it's all over, a dialog box asks you to restart the computer; click Restart. When the machine comes to, it's a much more functional Windows Mac. (And it has an online Boot Camp Help window waiting for you on the screen.)

Note: Once you're running Windows, you might wonder: How am I supposed to right-click? I don't have a two-button mouse or two-button trackpad!

Yes, you do. See page 524 for a panoply of options.

Forth and Back, Windows/Mac

From now on, your main interaction with Boot Camp will be telling it what kind of computer you want your Mac to be today: a Windows machine or a Mac.

Presumably, though, you'll prefer one operating system *most* of the time. Figure 8-2 (top and middle) shows how you specify your favorite.

Tip: If you're running Windows and you just want to get back to Mac OS X right now, you don't have to bother with all the steps shown in Figure 8-2. Instead, click the Boot Camp system-tray icon and, from the shortcut menu, choose Restart in Mac OS X.

From now on, each time you turn on the Mac, it starts up in the operating system you've selected.

If you ever need to switch—when you need Windows just for one quick job, for example—press the Option key as the Mac is starting up. You'll see something like the icons shown in Figure 8-2 (bottom).

Keyboard Translation Guide

Now, if you really want to learn about Windows, you need *Windows 7: The Missing Manual.*

Figure 8-2:
Top: To choose your preferred operating system—the one that starts up automatically unless you intervene—choose ⌘→*System Preferences. Click Startup Disk, and then click the icon for either Mac OS X or Windows. Next, either click Restart (if you want to switch right now) or close the panel. The identical controls are available when you're running Windows, thanks to the new Boot Camp Control Panel.*

Middle: To open the Boot Camp control panel, choose its name from its icon in the Windows system tray.

Bottom: This display, known as the Startup Manager, appears when you press Option during startup. It displays all the disk icons, or disk partitions, that contain bootable operating systems. Just click the name of the partition you want, and then click the Continue arrow.

But suggesting that you go buy *another* book would be tacky. So here's just enough to get by.

First of all, a Mac keyboard and a Windows keyboard aren't the same. Each has keys that would strike the other as extremely goofy. Still, you can trigger almost any keystroke Windows is expecting by substituting special Apple-keystrokes, like this:

Windows keystroke	Apple keystroke
Ctrl+Alt+Delete	Control-Option-Delete
Alt	Option
⊞ key	⌘
Backspace	Delete
Delete (forward delete)	⌦ (on laptops, Fn-Delete)
Enter	Return or Enter
Num lock	Clear (laptops; Fn-F6)
Print Screen	F14 (laptops: Fn-F11)
Print active window	Option-F14 (laptops: Option-Fn-F11)

The keyboard shortcuts in your programs are *mostly* the same as on the Mac, but you have to substitute the Ctrl key for the ⌘ key. So in Windows programs, Copy, Save, and Print are Ctrl+C, Ctrl+S, and Ctrl+P.

Similarly, the Alt key is the Windows equivalent of the Option key.

Tip: You know that awesome two-finger scrolling trick on Mac laptops? It works when you're running Windows, too.

Accessing Mac Files from Windows—and Vice Versa

When you've started up in one operating system, it's easy to access documents that "belong" to the other one. For example:

- When you're running Mac OS X, you can get to the documents you created while you were running Windows, which is a huge convenience. Just double-click the Windows disk icon (called NO NAME or Untitled), and then navigate to the Documents and Settings→[your account name]→My Documents (or Desktop).

  You can only copy files *to* the Mac side, or open them without the ability to edit them.

Tip: You can rename the Windows disk, if you want, so it doesn't say NONAME the rest of its life—as long as you do it while you're running Windows.

- When you're running Windows, you can get to your Mac documents, too. Click Start→Computer. In the resulting window, you'll see an icon representing your Mac's hard drive partition. Open it up.

  You can see and open these files. But if you want to edit them, you have to copy them to your Windows world first—onto the desktop, for example, or into a folder.

(The Mac partition is "read-only" in this way, Apple says, to avoid the possibility that your Mac stuff could get contaminated by Windows viruses.)

> **Tip:** If you did want to edit Mac files from within Windows, one solution is to buy a $50 program called MacDrive (*www.mediafour.com*). Another solution: Use a disk that both Mac OS X and Windows "see," and keep your shared files on *that*. A flash drive works beautifully for this. So does a shared drive on the network.

Windows in a Window

The problem with Boot Camp is that every time you switch to or from Windows, you have to close down everything you were working on and restart the computer—and reverse the process when you're done. You lose 2 or 3 minutes each way. And you can't copy and paste between Mac and Windows programs.

There is another way: an $80 utility called Parallels Desktop for Mac (*www.parallels.com*), and its rival, VMware Fusion (*www.vmware.com*). These programs let you run Windows and Mac OS X *simultaneously;* Windows hangs out in a window of its own, while the Mac is running Mac OS X (Figure 8-3). You're getting about 90 percent of Boot Camp's Windows speed—not fast enough for 3-D games, but plenty fast for just about everything else.

UP TO SPEED

Removing Windows

Maybe you're a switcher who held onto Windows because you were worried that you'd need it. Maybe you're finished with the project, the job, or the phase of life that required you to use Windows on your Mac. But one way or another, there may come a time when you want to get rid of your Windows installation and reclaim all the hard drive space it was using.

You can, and better yet, the process doesn't touch anything that's already on the Mac side. You don't have to erase your entire hard drive or anything—Mac OS X simply erases what's on the Windows partition of your hard drive, and then adds that disk space back to your main, *Mac* partition.

To do this, start by making sure you've rescued anything worth saving from the Windows side of your computer—it's about to be erased.

Start up in Mac OS X, quit all open programs, and make sure nobody's logged in but you. Now open up the Boot Camp Assistant program in your Applications→Utilities folder.

On the Select Task screen, click "Create or remove a Windows partition." On the next screen, you're warned: "The Windows volume and all of its contents will be permanently lost." But you knew that. Click Restore.

That's all there is to it.

Special notes for special setups: If you installed Windows on a separate hard drive, rather than a partition of your main hard drive, don't bother with all this. Just erase the Windows hard drive using Disk Utility, as described on page 611, and format it as a Mac drive.

On the other hand, if your Mac has more than one internal hard drive and you created a Windows partition on one of them (rather than taking it over completely), then open Boot Camp Assistant as described above. Click the partition with Windows on it, and then click "Restore to a single Mac OS partition." Then click Continue.

Once again, you have to supply your own copy of Windows for the installation process. This time, though, it can be any version of Windows, all the way back to Windows 3.1—or even Linux, FreeBSD, Solaris, OS/2, or MS-DOS.

Having virtualization software on your Mac is a beautiful thing. You can be working on a design in iWork, duck into a Microsoft Access database (Windows only), look up an address, copy it, and paste it back into the Mac program.

And what if you can't decide whether to use Boot Camp (fast and feature-complete, but requires restarting) or Parallels/Fusion (fast and no restarting, but no 3-D games)? No problem—install both. They coexist beautifully on a single Mac and can even use the same copy of Windows.

Together, they turn the Macintosh into the Uni-Computer: the single machine that can run nearly 100 percent of the world's software catalog.

Virtualization Tip-o-Rama

Mastering Parallels or Fusion means mastering Windows, of course, but it also means mastering these tips:

Figure 8-3:
The strangest sight you ever did see: Mac OS X and Windows XP. On the same screen. At the same time. Courtesy of VMware Fusion. Parallels is very similar.

- You don't *have* to run Windows in a window. With one keystroke, you can make your Windows simulator cover the entire screen. You're still actually running two operating systems at once, but the whole Mac world is hidden for the moment so you can exploit your full screen. Just choose View→Full Screen.

Tip: Or use the keystroke Control-⌘-F (Parallels) or Control-⌘-Return (Fusion) to enter and exit Full Screen mode. (These keystrokes tend to change from version to version. You've been warned.)

- Conversely, both Parallels and Fusion offer something called *Coherence* or *Unity* mode, in which there's no trace of the Windows desktop. Instead, each Windows program floats in its own disembodied window, just like a Mac program; the Mac OS X desktop lies in the background.

Tip: In Fusion's Unity mode and Parallels' Coherence mode, you can access your Computer, Documents, Network, Control Panel, Search, and Run commands right from Fusion's or Parallels' Dock icon or launch palette, so you won't even care that there's no Start menu.

In Parallels, press Control-⌘-Enter to enter or exit Coherence mode. In Fusion, hit Control-⌘-U for Unity mode.

Tip: In Fusion, in Unity mode, you can use the usual Mac keystrokes for Cut, Copy, and Paste within Windows applications (⌘-X, ⌘-C, and ⌘-V). In Parallels, on the other hand, you can remap *all* Windows Ctrl-key shortcuts to the ⌘ key in Preferences.

- To send the "three-fingered salute" when things have locked up in Windows (usually Ctrl+Alt+Delete), press Control-Option-Delete (Fusion) or Control-Fn-Alt-Delete (Parallels). Or use the Send Control-Alt-Delete command in the menus.

- You can drag files back and forth between the Mac and Windows universes. Just drag icons into, or out of, the Windows window.

- If you have a one-button mouse, you can "right-click" in Parallels by Control-Shift-clicking. In Fusion, Control-click instead. On Mac laptops, you can right-click by putting two fingers on the trackpad as you click.

- When you quit the virtualization program, you're not really shutting down the PC; you're just *suspending* it, or putting it to sleep. When you double-click the Parallels/VMware icon again, everything in your Windows world is exactly as you left it.

POWER USERS' CLINIC

Beyond the Big Names

Parallels and VMware Fusion are bloodthirsty rivals. New versions tumble out with alarming frequency, each designed to one-up the competitor's.

Both also let you specify which program—Mac or Windows—opens when you double-click documents of specific types (like .jpeg or .doc). That's yet another way Windows becomes a full player on the Mac team.

Still, these aren't the only options. Several efforts are afoot to create software that lets you run Windows software without Windows. The most promising one is a $60 program called CrossOver Impersonator (*www.codeweavers.com*). It's a commercialized version of Wine, a Unix-based Windows simulator.

Sure enough, CrossOver-compatible Windows programs open up and run in Mac OS X just as though they were real Mac programs—without your having to own, install, or fire up a copy of Windows itself.

Unfortunately, the list of compatible programs is tiny. The CrossOver Web site lists over 9,000 Windows apps that work, but only about 1,000 of them work perfectly. Still, you owe it to yourself to check the list to see if what you need is CrossOver-friendly.

- Your entire Windows universe of files, folders, and programs is represented by a single file on your hard drive. In Parallels, it's in your Home→Documents→Parallels folder. In Fusion, it's in your Home→Documents→Virtual Machines folder.

That's super convenient, because it means you can back up your entire Windows "computer" by dragging a single icon to another drive. And if your Windows world ever gets a virus or spyware infestation, you can drag the entire thing to the Trash—and restore Windows from that clean backup.

Windows via OnLive Desktop

Parallels and VMWare are useful and powerful, all right. But they're memory hogs, disk-space pigs, and sluggish to start up and shut down.

On the horizon, however, there's a newer Windows-on-Mac alternative that spares you the disk, memory, and speed penalties. It's called OnLive Desktop (*www.onlive.com*).

It's a Mac app. When you open it, you see a standard Windows 7 desktop, right there on your Mac. The full, latest versions of Word, Excel, PowerPoint, Internet Explorer and Adobe Reader are set up and ready to use: no installation, no serial numbers, no pop-up balloons nagging you to update this or that. It may be the least annoying version of Windows you've ever used.

The PC that's driving your Mac Windows experience is, in fact, a "farm" of computers at one of three data centers thousands of miles away. Every time you click your mouse or press a key, you're sending signals to those distant computers. The screen image is blasted back to your Mac with astonishingly little lag.

OnLive offers various plans with various features. It's free to use Word, Excel, and PowerPoint. For $10 a month, the company says that you'll be able to use whatever Windows software you want.

At this writing, the Mac version of OnLive is still in the works—the iPad version works beautifully. Once it's available, hold onto your hat: You'll have a super fast, virus-free, always-updated Windows world available to your Mac whenever you need it.

Life with Microsoft Exchange

In the corporate world, Microsoft Exchange is the 800-pound gorilla. It's the networking software that runs the email, address book, and calendars for hundreds or thousands of employees. All of this communicates with a central master database whose heart beats away in some closet or back room at your company's headquarters.

For years, Macs have been second-class citizens in Corporate America. As long as they couldn't talk to the Exchange brain, they weren't much use outside the graphic-design department. (You could buy add-on software or muck with workarounds, but you always felt like a weirdo.)

Now, however, Exchange compatibility is built in. In iCal, your company's Exchange calendar shows up. In Address Book, your company's names and addresses show up.

In Mail, you can get all your corporate email. Best of all, this information shows up side by side with your own personal data, so you can have it all in one place. All the conveniences of Mac OS X now apply to your corporate email: Spotlight, Quick Look, data detectors, and so on.

If you're lucky—that is, if your company is using Exchange 2007 or later (Service Pack 1, Update Rollup 4 and later)—setting this up could not be easier.

Connecting to Exchange

To connect to your company's Exchange system, open Mail (Chapter 12). Choose Mail→Preferences. Click the **+** below the list of email accounts; proceed as shown in Figure 8-4.

Note: You can also set up your Exchange information in the new System Preferences→Mail, Contacts & Calendars pane. Just click the big Microsoft Exchange button to begin.

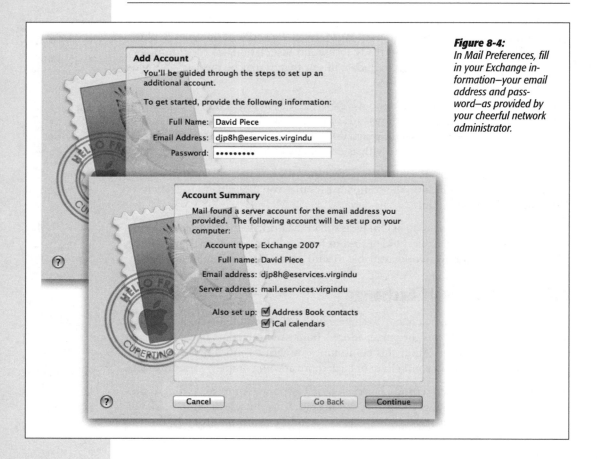

Figure 8-4:
In Mail Preferences, fill in your Exchange information—your email address and password—as provided by your cheerful network administrator.

When you click Continue, one of two things happens:

- You're treated to a message that says, "Mail found a server account for the email address you provided. The following account will be set up on your computer." You're all set.

   That box offers an "Also set up" item, featuring two delicious checkboxes: "Address Book contacts" and "iCal calendars." Hard to think why you'd want to turn these off; they'll do all the work for you.

- Your Mac doesn't find the server. In that case, either (a) your company doesn't use Exchange 2007 or later, or (b) your network geek hasn't turned on Exchange Autodiscover. In that case, you have no choice but to call that person over to your desk and either (a) harangue him for not turning on Autodiscover, or (b) have him fill in the server address and other boxes by hand.

Exchange in Mail

Once everything is set up, open Mail. If you have a lot of mail, it may take a moment (or several) for Mail to synchronize with the Exchange server and display your messages. But it gets there eventually.

Your Exchange account appears with its own heading, beneath your personal accounts (Figure 8-5).

Figure 8-5:
Once everything is hooked up, a new heading appears in Mail (left), iCal (middle), and Address Book (right), named after your Exchange account. That's your corporate life, which you can hide and show at will.

Now you can send and receive email, create notes and to-do items, respond to emailed invitations, and so on. All the Mail features described in Chapter 12 are ready to go: Spotlight can search all your accounts simultaneously, Smart Folders can round up messages from one account or all of them, Quick Look can show you attachments without your having to open them in a separate program, and so on.

Exchange in iCal

Your corporate appointments now show up in the Mac's calendar program (Chapter 16), neatly filed under their own heading in the Calendars list (Figure 8-5, middle). Each appointment category shows up with its own checkbox, as usual, so you can hide and show them as you see fit—even when they're mixed right in with your personal agenda.

The big payoff here is scheduling meetings. When you click "Invite to an appointment, iCal can show you a graph of your coworkers' free time, and open slots for your conference room, so you can find a time when they're free.

Exchange in Address Book

Your company's Global Address Lists show up in Address Book as a group on the Groups page (choose View→Groups, or click the two-silhouette bookmark), as shown at right in Figure 8-5. You can work with your contacts on the server just as you would with your own addresses: Put them in groups, click an address to see where it is in Google Maps, and so on. When you're addressing an email message or a calendar invitation, the autocomplete feature now proposes names from both your personal and corporate address books.

Hardware on the Mac

M ost of the discussion in this book so far has covered *software*—not only the Mac OS X operating system that may be new to you, but also the programs and documents you'll be using on it. But there's more to life with a computer than software. This chapter covers the finer points of using Macintosh-compatible printers, cameras, disks, monitors, and keyboards.

Printers and Printing

Printing has always been one of the Mac's strong suits—and you're about to find out why.

Setting Up a Printer

1. **Connect the printer to the Mac, and then turn the printer on.**

   Inkjet printers connect to your USB jack. Laser printers hook up either to your USB jack or to your network (Ethernet or wireless).

2. **Open the document you want to print. Choose File→Print. In the Print dialog box, choose your printer's name from the Printer pop-up menu (or one of its submenus, if any, like Nearby Printers). See Figure 9-1.**

   Cool! Wasn't that easy? Very nice how the Mac autodiscovers, autoconfigures, and autolists almost any USB, FireWire, Bluetooth, or Bonjour printer.

   Have a nice afternoon. The End.

   Oh—unless your printer *isn't* listed in the Printer pop-up menu. In that case, read on.

Note: "Nearby Printers" refers to printers that aren't connected directly to your Mac, but are accessible anyway: a printer connected to an Apple Time Capsule or an AirPort base station, certain network printers that speak Bonjour, or printers connected to other Macs that you've shared, as described later in this chapter.

3. **From the Printer pop-up menu (Figure 9-1, top), choose Add Printer.**

   A special setup window opens (Figure 9-1, bottom), which is even better at auto-detecting printers available to your Mac. If you see the printer's name here, click it and then click Add (Figure 9-1, bottom).

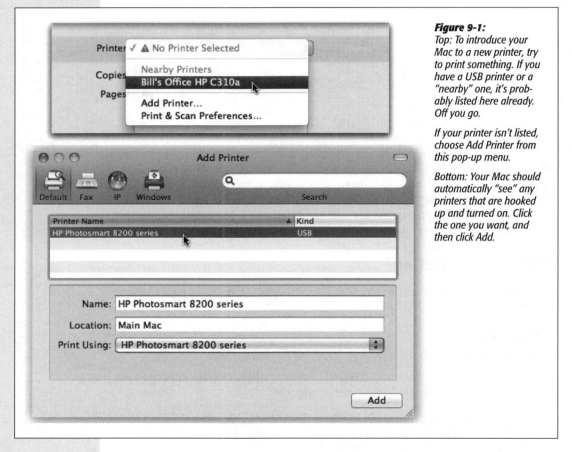

Figure 9-1:
Top: To introduce your Mac to a new printer, try to print something. If you have a USB printer or a "nearby" one, it's probably listed here already. Off you go.

If your printer isn't listed, choose Add Printer from this pop-up menu.

Bottom: Your Mac should automatically "see" any printers that are hooked up and turned on. Click the one you want, and then click Add.

You're all set. Have a good time.

Unless, of course, your printer *still* isn't showing up. Proceed to step 4.

4. **Click the icon for the *kind* of printer you have: Default, IP, or Windows.**

   Default usually does the trick, especially if you have an inkjet printer. Choose IP if you have a network printer that's not showing up in Default—especially if you have an old AppleTalk printer. And choose Windows if there's a Windows-only printer out there on your office network.

After a moment, the names of any printers that are turned on and connected appear in the printer list. For most people, that means only one printer—but one is enough.

5. **Click the name of the printer you want to use.**

As an optional step, you can open the Print Using pop-up menu at the bottom of the dialog box. Choose "Select a driver to use," and then, in the list that appears, choose your particular printer's model name, if you can find it. That's how your Mac knows what printing features to offer you when the time comes: double-sided, legal size, second paper tray, and so on.

6. **Click Add.**

After a moment, you return to the main Printer Browser window (Figure 9-1, top), where your printer now appears. You're ready to print.

Note: If you still don't see your printer's name show up, ask yourself: Is my Mac on a corporate network? Does the network have an LPR (Line Printer Remote) printer? If you and your company's network nerd determine that the printer you want to use is, in fact, an LPR printer, then click IP Printing at the top of the Printer Browser dialog box. Fill in the appropriate IP address and other settings, as directed by your cheerful network administrator.

Printer Preferences

If you're lucky enough to own several printers, repeat the steps above for each one. Eventually, you'll have introduced the Mac to all the printers available to it, so all their names show up in the printer list.

To see the printer list so far, open System Preferences→Print & Scan. You can have all kinds of fun here (Figure 9-2):

- **Choose a default printer.** As indicated by the Default Printer pop-up menu, Mac OS X intends, conveniently enough, to use whichever printer you used for the last printout for the next one. Most people, after all, don't switch printers much.

  Still, you can choose one particular printer from this pop-up menu to set it as the default printer—the one the Mac uses unless you intervene by choosing from the Printer pop-up menu in the Print dialog box (Figure 9-1).

- **Create desktop printer icons.** *This* handy, little-known feature gives you drag-and-drop access to your printers.

  From the Print & Scan pane of System Preferences, just drag a printer's icon out of the window and onto the desktop (or wherever you like). Repeat for your other printers. From now on, you can print a document on a certain printer just by dragging the document's icon onto the appropriate printer icon.

- **Check the ink level.** Click a printer, and then click Options & Supplies, to see how your inkjet ink or laser-printer toner level is. That way, you won't be caught short when you're on a deadline and your printer is out of ink. You now get a bright yellow "low ink" warning in the dialog box that appears when you print.

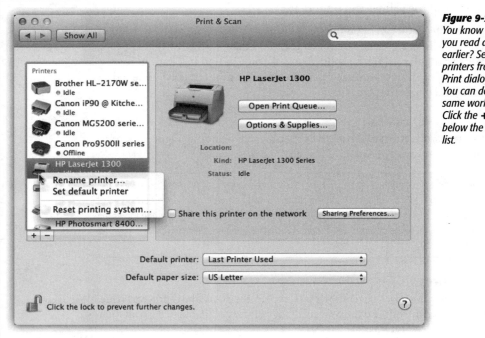

Figure 9-2:
You know that stuff you read about earlier? Setting up printers from the Print dialog box? You can do the same work here. Click the + button below the left-side list.

Making the Printout

You can't miss the Print dialog box. It appears, like it or not, whenever you choose File→Print in one of your programs.

The options you encounter depend on the printer you're using. They also depend on whether or not you *expand* the dialog box by clicking the Show Details button. That reveals a *lot* of useful options, including a handy preview; see Figure 9-3.

If you expand the box, the options you find vary by printer. But here are the common options:

- **Printer.** If you have more than one printer connected to your Mac, you can indicate which you want to use for a particular printout by choosing its name from this pop-up menu.

- **Presets.** Here's a way to preserve your favorite print settings: Once you've proceeded through this dialog box, specifying the number of copies, which printer trays you want the paper taken from, and so on, you can choose Save As from the pop-up menu, and then assign your settings set a name (like "Borderless, 2 copies"). Thereafter, you'll be able to recreate that elaborate suite of settings simply by choosing its name from this pop-up menu.

• **Copies.** Type the number of copies you want printed. The Collated checkbox

Figure 9-3:
Bottom: Most of the time, all you want is one darned copy of what's on your screen. So the standard Print dialog box is spartan indeed: You get a preview that you can page through; page controls; and a Print button.

Top: But when you expand the box by clicking Show Details, you get a new world of options. You can specify which orientation you want for the printout, how much you want it reduced or magnified, and so on. On the Layout pane, you can save paper by choosing a higher number from the Pages per Sheet pop-up menu.

controls the printing order for the various pages. For example, if you print two copies of a three-page document, the Mac generally prints the pages in this order: 1, 2, 3, 1, 2, 3. If you turn off Collated, on the other hand, it prints in this order: 1, 1, 2, 2, 3, 3.

- **Pages.** You don't have to print an entire document—you can print, say, only pages 2 through 15.

Tip: You don't have to type numbers into both the From and To boxes. If you leave the first box blank, the Mac assumes that you mean "from page 1." If you leave the second box blank, the Mac understands that you mean "to the end." To print only the first three pages, in other words, leave the first box blank and type 3 into the second box. (These page numbers refer to the physical pages you're printing, not to any fancy numbering you've set up in your word processor. As far as the Print dialog box is concerned, the first printed page is page 1, even if you've told your word processor to label it page 455.)

- **Paper Size, Orientation.** Somebody at Apple finally realized how frustrating it was to have to open the Page Setup dialog box to change the paper-size and orientation settings, and then open the Print dialog box for other settings. Now, in most programs, these controls are duplicated right in the Print dialog box for your convenience.

- **PDF.** A *PDF* file, of course, is an Adobe Reader (Acrobat) document—a file that any Mac, Windows, Linux, or Unix user can view, read, and print using either Preview or the free Adobe Reader (included with every PC and Mac operating system).

  You can easily save any document as a PDF file instead of printing it—a truly beautiful feature that saves paper, ink, and time. The document remains on your hard drive, and the text inside is even searchable using Spotlight.

  And that's just the beginning. Apple has added a long list of additional PDF options (like password-protected PDFs, emailed ones, and so on). But Apple faced a design quandary: How could it offer a new list of PDF-related options without junking up the Print dialog box?

  Its solution was a strange little item called a pop-up *button,* shown in Figure 9-3, bottom. Use it like a pop-up menu. The command you'll use most often is probably Save as PDF, which turns the printout into a PDF file instead of sending it to the printer. For details on the other PDF-related options here, see page 271.

If you examine the unnamed pop-up menu just below the Presets pop-up menu, you'll find dozens of additional options. They depend on your printer model and the program you're using at the moment, but here are some typical choices:

- **Layout.** As described in Figure 9-3, you can save paper and ink or toner cartridges by printing several miniature "pages" on a single sheet of paper.

- **Paper Handling.** You can opt to print your pages in reverse order so that they stack correctly, or you can print just odd or even pages so that you can run them through again for double-sided printing.

- **Paper Feed.** If you chose the correct printer model when setting up your printer, then this screen "knows about" your printer's various paper trays. Here's where you specify which pages you want to come from which paper tray. (By far the most popular use for this feature is printing the first page of a letter on company letterhead, and the following pages on blank paper from a second tray.)

- **Cover Page.** Yes, that throwaway info page has made its way from the fax world into the hard-copy world.

- **Scheduler.** This option lets you specify *when* you want your document to print. If you're a freelancer, sitting at home with an inkjet on your desk, you might not immediately grasp why anyone wouldn't want the printouts *right now.* But try printing a 400-page catalog in a big office where other people on the network might conceivably resent you for tying up the laser printer all afternoon, and you'll get the idea.

- **ColorSync.** Most color printers offer this panel, where you can adjust the color settings—to add a little more red, perhaps. This is also where you indicate whose *color-matching system* you want to use: Apple's ColorSync, your printer manufacturer's, or none at all.

Then, below the light-gray line in this pop-up menu, you'll find a few options that are unique to the chosen printer or program. Some HP printers, for example, offer Cover Page, Finishing, and other choices. Other likely guest commands:

- **Quality & Media** (inkjet printers only). Here's where you specify the print quality you want, the kind of paper you're printing on, and so on. (The name of this panel varies by manufacturer.)

- **[Program Name].** Whichever program you're using—Mail, Word, Pages, or anything else—may offer its own special printing options on this screen.

- **Summary.** This command summons a text summary of all your settings so far.

Tip: Here's one for the technically inclined. Open your Web browser and enter this address: *http://127.0.0.1:631.* You find yourself at a secret "front end" for CUPS (Common Unix Printing System), the underlying printing technology for Mac OS X. This trick lets your Mac communicate with a huge array of older printers that don't yet have Mac OS X drivers. Using this administration screen, you can print a test page, stop your printer in its tracks, manage your networked printers and print jobs, and more—a very slick trick.

Printing

When all your settings look good, click Print (or press Return) to send your document to the printer.

Managing Printouts

After you've used the Print command, you can either sit there until the paper emerges from the printer, or you can *manage* the printouts-in-waiting. That option is attractive primarily to people who do a lot of printing, have connections to a lot of printers, or share printers with many other people.

Start by opening the printer's window. If you're already in the process of printing, just click the printer's Dock icon. If not, open →System Preferences→Print & Scan, click the printer's name, and then click Open Print Queue.

At this point, you see something like Figure 9-4: The printouts that will soon be sliding out of your printer appear in a tidy list.

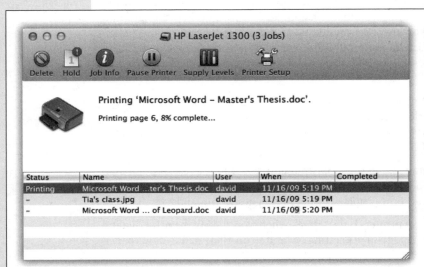

Figure 9-4:
Waiting printouts appear in this window. You can sort the list by clicking the column headings (Name or Status), make the columns wider or narrower by dragging the column-heading dividers horizontally, or reverse the sorting order by clicking the column name a second time. The Supply Level button opens a graph that shows how much ink each cartridge has remaining (certain printer models only).

Here are some of the ways in which you can control these waiting printouts, which Apple collectively calls the *print queue:*

- **Delete them.** By clicking an icon, or ⌘-clicking several, and then clicking the Delete toolbar button, you remove items from the list. Now they won't print.

- **Pause them.** By highlighting a printout and then clicking the Hold button, you pause that printout. It doesn't print out until you highlight it again and then click the Resume button. (Other documents continue to print.) This pausing business could be useful when, for example, you need time to check or refill the printer, or when you're just about to print your letter of resignation as your boss drops by. (Maybe to offer you a promotion.)

- **Halt them all.** You can stop all printouts from a printer by clicking Pause Printer. (They resume when you click the button again, which now says Resume Printer.)

You can't rearrange printouts by dragging them in the queue list. But remember that you can resequence the printing order by choosing the Scheduler option; you can also drag waiting printouts *between* these lists, shifting them from one printer to another.

Tip: As you now know, the icon for a printer's queue window appears automatically in the Dock when you print. But it also *stays* in the Dock for the rest of the day; it doesn't disappear when the printing is complete.

If you wish it would, Control-click (or right-click) the printer's Dock icon; from the shortcut menu, choose Auto Quit.

Printer Sharing

Printer sharing is for people (or offices) with more than one Mac, connected to a network, who'd rather not buy a separate printer for each machine. Instead, you connect the printer to one Mac, flip a couple of software switches, and then boom: The other Macs on the network can send their printouts to the printer without actually being attached to it—even wirelessly, if they're on an AirPort network.

Note: Of course, this feature is most useful when you're sharing printers that can hook up to only one Mac at a time, like USB inkjet photo printers. Office laser printers are often designed to be networked from Day One.

Setting up printer sharing is easy; see Figure 9-5, top. Then, to make a printout from across the network, see the instructions in Figure 9-5, bottom.

Tip: You can control *which* account holders on your network are allowed to use the printer you've shared. You know that idiot in Accounting who's always using up your cartridges by printing 200-page documents? Cut that sucker off! Just add the lucky guests' names to the Users column in System Preferences→Sharing→Printer Sharing, as shown in Figure 9-5.

Figure 9-5:
Top: On the Mac with the printer, open the Sharing panel of System Preferences. Turn on Printer Sharing, and then turn on the checkboxes for the printers you want to share. Switch to the Print & Scan pane, and turn on "Share this printer on the network" for the printer(s) you want to share.

Bottom: To use a shared printer elsewhere on the network, open the document you want to print, and then choose File→Print. In the Print dialog box, the shared printer is clearly identified under the Nearby Printers heading.

If you install Bonjour for Windows (a free download from this book's "Missing CD" page at *www.missingmanuals.com*) onto your old PC, you can even print to your Mac's shared printer from it, too.

Tip: Of course, your Mac (the one attached to the printer) must be turned on in order for the other computers to print. In part, that's because the documents-in-waiting from other people pile up on *your* hard drive.

Faxing

Apple giveth, and Apple taketh away. And in Lion, Apple hath taken out faxing.

Apple has never been afraid to abandon technologies that strike it as obsolete, and faxing is no different. Heck, Lion can't even fax if you own one of Apple's own USB fax modems.

If you still need to fax, you have a couple of options. First, you can sign up for a service like eFax or Faxaway, which let you send and receive faxes online; they come to you by email. Second, you're welcome to buy a non-Apple fax modem, some of which work fine in Lion. Whatever you buy comes with its own software and instructions.

PDF Files

As a PC veteran, you've probably run into PDF (portable document format) files already. Many a software manual, Read Me file, and downloadable "white paper" comes in this format. In Windows, you needed the free program called Acrobat Reader to open or print these files, and some not-free-at-all software program to *create* them.

PDF files, however, are one of Mac OS X's common forms of currency. In fact, you can turn *any document* (in any program with a Print command) into a PDF file—a trick that once required the $250 program called Adobe Acrobat Distiller.

Note: Mac OS X alone creates *screen-optimized* PDF files: compact, easy-to-email files that look good onscreen but don't have high enough resolution for professional printing. For high-end purposes and more optimization for specific uses (Web, fancy press machines, and so on), you still need a program like Adobe Acrobat, Illustrator, or InDesign.

But why would you want to create PDFs? What's the big deal about them? Consider these advantages:

- **Other people see your layout.** When you distribute PDF files to other people, they see precisely the same fonts, colors, page design, and other elements that you put in your original document. And here's the kicker: They get to see all of this even if they don't *have* the fonts or the software you used to create the document. (Contrast with the alternative. Say you're sending somebody a Microsoft Word document. If your correspondent doesn't have precisely the same fonts you have, then he'll see a screwy layout. And if he doesn't have Word or a program that can open Word files, he'll see nothing at all.)

- **It's universal.** PDF files are very common in the Macintosh, Windows, Unix/Linux, and even smartphone worlds. When you create a PDF file, you can distribute it (by email, for example) without worrying about what kinds of computers your correspondents are using.

- **It has very high resolution.** PDF files print at the maximum quality of any printer. A PDF file prints great both on cheapo inkjets and on high-quality image-setting gear at professional print shops. (Right now you're looking at a PDF file that was printed at a publishing plant.)

- **You can search it.** A PDF file may look like a captured graphic, but behind the scenes, its text is still text; Spotlight can find a PDF word in a haystack in a matter of seconds. That's an especially handy feature when you work with electronic software manuals in PDF format.

Opening PDF Files

There's nothing to opening up a PDF file: Just double-click it. Preview takes over from there and opens the PDF file on your screen. (Or highlight its icon in the Finder and tap the space bar for a Quick Look at it.)

Creating PDF Files

Opening, schmopening—what's really exciting in Mac OS X is the ability to create your *own* PDF files. The easiest way is to click the PDF pop-up button in the standard Print dialog box (Figure 9-6). When you click it, you're offered a world of interesting PDF-creation possibilities:

- **Open PDF in Preview** lets you convert whatever document you're on the verge of printing into a frozen PDF document that opens into Preview for your inspection. The point here is that you can have a look at it *before* you print it.

- **Save as PDF** saves your document to the disk as a PDF document instead of printing it.

Figure 9-6:
The PDF button is crawling with neat ways to process a document while it's still open–and you can add to this pop-up button's list, too. For example, you can create even more elaborate pathways for documents you want to print or convert to PDF using an Automator workflow, if you're handy with that sort of programming.

- **Save PDF as PostScript** gives you a PostScript file instead of a PDF. (PostScript is a format preferred by some designers and print shops. It consists of highly precise "what to draw" instructions for PostScript laser printers.)

- **Fax PDF** *faxes* a document instead of printing it, in the unlikely event that you have a Lion-compatible fax modem.

- **Save PDF to iTunes** converts the document into a PDF file and stores it in, of all places, iTunes. (Yes, iTunes can manage PDF documents.)

- **Mail PDF** generates a PDF file and then attaches it to an outgoing message in Mail. Great for exchanging layout-intensive documents with collaborators who don't have the same fonts, layout software, or taste as you.

- **Save PDF to Web Receipts Folder** is one of the simplest and sweetest features in all of Mac OS X.

  You use it when you've just ordered something on a Web site, and the "Print this receipt" screen is staring you in the face. Don't waste paper and ink (and, later, time trying to find it!). Instead, use this command. You get a perfectly usable PDF version, stored in your Home→Documents→Web Receipts folder, where you can use Spotlight to find it later, when you need to consult or print it because your gray-market goods never arrived.

Note: You may see other commands here, too, as you install other companies' software programs

---

Fonts—and Font Book

Mac OS X type is all smooth, all the time. Fonts in Mac OS X's formats—called TrueType, PostScript Type 1, and OpenType—always look smooth onscreen and in printouts, no matter what the point size.

Mac OS X also comes with a program that's *just* for installing, removing, inspecting, and organizing fonts. It's called Font Book (Figure 9-7), and it's in your Applications folder.

Where Fonts Live

Brace yourself. In Mac OS X, there are *three* Fonts folders. The fonts you actually see listed in the Fonts menus and Font panels of your programs are combinations of these Fonts folders' contents.

Here's a rundown:

- **Your private fonts (your Home folder→Library→Fonts).** This Fonts folder sits right inside your own Home folder. You're free to add your own custom fonts to this folder. Go wild—it's your font collection and yours alone. Nobody else who uses the Mac can use these fonts; they'll never even know that you have them.

Note: Your Home→Library folder is ordinarily hidden. The quickest way to see it is to press Option as you choose View→Library in the Finder.

- **Main font collection (Library→Fonts).** Any fonts in this folder are available to everyone to use in every program. (As with most features that affect everybody who shares your Macintosh, however, only people with Administrator accounts can change the contents of this folder.)

Figure 9-7:
Each account holder can have a separate set of fonts; your set is represented by the User icon. You can drag fonts and font families among the various Fonts folders represented here—from your User account folder to the Computer icon, for example, making them available to all account holders.

- **Essential system fonts (System→Library→Fonts).** This folder contains the 35 fonts that the Mac itself needs: the typefaces you see in your menus, dialog boxes, icons, and so on. You can open this folder to *see* these font suitcases, but you can't do anything with them, such as opening, moving, or adding to them. Remember that, for stability reasons, the System folder is sealed under glass forever. Only the *superuser* can touch these files (ask a Unix geek)—and even that person would be foolish to do so.

With the exception of the essential system fonts, you'll find an icon representing each of these locations in your Font Book program, described next.

Note: And just to make life even more exciting, Adobe's software installers may donate even *more* fonts to your cause, in yet *another* folder: your Home→Application Support folder.

Font Book: Installing and Managing Fonts

One of the biggest perks of Mac OS X is its preinstalled collection of over 50 great-looking fonts—"over $1,000 worth," according to Apple, which licensed many of them from type companies. In short, fewer Mac users than ever will wind up buying and installing new fonts.

But when you do buy or download new fonts, you're in luck. There's no limit to the number of fonts you can install.

Looking over your fonts

Right off the bat, Font Book is great for looking at samples of each typeface. For example, click Computer, click the first font name, and then press the ↓ key. As you walk down the list, the rightmost panel shows you a sample of each font (Figure 9-7).

You can also click any font family's flippy triangle (or highlight its name and then press →) to see the font *variations* it includes: Italic, Bold, and so on.

Tip: When you first open Font Book, the actual text of the typeface preview (in the right panel) is pretty generic. Don't miss the Preview menu, though. It lets you substitute a full display of every character (choose Repertoire)—or, if you choose Custom, it lets you type your *own* text.

Printing a reference sheet

You can print a handy, whole-font sampler of any font. Click its name and then choose File→Print. In the Print dialog box, click the Show Details button to expand the dialog box, if necessary. You can then use the Report Type pop-up menu to choose from three reference-sheet styles. When everything looks good, click Print.

Eliminating duplicates

A bullet (•) next to a font's name is Font Book's charming way of trying to tell you that you've got copies of the same font in more than one of your Fonts folders. You might have one version of Comic Sans in your own Home→Library→Fonts folder, for example, and another in your Mac's main Fonts folder.

Click the one you want to keep, and then choose Edit→Resolve Duplicates. Font Book turns off all *other* copies, and the bullet disappears.

Adding, removing, and hiding fonts

Here's what you can do with Font Book:

- **Install a font.** When you double-click a font file's icon in the Finder, Font Book opens and presents the typeface for your inspection pleasure. If you like it, click Install Font. You've just installed it into *your account's* Fonts folder so that it appears in the Font menus of all your programs. (If you'd rather install it so that it appears in *all* account holders' Fonts menus, see Figure 9-7.)

- **Remove a font.** Removing a font from your machine is easy: Highlight it in the Font Book list, and then press the Delete key. (You're asked to confirm the decision.)

Before taking such a drastic and permanent step, however, keep in mind that you can simply *disable* (hide) the font instead. Read on.

- **Disable a font.** When you disable a font, you're simply hiding it from your programs. You might want to turn off a font so that you can use a different version of it (bearing the same name but from a different type company, for example), or to make your Font menus shorter, or to make programs like Microsoft Word start up faster. You can always turn a disabled font back on if you ever need it again.

Tip: How's this for a sweet feature? Mac OS X can activate fonts *automatically* as you need them. When you open a document that relies on a font it doesn't have, Mac OS X activates that font and keeps it available until that particular program quits.

Actually, it does better than that. If it doesn't see that font installed, it *searches your hard drive* on a quest to find the font—and then it asks you if you want it installed, so the document will look right.

To disable a font, just click it or its family name, and then click the checkbox button beneath the list (or press Shift-⌘-D). Confirm your decision by clicking Disable in the confirmation box. (Turn on "Do not ask me again" if you're the confident sort.)

The font's name now appears gray, and the word "Off" appears next to it, making it absolutely clear what you've just done. (To turn the font on again, highlight its name, and then click the now-empty checkbox button, or press Shift-⌘-D again.)

Note: When you install, remove, disable, or enable a font using Font Book, you see the changes in the Font menus and panels of your *Cocoa* programs immediately. You won't see the changes in open Carbon programs, however, until you quit and reopen them.

Font collections

A *collection*, like any of the ones listed in the first Font Book column, is a subset of your installed fonts. Apple starts you off with collections called things like PDF (a set of standard fonts used in PDF files) and Web (fonts you're safe using on Web pages—that is, fonts that are very likely to be installed on the Macs or Windows PCs of your Web visitors).

But you can create collections called, for example, Headline or Sans Serif, organized by font type. Or you can create collections like Brochure or Movie Poster, organized by project. Then you can switch these groups of fonts on or off at will.

To create a new collection, click the leftmost **+** button to create a new entry in the Collections column, whose name you can edit. Then click one of the font storage locations—User or Computer—and drag fonts or font families onto your newly created collection icon. (Recognize this process from playlists in iTunes, or albums in iPhoto?) Each font can be in as many different collections as you want.

To remove a font from the collection, click its name, and then press Delete. You're not actually removing the font from your Mac, of course—only from the collection.

Font libraries

Don't get confused; a font *library* is not the same as a font *collection*.

A font library is a set of fonts *outside* Font Book that you can install or uninstall on the fly. They don't have to be in any of your Fonts folders; Font Book can install them from wherever they happen to be sitting on your hard drive (or even on the network). Font Book never copies or moves these font files as you install or remove them from libraries; it simply adds them to your Font menus by referencing them right where they sit.

Tip: That can be a handy arrangement if you periodically work on different projects for different clients. Why burden your day-to-day Font menu with the 37 fonts used by *Beekeeper Quarterly* magazine, when you need to work with those fonts only four times a year?

Once you've added some fonts to a library, you can even set up collections *within* that library.

To create a library, choose File→New Library; the library appears in the Collection list at the left side of Font Book. Now you can drag fonts into it right from the Finder, or set up collections inside it by highlighting the library's icon and choosing File→New Collection.

Figure 9-8:
The Fonts panel, generally available only in Cocoa programs, offers elaborate controls over text color, shadow, and underline styles.

See the handy font sample shown here above the font lists? To get it, choose Show Preview from the ✿ pop-up menu. Or use the mousy way: Place your cursor just below the title bar (where it says Fonts) and drag downward.

The Fonts Panel

In long-established programs like Microsoft Word, choosing fonts works exactly as you're probably used to: You choose a typeface name from the Font menu or from a formatting palette or toolbar.

Things get much more interesting when you use more recently written programs, like TextEdit, iMovie, Pages, Keynote, Numbers, iPhoto, and Mail. They offer a standard Mac OS X feature called the Fonts panel. If you're seated in front of your Mac OS X machine now, fire up TextEdit or Pages and follow along.

Choosing fonts from the Fonts panel

Suppose you've just highlighted a headline in TextEdit, the Mac's built-in word processor, and now you want to choose an appropriate typeface for it.

In TextEdit, you open the Fonts panel (Figure 9-8) by choosing Format→Font→Show Fonts (⌘-T). Just as in Font Book, the first column lists your Collections. The second column, Family, shows the names of the actual fonts in your system. The third, Typeface, shows the various style variations—Bold, Italic, Condensed, and so on—available in that type family. (Oblique and Italic are roughly the same thing; Bold, Black, and Ultra are varying degrees of boldface.)

The last column lists a sampling of point sizes. You can use the Size slider, choose from the point-size pop-up menu, or type any number into the box at the top of the Size list.

Designing collections and favorites

At the bottom of the Fonts panel, the ✿ menu offers a few useful customization tools:

- **Add to Favorites.** To designate a font as one of your favorites, specify a font, style, and size by clicking in the appropriate columns of the Fonts panel. Then use this command.

  From now on, whenever you click Favorites in the Collections column, you'll see a list of the typefaces you've specified.

- **Show Preview.** The Fonts panel is great and all that, but you may have noticed that, until you choose this option, it doesn't actually *show* you the fonts you're working with—something of an oversight in a window designed to help you find your fonts. See Figure 9-8 for details. (Choose this command again—now called Hide Preview—to get rid of the preview.)

Tip: Once you've opened the Preview pane, feel free to click the different sizes, typeface names, and family names to see the various effects.

- **Hide Effects.** The "toolbar" of the Fonts panel lets you create special text effects—colors, shadows, and so on—as shown in Figure 9-8. This command hides that row of pop-up buttons.

- **Color.** Opens the Color Picker, so you can specify a color for the highlighted text in your document.

- **Characters.** Opens the Character palette, so you can choose a symbol without having to remember the crazy keyboard combo that types it.

- **Typography.** Opens the Typography palette (see Figure 9-9).

- **Edit Sizes.** The point sizes listed in the Fonts panel are just suggestions. You can actually type in any point size you want. By choosing this command, in fact, you can edit this list so that the sizes you use most often are only a click away.

- **Manage Fonts.** Opens Font Book, described earlier in this chapter.

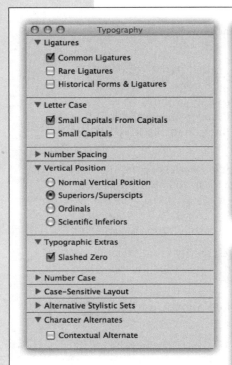

Figure 9-9:
The Typography palette is a collapsible menagerie of fancy type effects, which vary by font. In this example, turning on Common Ligatures creates fused letter pairs like fl and fi; the Small Capitals option created the "Do Not Drink" style; and so on.

Digital Cameras

Just like Windows XP and later versions, Mac OS X is extremely camera-friendly. The simple act of connecting a digital camera to its USB cable stirs Mac OS X into action—namely, it opens iPhoto, Apple's digital-photo shoebox program.

If it's a digital *video* camera you plugged in, Mac OS X opens iMovie instead. (Both of these programs are described in this book's free 85-page iLife Appendix, which you can download from this book's "Missing CD" at *www.missingmanuals.com.*)

Disks

Floppy drives disappeared from Macs beginning in 1997—and these days, they're absent from most Windows PCs, too.

In the meantime, there are all kinds of other disks you can connect to a Mac these days: CDs and DVDs, hard drives, iPods, USB flash drives, and so on.

When you insert a disk, its icon shows up in two or three places (depending on your settings in Finder Preferences): on the right side of the screen, in the Computer window, and in the Sidebar (page 39). To see what's on a disk you've inserted, double-click its icon.

Tip: You can make the Mac work like Windows, if you choose. For example, to open a single window containing icons of all currently inserted disks, choose Go→Computer (which produces the rough equivalent of the My Computer window).

To save you that step, though, you can tell Mac OS X to put disk icons on the desktop, too. Just choose Finder→Preferences, click General, and turn on the top checkboxes—"Hard disks," "External disks," and "CDs, DVDs, and iPods."

To remove a disk from your Mac, use one of these methods:

- Hold down the ⏏ key on your keyboard. Mac keyboards, both on laptops and desktops, have a special Eject key (⏏), usually in the upper-right corner. Hold it down for a moment to make a CD or DVD pop out. (If you don't have an ⏏ key, hold down F12 instead.)

- Drag its icon onto the Trash icon. For years, this technique has confused and frightened first-time Mac users. Their typical reaction: Doesn't the Trash mean "delete"? Yes, but only when you drag *file or folder* icons there—not *disk* icons. Dragging a disk icon into the Trash (at the end of the Dock) makes the Mac spit the disk out. (If you drag a *disk image* icon or the icon of a networked disk, this maneuver *unmounts* them—that is, gets them off your screen.)

  The instant you begin dragging a disk icon, the Trash icon on the Dock changes form, as though to reassure the novice that dragging a disk icon there will only eject the disk. As you drag, the wastebasket icon morphs into a giant-sized ⏏ logo.

- Highlight the disk icon, and then choose File→Eject (or press ⌘-E). The disk pops out.

- Right-click the disk icon. Choose Eject from the shortcut menu.

- Click the ⏏ button next to a disk's name in the Sidebar.

Any of these techniques also work to get network disks and disk images off your screen.

Startup Disks

When you turn the Mac on, it hunts for a *startup disk*—that is, a disk containing a System folder. If you've ever seen the dispiriting blinking folder icon on a Mac's screen, you know what happens when the Mac *can't* find a startup disk. It blinks like that forever, or until you find and insert a disk with a viable System folder on it.

Usually, a startup disk is a hard drive or a DVD. (Not all external USB disks are capable of starting up the Mac, but any internal hard drive can, and any external FireWire or Thunderbolt hard drive can.) You can even put a stripped-down, emergency copy of Lion onto a flash drive and start up your Mac that way; see page 638.

Selecting a startup disk

It's perfectly possible to have more than one startup disk simultaneously attached to your Mac. Some veteran Mac fans deliberately create other startup disks—using external hard drives, for example—so that they can easily start the Mac up from a backup disk, or from a different version of the OS. If you use Boot Camp to run Windows on your Mac (Chapter 9), your Windows partition acts like a different startup disk, too.

Only one System folder can be operational at a time. So how does the Mac know which to use as its startup disk? You make your selection in the Startup Disk pane of System Preferences (Figure 9-10).

Tip: If you're in a hurry to start the machine up from a different disk, just click the disk icon and then click Restart in the System Preferences window. You don't have to close the System Preferences window first.

Figure 9-10:
In the Startup Disk pane of System Preferences, the currently selected disk–the one that will be "in force" the next time the machine starts up–is always highlighted. You also see the System folder's version, the name of the drive it's on, and its actual name.

Erasing a disk

Mac OS X doesn't have an Erase Disk command at the desktop. When you want to erase a disk (such as a DVD-RW disc), you're supposed to use Disk Utility, which sits in your Applications→Utilities folder. This is the same program you use to erase, repair, or subdivide *(partition)* a hard drive.

Once you've opened Disk Utility, click the name of the disk (in the left-side list), click the Erase tab, and then click the Erase button.

You won't be able to do so, though, if:

- The disk is a standard CD-ROM, DVD, a previously recorded CD-R disc, or a disk elsewhere on the network.

- You're trying to erase the startup disk. You can't wipe out the disk that contains the currently running System folder any more than you can paint the floor directly beneath your feet. (To erase your built-in hard drive, for example, you must start up from the Mac OS X DVD.)

Burning CDs and DVDs

Burning a CD or DVD is great for backing up stuff, transferring stuff to another computer (even a Windows PC), mailing to somebody, or offloading (archiving) older files to free up hard drive space. You can buy blank CDs and DVDs incredibly cheaply in bulk—$20 for 100 CDs, for example—via the Web.

You can burn a disc in either of two ways: with the blank disc inserted or without.

Burn Folders: Without the Disc

The *burn folder* is a special folder that you fill up by dragging file and folder icons to it. Then, when you're ready to burn, you just insert the blank disc and go.

The burn-folder concept has a lot going for it:

- **No wasted hard drive space.** When you use a burn folder, you're not using up any additional disk space as you load up a disc with files and folders. Instead, the Mac just sets aside *aliases* of the files and folders you want to burn. Aliases take up negligible hard drive space. When you finally burn the disc, the designated material is copied directly onto the CD or DVD.

- **Easy reuse.** You can keep a burn folder on your desktop, prestocked with the folders you like to back up. Each time you burn a disc, you get the latest version of those folders' contents, and you're saved the effort of having to gather them each time.

- **Prepare ahead of time.** You can get a CD or DVD ready to burn without having a blank disc on hand.

Here's how you use burn folders:

1. **Create a burn folder.**

To make a burn folder appear on your desktop, choose File→New Burn Folder. To create one in any other window, Control-click (or right-click) a blank spot inside that window and, from the shortcut menu, choose New Burn Folder.

Either way, a new folder appears, bearing the universal Mac "burn" symbol (☢).

2. **Rename it.**

   Its name is highlighted, so you can just start typing to rename it. Press Return when you're finished.

3. **Load up the folder by dragging files and folders onto it.**

   If you double-click the burn folder to open its window (Figure 9-11), you'll notice that you're not actually copying huge files. You're simply making a list of aliases.

Tip: At the bottom of the burn folder's window, the "minimum disc size" display keeps track of how much stuff you've loaded up so far, so you can gauge if it will fit on one disc.

Figure 9-11:
Top: A burn folder looks like any ordinary folder—except that it has that radioactive logo on it. You can drag files and folders right into its window; Mac OS X displays only aliases for now, but when you burn the disc, the actual files and folders will be there.

If you open the burn folder, you find an unusual strip across the top. Its most important feature is the Burn button at the right.

Bottom: Ready to proceed, Captain.

4. **Decorate the window, if you like.**

   You can choose list view or icon view; you can drag the icons into an arrangement you like; you can change the background color of the window; and so on. One nice feature of the Mac (which is not available on The Other OS) is that the look of a window is preserved when you burn it to CD.

5. **Click the Burn button in the upper-right corner of the window, or choose File→ Burn Disc.**

   The message shown at bottom in Figure 9-11 appears.

6. **Insert a blank disc.**

   If you have a slot-loading Mac, slip the disc into the slot. If your Mac has a sliding CD/DVD tray instead, open it first by pressing the button on the tray, or pressing your ▲ key for about a second.

Tip: Once you've inserted a CD or DVD into your tray, you can close it either by pushing gently on the tray or by pressing the ▲ key again.

   One last confirmation box appears, where you can name the disc and choose a burning speed for it.

7. **Click Burn (or press Return).**

   The Mac's laser proceeds to record the CD or DVD, which can take some time. Feel free to switch into another program and continue using your Mac. When it's all over, you have a freshly minted CD or DVD, whose files and folders you can open on any Mac or Windows PC.

When you have a blank disc on hand

If you have a blank disc ready to go, burning is even simpler.

Start by inserting the disc. After a moment, the Mac displays a dialog box asking, in effect, what you want to do with this blank disc (unless you've fiddled with your preference settings). See Figure 9-12 for instructions.

Figure 9-12:
Choose Open Finder if you plan to copy regular Mac files onto the CD or DVD, or Open iTunes if you plan to burn a music CD using iTunes. (Click "Make this action the default" if you figure you'll always answer this question the same way.) Click OK.

To burn the disk, drag its icon onto the ❖ icon in the Dock, or choose File→Burn Disc.

If you choose Open Finder, the disc's icon appears on the desktop after a moment; its icon also appears in the Sidebar, complete with the burn symbol (❖).

At this point, you can begin dragging files and folders onto the disc's icon, or (if you double-click the icon) into its window. You can add, remove, reorganize, and rename the files on it just as you would in any standard Finder window. All you're really doing is dragging aliases around; the real files are left untouched on your hard drive. You can also rename the CD or DVD itself, just as you would a file or folder.

When the disc's icon contains the files and folders you want to immortalize, do one of these things:

- Choose File→Burn [the disc's name].

- Click the ✪ button next to the disc's name in the Sidebar.

- Click the Burn button in the upper-right corner of the disc's window.

- Drag the disc's icon toward the Trash icon in the Dock. As soon as you begin to drag, the Trash icon turns into the yellow ✪ logo. Drop the disc's icon onto it.

- Control-click (or right-click) the disc's icon; from the shortcut menu, choose Burn [the disc's name].

In any case, a dialog box now appears. Click Burn. When the recording process is over, you'll have yourself a DVD or CD that works in any Mac or PC.

Here are a few final notes on burning CDs and DVDs at the desktop:

- Not sure what kinds of discs your Mac can burn? Choose ⌘→About This Mac, and click More Info. In the resulting dialog box, click the Storage tab. There it is, plain as day: a list of the formats your machine can read and write (that is, burn). For example, you might see: "CD-Write: -R, -RW. DVD-Write: -R, -RW, +R, +RW."

- If you do a lot of disc burning, a full-fledged CD-burning program like Toast (*www. roxio.com*) adds myriad additional formatting options that let you make startup CDs, video CDs, and so on.

- When you insert a CD-*RW* or DVD-*RW* disc that you've previously recorded, the box shown in Figure 9-12 doesn't appear. Instead, the disc's icon simply appears on the desktop as though it's an ordinary CD. Before you can copy new files onto it, you must erase it using Disk Utility, as described in the previous section.

- The discs that your Mac burns work equally well on Macs and Windows (or Linux) PCs. If you plan to insert a CD or DVD into a PC, however, remember that Windows doesn't permit certain symbols in a Windows filename (\ / : * ? " < > |). You'll run into trouble if any of your file names contain these symbols. In fact, you won't be able to open any folders on your disc that contain illegally named files.

iTunes: The Digital Jukebox

As a Windows veteran, you may already be familiar with iTunes.

iTunes, in your Applications folder, is the ultimate software jukebox (Figure 9-13). It can play music CDs, tune in to Internet radio stations, load up your iPod, iPhone, or iPad, and play back digital sound files (including the Internet's favorite format, MP3 files) and other popular audio formats. It can also turn selected tracks from your music CDs *into* MP3 files, so that you can store favorite songs on your hard drive to play back anytime—without having to dig up the original.

iTunes also lets you record your own custom audio CDs that contain only the good songs. Finally, of course, iTunes is the shop window for the online iTunes Store, which sells music, TV shows, movies, and iPhone/iPad apps.

Figure 9-13:
When the Library icon is selected in the Source list, you can click the Browse button (upper right) to produce a handy, supplementary view of your music database, organized like a Finder column view. It lets you drill down from a performer's name (left column) to an album by that artist (right column) to the individual songs on that album (bottom half, beneath the browser panes).

Source list · Progress/Status · View

New Playlist · Show/Hide Album cover · Start/Stop Show/Hide
Shuffle · Repeat · Genius playback · Sidebar

iTunes can also burn *MP3 CDs,* music CDs that fit much more than the usual 74 or 80 minutes of music onto a disc (because they store songs in MP3 format instead of AIFF). Not all CD players can play MP3 discs, however, and the sound quality is slightly lower than standard CDs.

The first time you run iTunes, you're asked (a) whether you want iTunes to be the program your Mac uses for playing music files from the Internet, (b) whether you want it to ask your permission every time it connects to the Internet, and (c) whether you want the program to scan your Home folder for all music files already on it. (You can decline to have your hard drive scanned at this time. Later, you can always drag it, or any other folder, directly into the iTunes window for automatic scanning.)

Tip: The following pages present a mini-manual on iTunes. For the full scoop, plus coverage of the iPod and the iTunes Store, consult *iPod: The Missing Manual.*

By now, the layout of iTunes should look familiar: a Source list at the left side, acting as a table of contents for the larger window to the right. It's the same layout used in Finder windows (the Sidebar), iPhoto, Image Capture, and other Apple programs.

The major headings in iTunes's list are Library, Store, Devices, Shared, Genius, and Playlists. (You may not see all of them.) Here's what they do.

Library

The items in this list represent all your music and videos: Music, Movies, TV Shows, Podcasts, and so on. They include both your own stuff—songs you copied off of music CDs, for example—and material you bought from the iTunes Store online.

Note: When you first open iTunes, it offers to search your hard drive for the kinds of files it can play—every song in formats like MP3, AIFF, WAV, AAC, and Apple Lossless, for example. It then copies all such files into your Home→Music→iTunes→iTunes Music folder. But you don't ever need to muck around in there; use iTunes to manage your collection instead.

When you click Music, the main iTunes window is organized much like a Finder window, with columns indicating the song length, artist, album, and so on. As always, you can rearrange these columns by dragging their headings, sort your list by one of these criteria by clicking its heading, reverse the sorting order by clicking the heading a second time, and so on.

Or click one of the View buttons next to the search box to display your music as a list, a list with album covers, a grid of album covers—or as Cover Flow, which lets you flip through album covers as though they're sitting in a record-store bin.

FREQUENTLY ASKED QUESTION

Autoplaying Music CDs

How do I make music CDs automatically play when they're inserted into the Mac?

First, make sure iTunes is slated to open automatically when you insert a music CD. You do that on the CDs & DVDs panel of System Preferences (use the "When you insert a music CD" pop-up menu).

Then all you have to do is make sure iTunes knows to begin playing automatically once it launches. Choose iTunes→Preferences, click the General icon if necessary; from the "When you insert a CD" pop-up menu, choose Begin Playing. Click OK.

From now on, whenever you insert a music CD, iTunes will open automatically and begin playing.

To find a particular song or video, just type a few letters into the Spotlight-ish search box above the list. iTunes hides all but the ones that match.

Store

The iTunes Store is easy to figure out. By clicking the tabs across the top of the window, you can search or browse for music, movies, TV shows, iPhone and iPad apps, free podcasts, not-free audiobooks, and more. Sure, you may go broke, but at least you'll be entertained.

Use the Search Music Store box (top-right corner) to find the songs or performers you're interested in. Double-click a song or video to hear or view a 60-second excerpt.

If you decide to buy a song, sign in with your Apple account (page 552). When you click the Buy button next to a song's name, iTunes downloads it to your Mac. Behind the scenes, it goes into your Home→Music→iTunes Music folder. But for your purposes, it shows up in the Store→Purchased category in the Source list for convenient access.

Devices

These icons represent other gadgets that iTunes can talk to. If you insert a CD, it shows up here. If you attach an iPod, iPad, or iPhone, its icon appears here, too. Click any one of these icons to see what's on it. And if you don't have *any* of these things attached, the Devices category doesn't appear at all.

Shared

You can share songs and playlists with up to five networked computers in either of two ways:

- **Stream the music and videos.** In this setup, the music someone else chooses to share with you is played over the network from that Mac to your Mac. You could, for example, tap into your roommates' jazz collection without getting up from your desk, and they can sample the zydeco and Tejano tunes from your World Beat playlist.

  To set this up, choose iTunes→Preferences→Sharing. Turn on "Share my library on my local network," and specify which playlists you want to share. You can require a password, if you like; set it up here. Then click OK.

  Suddenly, your copy of iTunes shows up in the Shared lists of your network buddies. They can expand the flippy triangles to see and play your movies and music files (but not your audiobooks).

- **Copy the music and videos to your Mac from another one.** In this scenario, you can enjoy the music and movies even when the original computer is turned off. This feature, called Home Sharing, even works between Macs and PCs.

Note: This Home Share feature even works between Macs and PCs.

To get started, sit at Computer A. Choose Advanced→Turn On Home Sharing. You're asked for your Apple account information. Click Create Home Share and then Done.

Now, if you open iTunes on Computer B, you'll see Computer A listed in the Shared category at left. Click it to see what's in *its* copy of iTunes. You can play that stuff—even sitting at Computer B—and copy it to Computer A. (Just drag the songs or videos you want into the appropriate category—Music, Movies, TV Shows, and so on—at the *top* of your Source list. Or, in the Show menu at the bottom of the iTunes window, choose "Items not in my library"; select the files you want to import, and then click Import.)

Note: There's some fine print. Up to five computers can do this Home Share business. They all have to sign in with the same Apple account, and they all have to be on the same network (meaning inside the same building).

Genius

Genius, according to Apple, assembles lists of "songs that sound great together," whatever that means. (It seems to mean "songs that have the same degree of rockiness.")

To get started, choose Store→Turn On Genius (unless it's already on); click Turn On Genius to dismiss the explanation screen; sign in with your Apple ID. Agree to the fine print.

Now click a song in your library that you want to serve as the anchor—the "seed" song—that you want to match. Then proceed in one of these three ways:

- **Create a Genius playlist.** Click the ❄ button at lower right. Presto: a new playlist, filed in your Source list under Genius. (Its name is Genius. Pure genius!) Play it to see how iTunes did at matching your original song's feel.

  At the top of the window, you can use the Limit To pop-up menu to specify how many songs are in this playlist, the Refresh button to try again matching your "seed" song, or the Save Playlist button to turn this iTunes guess into a proper playlist.

- **Create a Genius mix.** There's also such a thing as a Genius *Mix,* which, unlike a playlist, never ends. It's more like a radio station, eternally plucking songs from your collection that all match one another (or, as Apple would say, "sound great together"). Just click Genius Mixes in the Source list; you'll see a couple of starter mixes to get you going. Click one to hear it.

- **Shop for Genius suggestions.** If you click a song name and then click the tiny, boxed ▶ button to the *right* of the ❄ button, you get a new Genius panel hugging the right side of the iTunes window. It shows other songs and albums from the iTunes store that Apple thinks you'd like, based on whatever song you clicked.

Playlists

Apple recognizes that you may not want to listen to *all* your songs every time you need some tunes. That's why iTunes lets you create *playlists*—folders in the Source list that contain, and play back, only certain songs (or videos). In effect, you can devise your own albums, like one called Party Tunes, another called Blind Date Music, and so on.

Creating playlists

To create a new playlist, click the **+** button in the lower-left corner of the window, or choose File→New Playlist (⌘-N). Alternatively, if you've already highlighted certain songs—by ⌘-clicking them or Shift-clicking them—you can choose File→New Playlist from Selection.

A new playlist appears as an icon in the Source list. You can rename this playlist by double-clicking it, and add songs to it by dragging them out of the main list into the icon.

Tip: Deleting a song from a playlist doesn't delete it from the Library (or your hard drive). Similarly, it's fine to add the same song to as many different playlists as you like, since you're not actually increasing the size of your Library. (You might be starting to pick up a running theme in Apple's software. Playlists work just like albums in iPhoto, or the Sidebar in the Finder.)

Smart playlists

Smart playlists constantly rebuild themselves according to criteria you specify. You might tell one smart playlist to assemble 45 minutes' worth of songs you've rated higher than four stars but rarely listen to, and another to list your most-often-played songs from the '80s.

Tip: To rate a song, make the window wide enough that you can see the Rating column. (If you don't see this column, Control-click any column heading and choose Rating from the list of options.) Then just click the Rating column for a selected song. The appropriate number of stars appears—one, two, three, four, or five—depending on the position of your click. You can change a song's rating as many times as you like—a good thing, considering the short shelf life of a pop hit these days.

Figure 9-14:
A smart playlist is a powerful search command for your iTunes database. You can set up certain criteria, like the hunt for particular Beatles tunes illustrated here. The "Live updating" checkbox makes iTunes keep this playlist updated as your collection changes, as you change your ratings, as your play count changes, and so on.

To make a smart playlist, choose File→New Smart Playlist (Option-⌘-N)—or just Option-click the ✛ button beneath the Source list. The dialog box shown in Figure 9-14 appears. The controls here are designed to set up a search of your music database. Figure 9-14, for example, illustrates how you'd find up to 74 minutes of Beatles tunes released between 1965 and 1968—that you've rated three stars or higher and that you've listened to no more than twice.

When you click OK, your smart playlist is ready to show off. When you click its name in the Source list, the main song list updates itself according to your criteria and any changes in your music collection. (Smart playlists get transferred to your iPod or iPhone but don't continue to update themselves there.)

Audio CDs

If you insert a music CD while iTunes is open, the songs on it immediately show up in the list.

At first, they may appear with the exciting names "Track 01," "Track 02," and so on. But after a moment, iTunes connects to the Internet and compares your CD with the listings at *www.gracenote.com,* a global database of music CDs and their contents. If it finds a match among the thousands of CDs there, it copies the album and song names into iTunes, where they reappear every time you use this particular CD.

You can play the CD just as you would anything else in iTunes: by tapping the space bar, for example.

Tip: If you connect an iTunes-compatible portable MP3 player to your Mac (the iPod isn't the only one), its name, too, shows up in the left-side Source list. You can add songs to your player (by dragging them onto its icon), rename or reorder them, and so on.

WORKAROUND WORKSHOP

iPod Independence

Out of the box, the iPod (or iPad, or iPhone) and iTunes come set for automatic synchronization. That is, as soon as you hook them together, iTunes sends your complete music library (the contents of your Library "folder" in iTunes) to the iPod. The iPod's songs and playlists always match the Mac's.

Apple's idea here was to ensure that you don't use the iPod as a convenient piracy machine. Your iPod gets its music from your Mac, it but can't put its songs onto a Mac.

At least that's the theory. But what if your hard drive self-destructs, vaporizing the 945 MP3 files that you've made from your paid-for CD collection? You legally own those copies. Shouldn't you have the right to retrieve them from your own iPod?

If you believe the answer is yes, a quick search at *www.download.com* for the word "iPod" will bring up a list of programs like Senuti (iTunes spelled backward, get it?), which let you copy music from the iPod to the Mac.

These programs know that the name of the super-secret music folder on the iPod, called *iPod_Control,* is invisible, which is why you can't see it on your desktop without the help of these utilities.

Copying (ripping) CD songs to your hard drive

Once you copy your favorite audio CDs onto your hard drive, you can play them whenever you like, without the original CD.

To *rip* a CD (as aficionados would say) like this, make sure only the songs you want to capture have checkmarks in the main list. Choose a format for the files you're about to create, if you like—MP3, for example, or AAC (better quality/size tradeoff, but less compatible with other gadgets)—by clicking the Import Settings button (Figure 9-15). Finally, click the Import CD button at the lower-right corner of the window.

Figure 9-15:
Watch the display at the top of the window to see how long the conversion is going to take, and which song iTunes is working on. As iTunes finishes processing each song, you see a small, circled checkmark next to its name in the main list to remind you that you've got it on board.

When it's all over, you'll find the imported songs listed in your Library. (Click Music in the left-side Source list.) From there, you can drag them into any other "folder" (playlist), as described above.

The iPod, iPhone, and iPad

Unless you're just off the shuttle from Alpha Centauri, you probably already know that the iPod is Apple's tiny, elegant music player. It, and its pals the iPhone and the iPad, are designed to integrate seamlessly with iTunes.

All you have to do is connect the i-gadget to the Mac via its white USB cable. The gizmo's icon shows up in the iTunes Source list. Click its icon to view its contents—and click the tabs (Music, TV Shows, Podcasts, and so on) to specify what Mac material you'd like copied over to it.

Playing with Playback

To play a song or video, double-click it. Or click iTunes's Play button (▶) or press the space bar. The Mac immediately begins to play the songs whose names have check-marks in the main list, or from the CD currently in your Mac.

Tip: The central display at the top of the window shows not only the name of the song and album, but also where you are in the song, as represented by the diamond in the horizontal strip. Drag this diamond, or click elsewhere in the strip, to jump around in the song.

To view the current music's sound levels, click the tiny triangle at the left side of this display to see a pulsing VU meter, indicating the various frequencies.

GEM IN THE ROUGH

Internet Radio and Podcasts

Audio CDs and MP3 files aren't the only sources of musical and spoken sound you can listen to as you work. iTunes also lets you tune in to hundreds of Internet-based radio stations, which may turn out to be the most convenient music source of all. They're free, they play 24 hours a day, and their music collections make yours look like a drop in the bucket. You can also download and listen to podcasts, which are like Web-distributed personal radio shows—some commercial (like NPR) and some homemade (sometimes *very* homemade).

For radio, click Radio in the left-side Source list. (If you don't see Radio there, choose iTunes→Preferences→ General, and turn on Radio.)

In the main list, if you're connected to the Inter-

net, you'll see categories like Blues, Classic Rock, Classical, and so on, as shown here. Click the flippy triangle to see a list of Internet radio stations in that category.

When you see one that looks interesting, double-click it. (The higher the number in the Bit Rate column, the better the sound quality.) Wait a moment for your Mac to connect

to the appropriate Internet site, and then let the music begin!

Without add-on shareware (like Audio Hijack Pro), there's no easy way to capture Internet broadcasts or to save them onto your hard drive. You can, however, drag a radio station's name into the Music list (in the Source list), or even a playlist, to make it easier to access later on. If you discover other Internet radio stations that sound interesting, choose Advanced→Open Stream, type in the station's Web address (URL), and press Return.

To grab a podcast, click iTunes Store in the Source list. At the top of the screen, click Podcasts. Now iTunes lets you browse a vast list of available podcasts. When you click one that looks promising, you can either listen to it on the spot, or—and here's the

real fun—click Subscribe.

Once you do that, a new icon called Podcasts appears in your Source list; click it to find the latest episodes of the podcasts you've subscribed to. Sync those babies to your iPod or iPhone, and you've got interesting material—or at least fresh material—to listen to every day of the week.

As music plays, you can control and manipulate the music and the visuals of your Mac in all kinds of interesting ways. Some people don't move from their Macs for months at a time.

Turning on visuals

Visuals are onscreen light shows that pulse, beat, and dance in sync to the music. (For real party fun, invite some people who grew up in the '60s to your house to watch.)

To summon this psychedelic display, choose View→Show Visuals, or just press ⌘-T. The show begins immediately—although it's much more fun if you choose View→Enter Full Screen (Control-⌘-F) so the show takes over your whole monitor. True, you won't get a lot of work done, but when it comes to stress relief, visuals are a lot cheaper than a hot tub.

Keyboard control

You can control iTunes's music playback using its menus, of course, but the keyboard can be far more efficient. Here are a few of the control keystrokes worth noting:

Function	Keystroke
Play, Pause	space bar
Next song/previous song	↑, ↓ or ←, →
Louder, quieter	⌘-↑, ⌘-↓
Rewind, fast-forward	Option-⌘-←, Option-⌘-→
Eject the CD	⌘-E
Turn visuals on	⌘-T
Turn visuals off	⌘-T or mouse click
Full-screen mode	Control-⌘-F
Exit full-screen visuals	⌘-T, ⌘-F, Esc, or mouse click

Playing with the graphic equalizer

If you choose Window→Equalizer, you get a handsome control console that lets you adjust the strength of each musical frequency independently.

Sound Check: Preventing ear-blast syndrome

Here's a clever touch: In iTunes→Preferences→Playback, you see a checkbox called Sound Check. Its function is to keep the playback volume of all songs within the same basic level so you don't have to adjust the volume to compensate for different recorded levels. (This setting, too, gets transferred to your iPod, iPad, or iPhone.)

Come to think of it, you could while away quite a few happy afternoons just poking through the Preferences dialog box. It grows richer with every successive version of iTunes.

Burning Music CDs

iTunes can record selected sets of songs, no matter what the original sources, onto a blank CD. When it's all over, you can play the burned CD on a standard CD player, just as you would a CD from the record store—but this time, you hear only the songs you like, in the order you like, with all the annoying ones eliminated.

Start by creating a playlist for the CD you're about to make. Click its icon in the left-side Source list to see the list you've built. Drag songs up or down in the list to change their playback order. Keep these points in mind:

- The readout at the bottom of the list shows how much time the songs will take.

- About 74 or 80 minutes of regular audio files fit on one CD. But if you make an *MP3 CD,* you can fit at least 10 times as much—12 hours of music on a single disc!

   The fine print: Not all CD players can play MP3 CDs (check the manual or the side of the CD player's box). Also note that your MP3 CD can't include songs you've bought in Apple's iTunes music store; iTunes won't convert them into the MP3 format.

   To burn an MP3 CD, see Figure 9-16.

- You can control how many seconds of silence iTunes leaves between tracks on your custom CD, too. Use the Gap Between Songs pop-up menu shown in Figure 9-16.

When everything is set up, click the Burn button in the playlist window. Specify your CD options (Figure 9-16), insert a blank CD into the Mac, and go read a book; the burning process takes some time. Feel free to work in other programs while iTunes chugs away.

Figure 9-16:
To burn an MP3 CD, click the playlist, insert a blank CD, and then click Burn Disc (lower-right corner of the window). This box appears. Here you can select MP3 CD. If you're burning a regular audio CD instead, you can specify how much gap you want between the songs.

DVD Movies

Watching movies on your Mac screen couldn't be simpler: Just insert a movie DVD. The Mac detects that it's a video DVD (as opposed to, say, one that's filled with files). Then, unless you've fiddled with your preference settings, the DVD Player program opens and begins playing the movie in full-screen mode. (Even the menu bar disappears. To make it reappear, move your cursor to near the top of the screen.)

Note: If DVD Player *doesn't* open automatically when you insert a DVD movie, you can open it yourself. It's in your Applications folder. (Then fix the problem, using the CDs & DVDs panel of System Preferences.)

Playing a Movie

Once DVD Player starts playing your movie, you can move your mouse to the bottom of the screen, at any time, to bring up the control bar, which is deconstructed in Figure 9-17.

Figure 9-17:
Top: Even in full-screen mode, you can control the playback and navigate the disc using the new, translucent, pop-up control bar.

One especially cool feature is new Player Settings button. It opens the Zoom controls window shown here, which gives you manual control over the width and height of the picture on your screen.

Don't miss the scrubber bar at the very bottom, either. It lets you scroll directly to any spot in the DVD.

Bottom: When you're not in full-screen mode, you get a separate, floating "remote control." It has most of the same controls, but they're arranged with a more 1999 sort of design aesthetic.

Scrubber bar

Languages, Subtitles

Eject DVD

Click to see elasped time/ time remaining

Picture controls

Exit full screen

Slo Mo
Frame Advance
Return to Movie

Subtitles
Language
Angle

Previous chapter/Next chapter
(Hold to scan backward/forward)

Or just use the keyboard controls, which appear here in this clip 'n' save cheat sheet:

Function	Keystroke
Play, Pause	space bar
Fast-forward, rewind	Shift-⌘-→, Shift-⌘-← (press repeatedly to cycle to 3, 8, 16, and 32 times normal speed)
Skip forward/back 5 seconds	Option-⌘-→, Option-⌘-←
Louder, quieter	⌘-↑, ⌘-↓
Mute/Unmute	Option-⌘-↓
Next/previous "chapter"	→, ←
Full-screen mode on/off	⌘-F
Half, normal, maximum size	⌘-1, ⌘-2, ⌘-3
Eject	⌘-E
Add a bookmark	⌘-= (equal sign)

Language Fun

Most Hollywood DVDs have been programmed with onscreen subtitles to help those with hearing impairments and people sitting in noisy bars. The Subtitle button offers a pop-up menu of alternative languages and subtitle options.

Tip: For real fun, turn on English subtitles but switch the soundtrack to a foreign language. No matter how trashy the movie you're watching, you'll gain much more respect from your friends and family when you tell them you're watching a foreign film.

Chapter Thumbnails

A standard Hollywood DVD comes programmed with chapters—invisible markers that let you jump from the beginning of one important scene to the next. To see

---

GEM IN THE ROUGH

Parental Controls

The DVD Parental Controls in Lion aren't much. You can't say, for example, "Don't play anything rated PG-13 or above"; you have to rate each DVD yourself, one at a time.

But that's better than nothing.

Insert the DVD you're worried about. Choose File→Get Disk Info. Click the Parental Controls tab.

Click the 🔒 button and enter your administrator's password. (Unless, of course, your 8-year-old is the administrator of this Mac instead of you, in which case this DVD is the least of your problems.)

Now you can select either "Always ask for authorization" or "Always allow to be played," depending on your feelings about the movie. Click OK.

All you've done so far, however, is to specify what happens when you turn on Parental Controls—and you haven't done that yet. Choosing Features→Enable Parental Control does the trick.

When Parental Controls are turned on, nobody can watch the "Always ask for authorization" DVDs without correctly inputting your administrator's password.

Which nobody knows except you. (Right?)

---

them in DVD Player, just move your mouse to the top of the screen. A row of chapter thumbnail images appears, which you can click to jump around in.

Keyboard

As you know by now, switching to the Mac entails switching your brain, especially when it comes to the old keyboard shortcuts. All of those Ctrl-key sequences become, on the Mac, ⌘-key sequences. (Check your Macintosh keyboard: The ⌘ key is right next to the space bar, usually on both sides.)

But plenty of other Mac keys may seem unfamiliar. For your reassurance pleasure, Chapter 1 offers a rundown of what they do.

Text-Navigation Keystrokes

In Windows, you may have grown accustomed to certain common keystrokes for navigating text—key combinations that make the insertion point jump to the beginning or end of a word, line, or document, for example.

Mac OS X programs offer similar navigation keystrokes, as you can see here:

Function	Windows keys	Mac keys
Move to previous/next word	Ctrl+←, Ctrl+→	Option-←, Option-→
Move to beginning/end of line	Home/End	Home/End*
Move to previous/next paragraph	Ctrl+↑, Ctrl+↓*	Option-↑, Option-↓*
Move to top/bottom of window	Home/End	Home/End (but see below)
Select all text	Ctrl+A	⌘-A
Select text, one letter at a time	Shift+↑, Shift+↓	Shift-↑, Shift-↓
Select text, one word at a time	Ctrl+Shift+arrow keys	Option-Shift-arrow keys
Undo	Ctrl+Z	⌘-Z
Cut, Copy, Paste	Ctrl+X, C, V	⌘-X, C, V
Close window	Alt+F4	⌘-W
Switch open programs	Alt+Tab	⌘-Tab
Hide all windows	⊞+D	F11

* in some programs

Incidentally, the keystroke for jumping to the *top or bottom* of a window varies, depending on the program. You need ⌘-Home/End in Microsoft Word, ⌘-up/down arrow in TextEdit and Stickies, and Home/End in iPhoto and Finder list windows.

Mouse

Most USB mice work as soon as you plug them into your Mac—even two-button, scroll-wheel mice. Using System Preferences, you can program your spare mouse buttons to invoke cool features like Exposé and the Dashboard.

That's not to say, however, that you shouldn't install your mouse's driver software. If your mouse *came* with such software (or if you find it on the manufacturer's Web site), you may well find that your mouse learns a few new tricks—making its "back" and "forward" buttons work properly in Safari, for example. Otherwise, a shareware program like USB Overdrive ($20, from *www.usboverdrive.com*) can unlock those features.

(For more on Mac mice, see page 19.)

Monitors

Your Mac can use standard monitors of the type found in the Windows world. Every Macintosh can drive *multiple* screens at the same time, too, meaning that you can generally use your old PC screen either as your Mac's main monitor or as a second, external screen.

If one of those arrangements appeals to you, the only complication might be the connector. Most PC screens, of course, have a standard VGA connector (or a more modern DVI connector) at the tip of their tails. Over the years, however, Apple has "standardized" on enough different screen-plug types to fill a catalog. There's been DVI, Mini-DVI, Micro-DVI, Mini DisplayPort—you get the idea.

For the proper fee, Apple will be happy to sell you whatever adapter cable you need to accommodate the monitor you've got.

Tip: It's even possible to connect *both* your Mac and your PC to the *same* monitor, and switch from one to the other at will. If this arrangement appeals to you, you'll need a so-called KVM switch (which also lets you switch your keyboard and mouse between your two computers). You can find KVM switches for sale at electronics stores, and online from manufacturers like Belkin (*www.belkin.com*).

In any case, once you've hooked up a second monitor or a projector, you can turn Mirroring on or off. Mirroring is when both screens show the same thing—a handy setup in classroom situations; turning it off lets one screen act as additional real estate, an annex to the first. (If you're giving a PowerPoint or Keynote slideshow, you might also want to turn off Mirroring so that your laptop's screen shows your private speaker notes, while the audience's screen shows only your luscious bullet points.)

You specify which mode you want using the Displays pane of System Preferences, or using the Displays menu-bar icon.

Scanners

If you own a scanner, chances are good that you won't be needing whatever special scanning software came with it. Instead, Mac OS X gives you two programs that can operate any standard scanner: Image Capture and Preview. In fact, the available controls are identical in both programs.

To scan in Image Capture, turn on your scanner and click its name in the left-side list. Put your photos or documents into the scanner.

Now you have a couple of decisions to make:

- **Separate and straighten?** If you turn on "Detect separate items" in the Scan Size menu, Mac OS X will perform a nifty little stunt indeed: It will check to see if you've put *multiple* items onto the scanner glass, like several small photos. (It looks for rectangular images surrounded by empty white space, so if the photos are overlapping, this feature won't work.)

  If it finds multiple items, Image Capture automatically straightens them, compensating for haphazard placement on the glass, and then saves them as individual files.

Figure 9-18:
When you use the Show Details button, you get a new panel on the right, where you can specify all the tweaky details for the scan you're about to make: resolution, size, and so on. See how the two photos have individual dotted lines around them? That's because Detect Separate Items is turned on. These will be scanned into two separate files.

- **Where to file.** Use the "Scan to" pop-up menu to specify where you want the newly scanned image files to land—in the Pictures folder, for example. You have some other cool options beyond sticking the scans in a folder; for example, you can send the resulting image to iPhoto, Preview, or Mail.

Once you've put a document onto it or into it, click Scan. The scanner heaves to life. After a moment, you see on the screen what's on the glass. It's simultaneously been sent to the folder (or post-processing task) you requested using the "Scan to" pop-up menu.

More power to you

As you can see, Apple has tried to make *basic* scanning as simple as possible: one click. That idiotproof method gives you very few options, however.

If you click Show Details before you scan, though, you get a special panel on the right side of the window that's filled with useful scanning controls (Figure 9-18).

Here are some of the most useful options:

- **Resolution.** This is the number of tiny scanned dots per inch. 300 is about right for something you plan to print out; 75 is standard for graphics that will be viewed on the screen, like images on a Web page.

- **Name.** Here, specify how you want each image file named when it lands on your hard drive. If it says *Scan,* then the files will be called *Scan 1, Scan 2,* and so on.

- **Format.** Usually, the file format for scanned graphics is TIFF. That's a very high-res format that's ideal if you're scanning precious photos for posterity. But if these images are bound for the Web, you might want to choose JPEG instead; that's the standard Web format.

- **Image Correction.** If you choose Manual from this pop-up menu, then, incredibly, you'll be treated to a whole expando-panel of color correction tools: brightness, tint, saturation, a histogram, and so on.

Opening the Details panel has another handy benefit, too: It lets you scan only a *portion* of what's on the scanner glass.

Once you've put the document or photo into the scanner, click Overview. Image Capture does a quick pass and displays on the screen whatever is on the glass. You'll see a dotted-line rectangle around the entire scanned image—unless you've turned on "Detect separate images," in which case you see a dotted-line rectangle around *each* item on the glass.

You can adjust these dotted-line rectangles around until you've enclosed precisely the portion of the image you want scanned. For example, drag the rectangles' corner handles to resize them; drag inside the rectangles to move them; drag the right end of the line inside the rectangle to rotate it; preview the rotation by pressing Control and Option.

Finally, when you think you've got the selection rectangle(s) correctly positioned, click Scan to trigger the actual scan.

Note: These instructions apply to the most common kind of scanner—the *flatbed* scanner. If you have a scanner with a document feeder—a tray or slot that sucks in one paper document after another from a stack—the instructions are only slightly different.

You may, for example, see a Mode or Scan Mode pop-up menu; if so, choose Document Feeder. You'll want to use the Show Details option described above. You may also be offered a Duplex command (meaning, "scan both sides of the paper"—not all scanners can do this).

Part Three:
Making Connections

3

Internet Setup & iCloud

As Apple's programmers slogged away for months on the massive Mac OS X project, there were areas where they must have felt like they were happily gliding on ice: networking and the Internet. For the most part, the Internet already runs on Unix, and hundreds of extremely polished tools and software chunks were already available.

There are all kinds of ways to get your Mac onto the Internet these days:

- **WiFi.** Wireless hot spots, known as WiFi (or, as Apple used to call it, AirPort), are glorious conveniences, especially if you have a laptop. Without stirring from your hotel bed, you're online at high speed. Sometimes for free.

- **Cable modems, DSL.** Over half of the U.S. Internet population connects over higher-speed wires, using *broadband* connections that are always on: cable modems, DSL, or corporate networks. (These, of course, are often what's at the other end of an Internet hot spot.)

- **Cellular modems.** A few well-heeled individuals enjoy the go-anywhere bliss of *USB cellular modems,* which get them online just about anywhere they can make a phone call. These modems are offered by Verizon, Sprint, AT&T, and so on, and usually cost $60 a month.

Note: A MiFi is sort of a cellular modem, too. It's a pocketable, battery-operated, portable hot spot. It converts the cellular signal into a WiFi signal, so up to five people can be online at once, while the MiFi itself sits happily in your pocket or laptop bag.

• **Tethering.** *Tethering* is letting your cellphone act as a glorified Internet antenna for your Mac, whether connected by a cable or a Bluetooth wireless link. You pay your phone company extra for this convenience.

• **Dial-up modems.** It's true: Their numbers are shrinking, but plenty of people still connect to the Internet using a modem that dials out over ordinary phone lines. The service is cheap, but the connection is slow.

This chapter explains how to set up each one of these. It also describes some of Mac OS X's offbeat Internet featurettes. It tackles Internet Sharing, which lets several computers in the same household share a single broadband connection; the system-wide Internet bookmarks known as *Internet location files*; and iCloud, Apple's suite of free online syncing tools.

Network Central and Multihoming

In this chapter, you'll be spending a lot of time in the Network pane of System Preferences (Figure 10-1). (Choose →System Preferences; click Network.) This list summarizes the ways your Mac can connect to the Internet or an office network—Ethernet, WiFi, Bluetooth, cellular modem card, VPN, and so on.

Multihoming
The *order* of the network connections listed in the Network pane is important. That's the sequence the Mac uses as it tries to get online. If one of your programs needs

Figure 10-1:
You set up all your network connections here, and you can connect to and disconnect from all your networks here. The listed network connections are tagged with color-coded dots. A green dot means turned on and connected to a network; yellow means the connection is working but some other setting is wrong (for example, your Mac can't get an IP address); red means there's no connection, or you haven't yet set up a connection.

Internet access and the first method isn't hooked up, then the Mac switches to the next available connection automatically.

In fact, Mac OS X can maintain multiple simultaneous network connections—Ethernet, WiFi, dial-up, even FireWire—with a feature known as *multihoming*.

This feature is especially relevant for laptops. When you open your Web browser, your laptop might first check to see if it's plugged into an Ethernet cable, which is the fastest, most secure type of connection. If there's no Ethernet, it looks for a WiFi network.

Here's how to go about setting up the connection-attempt sequence you want:

1. **Open System Preferences. Click the Network icon.**

   The Network Status screen (Figure 10-1) brings home the point of multihoming: You can have more than one network connection operating at once.

2. **From the ✿ pop-up menu, choose Set Service Order.**

   Now you see the display shown in Figure 10-2. It lists all the ways your Mac knows how to get online, or onto an office network.

Figure 10-2:
The key to multihoming is sliding the network connection methods' names up or down. Note that you can choose a different connection sequence for each location. (Locations are described later in this chapter.)

3. **Drag the items up and down the list into priority order.**

   If you have a wired broadband connection, for example, you might want to drag Built-in Ethernet to the top of the list, since that's almost always the fastest way to get online.

4. **Click OK.**

   You return to the Network pane of System Preferences, where the master list of connections magically re-sorts itself to match your efforts.

Your Mac will now be able to switch connections even in real time, during a single Internet session. If lightning takes out your Ethernet hub in the middle of your Web surfing, your Mac will seamlessly switch to your WiFi network, for example, to keep your session alive.

All right, then: Your paperwork is complete. The following pages guide you through the process of setting up these various connections.

Broadband Connections

If your Mac is connected wirelessly or, um, *wirefully* to a cable modem, DSL, or office network, you're one of the lucky ones. You have a high-speed broadband connection to the Internet that's always available, always on. You never have to wait to dial.

Automatic Configuration

Most broadband connections require *no setup whatsoever*. Take a new Mac out of the box, plug in the Ethernet cable to your cable modem—or choose a wireless network from the 🛜 menulet—and you can begin surfing the Web instantly.

That's because most cable modems, DSL boxes, and wireless base stations use *DHCP*. It stands for *dynamic host configuration protocol,* but what it means is: "We'll fill in your Network pane of System Preferences automatically." (Including techie specs like IP address and DNS Server addresses.)

Manual Configuration

If, for some reason, you're not able to surf the Web or check email the first time you try, it's remotely possible that your broadband modem or your office network *doesn't* offer DHCP. In that case, you may have to fiddle with the Network pane of System Preferences.

Figure 10-3:
Here's the setup for a cable-modem account with a static IP address, which means you have to type in all these numbers yourself.

On the Network pane, click your Internet connection (Wi-Fi, Built-in Ethernet, cellular modem, whatever). Click Advanced; click TCP/IP. Now you see something like Figure 10-3. Don't be alarmed by the morass of numbers and periods—it's all in good fun. (If you find TCP/IP fun, that is.)

To get the information to fill in here, you can call your Internet provider (cable or TV company) for help—or you can copy your Windows configuration onto the Mac. Read on.

Settings from Windows 2000, XP, Vista, or Windows 7

Your first task is to get to the Properties dialog box for your connection:

- **Windows 2000.** Choose Start→Settings→Network and Dial-up Connections.

- **Windows XP.** Choose Start→Control Panel. Open Network Connections.

- **Windows Vista.** Choose Start→Control Panel. Open Network and Sharing Center. Click "Manage network connections."

- **Windows 7.** Choose Start→Control Panel. Open Network and Sharing Center. Click "Change adapter settings."

You wind up with a window full of icons that represent the various ways you can connect (3G Connection, Wireless Network Connection, Local Area Connection—that is, Ethernet cable—and so on).

Figure 10-4:
Here's another way to fill in your Mac's network settings: copy them, blank by blank, from your old Windows PC.

Continue by right-clicking the icon for your broadband connection; from the shortcut menu, choose Properties. (In Windows Vista, you get an "Are you sure?" box at this point; click Continue.)

In the resulting dialog box, click the row that says "Internet Protocol (TCP/IP)."

If the resulting screen says "Obtain an IP address automatically" (see Figure 10-4), then leave Using DHCP selected in the Mac's Configure pop-up menu; your Mac should teach itself the correct settings automatically.

If the Windows screen says, "Use the following IP address" instead, then select Manually from the Mac's Configure pop-up menu, and copy the relevant numbers into the Mac's Network panel (see Figure 10-4).

Similarly, if the Internet Protocol (TCP/IP Properties) dialog box says, "Use the following DNS server addresses," then type the numbers from the "Preferred DNS server" and "Alternate DNS server" boxes into the Mac's DNS Servers text box. (Press Return to make a new line for the second number.)

Note: If your Mac plugs directly into the cable modem (that is, you don't use a router), then you'll have to turn the cable modem or DSL box off and then on again when you've switched from the PC to the Mac.

Settings from Windows 98, Windows Me

Choose Start→Settings→Control Panel. In the Control Panel window, double-click Network. Double-click the TCP/IP row that identifies how your PC is connected to the broadband modem. (It may say "TCP/IP→3Com Ethernet Adapter," for example.)

Click the IP Address tab. If it says "Specify an IP address," then copy the IP Address and Subnet Mask numbers into the same ones on the Mac's Network panel. Then click the Gateway tab, and copy the "Installed gateway" number into the Mac's Router box.

Finally, click the DNS Configuration tab. Copy the strings of numbers you see here into the Mac's DNS Servers text box. (Press Return to make a new line for the second number, if necessary.)

Applying the settings

That's all the setup; on the Mac, in the Network pane of System Preferences, click Apply. If your settings are correct, you're online, now and forever. You never have to worry about connecting or disconnecting.

Ethernet Connections

The beauty of Ethernet connections is that they're super-fast and super-secure. No bad guys sitting across the coffee shop, armed with shareware "sniffing" software, can intercept your email and chat messages, as they theoretically can when you're on wireless.

And 99 percent of the time, connecting to an Ethernet network is as simple as connecting the cable to the Mac. That's it. You're online, quickly and securely, and you never have to worry about connecting or disconnecting.

WiFi Connections

WiFi is the friendlier term for *802.11 wireless networking technology*. It's the radio-wave technology that lets your Mac communicate with a wireless base station up to 300 feet away, much like a cordless phone. Doing so lets you surf the Web from your laptop in a hotel room, for example, or share files with someone across the building from you.

Chapter 14 has much more information about *setting up* a WiFi network. The real fun begins, however, when it comes time to *join* one.

Sometimes you just want to join a friend's WiFi network. Sometimes you've got time to kill in an airport, and it's worth a $7 splurge for half an hour. And sometimes, at some street corners in big cities, WiFi signals bleeding out of apartment buildings might give you a choice of several free hot spots to join.

Your Mac joins WiFi hot spots like this:

- First, it sniffs around for a WiFi network you've used before. If it finds one, it connects quietly and automatically. You're not asked for permission, a password,

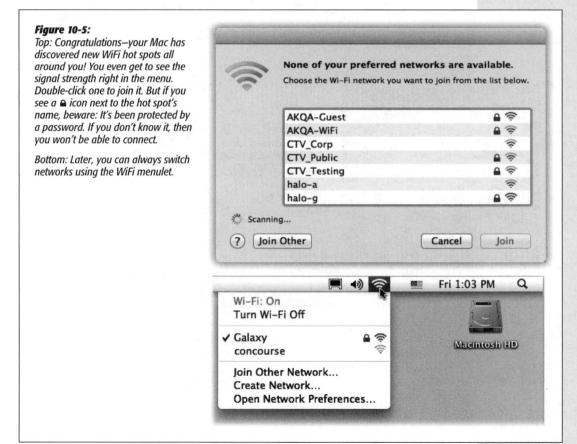

Figure 10-5:
Top: Congratulations—your Mac has discovered new WiFi hot spots all around you! You even get to see the signal strength right in the menu. Double-click one to join it. But if you see a 🔒 icon next to the hot spot's name, beware: It's been protected by a password. If you don't know it, then you won't be able to connect.

Bottom: Later, you can always switch networks using the WiFi menulet.

or anything else; you're just online. (It's that way, for example, when you come home with your laptop every day.) For details on this memorization feature, see the box on the facing page.

• If the Mac can't find a known hot spot, but it detects a new hot spot or two, a message appears on the screen, displaying their names (see Figure 10-5). Double-click one to connect.

Tip: If you don't *want* your Mac to keep interrupting you with its discoveries of new hot spots—it can get pretty annoying when you're in a taxi driving through a city—you can shut them off. In System Preferences, click Network, click Wi-Fi, and then turn off "Ask to join new networks."

• If you're in the presence of a commercial hot spot—one that requires payment or reading some kind of insipid legal agreement—Lion opens a miniature Web page, shoving it right into your face, even if your Web browser isn't open; see Figure 10-6.

Figure 10-6:
Lion auto-opens a page like this whenever it senses that you're in a commercial WiFi network, one that requires you to sign in. (That's a big improvement from the old way, where you'd join a network and then have no clue that you wouldn't be able to get any further until you opened up your Web browser to find that login screen.)

• If you missed the opportunity to join a hot spot when the message appeared, or if you joined the wrong one or a non-working one, then you have another chance. You can always choose a hot spot's name from the 🛜 menulet, as shown in Figure 10-5. A 🔒 icon indicates a hot spot that requires a password, so you don't waste your time trying to join it (unless, of course, you *have* the password).

Tip: It always takes a computer a few seconds—maybe 5 or 10—to connect to the Internet over WiFi. In Mac OS X, the 📶 menulet itself *pulses,* or rather ripples, with a black-and-gray animation to let you know you're still in the connection process. It's an anti-frustration aid. (Oh, and also, each hot spot's signal strength appears right in the menulet.)

Before you get too excited, though, some lowering of expectations is in order. There are a bunch of reasons why your 📶 menulet might indicate that you're in a hot spot, but you can't actually get online:

- **It's locked.** If there's a 🔒 next to the hot spot's name in your 📶 menulet, then the hot spot has been password protected. That's partly to prevent hackers from "sniffing" the transmissions and intercepting messages, and partly to keep random passersby like you off the network.

- **The signal isn't strong enough.** Sometimes the WiFi signal is strong enough to make the hot spot's name show up in your 📶 menu but not strong enough for an actual connection.

- **You're not on the list.** Sometimes, for security, hot spots are rigged to permit only *specific* computers to join, and yours isn't one of them.

- **You haven't logged in yet.** Commercial hot spots (the ones you have to pay for) don't connect you to the Internet until you've supplied your payment details on a special Web page that appears automatically when you open your browser, as described below.

POWER USERS' CLINIC

The Super-Secret Hot-Spot Management Box

If you open System Preferences→Network, click Wi-Fi in the left-side list, and then click Advanced, you see the dialog box shown here. It lets you manage the list of WiFi hot spots that Mac OS X has memorized on your travels.

For example, you can delete the old ones. Or you can drag the hot spots' names up and down the list to establish a priority for making connections when more than one is available.

Ordinarily, Mac OS X memorizes the names of the various hot spots you join on your travels. It's kind of nice, actually,

because it means you're interrupted less often by the "Do you want to join?" box.

But if you're alarmed at the massive list of hot spots Mac OS X has memorized—for privacy reasons, say—here's where you turn off "Remember networks this computer has joined."

Finally, for added security on your Mac, you can turn on checkboxes that prevent the unauthorized from making changes (creating computer-to-computer networks, changing networks, turning WiFi on or off) without an administrator's password.

• **The router's on, but the Internet's not connected.** Sometimes wireless routers are broadcasting, but their Internet connection is down. It'd be like a cordless phone that has a good connection back to the base station in the kitchen—but the phone cord isn't plugged into the base station.

Commercial Hot Spots

Choosing the name of the hot spot you want to join is generally all you have to do—if it's a *home* WiFi network.

Unfortunately, joining a *commercial* WiFi hot spot—one that requires a credit card number (in a hotel room or airport, for example)—requires more than just connecting to it. You also have to *sign into* it before you can send so much as a single email message.

To do that, open your Web browser—if, in fact, Lion doesn't auto-open the sign-up screen. You'll see the "Enter your payment information" screen either immediately or as soon as you try to open a Web page of your choice. (Even at free hot spots, you might have to click OK on a welcome page to initiate the connection.)

Figure 10-7:
In System Preferences→Network, click your cellular modem's icon (below). Click Connect to get online— or, better yet, turn on "Show WWAN status in menu bar." (It stands for wireless wide-area network, if that helps.) Next time, you'll be able to connect by choosing Connect from this menulet (above) instead of lumbering off to System Preferences.

Supply your credit card information or (if you have a membership to this WiFi chain, like Boingo or T-Mobile) your name and password. Click Submit or Proceed, try *not* to contemplate how this $8 per hour is pure profit for somebody, and enjoy your surfing.

Cellular Modems

WiFi hot spots are fast and usually cheap—but they're hot *spots*. Wander 150 feet away, and you're offline.

No wonder laptop luggers across America are getting into *cellular* Internet services. All the big cellphone companies offer USB sticks that let your laptop get online at high speed *anywhere* in major cities. No hunting for a coffee shop; with cellular Internet service, you can check your email while zooming down the road in a taxi. (Outside the metropolitan areas, you can still get online wirelessly, though much more slowly.)

Verizon, Sprint, and AT&T all offer cellular Internet networks with speeds approaching a cable modem's. So why isn't the world beating a path to this delicious technology's door? Because it's expensive—$60 a month on top of your phone bill.

To get online, insert the USB stick; it may take about 15 seconds for the thing to latch onto the cellular signal.

Now you're supposed to make the Internet connection using the special "dialing" software provided by the cellphone company. Technically, though, you may not need it. You can start and stop the Internet connection using the menulet—no phone-company software required (see Figure 10-7).

Tethering

If you have an iPhone, Android phone, or another app phone, you don't even need a cellular modem; you've already got one. Most app phones nowadays offer *tethering,* where the cellphone tunes into the Internet for the benefit of your laptop (or even desktop computer). The phone connects to your laptop either with a USB cable or wirelessly (Bluetooth or WiFi).

The nice part is that you can get online almost anywhere there's cellphone coverage. The less-nice part is that the connection isn't always blazing fast, and you have to pay your cellphone company for the privilege. (It's usually $20 or $30 on top of your regular monthly phone plan; for that, you're allowed to send and receive 2 gigabytes of data each month. If you go over the limit, you pay overage fees. Good luck figuring that out.)

Here's a typical example: Suppose you have an iPhone. You open Settings→General→Network→Personal Hotspot. You turn it on. You assign a password to your private little hot spot. The iPhone asks how you'll be connecting to the phone; let's say you tap Wi-Fi.

Now, on your laptop, you choose your iPhone's name from the 🛜 menulet. You enter your hot-spot password (just this time—later, your laptop will remember), and presto: Your laptop is online. A bright blue "Personal Hotspot: 1 Connection" banner appears on your iPhone to remind you, and your 📶 menulet changes to become the International Symbol for Apple Tethering: ♋.

Now, tethering eats up your phone's battery like crazy; you'll be lucky to get 3 hours out of it. So you probably shouldn't count on watching Netflix on your laptop via your phone.

But for email, emergency Web checks, and other mobile crises, tethering is a convenient, useful feature. And when you're on the road for a couple of weeks, it's a heck of a lot cheaper than paying your hotel $13 a night for WiFi.

Dial-Up Modem Connections

If you ask Apple, dial-up modems are dead. Macs don't even come with built-in modems anymore. You can get a non-Apple USB modem for $50, but clearly, Apple is trying to shove the trusty dial-up technology into the recycling bin.

Still, millions of people never got the memo. If you're among them, you need to sign up for Internet service. Hundreds of companies, large and small, would love to become your *Internet service provider* (ISP), generally charging $20 or so per month for the privilege of connecting you to the Internet.

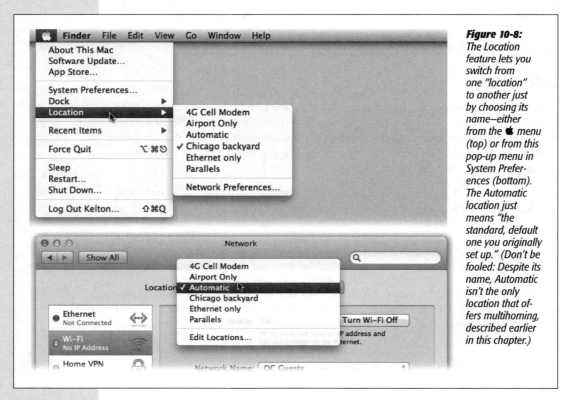

Figure 10-8:
The Location feature lets you switch from one "location" to another just by choosing its name—either from the menu (top) or from this pop-up menu in System Preferences (bottom). The Automatic location just means "the standard, default one you originally set up." (Don't be fooled: Despite its name, Automatic isn't the only location that offers multihoming, described earlier in this chapter.)

Once you've selected a service provider, you plug its settings into the Network pane of System Preferences. You get the necessary information directly from your ISP by consulting either its Web page, the instruction sheets that came with your account, or a help-desk agent on the phone.

Further details on Mac OS X's dial-up modem setup are in the free appendix to this chapter, "Setting Up a Dial-Up Connection." It's available on this book's "Missing CD" page at *www.missingmanuals.com*.

Switching Locations

If you travel with a laptop, you know the drill. You're constantly opening up System Preferences→Network so you can switch between Internet settings: Ethernet at the office, WiFi at home. Or maybe you simply visit the branch office from time to time, and you're getting tired of having to change the local access number for your ISP each time you leave home (and return home again).

The simple solution is the →Location submenu, which appears once you've set up more than one Location. As Figure 10-8 illustrates, all you have to do is tell it where you are. Mac OS X handles the details of switching Internet connections.

Creating a New Location

To create a *Location,* which is nothing more than a set of memorized settings, open System Preferences, click Network, and then choose Edit Locations from the Location pop-up menu. Continue as shown in Figure 10-9.

Tip: You can use the commands in the menu to rename or duplicate a Location.

Figure 10-9:
When you choose Edit Locations, this list of existing Locations appears; click the + button. A new entry appears at the bottom of the list. Type a name for your new location, such as Chicago Office or Dining Room Floor.

When you click Done, you return to the Network panel. Take this opportunity to set up the kind of Internet connection you use at the corresponding location, just as described on the first pages of this chapter.

If you travel regularly, you can build a *list* of Locations, each of which "knows" the way you like to get online in each city you visit.

A key part of making a new Location is putting the various Internet connection types (Ethernet, Wi-Fi, Modem, Bluetooth) into the correct order. Your connections will be slightly quicker if you give the modem connection priority in your Hotel setup, the WiFi connection priority in your Starbucks setup, and so on.

You can even turn off some connections entirely. For example, if you use nothing but a cable modem when you're at home, you might want to create a location in which *only* the Ethernet connection is active. Use the Make Service Inactive command in the ✿ menu.

Conversely, if your laptop uses nothing but WiFi when you're on the road, your Location could include *nothing* but the Wi-Fi connection. You'll save a few seconds each time you try to go online, because your Mac won't bother hunting for an Internet connection that doesn't exist.

Making the Switch

Once you've set up your various Locations, you can switch among them using the 🍎→Location submenu, as shown in Figure 10-8. As soon as you do so, your Mac is automatically set to get online the way you like.

Tip: If you have a laptop, create a connection called Offline. From the Show pop-up menu, choose Network Port Configurations; make *all* the connection methods in the list inactive. When you're finished, you've got yourself a laptop that will *never* attempt to go online. It's the laptop equivalent of Airplane Mode on a cellphone.

Internet Sharing

If you have cable modem or DSL service, you're a very lucky individual. You get terrific Internet speed and an always-on connection. Too bad only one computer in your household or office can enjoy these luxuries.

It doesn't have to be that way. You can spread the joy of high-speed Internet to every Mac (and PC) on your network in either of two ways:

- **Buy a router.** A *router* is a little box, costing about $50, that connects directly to the cable modem or DSL box. In most cases, it has multiple Internet jacks so you can plug in several Macs, PCs, and/or wireless base stations. As a bonus, a router provides excellent security, serving as a firewall to keep out unsolicited visits from hackers on the Internet.

- **Use Internet Sharing.** Mac OS X's Internet Sharing feature is the software version of a router: It distributes a single Internet signal to every computer on the network. But unlike a router, it's free. You just fire it up on the one Mac that's connected directly to the Internet—the *gateway* computer.

  But there's a downside: If the gateway Mac is turned off or asleep, the other machines can't get online.

Most people use Internet Sharing to share a broadband connection like a cable modem or DSL. But there are other times when it comes in handy. If you have a cellular modem, for example, you might want to share its signal via WiFi so the kids in the backseat can get online with their iPod Touches. You could even share a tethered Bluetooth cellphone's Internet connection with a traveling companion who needs a quick email check.

The only requirement: The Internet-connected Mac must have some *other* kind of connection (Ethernet, WiFi, Bluetooth, FireWire) to the Macs that will share the connection.

Turning On Internet Sharing

To turn on Internet Sharing on the gateway Mac, open the Sharing panel of System Preferences. Click Internet Sharing, as shown in Figure 10-10, but don't turn on the checkbox yet.

Figure 10-10:
Ka-ching! You and your buddy just saved money. In this example, a USB cellular modem (Sierra) is getting this Mac online. But it's sharing that Internet connection with other Macs via WiFi. They can get online, too, even though they're not directly connected to the USB modem.

Before you do that, you have to specify (a) how the gateway Mac is connected to the Internet, and (b) how it's connected to the other Macs on your network:

- **Share your connection from.** Using this pop-up menu, identify how *this Mac* (the gateway machine) connects to the Internet—via Built-in Ethernet, Wi-Fi, cellular modem, or Bluetooth DUN (dial-up networking—that is, tethering to your cellphone).

- **To computers using.** Using these checkboxes, specify how you want your Mac to rebroadcast the Internet signal to the others. (It has to be a *different* network channel. You can't get your signal via WiFi and then pass it on via WiFi.)

Note: Which checkboxes appear here depends on which kinds of Internet connections are turned on in the Network pane of System Preferences. If the gateway Mac doesn't have WiFi circuitry, for example, or if WiFi is turned off in the current configuration, the Wi-Fi option doesn't appear.

Now visit each of the other Macs on the same network. Open the Network pane of System Preferences. Select the network method you chose in the second step above: Wi-Fi, Built-in Ethernet, or FireWire. Click Apply.

If the gateway Mac is rebroadcasting using WiFi—by far the most common use of this feature—you have one more step. In your 📶 menulet, you'll see a strange new "hot spot" that wasn't there before, bearing the name of the gateway Mac. (It might say, for example, "Casey's MacBook Air.") Choose its name to begin your borrowed Internet connection.

As long as the gateway Mac remains on and online, both it and your other computers can get onto the Internet simultaneously, all at high speed, even Windows PCs. You've

---

POWER USERS' CLINIC

Internet Sharing as a Bridge

Ordinarily, only one Mac has Internet Sharing turned on: the one that's connected directly to the Internet.

But sometimes, you might want another Mac "downstream" to have it on, too. That's when you want to *bridge* two networks.

Consider the setup shown here. There are really two networks: one that uses WiFi, and another connected to an Ethernet hub.

If you play your cards right, all these Macs can get online simultaneously, using a single Internet connection.

Set up the gateway Mac so that it's a WiFi base station, exactly

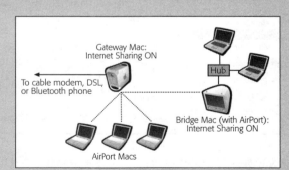

Gateway Mac: Internet Sharing ON

To cable modem, DSL, or Bluetooth phone

Hub

Bridge Mac (with AirPort): Internet Sharing ON

AirPort Macs

as described on these pages.

Start setting up the *bridge* Mac the way you'd set up the other WiFi Macs—with Wi-Fi selected as the primary connection method, and Using DHCP turned on in the Network panel.

Then visit the bridge Mac's Sharing panel. Turn on Internet Sharing here, too, but this time select "To computers using: Built-in Ethernet."

The bridge Mac is now on both networks. It uses the WiFi connection as a bridge to the gateway Mac and the Internet—and its Ethernet connection to share that happiness with the wired Macs in its own neighborhood.

---

created a *software* base station. The Mac itself is now the transmitter for Internet signals to and from any other WiFi computers within range.

Tip: Now that you know how to let a wireless Mac piggyback on a wired Mac's connection, you can let a wired Mac share a *wireless* connection, too. Suppose, for example, that you and a buddy both have laptops in a hotel lobby. You're online, having paid $13 to use the hotel's WiFi network. If you set up Internet Sharing appropriately, your buddy can connect to your Mac via an Ethernet cable or even a FireWire cable and surf along with you—no extra charge.

---

iCloud

Apple's free iCloud service—formerly MobileMe, formerly .Mac, formerly iTools—offers a long list of very useful features. You don't have to sign up, but you owe it to yourself to know what's available.

So what is iCloud? Mainly, it's these things:

- **A synchronizing service.** It keeps your calendar, address book, and documents updated and identical on all your gadgets: Mac, PC, iPhone, iPad, iPod Touch.

- **An online locker.** Anything you buy from Apple—music, TV shows, ebooks, and apps—is stored online, for easy access at any time. For example, whenever you buy a song or a TV show from the online iTunes store, it appears automatically on all your i-gadgets and computers. Your photos are stored online, too.

- **Back to My Mac.** This option lets you grab files from one of your other Macs across the Internet. See page 500.

- **Find My iPhone—and Mac.** Find My iPhone pinpoints the current location of your iPhone or iPad on a map. In other words, it's great for helping you find your i-gadget if it's been stolen or lost.

  You can also make your lost gadget start making a loud pinging sound for a couple of minutes by remote control—even if it was set to Vibrate mode. That's brilliantly effective when your phone has slipped under the couch cushions. In dire situations, you can even erase the phone by remote control, preventing sensitive information from falling into the wrong hands.

  In iCloud, this feature can find your *Mac,* too. That might seem like a silly idea; how often do you misplace your iMac? But 75 percent of all computers Apple sells are laptops.

- **Automatic Backup.** iCloud can back up your iPhone, iPad, or iPod Touch—completely, automatically, and wirelessly (over WiFi, not over cellular connections). It's a quick backup, since iCloud backs up only the changed data.

  If you ever want to set up a new i-gadget, or if you want to restore everything to an existing one, life is sweet. Once you're in a WiFi hot spot, all you have to do is re-enter your Apple ID and password in the setup assistant that appears when

---

you turn the thing on. Magically, your gadget is refilled with everything that used to be on it.

Note: Well, *almost* everything. You get back everything you've bought from Apple (music, apps, books); photos and videos in your Camera Roll; settings, including the layout of your Home screen; text messages; and ringtones. Your mail and anything that came to the gadget from your computer (like music from iTunes and photos from iPhoto) have to be reloaded.

Figure 10-11:
To switch among iCloud features, click the ⬭ button that always appears in the upper-left corner of each feature's screen (like the calendar, shown at top). That summons the icons for the major iCloud Web-based features: email, address book, calendar, Find My iPhone (and Macs and iPads and iPhone Touches), and iWork.

Much of this is based on the central Web site *www.icloud.com* (Figure 10-11).

Starting Up iCloud

iCloud has certain requirements. Your Mac needs Mac OS X 10.7.2 or later, plus iPhoto version 11 or later, and iTunes version 10.5 or later. Your iPhone/iPad/iPod Touch needs iOS 5 or later. On a PC, iCloud requires Windows Vista or later, Outlook 2007 or later, and Apple's free iCloud Control Panel.

Once you have all of this, your iCloud adventure begins in System Preferences; click the iCloud icon. Enter your Apple ID and password (page 552). Click Sign In.

Now the preference pane invites you to turn on two of the biggest iCloud features:

• **Use iCloud for contacts, calendars, and bookmarks.** It's hard to imagine that you'd turn off this option—it's the single most important iCloud feature—but this is the on/off switch if you're some kind of heretic.

• **Use Find My Mac.** This is the "find my lost laptop on a map" feature described earlier in this chapter. Click Next, and then confirm that you *really* want to use Find My Mac.

Figure 10-12:
The headquarters of iCloud's features. You'll find a nearly identical panel on your iPhone, iPad, or iPod Touch (in Settings→iCloud).

At last you arrive at the screen you'll see when you open the iCloud pane on System Preferences from now on (Figure 10-12).

Let your grand tour of iCloud's motley features begin.

iCloud Sync

For many people, this may be the killer app for iCloud right here: The *icloud.com* Web site, acting as the master control center, can keep multiple Macs, Windows PCs, and iPhones/iPads/iPod Touches synchronized. There's both a huge convenience factor—all your stuff is always on all your gadgets—and a safety/backup factor, since you have duplicates everywhere.

It works by storing the master copies of your stuff—email, notes, contacts, calendars, Web bookmarks, and documents—on the Web. (Or "in the cloud," as the product managers would say.)

Whenever your Macs, PCs, or i-gadgets are online, they connect to the mother ship and update themselves. Edit an address on your iPhone, and shortly thereafter, you'll find the same change in Address Book (on your Mac) and Outlook (on your PC). Send an email reply from your PC at the office and you'll find it in your Sent Mail folder on the Mac at home. Add a Web bookmark anywhere and find it everywhere else. Edit a spreadsheet in Numbers on your iPad, find the same numbers updated on your Mac.

Actually, there's another place where you can work with your data: on the Web. At *www.icloud.com,* you can log in to find Web-based clones of iCal, Address Book, Mail, and iWork.

To set up syncing, open System Preferences→iCloud. Turn on the checkboxes of the stuff you want to be synchronized all the way around:

- **Mail & Notes.** "Mail" refers to your actual email messages, plus your account settings and preferences from Mac OS X's Mail program. "Notes" refers to the notes you enter in Mail's Notes feature (Chapter 11). How great to make a reminder for yourself on one Mac and have it reminding you later on another one.

- **Calendars, Contacts.** This is a big one. There's nothing as exasperating as realizing that the Address Book you're consulting on your home Mac is missing somebody you're *sure* you entered—on your computer at work. This option keeps all your Macs' Address Books and iCal calendars synchronized. Delete a phone number at work, and you'll find it deleted on your Mac at home, too. Enter an appointment on your iPhone, and you'll find the calendar updated everywhere else.

- **Bookmarks.** If a Web site is important enough to merit bookmarking while you're using your laptop, why shouldn't it also show up in the Bookmarks menu on your desktop Mac at home, your iPhone, or your PC at work? This option syncs your Safari Reading List, too.

- **Photo Stream.** See the page 324.

- **Documents and Data.** Some programs are available for more than one machine—including Apple's own iWork suite (Numbers, Pages, Keynote). Those programs are available for Mac, iPhone/iPod Touch, and iPad.

In that delicious situation, you can create or edit a document on *one* kind of machine, and marvel as iCloud automatically syncs it with all your *other* devices.

When you fire up one of the iWork programs on an i-gadget, the startup screen offers two buttons: Later (don't connect to iCloud now) or Use iCloud (copy your work wirelessly to iCloud, so your other computers and gadgets can get at it).

From now on, you don't have to do anything special; any document you create or edit appears automatically on your other iCloud-connected machines. If you have iWork for your Mac, your documents are auto-synced to iCloud *if* you've turned on this checkbox in System Preferences.

Figure 10-13:
To see the documents your i-gadgets have stored online, log into iCloud.com. Click the ☁ icon, if necessary, and switch to the iWork mode.

To download one of your mobilely created files, point to its icon and click Download. To upload files from your Mac to your mobile gadgets, drag them into this window from the Finder, or choose Upload from the ✿ menu.

On your computer, though, the syncing isn't quite so automatic; you're supposed to use the iWork page of iCloud.com to upload and download Keynote, Numbers, and Pages files to and from your mobile gadgets. See Figure 10-13.

- **Back to My Mac.** See page 500 for details.
- **Find My Mac.** Read on.

To set up syncing, turn on the checkboxes for the items you want synced.

Note: You may notice that there are no checkboxes here for syncing stuff you buy from Apple, like books, movies, apps, and music. They're not so much *synced* as they are *stored* for you online. You can download them at any time to any of your machines.

After the first sync with the first machine, you can turn on the checkboxes on the other computers and gadgets, too, in effect telling them to participate in the great data-sharing experiment.

Photo Stream

Every time a new photo enters your life—when you take a picture with an i-gadget, for example, or import one onto your computer—it gets added to your Photo Stream. In other words, it appears automatically on all your *other* iCloud machines. Here's where to find them:

- **iPhone, iPad, iPod Touch.** Open your Photos app. There it is: a new listing called Photo Stream. It shows the most recent 1,000 photos you've taken with any of your *other* i-gadgets, or that you've imported to your computer from a scanner or digital camera.

  Now, Apple realizes that your i-gadget doesn't have nearly as much space available as your Mac or PC; you can't yet buy an iPad with 750 gigabytes of storage. That's why, on your iPhone/iPad/iPod, your Photo Stream consists of just the last 1,000 photos. (There's another limitation, too: The iCloud servers store your photos for 30 days. As long as your gadgets go online at least once a month, they'll remain current with the photo stream.)

Figure 10-14:
Left: Why, look! It's photos you imported onto your Mac at home. How'd they get here on the iPhone? iCloud!

Middle: To rescue one of these photos from the 1,000-Photo Rule, open it. Then tap the ⬆ button.

Right: Finally, tap Save to Camera Roll. Now, even after that photo disappears from the Photo Stream, having been displaced by the 1,001st incoming photo, you'll still have your permanent copy.

Once a photo arrives, you can save it to your Camera Roll, where it's permanently saved. See Figure 10-14.

Note: Photo Stream doesn't sync over the cellular airwaves. It sends photos around only when you're in a WiFi hot spot or connected to a wired network.

- **On the Mac or PC.** In iPhoto (Mac), your Photo Stream photos appear in a new album called, of course, Photo Stream. On a Windows PC, you get a Photo Stream folder in your Pictures folder.

  You don't have to worry about that 30-day, 1,000-photo business. Once pictures appear here, they're here until you delete them.

  This, in its way, is one of the best features in all of iCloudland, because it means you don't have to sync your iPhone over a USB cable to get your photos onto your computer. It all happens automatically, wirelessly over WiFi.

- **Apple TV.** When you're viewing your photos on an Apple TV, a new album appears there called Photo Stream. There they are, ready for showing on the big plasma.

If you bought your gadget/photo software/Apple TV before iCloud's debut, of course, you'll need a software update to add the Photo Stream feature.

Find My Mac, Find My iPhone

Did your laptop get stolen? Did you leave your iPhone somewhere? Has that mischievous 5-year-old hidden your iPad again?

Now you can check into iCloud.com to see exactly where your Mac, iPhone, or iPad is. You can even make it beep loudly for 2 minutes, so you can figure out which couch cushion it's under, or which jacket pocket you left it in. If the missing item is an iPad or an iPhone, you can make it beep even if the ringer switch is off, and even if the phone is asleep. You can also make a message pop up on the screen; if you actually left the thing in a taxi or on some restaurant table, you can use this feature to plead for its return. The bottom line: If you ever lose your Apple gear, you have a fighting chance at getting it back.

(That's *if* it's online, and *if* you turned on Find My Mac in the iCloud panel of System Preferences.)

If an ethical person finds your phone, you might get it back. If it's a greedy person who says, "Hey, cool! A free iPhone!" then maybe you can bombard him with so many of these messages that he gives it back in exasperation.

If not, you can either lock the gadget with a password (yes, by remote control) or even avail yourself of one more amazing last-ditch feature: Remote Wipe.

That means *erasing your data by remote control*, from wherever you happen to be. The evil thief can do nothing but stare in amazement as the phone, tablet, or Mac suddenly erases itself, winding up completely empty.

(If you ever get the device back, you can just sync with iTunes, and presto! Your stuff is back—at least everything since your last sync.)

To set up your Mac so you can find it remotely, open System Preferences→iCloud. Make sure Find My Mac is turned on. That's all there is to it.

Later, if the worst should come to pass and you can't find your Mac, go to any computer and call up *www.icloud.com*. Log in with your Apple name and password.

Click the ⌂ icon at upper left; in the list of iCloud features, click Find My iPhone. If you're asked for your password again, type it; Apple wants to make sure it's really, *really* you who's messing around with your account settings.

Finally, in the panel on the left side, click the name of your Mac.

Immediately, the Web site updates to show you, on a map, the current location of your Macs (and iPhones, iPod Touches, and iPads); see Figure 10-15.

Figure 10-15:
The location process can take a couple of minutes. You can zoom into or out of the map, click Satellite to see an overhead photo of the area, or click Hybrid to see the photo with street names superimposed.

Note: If they're not online, or if they're turned all the way off, you won't see their current locations. If your Mac is asleep, you won't find it, although if your i-gadget is asleep, you will.

If just knowing where the thing *is* isn't enough to satisfy you, click the little pushpin that represents your Mac, and try one of these three buttons:

- **Display Message or Play Sound.** Click this button, type a message, and then click Send. Instantly, that message appears on the Mac's screen, wherever it is, no matter what app was running. Whoever's using it can't miss it, can't even do anything without dismissing the message.

  When it's all over, Apple sends an email confirmation to your @me.com address.

- **Lock.** What if you worry about the security of your Mac's info, but you don't want to erase it completely and just want to throw a low-level veil of casual protection over the thing? Easy: Lock it by remote control. The Lock button lets you make up a four-digit passcode. Without it, the sleazy crook can't get into your Mac without erasing it.

- **Remote Wipe.** This is the last-ditch security option, for when your immediate concern isn't so much the Mac as all the private stuff that's on it. Click this button, confirm the dire warning box, and click Erase All Data. By remote control, you've just erased everything from your Mac, wherever it may be. (If it's ever returned, you can restore it from your Time Machine backup.)

UP TO SPEED

iTunes in the Cloud

Anything you've ever bought from the iTunes music store is now available for playing on any Apple gadget you own. We get it.

A lot of people, however, have music in their collections that *didn't* come from the iTunes store. Maybe they ripped some audio CDs into their computers. Maybe they acquired some music from, ahem, a friend.

What a sad situation! You've got some of your music available with you on any computer or mobile gadget, and some that's stranded at home on your computer.

Enter iTunes Match. It's an Apple service that lets you store your *entire* collection, including songs that didn't come from Apple, online, for $25 a year.

The iTunes software analyzes the songs in your collection. If it finds a song that's also available in iTunes, then—*bing!*—that song becomes available for your playback pleasure, without your actually having to transfer your copy to Apple. Apple says, in effect: "Well, our copy of the song is just as good as yours, so you're welcome to listen to our copy on any of your machines."

Truth is, in fact, Apple's copy is probably *better* than your copy. You get to play back the song at iTunes' 256-Kbps quality, no matter how grungy your own copy was.

If there's a song or two in your collection that are *not* among Apple's 20 million tracks, you can upload them to Apple.

The advantages of forking over the $25 a year are (a) you can listen to *all* your music from any computer/phone/tablet, (b) using the song-matching system saves you hours or days of uploading time, and (c) that audio-quality upgrade.

The disadvantage: You're paying $25 a year.

Once you've wiped the Mac, you can no longer find it or send messages to it using Find My Mac.

Email

Apple offers an email address as part of each iCloud account. Of course, you already *have* an email account. So why bother? The first advantage is the simple address: *YourName@me.com.*

Second, me.com addresses are integrated into Mac OS X's Mail program, as you'll see in the next chapter. And, finally, you can read your me.com email from any computer anywhere in the world, via the iCloud.com Web site, or on your iPhone/iPod Touch/iPad.

To make things even sweeter, your me.com mail is completely synced. Delete a message on one gadget, and you'll find it in the Deleted Mail folder on another. Send a message from your iPad, and you'll find it in the Sent Mail folder on your Mac. And so on.

Books, Music, Apps, Movies: The Locker in the Sky

Apple, as if you hadn't noticed, has become a big seller of multimedia files. It has the biggest music store in the world. It has the biggest app store, for both i-gadgets and Macs. It sells an awful lot of TV shows and movies. Its ebook store, iBooks, is no Amazon.com, but it's chugging along.

When you buy a song, movie, app, or book, you've always been allowed to copy it to all your other Apple equipment—no extra charge. But iCloud automates, or at least

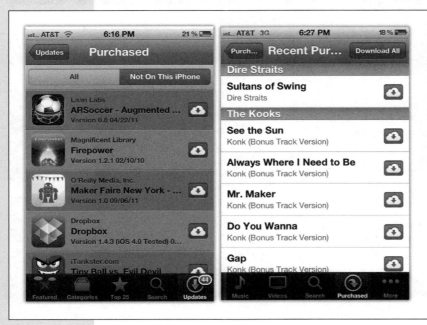

Figure 10-16:
Anything you've bought from Apple, like apps (left), music (right), TV shows, and ebooks, is always available to you, from any Mac or i-gadget, for redownloading from the great Apple locker in the sky. Tap the cloud-with-arrow button to download something to the machine you're using now.

formalizes, that process. Once you buy something, it's added to a tidy list of items that you can download to all your *other* machines.

Here's how to grab them:

- **iPhone, iPad, iPod Touch.** Open the App Store icon (for apps), the iBooks program (for books), or the iTunes app (for songs or TV shows; tap the category you want). Tap Updates. Tap Purchased. Tap Not on My iPhone (see Figure 10-16).

  There they are: all the items you've bought on your *other* machines using the same Apple ID. To download anything listed here onto *this* machine, tap the ☁ button. Or tap an album name to see the list of songs on it so you can download just *some* of those songs.

  You can save yourself all that tapping by opening Settings→Store and turning the Automatic Downloads switches to On (for Music, Apps, and Books). From now on, whenever you're in WiFi, stuff you've bought on other Apple machines gets downloaded to this one *automatically*, in the background.

Note: Any bookmark you set in an iBooks book is synced to your other gadgets, too. The idea, of course, is that you can read a few pages on your phone in the doctor's waiting room, and then continue on your iPad from the same page on the train ride home.

- **Mac or PC.** Open the App Store program (for apps) or the iTunes app (for songs, TV shows, books, and movies). Under the Store heading, there they are: individual subheadings for each gadget you've used to buy stuff: "Purchased on iPhone," "Purchased on Mom's iPad," and so on. Or just click Purchased to view the entire list. There are all your purchases, ready to open or redownload if necessary.

Tip: To make this automatic, open iTunes. Choose iTunes→Preferences→Store. Under Automatic Downloads, turn on Music, Apps, and Books, as you see fit. Click OK.

SWITCHING TO THE MAC: THE MISSING MANUAL

Mail & Address Book

You know how every copy of Windows comes with a free, basic email program like Outlook Express or Windows Mail? Well, every copy of Mac OS X comes with Mail, a slightly fancier email program that's also free. Mail is a surprisingly complete, refreshingly attractive program, filled with shortcuts and surprises. Together with the high-octane Address Book program included with Mac OS X, you may never pine for your Windows setup again.

Note: This chapter assumes that you've already transferred your email, addresses, and email account settings to Mail and the Address Book, as described in Chapter 6.

Checking Your Mail

You get new mail and send mail you've already written using the Get Mail command. You can trigger it in any of several ways:

- Click the ✉ button on the toolbar.
- Choose Mailbox→Get All New Mail (or press Shift-⌘-N).

Note: If you have multiple email accounts, you can also use the Mailbox→Get New Mail submenu to pick just *one* account to check for new mail.

- Right-click Mail's Dock icon, and choose Get New Mail from the shortcut menu. (You can use this method from within any program, as long as Mail is already open.)

• Wait. Mail comes set to check your email automatically every few minutes. To adjust its timing or to turn this feature off, choose Mail→Preferences, click General, and then choose a time interval from the "Check for new messages" pop-up menu.

Now Mail contacts the mail servers listed in the Accounts pane of Mail's preferences, retrieving new messages and downloading any files attached to those messages. It also *sends* any outgoing messages that couldn't be sent when you wrote them.

The Mailboxes List

The mailboxes panel, the leftmost list on the screen, isn't just for mailboxes. Categories like Reminders and RSS Feeds can appear there, too, as shown in Figure 11-1. But the top half of this gray-blue column on the left side lists all your email accounts' folders (and subfolders, and sub-subfolders) for easy access. Mail looks quite a bit like iTunes (and iPhoto, and the Finder)—except here you have mailboxes where your iTunes Library and connected iPods would be.

Tip: You can also collapse or expand the various sections of the mailboxes list (On My Mac and Reminders, for example) by clicking the Hide or Show button next to each one. That button doesn't appear, however, until you *point* to the section title (like Mailboxes or On My Mac).

Figure 11-1:
Click an icon in the mailboxes column to see its contents in the messages list. The messages list shows you the first couple of lines of each message, along with photos of the senders, if available in your Address Book. Click one of the column headings (From, Subject, and so on) to sort your mail collection by that criterion.

Under the Mailboxes heading, you may find these folders:

• **Inbox** holds mail you've received. If you have more than one email account, you can expand the triangles to see separate folders for each of your accounts. You'll see this pattern repeated with the Sent, Junk, and other mailboxes, too—separate accounts have separate subheadings.

Tip: If Mail has something to tell you about your Inbox (like, for instance, that Mail can't connect to it), a tiny warning triangle (⚠) appears on the right side of the Mailboxes heading. Click it to see what Mail is griping about.

If you see a wavy ⚡ icon, that's Mail's way of announcing that you're offline. Click the icon to try to connect to the Internet.

- **Outbox** holds mail you've written but haven't yet sent (because you were on an airplane when you wrote it, for example). If you have no mail waiting to be sent, the Outbox disappears.

- **Drafts** holds messages you've started but haven't yet finished and don't want to send just yet.

- **Sent,** unsurprisingly, holds copies of messages you've sent.

- **Trash** works a lot like the Trash on your desktop, in that messages you put there don't actually disappear. They remain in the Trash folder until you permanently delete them or move them somewhere else—or until Mail's automatic trash-cleaning service deletes them for you.

- **Junk** appears automatically when you use Mail's spam filter, as described later in this chapter.

- **Reminders.** Any Notes you've jotted down while working in Mail are here. If you've flagged any messages, the flag headings appear here, too. (Notes and flags are both described later in this chapter.)

- **RSS Feeds.** Who needs to bop into a Web browser to keep up with the news? Mail brings it right to you while you're corresponding, as described in a moment.

- **Mail Activity.** You don't need to summon a separate window to see how much more of that message with the giant attachment the program still has to send. To reveal the Mail activity panel, click the tiny ▣ icon below the Mailboxes list.

Tip: You can drag the mailboxes up and down in the list. Sweet.

Tailoring the Look of Mail

In a program made for managing lists and reading messages, you need all the room you can get. In Mail, you can choose either the Lion layout (three columns) or the Classic layout (list above, message below). The following pages offer advice in modifying the design of either layout.

Tweaking the Lion layout
The Lion layout is the three-column view shown at top in Figure 11-2.

Here's some of the plastic surgery you can perform:

- **Try full-screen mode.** Click the ⬈ in the upper-right corner of the window to make the Mail window expand to fill your monitor. (See page 11 for details on

Standard view (three columns)   Standard view (folder column hidden)

Classic view

Figure 11-2:
In Lion, Mail can have several different layouts. In the new, standard three-column view (top), all your information sources—mailboxes, Notes, and RSS feeds—are grouped tidily in the far-left column. You can hide that column, though, so that you have more space for reading (middle). You can also return to the pre-Lion layout (bottom), in which the messages list is above the message body.

full-screen mode.) Full-screen is a natural for space-hungry email, especially on a small screen (like the 11-inch MacBook Air).

- **Install folders onto the Favorites bar.** You can drag any icon in the mailboxes list onto the Favorites toolbar, where it becomes a button or a pop-up menu. The button works exactly like a folder: For example, you can drag a message onto one to file it there, or you can click one of these folder buttons (or use its pop-up menu) to see what's inside.

  The Favorites bar comes with starter buttons already installed, like Inbox, Sent, Notes, and so on. But you can, and should, install your *own* favorites there, and remove the ones you don't want. (To move a button around, ⌘-drag it. To get rid of it, just drag it away from the toolbar.)

Tip: You can also hide this new Favorites bar whenever you feel the urge. Choose View→Hide Favorites Bar, of course.

- **Hide the mailboxes panel completely.** To do that, click the ⊡ button above it. Now you have much more screen space to work with.

Tip: Hey, here's a thought! *Combine* the previous two ideas. Install the most important folders onto the Favorites bar, so you can get at them, and *then* hide the mailboxes list. Now you have easy access to the most important folders, but your mailboxes list isn't eating up a lot of screen space. This glorious, space-efficient result is shown back in Figure 11-2, center.

- **Label the toolbar buttons.** Out of the box, the buttons on the toolbar (✉, 🗑, and so on) have no labels. But if you right-click the toolbar, you get a pop-up menu that offers you other styles for those buttons: Icon & Text, Icon Only, Text Only (which is *very* space-efficient), and None (which is even more space-efficient—provided you know the keyboard shortcuts for all the buttons you've just hidden away).

- **Change the type size/icon size for the folders in the mailboxes panel.** To do that, open System Preferences→General. Use the "Sidebar icon size" pop-up menu to choose Small, Medium, or Large.

Note: Whatever size you choose here also affects the font and icon sizes in the *Finder window Sidebar.* Apple figures that if you're that eagle eyed (or that vision impaired), you'll want the same size adjustment in both apps.

- **Redesign the New Message window.** What signature do you want stamped on every outgoing message? Do you want the "Cc:" and "Bcc:" lines to show up? How about the Priority pop-up menu?

  You can make all these settings using the little ⊟▾ menu in the New Message window; see Figure 11-3.

- **Adjust the message window width.** Drag the very right edge of the window inward or outward to adjust the width of the message itself. Double-click the edge of the messages list to hide the *message* completely. Now you have only the mailboxes list and the very wide messages list; to read a message, you have to double-click it to open it into a new window. (Double-click the right edge of the window to restore the message-reading pane.)

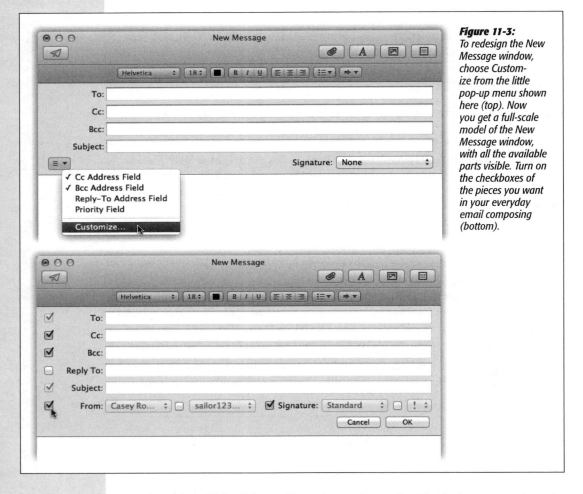

Figure 11-3:
To redesign the New Message window, choose Customize from the little pop-up menu shown here (top). Now you get a full-scale model of the New Message window, with all the available parts visible. Turn on the checkboxes of the pieces you want in your everyday email composing (bottom).

- **Adjust the width of the mailboxes or messages list.** Similarly, you can drag the right edges of the first two columns to adjust their width. Or double-click the right edge to make the column exactly as wide as Mail thinks it should be.

- **Change what morsels show up in the messages list.** The messages list (center column) usually shows the sender's name, subject line, and the first few lines of the message itself (an iPhone/iPad feature brought to the Mac). But you can add additional info displays to the list—message size, mailbox, date sent, and so on—by choosing from the View→Message Attributes submenu.

- **Change what details show up in the header.** The *header* is the top part of a message, where you see the details of how the message reached you. Ordinarily, Mail shields you from the geekiest details of the header; if you really want to see it all, choose View→Message→All Headers.

  But if you'd rather, you can tailor the standard header so that Mail always shows you exactly the information you want. In Mail→Preferences→Viewing, use the "Show header detail" pop-up menu to choose Custom. Now you can add just the details you always want to see: Attachments, BCC, CC, Flag, From, Reply-To, Resent-CC, and so on.

- **Control how many lines of preview text appear.** In Mail→Preferences→Viewing, you can use the List Preview pop-up menu to control how many lines of each message you want to appear, in light gray, as a preview of what's in the message itself. You can choose up to five lines, or choose None to hide the preview completely.

- **Sort the messages.** Use the "Sort by" pop-up menu above the messages list (by Date, by Attachment, by Unread, and so on). Use the bottom two commands—Ascending or Descending—to control *which way* the sorting goes (A to Z, Z to A, or whatever).

Tweaking the Classic layout

Out of the box, Mail assumes a new three-column layout (Figure 11-2, top): mailboxes list at left, messages list in the middle, and the message itself at right.

But if you hate it, you can use the older layout, shown at bottom in Figure 11-2, by choosing Mail→Preferences→Viewing and turning on "Show Classic layout."

You have a bunch of customization options here, too:

- **Adjust the columns.** You can make a column in the messages list narrower or wider by dragging the right edge of its column *heading*, or rearrange the columns by dragging their titles. Similarly, you can *sort* your email by clicking these column headings, exactly as in the Finder. Click a second time to reverse the sorting order. You can also control *which* columns appear using the commands in the View→Columns menu.

- **Hide the message body.** You can get rid of the message-reading pane altogether by double-clicking the divider line, double-clicking just above the vertical scroll bar, or dragging the divider line's handle all the way to the bottom of the screen. Bring it back by dragging the divider line up from the bottom.

- **Control the mailboxes pane.** Drag the thin vertical line that separates this tinted column from the white messages area to make the column wider or narrower. You can make the column disappear or reappear by choosing View→Hide Mailbox List (or View→Show Mailbox List), or by pressing Shift-⌘-M.

The toolbar

In either layout—Lion or Classic—you have full control over the toolbar, which works much like the Finder toolbar. You can rearrange or remove icon buttons (by ⌘-dragging them); add interesting new buttons to the toolbar (by choosing View→ Customize Toolbar); change its display to show just text labels or just icons (choose View→Customize Toolbar, and then use the Show pop-up menu); or hide the toolbar entirely (using the View→Hide Toolbar command).

Tip: Even when the toolbar is hidden, you can still hit Option-⌘-F to use the search box. (Press ⌘-F by itself to search the *current message.)*

Writing Messages

To send an email, click [✏️] in the toolbar or press ⌘-N. The New Message form, shown in Figure 11-4, opens. Here's how you go about writing a message:

1. **In the "To:" field, type the recipient's email address.**

   If somebody is in your Address Book, type the first couple of letters of the name or email address; Mail automatically completes the address. (If the first guess is wrong, type another letter or two until Mail revises its guess.)

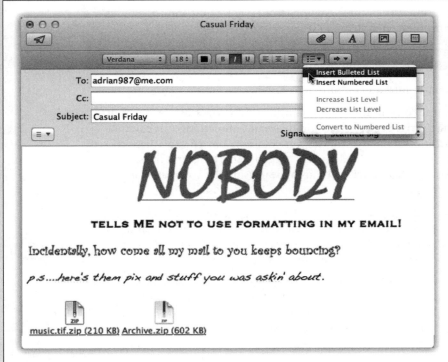

Figure 11-4:
If you want to use formatting, click the Show Format Bar icon ([A]) on the toolbar to open the Format bar—a strip of buttons for font, style, color, justification, bulleted lists, indentation, and so on. (The Format menu contains menu versions of the same stuff.)

Tip: If Mail constantly tries to autofill in the address of someone you don't really communicate with, you can zap that address from its memory by choosing Window→Previous Recipients. Click the undesired address, and then click Remove From List.

As in most dialog boxes, you can jump from blank to blank (from "To:" to "Cc:," for example) by pressing Tab. To send this message to more than one person, separate the addresses with commas: *bob@earthlink.net, billg@microsoft.com,* and so on.

Tip: If you send most of your email to addresses within the same organization (like *reddelicious@apple.com, grannysmith@apple.com,* and *winesap@apple.com*), Mail can automatically turn all *other* email addresses red. It's a feature designed to avoid sending confidential messages to outside addresses.

To turn this feature on, choose Mail→Preferences, click Composing, turn on "Mark addresses not ending with," and then type the "safe" domain (like *apple.com*) into the blank.

2. **To send a copy to other recipients, enter their addresses in the "Cc:" field.**

UP TO SPEED

Bcc:, Reply-To, and Priority

A blind carbon copy is a secret copy. This feature lets you send a copy of a message to somebody secretly, without any of the other recipients knowing that you did so. To view this field when composing a message (if it's not already visible), choose View→Bcc Address Field.

You can use the "Bcc:" field to quietly signal a third party that a message has been sent. For example, if you send your coworker a message that says, "Chris, it bothers me that you've been cheating the customers," you could Bcc your supervisor to clue her in without getting into trouble with Chris.

The "Bcc:" box is useful in other ways, too. Many people send email messages (corny jokes, for example) to a long list of recipients. You, the recipient, have to scroll through the long list of names the sender placed in the "To:" or "Cc:" field.

But if the sender used the "Bcc:" field to hold all the recipients' email addresses, you won't see anybody else's names at the top of the email. In the "To:" box, you might see the sender's name, or "undisclosed recipients," or nothing at all. (Spammers have also learned this trick, which is why it usually looks like you're the only recipient of a junk message when there are actually millions of other people who received the same message.)

Another hidden field you can add to your messages is *Reply-To.* (Choose View→Reply-To Address Field.) That field has one simple purpose: to make the recipient's email program reply to a different email address than the one you sent the message from.

For example, if your business email address isn't working but you absolutely *have* to send a field report to your boss, you can send the message from your personal email account but put your business address in the Reply-To field. That way, when your boss emails you back to congratulate you, the email goes to your business account.

Finally, if you click the ⊟▾ on the left side of an email message and choose Customize, you can enable one more hidden header option: Priority. (It's the pop-up menu with an exclamation mark in it.) If you turn on the checkbox next to that pop-up menu and click OK, then all your email messages let you set how important they are on a three-tiered scale.

The good part about this system is that it lets your recipient see that an email you've sent is, for example, urgent. The bad part is that not every email program displays the priority of email—and even if your recipient's email program *does* display your message's priority, there's no guarantee that it'll make him respond any faster.

Cc stands for *carbon copy*. Getting an email message where your name is in the "Cc:" line implies: "I sent you a copy because I thought you'd want to know about this correspondence, but I'm not expecting you to reply."

Tip: If Mail recognizes the address you type into the "To:" or "Cc:" box (because it's someone in your Address Book, for instance), then the name turns into a shaded, round-ended box button. In addition to looking cool, these buttons sprout a ▾ when you point to them; when you click there, you get a list of useful commands (including Show Contact Card).

These buttons are also drag-and-droppable. For example, you can drag one from the "To:" field to the "Cc:" field, or from Address Book to Mail.

---

3. Type the topic of the message in the Subject field.

It's courteous to put some thought into the subject line. (Use "Change in plans for next week," for instance, instead of "Yo.") On the other hand, don't put the *entire* message into the subject line, either.

4. Specify an email format.

There are two kinds of email: *plain text* and *formatted* (which Apple calls Rich Text— not to be confused with Rich Text Format word processing format, which is very different). Plain text messages are faster to send and open, are universally compatible with the world's email programs, and are greatly preferred by many veteran computer fans. And even though the message itself is plain, you can still attach pictures and other files.

By contrast, formatted messages sometimes appear without any formatting at all in some email programs.

To control which kind of mail you send on a message-by-message basis, choose from the Format menu either Make Plain Text or Make Rich Text. To change the factory setting for new outgoing messages, choose Mail→Preferences; click the Composing icon; and choose from the Message Format pop-up menu.

Tip: If you plan to send formatted mail, remember that your recipients won't see the fonts you use unless their machines have the same ones installed. Bottom line: For email to Mac and Windows owners alike, stick to universal choices like Arial, Times, and Courier.

---

5. Type your message in the message box.

You can use all standard editing techniques, including copy and paste, drag and drop, and so on. If you selected the Rich Text style of email, you can use word processor–like formatting (Figure 11-4).

As you type, Mail checks your spelling, using a dotted underline to mark questionable words. You can read much more about Mac OS X's built-in spelling/grammar checker (and typing expander) in Chapter 5.

If you're composing a long email message, or if it's one you don't want to send until later, click the Save as Draft button, press ⌘-S, or choose File→Save. You've just saved the message in your Drafts folder. It'll still be there the next time you open Mail. To reopen a saved draft later, click the Drafts icon in the mailboxes column and then double-click the message you want to work on.

6. **Click Send** ⌑ **(or press Shift-⌘-D).**

   Mail sends the message.

Tip: To resend a message you've already sent, click it and then choose Message→Send Again, or press Shift-⌘-D.

If you'd rather have Mail place each message you write in the Outbox folder instead of connecting to the Internet when you click Send, choose Mailbox→Take All Accounts Offline. While you're offline, Mail refrains from trying to connect, which is a great feature when you're working on a laptop at 39,000 feet and didn't feel like paying for WiFi. (Choose Mailbox→Take All Accounts Online to reverse the procedure.)

Attaching Files to Messages

Sending little text messages is fine, but it's not much help when you want to send somebody a photograph, a sound, or a Word document. To attach a file to a message you've written, use one of these methods:

- Drag the icons you want to attach directly off the desktop (or out of a folder) and into the New Message window. There your attachments appear with their own hyperlinked icons (visible in Figure 11-4), meaning that your recipient can simply click to open them.

Tip: Exposé was *born* for this moment. Hit ⌘-F3 to make all open windows flee to the edges of the screen, revealing the desktop. Root around until you find the file you want to send. Begin dragging it; without releasing the mouse, press ⌘-F3 again to bring your message window back into view. Complete your drag into the message window.

Mail makes it look as though you can park the attached file's icon (or the full image of a graphics file) *inside* the text of the message, mingled with your typing. Don't be fooled, however; on the receiving end, all the attachments will be clumped together at the end of the message (unless your recipient also uses Mail or you've sent pictures with Stationery).

- Drag the icons you want to attach from the desktop onto Mail's *Dock icon.* Mail dutifully creates a new outgoing message, with the files already attached.

- Click the (⬚) on the New Message toolbar, choose File→Attach Files, or press Shift-⌘-A. The standard Open File sheet now appears so you can navigate to and select the files you want to include. (You can choose multiple files simultaneously in this dialog box. Just ⌘-click or Shift-click the individual files you want as though you were selecting them in a Finder window.)

Once you've selected them, click Choose File (or press Return). You return to the New Message window, where the attachments' icons appear, ready to ride along when you send the message.

To remove an attachment, drag across its icon to highlight it, and then press the Delete key. (You can also choose Message→Remove Attachments.)

Signatures

Signatures are bits of text that get stamped at the bottom of your outgoing email messages. A signature might contain a name, a postal address, a pithy quote, or even a scan of your *real* signature.

You can customize your signatures, as shown in Figure 11-5, by choosing Mail→Preferences→Signatures. Here's what you should know:

- **To build up a library of signatures that you can use in any of your accounts:** Select All Signatures in the leftmost pane, and then click the **+** button to add each new signature (Figure 11-5). Give each new signature a name in the middle pane, and then customize the signatures' text in the rightmost pane.

Attachment Tricks

Nowadays, what's attached to an email message is often more important than the message itself. You might send a PowerPoint file to a coworker or send your aunt a picture of your new dog, for example, without bothering to write anything more than "See attached" in the body of the message.

That's why it's such a pain when email attachments don't go through properly—or when they're too big to send at all. Luckily, Mac OS X provides three tools for making attachments smaller and more compatible with Windows, so you'll never get another angry "I *can't* see attached!" reply again.

If you're sending images along with your message, you can shrink them down right in Mail. Use the Image Size pop-up menu in the lower-right corner of the window to pick a smaller size for the images (like Medium or Small).

You can keep tabs on the total size of your attachments in the lower-left corner of the window, too. Ideally, you should keep the total under 2 MB, so dial-up sufferers don't get annoyed—and so your message doesn't get rejected by your recipient's ISP for being too big.

Use the Finder to compress big files before you send them. It makes the Finder creates zip-compressed files, which gener-

ally take up much less space than the originals.

You can pick from two different formats for your attachments: normal or Windows-friendly. Normal attachments open correctly on both Macs and PCs. Trouble is, a normal attachment may show up on a PC accompanied by a useless second attachment whose name starts with "._" (which can frustrate your recipients).

Windows-friendly attachments, on the other hand, always work correctly on PCs—but when sent to Macs, they lose minor details like color labels and originating Web site information.

Bottom line: Unless you work in an all-Mac company, stick with the Windows-friendly setting.

To use the Windows-friendly setting for an open message, choose Edit→Attachments→Send Windows-Friendly Attachments. (If no message is open, the command says *Always* Send Windows-Friendly Attachments instead). You can also adjust the setting on a per-email basis using the Send Windows-Friendly Attachments checkbox at the bottom of the attachment dialog box.

Tip: If you ever get tired of a signature, you can delete it forever by selecting All Signatures→[your signature's name], clicking the — button, and then clicking OK.

- **To make a signature available in one of your email accounts:** Drag the signature's name from the middle pane onto the name of the account in the leftmost pane. In other words, you can make certain signatures available to only your work (or personal) account, so you never accidentally end up appending your secret FBI contact signature to the bottom of a birthday invitation you send out.

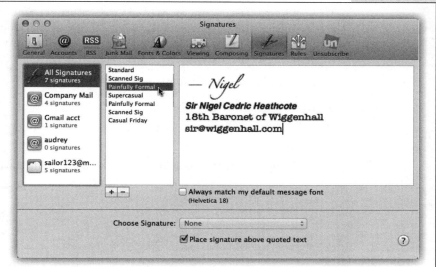

Figure 11-5:
After naming your signature in the middle pane and typing the text on the right, don't miss the Format menu, which you can use to dress up your signature with colors and formatting. You can even paste a picture into the signature box. Click OK when you're finished. (You can use formatted signatures only when sending Rich Text messages.)

- **To assign a particular signature to one account:** In the left pane, click an account; pick from the Choose Signature pop-up menu. Each time you compose a message from that account, Mail inserts the signature you selected.

Tip: To make things more interesting for your recipients, pick At Random; Mail selects a different signature each time you send a message. Or, if you're not that much of a risk-taker, choose In Sequential Order; Mail picks the next signature in order for each new message you write.

Remember that you can always change your signature on a message-by-message basis, using the Signature pop-up menu in any new email message.

- **To use the signature feature as a prefix in replies:** Turn on "Place signature above quoted text." If you turn on this setting, your signature gets inserted *above* any text that you're replying to, rather than below. You'd use this setting if your "signature" said something like, "Hi there! You wrote this to me!"

Tip: If you're into consistent typographical styling, also turn on "Always match my default font." That setting makes sure that any messages you send contain the signature in the same font as the rest of the message, lending it an air of professionalism.

Stationery

Suppose you have an occasion where you *want* to jazz up your mail, like an invitation to a bridal shower or a mass-mail update as you get your kicks down Route 66.

These messages just cry out for Mail's *Stationery* feature. Stationery means colorful, predesigned mail templates that you make your own by dragging in photos from your own collection. Those fancy fonts and graphics will certainly get people's attention when they open the message.

Here's how to make a stylized message with Mail Stationery:

1. **Create a new message.**

   Click File→New Message, press ⌘-N, or click the ☑ button on the Mail window toolbar.

2. **On the right side of the toolbar in the New Message window, click the ▣ button.**

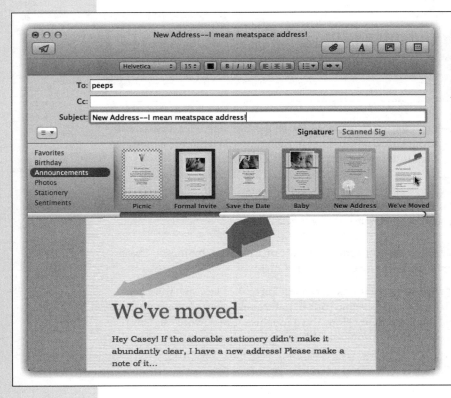

Figure 11-6:
To use Stationery, start by clicking a template, and then add your own text in place of the generic copy that comes with the template.

A panel opens up, showing you all the available templates, in categories like Birthday and Announcements (Figure 11-6).

3. **Click a category, and then click a stationery thumbnail image to apply it to your message.**

   The body of your message changes to take on the look of the template.

4. **If you like what you see, click the ▣ button on the toolbar again to fold up the stationery-picker panel.**

   Now, Apple's canned stationery looks fantastic. The only problem is, the photos on most of the templates are pictures of *somebody else's* family and friends. Unless you work for Apple's modeling agency, you probably have no clue who they are.

   Fortunately, it's easy enough to replace those placeholder photos with your *own* snaps.

5. **Add and adjust pictures.**

   Click the Photo Browser icon (▣) on the toolbar to open up a palette that lists all the photos you've stored in iPhoto, Aperture, and Photo Booth.

Tip: If you don't keep your pictures in any of those programs, you can drag any folder of pictures onto the Photo Browser window to add them.

Now you can drag your own pictures directly onto Apple's dummy photos on the stationery template. They replace the sunny models. You don't have to know a lick of HTML to use the templates—it's all drag, drop, and type, baby.

To resize a photo in the template, double-click it. A slider appears that lets you adjust the photo's size within the message. Drag the mouse around the photo window to reposition the picture relative to its frame.

6. **Select the fake text and type in what you really want to say.**

   As you type over the dummy text, your words are autoformatted to match the template design.

Once you've got your message looking the way you want it, address it just as you would any other piece of mail, and then click the Send ◁ button to get it on its way.

Tip: You're not stuck with Apple's designs for your stationery templates; you can make your own. Just make a new message, style the fonts and photos the way you want them, and then choose File→Save as Stationery. You can now select your masterwork in the Custom category, which appears down at the end of the list in the stationery-picker panel.

If you decide that the message would be better off as plain old text, click Show Stationery on the message window. In the list of template categories, click Stationery and then Original to strip the color and formats out of the message.

Reading Email

Mail puts all incoming email into your Inbox; the statistic after the word *Inbox* lets you know how many messages you haven't yet read. New messages are also marked with light-blue dots in the main list.

Tip: The Mail icon in the Dock also shows you how many new messages you have waiting; it's the number in the red circle. In Mail→Preferences→General, you can specify *which* mailbox it's tallying up—or have it tally up all of them.

Click the Inbox folder to see a list of received messages. If it's a long list, press Control-Page Up and Control-Page Down to scroll. (Page Up and Page Down without the Control key scroll the message pane instead.

Tip: If you ⌘-click more than one mailbox folder, you can combine them (and their total-message counts) into one unified messages list.

Click the name of a message once to read it in the message window, or double-click a message to open it into a separate window. (If a message is already selected, pressing Return also opens its separate window.)

When you click the name of a message in the messages list (or press the ↑ and ↓ keys to highlight successive messages in that list), you see the message itself, along with any attachments, in the message pane.

Tip: Instead of reading your mail, you might prefer to have Mac OS X read it *to* you, as you sit back in your chair and sip a strawberry daiquiri. Highlight the text you want to hear (or choose Edit→Select All), and then choose Edit→Speech→Start Speaking. You'll hear the message read aloud, in the voice you've selected on the Speech pane of System Preferences (Chapter 15). To stop the insanity, choose Edit→Speech→Stop Speaking.

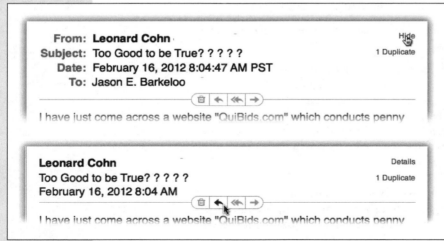

Figure 11-7:
The little blue Hide button, new in Lion, pares down all this gunk (top) to a simpler look—sender, subject, date. (Click Details to expand the header again.) Bottom: If you point to the header without clicking, you get to see the ghosts of four useful buttons: Trash, Reply, Reply All, and Forward.

At the top of each message, you see the *header*—a bunch of details like date, subject, to/from addresses, and so on. Figure 11-7 has more on headers.

Once you've viewed a message, you can respond to it, delete it, print it, file it, and so on. The following pages should get you started.

Conversation View

Threading is one of the most useful mail-sorting methods to come along in a long time. It groups all messages that are part of the same back-and-forth conversation as a *single item* in the main messages list. (In this discussion, let's call that one item the *main message.* In Mail, it's always the most recent message in the conversation.)

Less sophisticated email programs figure out which messages go together by matching only their subject lines. But Mail is much smarter; it also studies the message headers, senders, recipients, and dates. Even if someone changes the subject line along the way, Mail still knows that a conversation is a conversation.

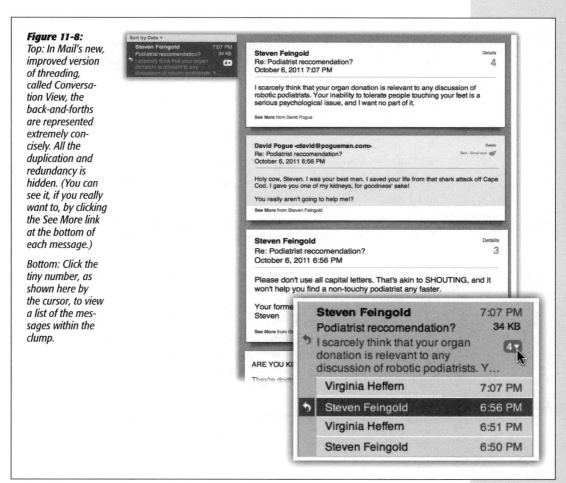

Figure 11-8:

Top: In Mail's new, improved version of threading, called Conversation View, the back-and-forths are represented extremely concisely. All the duplication and redundancy is hidden. (You can see it, if you really want to, by clicking the See More link at the bottom of each message.)

Bottom: Click the tiny number, as shown here by the cursor, to view a list of the messages within the clump.

In Lion, Apple has taken threading to new heights of usefulness. As shown in Figure 11-8, Conversation View, as it's now called, hides all the usual awful indents, repetitions, forwards of forwards, and so on. You see only neatly numbered scrolling blocks, each representing the *newly added* text in each back-and-forth.

To turn on threading, choose View→Organize by Conversation. Each main message in the messages list sprouts a little numbered badge, like "3 ▾," to indicate messages that have been clustered together (Figure 11-8).

Note: When Organize by Conversation is turned on, you might be wondering: What happens to chronological order? In other words, if the messages in a certain thread took place over several days or weeks, where does Mail wind up listing them when it sorts your messages list by date?

Answer: They're all clumped together in the main message—the *most recent* message. That is, if the messages on a certain topic arrived July 1, 4, 7, and 11, you'll find all four grouped with the July 11 message. They're essentially pulled *out* of the chronological list to join the latest one, for your reviewing pleasure.

Here are some powerful ways to use threading:

- **View all the messages in a conversation** by clicking the main message in the messages list. In the message pane, you see all the back-and-forths, minus the duplication and the replies to replies.

- **Expand a list of the messages in a conversation** by clicking the small gray number-of-messages badge—or by clicking the main message and then pressing the → key. A tiny message-conversation list sprouts out of the one listed message, as shown in the inset in Figure 11-8. (Or you can make *all* conversations display their sub-messages like this; to do that, choose View→Expand All Conversations.)

  Once you've expanded the mini-list, you can walk through it by pressing the ↑ and ↓ keys.

  The messages from the current mailbox are numbered—those are the big gray digits in the upper-right corner. Those numbers help you figure out where you are in all the back-and-forths.

- **Examine messages from multiple mailboxes.** Normally, conversations display only messages held in the *same* mailbox, but that's not especially convenient when you want to see, for example, both messages you've received (from your Inbox) and your replies (from your Sent box). To work around that problem, click the Show Related Messages (⬚) button in the toolbar (or turn on "Include related messages" in Mail→Preferences→Viewing). These options mean, "Include messages in *other* mailboxes, too, like Sent messages—not just this one mailbox." Now your conversations seamlessly combine related messages from all mailboxes.

Note: When "Include related messages" is turned on, the related messages do *not* display the big gray numbers in the corner—only the ones in the current mailbox sprout numbers.

- **Move all the messages in a conversation to a new mailbox** by dragging the main message. You might find this useful, for example, when you've just finished a project and want to file away all the email related to it quickly. You can even delete all the messages in a thread at once by deleting its main entry.

Note: If you just drag *one* message of a conversation to a different folder, though, it becomes a "related" message, no longer numbered, as described in the previous Note.

- **Send someone all the messages in a thread** by selecting the main message and then clicking Forward as usual. Mail automatically copies all the messages of the thread into a new message, putting the oldest at the top. You might find this useful, for instance, when you want to send your boss all the correspondence you've had with someone about a certain project.

- **Manipulate an individual message in a conversation** by first clicking it in the message-reading pane. For example, if you have five messages in a conversation and you want to forward only the juicy one, which happens to be message #2, click #2 and then use the Forward command—or Reply, Delete, or whatever. (You can also click one of the four light-gray buttons that appear when you point to the message header—Delete, Reply, Reply All, Forward.)

Tip: In Mail→Preferences→Viewing, you'll find a bunch of fine-tuning tweaks that apply to conversations. For example, you can ask that messages that are part of the same conversation show up highlighted in a color you choose—even when conversation grouping is turned *off*. And you can request that, when a conversation message is clicked in the messages list, the resulting messages are shown in reverse chronological order—oldest at the top.

Adding the Sender to Your Address Book

When you choose the Message→Add Sender to Address Book command, Mail memorizes the email address of the person whose message is on the screen. In fact, you can highlight a huge number of messages and add *all* the senders simultaneously using this technique.

Thereafter, you'll be able to address a new message to somebody just by typing the first few letters of her name or email address.

Data Detectors

Data detectors are described on page 190. They're what you see when Mac OS X recognizes commonly used bits of written information: a physical address, a phone number, a date and time, a flight number, and so on. With one quick click, you can send that information into the appropriate Mac OS X program, like iCal, Address Book, the Flight Tracker widget in Dashboard, or your Web browser (for looking an address up on a map).

This is just a public-service reminder that data detectors are especially useful—*primarily* useful, in fact—in Mail. Watch for the dotted rectangle that appears when you point to a name, address, date, time, or flight number.

Opening Attachments

Just as you can attach files to a message, so can people send files to you. Sometimes they don't even bother to type a note; you wind up receiving an empty email message with a file or two attached. Only the presence of the file's icon in the message body tells you there's something attached.

Tip: In Classic view, Mail doesn't ordinarily indicate the presence of attachments in the messages list. It can do so, however. Just choose View→Columns→Attachments. A new column appears in the messages list—at the far right—where you see a paper-clip icon and the number of file attachments listed for each message.

Mail stores downloaded files in a hidden folder on your hard drive. To bring them out into the open, you must proceed in one of these ways:

- Click the Quick Look button in the message header. Instantly, you're treated to a nearly full-size preview of the file's contents. Yes, Quick Look has come to email. It works exactly as described in Chapter 2.

Tip: If the attachments are pictures, clicking Quick Look gives you a full-screen slideshow of every attached image.

If you jiggle the mouse a little during the slideshow, you get a useful row of slideshow-control buttons along the bottom of the screen, too.

- Click the Save button in the message header to save it to your Downloads folder, nestled within easy reach in the Dock. (It's a pop-up menu, which is handy if there's more than one attachment. You can either save *all* attachments at once or choose from the pop-up menu to save them individually.)

Tip: If you don't want to use the Downloads folder, you can choose a new autosave location for attachments by choosing Mail→Preferences→General→Downloads folder.

- Drag the attachment icon (it appears at the bottom of the message) out of the message window and onto any visible portion of your desktop, or any visible folder window.

- Double-click the attachment's icon, or single-click the blue link underneath the icon. If you were sent a document (a photo, Word file, or Excel file, for example), it now opens in the corresponding program.

Note: After the attachment is open, use the File→Save As command to save the file into a folder of your choice. Otherwise, any changes you make to the document will be lost.

- Control-click (or right-click) the attachment's icon at the bottom of the message. From the shortcut menu, you can open it, save it, Quick Look it, and so on.

Replying to a Message

To answer a message, click the Reply ← button on the message toolbar (or choose Message→Reply, or press ⌘-R). If the message was originally addressed to multiple recipients, you can send your reply to everyone simultaneously by clicking Reply All ← instead (Shift-⌘-R).

A new message window opens, already addressed. As a courtesy to your correspondent, Mail places the original message at the bottom of the window, set off by a vertical bar, as shown in Figure 11-9.

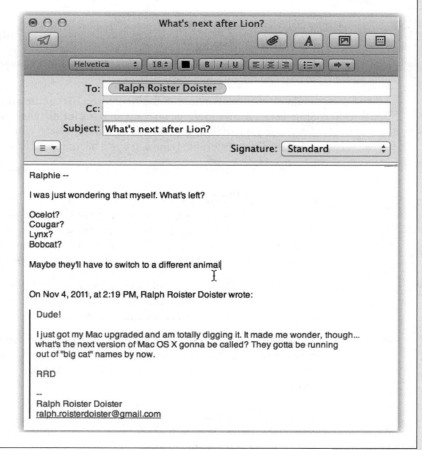

Figure 11-9:
If you highlight some text before clicking Reply, Mail pastes only that portion of the original message into your reply. That's a great convenience to your correspondent, who now knows exactly which part of the message you're responding to.

In Mail messages formatted with Rich Text, a reply includes the original message, marked in a special color (which you can change in Mail→Preferences) and with a vertical bar to differentiate it from the text of your reply. (In plain-text messages, each line of the reply is >denoted >with >brackets, although only your recipient will see them.)

The original sender's name is automatically placed in the "To:" field. The subject is the same as the original subject with the addition of Re: (shorthand for "regarding"). You're now ready to type your response.

At this point, you can add or delete recipients, edit the subject line or the original message, attach a file, and so on.

Tip: Use the Return key to create blank lines in the original message. Using this method, you can splice your own comments into the paragraphs of the original message, replying point by point. The brackets preceding each line of the original message help your correspondent keep straight what's yours and what's hers.

When you're finished, click Send (⌧).

Forwarding Messages

Instead of replying to the person who sent you a message, you may sometimes want to pass the note on to a third person.

To do so, click the Forward ➜ toolbar button (or choose Message→Forward, or press Shift-⌘-F). A new message opens, looking a lot like the one that appears when you reply. You may wish to precede the original message with a comment of your own, along the lines of: "Frank: I thought you'd be interested in this joke about your mom."

Finally, address it as you would any outgoing piece of mail.

Redirecting Messages

A *redirected* message is similar to a forwarded message, with one useful difference: When you forward a message, your recipient sees that it came from you. When you redirect it, your recipient sees the *original* writer's name as the sender. In other words, a redirected message uses you as a low-profile relay station between two other people.

Treasure this feature. Plenty of email programs don't offer a Redirect command at all. You can use it to transfer messages from one of your own accounts to another, or to pass along a message that came to you by mistake.

To redirect a message, choose Message→Redirect, or press Shift-⌘-E. You get an outgoing copy of the message—this time without any quoting marks. (You can edit redirected messages before you send them, too, which is perfect for April Fools' Day pranks.

Printing Messages

Sometimes there's no substitute for a printout. Choose File→Print, or press ⌘-P to summon the Print dialog box.

Filing Messages

Mail lets you create new mailboxes (mail folders) in the mailboxes list. You might create one for important messages, another for order confirmations from Web shopping, still another for friends and family, and so on. You can even create mailboxes *inside* these mailboxes, a feature beloved by the hopelessly organized.

Mail even offers *smart mailboxes*—self-updating folders that show you all your mail from your boss, for example, or every message with "mortgage" in its subject. It's the same idea as smart folders in the Finder or smart playlists in iTunes: folders whose contents are based around criteria you specify (Figure 11-10).

Figure 11-10:
Mail lets you create self-populating folders. In this example, the "New Mail from Mom" smart mailbox will automatically display all messages from her that you've received in the past week.

The commands you need are all in the Mailbox menu. For example, to create a new mailbox folder, choose Mailbox→New Mailbox, or click the **+** button at the bottom of the mailboxes column. To create a smart mailbox, choose Mailbox→New Smart Mailbox.

Mail asks you to name the new mailbox. If you have more than one email account, you can specify which one will contain the new folder. (Smart mailboxes, however, always sit outside your other mailboxes.)

Tip: If you want to create a folder-inside-a-folder, use slashes in the name of your new mailbox. (If you use the name *Cephalopods/Squid,* for example, then Mail creates a folder called Cephalopods, with a subfolder called Squid.) You can also drag the mailbox icons up and down in the drawer to place one inside another.

None of those tricks work for smart mailboxes, however. The only way to organize smart mailboxes is to put them inside a smart mailbox *folder,* which you create using Mailbox→New Smart Mailbox Folder. You might do that if you have several smart mailboxes for mail from your coworkers ("From Jim," "From Anne," and so on) and want to put them together in one collapsible group to save screen space.

When you click OK, a new icon appears in the mailboxes column, ready for use.

You can move a message (or group of messages) into a mailbox folder in any of three ways:

• Drag it out of the messages list onto a mailbox icon.

- Highlight one or more messages, and then choose from the Message→Move To submenu, which lists all your mailboxes.

- Right-click a message, or one of several that you've highlighted. From the resulting shortcut menu, choose Move To, and then, from the submenu, choose the mailbox you want.

Of course, the only way to change the contents of a *smart* mailbox is to change the criteria it uses to populate itself. To do so, double-click the smart mailbox icon and use the dialog box that appears.

Flagging Messages

Sometimes you'll receive email that prompts you to some sort of action, but you may not have the time (or the fortitude) to face the task at the moment. ("Hi there... it's me, your accountant. Would you mind rounding up your expenses for 1999 through 2011 and sending me a list by email?")

That's why Mail lets you *flag* a message, summoning a little flag icon in a new column next to the message's name. In fact, in Lion, you can now use seven differently *colored* flags.

These indicators can mean anything you like—they simply call attention to certain messages.

Once you've applied some flags, you can use their power in all kinds of ways. For example, you can sort your mail list by flag color (choose Sort by Flags at the top of the messages list). You can search for flagged messages using the search box. Better yet, you can view all messages with a certain flag color—magically rounded up from

---

UP TO SPEED

All the Little Symbols

The left edge of the messages list shows little symbols that let you know at a glance how you've processed certain messages. The most common one is, of course, the light-blue dot (●), which means "new message." (After reading a message, you can mark it once again as an *unread* message by choosing Message→Mark→As Unread [Shift-⌘-U]—or by Control-clicking the message's name and then choosing Mark→As Unread from the shortcut menu.)

You might also see these symbols, which represent messages you've replied to (↩), forwarded (➡), redirected (⤳), or flagged (⚑).

A well-guarded secret, however, is that the "replied to" and "forwarded" symbols aren't just indicators—they're also *buttons*.

When you see one of these symbols next to your original message, click it to jump straight to your reply (or forwarded message). You're spared the trouble of having to search through all your mailboxes.

Incidentally, you may have noticed that Mail marks a message as having been read the moment you click it. You can change it back to unread by using its shortcut menu—but there's also a more permanent workaround.

If you hide the message pane by double-clicking the divider bar to its right (or, in Classic view, above it), Mail no longer marks messages "read" just because you clicked them in the list.

---

all your different accounts and mailboxes—by clicking the corresponding icon in the Flagged folder of the mailboxes list.

Tip: Just in case you don't find "Red," "Orange," "Yellow," and so on to be the most descriptive possible flag names, you can change them.

First, though, make sure you've applied a couple of flags to different messages already. That's necessary to make the new Flagged mailbox appear in the mailboxes list. If you open the flippy triangle, you'll see the names of the flags you've applied so far. You can change a flag's name just the way you'd name a file—start by double-clicking it.

To flag a message in this way, select the message (or several messages) and then choose one of the colored flags in the Message→Flag submenu. Or Control-click (right-click) the message's name in the list and, from the shortcut menu, choose one of the seven flag colors. (To clear the flags, repeat the procedure, but use the Message→Flag→Clear Flag command instead.)

If you're using only one flag to simply mean "flag this," and you don't need all the colors, you can also press Shift-⌘-L.

Finding Messages

When you deal with masses of email, a fast, powerful search command is essential. In Lion, Mail's search command has grown deeper and better.

The box in the upper-right corner of the main mail window is Mail's own private Spotlight. You can use it to hide all but certain messages, as shown in Figure 11-11.

Figure 11-11:
You can jump to the search box by clicking or by pressing Option-⌘-F. As you type, Mail shrinks the list of messages—and simultaneously displays a list of suggestions. You can fine-tune your results using the mailbox buttons you've installed on the Favorites bar. To return to the full messages list, click the tiny ⊗ at the right side of the search box.

This search box is powerful indeed. In fact, it incorporates the same pop-up suggestions lists and "search tokens" as regular file searching in the Finder (page 117). Here's how it works:

1. **Press Option-⌘-F (or click in the search box).**

   The cursor jumps up there.

2. **Start typing what you're looking for.**

   As you type, the messages list changes to show only the matching messages from all your mail folders.

   If you see the message you're looking for, great. Click it, and off you go.

   But this initial search is a pretty broad one. Mail is rounding up messages that match your search term *in any way*. If you type *veg,* you see messages from Murray Vegelstein, messages from vegan@militanteaters.org, and messages with the subject line "HOT DEALS IN VEGAS." All of them in one big stew.

   To help you sort through it, Mail produces a new Suggestions list, which sprouts from the search box. As in the Finder, it's Mail's way of asking what sort of *thing* your search term is. Is it a person? A subject? The status of a message? A date? Figure 11-11 shows the idea.

3. **Click the suggestion you want.**

   Mail filters the list. For example, if you click Murray Vegelstein, you'll see *only* the messages to or from Murray.

4. **Edit the search token.**

   The *search token* is the little bubble that appears in the search box after you've clicked one of the suggestions. You can click the little ▾ in the search token to change it. For example, if you've clicked somebody's name, that pop-up menu says To, From, or Entire Message (including the header and the body).

   You can also type more into the search box to add *another* search token. For example, the first token might limit the search to messages from one person; you could then create another one that limits the search to a certain date.

POWER USERS' CLINIC

Secrets of the Mailbox Files

Mail keeps your messages in a series of mailbox folders in your Home→Library→Mail folder, inside folders (Outbox, Deleted Messages, and so on) named for each account.

Knowing this permits you to perform a number of interesting tricks. First of all, now you know what files to back up for safekeeping. (To see the invisible Library folder, press Option as you choose Go→Library in the Finder.)

Second, if you have messages on an old Mac that you'd like to copy to your new one, now you know where they're stored.

Tip: Once you've built up a complicated search like this, save yourself the effort next time by *saving* that search. Click the Save button just below the search box. You get the Smart Mailbox dialog box, already filled out with the search setup you've specified. All you have to do is give it a name and click OK to transform your search into a smart mailbox that you can open anytime.

You've done a lot of refining of this search. But you still haven't limited your results by *account or folder.* Mail is showing you results from either *all* mailboxes, or from only the most recent mailbox you've searched. Fortunately, your Favorites bar has now sprouted two new buttons: one called All, and one that names the folder you most recently clicked.

5. **Click a button on the Favorites bar to change which mailbox is being searched.**

The results list updates itself.

Tip: If you ⌘-click *several* mail folders before you search, you can limit the search to that particular *set* of mailboxes. (In that case, you see a button on the Favorites bar called Selected Mailboxes.)

When you're finished hunting around, you can empty out the search box, and get back to your regularly scheduled lists of email, by clicking any other mailbox, or by clicking the ⊗ button at the right end of the search box.

- In Mail→Preferences→General, you can specify whether or not you want Mail to include the Trash folder, Junk folder, and encrypted messages when you search all mailboxes.

- Notes show up in the search results, too.

- You can also search for certain text *within* an open message. Choose Edit→Find→ Find (or press ⌘-F) to bring up the Find dialog box.

Deleting Messages

Sometimes it's junk mail. Sometimes you're just done with it. Either way, it's a snap to delete a selected message, several selected messages, or a message that's currently before you on the screen. You can press the Delete key, click the 🗑 button on the toolbar, choose Edit→Delete, or drag messages out of the list window and into your Trash mailbox—or even onto the Dock's Trash icon.

Tip: If you delete a message by accident, the Undo command (Edit→Undo or ⌘-Z) restores it.

All these commands move the messages to the Trash folder. If you like, you can then click its icon to view a list of the messages you've deleted. You can even rescue messages by dragging them back into a mailbox (back to the Inbox, for example).

Emptying the Trash folder

Mail doesn't vaporize messages in the Trash folder until you "empty the trash," just like in the Finder. You can empty the Trash folder in any of several ways:

- Click a message (or several) within the Trash folder list, and then click the 🗑 icon on the toolbar (or press the Delete key). Now those messages are *really* gone.

- Choose Mailbox→Erase Deleted Items (Shift-⌘-Delete). (If you have multiple accounts, choose Erase Deleted Items→In All Accounts.)

- Right-click the Trash mailbox icon, and then choose Erase Deleted Items from the shortcut menu. Or choose the same command from the ✿ pop-up menu at the bottom of the window.

- Wait. Mail will permanently delete these messages automatically after a week.

If a week is too long (or not long enough), you can change this interval. Choose Mail→Preferences, click Accounts, and select the account name from the list at left. Then click Mailbox Behaviors, and change the "Permanently erase deleted messages when" pop-up menu. If you choose Quitting Mail from the pop-up menu, then Mail will take out the trash every time you quit the program.

Turning deleted mail invisible

Mail offers another—and very unusual—method of deleting messages that doesn't involve the Trash folder at all. Using this method, pressing the Delete key (or clicking the 🗑 toolbar button) simply hides the selected message in the list. Hidden messages remain hidden, but they don't go away for good until you use the Mailbox→Rebuild command.

If this arrangement sounds useful, choose Mail→Preferences; click Accounts and then select the account from the list on the left; click Mailbox Behaviors; and then turn off the checkbox called "Move deleted messages to a separate folder" or "Move deleted messages to the Trash mailbox." (The checkbox's wording depends on what kind of account you have.) From now on, messages you delete vanish from the list.

They're not really gone, however. You can bring them back, at least in ghostly form, by choosing View→Show Deleted Messages (or pressing ⌘-L). Using this system, in other words, you never truly delete messages; you just hide them.

At first, you might be concerned about the disk space and database size involved in keeping your old messages around forever like this. Truth is, Mac OS X is perfectly capable of maintaining many thousands of messages in its mailbox databases—and with the sizes of hard drives nowadays, a few thousand messages aren't likely to make much of a dent.

Meanwhile, there's a huge benefit to this arrangement. At some point, almost everyone wishes he could resurrect a deleted message—maybe months later, maybe years later. Using the hidden-deleted-message system, your old messages are always around for reference. (The downside to this system, of course, is that SEC investigators can use it to find incriminating mail that you thought you'd deleted.)

When you do want to purge these messages for good, you can always return to the Mailbox Behaviors dialog box and turn the "Move deleted mail to a separate folder" checkbox back on.

Archiving messages

There's one final option for getting unwanted messages out of your hair: *archiving*. It just means, "Get it out of my sight for now." Archiving sweeps the selected message into a folder called Archived, where it will stay until you deal with it further (by moving or deleting it). There's one of these folders per account.

To archive a selected message, a group of selected messages, or a conversation, choose Message→Archive, or click the Archive icon on the toolbar.

Message Rules

Once you know how to create folders, the next step in managing your email is to set up a series of *message rules* (filters) that file, answer, or delete incoming messages automatically based on their contents (such as their subject, address, and/or size). Message rules require you to think like the distant relative of a programmer, but the mental effort can reward you many times over. Message rules turn Mail into a surprisingly smart and efficient secretary.

Setting up message rules

Here's how to set up a message rule:

Figure 11-12:
Top: Message rules can screen out junk mail, serve as an email answering machine, or call important messages to your attention. All mail message rules you've created appear in this list. (The color shading for each rule is a reflection of the colorizing options you've set up, if any.)

Bottom: Double-click a rule to open the Edit Rule dialog box, where you can specify what should set off the rule and what it should do in response.

1. **Choose Mail→Preferences. Click the Rules icon.**

   The Rules pane appears, as shown at top in Figure 11-12.

2. **Click Add Rule.**

   Now the dialog box shown at bottom in Figure 11-12 appears.

3. **Use the criteria options (at the top) to specify how Mail should select messages to process.**

   For example, if you'd like the program to watch out for messages from a particular person, you would set up the first two pop-up menus to say "From" and "Contains," respectively.

   To flag messages containing *loan, $$$$, XXXX, !!!!,* and so on, set the pop-up menus to say "Subject" and "Contains."

   You can set up *multiple* criteria here to flag messages whose subjects contain any one of those common spam triggers. (If you change the "any" pop-up menu to say "all," then *all* the criteria must be true for the rule to kick in.)

4. **Specify which words or people you want the message rule to watch for.**

   In the text box to the right of the two pop-up menus, type the word, address, name, or phrase you want Mail to watch for—a person's name, or *$$$$,* in the previous examples.

5. **In the lower half of the box, specify what you want to happen to messages that match the criteria.**

   If, in steps 1 through 4, you've told your rule to watch for junk mail containing *$$$$* in the subject line, here's where you can tell Mail to delete it or move it into, say, a Junk folder.

   With a little imagination, you'll see how the options in this pop-up menu can do absolutely amazing things with your incoming email. Mail can colorize, delete, move, redirect, or forward messages—or even play a sound when you get a certain message.

   By setting up the controls as shown in Figure 11-12, for example, you'll have specified that whenever your mother sends something to you that mentions a visit, you'll hear a specific alert noise as the email is highlighted in a bright red, so it will jump out at you in the Inbox.

6. **In the very top box, name your mail rule. Click OK.**

   Now you're back to the Rules pane (Figure 11-12, top). Here you can choose a sequence for the rules you've created by dragging them up and down. Here, too, you can turn off the ones you won't be needing at the moment, but may use again one day.

Tip: Mail applies rules as they appear, from top to bottom, in the list. If a rule doesn't seem to be working properly, it may be that an earlier rule is intercepting and processing some messages before the "broken" rule even sees them. To fix this, try dragging the rule (or the interfering rule) up or down in the list.

The Anti-Spam Toolkit

Spam, the junk that now makes up more than 80 percent of email, is a problem that's only getting worse. Luckily, you, along with Mail's advanced spam filters, can make it better—at least for *your* email accounts.

Using the Junk Mail Filter

You'll see the effects of Mail's spam filter the first time you check your mail: A certain swath of message titles appears in brown. These are the messages that Mail considers junk.

Note: Out of the box, Mail doesn't apply its spam-targeting features to people whose addresses are in your Address Book, to people you've emailed recently, or to messages sent to you *by name* rather than just by email address. You can adjust these settings in the Mail→Preferences→Junk Mail tab.

During your first couple of weeks with Mail, your job is to supervise Mail's work. That is, if you get spam that Mail misses, click the message, and then click the Junk button on the toolbar. On the other hand, if Mail flags legitimate mail as spam, slap it gently on the wrist by clicking the Not Junk button. Over time, Mail gets better and better at filtering your mail.

The trouble with this so-called Training mode is that you're still left with the task of trashing the spam yourself, saving you no time whatsoever.

Once Mail has perfected its filtering skills to your satisfaction, though, open Mail's preferences, click Junk Mail, and then click "Move it to the Junk mailbox." From now on, Mail automatically files what it deems junk into a Junk mailbox, where it's much easier to scan and delete the messages en masse.

Tip: Don't miss the "Trust Junk Mail headers" option in the Junk Mail pane of the Preferences window. If you turn on that checkbox, Mail takes your Internet provider's word that certain messages are spam, giving you a *double* layer of spam protection.

More Anti-Spam Tips

The Junk filter goes a long way toward cleaning out the spam from your mail collection—but it doesn't catch everything. If you're overrun by spam, here are some other steps you can take:

- **Rules.** Set up some message rules, as described on the preceding pages, that autoflag as spam messages that have subject lines containing trigger words like "Viagra," "Herbal," "Mortgage," "Refinance," "Enlarge," "Your"—you get the idea.

- **Create a private account.** If you're overrun by spam, consider sacrificing your current address, using it for the public areas of the Internet, like chat rooms, online shopping, Web site and software registration, and newsgroup posting. Reserve a separate email account for person-to-person email.

  Spammers use automated software robots that scour every public Internet message and Web page, recording email addresses they find. (In fact, that's probably how they got your address in the first place.)

  Using this technique, at least you're now restricting the junk mail to a secondary mail account.

- **For goodness' sake, don't** *order* **anything sold by the spammers.** If only one person in 500,000 does so, the spammer makes money.

RSS Feeds

Mail gets more than *mail.* It also helps you keep yourself up to date with the world outside—and within your own little corner of it.

For example, the ability to subscribe to those constantly updating news summaries known as *RSS feeds* has saved a lot of people a lot of time over the years. After all, why waste precious minutes looking for the news when you can make the news find you?

In fact, you don't even have to waste the seconds it would take to switch from your Inbox to your browser or dedicated RSS program to get a fresh dose of headlines. With Mail, they can appear right in the message window, making it easy to find out which political candidate shot his foot off while it was still in his mouth.

In fact, if you find it too exhausting to click the RSS icon in the mailboxes list, you can choose instead to have all your RSS updates land right in your Inbox along with all your other messages.

Adding RSS Feeds

With just a few clicks, you can bring the news of the world right in with the rest of your mail. Choose File→Add RSS Feeds, and then proceed as shown in Figure 11-13.

Tip: As you turn on the feeds you want to see in Mail, ⌘-click to select a bunch of feeds at once.

If you want the RSS headlines to appear in your Inbox like regular email messages, then turn on Show in Inbox. Finally, once you've chosen the feeds you want to see, click Add. Your feeds now appear wherever you told them to go: to either the Inbox or the mailboxes column.

Now, in the RSS category of your mailboxes list, you see the names of your RSS feeds; the number in the small gray circle tells you how many unread headlines are in the list. If a feed headline intrigues you enough to want more information, click "Read More…" to do just that. Safari pops up and whisks you away to the Web site that sent out the feed in the first place.

Tip: Click the ↑ button next to a feed's name to move all its updates into your Inbox; there, they appear with the same blue RSS label, but they behave as though they're an Inbox category, to spare you having to flip back and forth between two distant areas of the mailboxes list.

If you *accidentally* click that arrow, and you don't really want 57 headlines from RollingStone.com peppering your daily dose of mail, click the feed's name and then click the ↓ next to it; it returns to the RSS section of the list. Alternatively, you can Control-click (or right-click) the feed name on the mailboxes list and turn off Show in Inbox from the shortcut menu.

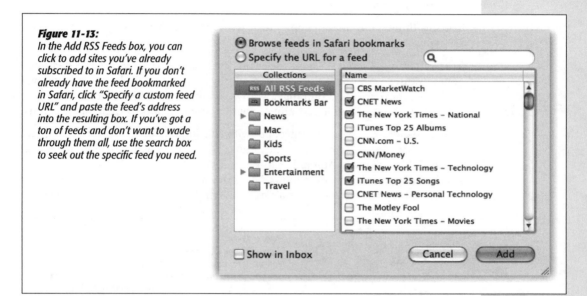

Figure 11-13:
In the Add RSS Feeds box, you can click to add sites you've already subscribed to in Safari. If you don't already have the feed bookmarked in Safari, click "Specify a custom feed URL" and paste the feed's address into the resulting box. If you've got a ton of feeds and don't want to wade through them all, use the search box to seek out the specific feed you need.

Managing Feeds

Now that you've got your feeds in Mail, you may want to fiddle around with them.

- **Updating.** You can change the frequency of your news updates by choosing Mail→Preferences→RSS→Check for Updates.

- **Sharing.** If you want to share the news with a friend, right-click a headline; from the shortcut menu, choose Forward (or Forward as Attachment) to pop the info into a new Mail message that you can send off to your pal.

- **Renaming.** You don't have to use the site's full name in your Mail window—after all, "WaPo" fits much better in the Mailboxes column than "Washington Post." To rename a feed, select it and then choose Mailbox→Rename Feed. Type in the new name and press Return.

- **Deleting.** After you've read a news item and are done with it, click the Delete button at the top of the window. You can tell Mail to dump all the old articles after a certain amount of time (a day, a week, a month) in Mail→Preferences→RSS→Remove Articles.

Or, to get rid of an RSS feed altogether, select it and then choose Maibox→Delete Feed.

Notes

No operating system is complete without Notes. You *have* to have a place for little reminders, phone numbers, phone messages, Web addresses, brainstorms, shopping-list hints—anything that's worth writing down, but too tiny to justify heaving a whole word processor onto its feet.

The silly thing is how many people create reminders for themselves by *sending themselves an email message.*

That system works, but it's a bit inelegant. Fortunately, Mac OS X has a dedicated Notes feature. As a bonus, it syncs automatically to the Notes folder of your iPhone's mail program, or to other computers, as long as you have an IMAP-style email account (one where the email stash sits online, as with a Gmail, Yahoo, or Exchange account).

Notes look like actual yellow notepaper with ruled lines, but you can style 'em, save 'em, and even send 'em to your friends. You can type into them, paste into them, and attach pictures to them. And unlike loose scraps of paper or email messages to yourself that may get lost in your mailbox, Notes stay obediently tucked in the Reminders section of the mailboxes list so you can always find them when you need them.

Figure 11-14:
They may look like little pads of scratch paper, but Mail Notes let you paste in Web addresses and photos alongside your typed and formatted text. If you want to share, click the Send ( ) button to have the entire Note plop into a new Mail message, ready to be addressed.

Tip: Ordinarily, Notes also appear in your Inbox, at the top. If you prefer to keep your Inbox strictly for messages, though, you can remove the Notes. Choose Mail→Preferences→Accounts→Mailbox Behaviors, and then turn off "Show notes in Inbox." The Notes will still be waiting for you in the mailboxes column, down in the Reminders area.

To create a Note, click the Note ( ) icon on the Mail toolbar. You can also choose File→New Note or press Control-⌘-N.

Once you have your Note, type your text and click the Fonts button ( ) at the top of the window to style it. To insert a picture, click the Attach ( ) button, and then find the photo or graphic you want to use on your Mac. Figure 11-14 shows an example.

Note: You can also attach other kinds of files to a Note—ordinary documents, for example. But you can't send such Notes to other people—only Notes with pictures.

When you're finished with your Note, just close its window. When you look for it in the Reminders category of the mailboxes list, you'll see that Mail used the first line of the Note as its subject.

To delete a Note for good, select it and press the Delete key.

Address Book

Address Book is Mac OS X's little-black-book program—an electronic Rolodex where you can stash the names, job titles, addresses, phone numbers, email addresses, and Internet chat screen names of all the people in your life. Address Book can also hold related information, like birthdays, anniversaries, and any other tidbits of personal data you'd like to keep at your fingertips.

The best part: It's *centralized.* This one address list appears everywhere: in Mail, iChat, and so on. And it synchronizes with your iPhone, iPad, and (via iCloud) your other computers.

In Lion, it's been completely redesigned to look more like (can you guess?) the same program on the iPhone/iPad, as shown in Figure 11-15.

Tip: If you need to see two people's cards simultaneously, double-click each one in the list. That makes them open into individual windows.

Once you make Address Book the central repository of all your personal contact information, you can call up this information in a number of convenient ways:

- **You can open Address Book and then search for a contact** by typing just a few letters in the search box.

- **Regardless of what program you're in,** you can use a single keystroke (the ⌽ key on aluminum keyboards) to summon the Address Book Dashboard widget. There you can search for any contact you want. When you're done, hide the widget with the same quick keystroke.

- **When you're composing messages in Mail,** Address Book automatically fills in email addresses for you when you type the first few letters.

Tip: If you choose Window→Address Panel (Option-⌘-A) from within Mail, you can browse all your addresses without even launching the Address Book program. Once you've selected the people you want to contact, just click the "To:" button to address an email to them—or, if you already have a new email message open, to add them to the recipients.

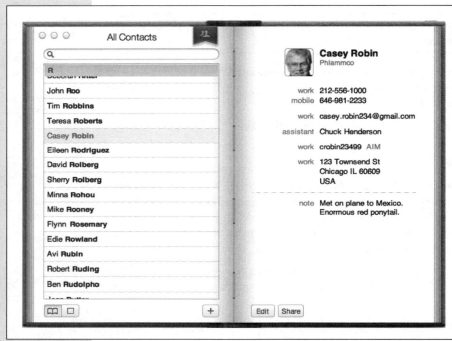

Figure 11-15:
Address Book is meant to look like a physical address book. On the left, the full list of names; on the right, the card for the one person whose name you've clicked. (You can hide the names list by choosing View→Card Only, or bring it back with View→List and Card.)

- **When you use iChat to exchange instant messages** with people in your Address Book, the pictures you've stored of them automatically appear in chat windows.

- **The free iCloud service can synchronize your contacts** to the Web so you can see them while you're away from your Mac.

- **Address Book can sync its information with an iPod, iPhone, or iPad,** giving you a "little black book" that fits in your shirt pocket, can be operated one-handed, and comes with built-in musical accompaniment. You can have that happen wirelessly, using iCloud, or wirefully, when you connect your iPod/iPhone/iPad to your Mac. (To set this up, open iTunes while your i-gadget is connected. Click the i-gadget's icon; on the Contacts or Info tab, turn on Synchronize Address Book Contacts.)

You can find Address Book in your Applications folder or in the Dock.

Importing Addresses

The easiest way to add people to Address Book is to import them from another service, like Yahoo or Exchange, or another program, like Microsoft Outlook (for Mac) or Entourage.

Importing from Yahoo, Google, Exchange, or another Internet service

Yeah, it's a big deal, baby: Address Book can synchronize its contacts with online Rolodexes that may be very important to you: Your Gmail (Google) contacts, Yahoo contacts, iCloud address book, or your company's Microsoft Exchange master address book (Figure 11-16).

Figure 11-16:
Address Book can sync your digital Rolodex with online contact managers like Yahoo and Google. Turn on the appropriate checkbox to enter your account name and password. For other account types, like Exchange, click the + button below the list to begin.

In Address Book, choose Address Book→Preferences→Accounts. There, staring you in the face, are checkboxes that let you sync your contacts with iCloud, Yahoo, Google. Turn on the checkbox you want, click Configure, agree to the legalese, enter your account information, and boom—you're done. Your Mac's Address Book is now synced with your online accounts. Change information in one place, and it's also changed in the other. (That's *if* you have no conflicts between the two.) Even their photos, if your online address book has them, show up in Address Book!

Tip: You can also enter this information in the Mail, Contacts & Calendars pane of System Preferences.

If some other online service maintains your address book, Address Book can sync with it, too, as long as it uses one of the standard sharing formats (Exchange, Card-DAV, or Lightweight Directory Access Protocol, known by the pros as LDAP). To teach Address Book about those, choose Address Book→Preferences→Accounts. Click the + button in the lower left, enter your account information on the resulting screen, click Create, and away you go.

Note: Address Book may display an advanced Account Settings screen, where you have to enter more detailed information. If you're a hands-on sort of nerd, you can also force this screen to open on your command. To do that, press Option; point to the Create button, which now says Continue. Click it.

Once you've set up an Address Book account, you can also change its settings, right there in the same Preferences dialog box. Specify how often you want your Mac to sync changes with the online account, for example.

Importing from another address-book program

Address Book can also slurp in contact info from other address-book or list programs, like Microsoft Outlook (Entourage), Palm Desktop, Excel, and others. Not directly, of course; that would be too easy. But most of those programs can *export* their information as an intermediary file in one of four popular formats: vCard, LDAP Interchange Format (LDIF), tab-delimited, or comma-separated value (CSV).

For example, Microsoft's programs can export addresses as vCards; Thunderbird can export in LDIF format; Excel can export tab-delimited or CSV files.

It's a fine art, this importing business; all kinds of things can go wrong. The fields (like Name, Street, Phone) may not be in the right order. Tab-separated export files may not have the right number of empty fields. And so on.

For best results, choose Address Book→Help, and search for "Importing contacts from other applications." The resulting page gives special tips for each kind of export/import file format. (Fortunately, if the fields are out of order, Address Book will offer you the chance to straighten them out.)

About vCards

Address Book exchanges contact information with other programs primarily through *vCards*. vCard is short for *virtual business card*. More and more email programs send and receive these electronic business cards, which you can identify by their .vcf file name extensions (if, that is, you've set your Mac to display these extensions).

If you ever receive an email with a vCard file attached, drag the .vcf file into your Address Book window to create an instant entry with a complete set of information. You can create vCards of your own, too. Just drag a name out of your Address Book and onto the desktop (or into a piece of outgoing mail).

Tip: In addition to letting you create vCards of individual entries, Address Book makes it easy to create vCards that contain several entries. To do so, ⌘-click the entries in the Name column that you want included, and drag them to the desktop. There they'll appear all together as a single vCard. You can even drag an item from the Group page to the desktop to make a vCard that contains all the group's entries.

Keep this trick in mind if you ever want to copy all your contacts from an old PC to a new Mac. By creating a single vCard containing all your contacts, you've made it trivial to import them into the copy of Address Book running on your new Mac.

Creating Address Cards

Each entry in Address Book is called a *card*—like a paper Rolodex card, with predefined spaces to hold all the standard contact information.

To add a new person, choose File→New Card, press ⌘-N, or click the **+** button beneath the Name column. Then type in the contact information, pressing the Tab key to move from field to field, as shown in Figure 11-17.

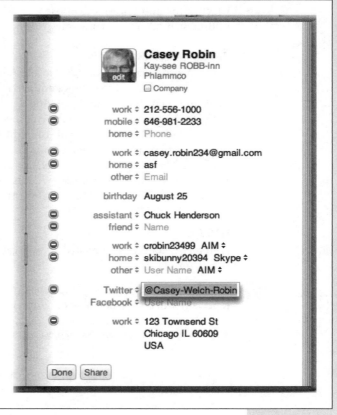

Figure 11-17:
If one of your contacts happens to have three office phone extensions, a pager number, two home phone lines, a cellphone, and a couple of fax machines, no problem—you can add as many fields as you need. Each time you fill up a phone, email, chat name, or address box, a new, empty one magically sprouts up to accommodate another one. Click a field's name to change its label; you can select one of the standard labels from the pop-up menu (Home, Work, and so on) or make up your own labels by choosing Custom.

Tip: If you find yourself constantly adding the same fields to new cards, check out the Template pane of Address Book's Preferences (Address Book→Preferences). There you can customize exactly which fields appear for new cards.

Figure 11-17 shows some unusual fields that you can plug into your address cards. The phonetic first/last name fields (shown at top) let you store phonetic spellings of hard-to-pronounce names. There's a Birthday field and a place to store a Twitter name, too. To add fields like these, choose from the Card→Add Field menu.

Each card also contains a free-form Note field at the bottom, where you can type any other random crumbs of information you'd like to store about the person (pet's name, embarrassing nicknames, favorite Chinese restaurant, and so on).

Editing an address

When you create a new address card, you're automatically in Edit mode, which means that you can add and remove fields and change the information on the card. To switch into Browse mode (where you can view and copy contact information but not change it), click the Edit button or choose Edit→Edit Card (⌘-L). You can also switch *out* of Browse mode in the same ways.

Adding addresses from Mail

You can also make new contacts in the Address Book right in Mail, saving you the trouble of having to type names and email addresses manually. Select a message in Mail, and then choose Message→Add Sender to Address Book (Shift-⌘-Y). Presto: Mac OS X adds a new card to the Address Book, with the name and email address fields already filled in. Later, you can edit the card in Address Book to add phone numbers, street addresses, and so on.

Tip: If you enter some people's birthdays in Address Book, they can show up automatically in iCal. To make that happen, open iCal, and then choose iCal→Preferences→General. Turn on "Show Birthdays calendar."

Groups

A *group* is a collection of related address cards, saved under a single descriptive name (see Figure 11-18).

Organizing your contacts into groups can make them much easier to find and use—especially when your database of addresses climbs into the hundreds.

Tip: When you send an email message to a group en masse, how does Mail know *which* email address to use for each person?

Because you've *told* it. In Address Book, choose Edit→Edit Distribution List. A special dialog box appears, listing everyone in each group, along with each person's complete list of email addresses. (Use the tiny pop-up menu above the list to choose Phone or Address; that way, you can also indicate the preferred phone number and mailing address.) Just click the preferred email address to make it bold.

To see your groups, choose View→Groups, press ⌘-3, or click the red bookmark at the top of the page that shows individuals' names.

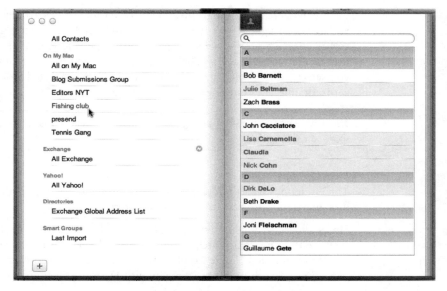

Figure 11-18:
If you regularly send out a family newsletter to 35 relatives, you might gather the address cards of all your assorted siblings, cousins, nieces, nephews, uncles, and aunts into a single group called Family. When addressing an outgoing message using Mail, you can type this group name to reach all your kin at once.

To create a group, click the **+** button at the bottom of the Group column in the Address Book window, or choose File→New Group (Shift-⌘-N.) Type a name for the newly spawned group icon in the Group column.

Now you have to fill up the group with the appropriate subset of names. There are three ways to do that:

- To turn a set of address cards into a group very quickly when you're in regular address-book mode (not Groups), select multiple entries from the Names column. You can do that either by Shift-clicking the names (to make contiguous selections) or by ⌘-clicking (for noncontiguous selections)—and then choose File→New Group From Selection. You end up with a new group containing all the selected names.

- While you're on the Groups page, click All Contacts at the top of the screen. Now your full names list appears on the right page; drag them directly onto the group names to put them there.

- If you're not on the Groups page, drag contacts up onto the Groups bookmark at the top of the page—leave the mouse button down as Address Book shows you the Groups page—and continue dragging onto the groups' name.

Note: You're not *moving* those names; in essence, you're just creating *aliases* of them, just as you might put songs in different playlists in iTunes. The only exception is Exchange accounts; those names can exist in only one group or folder at a time.

Once you've created some groups, you can even add groups to *other* groups, as though you were nesting folders. You might find it useful to keep a Nieces group and a Nephews group, for example, but to keep both groups inside a master Family group. To do this, create the two groups. Then drag each onto the Family group. Now, whenever you select Family, you'll see both Nieces and Nephews listed among the rest of the cards; double-click either group to see its members.

Tip: If, while viewing the list of groups, you Option-click someone's name in the main list, Address Book shows you all the groups and folders that person belongs to.

Smart groups

The Finder has smart folders, Mail has smart mailboxes, and iTunes has smart playlists; inevitably, Address Book has smart *groups*.

Smart address groups, like smart folders in the Finder, automatically populate themselves with items that match criteria you specify. For example, you might create a smart group called "Apple Employees" that lists all your contacts with "apple.com" in their email addresses. Or when you visit Detroit, you could whip up a group that lists everyone you know who lives there.

To create a smart group, choose File→New Smart Group (Option-⌘-N). Then use the resulting dialog box (which looks a lot like Mail's smart mailbox dialog box) to specify how you'd like the smart group to fill itself.

Once you're done, you can use your new smart group much like you'd use a regular group. You can't add contacts to a smart group yourself, of course, but you can still send an email to all the members of a smart group, for example, or drag one to the Finder to create a composite vCard.

Removing someone from a group

To take someone out of a group, first click the group name, and then click the person's name in the Name column and press the Delete key. If you want to remove the person from Address Book *itself*, click Delete in the resulting dialog box. Otherwise, just click Remove from Group or press Return. Address Book keeps the card but removes it from the currently selected group.

Note: If you selected All Contacts in the Group column, rather than a specific group, you don't get a Remove from Group option. Instead, the Mac just asks you to confirm that you do, in fact, want to permanently remove the card.

Adding Pictures

You can dress up each Address Book entry with a photo. Whenever you're editing somebody's address book card, drag a digital photo—preferably 64 pixels square, or a multiple of that—onto the empty headshot square; the image shows up. Or double-click the picture well; now you can either browse to a picture on your hard drive by clicking Choose, or, if this person is *with* you, take a new photo by clicking the camera icon. (Don't miss the swirly button next to it, which lets you apply nutty Photo Boothish effects.) At that point, you can enlarge, reposition, and crop the new photo. Click Set when you're done.

Tip: If you use iPhoto, and you've used its Faces feature to tag photos with who's in them, this process is a lot easier. Click the little Faces icon ▣ to view all the people iPhoto knows about, which should save you some time. You can crop or zoom as usual.

You don't necessarily have to use a photo, of course. You could add any graphic that you want to represent someone, even if it's a Bart Simpson face or a skull and crossbones. You can use any standard image file in an address card—a JPEG, GIF, PNG, TIFF, or even a PDF.

From now on, if you receive an email from that person, the photo shows up right in the email message.

Tip: If you've got snapshots in iPhoto, it's particularly easy to add a picture to any address card. Just drag a picture directly from the main iPhoto window to the picture frame on the address card to insert it.

Replacing and removing a picture

To replace a photo on an address card, just drag a new image on top of the old one. If you want to get rid of an existing picture without replacing it, select the card, and then choose Card→Clear Custom Image (or, in Edit mode, select the picture and press Delete).

Finding an Address

You can search for an Address Book entry inside the currently selected group by typing a few letters of a name (or address, or any other snippet of contact information) in the search box. To search *all* your contacts instead of just the current group, click All Contacts in the Group list.

Tip: You can press ⌘-F to jump directly to the search field and start typing. Your savings: one mouse click.

With each letter you type, Address Book filters your social circle and displays the number of matches at the bottom. The matching records themselves appear in the Name column, the first of the matching card entries appears in the far-right pane, and the matching text itself appears highlighted in the matching card.

If Address Book finds more than one matching card, use the ↓ and ↑ keys, or Return and Shift-Return, to navigate through them.

Once you've found the card you're looking for, you can perform some interesting stunts. If you click the label of a phone number ("home" or "office," for example), you see the Show in Large Type option: Address Book displays the number in an absurdly gigantic font that fills the entire width of your screen, making it possible to read the number as you dial from across the room. You can also click the label of an email address to create a preaddressed email message, or click a home page to launch your Web browser and go to somebody's site.

Tip: That same pop-up menu lists FaceTime. That is, you can begin a FaceTime video call right from the Address Book.

You can also copy and paste (or drag) address card info into another program or convert it into a Sticky Note.

Tip: Once you find a street address in your Address Book, you can find those coordinates on a map by Control-clicking (or right-clicking) the address's *label* and choosing Map This Address from the shortcut menu, as shown in Figure 11-19. Your Web browser obediently leaps up to display the address on a Google map.

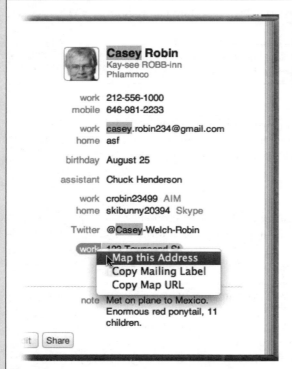

Figure 11-19:
The options that become available when you click the field labels on an address card vary according to field type. Pop-up menus let you send email, open a Web page, or view a map, depending on the type of field you've clicked.

Changing the Address Book Display

You can't do much to customize Address Book's appearance, but the preferences pane (Address Book→Preferences) gives you at least a couple of options in the General pane that are worth checking out:

- **Show first name.** Choose to have names displayed with the first name followed by the last name, or vice versa.

- **Sort By.** Sort the entries in Address Book by either first or last name.

Printing Options

When you choose File→Print and click Show Details, the Style pop-up menu offers four ways to print whatever addresses are selected at the moment:

- **Mailing Labels.** This option prints addresses on standard sheets of sticky mailing labels—Avery, for example—that you buy at office-supply stores.

Tip: As you manipulate settings, you can see your changes in the preview pane on the left. If the preview is too small for you to see, use the Zoom slider. (It doesn't affect your printout.)

- **Envelopes.** This feature is great if you have bad handwriting; rather than hand addressing your envelopes, you can have Address Book print them out for you. Use the Layout pop-up menu to pick the size of your envelopes—it's usually listed on the outside of the envelope box.

Note: Both the Mailing Labels and Envelopes options print *only* the contacts for which you have, in fact, entered physical mailing addresses.

- **Lists.** If all you want is a paper backup of your Address Book entries, use this setting. In the Attributes list, turn on the checkboxes of the fields you want printed—just name and phone number, for example.

- **Pocket Address Book.** This feature prints out a convenient *paper* address book from your virtual one. If you pick Indexed from the Flip Style pop-up menu, then each page's edge will even list the first letters of the last names listed on the page, making it a cinch to find the page with the address you want. (Here again, you can pick which fields you'd like to include—phone numbers, addresses, and so on.)

As you fiddle with the options presented here, you get to see a miniature preview, right in the dialog box, that shows what you're going to get.

No matter which mode you choose, the only cards that print are the ones that were selected when you chose File→Print. If you want to print *all* your cards, therefore, click All in the Group column before you print.

Tip: You can combine the smart-groups feature with the printing features in one clever way: to print yourself a portable phone book when you're heading off for a visit to a different city. That is, set up a smart group that rounds up everyone you know who lives in Chicago, and then print that as a pocket address book.

Address Book Backups

Your Address Book may represent *years* of typing and compiling effort. Losing all that information to a corrupted database or a hard drive crash could be devastating. Here are three ways to protect your Address Book data:

- **Back up your entire Address Book database.** Choose File→Export→Address Book Archive. Store the resulting backup file on another drive, if you like. Later, you can use the File→Import command to find that data and slurp it back in.

- **Turn on iCloud syncing.** An iCloud account has its privileges—and one of them is automatic synchronizing with the iCloud mother ship online.

- **Back up your whole Mac with Time Machine.** Chapter 5 tells you how.

Safari & iChat

A pple's most obvious Internet-friendly creation is Safari, a smartly designed window to the Web (available for both Mac OS X and, believe it or not, Windows). This chapter is all about Safari—the compass icon in the Dock points the way to your Internet adventure—and iChat, the unsung superstar of the chat-and-conferencing universe.

Browsing Basics

You probably know the drill when it comes to Web browsers. When you click a *link* (*hyperlink*) or a picture button, you're transported from one Web page to another. One page might be the home page of General Motors; another might contain critical information about a bill in Congress; another might have baby pictures posted by a parent in Omaha.

Scrolling

You'll rarely do more page scrolling than you do in a Web browser. Scrolling is a *constant* activity.

Fortunately, Apple gives you about 11,339 different ways to do it.

You can use the regular scroll gesture (two fingers on the trackpad). You can also press your ↑ and ↓ keys to scroll one line at a time. Page Up and Page Down scroll in full-screen increments, while Home and End whisk you to the top or bottom of the current Web page. And if your mouse has a scroll wheel, it works, too. (Hold Shift while you're rolling the wheel to scroll *horizontally*.)

But maybe the best way of all is to *tap the space bar* each time you want to see more. Press Shift-space to scroll *up*. (The space bar serves its traditional, space-making function only when the insertion point is blinking in a text box or the address bar.)

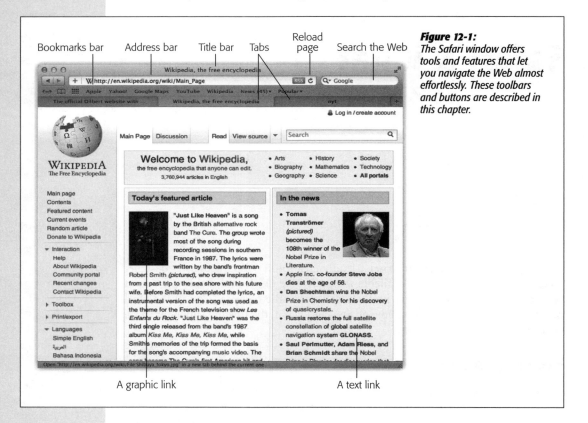

Figure 12-1:
The Safari window offers tools and features that let you navigate the Web almost effortlessly. These toolbars and buttons are described in this chapter.

Bookmarks bar   Address bar   Title bar   Tabs   Reload page   Search the Web

A graphic link   A text link

Safari Toolbars

Many of Safari's most useful controls come parked on toolbars and buttons that you can summon or hide by choosing their names from the View menu. Here's what they do:

Toolbar (address bar)

The main bar, the one where your current Web address appears, is what the View menu simply calls the toolbar. When you type a new Web page address (URL) into this strip and press Return, the corresponding Web site appears.

Because typing out Internet addresses is so central to the Internet experience and such a typo-prone hassle, the address bar is rich with features that minimize keystrokes. For example:

• **You don't have to click the address bar before typing;** just press ⌘-L.

- **You can highlight the entire address** (so it's ready to be typed over with a new one) by clicking the very upper or lower edge of the address bar text box. Alternatively, you can click the small icon just to the left of the current address, or triple-click the address bar, or press ⌘-L.

- **You don't have to type out the whole Internet address.** You can omit the *http://*, *www,* and *.com* portions; Safari fills in those standard address bits for you. To visit *NYTimes.com,* for example, a speed freak might press ⌘-L to highlight the address bar, type *nytimes,* and then press Return.

- **When you begin to type into the address bar,** the AutoComplete feature compares what you're typing against a list of Web sites that you've recently visited (labeled History) or that you've saved as bookmarks. Safari displays a drop-down list of Web addresses that seem to match what you're typing. To spare yourself the tedium of typing out the whole thing, click the correct complete address with your mouse,

---

GEM IN THE ROUGH

Let AutoFill Do the Typing

Safari can also remember user names, passwords, and other information you type into the text boxes you encounter in your Web travels.

To turn on this great feature, visit the Safari→Preferences→ AutoFill tab. If you turn on "Using info from my Address Book card," then whenever you're supposed to fill in your shipping address on a Web form, you can click the AutoFill button in the address bar to have Safari fill in the blanks for you automatically. (If you don't see the AutoFill button, choose Edit→AutoFill Form to do the deed instead.)

Alternatively, just click a text box–Name, for example–and start typing. As soon as Safari recognizes a familiar scrap of your contact information, it displays a new, Lionized pop-up suggestion below the text box, as shown here. To accept the suggestion, click it (or press the ↓ arrow key and then press Return). To decline it, press Return, or just keep typing.

If, in Preferences, you turn on "User names and passwords," then each time you type a password into a Web page, Safari

offers to memorize it for you. It's a great time- and brain-saver, even though it doesn't work on all Web sites. (Of course, use it with caution if you share an account on your Mac with other people.)

When you want Safari to "forget" your passwords–for security reasons, for example–revisit that Safari→Preferences→AutoFill tab. Click one of the Edit buttons, and then delete the Web site names for which your information has been stored.

Turn on Other Forms if you'd like Safari to remember the terms you've typed into search engines, shopping sites, online gaming sites, and so on.

Finally, there's a handy little timesaving feature that's new in Lion: The first time you log into your Gmail, Yahoo, or AOL email account, Safari pops up a message that invites you to use that account as the source of your mail, calendar, and chat information for Mail, iCal, and iChat. If you click Add Account, Lion opens the corresponding app and fills in the account information automatically, based on what you just typed while logging in.

---

or use the ↓ key to reach the desired listing and then press Return. The complete address you select pops into the address bar.

Tip: Even with this bar hidden, you can briefly summon it by pressing ⌘-L. Type the address you want and then press Return to make the bar disappear again. That's good news for people with small screens—and for Mac trivia collectors.

Toolbar buttons

You can summon or dismiss the individual buttons on the address bar, in effect customizing it (Figure 12-2).

Figure 12-2:
To summon this toolbar-tailoring screen, choose View→Customize Toolbar. Then drag the buttons you want directly onto the address bar. Some of them lack text labels once installed, but all offer tooltip labels that you can read by pointing to the button without clicking.

It's worth putting some thought into this tailoring, because some of these buttons' functions are really handy. So here's a catalog of your options:

- **Back/Forward.** Click the Back button (◀) to revisit the page you were just on. *Keyboard shortcut:* Delete, or ⌘-←, or ⌘-[, or a two-finger swipe left on the trackpad. (On a Mighty Mouse, that's a *one*-finger swipe.)

  Once you've clicked ◀, you can then click the ▶ button (or press ⌘-→, or ⌘-], or a two-finger swipe to the *right*) to return to the page you were on before you clicked the Back button. Click and hold the ◀ or ▶ button for a drop-down list of *all* the Web pages you've visited during this online session.

  That pop-up menu lists the sites by name, as in "The New York Times—Breaking News, World News & Multimedia." To view the actual *addresses* instead, Option-click (and hold the mouse down on) the ◀ or ▶ button.

- **Reading List.** This button hides or shows the Reading List, described on page 385.

- **Top Sites.** This feature opens up the highly visual dashboard shown in Figure 12-3. These thumbnails represent what Safari has determined are your favorite Web sites, as calculated by how often and how recently you've visited them.

- **Home.** Click to bring up the Web page you've designated as your home page (in the Safari→Preferences→General tab).

Figure 12-3:
You can open the Top Sites display either by clicking the Top Sites button on the toolbar or by choosing History→Top Sites. Click a page to revisit it; a star in the corner means, "This page has changed since your last visit."

- **New Tab.** Creates a new tab (embedded window), described later in this chapter.

- **History.** Click to open the list of Web sites you've visited recently in a window—a much easier-to-navigate display than the History *menu*.

- **Bookmarks, Add Bookmark.** When you find a Web page you might like to visit again, click Add Bookmark. You can also press ⌘-D, choose Bookmarks→Add Bookmark, or drag the tiny Web-page icon from the address bar directly onto your Bookmarks bar.

  As shown in Figure 12-4, Safari offers to add this Web page's name (or a shorter name that you specify for it) either to the Bookmarks menu or to the Bookmarks bar (described below). The next time you want to visit that page, just select its name in whichever location you chose.

Tip: Press Shift-⌘-D to add the bookmark to the menu instantly—no questions asked, no dialog box presented.

The ⌸ (Bookmarks) button opens the Bookmarks editing window (Figure 12-4). Here you can rearrange the names in your Bookmarks menu easily, or peruse them by scrolling through their giant Cover Flow thumbnails—a great feature in a Web browser, because a visual representation of a page is a lot more helpful than some Web address.

(Even without the ⌸ button, you can get there by choosing Bookmarks→Show All Bookmarks or by pressing Option-⌘-B.)

Figure 12-4:
Top: Once you've got a juicy Web page on the screen, you can drag its page-logo icon (left end of the address bar) from the toolbar directly onto the Bookmarks bar or menu.

Second from top: Safari realizes that you may prefer a shorter name to appear on the space-limited bar, so it offers you the chance to type in a new label.

Third from top: When you click OK, the button appears on the bar. (You can also drag any link to the bar, such as a blue underlined phrase from a Web page, or even an icon from your desktop!) To remove a button, drag it off the bar.

Bottom: Click the ⌸ icon (left end of toolbar) to open the Organize Bookmarks window. Here you can drag names up or down to rearrange the list, or drag them into a submenu in the Bookmarks menu. (Create a submenu by clicking the + button below the list.) You can edit a bookmark by clicking once on its name or URL, or delete one by pressing Delete.

In the resulting organization window, drag the bookmarks up and down. Figure 12-4 also shows you how to perform more dramatic management tasks, like editing, renaming, or deleting bookmarks.

- **Bookmarks Bar.** Hides or shows the horizontal toolbar that lists your favorite bookmarks. (The equivalent of choosing View→Bookmarks Bar.)

- **AutoFill.** Click this button to make Safari fill in Web order forms with your name, address, and other information. See the box on page 379.

- **Zoom.** You can adjust the size of a Web page's text using these buttons. When you visit a Web site designed for Windows computers—whose text often looks too small on Mac screens—you can use these buttons to bump up the size. The keyboard shortcuts are ⌘-plus or ⌘-minus.

- **Open in Dashboard.** This icon is the key to creating Dashboard *Web clips*, as described on page 153. Click this button, and then select the part of the page you want to widgetize. It's the equivalent of the File→Open in Dashboard command.

- **Mail.** Opens a new, outgoing email message in your email program. The subject line contains the *name* of the site you were visiting; the body contains a link to it. You can address the message, add a comment ("Re: your comment that 'no expert' recommends trampolines for children"), and send it.

- **Print.** You can add a printer icon to Safari for point-and-click paper action if you don't want to bother with ⌘-P.

POWER USERS' CLINIC

Customizing Top Sites

Ordinarily, the Top Sites display changes over time, as your tastes and your activity change. But you can override Safari's attempt to curate this page in various ways. For example, you can pin a certain site so that it never leaves the Top Sites screen, or you can manually add a page.

It all happens when you click the Edit button in the lower left. Each thumbnail sprouts two buttons in the corner: the X button (this page will never again appear on Top Sites) and the thumbtack button (this page will always appear in Top Sites, even if you don't visit it much).

To add a new page to the Top Sites display, first open that page in another Safari window. Then highlight its address in the address bar and drag it right onto the Top Sites page. You can also drag a Web link from an email message, text document, Web page, or any other source to the Top Sites page.

You can reorder the thumbnails, too, just by dragging them around on this screen.

Finally, you can change the thumbnail size on this Edit screen, too. Use the Small/Medium/Large control in the lower right; the smaller the thumbnails, the more of them fit (24, 12, or six, respectively).

Tip: Safari automatically shrinks your printouts, if necessary, by up to 10 percent, if doing so will avoid printing a second page with just one or two lines of text on it. Nice.

- **Downloads.** Here's that awesome new Downloads button described at the beginning of this chapter.

- **Web Inspector.** This button is intended for Web designers and programmers (it appears only if you've visited Safari→Preferences and turned on "Show Develop menu in menu bar"). Clicking it opens a technical-looking window that lists everything on the current Web page: documents, style sheets, and scripts. Using the buttons across the top, you can also view statistics like how long each resource takes to load, and how much bandwidth (Internet data) this page requires.

- **Report Bug.** This insect-shaped button opens a tiny "Dear Apple" box, where you can tell Apple about a Safari feature or Web page that doesn't work. If you click Options, you can even send Apple a screen illustration of, for example, a screwy Web page layout that Safari delivered.

- **Address Bar/Stop/Reload.** Yep, it's the address bar, where you type in the Web address you want to call out.

  The Stop/Reload button is built into the address bar, at the right end. Click the Stop button (or Esc, or ⌘-period) to interrupt the downloading of a Web page you've just requested—if you've made a mistake, for instance.

  Once a page has finished loading, the Stop button turns into a Refresh button. Click this circular arrow (or press ⌘-R) if a page doesn't look or work quite right, or if you want to see the updated version of a Web page (such as a breaking-news site) that changes constantly. Safari redownloads the Web page and reinterprets its text and graphics.

- **Search.** Here's one of Safari's most profoundly useful features—a search box that automatically sends your search request to Google, Yahoo, or Bing, the three most popular Web-page search pages. Press Option-⌘-F to deposit your insertion point inside this rounded text box, type something you're looking for—*phony baloney,* say—and then press Return. Safari takes you directly to the Google results page.

Tip: The tiny ▾ at the left end of the search box is a pop-up menu. It offers two categories of listings, in hopes of saving you time and typing: First is Suggestions (you may notice that these pop up automatically *as you type* into the search box, too). These suggestions come from Google's own Suggest feature. The second category: your most Recent Searches. At the bottom: your choice of Google, Yahoo, or Bing.

Bookmarks Bar

The Bookmarks menu is one way to maintain a list of Web sites you visit frequently. But opening a Web page from that menu requires *two mouse clicks*—an exorbitant expenditure of energy. The Bookmarks bar (View→Bookmarks Bar), on the other hand, lets you summon a few *very* favorite Web pages with only one click.

Figure 12-4 illustrates how to add buttons to, and remove them from, this toolbar.

Tip: As shown in Figure 12-4, you can drag a link from a Web page onto your Bookmarks bar. But you can also drag a link directly to the desktop, where it turns into an *Internet location file.* Thereafter, to launch your browser and visit the associated Web page whenever you like, just double-click this icon.

Better yet, stash a few of these icons in your Dock or Sidebar for even easier access.

Status Bar

The Status bar at the bottom of the window tells you what Safari is doing (such as "Opening page..." or "Done"). When you point to a link without clicking, the Status bar also tells you which URL will open if you click it. For those two reasons, it's a very useful strip, but it doesn't appear when you first run Safari. You have to summon it by choosing View→Show Status Bar.

Tips for Better Surfing

Safari is filled with shortcuts and tricks for better speed and more pleasant surfing. For example:

Reader

How can people read Web articles when there's Times-Square blinking going on all around them? Fortunately, you'll never have to put up with that again.

The Reader button in the address bar is amazing. With one click (or press Shift-⌘-R), it eliminates *everything* from the Web page you're reading except the text and photos. No ads, blinking, links, banners, promos, or anything else.

The text is also changed to a clean, clear font and size, and the background is made plain white. Basically, it makes any Web page look like a printed book page or a Kindle page, and it's glorious (Figure 12-5).

To exit Reader, press the same keyboard shortcut, or click the Reader button again.

Best. Feature. Ever.

The Reading List

The Reading List is a hide-able panel at the left side of the screen that lists Web pages you want to read later (Figure 12-6).

The Reading List doesn't actually store the pages on the Mac; it basically stores a link to the page, just like a bookmark. You can't read it later unless you're actually online.

It does have some advantages over bookmarks, though. For example, it's faster to flag a Web page you like—you don't have to make up a name or location for it, as with a bookmark. The Reading List keeps track of what you've read; you can use the All/Unread buttons at the top of the list to view everything, or just what you haven't yet read. You might treat the Reading List as a list of pages you'll want to read *once* later, and use bookmarks for pages you like to revisit *frequently.*

Tip: To make matters even sweeter, iCloud synchronizes your Reading List among your Mac, iPhone, iPad, and so on—as long as you've turned on bookmark syncing. It's as though the Web always keeps your place.

To add a page to the Reading List, use one of these techniques:

- **Shift-click a link.** That simple trick adds the linked page to the Reading List. You haven't even had to *visit* the page itself (only the link to it), or even to open the Reading List itself.

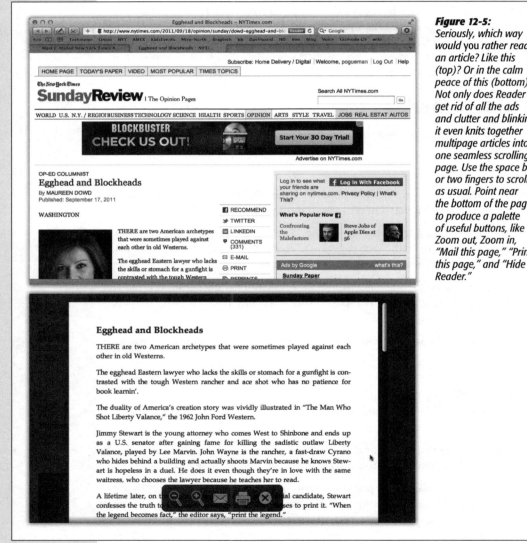

Figure 12-5:
Seriously, which way would you *rather read an article? Like this (top)? Or in the calm peace of this (bottom)? Not only does Reader get rid of all the ads and clutter and blinking, it even knits together multipage articles into one seamless scrolling page. Use the space bar or two fingers to scroll, as usual. Point near the bottom of the page to produce a palette of useful buttons, like Zoom out, Zoom in, "Mail this page," "Print this page," and "Hide Reader."*

- **Use the menu.** If you're already *on* the page you might want to read later, choose Bookmarks→Add to Reading List, or press Shift-⌘-D.

- **Use the Reading List.** If the Reading List is already open, just click Add Page to add the current page to the list.

Once you've added a page to the Reading List, you can get to it by clicking the ↩ button on the toolbar, or by choosing View→Show Reading List, or by pressing Shift-⌘-L.

To read the pages you've flagged for the Reading List, you can press Option-⌘-↓ or Option-⌘-↑ to move up and down your list.

Tip: If you're reading one article in your Reading List using the Reader feature and then select another article, it, too, will appear in Reader.

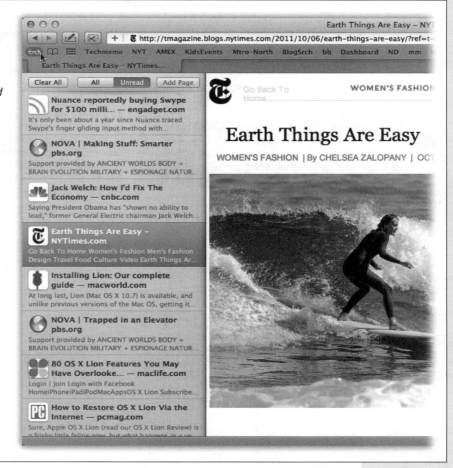

Figure 12-6:
To revisit a page you've set aside in the Reading List, just click it. Screen out the pages you've already read by clicking the Unread tab at the top. Delete an entry by clicking the ⊗ button that appears at the right side when you point there.

Full Screen and Gestures

If any app is going to remind you of an iPhone/iPad, it's Safari. Once you enter full-screen mode by clicking the ⬚ button at upper right (see page 11), it's almost exactly like surfing the Web on the iPad. For example:

- **Zoom in and out with pinch and spread.** That is, put two fingers on your trackpad and spread them to magnify the Web page, or pinch to zoom out. Great when the type is a little too small.

- **Magnify just a block with a two-finger double-tap.** Most Web pages are subdivided into various rectangles of text or graphics. Just as on the iPhone/iPad, you can double-tap (with *two* fingers on your trackpad) to magnify only one single block of text or graphics. Repeat the process to zoom back out to regular size. (Note that this is *tapping*, not *clicking*.)

- **Use a two-finger swipe for Back and Next.** This one's really juicy. With two fingers on your trackpad, swipe left or right instead of clicking the ◀ or ▶ buttons. The great part is that if you do this *slowly*, you pull the previous or next page onto the screen *gradually*, giving you a chance to peek at the page without actually moving to it.

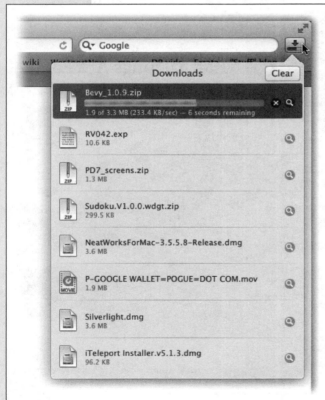

Figure 12-7:
Click the Downloads (⬛) button to view this list of recent downloads. Double-click an icon to open the download. Click the ◉ button to jump to the file wherever it's sitting in the Finder. To remove an item from the list, click it and then press Delete. (The Clear button erases the whole list.) You can also drag an item out of this list and onto the desktop to park it there.

Note: Each time you open Safari, it brings up whatever pages you had open last. That's part of Lion's auto-resume feature (page 138).

The Download Manager

When you click a link to download something from a Web page, it *visibly* flies to the upper-right corner of the Safari window, where the Downloads button 🅾 appears. You can then monitor the progress of the download at a glance—because the Downloads button *fills up* with blue as the download completes.

As Figure 12-7 shows, you can also view and manipulate a list of everything you've downloaded recently, all without leaving the comfort of whatever page you're on.

To pause downloading, click the ⊗ button next to the download's name. Later, you can generally pick up from where you left off by clicking the Resume (⏻) button.

> **Tip:** In Safari→Preferences→General, you can opt to have your download listings removed from the Downloads window as soon as they've been successfully downloaded.

Graphics Worth Saving

When you see a picture you'd like to keep, right-click it and choose Save Image to Downloads (or Add Image to iPhoto Library, or just Save Image As) from the shortcut menu. Safari stores it as a new graphics file, freed from its birthplace on the Web. (You can specify where Safari saves downloaded pictures on the Safari→Preferences→General tab. In that case, the shortcut menu's wording changes to say, for example, "Save Image to 'Pictures.'")

> **Tip:** You can also save a graphic to the desktop just by dragging it there, right out of the Safari window.

SnapBack

The little orange SnapBack button (◀), which sometimes appears at the right end of the address bar or search box, takes you instantly back to your last page of search results.

The point here is that, after burrowing from one link to another in pursuit of some Google result or Amazon listing, you can return to your starting point without having to mash the Back button over and over again. (The SnapBack button doesn't appear until you've actually clicked away from the first page you visited.)

Stifle Pop-Ups and Pop-Unders

The world's smarmiest advertisers inundate us with *pop-up* and *pop-under* ads—nasty little windows that appear in front of the browser window or, worse, behind it, waiting to jump out the moment you close your current window. They're often deceptive, masquerading as error messages or dialog boxes, and they'll do absolutely anything to get you to click inside them.

If this kind of thing is driving you crazy, choose Safari→Block Pop-Up Windows, so that a checkmark appears next to the command. It's a war out there—but at least you now have some ammunition.

Note: This feature doesn't squelch small windows that pop up when you click a link–only windows that appear unbidden.

Even unbidden windows, however, are sometimes legitimate (and not ads)–notices of new banking features, warnings that the instructions to use a site have changed, and so on. Safari can't tell these from ads and stifles them, too. So if a site you trust says, "Please turn off pop-up blockers and reload this page," then you know you're probably missing out on a *useful* pop-up message.

And one more thing: These days, the evildoers of the Internet have begun to attract your attention using other programming tricks that don't work by creating new windows (instead, they create new layers in your browser window). There's not much you can do about those nuisances.

Five Ways to Magnify a Page

If it seems as though a lot of Web sites are designed with type that's too small to read, it's not just you and your aging eyes. Often, it has to do with the high resolution of today's screens, which work by packing their pixels together more tightly—and making everything look smaller.

Fortunately, Safari is extremely well equipped to help you with this problem. In fact, it offers many solutions:

- **Enlarge the screen.** Press ⌘-plus or ⌘-minus to enlarge or reduce the entire Web page. Or use the two-finger "spread" gesture on your laptop trackpad. Or use the Zoom button, if you've added it to your toolbar. The advantage of this method is that the whole Web page's layout remains proportional.

- **Magnify a block.** Double-tap (not click) with *two fingers* on your trackpad to zoom into one block of text or graphics on a page.

- **Blow up just the text.** If you turn on View→Zoom Text Only, then all those shortcuts serve to magnify or shrink *only the text* on your page. Graphics remain at their original size. You're now distorting the original layout, but you're maximizing the amount of reading you can do before you have to scroll.

- **Zoom in the usual way.** You know the Control-key zooming technique described on page 541? It's not the same thing as the ⌘-plus or ⌘-minus tricks, which keep the window frame and menu at normal size. The Control-key zooming technique magnifies *everything*—the entire screen, menus and all. It also doesn't keep text as sharp as the ⌘-plus/⌘-minus trick.

- **Specify a minimum type size.** This may be the best option of all, because it saves you all that zooming. Open Safari→Preferences→Advanced, and set the "Never use font sizes smaller than" option to, for example, 14 points. Now *every* Web page shows up with legible text. (Except a few oddballs that use weird coding to prevent text-size changing.)

Keyboard Control

Efficiency freaks generally prefer keyboard shortcuts to using the mouse, so Safari is filled with them.

Press Tab to jump from one text box or pop-up menu to the next on your Web page. Add the Option key to jump from one *link* to another (and when you highlight a link, press Return to "click" it).

Tip: For a shockingly complete list of Safari's keyboard shortcuts, open the Help menu. In the search box at the top of the menu, type *Safari shortcuts.* Wait a moment. Click "Safari shortcuts" in the list of Help topics.

Viewing Web Pages Offline

You don't have to be connected to the Net to read a favorite Web page. You can save it on your hard drive so you can peruse it later—on your laptop during your commute, for example—just by choosing File→Save As.

At that point, to save the *entire* page, along with all its images, movies, and so on, choose Web Archive from the Format pop-up menu. (Choose Page Source only if you intend to *edit* the raw HTML Web documents and then repost them, or if you just want to study the underlying code.)

Tip: When you buy something online, don't waste paper by printing out the "This is your receipt" page. Instead, choose File→Print and, from the PDF pop-up button, choose Save PDF to Web Receipts Folder. Safari saves the page as a PDF file into a tidy folder (in your Home→Documents folder) called Web Receipts. Nice touch!

Where Am I?

Occasionally, you may wish you could view a little map that marks the path of the current Web page within its site. Ah, but Safari has already thought of that. See Figure 12-8.

Figure 12-8:
If you ⌘-click the title bar (centered just above the address bar), Safari displays the "ladder" that shows the Web site's internal folder structure. That can be handy when you want to jump to this page's "parent" page.

Sending a Page to a Friend

Safari provides two ways of telling a friend about the page you're looking at. You might find that useful when you come across a particularly interesting news story, op-ed piece, or burrito recipe.

- **The send-the-whole-page method.** While looking at a page, choose File→Mail Contents of This Page (⌘-I) to open a new Mail message with a copy of the *actual* Web page in the body. Address the message and click Send.

- **The send-a-link method.** To send just a *link* to the page you're looking at, choose File→Mail Link to This Page (Shift-⌘-I). Then proceed as usual, addressing the message and clicking Send.

  Links take only a split second for your recipient to download, and they're guaranteed to display properly in all email programs. All your recipients have to do is click the link to open it in their Web browsers.

Expanding Web Forms

If the customer-service comment form on that corporate Web site doesn't give you enough room to rant properly, you can resize the text box right on the page—a *very* welcome feature. Figure 12-9 tells all.

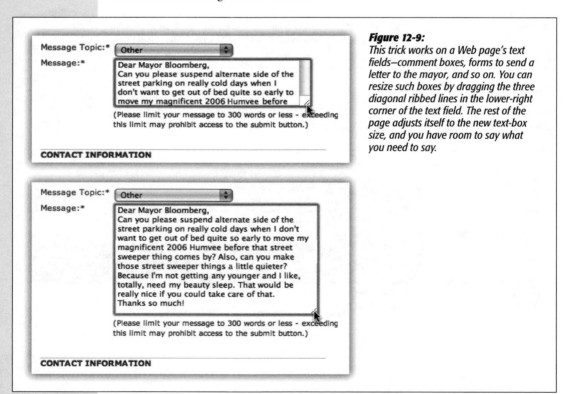

Figure 12-9:
This trick works on a Web page's text fields—comment boxes, forms to send a letter to the mayor, and so on. You can resize such boxes by dragging the three diagonal ribbed lines in the lower-right corner of the text field. The rest of the page adjusts itself to the new text-box size, and you have room to say what you need to say.

Designate Your Start Page

What's the first thing you see when you open Safari? Is it the Apple news Web site? Is it the Top Sites display (Figure 12-3)?

Actually, that's up to you.

Choose Safari→Preferences→General tab. Here, the "New windows open with" pop-up menu offers choices like these:

- **Top Sites.** The thumbnail view of your favorites sites makes a great starting point.

- **Home Page.** If you choose this option, then Safari will open up with whatever page you've specified in the "Home page" box. Google—or its news page, *http://news.google.com*—is a good starting place. So is your favorite newspaper home page, or maybe *www.dilbert.com* for today's Dilbert cartoon.

If you're already *on* the page you like, just click Set to Current Page.

FREQUENTLY ASKED QUESTION

Erasing Your Tracks—and Private Browsing

So, about this History menu: I'd just as soon my wife/husband/boss/parent/kid not know what Web sites I've been visiting. Must that History menu display my movements quite so proudly?

Some people find it creepy that Safari maintains a complete list of every Web site they've seen recently, right there in plain view of any family member or coworker who wanders by.

To delete just one particularly incriminating History listing, click the 🕮 icon at the left end of the Bookmarks bar; in the resulting Bookmarks organizer window, click History. Expand the relevant date triangle, highlight the offending address, and then press your Delete key. Click 🕮 again to return to normal browsing. You've just rewritten History!

Or, to erase the entire History menu, choose History→Clear History.

Of course, the History menu isn't the only place where you've left footprints. If you choose Safari→Reset Safari instead, you also erase all other shreds of your activities: any cookies (Web-page preference files) you've accumulated, your list of past downloads, the cache files (bits of the Web pages that a browser stores on your hard drive to save time when you return to the page they came from), and so on. This is good information to know; after all, you might be nominated to the Supreme Court someday.

That's a lot of work just to cover my tracks; it also erases a lot of valuable cookies, passwords, and History entries I'd like to keep. Is all that really necessary just so I can duck in for an occasional look at the Hot Bods of the Midwestern Tax Preparers' Association Web site?

No, it's not. A feature called private browsing lets you surf without adding any pages to your History list, searches to your Google search box, passwords to Safari's saved password list, or autofill entries to Safari's memory. (Apple says this feature is intended for use at public Macs, where you don't want to reveal anything personal to subsequent visitors. Ha!)

The trick is to choose Safari→Private Browsing before you start browsing. Once you OK the explanation box, Safari records nothing while you surf. As you'd hope, Lion won't use auto-resume the next time you open Safari, either—that is, the last page you'd opened won't reopen automatically

When you're ready to browse "publicly" again, choose Safari→Private Browsing once more so the checkmark goes away. Safari again begins taking note of the pages you visit—but it never remembers the earlier ones.

In other words, what happens in Private Browsing stays in Private Browsing.

- **Empty Page.** Some people prefer this setup, which makes Safari load very quickly when you first open it. Once this empty window opens, *then* you can tell the browser where you want to go today.

- **Bookmarks.** Whenever you open a new window or launch Safari, you see your full list of bookmarks. You can then choose exactly which page you want to open.

- **Tabs for Bookmarks Bar.** This intriguing option creates a row of tabs in a single window—one for *every* icon on your Bookmarks bar. The idea, of course, is to have not just one favorite Web page waiting for you in the morning, but *all* the ones you visit frequently, preloaded and ready to go.

- **Choose Tabs folder.** This option is similar to Tabs for Bookmarks Bar, except that it starts you off with tabs for *any* random bunch of Web sites—not just the ones on your Bookmarks bar. The trick is to build a *folder* full of bookmarks, and choose *that* as the basis for your auto-opening tabs.

Note: An identical pop-up menu is available for "New tabs open with." That is, you can specify one starter-page preference for new *tabs,* and another for new *windows.*

Finding Text on Web Pages

Some pages are so long, dense, or poorly designed that finding the words *on* the page needs a whole 'nother search engine. Safari's search-within-the-page function shines a light on the words or phrase you're seeking.

To use it, press ⌘-F and then type your search word into the Find box (Figure 12-10). As Safari locates the word or words, it displays them within a bright yellow box and

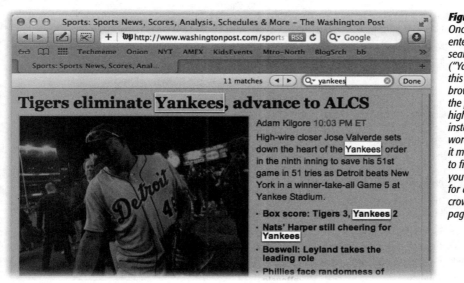

Figure 12-10:
Once you enter your search word ("Yankees," in this case), the browser dims the page and highlights every instance of that word—making it much easier to find what you're looking for across a crowded Web page.

dims the background of the rest of the page. The Find bar also tells you how many times the word or phrase occurs on the page; you can jump to each instance. Click the ✪ to start over with new search terms, or click Done to close the Find box and return to your normal browsing activity.

The History Menu

The History menu lists the Web sites you've visited in the past week or so, neatly organized into subfolders like Earlier Today and Yesterday. (A similar menu appears when you click *and hold* the ◀ or ▶ button.) These are great features if you can't recall the URL for a Web site you remember having visited recently.

Tip: See Safari's Help menu? It features a search box that lets you search all the *menu commands* in Safari—including Safari's History menu. That's just a *crazy* powerful feature. It means you can re-find a site without having to hunt through all the History submenus manually; just search for a word you remember in the title.

You can also view your History in a more expansive view—in Cover Flow view, in fact—by clicking the 🕮 at the left end of your toolbar. You enter the Bookmarks-management view, described in Figure 12-4.

Figure 12-11:
If you're having trouble reading the tiny type in a PDF, point your mouse to the bottom of it to invoke Safari's PDF toolbar. You can zoom out, zoom in, open the file in the Mac's Preview program, or even download it from the Web site with a well-placed click.

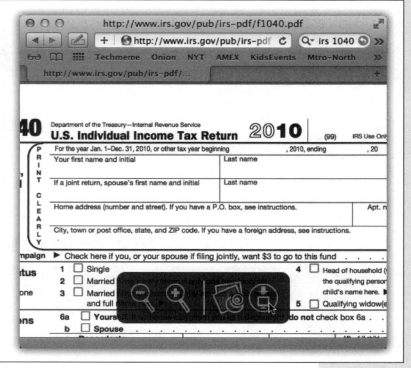

Tip: Having History available in the Bookmarks window is very handy, because you can drag a Web page from your History into your Bookmarks menu, folder, or bar. That is, you can bookmark a Web site long after your initial visit.

PDF Pages Online

PDF files are all over the Web as, among other things, forms to download, online brochures, and scanned book pages. But they aren't always especially readable in a browser window.

Unless, that is, you're using Safari. The next time you're squinting at a PDF in the window, point to the bottom edge of the document; you'll see a toolbar like the one in Figure 12-11 appear. With these four icons, you can zoom out, zoom in, open the file in Preview, or save the PDF file to your Downloads folder.

Tabbed Browsing

Beloved by hardcore surfers the world over, *tabbed browsing* is a way to keep a bunch of Web pages open simultaneously—in a single, neat window. Figure 12-12 illustrates.

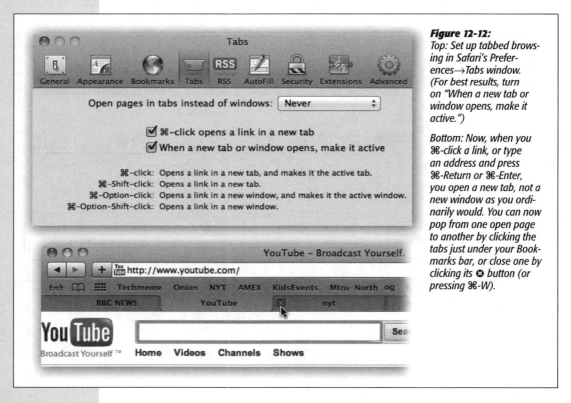

Figure 12-12:
Top: Set up tabbed browsing in Safari's Preferences→Tabs window. (For best results, turn on "When a new tab or window opens, make it active.")

Bottom: Now, when you ⌘-click a link, or type an address and press ⌘-Return or ⌘-Enter, you open a new tab, not a new window as you ordinarily would. You can now pop from one open page to another by clicking the tabs just under your Bookmarks bar, or close one by clicking its ⊗ button (or pressing ⌘-W).

Turning on tabbed browsing unlocks a whole raft of Safari shortcuts and tricks, which are just the sort of thing power surfers gulp down like Gatorade:

- If there's a certain set of Web sites you like to visit daily, put the bookmarks into one folder, using Bookmarks→Add Bookmark Folder and the Bookmarks organizer window (Figure 12-12). You can then load all of them into a single tabbed window, simply by selecting the resulting "folder" in the Bookmarks menu—or the Bookmarks bar—and choosing Open in Tabs from the submenu.

 The beauty of this arrangement is that you can start reading the first Web page while all the others load into their own tabs in the background.

Tip: Click the ⌂ icon at the left end of the Bookmarks bar. In the Bookmarks organizer, click the Bookmarks Bar item in the left-side list. Now you can see an Auto-Click checkbox for each listed folder.

If you turn on this checkbox, you'll be able to open all the bookmarks in that folder into tabs, all at once, merely by clicking the folder's name in the Bookmarks bar. (If you want to summon the *normal* menu from the folder, just hold the mouse button down.)

- A variation on a theme: When you have a bunch of pages open in tabs, you can drag the tabs across the window to rearrange the order. When you have them the way you want them, right-click a tab, and then choose Add Bookmark for These [*Number*] Tabs from the shortcut menu. You can save your saved tabs to the Bookmarks bar and load all those pages with one click.

- If you Option-click a tab's ⊗ button, you close all the tabs *except* the one you clicked. The same thing happens if you hold down Option and choose File→Close Other Tabs, or if you press Option-⌘-W.

- If you Option-⌘-click a link, it opens in a separate window, rather than a new tab. (When tabbed browsing is turned *off,* just ⌘-click a link to open a new window.)

- If you find yourself with a bunch of separate browser windows all over your screen, you can neatly consolidate them all into one nicely tabbed Safari window by choosing Window→Merge All Windows.

- If you Shift-⌘-click a link, Safari opens that page in a tab *behind* the one you're reading. That's a fantastic trick when you're reading a Web page and see a reference you want to set aside for reading next, but you don't want to interrupt whatever you're reading now.

Note: When you log into Gmail, Yahoo Mail, or another popular mail service, Safari cheerfully offers to set up that account for you in Mail (and iCal and iChat), so you don't have to visit the Web to do your email, check your calendar, and conduct chats. Thanks for saving us the time, Apple!

RSS: The Missing Manual

Web browsing these days entails a constant battle against intrusive advertising and annoying animations. And with the proliferation of Web sites of every kind—from news sites to personal blogs—just reading your favorite sites can become a full-time job.

Enter RSS, a technology that lets you subscribe to *feeds*—summary blurbs provided by thousands of sources around the world, from Reuters to Apple to your nerdy next-door neighbor. You use a program like Safari to "subscribe" to updates from such feeds and then read any new articles or postings at your leisure (Figure 12-13).

The result: You spare yourself the tedium of checking for updates manually, plus you get to read short summaries of new articles without ads and blinking animations. And if you want to read a full article, you can click its link in the RSS feed to jump straight to the main Web site.

Note: RSS stands for either Rich Site Summary or Really Simple Syndication. Each abbreviation explains one aspect of RSS—either its summarizing talent or its simplicity.

News source   Headline   Date/time posted   RSS button   Article count

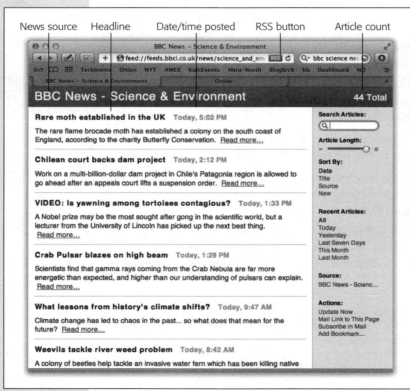

Figure 12-13:
The Article Length slider controls how much text appears for each RSS blurb; if you drag it all the way to the left, you're left with nothing but headlines. To change the number and order of the articles being displayed, use the sorting options on the right. And if you feel a sudden desire to tell your friends about an amazing RSS feed you've just discovered, use the Mail Link to This Page link in the lower-right section of the window.

Viewing an RSS Feed

So how do you sign up for these free, automatic RSS "broadcasts"? Watch your address bar as you're surfing the Web. When you see an RSS button appear, Safari is telling you, "This site has an RSS feed available."

To see what the fuss is all about, click that button. Safari switches into RSS-viewing mode, shown in Figure 12-13.

At this point, you have two choices:

- **Add the RSS feed as a bookmark.** Use the Bookmarks→Add Bookmark command, and add the feed to your Bookmarks menu, Bookmarks bar, or Mail as you would any Web page. From now on, you'll be able to see whether the RSS feed has had

---

FREQUENTLY ASKED QUESTION

Cookie Control—and Privacy Control

Help! I'm afraid of cookies! The cookies are trying to watch me!

Cookies are something like Web page preference files. Certain Web sites—particularly commercial ones like Amazon. com—deposit them on your hard drive like little bookmarks so that they'll remember you the next time you visit. Most cookies are perfectly innocuous—and, in fact, are extremely helpful, because they help Web sites remember your tastes. Cookies also spare you the effort of having to type in your name, address, credit card number, and so on, every time you visit these Web sites.

But fear is widespread, and the media fans the flames with tales of sinister cookies that track your movements on the Web. If you're worried about invasions of privacy, Safari is ready to protect you.

Once the browser is open, choose Safari→Preferences→ Privacy tab. The buttons in this dialog box are like a paranoia gauge. If you click Always, you create an acrylic shield around your Mac. No cookies can come in, and no cookie

information can go out. You'll probably find the Web a very inconvenient place; you'll have to re-enter your information upon every visit, and some Web sites may not work properly at all.

A less-drastic choice is "From third parties and advertisers," which accepts cookies from sites you want to visit but blocks cookies deposited on your hard drive by sites you're not actually visiting—cookies an especially evil banner ad gives you, for example.

Note, too, the Details button. It reveals the shockingly complete list of every cookie you've accumulated so far—and offers you the chance to delete the ones that don't look so savory.

While you're in there, horrified at the number of cookies, notice that there's other stuff Web sites have dumped onto your Mac. There are things like cache files (see the previous sidebar box) and local storage files (data that Web applications leave behind on your hard drive—something like cookies, except that Web sites can't retrieve this information later). All of it is available for your removal.

---

any new articles posted—without actually having to visit the site. Figure 12-14 (top) has the details.

- **Close the RSS feed altogether.** To do so, just click the RSS button again. You're left back where you started, at whatever Web page you were visiting.

Figure 12-14:
Top: Want to specify when Safari should check for updates to your RSS bookmarks? In Safari→Preferences, click RSS. Turn on Bookmarks Bar and Bookmarks Menu. (If you're an especially impatient person, select "Every 30 minutes" from the "Check for updates" pop-up menu.)

Bottom: Next to your RSS feeds' names, a number tells you how many new articles are waiting for you. If you have a bookmark folder containing several RSS feeds in it (here, Potato News), the number reflects the total number of new articles in that folder's feeds.

RSS Tricks

RSS is a tremendously flexible and powerful technology, especially in Safari. The fun never ends, as these tricks illustrate.

Creating RSS summaries

If you create a new bookmark folder and fill it with RSS feeds, you can see the *total* number of new articles right next to the folder's name (Figure 12-14, bottom). You might create a folder of Mac news feeds, for instance, so you know whenever there's an important event in the Mac world.

From then on, by clicking the folder's name (and opening its pop-up menu), you can see which feeds have new articles; they're the ones with numbers next to their names. If you ⌘-click a bookmark folder's name—in the Bookmarks bar—Safari shows you *all* the feeds, neatly collated into one big, easily digestible list for your perusing pleasure. (If you're billing by the hour, you can also choose View All RSS Articles from the folder's pop-up menu to achieve the same effect.)

Tip: To make the merged list more useful, click New under the Sort By heading. Now Safari displays any new articles at the top of the list, regardless of what site they came from, so you don't have to hunt through the list for new articles yourself.

The personal clipping service

The search box at the right of any RSS-viewing window works as you'd expect: It narrows down the list of articles to only those that contain your search terms.

But that's barely scratching the surface of the search field's power. If you've adopted the feed-merging trick described above, the Search box can search *several* feeds at once—perfect, for example, if you want to see all the news from Mac sites that has to do with iTunes.

You can then save the search itself as a bookmark. Use the Bookmark This Search link at the lower-right corner of the window. Give the bookmark a name, choose where it should appear in Safari, and then click Add.

You've just turned Safari into a high-tech personal clipping service. With one click on your new bookmark, you can search all your favorite news sources simultaneously— the feeds you've selected—for the terms you want. You've just saved yourself *hours* of daily searching—not to mention the expense of a real clipping service.

Tip: If you find RSS feeds completely addictive in Safari, you'll love them in Mail—where you can display them right in the program's window or have them land in your Inbox like regular messages. Flip back to page 362 if you skipped that chapter.

GEM IN THE ROUGH

Safari Extensions

Safari extensions are fantastic. They're little add-on, plug-in features, written by other people, that can make the Web a much better place.

Consider, for starters, the terrific ClickToFlash. Basically, it blocks all the Flash animations that turn Web pages into a blinking, flashing, animated mess. Anytime you'd normally see a Flash animation, you just get an empty gray box. And if you want to see that Flash? If it is, for example, a video you were hoping to watch? Well, as the name suggests, you just click inside the empty box to make the Flash load.

(You can also tell ClickToFlash not to block Flash on certain favorite Web sites.)

Another great one is A Cleaner YouTube, which presents each YouTube video on a simple, pure, plain white page, without the 50,000 elements of clutter and chaos. Facebook Cleaner is similar, but for Facebook.

You can find these and many other great Safari extensions at Apple's extensions gallery, *https://extensions.apple.com*.

The RSS screen saver

In the System Preferences→Desktop & Screen Saver→Screen Saver tab, you'll find the RSS Visualizer screen saver. When you click Options and select an RSS feed (and enable screen savers), you set up Mac OS X to get news from that feed whenever you're away from your Mac. When the screen saver comes on, you're treated to a three-dimensional animation of the news from that site—along with astonished gazes from your coworkers.

If a news story grabs your interest, press the number key mentioned at the bottom of the screen. The screen saver fades out, and Safari displays the associated article.

Make feeds open automatically

You can also make an RSS feed—or a list of feeds—your Safari starting page. Open the feeds you want, choose Safari→Preferences→General tab, click Set to Current Page, and choose Home Page from the "New windows open with" pop-up menu.

You've just made yourself a fantastic imitation of newspaper headlines, but tailored to *your* interests with spectacular precision: The Francis J. McQuaid Times (or whatever your name is).

Tip: If you've turned on tabbed browsing, you can ⌘-click headlines. That makes the full articles open in background tabs while you continue to read the headlines.

Articles in this Safari-newspaper arrangement are timelier than anything you could read in print—and they're completely free. If you miss a day of reading the headlines, no problem; they stick around for days and disappear only once you've read them. And finally, when you're done reading, you don't have to worry about recycling your "newspaper." No trees were harmed in the making of this publication.

Welcome to the future of news: customized, free, up-to-date, and paperless.

Tip: To find more RSS feeds, just watch for the appearance of the blue RSS button in the address bar.

By the way, Safari isn't the only RSS reader. A lot of people adore Google Reader for the same purpose *(www.google.com/reader)*.

---

iChat

Somewhere between email and the telephone lies the joyous communication tool called instant messaging. Plenty of instant messenger programs run on the Mac, but Mac OS X comes with its very own instant messenger program called iChat. It's built right into the system and ready to connect to your friends on the Yahoo, AIM, Jabber, Facebook, or Google Talk networks.

iChat does six things very well:

- **Instant messaging.** If you don't know what instant messaging is, there's a teenager near you who does.

Instant messaging combines the privacy of email and the immediacy of the phone. You type messages in a chat window, and your friends type replies back to you in real time.

In this regard, iChat is a lot like the popular standalone messenger apps from AOL and Yahoo. But iChat lets you type back and forth with anyone from the AOL, Yahoo, Google Talk, and Facebook chat networks, all in a single program, which is a huge advantage. And iChat's visual design is pure Apple.

- **Free long distance.** If your Mac has a microphone, and your buddy's does, too, the two of you can also chat *out loud,* by talking, using the Internet as a free long-distance phone. Wait, not just the two of you—the *10* of you, thanks to iChat's party-line feature.

- **Free videoconferencing.** If you and your buddies all have fast Internet connections and cameras—like the ones built into most Mac models—or even camcorders, up to four participants can join in *video* chats, all onscreen at once, no matter where they happen to be in the world. This jaw-dropping visual stunt can bring distant collaborators face to face without plane tickets—and it costs about $99,900 less than professional videoconferencing gear.

- **File transfers.** Got an album of high-quality photos or a giant presentation file that's too big to send by email? Forget about using some online file-transfer service or networked server; you can drag that monster file directly to your buddy's Mac, through iChat, for a direct machine-to-machine transfer. (It lands in the other Mac's Downloads folder.)

- **Presentations.** You can open up most kinds of documents, at nearly full size, to show your video buddy, right there in the iChat window, without actually having to transfer them. That's iChat Theater.

- **Screen sharing.** Next time some parents or neighbors are throwing themselves upon your mercy for tech support, remember this: iChat lets you see their screen, and even control it, from across the Internet. Or you can volunteer your own screen for sharing, so you can demonstrate things to them.

To start up iChat, go to Applications→iChat, or just click iChat's Dock icon. This section covers how to use iChat to communicate by video, audio, and text with your online pals.

Many Chat Networks

iChat lets you reach out to chat partners on several different networks:

- **The AIM network.** If you've signed up for a free AOL Instant Messenger (AIM) account, you can chat with anyone in the 150 million-member AOL Instant Messenger network.

- **The Yahoo Messenger network.** Yes, kids, it's true: you can chat with your Yahoo account, too, with all your Yahoo buddies.

- **The Jabber network.** Jabber is a chat network whose key virtue is its *open-source* origins. In other words, it wasn't masterminded by some corporate media behemoth; it's an all-volunteer effort, joined by thousands of programmers all over the world. There's no one Jabber chat program (like AOL Instant Messenger). There are dozens, available for Mac OS X, Windows, Linux, Unix, iPhone, Palm organizers, and so on. They can all chat with one another across the Internet in one glorious frenzy of typing.

  And now there's one more program that can join the party: iChat.

- **Google Talk.** Evidently, Google felt that there just weren't enough different chat programs, because it released its own in 2005.

  Behind the scenes, it uses the Jabber network, so Google Talk doesn't really count as a different network. But it does mean you can use iChat to converse with all those Google Talkers, too.

- **Your own local network.** Thanks to the Bonjour network-recognition technology, you can communicate with other Macs on your own office network without signing up for anything at all—and without being online. This is a terrific feature when you're sitting around a conference table, idly chatting with colleagues using your wireless laptop (and the boss thinks you're taking notes). It's also handy when you want to type little messages throughout the day to a family member downstairs, or a roommate 15 feet away.

In iChat, your contacts from all of these services are consolidated into a single buddy list.

You log into each network separately using the iChat→Accounts submenu, but you can be logged into all of them at once. This is a great option if your friends are spread out among different chat networks.

Note: If you're on AOL's AIM service or Yahoo's Messenger service, why would you want to use iChat instead of those companies' dedicated chat programs? Easy: Because iChat is a nice, cleanly designed program that's free of advertisements, chatbots, and clunky interface elements.

On the other hand, there are some great chat apps that iChat can't touch. One is the popular Adium, a single program that works with iChat's chat services and many others, including MSN and ICQ. And then, of course, there's Skype, the granddaddy of all chat programs, which offers audio and video chats like iChat, but happily connects to Skype running on Windows, iPhone, Android phones, and so on.

Chatting and videoconferencing work identically on all of these networks. Keep that in mind as you read the following pages.

Setting Up Your Chat Account(s)

When you open iChat for the first time, you see the Welcome to iChat window (Figure 12-15, top). This is the first of several screens in the iChat setup sequence, during which you're supposed to tell it which kinds of chat accounts you have and set up your camera, if any.

An account is a name and password. Fortunately, these accounts are free, and there are several ways to acquire one.

Figure 12-15:
The iChat setup assistant gives you the chance to input your account names and passwords if you already have them. Sometimes (Mac. com, me.com, AIM), you get the chance to create an account on the spot. Otherwise, you're expected to have a name and password (for Google Talk, Yahoo, or Jabber) already.

iChat

Welcome to iChat

The first personal video conferencing system that makes it easy to keep in touch with friends, family, and colleagues around the world is now even better.

Using silly funhouse effects and amazing backdrop effects, transform your video in real–time and bring the fun of Photo Booth to video conferencing. With iChat Theater,

iChat

Account Setup

iChat supports me.com, Mac.com, AIM, Yahoo!, Google Talk, and Jabber accounts.

To skip this step, click Continue.

Account Type: AIM

Username:

Password:

Get an iChat Account...

On the second setup screen, you're offered a pop-up menu that lists the different kinds of accounts iChat offers: AIM, me.com, Mac.com, Jabber, or Yahoo.

If you already have one of these accounts, enter your name and password and click Continue. (If you're an America Online member, your existing screen name and password work for AIM purposes.)

If you don't have one, it's easy enough to get one. If you've chosen me.com, Mac.com, or AIM, you can click Get an iChat Account to sign up for a free account on the spot. Jabber, Google Talk, and Yahoo accounts assume that you've signed up for an account on your own (at *gmail.com* or *yahoo.com*, for example).

You can also input account information later—the setup assistant isn't your only opportunity. You can do it in either of two places:

• In System Preferences, click Mail, Contacts & Calendars, described in Chapter 15.

• In iChat, choose iChat→Preferences, click the Accounts button, click the **+** button, and proceed as shown in Figure 12-15, bottom.

Once you've set up your accounts, you can activate or deactivate them either in iChat→Preferences→Accounts or by using the iChat→Accounts submenu. You might want to deactivate an account when, for example, you don't want to be bugged by the rabble on that particular service.

Note: Incidentally, it's possible to get good mileage out of iChat even if you don't have a chat account. iChat comes ready to connect you with other people in your building, over the office network, thanks to a technology called Bonjour. You can't add names to your Bonjour list; anyone who's on the network and running iChat appears there automatically.

The Buddy List

Once you've entered your account information, you're technically ready to start chatting. All you need now is a chatting companion, or, in instant-messaging circles, a buddy. iChat comes complete with a newly unified iChat Buddies window where you can house the chat "addresses" for all your chat partners from all the different chat services, in a single list.

Tip: If you like, you can give each service (AIM, Yahoo, and so on) its own separate buddy list window. To do that, choose iChat→Preferences→General; turn off "Show all my accounts in one list." Now you can use the Window menu to reveal each service's buddy list separately.

A tiny icon appears next to each name in your list, indicating that person's availability to chat—and what kinds of multimedia chats are available. A phone icon means "equipped for an audio chat"; a camcorder means "equipped for a video chat." The little colored dots mean "available" (green), "away" (red), "idle" (orange), and "undetermined—probably on a cellphone" (gray). A little .ᴬᴵ icon means you're chatting with someone on a cellphone.

Making a List

When you start iChat, your buddy list automatically appears (Figure 12-16). If you don't see it, choose iChat Buddies from the Window menu.

Adding a buddy to this list entails knowing that person's account name/address (for example, *bunnyface23@aim.com* or *harold1968@yahoo.com*).

Once you have it, click the **+** button in the bottom-left corner of the iChat Buddies window; in the resulting window, click Add Buddy.

Down slides a sheet attached to the buddy list window, offering a window into the Address Book program (Chapter 16). Using the "Add to" pop-up menu, choose the service you want to use for chatting with this person (Yahoo, Google, AIM, whatever).

Tip: As you accumulate buddies, your buddy list may become crowded. If you choose View→Show Offline Buddies (so that the checkmark disappears), then only your currently online buddies show up in the buddy list—a much more meaningful list for the temporarily lonely.

If your companion's chat address is already in Address Book, then double-click the person's name, or click it and then click Add.

If not, enter your pal's chat address in "Account name." Enter this person's real first and last names in the appropriate boxes, if you like.

Tip: Just to make things more complicated—er, flexible—iChat lets you organize buddies into groups, like Work, Family, and Fantasy Badminton League. Use the "Add to group" pop-up menu here to specify which group you want—or just choose Buddies to leave the new person in the general sloshing bucket of humanity.

When everything looks good, click Add.

Broadcasting Your Status

Using the pop-up menu just below your name (Figure 12-16, right), you can display your current mental status to *other* people's chat programs. You can announce that you're Available, Away, On the Phone, Drunk, and so on. (You have to choose Edit Status Menu for that last one; see Figure 12-16, right.)

Figure 12-16:
Left: The new Lion buddy list combines all your contacts from all chat services. Each chat account has its own status menu at the top.

Right: You can also choose Edit Status Menu to set up more creative alternatives to "Available" and "Away."

Announce that you're available to chat, or display your current iTunes track

Choose your own buddy icon

Status indicators

Control-click for common commands (like "Invite to Audio Chat")

Capable of video chat

Invite for text, audio, or video chats (or screen sharing)

Add buddy

Better yet, if you have music playing in iTunes, you can tell the world what you're listening to by choosing Current iTunes Song. (Your buddy can even click that song's name to open its screen on the iTunes Store, all for instant purchase gratification.)

For some people, by far the juiciest status option is Invisible (available for me.com and AIM accounts only). It's like a Star Trek cloaking device for your onscreen presence. Great for stalkers!

You can display the same status to your friends on all the different chat networks—Available, say, or Out to Lunch. Or you can set the status for each account separately, so that the lowlifes on Yahoo believe you to be "In a meeting" but the sophisticates on AIM realize that you're "Available."

To control whether your status message appears identically to all services, choose Use Same Status for All Accounts from the Status pop-up menu (Figure 12-16, right).

If you become a hardcore chataholic, don't miss the options in iChat→Preferences→General. Here you can set up automatic status changes. For example, "Set my status to Away after the computer is inactive" changes your status to Away when you haven't touched your Mac in 15 minutes, or when the Mac goes to sleep or the screen saver kicks in. That way, people seeking your witty repartee won't think you're just ignoring them.

You can also select what happens when you return to your computer after your status has been set to Away.

Let the Chat Begin

As with any conversation, somebody has to talk first. In chat circles, that's called *inviting* someone to a chat.

Figure 12-17:
You're being invited to a chat! Your buddy wants to have a typed chat (top left) or a spoken one (top right). To begin chatting, click the invitation window, type a response in the bottom text box if you like (for text chats), and click Accept (or press Return). Or click Block to lock out the person sending you messages—a good trick if someone's harassing you.

They Invite You

If someone invites you to chat, iChat opens automatically and displays an invitation message like the one in Figure 12-17. If the person initiating a chat isn't already in your buddy list, the note says, "[service] Message from [name of the person]."

(If you've set your status to Offline, on the other hand, you won't see those messages invitations. You'll see me.com and AIM invitations once you're online again, but if the invites come from the other services, you've missed out.)

You Invite Them

To begin a chat:

- **One-to-one typed conversations (instant messaging).** To message someone, double-click the person's name, type a quick invite ("You there?"), and press Return. You've just triggered what Apple calls an instant messaging session, which is a one-to-one affair.

Tip: If this person is on more than one chat network, open the flippy triangle and choose the account you want to use. The flippy triangle is in the little strip called the Recipient bar; if you don't see it, choose View→Show Recipient Bar.

- **Multiperson typed conversations (chat).** To start a chat instead, click someone's name in the buddy list and then choose Buddies→Invite to Chat. Now, each time you click the **+** button at the bottom of the Participants list, you choose another person to invite. (Or ⌘-click each name in the buddy list to select several people at once and then click the ⬛*A* button below the list to start the text chat.) Everyone sees all the messages anyone sends, and anyone can add new participants.

GEM IN THE ROUGH

Making iChat Auto-Answer

When you invite another Mac owner to a video chat, someone has to be sitting in front of it to accept your invitation. That's an important privacy feature, of course, because it prevents total strangers from peeking in on you when you're walking around in your underwear.

But having to have a live human at the other end is kind of a bummer if you just want to peek in on your house, your kids, or your spouse

while you're away, using your Mac's built-in camera as a sort of security cam or nannycam.

To do that, choose iChat→ Preferences→Alerts, From the Event pop-up menu, choose Video Invitation , then turn on "Run an AppleScript script." From the adjoining pop-up menu, choose Auto Accept.applescript.

From now on, iChat will love all your buddies and accept their invites immediately.

CHAPTER 12: SAFARI & ICHAT   **409**

- **Audio or video chats.** To start an audio or video chat, click the microphone or movie-camera icon in your buddy list.

To initiate a chat with someone who isn't in the buddy list, choose File→New Chat. Type the account name, and then click OK to send the invitation.

Text Chatting

A typed chat works like this: Each time you or your chat partner types something and then presses Return, the text appears on both of your screens (Figure 12-18).

Figure 12-18:
As you chat, your comments always appear on the right. If you haven't yet created a custom icon, you'll look like a blue globe or an AOL running man. You can choose a picture for yourself either in your own Address Book card or right in iChat. And Web links your pals paste into messages are perfectly clickable—your Web browser leaps right up to take you to the site your friend has shared.

iChat displays each typed comment next to an icon, which can be any of these three things:

- **A picture the other person added.** If the buddy added her own picture—to her own copy of iChat, a Jabber program, AOL Instant Messenger, or Yahoo Messenger—it will be transmitted to you, appearing automatically in the chat window. Cool!

- **A picture you added.** If you've added a picture of that person to the buddy list or Address Book, you see it here instead. (After all, your vision of what somebody looks like may not match his own self-image.)

- **Generic.** If nobody's done icon-dragging of any sort, you get a generic silhouette icon.

To choose a graphic to use as your own icon, click the square picture to the right of your own name at the top of the buddy list. From the pop-up palette of recently selected pictures, choose Edit Picture to open a pop-up image-selection palette, where you can take a snapshot with your Mac's camera or choose a photo file from your hard drive. Feel free to build an array of graphics to represent yourself—and to change them in midchat, using this pop-up palette, to the delight or confusion of your conversation partner.

Tip: When you minimize the iChat message window, its Dock icon displays the icon of the person you're chatting with—a handy reminder that she's still there.

In-Chat Fun

Typing isn't the only thing you can do during a chat. You can also perform any of these stunts:

- **Open the drawer.** Choose View→Show Chat Participants to hide or show the "drawer" that lists every person in your current group chat. To invite somebody new to the chat, click the **+** button at the bottom of the drawer, or drag the person's icon out of the buddy list window and into this drawer.

- **Format your text.** You can press ⌘-B or ⌘-I to make your next typed utterance bold or italic. Or change your color or font by choosing Format→Show Colors or Format→Show Fonts, which summons the standard Mac OS X color or font palettes. (If you use some weird font that your chat partners don't have installed, they won't see the same typeface.)

- **Insert a smiley.** When you choose a face (like Undecided, Angry, or Frown) from this quick-access menu of smiley options (at the right end of the text-reply box), iChat inserts it as a graphic into your response.

  On the other hand, if you know the correct symbols to produce smileys—that :) means a smiling face, for example—you can save time by typing them instead of using the pop-up menu. iChat converts them into smiley icons on the fly, as soon as you send your reply.

- **Send a file.** Choosing Buddies→Send File lets you send a file to *all* the participants in your chat.

  Better yet, just drag the file's icon from the Finder into the box where you normally type. (This trick works well with pictures, because your conversation partner sees the graphic right in his iChat window.)

  This is a fantastic way to transfer a file that would be too big to send by email. A chat window never gets "full," and no attachment is too large to send.

  This method halves the time of transfer, too, since your recipients get the file as you upload it. They don't have to wait 20 minutes for you to send the file, and then another 20 minutes to download it, as they would with email or FTP.

  If you have multiple conversations taking place—and are flinging files around to a bunch of people—you can keep an eye on each file's progress with the File Transfer Manager. Choose Window→File Transfers (or press Option-⌘-L) to pop open an all-in-one document delivery monitor.

Tip: If you've opened the Participants drawer (View→Show Chat Participants), you can drag files from the Finder onto individual participants' names in this drawer to send files directly to them. (You can also drag files onto names in your buddy list.)

- **Send an Instant Message.** Not everything in a chat session has to be "heard" by all participants. If you choose Buddies→Send Instant Message, you get a private chat window, where you can "whisper" something directly to a special someone behind the other chatters' backs.

- **Send Email.** If someone messages you, "Hey, will you email me directions?" you can do so on the spot by choosing Buddies→Send Email. Your email program opens up automatically so you can send the note along; if your buddy's email address is part of his Address Book info, the message is even preaddressed.

- **Send a text message to a cellphone.** If you're using an AIM screen name or me.com account, you can send text messages directly to your friends' cellphones (in the United States, anyway). Choose File→New SMS. In the box that pops up, type the full cellphone number, without punctuation, like this: 2125551212.

  Press Return to return to the chat window. Type a very short message (a couple of sentences, tops), and then press Return.

Tip: If iChat rudely informs you that your own privacy settings prevent you from contacting "this person," choose iChat→Preferences, click Accounts, click your chat account, switch to Security tab and then turn on "Allow anyone."

Obviously, you can't carry on much of an interactive conversation this way. The only response you get is from AOL's computers, letting you know that your message has been sent. But what a great way to shoot a "Call me!" or "Running late—see you tonight!" or "Turn on Channel 4 right now!!!" message to someone's phone.

On the other hand, if you're going to be away from your Mac for a few hours, you can have iChat forward incoming chat messages to your cellphone. Choose

---

UP TO SPEED

The Chat Transcript

Every now and then, you wish you could preserve a chat for all time—for example, a particularly meaningful conversation with a friend, lover, or customer-service agent.

On the iChat→Preferences→Messages panel, you can turn on "Save chat transcripts to" (and choose a folder on your hard drive). From now on, the text of your conversations is automatically saved in that folder. To view a chat later, double-click its icon. It opens within iChat, compete with all its colors and formatting.

While you're at it, you might also want to turn on "In new chat windows, show." What that means is, the next time you chat with someone, your last chat message with that buddy (or your last five, 25, 100, or 250) pop up automatically in a new window, for your reference. (Bonus tip: Edit→Mark Transcripts stamps the current date and time on each transcript.)

Even if you don't turn on this checkbox, you can save individual chats in progress by choosing File→Save a Copy As.

---

iChat→Preferences→Accounts and click Configure AIM Mobile Forwarding. In the resulting window, fill in your own cellphone number, so the incoming messages know where to go.

Popping the Balloons

The words you might have for iChat's word-balloon design might be "cute" and "distinctive." But it's equally likely that your choice of adjectives includes "juvenile" and "annoying."

Fortunately, behind iChat's candy coating are enough options tucked away in the View menu that you'll certainly find one that works for you (see Figure 12-19).

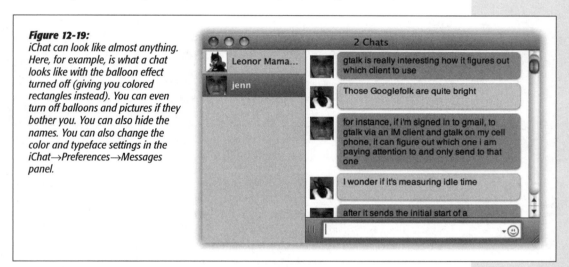

Figure 12-19:
iChat can look like almost anything. Here, for example, is what a chat looks like with the balloon effect turned off (giving you colored rectangles instead). You can even turn off balloons and pictures if they bother you. You can also hide the names. You can also change the color and typeface settings in the iChat→Preferences→Messages panel.

You can even change iChat's white background to any image using View→Set Chat Background. Better yet, find a picture you like and drag it into your chat window; iChat immediately makes it the background of your chat. To get rid of the background and revert to soothing white, choose View→Clear Chat Background.

Audio Chats

iChat becomes much more exciting when you exploit its AV Club capabilities. Even over slow Internet connections, you can conduct audio chats, speaking into your microphone and listening to the responses from your speaker.

If you have a broadband connection, though, you get a much more satisfying experience: Up to 10 of you can join in one massive, free conference call from across the Internet.

A telephone icon next to a name in your buddy list tells you that the buddy has a microphone and is ready for a free Internet "phone call." If you see what appear to be stacked phone icons, then your pal's Mac has enough horsepower to handle a multiple-person conference call.

To begin an audio chat, you have three choices:

- Click the telephone icon next to the buddy's name.

- Highlight someone in the buddy list, and then click the telephone icon at the bottom of the list.

- If you're already in a text chat, choose Buddies→Invite to Audio Chat.

Once your invitation is accepted, you can begin speaking to each other. The bars of the sound-level meter let you know that the microphone—which you've specified in the iChat→Preferences→Audio/Video tab—is working.

Tip: Although the audio is full duplex (you can hear and speak simultaneously, like a phone but unlike a walkie-talkie), there may be a delay, like you're calling overseas on a bad connection. If you can't hear anything at all, check out iChat's Help system, which contains some suggestions.

Video Chats

If you and your partner both have broadband Internet connections, even more impressive feats await. You can conduct a free video chat with up to four people, who show up on three vertical panels, gorgeously reflected on a shiny black table surface. This isn't the jerky, out-of-audio-sync, Triscuit-sized video of days gone by. If you've got the Mac muscle and bandwidth, your partners are as crisp, clear, bright, and smooth as television—and as big as your screen, if you like.

People can come and go; as they enter and leave the "videosphere," iChat slides their glistening screens aside, enlarging or shrinking them as necessary to fit on your screen.

Equipment Requirements

Everyone in a video chat has to be on the same service (me.com/AIM or Jabber), and everyone needs pretty high-horsepower computers and Internet connections.

Tip: For better audio quality during your video calls—both hearing and broadcasting—wear a headset. For example, you can pair a wireless Bluetooth headset with your Mac in iChat→Preferences→Audio/Video→Set Up Bluetooth Headset. This fires up the Mac's Bluetooth Setup Assistant program to guide you through the process.

After you get your Bluetooth headset married to your Mac, go to $\bullet$→System Preferences→Output and select your headset in the list.

For example, your Mac needs a video camera (like the one that came built in), a camcorder, or a FireWire version of one of those golf-ball Webcams.

You need pretty decent Internet speeds, too.

Note: As you're beginning to appreciate, iChat's system requirements are all over the map. Some features require very little horsepower; others require tons. To find out exactly which features your Mac can handle, choose Video→Connection Doctor; from the Show pop-up menu, choose Capabilities. There's a little chart of all iChat features, showing checkmarks for the ones your Mac can manage.

Starting the Video Call

If you see a camcorder icon next to a buddy's name, you can have a full-screen, high-quality video chat with that person, because they, like you, have a suitable camera and a high-speed Internet connection. If you see a stacked camcorder icon, then that person has a Mac that's capable of joining a four-way video chat.

To begin a video chat, click the camera icon next to a buddy's name, or highlight someone in the buddy list and then click the camcorder icon at the bottom of the list. Or, if you're already in a text chat, choose Buddies→Invite to Video Chat.

A window opens, showing you. This Preview mode is intended to show what your buddy will see. (You'll probably discover that you need some kind of light in front of you to avoid being too shadowy.) As your buddies join you, they appear in their own windows (Figure 12-20).

Figure 12-20:
That's you in the smaller window. To move your own miniwindow, click a different corner, or drag yourself to a different corner. If you need to blow your nose or do something else unseemly, Option-click the microphone button to freeze the video and mute the audio. Click again to resume.

And now, some video-chat notes:

- If your conversation partners seem unwilling to make eye contact, it's not because they're shifty. They're just looking at *you*, on the screen, rather than at the camera—and chances are you aren't looking into your camera, either.

- Don't miss the Video→Enter Full Screen command! Wild.

- If you're the one who started the call, you can add more people by clicking the + button in the chat window, or dragging a buddy's name into the window. (If that person doesn't have a camera, she can still enjoy audio or typing privileges.)

- You can have video chats with Windows computers, too.

- You can capture a still "photo" of a video chat by ⌘-dragging the image to your desktop, or by choosing Video→Take Snapshot (Option-⌘-S). Or just use the Copy command (⌘-C) to copy an image of the chat to the Clipboard, ready for pasting in another program.

- This cutting-edge technology can occasionally present cutting-edge glitches. The video quality deteriorates, the transmission aborts suddenly, the audio has an annoying echo, and so on. iChat Help offers a number of tips; the Video→Connection Doctor can identify your network speed. (iChat video likes lots of network speed.)

Tip: If the iChat video seems to be struggling too much to be worthwhile, consider using FaceTime instead (page 552). It's designed to deliver good video quality over less-beefy Internet connections.

- Just as you can save your typed transcripts of instant message conversations, you can record your audio and video chats. Once you start a chat, choose Video→Record Chat. Your buddy is asked if it's OK for you to proceed with the recording (to ward off any question of those pesky wiretapping laws); if permission is granted, then iChat begins recording the call.

  When you've got what you want, click Stop. Your recordings are automatically saved into Home→Documents→iChats (AAC files for audio conversations, MPEG-4 files for video chats). From there, you can drag them into iTunes to play or sync them up with an iPod or iPhone. Yes, you can now relive those glorious iChat moments when you're standing in line at the grocery store.

Bluescreen Backdrops and Video FX

If your video chats look like a bunch of cubicle-dwellers sitting around chatting at their desks, you can liven things up with one of iChat's most glamorous and jaw-dropping features: photo or video *backgrounds* for your talking head. Yes, now you can make your video chat partners think you're in Paris, on the moon, or even impersonating a four-panel Andy Warhol silkscreen.

Note: The iChat and Photo Booth backdrop effects require bandwidth, man, serious bandwidth—at least 128 Kbps for both upload and download speeds.

Here's how to prepare your backdrop for a video chat that's under way:

1. **Click Effects. (Or choose Video→Show Video Effects).**

   The Effects box appears, looking a lot like the one in Photo Booth (Chapter 16); visual backdrops are the same. Click the various squares to see how each effect will transform you in real time.

   The first three pages of effects all do video magic on you and everything else in the picture. The second two pages of effects, however, don't do anything to your image. Instead, they replace the background.

   This is the really amazing part. In TV and movies, replacing the background is an extremely common special effect. All you have to do is set up a perfectly smooth, evenly lit, shadowless blue or bright green backdrop behind the subject. Later, the computer replaces that solid color with a new picture or video of the director's choice.

   iChat, however, creates exactly the same special effect (Figure 12-21) without requiring the bluescreen or the greenscreen. Read on.

Figure 12-21:
Top left: You have plenty of backgrounds to choose from for your next video chat. Click an effect to add it to your chat window. Click the small arrows at the bottom of the window to advance or retreat through the various effects styles. Click the Original square in the middle of the window to erase the effect and start again from scratch.

Lower right: Let the live bluescreen action begin!

2. **Click the background effect you want.**

   Suppose, for example, that you've clicked the video loop showing the Eiffel Tower with people walking around. At this point, a message appears on the screen that says, "Please step out of the frame."

3. **Duck out of camera range (or move off to one side).**

   See, iChat intends to memorize a picture of the *real* background—without you in it. When you return to the scene, your high-horsepower Mac then compares each pixel of its memorized image with what it's seeing now. Any differences, it concludes, must be *you*. And *that* is how it can create a bluescreen effect without a bluescreen.

Note: To make this work, both the camera and the background must be perfectly still. If the lighting or the visuals shift or change in any way, you may get some weird, glitchy effects where your real background bleeds through.

---

4. **When the screen says, "Background detected," step back into the frame.**

   Sacré bleu! You're now in virtual Paris. Go ahead and start the video chat with your friends, and don't forget your beret.

   If you want to clear out the background or change it, click the Original square in the middle of the Effects palette and then choose a different backdrop. (You can also change backdrops in midchat by clicking Effects again.)

   If things get too weird and choppy onscreen, you can restore the normal background by choosing Video→Reset Background. (That's also handy if you suddenly have to have a video talk with your boss about your excessive use of iChat while he's away on his business trip.)

Tip: You can use one of your own photos or video clips as iChat backdrops, too. In the Video Effects box, click the arrows on the bottom until you get to the screen with several blank User Backdrop screens. Next, drag a photo or video from the desktop directly onto one of the blank screens. Click it just like you would any of Apple's stock shots.

Juggling Chats and Windows

Once you become an iChat addict, you often wind up with multiple chats in progress. These days, iChat contains all your conversations in a single window, as shown in Figure 12-22.

If you prefer to wind up with screens overflowing with individual chat windows, choose iChat→Preferences→Messages and turn off "Collect chats in a single window." At that point, if you ever decide that your archipelago of windows is getting out of control, choose Window→Merge All Chat Windows. Now all your windows are consolidated into one.

Tip: You can press Control-Tab to switch from chat to chat in a multi-chat window. Add the Shift key to move the other way.

You can also add one window to another one (or to an existing unified multi-chat window). Click inside it, choose View→Show Tab Bar, and then drag the tab into the other window.

To liberate a window from a multi-chat window, drag its tab away from the multi-chat window.

Figure 12-22:
Once you've unified your chats, you can click the different tabs to switch chats. Drag tabs vertically to rearrange the chats. You can also copy and paste (or drag highlighted text) between chats. The little cartoon balloon lets you know when one of your not-in-the-foreground buddies is saying something.

Sharing Your Screen

As you've seen already in this chapter, iChat lets you share your thoughts, your voice, and your image with the people on your buddy list. And now, for its next trick, it lets you share…your computer.

iChat's screen-sharing feature lets you not only *see* what's on a faraway buddy's screen, but control it, taking command of the distant mouse and keyboard. (You can share your screen with the other guy, too.)

You can open folders, create and edit documents, and copy files on the shared Mac screen. Sharing a screen makes collaborating as easy as working side by side around the same Mac, except now you can be sitting in San Francisco while your buddy is banging it out in Boston.

And if you're the family tech-support specialist—but the family lives all over the country—screen sharing makes troubleshooting a heckuva lot easier. You can now jump on your Mom's shared Mac and figure out why the formatting went wacky in her Word document, without her having to attempt to *explain* it to you over the phone. ("And then the little thingy disappeared and the doohickey got scrambled…")

Tip: Once you're controlling someone else's screen remotely, your keyboard shortcuts operate their Mac instead of yours. Press ⌘-Tab to bring up the application switcher, hit ⌘-Q to quit a program, use all the Mission Control and Spotlight shortcuts, and so on.

To make iChat screen sharing work, you and your buddy must both be running Macs with Mac OS X 10.5 (Leopard) or later. On the other hand, you can share over any account type: AIM, iCloud, Google Talk, Yahoo, Jabber, or Bonjour.

To begin, click the sharee's name in your buddy list.

- To share your screen, choose Buddies→Share My Screen with [person's name].

- To see her screen, choose Buddies→Ask to Share [person's name]'s Screen.

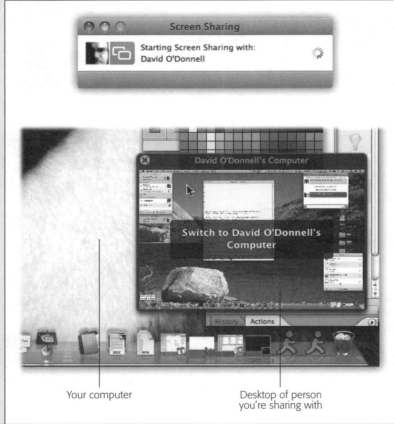

Figure 12-23:
Top: You either send or receive an invitation to start sharing your screen, but make sure you know with whom you're dealing before accepting the offer and starting the sharing process.

Bottom: When you're sharing someone else's screen, you have the option to click back and forth between the two Mac screens.

Your computer

Desktop of person you're sharing with

Note: Similar commands are available in the Screen Sharing pop-up button—the two overlapping squares at the bottom of the Buddies window.

Once the invitation is accepted, the sharing begins, as shown in Figure 12-23. To help you communicate further, iChat politely opens up an audio chat with your buddy so you can have a hands-free discussion about what you're doing on the shared machine.

If you're seeing someone else's screen, you see his Mac desktop in full-screen view, right on your own machine. You also see a small window showing your own Mac; click it to switch back to your own desktop.

Tip: To copy files from Mac to Mac, drag them between the two windows. Files dragged to your Mac wind up in your Downloads folder.

To bail out, press Control-Esc on the Mac's keyboard.

iChat Theater

iChat Theater turns the chat window into a presentation screen for displaying and narrating your own iPhoto or Keynote slideshows, QuickTime movie files, and even text documents. Your buddy, on the other end of the iChat line, sees these documents at nearly full size—with you in a little picture-in-picture screen in the corner.

All you need is:

- **Some stuff to show off.** iChat Theater can display exactly the same kinds of files that Quick Look (Chapter 2) can display: Word, Excel, and PowerPoint documents; photos; text and HTML files; PDF files; audio and movie files; fonts; vCards; Pages; Numbers; Keynote and TextEdit documents, and so on.

- **A zippy broadband Internet connection.** iChat Theater likes 384 kilobits per second or faster; check with your Internet provider if you aren't sure of your connection speed.

To get the show running, you can take one of two approaches.

- **If a video chat is under way,** you can just drag the file(s) you want to share into the video window. iChat asks if you want to send the file to the person or share it with iChat Theater (Figure 12-24, top). Click iChat Theater, of course.

- If no video chat is in progress, choose File→Share a File in iChat Theater. Locate the file you want to present on your hard drive. When iChat asks you to start a video chat with the buddy who's going to be your audience, click the video-camera icon next to that person's name (or choose Video→Invite to Video Chat).

When your friend accepts, the curtain goes up, as shown the bottom of Figure 12-24. The file you're sharing takes center stage (er, window) and your buddy appears in a little video window off to the side. Click the ▣ button to expand the view to full screen.

Actually, iChat offers two other ways for the two of you to join in harmonious digital unity:

- **Share a slideshow.** Sharing picture albums is one menu command away: Choose File→Share iPhoto with iChat Theater. When the Media Browser pops up, pick the album you want to present. The first picture in the selected album appears in the iChat window before iPhoto itself opens, so you can use iPhoto's nice controls for cruising forward (or backward) through your album.

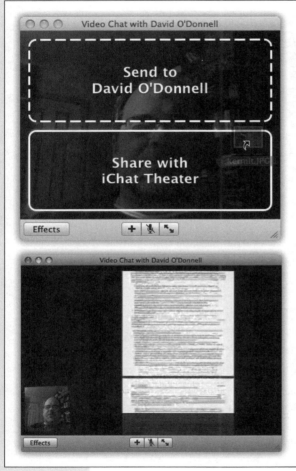

Figure 12-24:
Top: You can start an iChat Theater session by choosing File→Share a File with iChat Theater, or as shown here, by simply dropping the file on an open video chat window and going for the iChat Theater option.

Bottom: Once you've started a Theater show in iChat, the shared file takes center stage so you both can look at it and discuss amongst yourselves.

- **Share a Web page.** "I'm telling you, Mom, their Web site says they're open until 10! Look, I'll show you!" Choose File→Share Webpage with iChat Theater. When the little text box appears, paste in (or type in) the Web address you want to share. When you click Share, your chat partner gets to see the Web site in question.

When the show is over, close the window to end the iChat Theater session.

Part Four:
Putting Down Roots

4

Accounts, Parental Controls & Security

I n an era when *security* is the hottest high-tech buzzword, Apple was smart to make security a focal point for Mac OS X. It was already virus-free and better protected from Internet attacks than Windows. But Mac OS X 10.7 is the most impenetrable Mac system yet, filled with new defenses against the dark arts. This chapter covers the whole range of them.

On the premise that the biggest security threat of all comes from other people in your home or office, though, the most important security feature in Mac OS X is the *accounts* system.

Introducing Accounts

The concept of *user accounts* is central to Mac OS X's security approach. Like the Unix under its skin (and also like recent versions of Windows), Mac OS X was designed from the ground up to be a *multiple-user* operating system. That is, you can set up your Mac OS X so that everyone must log in—click his name and type his password—when the computer turns on (Figure 13-1).

Upon doing so, you discover the Macintosh universe just as you left it, including these elements:

- Your documents, files, and folders.

- Your preference settings in every program you use: Web browser bookmarks and preferred home page; desktop picture, screen saver, and language; icons on the desktop and in the Dock—and the size and position of the Dock itself; and so on.

- Email account(s), including personal information and mailboxes.

- Your personally installed programs and fonts.

- Your choice of programs that launch automatically at startup.

This system lets different people use it throughout the day without disrupting one another's files and settings. It also protects the Mac from getting fouled up by mischievous (or bumbling) students, employees, and hackers.

Figure 13-1:
When you set up several accounts, you don't turn on the Mac so much as sign into it. A command in the menu called Log Out summons this sign-in screen, as does the Accounts menu described later in this chapter. Click your own name, and type your password (if any), to get past this box and into your own stuff.

Casey McUser   Dale McRobin   Robin McCasey

If you're the only person who uses your Mac, you can safely skip most of this chapter. The Mac never pauses at startup time to demand the name and password you made up when you installed Mac OS X, because Apple's installer automatically turns on something called *automatic login*. You *will* be using one of these accounts, though, whether you realize it or not.

Furthermore, when you're stuck in line at the Department of Motor Vehicles, you may find the concepts presented here worth skimming, as certain elements of this multiple-user system may intrude upon your solo activities—and figure in the discussions in this book—from time to time.

Tip: Even if you don't share your Mac with anyone and don't create any other accounts, you might still be tempted to learn about the accounts feature because of its ability to password-protect the entire computer. All you have to do is to turn *off* the automatic login feature described on page 443. Thereafter, your Mac is protected from unauthorized fiddling when you're away from your desk or if your laptop is stolen.

The First Account

When you first installed Mac OS X, whether it was 10.7 or an earlier version, you were asked for a name and a password. You were creating the first *user account* on your Macintosh. Since that fateful day, you may have made a number of changes to your desktop—adjusted the Dock settings, set up your folders and desktop the way you like them, added some bookmarks to your Web browser, and so on—without realizing that you were actually making those changes only to *your account.*

You've probably been saving your documents into your own Home folder, which is the cornerstone of your account. This folder, generally named after you and stashed in the Users folder on your hard drive, stores not only your own work, but also your preference settings for all the programs you use, special fonts you've installed, your own email collection, and so on.

Now then: Suppose you create an account for a second person. When she turns on the computer and signs in, she finds the desktop exactly the way it was factory-installed by Apple—stunning outer-space desktop picture, Dock along the bottom, and so on. She can make the same kinds of changes to the Mac that you've made, but nothing she does affects *your* environment the next time you log in.

In other words, the multiple-accounts feature has two components: first, a convenience element that hides everyone else's junk; and second, a security element that protects both the Mac's system software and everybody's work.

Creating an Account

Suppose somebody new joins your little Mac family—a new worker, student, or love interest, for example. And you want to make that person feel at home on your Mac.

Begin by opening System Preferences (Chapter 15). In the System Preferences window, click Users & Groups. You've just arrived at the master control center for account creation and management (Figure 13-2).

To create a new account, start by unlocking the Users & Groups panel. That is, click the 🔒 at lower left, and fill in your own account name and password.

Now you can click the **+** button beneath the list of accounts. The little panel shown at bottom in Figure 13-2 appears.

Phase 1: Choose an Account Type

As though this business of accounts and passwords weren't complicated enough already, Mac OS X offers several *types* of accounts. And you're expected to specify *which* type each person gets at the moment you create an account.

To do that, open the New Account pop-up menu (Figure 13-2, bottom). Its five account types are described on the following pages.

Administrator accounts

If this is your own personal Mac, then just beneath your name on the Users & Groups pane of System Preferences, it probably says *Admin*. This, as you could probably guess, stands for Administrator.

Because you're the person who originally installed Mac OS X, the Mac assumes that you are its *administrator*—the technical wizard in charge of it. You're the teacher, the

Figure 13-2:
Top: The screen lists everyone who has an account. From here, you can create new accounts or change passwords. If you're new at this, there's probably just one account listed here: yours. This is the account Mac OS X created when you first installed it. You, the all-wise administrator, have to click the ⚿ to authenticate yourself before you can start making changes.

Bottom: In the account-creation process, the first step is choosing which type of account you want to create.

parent, the resident guru. You're the one who will maintain this Mac. Only an administrator is allowed to install new programs into the Applications folder; add fonts that everybody can use; make system-wide changes in System Preferences (including Network, Date & Time, Energy Saver, and Startup Disk); create, move, or delete folders outside of your Home folder; decide who gets to have accounts on the Mac; open, change, or delete anyone else's files, and so on.

You'll find certain settings all over Mac OS X that you can change *only* if you're an administrator—including many in the Users & Groups pane itself. Administrator status also plays an enormous role when you want to network your Mac to other kinds of computers, as described in the next chapter.

As you create accounts for other people who'll use this Mac, you're offered the opportunity to make each one an administrator just like you. Needless to say, use discretion. Bestow these powers only upon people as responsible and technically masterful as yourself.

Standard accounts

Most people, on most Macs, are ordinary *Standard* account holders. These people have everyday access to their own Home folders and to the harmless panes of System Preferences, but most other areas of the Mac are off limits. Mac OS X won't even let them create new folders on the main hard drive, except inside their own Home folders (or in the Shared folder described on page 446).

A few of the System Preferences panels display a padlock icon (🔒). If you're a Standard account holder, you can't make changes to these settings without the assistance of an administrator. Fortunately, you aren't required to log out so that an administrator can log in and make changes. You can just call the administrator over, click the padlock icon, and let him type in his name and password (if, indeed, he feels comfortable with you making the changes you're about to make).

Managed accounts with Parental Controls

A *Managed* account is the same thing as a Standard account—except that you've turned on Parental Controls. (These controls are described later in this chapter.) You can turn a Managed account into a Standard account just by turning off Parental Controls, and vice versa.

That is, this account usually has even fewer freedoms—because you've limited the programs this person is allowed to use, for example. Use a Managed account for children or anyone else who needs a Mac with rubber walls.

Sharing Only account

This kind of account is extremely useful—*if* your Mac is on a network (Chapter 14).

See, ordinarily, you can log in and access the files on your Mac in either of two ways:

- In person, seated in front of it.
- From across the network.

This arrangement was designed with families and schools in mind: lots of people sharing a *single* Mac.

This setup gets a little silly, though, when the people on a home or office network all have their *own* computers. If you wanted your spouse or your sales director to be able to grab some files from you, you'd have to create full-blown accounts for them on *your* Mac, complete with utterly unnecessary Home folders they'd never use.

That's why the *Sharing Only* account is such a great idea. It's available *only* from across the network. You can't get into it by sitting down at the Mac itself—it has no Home folder!

Finally, of course, a Sharing Only account holder can't make any changes to the Mac's settings or programs.

In other words, a Sharing Only account exists *solely* for the purpose of file sharing on the network, and people can enter their names and passwords *only* from other Macs.

Once you've set up this kind of account, all the file-sharing and screen-sharing goodies described in Chapter 14 become available.

Group

A *group* is just a virtual container that holds the names of other account holders. You might create one for your most trusted colleagues, another for those rambunctious kids, and so on—all in the name of streamlining the *file-sharing privileges* feature described on page 105. The box on the facing page covers groups in more detail.

The Guest account

The *Guest* account is great for accommodating visitors, buddies, or anyone else who's just passing through and wants to use your Mac for a while. If you let such people use the Guest account, your own account remains private and un-messed-with.

Note: The Guest account isn't listed among the account *types* in the New Account pop-up menu (Figure 13-2). That's because there's only *one* Guest account; you can't actually create additional ones.

But it's still an account type with specific characteristics. It's sitting right there in the list of accounts, from Day One.

Any changes your guest makes while using your Mac are automatically erased when she logs out. Files are deleted, email is nuked, setting changes are forgotten.

The Guest account is permanently listed in the Users & Groups panel of System Preferences. Ordinarily, though, you don't see it in the login screen list; if you're normally the only person who uses this Mac, you don't need to have it staring you in the face every day.

So to use the Guest account, bring it to life by turning on "Allow guests to log into this computer." You can even turn on the parental controls described earlier in this chapter by clicking Open Parental Controls, or permit the guest to exchange files with your Mac from across the network (Chapter 14) by turning on "Allow guests to connect to shared folders."

Just remember to warn your vagabond friend that once he logs out (and acknowledges the warning), all traces of his visit are wiped out forever.

At least from your *Mac*.

Phase 2: Name, Password, and Status

All right. So you clicked the **+** button. And from the New Account pop-up menu, you chose the type of account you wanted to create.

Now, on the same starter sheet, it's time to fill in the most critical information about the new account holder:

- **Name.** If it's just the family, this could be "Chris" or "Robin." If it's a corporation or a school, you probably want to use both first and last names.

POWER USERS' CLINIC

Creating Groups

Changing permissions settings on a networked Mac, or one with a lot of account holders, is easier if you sweep all your minions into subsets called groups.

This process used to require a complicated series of Unixy steps that, if not performed carefully, could seriously foul up your Mac.

But in Mac OS X, you can create a group as easily as you'd create an account. And in the same place: the Users & Groups pane of System Preferences.

Click the tiny 🔒 in the lower-left corner. When prompted, type in your administrator's name and password, and then click OK. The Mac is just making sure that somebody with a clue is at the helm.

Now click the **+** button as though you were about to create a new account. But from the New Account pop-up menu (shown at bottom in Figure 13-2), choose Group. Type a name for the new group (Accounting, Kids, or whatever), and then click Create Group.

Now you see something like the list shown here: checkboxes for all this Mac's account holders. Turn on the checkboxes for the ones you consider worthy of being a part of this group.

You can create as many groups as you like. Later, when it comes time to share a folder or file, you'll save time by choosing a group name instead of setting these permissions one person at a time.

- **Account Name.** You'll quickly discover the value of this Account Name, particularly if your name is, say, Alexandra Stephanopoulos. It's meant to be an abbreviation of your actual name.

  When you sign into your Mac in person, you can use either your full name or account (short) name. But when you access this Mac by dialing into it or connecting from across the network (as described in the next chapter), the short version is more convenient.

  As soon as you tab into this field, the Mac proposes a short name for you. You can replace the suggestion with whatever you like. Technically, it doesn't even have to be shorter than the "long" name, but spaces and most punctuation marks are forbidden.

- **Password, Verify.** Here's where you type this new account holder's password (Figure 13-2). In fact, you're supposed to type it twice, to make sure you didn't introduce a typo the first time. (The Mac displays only dots as you type, to guard against the possibility that somebody is watching over your shoulder.)

  The usual computer book takes this opportunity to stress the importance of a long, complex password—a phrase that isn't in the dictionary, something that's made up of mixed letters and numbers. This is excellent advice if you create sensitive documents and work in a big corporation.

  But if you share the Mac only with a spouse or a few trusted colleagues in a small office, you may have nothing to hide. You may see the multiple-users feature more as a convenience (keeping your settings and files separate) than a protector of secrecy and security. In these situations, there's no particular urgency to the mission of thwarting the world's hackers with a convoluted password.

  In that case, you may want to consider setting up *no* password—leaving both password blanks empty. Later, whenever you're asked for your password, just leave the Password box blank. You'll be able to log in that much faster each day.

- **Password Hint.** If your password is the middle name of the first person who ever kissed you, for example, your hint might be "middle name of the first person who ever kissed me."

  Later, if you forget your password, the Mac will show you this cue to jog your memory.

When you finish setting up these essential items, click Create User. If you left the password boxes empty, the Mac asks for reassurance that you know what you're doing; click OK.

You then return to the Users & Groups pane, where you see the new account name in the list at the left side.

Here, three final decisions await your wisdom:

- **Apple ID.** Since the Apple ID (page 552) is growing in importance and features—App Store, iTunes Store, email address, Web site, iCloud, syncing, and so on—it's convenient to associate each account with its own Apple ID.

Tip: "Allow user to reset password using Apple ID" means that if this person ever forgets his password, he'll be offered, on the login screen, a chance to recover it by entering his Apple ID.

- **Allow user to administer this computer.** This checkbox lets you turn ordinary, unsuspecting Standard or Managed accounts into Administrator accounts, as described above. You know—when your kid turns 18.

- **Enable Parental Controls.** "Parental Controls" refers to the Mac OS X feature that limits what your offspring are allowed to do on this computer—and how much time a day they're allowed to spend glued to the mouse. Details are on page 435.

Phase 3: Choose a Picture

The usual Mac OS X sign-in screen (Figure 13-1) displays each account holder's name, accompanied by a little picture.

When you click the sample photo, you get a pop-up menu of Apple-supplied graphics; you can choose one to represent you. It becomes not only your icon on the sign-in screen, but also your "card" photo in Mac OS X's Address Book program and your icon in iChat.

Figure 13-3:
Once you've selected a photo to represent yourself (left), you can adjust its position relative to the square "frame" (right), or adjust its size by dragging the slider. Finally, when the picture looks correctly framed, click Set. (The next time you return to the Images dialog box, you can recall the new image using the Recent Pictures pop-up menu.)

If you'd rather supply your *own* graphics file—a digital photo of your own head, for example—then choose Edit Picture from the pop-up menu. As shown in Figure 13-3, you have several options:

- **Drag a graphics file directly into the "picture well" (where the kitten appears top in Figure 13-3).** Use the cropping slider below the picture to frame it properly.

- **Click Choose.** You're shown a list of what's on your hard drive. Find and double-click the image you want.

- **Take a new picture.** If your Mac has a built-in camera above the screen, or if you have an external Webcam or a camcorder hooked up, then click the little camera button. The Mac counts down from 3 with loud beeps to help you get ready and then takes the picture.

In each case, click Set to enshrine your icon forever (or until you feel like picking a different one).

Phase 4: Startup Items

There's one additional setting that your account holders can set up for themselves: which programs or documents open automatically upon login. (This is one decision an administrator *can't* make for other people. It's available only to whoever is logged in at the moment.)

To choose your own crew of self-starters, open System Preferences and click Users & Groups. Click your account. Click the Login Items tab. As shown in Figure 13-4, you

Figure 13-4:
You can add any icon to the list of things you want to start up automatically. Click the + button to summon the Open dialog box, where you can find the icon, select it, and then click Choose. Better yet, if you can see the icon in a folder or a disk window (or on the desktop), just drag it into this list. To remove an item, click it in the list and then click the − button.

can now build a list of programs, documents, disks, and other goodies that automatically launch each time you log in. You can even turn on the Hide checkbox for each one so that the program is running in the background at login time, waiting to be called into service with a quick click.

Don't feel obligated to limit this list to programs and documents, by the way. Disks, folders, servers on the network, and other fun icons can also be startup items, so that their windows are open and waiting when you arrive at the Mac each morning.

Tip: Here's a much quicker way to add something to the Login Items list: Control-click (or right-click) its Dock icon and choose Open at Login from the shortcut menu.

Parental Controls

If you're setting up a Standard/Managed account, the Parental Controls checkbox affords you the opportunity to shield your Mac—or its very young, very fearful, or very mischievous operator—from confusion and harm. This is a helpful feature to remember when you're setting up accounts for students, young children, or easily intimidated adults. (This checkbox is available for Admin accounts, too, but turning it on produces a "Silly rabbit—this is for kids!" sort of message.)

You can specify how many hours a day each person is allowed to use the Mac, and declare certain hours (like sleeping hours) off-limits. You can specify exactly who your kids are allowed to communicate with via email (if they use Mail) and instant messaging (if they use iChat), what Web sites they can visit (if they use Safari), what programs they're allowed to use, and even what words they can look up in the Mac OS X Dictionary.

Here are all the ways you can keep your little Managed account holders shielded from the Internet—and themselves. For sanity's sake, the following discussion refers to the Managed account holder as "your child." But some of these controls—notably those in the System category—are equally useful for people of *any* age who feel overwhelmed by the Mac, are inclined to mess it up by not knowing what they're doing, or are tempted to mess it up deliberately.

Note: If you apply any of these options to a Standard account, then the account type listed on the Users & Groups panel changes from "Standard" to "Managed."

To begin, click Open Parental Controls at the bottom of the Users & Groups pane. Click Enable Parental Controls, if necessary. Now you should see the screen shown in Figure 13-5.

Apps Tab

On this tab (Figure 13-5), you can limit which programs your Managed-account flock is allowed to use. (Limiting what people can do to your Mac when you're not looking is a handy feature under any shared-computer circumstance. But if there's one word tattooed on its forehead, it would be "Classrooms!")

Figure 13-5:
In the Parental Controls window, you can control the capabilities of any account holder on your Mac. If you turn on Limit Applications, then the lower half of the Apps tab window lets you choose applications (those from the Mac App Store and others), and even Dashboard widgets, by turning on the boxes next to their names. (Expand the flippy triangles if necessary.) Those are the only programs the account holder will be allowed to use. The Search box helps you find certain programs without knowing their categories.

At the bottom of the dialog box shown in Figure 13-5, you see a list of all the programs you've bought from the Mac App Store, all other programs, all Dashboard widgets, and all the apps in your Utilities folder. Only checked items will show up in the account holder's Applications folder. (If you don't see a program listed, then use the search box, or drag its icon from the Finder into the window.)

Use Simple Finder

If you're *really* concerned about somebody's ability to survive the Mac—or the Mac's ability to survive somebody—turn on Use Simple Finder. Then turn on the checkboxes of the programs that person is allowed to use.

Suppose you've been given a Simple Finder account. When you log in, you discover the barren world shown in Figure 13-6. There are only three menus (, Finder, and File), a single onscreen window, no hard drive icon, and a bare-bones Dock. The only folders you can see are in the Dock. They include these:

- **My Applications.** This folder holds aliases of the applications that the administrator approved. They appear on a strange, fixed icon view called "pages." List and column views don't exist. As a Simple person, you can't move, rename, delete, sort, or change the display of these icons—you can merely click them. If you have too many to fit on one screen, you get numbered page buttons beneath them, which you can click to move from one set to another.

Figure 13-6:
The Simple Finder doesn't feel like home—unless you've got one of those spartan, space-age, Dr. Evil–style pads. But it can be just the ticket for less-skilled Mac users, with few options and a basic one-click interface. Every program in the My Applications folder is actually an alias to the real program, which is safely ensconced in the off-limits Applications folder.

- **Documents.** Behind the scenes, this is your Home→Documents folder. Of course, as a Simple Finder kind of soul, you don't *have* a visible Home folder. All your stuff goes in here.

- **Shared.** This is the same Shared folder described on page 446. It's provided so that you and other account holders can exchange material. However, you can't open any of the folders here, only the documents.

- **Trash.** The Trash is here, but you won't use it much. Selecting or dragging any icon is against the rules, so you're left with no obvious means of putting anything into your Trash.

The only program with its own icon on the Dock is the Finder.

To keep things extra-simple, Mac OS X permits only one window at a time to be open. It's easy to open icons, too, because *one* click opens them, not two.

The File menu is stunted, offering only a Close Window command. The Finder menu gives you only two options: About Finder and Run Full Finder. (The latter command prompts you for an administrator's user name and password, and then turns back into the regular Finder—a handy escape hatch. To return to Simple Finder, just choose Finder→Return to Simple Finder.)

The menu is *really* bare-bones: You can Log Out, Force Quit, or go to Sleep. That's it. And there's no trace of Spotlight.

Otherwise, you can essentially forget everything else you've read in this book. You can't create folders, move icons, or do much of anything beyond clicking the icons that your benevolent administrator has provided. It's as though Mac OS X moved away and left you the empty house:

Although the Simple Finder is simple, any program (at least, any that the administrator has permitted) can run from Simple Finder. A program running inside the Simple Finder still has all its features and complexities—only the Finder has been whittled down to its essence.

In other words, Simple Finder is great for streamlining the Finder, but novices won't get far combating their techno-fear until the world presents us with Simple iMovie, Simple Mail, and Simple Microsoft Word. Still, it's better than nothing.

GEM IN THE ROUGH

Logs

On the Apps tab of the Parental Controls panel, you'll find a button called Logs. That, my friends, is Big Brother Central.

It gives you a complete rundown of what your kids have been up to. Its four categories—Websites Visited, Websites Blocked, Applications, and iChat— are extremely detailed. For example, in Applications, you can see exactly which programs your kids tried to use when, and how much time they spent in each one.

It's spying, sure, but it's for the good of the child. (Right?) Use the pop-up menus at the top to change the time period being reported (Today, This Week, or whatever)

and how they're grouped in the list—by date or by application/Web site.

If you see something that you really think should be off limits—a site in the Websites Visited list, an application, an iChat session with someone—click its name and then click Restrict. You've just nipped that one in the bud.

Conversely, if the Mac blocked a Web site that you think is really OK, click its name in the list, and then click Allow. (And if you're wondering what a certain Web page *is,* click it and then click Open.)

Web Tab

This feature is designed to limit which Web sites your kid is allowed to visit.

Frankly, trying to block the racy stuff from the Web is something of a hopeless task; if your kid doesn't manage to get around this blockade by simply using a different browser, then he'll just see the dirty pictures at another kid's house. But at least you can enjoy the illusion of taking a stand, using approaches with three degrees of severity:

- **Allow unrestricted access to Web sites.** No filtering. Anything goes.

- **Try to limit access to adult Web sites automatically.** Those words—"try to"—are Apple's way of admitting that no filter is foolproof.

  In any case, Mac OS X analyzes what's on a Web page that you try to call up and filters out Web sites with naughty material. These sites won't appear in Safari while this account holder is logged in. By clicking Customize and then editing the "Always allow" and "Never allow" lists, you can override its decisions on a site-at-a-time basis.

- **Allow access to only these Web sites.** This is the most restrictive approach of all: It's a *whitelist,* a list of the *only* Web sites your youngster is allowed to visit. It's filled with kid-friendly sites like Disney and Discovery Kids, but of course you can edit the list by clicking the **+** and **−** buttons below the list.

People Tab

Here you can control your kid's access to two realms of people: those on email and those on iChat. Turn on the checkboxes at the top as you feel it's necessary.

Then build a list of email and chat addresses, corresponding to the people you feel comfortable letting your kid exchange emails and chats with. Click the **+** button below the list, type the address, and then press Return. Lather, rinse, repeat.

Tip: No, you can't drag cards in from your Address Book; that would be much too simple. But after clicking the **+** button to create a new row in the list (in Edit mode), you can drag *just the email address* out of an Address Book card you've opened up. Or expand the resulting dialog box (click the ▾ button) and double-click someone in your Address Book.

For reasons explained in a moment, turn on "Send permission requests to" and plug in your own email address.

Now then: When your youngster uses Apple's Mail program to send a message to someone who's *not* on the approved list, or tries to iChat with someone not on the list, she gets the message shown at top in Figure 13-7. If she clicks Ask Permission, then *your* copy of Mail shortly receives a permission-request message; meanwhile, the outgoing message gets placed in limbo in her Drafts folder.

If you add that person's address to the list of approved correspondents (Figure 13-7, bottom), then the next time your young apprentice clicks the quarantined outgoing message in her Drafts folder, the banner across the top lets her know that all is well—and the message is OK to go out.

> **Note:** This feature doesn't attempt to stop email or chat using *other* programs, like Microsoft Outlook or Skype. If you're worried about your efforts being bypassed, block access to those programs using the Permitted Applications list described above.

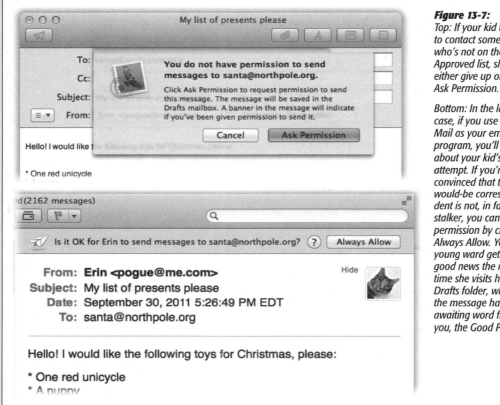

Figure 13-7:
Top: If your kid tries to contact someone who's not on the Approved list, she can either give up or click Ask Permission.

Bottom: In the latter case, if you use Mail as your email program, you'll know about your kid's attempt. If you're convinced that the would-be correspondent is not, in fact, a stalker, you can grant permission by clicking Always Allow. Your young ward gets the good news the next time she visits her Drafts folder, where the message has been awaiting word from you, the Good Parent.

When your underling fires up iChat or Mail, she'll discover that her buddy list is empty except for the people you've identified.

Handling the teenage hissy fit is your problem.

Time Limits

Clever folks, those Apple programmers. They must have kids of their own.

They realize that some parents care about *how much* time their kids spend in front of the Mac, and that some also care about *which* hours (Figure 13-8):

- **How much time.** In the "Weekday time limits" and "Weekend time limits" sections, turn on "Limit computer use to," and then adjust the slider.

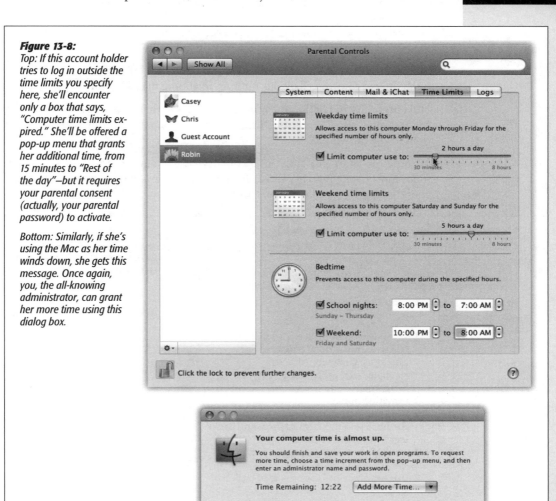

Figure 13-8:
Top: If this account holder tries to log in outside the time limits you specify here, she'll encounter only a box that says, "Computer time limits expired." She'll be offered a pop-up menu that grants her additional time, from 15 minutes to "Rest of the day"—but it requires your parental consent (actually, your parental password) to activate.

Bottom: Similarly, if she's using the Mac as her time winds down, she gets this message. Once again, you, the all-knowing administrator, can grant her more time using this dialog box.

- **Which hours.** In the "Bedtime" section, turn on the checkbox for either "School nights" or "Weekend," and then set the hours of the day (or, rather, night) when the Mac is unavailable to your young account holder.

  In other words, this feature may have the smallest pages-to-significance ratio in this entire book. Doesn't take long to explain it, but it could bring the parents of Mac addicts a lot of peace.

Tip: When Time Limits have been applied, your little rug rats can now check to see how much time they have left to goof off on the Mac before your digital iron fist slams down. When they click the menu-bar clock (where it now says the current time), a menu appears, complete with a readout that says, for example, "Parental Controls: Time Remaining 1:29." Good parenting comes in many forms.

Other Tab

This tab offers a few miscellaneous options, including the following:

- **Hide profanity in Dictionary.** Mac OS X comes with a complete electronic copy of the *New Oxford American Dictionary.* And "complete," in this case, means "it even has swear words."

  Turning on "Hide profanity in Dictionary" is like having an Insta-Censor™. It hides most of the naughty words from the dictionary whenever your young account holder is logged in (Figure 13-9).

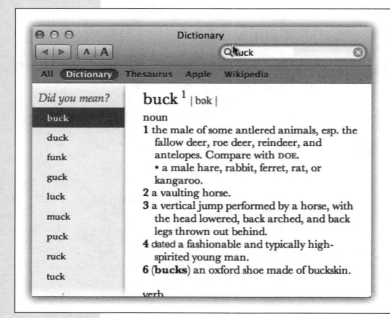

Figure 13-9:
Something's missing from the Dictionary when the Parental Control tool is turned on: dirty words.

- **Limit printer administration.** When this checkbox is on, your underlings aren't allowed to change your Mac's printer settings. You wouldn't want them deleting or installing any printers, would you?

- **Limit CD and DVD burning.** When you first create Standard accounts, their holders are free to burn CDs or DVDs. But in a school lab, for example, you might want to turn off the ability to burn discs (to block software piracy). That's why this box is here.

• **Disable changing the password.** Pretty self-explanatory. This option prevents your unruly minions from changing their passwords. That's your job, after all.

Editing Accounts

If you're an administrator, you can change your own account in any way you like.

If you have any other kind of account, though, you can't change anything but your picture, password, Apple ID, and login items. If you want to make any other changes, you have to ask an admin to log in, make the changes you want made to your account, and then turn the computer back over to you.

Deleting Accounts

Hey, it happens: Somebody graduates, somebody gets fired, somebody dumps you. Sooner or later, you may need to delete an account from your Mac.

When that time comes, click the account name in the Users & Groups list and then click the **−** button beneath the list. Mac OS X asks what to do with all the dearly departed's files and settings:

• **Save the home folder in a disk image.** This option represents the "I'll be back" approach. Mac OS X preserves the deleted account holder's folders on the Mac, in a tidy digital envelope that won't clutter your hard drive and can be reopened in case of emergency.

   In the Users→Deleted Users folder, you find a disk image file (.dmg). If you double-click it, a new, virtual disk icon named for the deleted account appears on your desktop. You can open folders and root through the stuff in this "disk," just as if it were a living, working Home folder.

   If fate ever brings that person back into your life, you can use this disk image to reinstate the deleted person's account. Start by creating a brand-new account. Then copy the contents of the folders in the mounted disk image (Documents, Pictures, Desktop, and so on) into the corresponding folders of the new Home folder.

• **Do not change the home folder.** This time, Mac OS X removes the *account*, in that it no longer appears in the Login list or in the Users & Groups panel of System Preferences—but it leaves the *Home folder* right where it is. Use this option if you don't intend to dispose of the dearly departed's belongings right here and now.

• **Delete the home folder.** The account and all its files and settings are vaporized forever, on the spot.

Setting Up the Login Process

Once you've set up more than one account, the dialog box shown in Figure 13-1 appears whenever you turn on the Mac, whenever you choose →Log Out, or whenever the Mac logs you out automatically. But a few extra controls let you, an administrator, set up either more or less security at the login screen—or, put another way, build in less or more convenience.

Open System Preferences, click Users & Groups, click the 🔒 and enter an admin password to prove your worthiness, and then click the Login Options button (Figure 13-10). Here are some of the ways you can shape the login experience for greater security (or greater convenience):

- **Automatic login.** This option eliminates the need to sign in at all. It's a timesaving, hassle-free arrangement if only one person uses the Mac, or uses it most of the time.

  When you choose an account holder's name from this pop-up menu, you're prompted for his password. Type it and click OK.

  From now on, the dialog box shown in Figure 13-1 won't appear *at all* at startup time. After turning on the machine, you, the specified account holder, zoom straight to your desktop.

  Of course, everybody else must still enter their names and passwords. (And how can they, since the Mac rushes right into the Automatic person's account at startup time? Answer: The Automatic thing happens only at startup time. The usual login screen appears whenever the current account holder logs out—by choosing 🍎→Log Out, for example.)

Figure 13-10:
These options make it easier or harder for people to sign in, offering various degrees of security. By the way: Turning on "Name and password" also lets you sign in as >console, a trouble-shooting technique for power users.

- **Display login window as.** Under normal circumstances, the login screen presents a list of account holders when you power up the Mac, as shown in Figure 13-1. That's the "List of users" option in action.

  If you're especially worried about security, however, you might not even want that list to appear. If you turn on "Name and password" (Figure 13-10), then each person who signs in must type both his name (into a blank that appears) *and* his password—a very inconvenient, but more secure, arrangement.

- **Show the Sleep, Restart, and Shut Down buttons.** Truth is, the Mac OS X security system is easy to circumvent. Truly devoted evildoers can bypass the standard login screen in a number of different ways: restarting in FireWire disk mode, restarting at the Unix Terminal, and so on. Suddenly, these no-goodniks have full access to every document on the machine, blowing right past all the safeguards you've so carefully established.

  One way to thwart them is to turn off this checkbox. Now there's no Restart or Shut Down button to tempt mischief-makers. That's plenty of protection in most homes, schools, and workplaces; after all, Mac people tend to be *nice* people.

- **Show password hints.** Mac OS X is kind enough to display your password hint ("middle name of the first person who ever kissed me") after you've typed your password wrong three times when trying to log in. This option lets you turn off that feature for an extra layer of security. The hint will never appear.

- **Show fast user switching menu as:** The Fast User Switching feature lets you switch to another account without having to log out of the first one.

  If you do turn on Fast User Switching, a new menu appears at the upper-right corner of your screen, listing all the account holders on the machine. Thanks to this pop-up menu, you can specify what that menu looks like. It can display the current account holder's full name (Name), the short name (Short Name), or only a generic torso-silhouette icon (Icon) to save space on the menu bar.

- **Use VoiceOver in the login window.** The VoiceOver feature (page 540) is all well and good if you're blind. But how are you supposed to log in? Turn on this checkbox, and VoiceOver speaks the features on the Login panel, too.

Signing In, Logging Out

Once somebody has set up your account, here's what it's like getting into, and out of, a Mac OS X machine. (For the purposes of this discussion, "you" are no longer the administrator—you're one of the students, employees, or family members for whom an account has been set up.)

Identifying Yourself

When you first turn on the Mac—or when the person who last used this computer chooses →Log Out—the login screen shown in Figure 13-1 appears. At this point, you can proceed in any of several ways:

- **Restart.** Click if you need to restart the Mac for some reason.

- **Shut Down.** Click if you're done for the day, or if sudden panic about the complexity of user accounts makes you want to run away. The computer turns off.

- **Log In.** To sign in, click your account name in the list. If you're a keyboard speed freak, you can also type the first letter or two—or press the up or down arrow keys—until your name is highlighted. Then press Return.

  Either way, the password box appears now (if a password is required). If you accidentally click the wrong person's name on the first screen, you can click Back. Otherwise, type your password, and then press Return (or click Log In).

  You can try as many times as you want to type the password. With each incorrect guess, the entire password box shudders violently from side to side, as though shaking its head no. (If you see a strange ⇪ icon in the password box, guess what? You've got your Caps Lock key on, and the Mac thinks you're typing an all-capitals password.)

  If you try unsuccessfully three times, your hint appears—if you've set one up. And if even that safety net fails, you can use your Apple ID as the key to resetting your password. See the box on page 450.

Once you're in, the world of the Mac looks just the way you left it (or the way an administrator set it up for you). Everything in your Home folder, all your email and bookmarks, your desktop picture and Dock settings—all of it unique to you.

Unless you're an administrator, you're not allowed to install any new programs (or, indeed, to put anything at all) into the Applications folder. That folder, after all, is a central software repository for *everybody* who uses the Mac, and the Mac forbids everyday account holders from moving or changing all such universally shared folders.

Logging Out

When you're finished using the Mac, choose →Log Out (or press Shift-⌘-Q). A confirmation message appears; if you click Cancel or press Esc, you return to whatever you were doing. If you click Log Out or press Return, you return to the screen shown in Figure 13-1, and the entire sign-in cycle begins again.

Tip: If you press Option as you choose →Log Out (or as you press Shift-⌘-Q), the confirmation box doesn't appear.

Sharing Across Accounts

It's all fine to say that every account is segregated from all *other* accounts. It's nice to know your stuff is safe from the prying eyes of your coworkers or family.

But what about collaboration? What if you *want* to give some files or folders to another account holder?

You can't just open up someone else's Home folder and drop it in there. Yes, every account holder has a Home folder (all in the Users folder on your hard drive). But if you try to open anybody else's Home folder, you'll see a tiny red ⊖ icon superimposed on almost every folder inside, telling you, "Look, but don't touch."

Fortunately, there are a couple of wormholes between accounts (Figure 13-11):

Figure 13-11:
Top: In other people's Home folders, the Public folder is available for your inspection. It contains stuff that other people have "published" for the benefit of their coworkers.

Middle: In the Public folder is the Drop Box, which serves the opposite purpose. It lets anyone else who uses this Mac hand in files to you; they, however, can't see what's in it.

Bottom: Inside the Users folder (to get there from a Home folder, press ⌘-↑) is the Shared folder, a wormhole connecting all accounts. Everybody has full access to everything inside.

- **The Shared folder.** Sitting in the Users folder is one folder that doesn't correspond to any particular person: Shared. Everybody can freely access this folder, inserting and extracting files without restriction. It's the common ground among all the account holders on a single Mac. It's Central Park, the farmers' market, and the grocery-store bulletin board.

- **The Public folder.** In your Home folder, there's a folder called Public. Anything you copy into it becomes available for inspection or copying (but not changing or deleting) by any other account holder, whether they log into your Mac or sign in from across the network.

- **The Drop Box.** And *inside* your Public folder is another cool little folder: the Drop Box. It exists to let *other* people give files to *you,* discreetly and invisibly to anyone else. That is, people can drop files and folders into your Drop Box, but they can't actually *open* it. This folder, too, is available both locally (in person) and from across the network.

Fast User Switching

Suppose you're logged in, and somebody else wants to duck into her account just for a second—to check email or a calendar, for example. What are you supposed to do—log out completely, closing all your documents and quitting all your programs, just so the interloper can look something up? Then afterward, you'd have to log back in and fire up all your stuff again, praying that your inspirational muse hasn't fled in the meantime.

Fortunately, that's all over now. Fast User Switching works just as it does in Windows: It lets Person B log in and use the Mac for a little while. All *your* stuff, Person A, simply slides into the background, still open the way you had it; see Figure 13-12.

When Person B is finished working, you can bring your whole work environment back to the screen without having to reopen anything. All your windows and programs are still open, just as you left them.

To turn on this feature, open the Users & Groups panel of System Preferences (and click the 🔒, if necessary, to unlock the panel). Click Login Options, and turn on the "Show fast user switching menu as" checkbox. (You can see this option in Figure 13-10.)

The only change you notice immediately is the appearance of your own account name in the upper-right corner of the screen (Figure 13-12, top). You can change what this menu looks like by using the "Show fast user switching menu as" pop-up menu.

That's all there is to it. Next time you need a fellow account holder to relinquish control so you can duck in to do a little work, just choose your name from the Accounts menu. Type your password, if one is required, and feel guiltless about the interruption.

And now, the finer points of Fast User Switching:

- To exit an open account, choose →Log Out as usual. Or just choose Login Window from the Accounts menu. It ensures that you can get to your own account no matter whose is running at the moment.

- Weirdly enough, a bunch of account holders can be using the same program simultaneously in their own parallel universes. Even if Microsoft Word was open in your account, Chris, Casey, and Robin can each open the same copy of the same program simultaneously when they fast-switch into their own accounts.

- You can't make changes to accounts (in System Preferences) that are still logged in. Nor, as you'd expect, can you turn off Fast User Switching while other people are logged in. Can't turn on FileVault, either.

- If you try to shut the Mac down or restart it while other people are logged in, a dialog box tells you, "There are currently logged in users who may lose unsaved

Figure 13-12:

Top: The appearance of the Accounts menu lets you know that Fast User Switching is turned on. The circled checkmark indicates people who are already logged in, including those who have been "fast user switched" into the background. The dimmed name shows who's logged in right now.

Bottom: When the screen changes from your account to somebody else's, your entire world slides visibly off-screen as though it's mounted on the side of a rotating cube—a spectacular animation made possible by Mac OS X's Quartz Extreme graphics software.

changes if you shut down this computer." And you're asked to type in an administrator's name and password to establish that you know what the heck you're doing.

- Remember the Shared folder (in the Users folder on the hard drive)? It's still the wormhole connecting all accounts. If you want to share a file with another account holder, put it there.

- Your account isn't anesthetized completely when it's switched into the background. In fact, it keeps on doing whatever you set it to doing. If you were downloading some big file, for example, it keeps right on downloading when the next guy logs in.

Five Mac OS X Security Shields

Mac OS X has a spectacular reputation for stability and security. At this writing, there still hasn't been a single widespread Mac OS X virus or spyware app.

The Forgotten-Password Survival Guide

Help—I forgot my password! And I never told it to anybody, so no one can help me!

No problem. Your administrator can simply open up System Preferences, click Users & Groups, click your account name, and then click Reset Password to reestablish the password.

But you don't understand. I am the administrator! And I'm the only account!

Lucky for you, Apple has provided you with not one, not two, but three safety nets. None of them work, however, unless your friendly neighborhood administrator (so, you) turned them on in advance.

First: On your third attempt to type your password correctly, the Mac shows you your password hint (if you have one, and if the administrator left the Hint option turned on).

Second: If the administrator has turned on the "Allow user to reset password using Apple ID" in System Preferences→Users & Groups, then you can click the ⑦ button right there in the Password box when you're logging in. A tiny message appears, letting you know that, "If you forgot your password, you can reset it using your Apple ID."

To proceed, click the ⊕ button to bring up the Reset Password dialog box. Enter your Apple ID and password, and

then click Reset Password. A message appears to let you know that changing your account password will also create a new Keychain (page 460Ø). (The old one is still around, ready to be unlocked if you remember the old password at some point.) Click OK. Now enter a new password (twice) and password hint, and then click Reset Password.

You've just reset your account password. Click Continue Log In to finish logging in with your new, improved, not-forgotten password.

Third: If the administrator has turned on FileVault, described later in this chapter, then you can use its recovery key to log in, in a pinch. It's a last-ditch, emergency, backup password.

If you have your recovery key, read on. (If not, and you opted to store it with Apple, call Apple tech support; they'll give it to you. If not, and you didn't store it with Apple, you're completely out of luck. Your hard drive is encrypted, and you can't do anything but erase it and kiss your files goodbye.)

Anyway, restart the Mac. On the login screen, click your name; then click the ? button. If the hint appears and it helps you out, great. If not, click "Reset it using your Recovery Key," type in your recovery key, and then praise the Apple gods that this final safety net actually worked.

The usual rap is, "Well, that's because Windows is a much bigger target. What virus writer is going to waste his time on a computer with 8 percent market share?"

That may be part of the reason Mac OS X is virus-free, but that's not the whole story:

- In Mac OS X, no program (like a virus) can install itself without your awareness. You're notified at every juncture when anything is trying to install itself on your Mac. In fact, every time you try to download something, either in Safari or Mail, that contains *executable code* (a program, in other words), a dialog box warns you that it could conceivably harbor a virus—even if your download is compressed as a .zip file (Figure 13-13).

Figure 13-13:
Lion makes darned sure that no program ever runs without your knowledge (which is how Windows PCs get viruses and spyware). It tries to protect you, for example, when you open a new program or when you first double-click any program that came from the Internet.

- Mac OS X doesn't let even an administrator touch the files that drive Mac OS X itself without pestering you to provide your password and grant it permission to do so. A Mac OS X virus could theoretically wipe out all your files, but it wouldn't be able to access anyone else's stuff—and it couldn't touch the operating system itself.

- Safari's Private Browsing mode means that you can freely visit Web sites without leaving any digital tracks—no history, no nothing (page 393).

Those are only a few tiny examples. Here are a few of Mac OS X's big-ticket defenses.

The Firewall

If you have a broadband, always-on connection, you're open to the Internet 24 hours a day. It's theoretically possible for some cretin to use automated hacking software to flood you with data packets or take control of your machine. Mac OS X's *firewall* feature puts up a barrier to such mischief. To turn it on, click the 🔒 on this pane, authenticate yourself, and then click Start.

Note: You don't need to turn on this firewall if your Mac connects to the Internet through a wired or wireless router (including the AirPort base station). Virtually every router already has a built-in firewall that protects your entire network. (Similarly, if you're using the Internet Sharing feature described on page 316, turn on the firewall only for the *first* Mac, the one connected right to the Internet.)

In short: Use the firewall only if your Mac is connected *directly* to a cable modem, DSL box, or dial-up modem.

Fortunately, it's not a *complete* barrier. One of the great joys of having a computer is the ability to connect to other computers. Living in a cement crypt is one way to avoid getting infected, but it's not much fun.

Therefore, you can turn the firewall on by opening System Preferences→Security→Firewall tab, authenticating, and clicking Start. But you can also fine-tune the blockade.

To do that, click Advanced; you see something like Figure 13-14 at top. As you can sort of tell, Lion lets you allow or block Internet connections individually for *each program* on your Mac. Here's what you'll find there:

- **Block all incoming connections.** This option might be better known as Paranoid Mode. You're allowed to do email and basic Web surfing and a few other deep-seated services that Mac OS X needs to get by. But all other kinds of network connections are blocked, including screen sharing, iTunes music sharing, and so on. This is a hard-core, meat-fisted firewall that, for most people, is more trouble than it's worth.

Figure 13-14:
Top: The Mac OS X firewall starts with a simple Start/Stop button. The fun stuff doesn't begin until you click the Advanced button at the bottom (it's covered up in this shot, but it's there).

Bottom: This pane lists the programs that have been given permission to receive communications from the Internet. At any point, you can change a program's Block/Allow setting, as shown here. You can also click the + button to navigate to your Applications folder and manually choose programs for inclusion.

Tip: As you can tell from the wording of this item, Mac OS X's firewall blocks only *incoming* connections, which covers most of the dangerous stuff. But if you'd also like your Mac to block *outgoing* Internet connections, you can install a shareware firewall program like Little Snitch. It's available on this book's "Missing CD" page at *www.missingmanuals.com.*

- **[List of individual programs].** If the firewall is on but you haven't turned on "Block all," then the Mac uses this list of individual programs and features to determine what's allowed to accept network connections.

  Above the horizontal line (Figure 13-14, bottom), features of Mac OS X itself are listed. They get added to this list automatically when you turn them on in System Preferences: File Sharing, Printer Sharing, and so on.

  Non-Apple programs can gain passage through your firewall, too. You can add one to the list manually by clicking the **+** button below the list and choosing it by hand; or you can simply respond to the request box that pops up whenever a new program wants to accept incoming Internet connections.

  Click Allow for each such request (unless, of course, you see a request for an app called SneakyPoisonVirus or something). As you do so, their names get added to the list of programs in this dialog box.

  For each program, you can use the pop-up menu beside its name to specify either "Allow incoming connections" or "Block incoming connections," depending on your level of paranoia.

Note: From time to time, some program will ask for permission to accept incoming messages from its mother ship online. If it's a program you trust, click Allow.

- **Automatically allow signed software to receive incoming connections.** *Signed* software means programs that Apple recognizes as coming from legitimate companies. Anything from Adobe or Microsoft, for example, has got to be OK, right? (Insert your own wisecrack here.)

  If this checkbox is *not* turned on, then each time you run a new program for the first time, you'll be interrupted so that the Mac can ask if it's OK to permit Internet connections. The "signed software" box cuts down on the interruptions, since well-known apps are assumed not to be viruses or spyware.

- **Enable stealth mode.** This is designed to slam shut the Mac's back door to the Internet. See, hackers often use automated hacker tools that send out "Are you there?" messages. They're hoping to find computers that are turned on and connected full time to the Internet. If your machine responds, and they can figure out how to get into it, they'll use it, without your knowledge, as a relay station for pumping out spam or masking their hacking footsteps.

  "Enable stealth mode," then, makes your Mac even more invisible on the network; it means your Mac won't respond to the electronic signal called a *ping*. (On the other hand, *you* won't be able to ping your machine, either, when you're on the road and want to know if it's turned on and online.)

FileVault

FileVault is one of Mac OS X's most powerful security features. Understanding what it does, however, may take a little slogging.

As you know, the Mac OS X accounts system is designed to keep people out of one another's stuff. Ordinarily, for example, Chris isn't allowed to go rooting through Robin's email and files.

Until FileVault came along, though, there were all kinds of ways to circumvent this protection system. A sneak or a show-off could start up the Mac in FireWire disk mode, for example, or even remove the hard drive and hook it up to a Linux machine or another Mac.

In each case, they'd then be able to run rampant through everybody's files, changing or trashing them with abandon. For people with sensitive or private files, the result was a security hole bigger than Oprah's bank account.

FileVault is an extra line of defense. When you turn on this feature, your Mac automatically *encrypts* (scrambles) *everything* on your startup hard drive. Every time you create or save a new file, it, too, is insta-encrypted.

Note: FileVault uses something called XTS-AES 128 encryption. How secure is that? It would take a password-guessing computer *149 trillion years* before hitting pay dirt. Or, in more human terms, slightly longer than two back-to-back Kevin Costner movies.

This means that unless someone knows (or can figure out) your password, FileVault renders your files unreadable for anyone but you and your computer's administrator—no matter what sneaky tricks they try to pull. (You can, if you like, authorize other account holders to get in, too.)

You won't notice much difference when FileVault is turned on. You log in as usual, clicking your name and typing your password. Only a slight pause as you log out indicates that Mac OS X is doing some housekeeping on the encrypted files: freeing up some space and/or backing up your home directory with Time Machine.

Tip: This feature is especially useful for laptop owners. If someone swipes or "borrows" your laptop, they can't get into your stuff without the password.

Here are some things you should know about FileVault's protection:

- **It's useful only if you've logged out.** Once you're logged in, the entire drive is unlocked and accessible. If you want the protection, log out before you wander away from the Mac.

- **An administrator can access your files, too.** According to Mac OS X's caste system, anyone with an Administrator account can theoretically have unhindered access to his peasants' files—even with FileVault on—if that administrator has the master password (the recovery key) described below.

- **FileVault 2 relies on the Recovery HD partition.** You can read about this secret Lion chunk of your hard drive on page 641. For now, the point is that if you've deliberately reformatted your hard drive in some nonstandard way, you may not be able to use FileVault 2.

- **FileVault can encrypt external drives, too—even flash drives.** The controls to do this, though, are in a totally different place—not in System Preferences at all. Instead, open Disk Utility (in your Utilities folder). Erase the external drive using Mac OS Extended (Journaled, Encrypted) format. (And, yes, you have to *erase* the drive before you can encrypt it.)

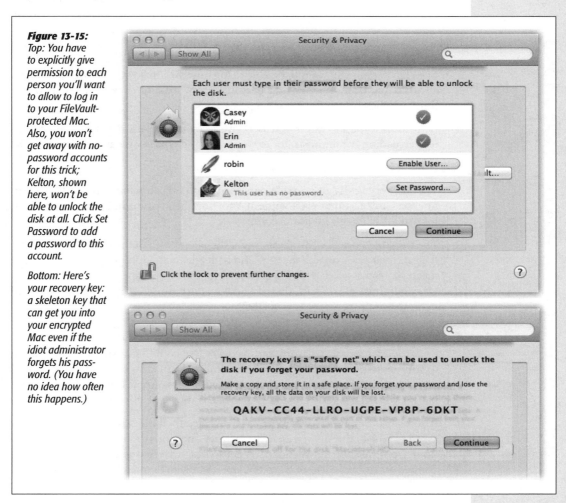

Figure 13-15:
Top: You have to explicitly give permission to each person you'll want to allow to log in to your FileVault-protected Mac. Also, you won't get away with no-password accounts for this trick; Kelton, shown here, won't be able to unlock the disk at all. Click Set Password to add a password to this account.

Bottom: Here's your recovery key: a skeleton key that can get you into your encrypted Mac even if the idiot administrator forgets his password. (You have no idea how often this happens.)

Note: Pre-Lion machines won't be able to access a drive you've encrypted in this way.

- **You can turn FileVault off at any time.** Just revisit the FileVault pane in System Preferences. (It takes time to decrypt your drive, but you can keep right on working.)

- **If you forget your password *and* your administrator forgets the recovery key, you're toast.** If this happens, your data is *permanently lost.* You have no choice but to erase your hard drive and start from scratch.

To turn FileVault on, proceed like this:

1. **In System Preferences, click Security & Privacy, and then click FileVault. Click the 🔒, authenticate yourself, and then click Turn On FileVault.**

   A list of account holders appears (Figure 13-15, top). The button next to each one, Enable User, might sound like you're about to lead someone into drug addiction, but it's actually your chance to specify who else can unlock the disk by logging in.

Note: If an account has *no* password, you have to add one first. Click the Set Password button that appears.

2. **For each person you want to be able to log into this Mac with her own password, click Enable User. Type in that person's password and click OK. When you're finished, click Continue.**

   (Anyone in this list to whom you *don't* give access can still use the Mac—but only after persuading an administrator to come over and type in his name and password.)

   Now, in huge type, the Mac displays your *recovery key*.

   The recovery key is an override password that gives an administrator full power to access any account, even without knowing the account holder's password, or to turn off FileVault for any account.

   The thinking goes like this: Yeah, yeah, the peons with Standard accounts forget their *account* passwords all the time. But with FileVault, a forgotten password would mean *the entire hard drive is locked forever*—so Apple gave you, the technically savvy administrator, a back door. (And you, the omniscient administrator, would *never* forget the recovery key—right?)

3. **Print or copy down the recovery key. Click Continue.**

   Because a forgotten password and recovery key could be absolutely devastating to your life, Apple handles this whole business like nuclear secrets (and so should you). Now, for example, a message appears that says, "Apple can store the recovery key for you." It's a really great idea to take advantage of this option.

   If you click "Store the recovery key with Apple," then the box expands and you're asked to type in the answers to three security questions (you can choose the questions from the pop-up menus): "What's your maternal grandmother's middle name?" for example. Don't mess this up; if you can't remember the answers, you won't get your recovery key from Apple.

4. **After answering the "Store recovery key" screen, click Continue. On the following screen, click Restart.**

When you log in again, the Mac begins the process of encrypting your entire hard drive. This process takes a long time (the FileVault pane in System Preferences shows you the estimated remaining time), but you can keep using your Mac in the meantime; in theory, you won't feel much of a slowdown at all while the encrypting is going on. You can even restart or shut down the computer.

You shouldn't notice any speed hit as you work with an encrypted disk, either. You'll notice only a few small security-related changes. For example, you'll be asked for your password every time you wake the computer or exit the screen saver.

Logout Options

As you read earlier in this chapter, the usual procedure for finishing up a work session is for each person to choose →Log Out. After you confirm your intention to log out, the login screen appears, ready for the next victim.

But sometimes people forget. You might wander off to the bathroom for a minute, but run into a colleague there who breathlessly begins describing last night's date and proposes finishing the conversation over pizza. The next thing you know, you've left your Mac unattended but logged in, with all your life's secrets accessible to anyone who walks by your desk.

You can tighten up that security hole, and many others, using the options in the Security & Privacy→General panel of System Preferences:

- **Require password [immediately] after sleep or screen saver begins.** This option gives you a password-protected screen saver that locks your Mac when you wander away. Now, whenever somebody tries to wake up your Mac after the screen saver has appeared (or when the Mac has simply gone to sleep), the "Enter your password" dialog box appears. No password? No access.

  The pop-up menu here (which starts out saying "immediately") is a handy feature. Without it, the person most inconvenienced by the password requirement would be *you,* not the evil snitch from Accounting; even if you just stepped away to the bathroom or the coffee machine, you'd have to unlock the screen saver with your password. It would get old fast.

  Instead, the password requirement can kick in only after you've been away for a more serious amount of time—5 minutes, 15 minutes, an hour, whatever. You can still put the Mac to sleep, or you can still set up your screen saver to kick in sooner than that. But until that time period has passed, you'll be able to wake the machine without having to log in.

- **Disable automatic login.** This is just a duplicate of the Automatic Login on/off switch described earlier. Apple figured that this feature really deserved *some* presence on a control panel called Security & Privacy.

- **Require an administrator password to access system preferences with lock icons.** Ordinarily, certain System Preferences changes require an administrator's approval—namely, the ones that affect the entire computer and everyone who uses it, like Date & Time, Users & Groups, Network, Time Machine, and Security & Privacy. If you're *not* an administrator, you can't make changes to these panels until an administrator has typed in her name and password to approve your change.

  However, once Mr. Teacher or Ms. Parent has unlocked *one* of those secure preference settings, they're *all* unlocked. Once the administrator leaves your desk, you can go right on making changes to the *other* important panels (Network *and* Time Machine *and* Security & Privacy) without the administrator's knowledge.

  Unless this "Require an administrator password" box is turned on, that is. In that case, an Administrative account holder has to enter her name and password to approve *each* of those System Preferences panes individually.

- **Log out after [60] minutes of inactivity.** You can make the Mac sign out of your account completely if it figures out that you've wandered off (and it's been, say, 15 minutes since the last time you touched the mouse or keyboard). Anyone who shows up at your Mac will find only the standard login screen.

- **Show a message when the screen is locked.** Whatever you type into this box will appear on the login screen (where you click your name in the list) or the screen saver. You might leave a little note here for other people who use the Mac. Or, on a laptop, you can add your name and phone number as contact information in case your laptop gets lost—and then found.

- **Disable remote control infrared receiver.** You can operate the playback functions of certain laptops and iMacs with a remote control, like Apple's tiny white one.

UP TO SPEED

Password Hell

In Mac OS X, you have quite a few different passwords to keep straight. Each one, however, has a specific purpose:

Account password. You type this password in at the normal login screen. You can't get into anyone else's account with it—only yours. Entering this password unlocks FileVault, too.

Administrator password. You're asked to enter this password whenever you try to install new software or modify certain system settings. If you're the only one who uses your computer (or you're the one who controls it), your administrator password *is* your account password. Otherwise, you're supposed to go find an administrator (the parent, teacher,

or guru who set up your account to begin with) and ask that person to type in his name and password once he's assessed what you're trying to do.

Recovery key. Think of this password as a master key. If anyone with FileVault forgets her account password, the administrator who knows the master password can unlock the account. This master password also lets an administrator change an account's password right at the login screen, whether FileVault is turned on or not.

Root password. This password is rarely useful for anything other than Unix-hacky power users.

If you're worried about some smart-aleck high-school kid interfering by, for example, pausing iTunes when you're trying to crunch some numbers, then turn this on. Now the Mac turns a deaf eye and ear to remote-control signals.

Note: *The Pair button here is handy when* more than one *Apple product is responding to remote-control signals—two different Macs sitting next to each other, for example, or one Mac and an Apple TV. Click Pair to "marry" one particular remote with this particular Mac.*

- **Automatically update safe downloads list.** This option refers to Apple's master list of viruses and spyware, which Mail and Safari block automatically. That list, of course, is changing all the time as Apple discovers new nasties; this option tells your Mac to update itself with Apple's master list automatically.

The Password Assistant

Plenty of software features require you to make up a password: Web sites, accounts, networked disks, and so on. No wonder most people wind up trying to use the same password in as many situations as possible. Worse, they use something easily guessable like their names, kids' names, spouse's names, and so on. Even regular English words aren't very secure, because hackers routinely use *dictionary attacks*—software that tries to guess your password by running through every word in the dictionary—to break in.

To prevent evildoers from guessing your passwords, Mac OS X comes with a good-password suggestion feature called the Password Assistant. It cheerfully generates one suggestion after another for impossible-to-guess passwords. (*recharges8@exchange-ability,* anyone?)

Fortunately, *you* won't have to remember most of them, thanks to the Keychain password-memorizing feature described at the end of this chapter. (The only password you have to memorize is your account password.)

See Figure 13-16 for details on the Password Assistant.

Figure 13-16:
Anyplace you're supposed to make up a password, including in the Users & Groups pane of System Preferences, a key icon appears. When you click it, the Password Assistant opens. Use the pop-up menu and the Length slider to specify how long and unguessable the password should be. The Quality graph shows you just how tough it is to crack this password.

(In the Type pop-up menu, you might wonder about FIPS-181. It stands for the Federal Information Processing Standards Publication 181, which sets forth the U.S. government's standard for password-generating algorithms.)

The Keychain

The information explosion of·the computer age may translate into bargains, power, and efficiency, but as noted above, it carries with it a colossal annoyance: the prolif-

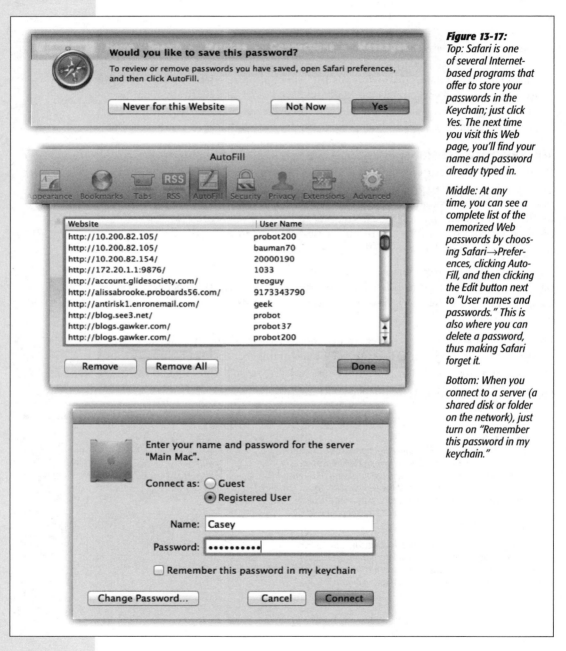

Figure 13-17:
Top: Safari is one of several Internet-based programs that offer to store your passwords in the Keychain; just click Yes. The next time you visit this Web page, you'll find your name and password already typed in.

Middle: At any time, you can see a complete list of the memorized Web passwords by choosing Safari→Preferences, clicking Auto-Fill, and then clicking the Edit button next to "User names and passwords." This is also where you can delete a password, thus making Safari forget it.

Bottom: When you connect to a server (a shared disk or folder on the network), just turn on "Remember this password in my keychain."

eration of *passwords* we have to memorize. Shared folders on the network, Web sites, FTP sites—each requires another password.

Apple has done the world a mighty favor with its *Keychain* feature. Whenever you log into Mac OS X and type in your password, you've typed the master code that tells the computer, "It's really me. I'm at my computer now." From that moment on, the Mac *automatically* fills in every password blank you encounter, whether it's a Web site in Safari, a shared disk on your network, a wireless network, an encrypted disk image, or an FTP (file-transfer) program like Transmit or Cyberduck. With only a few exceptions, you can safely forget *all* your passwords except your login password.

These days, all kinds of programs and services know about the Keychain and offer to store your passwords there. For example:

- In Safari, whenever you type your name and password for a certain Web page and then click OK, a dialog box asks: "Would you like to save this password?" (See Figure 13-17, top.)

Note: This offer is valid only if, in Safari→Preferences→AutoFill tab, "User names and passwords" is turned on. If not, the "Would you like to save this password?" message never appears.

Note, too, that some Web sites use a nonstandard login system that also doesn't produce the "Would you?" message. Unless the Web site provides its own "Remember me" or "Store my password" option, you're out of luck; you'll have to type in this information with every visit.

- When you connect to a shared folder or disk on the network, the opportunity to save the password in your Keychain is equally obvious (Figure 13-17, bottom).

- You also see a "Remember password (add to Keychain)" option when you create an encrypted disk image using Disk Utility.

- Mac email programs, like Mail and Entourage/Outlook, store your email account passwords in your Keychain. So do FTP programs; check their Preferences dialog boxes.

- Your iCloud account information is stored in the Keychain, too (as you entered it on the iCloud pane of System Preferences).

- A "Remember password" option appears when you type in the password for a wireless network or an AirPort base station.

- The iTunes program memorizes your iTunes Store password, too.

Locking and unlocking the Keychain

If you work alone, the Keychain is automatic, invisible, and generally wonderful. Login is the only time you have to type a password. After that, the Mac figures, "Hey, I know it's you; you proved it by entering your account password. That ID is good enough for me. I'll fill in all your other passwords automatically." In Apple parlance, you've *unlocked* your Keychain just by logging in.

But there may be times when you want the Keychain to *stop* filling in all your passwords, perhaps only temporarily. Maybe you work in an office where someone else might sit down at your Mac while you're getting a candy bar. You can use any of these methods. Each requires the Keychain Access program (in your Applications→Utilities folder):

- **Lock the Keychain manually.** In the Keychain Access program, choose File→"Lock Keychain 'login' " (⌘-L), or just click the big 🔒 button in the toolbar (Figure 13-18).

- **Choose "Lock Keychain 'login'" from the Keychain menulet.** To put the Keychain menulet on your menu bar, open Keychain Access, choose Keychain Access→Preferences→General. Turn on "Show keychain status in menu bar."

- **Lock the Keychain automatically.** In the Keychain Access program, choose Edit→Change Settings for Keychain [your name]. The resulting dialog box lets you set up the Keychain to lock itself, say, 5 minutes after the last time you used your Mac, or whenever the Mac goes to sleep. When you return to the Mac, you're asked to re-enter your account password in order to unlock the Keychain, restoring your automatic-password feature.

Figure 13-18:
In the main Keychain list, you can double-click a listing for more details about a certain password—including the actual password it's storing. To see the password, turn on "Show password." The first time you try this, you're asked to prove your worthiness by entering your Keychain password (usually your account password). If you then click Always Allow, you won't be bothered for a password-to-see-this-password again.

Whenever the Keychain is locked, Mac OS X no longer fills in your passwords.

Note: As noted above, you unlock your Keychain using the same password you use to log into Mac OS X, but that's just a convenience. If you're really worried about security, you can choose Edit→Change Password for Keychain [your name], thereby establishing a *different* password for your Keychain, so that it no longer matches your login password.

Of course, doing so also turns off the automatic-Keychain-unlocking-when-you-log-in feature.

Managing Keychain

To take a look at your Keychain, open the Keychain Access program. By clicking one of the password rows, you get to see its attributes—name, kind, account, and so on (Figure 13-18).

Tip: The primary purpose of the Keychain is, of course, to type in passwords for you automatically. However, it's also an excellent place to record all kinds of private information just for your own reference: credit card numbers, ATM numbers, and so on. Simply choose File→New Password Item (if it's a name and password) or File→New Secure Note Item (if you just want to type a blob of very, very private text).

No, the Mac won't type them in for you automatically anywhere, but it will maintain them in one central location that is, itself, password-protected.

Multiple Keychains

By choosing File→New Keychain, you can create more than one Keychain, each with its own master password. On one hand, this might defeat the simplicity goal of the Keychain. On the other hand, it's conceivable that you might want to encrypt all your business documents with one master password and all your personal stuff with another, for example.

If you do have more than one Keychain, you can view all of them by clicking the little Show Keychains button at the lower-left corner of the Keychain Access window; now you see a list of all your Keychains (including some maintained by Mac OS X itself). Click their names to switch among them.

Keychain files

Keychains are represented by separate files in your Home→Library→Keychains folder. Knowing that can be handy when you want to delete a Keychain or copy it to another Mac—your laptop, for example. (Then again, the File→Export command may be even more convenient.)

Two Mac OS X Privacy Shields

The Privacy tab in the Security & Privacy pane of System Preferences harbors two fairly random privacy-related options:

Send Diagnostic & Usage Data to Apple

If you turn on this box, your Mac will automatically and quietly send data to Apple about what's going on with your Mac (anonymously, of course—Apple won't know it's you). The transmissions include details about crashes and freezes, what programs and hardware you use, what software versions and peripherals you have, and so on.

None of this is transmitted unless you turn this box on.

Incidentally, you have another chance to turn on automatic reporting: when a program, or your Mac, crashes. At that time, a message invites you to send a crash report to Apple; you can click either OK or No Thanks. You can also turn on "Don't ask me again," which makes your OK or No Thanks decision permanent. (What you're actually doing with that "Don't ask me again" option, of course, is changing the status of this checkbox here in the Security & Privacy pane of System Preferences. That's how you can change your mind later.

Tip: Want to *see* the sort of information being sent? Open the Console app in Applications→Utilities. In the toolbar, click Show Log List, if necessary. Next to Diagnostic and Usage Information, click Show, if necessary. Under the subheadings here, you can read the sort of reports that Apple gets if you permit automatic sending. (*Understanding* the gobbledygook is another story.)

Enable Location Services

Location Services means "knowing where I am." It's the feature that lets your laptop figure out its own time zone automatically, for example, or that lets a weather Web site show your *local* weather the first time you visit.

Every time a program wants to use your current location for its own features, you'll be asked about it. (The Mac figures out your location based on its proximity to known WiFi networks.) Each time you say OK, the program that did the asking installs its own name into the list here.

You can turn off the checkboxes of the programs you'd rather didn't where you are, or you can turn off location tracking altogether by turning off the "Enable location services" box.

Networking, File Sharing & Screen Sharing

Networks are awesome. Once you've got a home or office network, you can copy files from one machine to another—even between Windows PCs and Macs—just as you'd drag files between folders on your own Mac. You can send little messages to other people's screens. Everyone on the network can consult the same database or calendar, or listen to the same iTunes music collection. You can play games over the network. You can share a single printer or cable modem among all the Macs in the office. You can connect to the network from wherever you are in the world, using the Internet as the world's longest extension cord back to your office.

In Mac OS X, you can even do *screen sharing,* which means that you, the wise computer whiz, can see what's on the screen of your pathetic, floundering relative or buddy elsewhere on the network. You can seize control of the other Mac's mouse and keyboard. You can troubleshoot, fiddle with settings, and so on. It's the next best thing to being there—often, a lot *better* than being there.

Note: This chapter concerns itself with *local* networking—setting up a network in your home or small office. But don't miss its sibling, Chapter 10, which is about hooking up to the somewhat larger network called the Internet.

Wiring the Network

Most people connect their computers using one of two connection systems: Ethernet or WiFi.

Ethernet Networks

Every Mac (except the MacBook Air) has an Ethernet jack (Figure 14-1). If you connect all the Macs and Ethernet printers in your small office to a central Ethernet hub, switch, or *router*—a compact, inexpensive box with jacks for five, 10, or even more computers and printers—you've got yourself a very fast, very reliable network. (Most people wind up hiding the hub in a closet and running the wiring either along the edges of the room or inside the walls.) You can buy Ethernet cables, plus the hub, at any computer store or, less expensively, from an Internet-based mail-order house; none of this stuff is Mac-specific.

Tip: If you want to connect only two Macs—say, your laptop and your desktop machine—you don't need an Ethernet hub. Instead, you just need a standard Ethernet cable. Run it directly between the Ethernet jacks of the two computers. (You don't need a special *crossover* Ethernet cable, as you did with Macs of old.) Then connect the Macs as described in the box on page 468.

Or don't use Ethernet at all; just use a FireWire cable or a person-to-person WiFi network.

Figure 14-1:
Every Mac except the Air has a built-in Ethernet jack (left). It looks like an overweight telephone jack. It connects to an Ethernet router or hub (right) via an Ethernet cable (also known as Cat 5 or Cat 6), which ends in what looks like an overweight telephone-wire plug (also known as an RJ-45 connector).

Ethernet jack   Ethernet hub

Ethernet is the best networking system for many offices. It's fast, easy, and cheap.

WiFi Networks

WiFi, known to the geeks as 802.11 and to many Apple fans as AirPort, means wireless networking. It's the technology that lets laptops get online at high speed in any WiFi "hot spot." Hot spots are everywhere these days: in homes, offices, coffee shops (notably Starbucks), hotels, airports, and thousands of other places.

Tip: At *www.jiwire.com,* you can type in an address or a city and learn exactly where to find the closest WiFi hot spots.

When you're in a WiFi hot spot, your Mac has a very fast connection to the Internet, as though it's connected to a cable modem or DSL.

WiFi circuitry comes preinstalled in every Mac. This circuitry lets your machine connect to your network and the Internet without any wires at all. You just have to be within about 150 feet of a *base station* or (as Windows people call it) an *access point*, which must in turn be physically connected to a network and Internet connection.

If you think about it, WiFi is a lot like a cordless phone, where the base station is, well, the base station, and the Mac is the handset.

The base station can take any of these forms:

- **AirPort base station.** Apple's sleek, white, squarish base stations ($100 to $180) permit as many as 50 computers to connect simultaneously.

  The less expensive one, the AirPort Express, is so small it looks like a small white power adapter. It also has a USB jack so you can share a USB printer on the network. It can serve up to 10 computers at once.

- **A Time Capsule.** This Apple gizmo is exactly the same as the AirPort base station, except that it also contains a huge hard drive so that it can back up your Macs automatically over the wired or wireless network.

UP TO SPEED

AirPort a, b, g, and n: Regular or Supersized?

In the short history of wireless networking, WiFi gear has come in several variants, bearing the absurdly user-hostile names 802.11b, 802.11g, 802.11a, 802.11n, and so on.

The difference involves the technical specs of the wireless signal. Original AirPort uses the 802.11b standard; AirPort Extreme uses 802.11g; the current AirPort cards and base stations use 802.11n.

So what's the difference? Equipment bearing the "b" label transfers data through the air at up to 11 megabits per second; the "g" system is almost five times as fast (54 megabits a second); and "n" is supposed to be four times as fast as that.

(Traditionally, geeks measure network speeds in megabits, not megabytes. If you're more familiar with megabytes, though, here's a translation: The older AirPort gear has a top speed of 1.4 megabytes per second, versus more than 6 megabytes per second for the AirPort Extreme stuff.)

(Oh, and while we're using parentheses here: The only place you'll get the quoted speeds out of this gear is on the moon. Here on earth, signal strength is affected by pesky things like air, furniture, walls, floors, wiring, phone interference, and antenna angles. Speed and signal strength diminish proportionally as you move away from the base station.)

Now, each successive version of the WiFi base station/laptop circuitry standard is backward-compatible. For example, you can buy a new, 802.11n base station, and still connect to it from your ancient 802.11g PowerBook. You won't get any greater speed, of course—that would require a laptop with an 802.11n transmitter—but you'll enjoy the greater range in your house.

It's important to understand, though, that even the most expensive, top-tier cable modem or DSL service delivers Internet information at only about half a megabyte per second. The bottleneck is the Internet connection, not your network. Don't buy newer AirPort gear thinking that you're going to speed up your email and Web activity.

Instead, the speed boost you get with AirPort Extreme is useful only for transferring files between computers and gadgets on your own network (like the bandwidth-hungry Apple TV)—and playing networkable games.

And one more note: All WiFi gear works together, no matter what kind of computer you have. There's no such thing as a "Windows" wireless network or a "Macintosh" wireless network. Macs can use non-Apple base stations, Windows PCs can use AirPort base stations, and so on.

- **A wireless broadband router.** Lots of other companies make less expensive WiFi base stations, including Linksys (*www.linksys.com*) and Belkin (*www.belkin.com*). You can plug the base station into an Ethernet router or hub, thus permitting 10 or 20 wireless-equipped computers, including Macs, to join an existing Ethernet network without wiring. (With all due non-fanboyism, however, Apple's base stations and software are infinitely more polished and satisfying to use.)

Tip: It's perfectly possible to plug a WiFi base station into a regular router, too, to accommodate both wired and wireless computers.

- **Another Mac.** Your Mac can also *impersonate* an AirPort base station. In effect, the Mac becomes a software-based base station, and you save yourself the cost of a separate physical base station.

  A few, proud people still get online by dialing via modem, which is built into some old AirPort base station models. The base station is plugged into a phone jack. Wireless Macs in the house can get online by triggering the base station to dial by remote control.

Tip: If you connect through a modern router or AirPort base station, you already have a great firewall protecting you. You don't have to turn on Mac OS X's firewall.

You use the AirPort Utility (in your Applications→Utilities folder) to set up your base station; if you have a typical cable modem or DSL, the setup practically takes care of itself.

Whether you've set up your own wireless network or want to hop onto somebody else's, Chapter 10 has the full scoop on *joining* WiFi networks.

Cell Networks

If you have an iPhone or a similar cellphone, you may be able to get your Mac online even when you're hundreds of miles from the nearest Ethernet jack or WiFi hot spot.

GEM IN THE ROUGH

Networking Without the Network

In a pinch, you can connect two Macs without any real network at all. You can create an Ethernet connection without a hub or a router—or an AirPort connection without a WiFi base station.

To set up the wired connection, just run a standard Ethernet cable between the Ethernet jacks of the two Macs. (You don't need to use an Ethernet crossover cable, as you did in days of old.)

To set up a wireless connection, from your 🛜 menulet, choose Create Network. Make up a name and password for your little private network, and then click OK. On the second Mac, choose 🛜→Join Network, enter the same private network name, and then click Join.

At this point, your two Macs belong to the same ad hoc micro-network. If you've shared some folders on the first Mac, its name (like "Casey's iMac") now appears in the Sidebar of the second Mac. Click it to see what's on it.

Thanks to *tethering,* your phone can act as an Internet antenna for your laptop, relying on the slow, expensive, but almost ubiquitous *cellular* network for its connection. Details are on page 313.

File Sharing: Three Ways

When you're done wiring (or not wiring, as the case may be), your network is ready. Your Mac should "see" any Ethernet or shared USB printers, in readiness to print (Chapter 9). You can now play network games or use a network calendar. And you can now turn on *File Sharing,* one of the most useful features of all.

In File Sharing, you can drag files back and forth between different Macs (or even PCs) on the network, exactly as though the other computer's folder or disk is a hard drive connected to your own machine. You can see the idea in Figure 14-2.

Figure 14-2:
Here's the master switch that makes your Public folder (and any other folders you designate) available to other people on the network. You can edit the Computer Name, if you like. Your Mac will appear on the network with this name. Make it nice and descriptive, such as Front Desk iMac.

The thing is, it's not easy being Apple. You have to write *one* operating system that's supposed to please *everyone,* from the self-employed first-time newbie to the network administrator for NASA. You have to design a networking system simple enough for the laptop owner who just wants to copy things to a desktop Mac when returning from a trip, yet secure and flexible enough for the network designer at a large corporation.

Clearly, different people have different attitudes toward the need for security and flexibility.

That's why Lion offers *three ways* to share files, striking three different positions along the Simplicity-to-Flexibility Spectrum:

- **The easiest way: AirDrop.** This Lion feature is dreamy—if there are other people in your house or office who have wireless Macs running Lion or Mountain Lion. Imagine this: You open the AirDrop folder, where you see everybody else's icons. To give someone a file, you drop its icon on that person's face. Done.

- **What used to be the easiest way: the Public folder.** Every account holder has a Public folder. It's free for anyone else on the network to access. Like a grocery store bulletin board, there's no password required. Super-convenient, super-easy.

  There's only one downside, and you may not care about it: You have to move or copy files *into* the Public folder before anyone else can see them. Depending on how many files you want to share, this can get tedious, disrupt your standard organizational structure, and eat up disk space.

- **The flexible way: any folder.** You can also make *any* file, folder, or disk available for inspection by other people on the network. This method means that you don't have to move files into the Public folder, for starters. It also gives you elaborate control over who is allowed to do what to your files. You might want to permit your company's executives to see *and* edit your documents, but allow the peons in Accounting just to see them. And Andy, that unreliable goofball in Sales? You don't want him even *seeing* what's in your shared folder.

  Of course, setting up all those levels of control means more work and more complexity.

The following pages tackle these three methods one at a time.

AirDrop

AirDrop is one of Mac OS X Lion's star attractions. It's a breakthrough in speed, simplicity, and efficiency. There's no setup, no passwords involved. It lets you copy files to someone else's Mac up to 30 feet away, instantly and wirelessly; you don't need an Internet connection or even a WiFi network. It works on a flight, a beach, or a sailboat in the middle of the Atlantic. It also works if you are on a WiFi network, doing other things online.

To give someone a file, you and your lucky recipient must each open your respective AirDrop window. To do that, you can click the AirDrop icon (at the top of the Sidebar in any Finder window), choose Go→AirDrop, or press Shift-⌘-R.

The window shown in Figure 14-3 appears. After a moment, it fills up with icons for everyone nearby who's running a wireless Lion Mac (and who's opened their AirDrop windows). They don't have to do anything else; their icons show up automatically.

All you have to do is drag a file or folder icon, or several, onto the icon of the intended recipient. When the Mac asks if you're sure, click Send or press Return. Now the message says, "Waiting for [the other Mac's name] to accept."

The recipient now sees a message that says, "[Other guy's Mac] wants to send you [the file's name]." And there are three options: Save and Open, Decline, and Save.

If the lucky winner clicks one of the Save buttons, the file transfer proceeds automatically. A progress bar wraps *around* the other person's icon in the AirDrop window—cute. The transfer is encrypted, so evildoers nearby have no clue what you're transferring (or even *that* you're transferring).

Figure 14-3:
Top: If there are other Lion Macs within about 30 feet, you see their logged-in users' icons here. Usually, the icons display the Mac owners' account pictures; but if they have facial photos in your Address Book, then you see those instead.

Bottom: Here's what you see if you're the recipient (and have clicked Save in the confirmation box). To find your newly arrived goodies, open your Downloads folder.

The file winds up in the other guy's Downloads folder.

Tip: The Downloads folder generally sits on the Dock, so it's easy to find. But your recipient can also choose Go→Downloads, or press Option-⌘-L, to jump there.

So if AirDrop is so great, why doesn't it wipe out all other forms of file transfer and save this book a bunch of pages? Because (a) it works only on *Macs running Lion (or later Mac OS X versions),* (b) it works only *wirelessly,* and (c) it's a one-way street. Other people can't *take* files from your Mac—you have to shove the files to them.

If you can get past those limitations, though, there's a lot of great stuff in AirDrop:

- If you see someone's name beneath her icon in the AirDrop window, that means that she's in your Address Book *and* has signed in with her Apple ID. That's an extra bit of confidence that she is who her icon says she is.

- AirDrop works by creating a temporary two-computer wireless network. That's why it works even if you're not in a WiFi hot spot. It does, however, require both computers to have WiFi turned *on,* which you can check by opening the 🛜 menu.

- If *you're* the one receiving a file, you can cancel a half-finished transfer by clicking the ⊗ button on the progress bar that wraps around the sender's icon in the AirDrop window. (Another way: If your Downloads folder is set to Stack view, you can click the ⊗ button in the corner of the file's icon.)

- AirDrop doesn't work unless both of you have opened your AirDrop windows in the Finder. If you close your AirDrop window, or even click outside that window, your Mac disappears from everyone else's AirDrop screens.

Sharing Your Public Folder

AirDrop is the simplest and happiest way to share files, no doubt about it. But it requires Lion on both Macs, it works only wirelessly, and it's a one-way street (you have to initiate the file handoff).

The next simplest file-sharing method eliminates all those limitations. It's the Public-folder method.

Inside your Home folder, there's a folder called Public. (Actually, inside *everybody's* Home folder is a folder called Public.)

Anything you put into this folder is automatically available to everyone else on the network. They don't need a password, they don't need an account on your Mac— they just have to be on the same network, wireless or wired. They can put files here *or* copy things out.

To make your Public folder available to your networkmates, you have to turn on the File Sharing master switch. Choose →System Preferences, click Sharing, and then turn on File Sharing (Figure 14-2).

Now round up the files and folders you want to share with all comers on the network and drag them into your Home→Public folder. That's all there is to it.

Note: You may notice that there's already something in your Public folder: a folder called Drop Box. It's there so that other people can give *you* files from across the network, as described later in this chapter.

So now that you've set up Public folder sharing, how are other people supposed to access your Public folder? See page 478.

Sharing Any Folder

If the Public-folder method seems too simple and restrictive, then you can graduate to the "share any folder" method. In this scheme, you can make *any* file, folder, or disk available to other people on the network.

The advantage here is that you don't have to move your files into the Public folder; they can sit right where you have them. And this time, you can set up elaborate *sharing privileges* (also known as *permissions*) that grant individuals different amounts of access to your files.

This method is more complicated to set up than that Public-folder business. In fact, just to underline its complexity, Apple has created two different setup procedures. You can share one icon at a time by opening its Get Info window; or you can work in a master list of shared items in System Preferences.

The following pages cover both methods.

The Get Info Method

Here's how to share a Mac file, disk, or folder disk using its Get Info window.

The following steps assume that you've turned on →System Preferences→Sharing→File Sharing, as shown in Figure 14-2.

1. **Highlight the folder or disk you want to share. Choose File→Get Info.**

   The Get Info dialog box appears (Figure 14-4). Expand the General panel, if it's not already visible.

Note: Sharing an entire disk means that every folder and file on it is available to anyone you give access to. On the other hand, by sharing only a folder or two, you can keep *most* of the stuff on your hard drive private, out of view of curious network comrades. Sharing only a folder or two does *them* a favor, too, by making it easier for them to find the files they're supposed to have. This way, they don't have to root through your entire drive looking for the folder they actually need.

2. **Turn on "Shared folder."**

   Enter your administrative password, if necessary.

Tip: To help you remember what you've made available to other people on the network, a gray banner labeled "Shared Folder" appears across the top of any Finder window you've shared. It even appears at the top of the Open and Save dialog boxes.

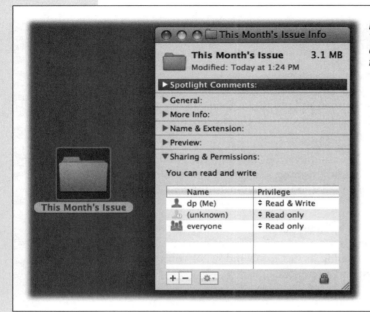

Figure 14-4:
The file-sharing permissions controls are here, in the Get Info box for any file, folder, or disk.

OK, this disk or folder is now shared. But with whom?

3. **Expand the Sharing & Permissions panel, if it's not already visible. Click the 🔒 icon and enter your administrator's password.**

   The controls in the Sharing & Permissions area spring to life and become editable. At the bottom of the Info panel is a little table. The first column can display the names of individual account holders, like Casey or Chris, or *groups* of account holders, like Everyone or Accounting Dept.

   The second column lists the *privileges* each person or group has for this folder.

   Now, the average person has no clue what "privileges" means, and this is why things get a little hairy when you're setting up folder-by-folder permissions. But read on; it's not as bad as it seems.

4. **Edit the table by adding people's names. Then set their access permissions.**

   At the moment, your name appears in the Name column, and it probably says Read & Write in the Privilege column. In other words, you're currently the master of this folder. You can put things in, and you can take things out.

If you just want to share files with *yourself*, so you can transfer them from one computer to another, you can stop here.

If you want to share files with *other* people—well, at the moment, the privileges for Everyone are probably set to "Read only." Other people can see this folder, but they can't do anything with it.

Your job is to work through this list of people, specifying *how much* control each person has over the file or folder you're sharing.

To add the name of a person or group, click the **+** button below the list. The list shown in Figure 14-5 appears.

Figure 14-5:
This list includes every account holder on your Mac, plus groups you've set up (page 430), plus the contents of your Address Book. One by one, you can add them to the list of lucky sharers of your files or folders—and then change the degree of access they have to the stuff you're sharing.

Now click a name in the list. Then, from the Privilege pop-up menu, choose a permissions setting.

- **Read & Write** has the most access of all. This person, like you, can add, change, or delete any file in the shared folder, or make any changes she likes to a document. Give Read & Write permission to people you trust not to mess things up.

- **Read only** means "Look, but don't touch." This person can see what's in the folder (or file) and can copy it, but he can't delete or change the original. It's a good setting for distributing company documents or making source files available to your minions.

- **Write only (Drop Box)** means that other people can't even open the folder. They can drop things *into* it, but it's like a mail slot: The letter disappears into the slot, and then it's too late for them to change their minds. As the folder's owner, you can do what you like with the deposited goodies. This drop-box effect is great when you want students, coworkers, or family members to be able to *turn things in* to you—homework, reports, scandalous diaries—without running the risk that someone else might see those documents. (This option doesn't appear for documents—only disks and folders.)

- **No access** is an option only for Everyone. It means that other people can see this file or folder's icon but can't do a thing with it.

Tip: Usually, you'll want the privileges for the folder to also apply to everything *inside* it; it would be a real drag to have to change the sharing privileges of the contents one icon as a time. That's why the ✿ menu at the bottom of the Get Info box has a command called "Apply to enclosed items."

---

5. **Close the Get Info window.**

Now the folder is ready for invasion from across the network.

The System Preferences Method

It's very convenient to turn on sharing one folder at a time, using the Get Info window. But there's another way in, too, one that displays *all* your shared stuff in one handy master list.

To see it, choose ●→System Preferences. Click Sharing. Click File Sharing (and make sure it's turned on).

Now you're looking at a slightly different kind of permissions table, shown in Figure 14-6. It has *three* columns:

Figure 14-6:
Hiding in System Preferences is a list of every disk and folder you've shared. To stop sharing something, click it and click the — button. To share a new disk or folder, drag its icon off the desktop, or out of its window, directly into the Shared Folders list.

- **Shared folders.** The first column lists the files, folders, and disks you've shared. You'll probably see that every account's *Public* folder is already listed here, since they're all shared automatically. (You can turn *off* sharing for a Public folder, too, just by clicking it and then clicking the − button.)

  But you can add more icons to this list. Either drag them into the list directly from the desktop or a Finder window, or click the **+** sign, navigate to the item you want to share, select it, and then click Add. Either way, that item now appears in the Shared Folders list.

- **Users.** When you click a shared item, the second column sprouts a list of *who* gets to work with it from across the network. You're listed here, of course, since it's your stuff. There's also a listing here for Everyone, which really means, "everyone *else*"—that is, everyone who's not specifically listed here.

  You can add to this list, too. Click **+** to open the person-selection box shown in Figure 14-5. It lists the other account holders on your Mac, and some predefined groups, as well as the contents of your Address Book.

Note: Most of the Address Book people don't actually have accounts on this Mac, of course. If you choose somebody from this list, you're asked to make up an account password. When you click Create Account, you've actually created a *Sharing Only* account on your Mac for that person, as described on page 429. When you return to the Accounts pane of System Preferences, you'll see that new person listed.

Double-click a person's name to add her to the list of people who can access this item from over the network, and then set up the appropriate privileges (described next).

To *remove* someone from this list, just click the name and then click the − button.

- **Users.** This *third* column lets you specify how much access each person in the *second* column has to this folder. Your choices, once again, are **Read & Write** (full access to change or delete this item's contents); **Read Only** (open or copy, but can't edit or delete); and **Write Only** (**Drop Box**), which lets the person put things *into* this disk or folder, but not open it or see what else is in it.

  For the Everyone group, you also get an option called **No Access,** which means that this item is completely off limits to everyone else on the network.

And now, having slogged through all these options and permutations, your Mac is ready for invasion from across the network.

Accessing Shared Files

The previous pages have described *setting up* a Mac so people at other computers can access its files. There's an easy, limited way (use the Public folder) and a more elaborate way (turn on sharing settings for each folder individually).

Now comes the payoff to both methods: sitting at another computer and *connecting* to the one you set up. There are two ways to go about it. You can use the Sidebar, or you can use the older, more flexible Connect to Server command. The following pages cover both methods.

Connection Method A: Use the Sidebar

Suppose, then, that you're seated in front of your Mac, and you want to see the files on another Mac on the network. Proceed like this:

1. **Open any Finder window.**

   In the Shared category of the Sidebar at the left side of the window, icons for all the computers on the network appear. See Figure 14-7.

Tip: The same Sidebar items show up in the Save and Open dialog boxes of your programs, too, making the entire network available to you for opening and saving files.

Figure 14-7:
Macs appear in the Sidebar with whatever names they've been given in System Preferences→Sharing. Their tiny icons usually resemble the computers themselves. Other computers (like Windows PCs) look like generic PCs.

If you *don't* see a certain Mac's icon here, it might be turned off, it might not be on the network, or it might have File Sharing turned off.

Note: Or it might not have the right file-sharing *type* turned on. To check, open System Preferences→Sharing; click Sharing, and then Options. You'll see checkboxes for AFP and SMB; your computers can't see each other if they don't have one of these options in common.

If you don't see any computers at all in the Sidebar, then *your* computer might not be on the network. Or maybe you've turned off the checkboxes for Connected Servers and Bonjour Computers in Finder→Preferences→Sidebar.

If there are a lot of computer icons in the Sidebar, or if you're on a corporate-style network that has the sub-chunks known as *workgroups*, you may also see an icon called All. Click it to see the full list of network entities that your Mac can see: not just individual Mac, Windows, and Unix machines, but also any "network neighborhoods" (limbs of your network tree). For example, you may see the names of network zones (clusters of machines, as found in big companies and universities).

Or, if you're trying to tap into a Windows machine, open the icon representing the *workgroup* (computer cluster) that contains the machine you want. In small office networks, it's usually called MSHOME or WORKGROUP. In big corporations, these workgroups can be called almost anything—as long as it's no more than 15 letters long with no punctuation. (Thanks, Microsoft.)

If you *do* see icons for workgroups or other network "zones," double-click until you're seeing the icons for individual computers.

Note: If you're a network nerd, you may be interested to note that Mac OS X can "see" servers that use the SMB/CIFS, NFS, FTP, and WebDAV protocols running on Mac OS X Server, Unix, Linux, Novell NetWare, and Windows servers (NT, 2000, XP, Vista, and Windows 7). But the Sidebar reveals *only* the shared computers on your *subnet* (your local, internal office network).

---

2. **Click the computer whose files you want to open.**

   In the main window, you now see the Public Folder icons for each account holder on that computer: Mom, Dad, Sissy, whatever, as shown in Figure 14-7. (They *may* have shared other folders with you, too.) If you have an account on the other computer, you'll see a folder representing *your* stuff, too. At this point, you're considered a guest.

Note: This amount of access depends on a setting in System Preferences→Users & Groups. Click the Guest account to see it: "Allow guests to connect to shared folders." That checkbox is usually turned on—but it's something to check if you can't seem to connect.

From here, the remaining instructions diverge, depending on whether you want to access *other* people's stuff or *your* stuff. That's why there are two alternative versions of step 3 here:

3a. **If you want to access the stuff that somebody else has left for you, double-click that person's Public folder.**

   Instantly, that folder's contents appear in the Finder window.

In this situation, you're only a guest. You don't have to bother with a password. On the other hand, the only thing you can generally see inside the other person's account folder is his Public folder.

Tip: Actually, you *might* see other folders here—if the account holder has specifically shared them *and* decided that you're important enough to have access to them.

One thing you'll find inside the Public folder is the Drop Box folder. This folder exists so that you can *give* files and folders to the other person. You can drop any of your own icons onto the Drop Box folder—but you can't open the Drop Box folder to see what *other* people have put there. It's one-way, like a mail slot in somebody's front door.

If you see anything else at all in the Public folder you've opened, then it's stuff the account holder has copied there for the enjoyment of you and your networkmates. You're not allowed to delete anything from the other person's Public folder or make changes to anything in it.

You can, however, open those icons, read them, or even copy them to *your* Mac— and then edit *your* copies.

3b. **To access your own Home folder on the other Mac, click the Connect As button (Figure 14-8). Sign in as usual.**

When the "Connect to the file server" box appears, you're supposed to specify your account name and password (from the Mac you're tapping into). This is the same name and password you'd use to log in if you were actually sitting at that machine.

Type your account name (long or short version) and password. And if you didn't set up a password for your account, then leave the password box empty.

POWER USERS' CLINIC

What You Can See

Precisely which other folders you can see on the remote Mac depend on what kind of account you have there: Guest, Standard, or Administrator. (See the previous chapter.)

If you're using the Guest account, you can see only the Public folders. The rest of the Mac is invisible and off limits to you. (You may see additional folders if somebody turned on sharing for them.)

If you have a Standard account, you can see other people's Public and Drop Box folders, plus your own Home folder. (Again, somebody may have made other folders available.)

If you're an administrator, you get to see icons for the account holders' Public folders and the hard drive itself to which you're connecting. In fact, you even get to see the names of any other disks connected to that Mac.

If you, O lucky administrator, open the hard drive, you'll discover that you also have the freedom to see and manipulate the contents of the Applications, Desktop, Library, and Users→Shared folders.

You can even see what folders are in other users' Home folders, although you can't open them or put anything into them.

Tip: The dialog box shown in Figure 14-8 includes the delightful and timesaving "Remember this password in my keychain" option, which makes the Mac memorize your password for a certain disk so you don't have to type it—or even see this dialog box—every darned time you connect. (If you have no password, though, the "Remember password" doesn't work. You'll have to confront—and press Return to dismiss—the "Connect to the file server" box every time.)

Figure 14-8:
You can sign into your account on another Mac on the network (even while somebody else is using that Mac in person). Click Connect As and then enter your name and password. Turn on "Remember this password in my keychain" to speed up the process for next time. The Change Password button lets you change your account password on the other machine. No matter which method you use to connect to a shared folder or disk, its icon shows up in the Sidebar.

When you click Connect (or press Return or Enter), the other Mac's icon shows up in your Sidebar, and its contents appear in the main window. (The other Mac's icon may also show up on the desktop, if you've turned on the Connected Servers option in Finder→Preferences→Sidebar.)

Tip: Once you've connected to a Mac using your account, the other Mac has a lock on your identity. You'll be able to connect to the other Mac over and over again during this same computing session, without ever having to retype your password.

In the meantime, you can double-click icons to open them, make copies of them, and otherwise manipulate them exactly as though they were icons on your own hard drive. Depending on what permissions you've been given, you can even edit or trash those files.

You can even use Spotlight to find files on that networked disk. If the Mac across the network is running Leopard, Snow Leopard, or Lion, in fact, you can search for words *inside* its files, just as though you were sitting in front of it. If not, you can still search for text in files' names.

Connection Method B: Connect to Server

The Sidebar method of connecting to networked folders and disks is practically effortless. It involves nothing more than clicking your way through folders—a skill that, in theory, you already know.

But the Sidebar method has its drawbacks. For example, the Sidebar doesn't let you type in a disk's network address. As a result, you can't access any shared disk *on the Internet* (an FTP site, for example), or indeed anywhere beyond your local subnet (your own small network).

Fortunately, there's another way. When you choose Go→Connect to Server, you get the dialog box shown in Figure 14-9. You're supposed to type in the address of the shared disk you want.

Figure 14-9:
The Sidebar method of connecting to shared disks and folders is quick and easy, but it doesn't let you connect to certain kinds of disks. The Connect to Server method entails plodding through several dialog boxes, but it can find just about every kind of networked disk.

GEM IN THE ROUGH

Faster Ways to Connect Next Time

If you expect that you might want to access a shared disk or folder again later, take a moment to make an alias of it. The easiest way is to press Option-⌘ as you drag it out of the window where it first appears.

Next time, you can bring it back to your screen just by double-clicking the alias. And if you turned on "Remember this password in my keychain," you won't even be asked for your name and password again.

Similarly, if you put an alias like this onto the Dock, you can bring it back to your screen later just by clicking its icon.

You can even drag the alias into the Login Items window described on page 435. Now the disk appears on your desktop automatically each time you log in—the most effortless arrangement of all.

For example, from here you can connect to:

- **Everyday Macs on your network.** If you know the IP address of the Mac you're trying to access (you geek!), you can type nothing but its IP address into the box and then hit Connect. Or you can just type its Bonjour name, something like this: *afp://upstairs-PowerMac.local/*.

Tip: To find out your Mac's IP address, open the Network pane of System Preferences. There, near the top, you'll see a message like this: "AirPort is connected to Tim's Hotspot and has the IP address 192.168.1.113." That's your IP address.

To see your Bonjour address, open the Sharing pane of System Preferences. Click File Sharing. Near the top, you'll see the computer name with ".local" tacked onto its name—and hyphens instead of spaces—like this: Little-MacBook.local.

After you enter your account password and choose the shared disk or folder you want, you're connected exactly as though you had clicked Connect As (Figure 14-8).

The next time you open the Connect to Server dialog box, Mac OS X remembers that address, as a courtesy to you, and shows it pre-entered in the Address field.

- **Macs across the Internet.** If your Mac has a permanent (static) IP address, the computer itself can be a server, to which you can connect from anywhere in the world via the Internet.

- **Windows machines.** Find out the PC's IP address or computer name, and then use this format for the address: *smb://192.168.1.34* or *smb://Cheapo-Dell*.

After a moment, you're asked to enter your Windows account name and password, and then to choose the name of the shared folder you want. When you click OK, the shared folder's contents appear in the window, ready to use, and the computer's icon appears in your Sidebar. (More on sharing with Windows PCs later in this chapter.)

Tip: If you know the name of the shared folder, you can add that after a slash, like this: *smb://192.168.4.23/sharedstuff*. You save yourself one dialog box.

- **NFS servers.** If you're on a network with Unix machines, you can tap into one of their shared directories using this address format: *nfs://Machine-Name/pathname*, where *Machine-Name* is the computer's name or IP address, and *pathname* is the folder path to the shared item you want.

- **FTP servers.** Mac OS X makes it simple to bring *FTP servers* onto your screen, too. (These are the drives, out there on the Internet, that store the files used by Web sites.)

In the Connect to Server dialog box, type the FTP address of the server you want, like this: *ftp://www.apple.com*. If the site's administrators have permitted *anonymous* access—the equivalent of a Guest account—that's all there is to it. A Finder window pops open, revealing the FTP site's contents.

If you need a password for the FTP site, however, you're now asked for your name
and password.

___

Tip: *You can eliminate that password-dialog-box step by using this address format:* ftp://yourname:your-
password@www.apple.com.

___

Once you type it and press Return, the FTP server's icon appears in the Sidebar.
Its contents appear, too, ready to open or copy.

- **WebDAV server.** This special Web-based shared disk requires a special address
format, something like this: *http://Computer-Name/pathname.*

In each case, once you click OK, you may be asked for your name and password.

And now, some timesaving features in the Connect to Server box:

- Once you've typed a disk's address, you can click **+** to add it to the list of server
favorites. The next time you want to connect, you can just double-click its name.

- The clock-icon pop-up menu lists Recent Servers—computers you've accessed
recently over the network. If you choose one of them from this pop-up menu, you
can skip having to type in an address.

___

Tip: *Like the Sidebar network-browsing method, the Connect to Server command displays each connected
computer as an icon in your Sidebar, even within the Open or Save dialog boxes of your programs. You
don't have to burrow through the Sidebar's Network icon to open files from them, or save files onto them.*

___

Figure 14-10:
*To disconnect
from a shared
network disk or
folder, click the
other comput-
er's icon in the
Sidebar. Then
click Disconnect
at the top-right
corner of the
window.*

Disconnecting Yourself

When you're finished using a shared disk or folder, you can disconnect from it as shown in Figure 14-10.

Disconnecting Others

In Mac OS X, you really have to work if you want to know whether other people on the network are accessing *your* Mac. You have to choose System Preferences→Sharing→File Sharing→Options. There you'll see something like, "Number of users connected: 1."

Maybe that's because there's nothing to worry about. You certainly have nothing to fear from a security standpoint, since you control what they can see on your Mac. Nor will you experience much computer slowdown as you work, thanks to Mac OS X's prodigious multitasking features.

Still, if you're feeling particularly antisocial, you can slam shut the door to your Mac. Just open System Preferences→Sharing and turn off File Sharing.

GEM IN THE ROUGH

Hello, Bonjour

Throughout this chapter, and throughout this book, you'll encounter rituals in which you're supposed to connect to another Mac, server, or printer by typing in its IP address (its unique network address).

But first of all, IP addresses are insanely difficult to memorize (192.179.248.3, anyone?). Second, networks shouldn't require you to deal with them anyway. If a piece of equipment is on the network, it should announce its presence, rather than making you specifically call for it by name.

Now you can appreciate the beauty of Bonjour (formerly Rendezvous), an underlying Mac OS X networking technology that lets networked gadgets detect one another on the network automatically and recognize one another's capabilities.

It's Bonjour at work, for example, that makes other Macs' names show up in your iTunes program so you can listen to their music from across the network. Bonjour is also responsible for filling up your Bonjour buddy list in iChat automatically, listing everyone who's on the same office network; for making shared Macs' names show up in the Sidebar's Shared list; and for making the names of modern laser printers from HP, Epson, or Lexmark appear like magic in the list of printers in the Print dialog box.

And if you're lucky enough to have (a) a TiVo Series 2 or later video recorder for your television, (b) a home network that connects it with your Mac, and (c) TiVo's Home Networking option, then you already know that your Mac's name magically appears on the TiVo screen. This allows you to play your iTunes music, or put on a slideshow of your iPhoto pictures, right on the TV. Once again, it's Bonjour at work.

It's even more tantalizing to contemplate the future of Bonjour. To quote the Zeroconf trade group (*www.zeroconf.org*), whose underlying technology forms the basis of Bonjour:

"The long-term goal of Zeroconf is to enable the creation of entirely new kinds of networked products, products that today would simply not be commercially viable because of the inconvenience and support costs involved in setting up, configuring, and maintaining a network to allow them to operate."

But that's just the beginning. If electronics companies show interest (and some have already), you may someday be able to connect the TV, stereo, and DVD player with just a couple of Ethernet cables, or even wirelessly, instead of a rat's nest of audio and video cables.

For most of us, that day can't come soon enough.

If anybody is, in fact, connected to your Mac at the time (*from* a Mac), you, the door-slammer, get to see the dialog box in Figure 14-11, which lets you send a little warning or farewell message to whoever's connected to your Mac.

If nobody is connected right now, your Mac instantly becomes an island once again.

Figure 14-11:
This dialog box asks you how much notice you want to give your coworkers that they're about to be disconnected, and what message to send them before the ax falls.

Networking with Windows

As a switcher (or adder), this topic might be especially interesting to you. It's true: Macs and Windows PCs can see each other on the network, with no special software (or talent) required.

In fact, you can go in either direction. Your Mac can see shared folders on a Windows PC, and a Windows PC can see shared folders on your Mac.

It goes like this.

Seated at the Mac, Seeing the PC

Suppose you have a Windows PC and a Mac on the same wired or wireless network. Here's how you get the Mac and PC chatting:

1. **On your Windows PC, share some files.**

   This isn't really a book about Windows networking (thank heaven), but here are the basics.

   Just as on the Mac, there are two ways to share files in Windows. One of them is super-simple: You just copy the files you want to share into a central, fully accessible folder. As long as nobody has turned off the Guest-access feature, no passwords, accounts, or other steps are required.

   In **Windows XP,** that special folder is the Shared Documents folder, which you can find by choosing Start→My Computer. Share it on the network as shown in Figure 14-12, top.

In **Windows Vista,** it's the Public folder, which appears in the Navigation pane of every Explorer window. (In Vista, there's one Public folder for the whole *computer,* not one per account holder.)

In **Windows 7,** there's a Public folder in each library. That is, there's a Public Documents, Public Pictures, Public Music, and so on.

The second, more complicated method is the "share any folder" method, just as in Mac OS X. In XP or Vista, you right-click the folder you want to share, choose Properties from the shortcut menu, click the Sharing tab, and turn on "Share this

Figure 14-12:
Top: To share a folder in Windows, right-click it, choose Properties, and then turn on "Share this folder on the network." In the "Share name" box, type a name for the folder as it will appear on the network. (No spaces are allowed).

Bottom: Back in the safety of Mac OS X, click the PC's name in the Sidebar. (If it's part of a workgroup, click All, and then your workgroup name first.)

Next, click the name of the shared computer. If the files you need are in a Shared Documents or Public folder, no password is required. You see the contents of the PC's Shared Documents folder or Public folder, as shown here. Now it's just like file sharing with another Mac.

If you want access to any other shared folder, click Connect As, and see Figure 14-13.

folder on the network" (Figure 14-12, top). In Windows 7, use the Share With menu at the top of any folder's window. See the box below for more details.

Repeat for any other folders you want to make available to your Mac.

2. **On the Mac, open any Finder window.**

The shared PCs may appear as individual computer names in the Sidebar, or you may have to click the All icon to see the icons of their *workgroups* (network clusters). Unless you or a network administrator changed it, the workgroup name is probably MSHOME or WORKGROUP. Double-click the workgroup name you want.

Tip: You can also access the shared PC via the Connect to Server command, as described on page 484. You could type into it *smb://192.168.1.103* (or whatever the PC's IP address is) or *smb://SuperDell* (or whatever its name is) and hit Return—and then skip to step 5. In fact, using the Connect to Server method often works when the Sidebar method doesn't.

TROUBLESHOOTING MOMENT

Windows 7 Tips

Windows 7 is the most Maclike version of Windows yet, but making it share nicely with the Mac still requires a few setup steps.

First, make sure you've shared everything you want to share on the Windows 7 machine. For example, suppose you want to share your entire personal folder (the equivalent of the Mac's Home folder).

To do that, choose Start→ [your name]. In the window that opens, choose "Share with"→"Specific people." In the resulting dialog box, you'll see that you are already permitted to access this folder, as shown here; unless you want to add someone else, just click Share and then Done.

Now, on the Mac, in the Finder, choose Go→Connect to Server. Type smb:// SuperDell, or whatever your PC's name is. (And how do you find that out? Open the Start menu; right-click Computer; from the shortcut menu, choose Properties. You'll see the

computer name in the middle of the resulting info screen.)

On the Mac, after typing the PC's name into the Connect to Server box, click Connect. After a moment, you're asked for your account name and password, as it appears on the *PC.*

Enter these credentials—turn on "Remember my password" if you want to be spared this rigmarole the next time—and then click Connect.

Now you're shown a list of disks and folders you shared on the Windows PC. Double-click the one you want. Presto: It appears in a Finder window, ready to access!

(If you discover you can copy stuff out of these folders but can't put stuff into them, check the sharing permissions on the Windows side.)

Finally, for heaven's sake, make an alias of the Windows folder or disk on the Mac so you can just double-click to open it the next time!

Now the names of the individual PCs on the network appear in your Finder window. (If you're running Windows 7, see the box on the facing page.)

3. **Double-click the name of the computer you want.**

If you're using one of the simple file-sharing methods on the PC, as described above, that's all there is to it. The contents of the Shared Documents or Public folder now appear on your Mac screen. You can work with them just as you would your own files.

If you're not using one of those simple methods, and you want access to individual shared folders, read on.

Note: In Windows XP Pro, the next step won't work unless you turn *off* Simple File Sharing. To do that, choose Tools→Folder Options in any Explorer window. Click the View tab and turn off "Use simple file sharing."

---

4. **Click Connect As.**

Figure 14-13:
Top: The PC wants to make sure you're authorized to visit it. Fortunately, you see this box only the very first time you access a certain Windows folder or disk; after that, you see only the box shown below.

Bottom: Here you see a list of shared folders on the PC. Choose the one you want to connect to, and then click OK. Like magic, the Windows folder shows up on your Mac screen, ready to use!

This button appears in the top-right corner of the Finder window; you can see it at bottom in Figure 14-12. Now you're asked for your name and password (Figure 14-13, top).

5. **Enter the name and password for your account on the PC, and then click OK.**

At long last, the contents of the shared folder on the Windows machine appear in your Finder window, just as though you'd tapped into another Mac (Figure 14-13, bottom). The icon of the shared folder appears on your desktop, too, and an Eject button (⏏) appears next to the PC's name in your Sidebar.

From here, it's a simple matter to drag files between the machines, open Word documents on the PC using Word for the Mac, and so on—exactly like you're hooked into another Mac.

Seated at the PC, Seeing the Mac

Cross-platformers, rejoice: Mac OS X lets you share files in *both directions*. Not only can your Mac see other PCs on the network, but they can see the Mac, too.

TROUBLESHOOTING MOMENT

When the Mac Doesn't See the PC

Are you having trouble getting your PC's icon to show up in your Finder's Sidebar?

Now, you can probably connect to the PC using the Mac's Go→Connect to Server command, but the Sidebar would be a lot more convenient.

And the problem is probably that the Mac doesn't know anything about Windows workgroups.

Even a lowly home PC is part of a workgroup (a corporate cluster), whether it knows it or not. And until your Mac is part of that very tiny club, it won't be able to see your PCs, and they won't be able to see it.

So if you're having no luck with this whole Mac-PC thing, try this. First, find out what your PC thinks its workgroup is. (It's usually either WORKGROUP or MSHOME.) Click Start, and then right-click Computer. From the shortcut menu,

choose Properties. In the resulting info screen, you'll see the workgroup's name.

Now, on the Mac, open System Preferences. Click Network. Click the connection you're using (like WiFi or Ethernet). Click Advanced. Click WINS.

Now you see the peculiar controls shown here. Type the workgroup name into the box (if indeed it's not already a choice in the Workgroup pop-up menu). Click OK, and then click Apply.

Now your Windows PCs show up in the Sidebar, like magic.

Still having trouble? Open System Preferences→Security→Firewall. Make sure your Mac's firewall is either turned off or at least not set to "Block all incoming connections."

On the Mac, open →System Preferences→Sharing. Click File Sharing (make sure File Sharing is turned on), and then click Options to open the dialog box shown in Figure 14-14.

Figure 14-14:
Prepare your Mac for visitation by the Windows PC. It won't hurt a bit. The system-wide On switch for invasion from Windows is the second checkbox shown here, in the System Preferences→Sharing→File Sharing→Options box.

Next, turn on the individual accounts of people you want to allow to connect from the PC. You'll be asked to enter their account passwords, too. Click Done when you're done.

Turn on "Share files and folders using SMB (Windows)." Below that checkbox, you see a list of all the accounts on your Mac. Turn on the checkboxes to specify *which* Mac user accounts you want to be able to access. You must type in each person's password, too. Click Done.

Before you close System Preferences, study the line near the middle of the window, where it says something like: "Other users can access your computer at afp://192.168.1.108 or MacBook-Pro." You'll need one of these addresses shortly.

Now, on **Windows XP,** open My Network Places; in **Windows Vista,** choose Start→Network; in **Windows 7,** expand the Network heading in the sidebar of any desktop window. If you've sacrificed the proper animals to the networking gods, your Mac's icon should appear in the network window, as shown in Figure 14-15, top.

Note: If you *don't* see your Mac here, proceed immediately to the box on the previous page.

Double-click the Mac's icon. Public-folder stuff is available immediately. Otherwise, you have to sign in with your Mac account name and password; Figure 14-15, middle, has the details.

In the final window, you see your actual Home folder—on a Windows PC! You're
ready to open its files, copy them back and forth, or whatever (Figure 14-15, bottom).

Figure 14-15:
*Top: Double-click
the icon of the Mac
you want to visit
from your Windows
machine (Vista is
shown here).*

*Middle: Type your
Mac's NetBIOS
name in all capitals
(or its IP address),
then a backslash,
and then your Mac
account short name.
(You can find out
your Mac's NetBIOS
name—that is, what
Windows calls it—on
the Network pane of
System Preferences.
Click Advanced, then
WINS.)*

*Enter your Mac
account's password,
too. Turn on "Remem-
ber my password" if
you plan to do this
again someday. Click
OK.*

*Bottom: Here's your
Mac Home folder—in
Windows! Open it up
to find all your stuff.*

If your Mac's icon *doesn't* appear, and you've read the box on page 490, wait a minute or two. Try restarting the PC. In Windows XP, try clicking "Microsoft Windows
Network" or "View workgroup computers" in the task pane.

If your Mac still doesn't show up, you'll have to add it the hard way. In the address
bar of any Windows window, type *macbook-pro\chris* (but substitute your Mac's
actual computer name and your short account name), taking care to use backslashes
(\), not normal slashes (/). You can also type your Mac's IP address in place of its
computer name.

In the future, you won't have to do so much burrowing; your Mac's icon should appear automatically in the My Network Places or Network window.

More Mac-Windows Connections

The direct Mac-to-Windows file-sharing feature of Mac OS X is by far the easiest way to access each other's files. But it's not the only way. Chapter 6 offers a long list of other options, from flash drives to Dropbox.

Screen Sharing

Mac OS X has answered the prayers of baffled beginners and exasperated experts everywhere. Now, when a novice needs help from a guru, the guru doesn't have to run all the way downstairs or down the hall to assist. Thanks to Mac OS X's screen-sharing feature, you can see exactly what's on the screen of another Mac, from across the network—and even seize control of the other Mac's mouse and keyboard (with the newbie's permission, of course).

(Anyone who's ever tried to help someone troubleshoot over the phone knows *exactly* how helpful this is. If you haven't, this small example may suffice: "OK, open the Apple menu and choose About This Mac." Pause. "What's the Apple menu?")

Nor is playing Bail-Out-the-Newbie the only situation when screen sharing is useful. It's also great for collaborating on a document, showing something to someone for approval, or just freaking each other out. It can also be handy when *you* are the owner of both Macs (a laptop and a desktop, for example), and you want to run a program that you don't have on the Mac that's in front of you. For example, you might want to adjust the playlist selection on the upstairs Mac that's connected to your sound system.

Or maybe you just want to keep an eye on what your kids are doing on the Macs upstairs in their rooms.

The controlling person can do *everything* on the controlled Mac, including running programs, messing around with the folders and files, and even shutting it down. You can even press keystrokes on *your* Mac—⌘-Tab, ⌘-space, ⌘-Option-Escape, and so on—to trigger the corresponding functions on the *other* Mac.

Mac OS X is crawling with ways to use screen sharing. You can do it over a network, over the Internet, and even during an iChat chat.

Truth is, the iChat method, described in Chapter 12, is much simpler and better than the small-network method described here. It doesn't require names or passwords, it doesn't require the same Mac OS X version on both Macs, it's easy to flip back between seeing the other guy's screen and your own, and you can transfer files by dragging them from your screen to the other guy's (or vice versa).

Then again, the small-network method described here is built right into the Finder and doesn't require logging into iChat.

In Lion, Apple gave screen sharing a serious makeover. It's got loads of new features; for example, you can now log into a distant Mac and control it as though you were logged into your own account—*while somebody else is using it* and seeing a totally different screen! Read on.

Other Mac: Give Permission in Advance

As always, trying to understand meta concepts like seeing one Mac's screen on the monitor of another can get confusing fast. So in this example, suppose that you're seated at Your Mac, and you want to control Other Mac.

Now, it would be a chaotic world if any Mac could randomly take control of any other Mac (although it sure would be fun). Fortunately, though, nobody can share your screen or take control of your Mac without your explicit permission.

To give such permission, sit down at Other Mac. Choose $\bullet$→System Preferences→Sharing, and then turn on Screen Sharing.

At this point, there are three levels of security to protect your Mac against unauthorized remote-control mischief:

- **Secure.** If you select All Users, then *anyone with an account on your Mac* will be able to tap in and take control anytime they like, even when you're not around. They'll just have to enter the same name and password they'd use if they were sitting in front of your machine.

    If "anyone" means "you and your spouse" or "you and the other two fourth-grade teachers," then that's probably perfectly fine.

GEM IN THE ROUGH

Logging In with an Apple ID

In the bad old days, you couldn't share your screen or your files with other people unless you first created full-blown accounts for them on your Mac. You know: a Home folder, Music and Movies folders, and so on. That was an awful lot of disk space sacrificed, just so other people could visit your Mac over the network.

Nowadays, you can create a Sharing Only account for them. They can now share your screen or your files without actually having a presence on your hard drive.

In Lion, there's even a third option: They can exploit your shared screen or shared folders just by logging in with their Apple IDs. This way, you don't even have to set up a name and password for them on your Mac, and they don't have to learn another name and password. They don't have an account on your Mac at all—just an Address Book card.

To set this up, open Address Book. Make sure there's a card

in there for the person who will be visiting your Mac over the network. Make sure, furthermore, that the card includes the email address that person uses as an Apple ID.

Now visit System Preferences→Sharing. Click Screen Sharing. As shown in Figure 14-16, click the **+** sign. In the panel that appears, click Address Book, and double-click the name of the prospective visitor. You're asked to enter a screen-sharing password for this person (twice) and then click Create Account.

The visitor should make sure he's registered his Apple ID in his own account details for System Preferences→Users & Groups.

If so, then the setup is ready. When he attempts to connect to your Mac, he'll be able to use the "Using an Apple ID" option as his credentials. No account on your Mac is necessary!

- **Securer.** For greater security, though, you can limit who's allowed to stop in. Click "Only these users" and then click the **+** sign. A small panel appears, listing everyone with an account on your Mac. Choose the ones you trust not to mess things up while you're away from your Mac (Figure 14-16).

Tip: You can permit people to see your Mac's screen remotely by entering their Apple ID and passwords. That's a lot simpler and less disk space than before, when each person had to have a full-blown *account* on your Mac, complete with Pictures folder, Movies folder, and so on. To set this up, see the handy box on the previous page.

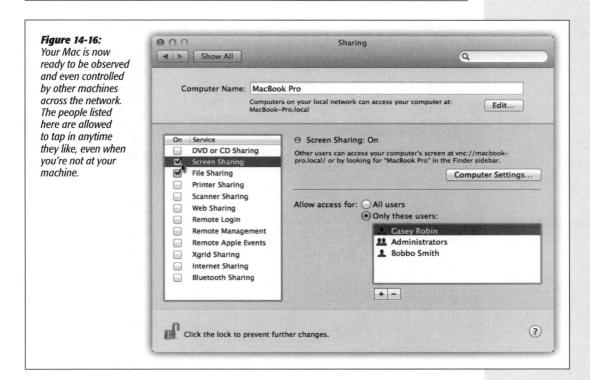

Figure 14-16:
Your Mac is now ready to be observed and even controlled by other machines across the network. The people listed here are allowed to tap in anytime they like, even when you're not at your machine.

- **Securest.** If you click "Only these users" and then don't add *anyone* to the list, then only people who have Administrator accounts on your Mac (page 428) can tap into your screen.

Alternatively, if you're only a *little* bit of a Scrooge, you can set things up so that they can request permission to share your screen—as long as you're sitting in front of your Mac at the time and feeling generous.

To set this up, click Computer Settings and then turn on "Anyone may request permission to share screen." Now your fans will have to request permission to enter, and you'll have to grant it (by clicking OK on the screen), in real time, while you're there to watch what they're doing.

Your Mac: Take Control

All right, Other Mac has been prepared for invasion. Now suppose you're the person on the other end. You're the guru, or the parent, or whoever wants to take control.

Sit at Your Mac elsewhere on your home or office network, and proceed like this:

1. **Open a Finder window. Expand the Shared list in the Sidebar, if necessary, so that you see the icon of Other Mac. Click it.**

   The dark strip at the top of the main window displays a button that wasn't there before: Share Screen (Figure 14-17, top).

Figure 14-17:
Top: Start by clicking Share Screen in the strip at the top of your Mac's window.

Middle: If you've been pre-added to the VIP list of authorized screen sharers, as already described, you can sign in with either your account name and password or your Apple ID. If not, you can request permission to share Other Mac's screen (provided the Mac owner has turned on that option in System Preferences→Sharing→Screen Sharing→Computer Settings). You'll be granted permission only if Other Mac's owner happens to be sitting in front of it at the moment and has opted to accept such requests.

Bottom: If you request permission, the other person (sitting at Other Mac) sees your request like this.

2. **Click Share Screen.**

Now you see the box shown at middle in Figure 14-17. It offers as many as three different ways for you to prove that you're not some East German teenage hacker. "By asking for permission" sends the other Mac's current operator a message asking if it's OK for you to take over.

Most of the time, people choose "As a registered user," meaning, "I have a regular account on the Other Mac."

But the "Using an Apple ID" option lets you enter an Apple ID and password instead, so the Other Mac's owner doesn't have to set up an account for you just so you can use screen sharing or file sharing. See the box on page 494.

Tip: In theory, you can also connect from across the Internet, assuming you left your Mac at home turned on and connected to a broadband modem. (You may also have to turn on a router feature called port forwarding. Let Google be your guide there.)

In this case, though, you'd begin by choosing Go→Connect to Server in the Finder; in the Connect to Server box, type in *vnc://123.456.78.90* (or whatever your home Mac's public IP address is). The rest of the steps are the same.

---

3. **If you have a user account on Other Mac, click "As a registered user" and log in. If your Apple ID will suffice, click "Using an Apple ID" and supply your sharing password.**

Your Mac, of course, *knows* your Apple ID already (because you've entered it in your account screen in System Preferences→User Accounts). It shows up here in the dialog box; all you have to do is enter your password.

4. **Click Connect.**

If you've signed in successfully, or if permission is granted, then you see the dialog box shown in Figure 14-18.

Figure 14-18:
The Mac wants to know if you want to view or control the screen that's in use right now by whoever's using Other Mac—or if you want to use the new "virtual display" option, where you take control of your account on the other Mac without disturbing the totally different activity of whomever is seated there.

If you choose "Connect to a virtual display," then you can use your account on the Other Mac even while somebody else is using her account. Simultaneously. Crazy stuff.

(The only evidence she'll have that you're rooting around behind the scenes is a tiny menu-bar icon that looks like this: ▣.)

Note: If *nobody* is using Other Mac at the moment, then it doesn't matter which option you click. And if you enter the name and password of the person who's already logged in at the Other Mac, then you don't see the dialog box in Figure 14-18. You just jump right into screen sharing, as shown in Figure 14-19.

---

5. **Click either "Ask to share the display" (to see the same thing as the Other Mac person) or "Connect to a virtual display" (to log into a different account and work independently).**

And now a weird and wonderful sight appears. As shown in Figure 14-19, your screen now fills with a *second* screen—from the other Mac. You have full keyboard and mouse control to work with that other machine exactly as though you were sitting in front of it.

Figure 14-19:
Don't be alarmed. You're looking at the Other Mac's desktop in a window on your Mac desktop. You have keyboard and mouse control, and so does the other guy (if he's there); when you're really bored, you can play King of the Cursor. (Note the Screen Sharing toolbar, which has been made visible by choosing View→Show Toolbar.)

Well, maybe not *exactly.* There are a few caveats and options.

- **Mismatched screen sizes.** If the other screen is *smaller* than yours, no big deal. It floats at actual size on your monitor, with room to spare. But if it's the same size as yours or larger, then the other Mac's screen gets shrunk down to fit in a window.

  If you'd prefer to see it at actual size, choose View→Turn Scaling Off. Of course, now you have to *scroll* in the Screen Sharing window to see the whole image.

Tip: Another way to turn scaling on and off is to click the "Fit screen in window" button on the Screen Sharing *toolbar* (shown in Figure 14-19).

- **Full-screen mode.** Screen Sharing is one of the programs that's been visited by the Lion fairy. There it is, in the upper-right corner: the ⬚ button. If you click it, then your view of Other Mac expands to fill your screen, edge to edge; now there's *no sign at all* that you're actually using a different computer.

- **The speed-vs.-blurriness issue.** Remember, you're asking the other Mac to pump its video display across the network—and that takes time. Entire milliseconds, in fact.

  So ordinarily, the Mac uses something called *adaptive quality,* which just means that the screen gets blurry when you scroll, quit a program, or do anything else that creates a sudden change in the picture. You can turn off this feature by choosing View→Full Quality. Now you get full sharpness all the time—but things take longer to scroll, appear, and disappear.

- **Observe Only.** In Observe Only (choose View→Switch to Observe Mode, or click the corresponding toolbar icon), your cursor turns white, and you give up all your typing and clicking powers. In other words, you're playing "look, but don't touch."

  This is a handy option when the person at Other Mac just wants to give you a slideshow or a presentation, or when you just want to watch what he's doing when you're on a troubleshooting hunt, or when he's freaked out by having you move the mouse or type stuff by remote control.

- **Manage the Clipboard.** You can actually *copy and paste* material from the remote-controlled Mac to your own—or the other way—thanks to a freaky little wormhole in the time-space continuum. In the Edit menu, choose Send Clipboard to put what's on *your* Clipboard onto *Other* Mac's Clipboard, or Get Clipboard to copy Other Mac's Clipboard contents onto *your* Clipboard. Breathe slowly and drink plenty of fluids, and your brain won't explode. (There are toolbar-button equivalents, too.)

Note: Unfortunately, there's no way to transfer *files* between Macs while screen sharing—only material you've copied *out* of documents. Use the iChat method described in Chapter 12 if you want to exchange files.

- **Quitting.** When you hit the ⌘-Q keystroke, you *don't* quit Screen Sharing; you quit whatever program is running on the other Mac! So when you're finished having your way with the other computer, choose Screen Sharing→Quit Screen Sharing to return to your own desktop (and your own sanity).

Variations on Screen Sharing

The steps above guide you through screen sharing between two Macs running Mac OS 10.5 or later. But screen sharing is based on a standard technology called VNC, and Mac OS X is bristling with different permutations.

Screen sharing through iChat

Two people who both have Mac OS 10.5 or later can perform exactly the same screen-sharing stunt *over the Internet.* No accounts, passwords, or setup are required—only the granting of permission by the other guy. Just initiate an iChat chat, and then proceed as described on page 419. It's really awesome.

Screen sharing with Back to My Mac

Back to My Mac is intended to simplify the nightmare of remote networking. It works only if:

- You use iCloud.

- You have at least two Macs, both running Mac OS 10.7.2 or later.

- On each one, you've entered your Apple ID into the Users & Groups pane of System Preferences, and logged in.

Once that's all in place, your Macs behave exactly as though they're on the same home network, even though they can be thousands of miles apart across the network.

To set it up, proceed as shown in Figure 14-20.

GEM IN THE ROUGH

Screen Sharing with Windows and Other Machines

The beauty of Apple's screen-sharing technology is that it isn't Apple's screen-sharing technology. It's a popular open standard called VNC (Virtual Network Computing).

Once you've turned on Screen Sharing on your Mac, any computer on earth with a free VNC client program—sort of a viewer program—can pop onto your machine for a screen share. VNC clients are available for Windows, Linux, pre-Leopard Macs, and even some cellphones. (Not all VNC programs work with the Lion version of screen sharing, alas; some require updates.)

To prepare your Mac for invasion, open the Sharing pane of System Preferences. Click Screen Sharing, and then click Computer Settings. Turn on "VNC viewers may control screen with password," and make up a password. (VNC doesn't know anything about Mac OS X account passwords, so you're making up one password for sharing your whole Mac.)

Give that password to the lucky few who have your trust. Let them plug your Mac's public IP address into their VNC clients—or let them connect over your office network, using the address displayed on the Screen Sharing pane (*vnc:// MacBook-Pro,* for example)—and let the sharing begin.

From now on, on your laptop in New Zealand, you see an entry for Back to My Mac in the Sharing section of your Sidebar. Click to see the icon of your Mac back at home. At this point, you can connect to it for file sharing by clicking Connect As or take control of it by clicking Share Screen.

Figure 14-20:
On the first Mac, open System Preferences. Click iCloud, and then turn on Back to My Mac. Close System Preferences. Repeat on each Mac, making sure they all have the same Apple ID account information.

In theory, Back to My Mac spares you an awfully long visit to networking hell (including having to turn on router port forwarding), because Apple has done all the configuration work for you.

In practice, not everyone can get Back to My Mac to work. Apple says the problems are related to firewalls, port-forwarding issues, and router incompatibilities. Apple also says you'll have the best luck on networks that involve only an AirPort base station—and not a hardware router.

All the technical details are available online. Visit *http://support.apple.com/kb/HT1109* to read about the Back to My Mac issues.

SWITCHING TO THE MAC: THE MISSING MANUAL

System Preferences

The hub of Mac customization is System Preferences. That is, it's the equivalent of the Windows Control Panel. Some of its panels are extremely important, because their settings determine whether or not you can connect to a network or go online to exchange email. Others handle the more cosmetic aspects of customizing Mac OS X.

This chapter guides you through the entire System Preferences program, panel by panel.

Tip: Only a system administrator (page 428) can change settings that affect everyone who shares a certain machine: most of its Network settings, Energy Saver settings, and so on. If you see a bunch of controls that are dimmed and unavailable, now you know why.

A tiny 🔒 in the lower-left corner of a panel is the other telltale sign. If you, a nonadministrator, would like to edit some settings, then call an administrator over to your Mac and ask him to click the 🔒, input his password, and supervise your tweaks.

The System Preferences Window

You can open System Preferences in dozens of ways:

- Choose its name from the menu.

- Press Option-volume key (◀, ◀), or ◀)) on the top row of the keyboard), Option-brightness key (☼ or ☀), or, on laptops that have them, Option-keyboard-brightness key (⸬ or ⸬). These tricks open the Sound and Displays panes, but you can then click Show All or press ⌘-L to see the full spread.

- If you know the name of the System Preferences panel you want, it's often quicker to use Spotlight (Chapter 3). To open the iCloud panel, for example, hit ⌘-space, type *iclo,* and then press Return.

- Turns out that if you put the System Preferences icon in your *Dock* (Chapter 2), you can open it *and* jump to a particular preference panel in one smooth move: Use your mouse to click-and-hold the System Preferences icon. You get a pop-up menu of every single System Preferences panel.

Suppose, then, that by hook or by crook, you've figured out how to open System Preferences. You'll notice that, at first, the rows of icons are grouped according to function: Personal, Hardware, and so on (Figure 15-1, bottom). But you can also view them in tidy alphabetical order, as shown at top in Figure 15-1. That can spare you the ritual of hunting through various rows just to find a certain panel icon whose name you

Figure 15-1:
You can view System Preferences icons alphabetically (top), rather than in rows of arbitrary categories (bottom); just choose View→Organize Alphabetically. Non-Apple preference panes appear in a category called Other (bottom).

Super-top-secret trick: The Show All button is actually a pop-up menu. At the bottom of it, there's a command called Customize. It makes checkboxes appear. You can turn off—and hide—hide the icons you never use. (You can still choose their names from the View menu.)

already know. (Quick, without looking: Which row is Date & Time in?) This chapter describes the various panels following this alphabetical arrangement.

Either way, when you click one of the icons, the corresponding controls appear. To access a different preference pane, you have a number of options:

- **Fast:** When System Preferences first opens, the insertion point is blinking in the System Preferences search box. (If the insertion point is *not* blinking there, then press ⌘-F.) Type a few letters of *volume, resolution, wallpaper, wireless,* or whatever feature you want to adjust. In a literal illustration of Spotlight's name, the System Preferences window darkens *except* for the icons where you'll find relevant controls (Figure 15-2). Click the name or icon of the one that looks the most promising.

Figure 15-2:
Even if you don't know which System Preferences panel contains the settings you want to change, Spotlight can help. Type into the box at the top, and watch as the "spotlight" shines on the relevant icons.

- **Faster:** Click the Show All icon in the upper-left corner of the window (or press ⌘-L, a shortcut worth learning). Then click the icon of the new panel you want.

- **Fastest:** Choose any panel's name from the View menu—or from the System Preferences Dock icon pop-up menu described above.

Here, then, is your grand tour of all 29 of the built-in System Preferences panes. (You may have a couple more or fewer, depending on your Mac model and whether you've installed any non-Apple panes.)

Bluetooth

Bluetooth is a short-range, low-power, wireless *cable-elimination* technology. It's designed to connect gadgets in pairings that make sense, like cellphone+earpiece, Mac+wireless keyboard, phone+portable speaker, or Mac+cellphone (for *tethering,* where you connect the Mac to the phone so the laptop can get online).

Now, you wouldn't want the guy in the next cubicle to be able to operate *your* Mac using *his* Bluetooth keyboard. So the first step in any Bluetooth relationship is *pair-*

ing, or formally introducing the two gadgets that will be communicating. Here's how that goes:

1. **Open System Preferences→Bluetooth (Figure 15-3).**

   Make sure the On checkbox is turned on. (The only reason to turn it off is to save laptop battery power.) Also make sure Discoverable is turned on; that makes the Mac "visible" to other Bluetooth gadgets in range.

   If you intend to send a file to another Mac, set up that other machine by visiting System Preferences→Sharing; turn on the Bluetooth Sharing checkbox.

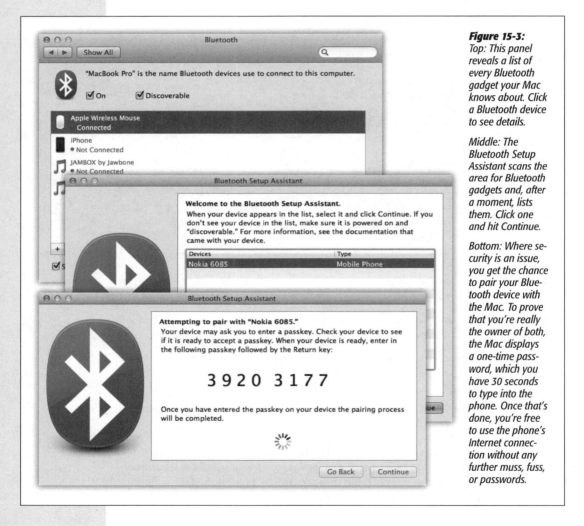

Figure 15-3:
Top: This panel reveals a list of every Bluetooth gadget your Mac knows about. Click a Bluetooth device to see details.

Middle: The Bluetooth Setup Assistant scans the area for Bluetooth gadgets and, after a moment, lists them. Click one and hit Continue.

Bottom: Where security is an issue, you get the chance to pair your Bluetooth device with the Mac. To prove that you're really the owner of both, the Mac displays a one-time password, which you have 30 seconds to type into the phone. Once that's done, you're free to use the phone's Internet connection without any further muss, fuss, or passwords.

2. **Click the + button below the list at left (or Set Up New Device, if you've never done this before).**

   The Bluetooth Setup Assistant opens. After a moment, it displays the names of all Bluetooth gadgets it can sniff out: nearby headsets, laptops, cellphones, and so on. Usually, it finds the one you're trying to pair.

3. **Click the gadget you want to connect to, and then click Continue.**

   If you're pairing a mobile phone or something else that has a keypad or keyboard, the Mac now displays a large, multiple-digit *passcode*. It's like a password, except you'll have to input it only this once, to confirm that *you* are the true owner of both the Mac and the gadget. (If it weren't for this passcode business, some guy next to you at the airport could enjoy free laptop Internet access through the cellphone in *your* pocket.)

   At this point, the phone, computer, or palmtop displays a message to the effect that you have 30 seconds to type that passcode. Do it. When the gadget asks if you want to pair with the Mac and connect to it, say yes. (If you're pairing one Mac with another, just click Continue on both machines; you *see* the same passcode on both but don't have to type it.)

When it's all over, click Done on the Mac that will do the sending. The new gadget is listed in the left-side panel, in the list of Bluetooth cellphones, headsets, and other stuff that you've previously introduced to this Mac.

CDs & DVDs

This handy pane is Apple's version of the Autoplay control panel in Windows. As shown in Figure 15-4, it lets you tell the Mac what it should do when it detects that you've inserted a CD or DVD. For example, when you insert a music CD, you probably want iTunes to open automatically so you can listen to the songs or convert them to MP3 or AAC files on your hard drive. Similarly, when you insert a picture CD (such as a Kodak Photo CD), you probably want iPhoto to open in readiness to import the

Figure 15-4:
You can tell the Mac exactly which program to launch when you insert each kind of disc, or tell it to do nothing at all.

pictures into your photo collection. And when you insert a DVD from Blockbuster, you probably want the Mac's DVD Player program to open.

For each kind of disc (blank CD, blank DVD, music CD, picture CD, or video DVD), the pop-up menu lets you choose options like these:

- **Ask what to do.** A dialog box appears that asks what you want to do with the newly inserted disc.

- **Open (iDVD, iTunes, iPhoto, DVD Player...).** The Mac can open a certain program automatically when you insert the disc. When the day comes that somebody writes a better music player than iTunes, or a better digital shoebox than iPhoto, then you can use the "Open other application" option.

- **Ignore.** The Mac won't do anything when you insert a disc except display its icon on the desktop. (If it's a blank disc, the Mac does nothing at all.)

Date & Time

Your Mac's conception of what time it is can be very important. Every file you create, save, or even open is stamped with this time, and every email you send or receive is marked with it. As you might expect, setting your Mac's clock is what the Date & Time pane is all about.

Date & Time Tab

Click the Date & Time tab. If your Mac is online, turn on "Set date & time automatically" and be done with it. Your Mac sets its own clock by consulting a scientific clock on the Internet. (No need to worry about daylight saving time, either; the time servers take that into account.)

If you're not online and have no prospect of getting there, you can also set the date and time manually. To change the month, day, or year, click the digit that needs changing and then either (a) type a new number, (b) press the ↑ or ↓ keys, or (c) click the little arrow buttons. Press the Tab key to highlight the next number. (You can also specify the day of the month by clicking a date on the minicalendar.)

To set the time of day, use the same technique—or, for more geeky fun, you can set the time by dragging the hour, minute, or second hands on the analog clock.

Finally, click Save. (If you get carried away with dragging the clock hands around and lose track of the *real* time, click the Revert button to restore the panel settings.)

Tip: If you prefer seeing 24-hour "military time" notation on your menu bar (that is, *17:30* instead of *5:30 p.m.*)—click the Clock tab and turn on "Use a 24-hour clock."

Note, however, that this affects only the menu bar clock. If you'd like to reformat the menu bar clock *and* all other dates (like the ones that show when your files were modified in list views), click the Open Language & Text button at the bottom of the Date & Time pane. Once there, click the Formats tab. There you'll see a Customize button for Times, which leads you to a whole new world of time-format customization.

Time Zone Tab

You'd be surprised how important it is to set the time zone for your Mac. If you don't do so, the email and documents you send out—and the Mac's conception of what documents are older and newer—could be hopelessly skewed.

Mac OS X can set its own time zone *automatically.* That's an especially useful feature if you're a laptop warrior who travels a lot.

Just turn on "Set time zone automatically using current location" (Figure 15-5). If possible, the Mac will think for a moment and then, before your eyes, drop a pin onto the world map to represent your location—and set the time zone automatically. (The world map dims to show that you can no longer set your location manually.)

Often, you'll be told that the Mac is "Unable to determine current location at this time." In that case, specify your location manually, as shown in Figure 15-5.

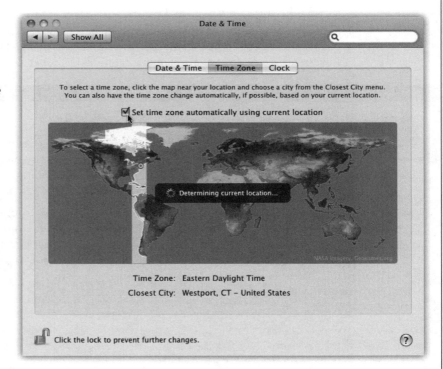

Figure 15-5:
To set your time zone the quick and dirty way, click a section of the map to indicate your general region of the world. To teach the Mac more precisely where you are in that time zone, use the Closest City pop-up menu. (Or, instead of using the pop-up menu with the mouse, you can also highlight the text in the Closest City box. Then start typing your city name until the Mac gets it.)

Clock Tab

In the Clock pane, you can turn the menu-bar clock on or off. You can choose between two different clock styles: digital (3:53 p.m.) or analog (a round clock face). You also get several other options for the digital clock display: whether to show seconds, designations for a.m. and p.m., the day of the week, a blinking colon, and a 24-hour clock.

If you decide you don't need all that information—if your menu bar is crowded enough as it is—you can always look up today's day and date just by *clicking* the time on your menu bar. A menu drops down revealing the complete date. The menu also lets you switch between digital and analog clock types and provides a shortcut to the Date & Time Preferences pane.

Desktop & Screen Saver

This panel offers two ways to show off Mac OS X's glamorous graphics features: *desktop pictures* and *screen savers*.

Desktop Pictures

Mac OS X Lion comes with an expanded collection of desktop pictures, ranging from *National Geographic*–style nature photos to plain solid colors. To install a new background picture, first choose one of the image categories in the list at the left side of the window, as shown in Figure 15-6.

Your choices include Desktop Pictures (muted, soft-focus swishes and swirls and a couple of nature shots); Nature (bugs, water, outer space); Plants (flowers, soft-focus leaves); Art (a new collection of famous paintings by Monet, Dégas, Seurat, and other

---

FREQUENTLY ASKED QUESTION

How the Mac Knows Where You Are

OK, I'll bite. To set my time zone automatically, the Mac has to know where I am. It doesn't have GPS. So how does it do that?

Metropolitan areas today are blanketed by overlapping WiFi signals. At a typical Manhattan intersection, you might be in range of 20 base stations. Each one broadcasts its own name and unique network address (its MAC address—nothing to do with Mac computers) once every second. Although you'd need to be within 150 feet or so to actually get onto the Internet, a laptop or phone can detect this beacon signal from up to 1,500 feet away.

A company called Skyhook had a huge idea: Suppose you could correlate all those beacon signals with their physical locations. Why, you'd be able to simulate GPS—without the GPS!

And so, since 2004, 500 full-time Skyhook employees have been driving every road, lane, and highway in major cities

around the world, measuring all those WiFi signals, noting their network addresses and locations. (Neither these vans nor the Mac ever has to connect to these base stations. They're just reading the one-way beacon signals.)

So far, Skyhook's database knows 50 million hot spots—and the precise longitude and latitude of each. The company licenses this information to companies, like Apple, that want to build location services into their gadgets.

To figure out where it is, the Mac sniffs around for WiFi base stations. If it finds any, it transmits their IDs back to Skyhook, which looks up those network addresses—and sends coordinates back to the Mac over the Internet.

That accuracy is good only to within 100 feet at best, and of course the Skyhook system fails completely once you're out of populated areas—or whenever your Mac doesn't have WiFi or an Internet connection. On the other hand, it works fast, and it works indoors, which GPS definitely doesn't.

---

canvas superheroes); Black & White (breathtaking monochrome shots); Abstract (swishes and swirls with wild colors); Patterns (a pair of fabric closeups); and Solid Colors (simple grays, blues, and greens).

Figure 15-6:
Using the list of picture sources at left, you can preview an entire folder of your own images before installing one as your new desktop picture. Use the + button to select a folder of assorted graphics—or, if you're an iPhoto veteran, click an iPhoto album name, as shown here. Clicking one of the thumbnails installs the corresponding picture on the desktop.

Using your own pictures

Of course, you may feel that decorating your Mac desktop is much more fun if you use one of your *own* pictures. You can use almost any graphics file: JPEG, GIF, TIFF, Photoshop, and even PDF. (Guess you could use the PDF option to help teach yourself your camera's user guide by staring at your desktop every morning.)

That's why icons for your own Pictures folder and iPhoto albums also appear here, along with a + button that lets you choose *any* folder of pictures. When you click one of these icons, you see thumbnail versions of its contents in the main screen to its right. Just click the thumbnail of any picture to apply it immediately to the desktop. (There's no need to remove the previously installed picture first.)

Making the picture fit

No matter which source you use to choose a photo of your own, you have one more issue to deal with. Unless you've gone to the trouble of editing your chosen photo so that it matches the precise dimensions of your screen (1280 × 800 pixels, for example), it probably isn't exactly the right size.

Fortunately, Mac OS X offers a number of solutions to this problem. Using the pop-up menu just to the right of the desktop preview well, you can choose options like Fill Screen (enlarges or reduces the image so that it fills every inch of the desktop without distortion, even if parts are chopped off) and Fit to Screen (photo appears as large as possible without distortion *or* cropping, but "letterbox bars" may appear).

Auto picture changing

The novelty of any desktop picture, no matter how interesting, is likely to fade after several months of all-day viewing. That's why the randomizing function is so delightful.

Turn on "Change picture" at the bottom of the dialog box. From the pop-up menu, specify when you want your background picture to change: "every day," "every 15 minutes," or, if you're *really* having trouble staying awake at your Mac, "every 5 seconds." (The option called "when waking from sleep" refers to the *Mac* waking from sleep, not you.)

Finally, turn on "Random order," if you like. If you leave it off, your desktop pictures change in alphabetical order by file name.

Now, at the interval you specified, your desktop picture changes automatically, smoothly cross-fading between the pictures like a slideshow. You may never want to open another window, because you'll hate to block your view of the show.

Screen Saver

On the Screen Saver panel, you can create your own screen-saver slideshows—an absolute must if you have an Apple Thunderbolt Display and a cool Manhattan loft apartment.

When you click a module's name in the Screen Saver list, you see a mini version of it playing back in the Preview screen. Click Test to give the module a dry run on your full screen. When you've had enough of the preview, just move the mouse or press any key. You return to the Screen Saver panel.

Apple provides a few displays to get you started, in two categories: Apple and Pictures. Click one to see a sample.

Tip: You can also create a screen saver from any *folder* full of photos on your hard drive. Click the **+** button and choose Add Folder of Pictures. The folder you select turns into a self-playing slideshow, complete with spectacular zooming and dissolving effects.

Now, no matter which pile of photos you choose for your slideshow screen saver, you can then choose from three presentation styles. They're represented by the three Display Style buttons just below the screen-saver preview:

- **Slideshow** displays one photo at a time; they slowly zoom and cut into each other.

- **Collage** sends individual photos spinning randomly onto the "table," where they lie until the screen is full.

- **Mosaic** will blow your mind; see Figure 15-7.

Tip: Click the Options button to specify the speed of the receding, the number of photos that become pixels of the larger photo, and whether or not you want the composite photos to appear in random order.

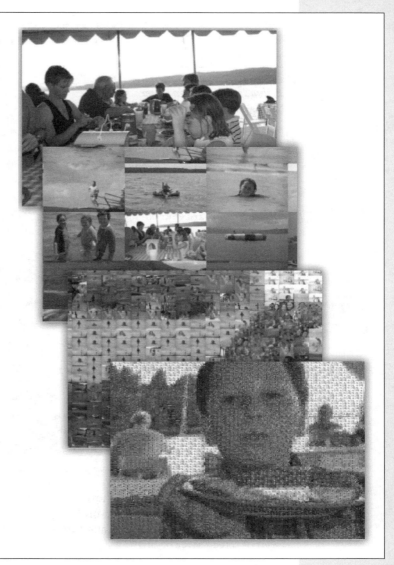

Figure 15-7:
This feeble four-frame sample will have to represent, on this frozen page, the stunning animated pullout that is the Mosaic screen saver.

It starts with one photo (top); your "camera" pulls back farther and farther, revealing that the photo is just one in a grid—a huge grid—composed of all your photos.

As you pull even farther back, each photo appears so small that it becomes only one dot of another photo—from the same collection!

And then that one starts shrinking, and the cycle repeats, on and on into infinity.

Whichever screen-saver module you use, you have two further options:

• **Use random screen saver.** If you can't decide which one of the modules to use, turn on this checkbox. The Mac chooses a different module each time your screen saver kicks in.

• **Show with clock.** This option just superimposes the current time on whatever screen saver you've selected. You'd be surprised at how handy it can be to use your Mac as a giant digital clock when you're getting coffee across the room.

Tip: You can find dozens more screen-saver modules from Apple. To look them over, click the **+** button below the list; choose Browse Screen Savers. You're taken to a Web page where you can choose from a selection of amazing add-on screen-saver modules.

Activating the screen saver

You can control when your screen saver takes over your monitor in a couple of ways:

• **After a period of inactivity.** Using the "Start screen saver" slider, you can set the amount of time that has to pass without keyboard or mouse activity before the screen saver starts. The duration can be as short as 3 minutes or as long as 2 hours, or you can drag the slider to Never to prevent the screen saver from ever turning on by itself.

• **When you park your cursor in the corner of the screen.** If you click the Hot Corners button, you can turn each corner of your monitor into a *hot corner* (Figure 15-8).

Figure 15-8:
Click the Hot Corners button to open this sheet, which lets you designate certain corners of your screen as instant-activation spots, or never-come-on spots. Sliding the mouse to the Start Screen Saver corner, for example, turns on your screen saver right away.

If you work in a business, or in a nosy family, it might be worth noting here that you can set things up so that your password is required to exit the screensaver. Visit System Preferences→Security & Privacy, and turn on "Require password immediately after sleep or screen saver begins."

Displays

Displays is the center of operations for all your monitor settings. Here you set your monitor's *resolution*, determine how many colors are displayed onscreen, and calibrate color balance and brightness.

Tip: You can open up this panel with a quick keystroke from any program on the Mac. Just press Option as you tap one of the screen-brightness keys on the top row of your keyboard.

The specific controls depend on the kind of monitor you're using, but here are the ones you'll most likely see:

Display Tab

This tab is the main headquarters for your screen controls. It governs these settings:

- **Resolutions.** All Mac screens today can make the screen picture larger or smaller, thus accommodating different kinds of work. You perform this magnification or reduction by switching among different *resolutions* (measurements of the number of dots that compose the screen). The Resolutions list displays the various resolution settings your monitor can accommodate: 800 × 600, 1024 × 768, and so on.

  When you use a low-resolution setting, such as 800 × 600, the dots of your screen image get larger, thus enlarging (zooming in on) the picture—but showing a smaller slice of the page. Use this setting when playing a small Web movie, for example, so that it fills more of the screen. (Lower resolutions usually look blurry on flat-panel screens, though.) At higher resolutions, such as 1280 × 800, the screen dots get smaller, making your windows and icons smaller, but showing more overall area. Use this kind of setting when working on two-page spreads in your page-layout program, for example.

Tip: You can adjust the resolution of your monitor without having to open System Preferences. Just turn on "Show displays in menu bar," which adds a Displays pop-up menu (a *menulet*) to the right end of your menu bar for quick adjustments. (If you choose Number of Recent Items—did Apple really mean for this command to say that?—then you can adjust how *many* common resolutions are listed in this menulet.)

- **Brightness.** This slider let you make the screen look good in the prevailing lighting conditions. Of course, most Apple keyboards have brightness-adjustment *keys,* so this software control is included just for the sake of completeness.

- **Automatically adjust brightness.** This option appears only if you have a Mac laptop with a light-up keyboard. In that case, your laptop's light sensor also dims the screen automatically in dark rooms—*if* this checkbox is turned on. (Of course, you can always adjust the keyboard lighting manually, by tapping the ·∴· and ·∵· keys.)

Arrangement Tab

From the dawn of the color-monitor era, Macs have had a terrific feature: the ability to exploit multiple monitors all plugged into the computer at the same time. Any Mac with a video-output jack (laptops, iMacs), or any Mac with a second or third video card (Mac Pros) can project the same thing on both screens (*mirror mode*); that's useful in a classroom when the "external monitor" is a projector.

Tip: The standard video card in a Mac Pro has jacks for two monitors. By installing more video cards, you can get up to *six* monitors going at once.

But it's equally useful to make one monitor act as an *extension* of the next. For example, you might have your Photoshop image window on your big monitor but keep all the Photoshop controls and tool palettes on a smaller screen. Your cursor passes from one screen to another as it crosses the boundary. To set this up, just hook up the monitor or projector and then choose Detect Displays from the Displays *menulet*.

When you open System Preferences, you see a different Displays window on each screen, so that you can change the color and resolution settings independently for each. Your Displays menulet shows two sets of resolutions, too—one for each screen.

If your Mac can show different images on each screen, then your Displays panel offers an Arrangement tab, showing a miniature version of each monitor. By dragging these icons around relative to each other, you can specify how you want the second monitor's image "attached" to the first. Most people position the second monitor's image to the right of the first, but you're also free to position it on the left, above, below, or even directly on top of the first monitor's icon (the last of which produces a video-mirroring setup). For the least likelihood of going insane, consider placing the real-world monitor into the same position.

For committed multiple-monitor fanatics, the fun doesn't stop there. See the microscopic menu bar on the first-monitor icon? You can drag that tiny strip onto a different monitor icon, if you like, to tell Displays where you'd like your menu bar to appear. (And check out how most screen savers correctly show different stuff on each monitor!)

Color Tab

This pane offers a list of *color profiles* for your monitor (or, if you turn off "Show profiles for this display only," for *all* monitors). Each profile represents colors slightly differently—a big deal for designers and photo types.

When you click Calibrate, the Display Calibrator Assistant opens to walk you through a series of six screens, presenting various brightness and color-balance settings in each screen. You pick the settings that look best to you; at the end of the process, you save your monitor tweaks as a ColorSync profile, which your Mac uses to adjust the screen for improved color accuracy.

Dock

See Chapter 2 for details on the Dock and its System Preferences pane.

Energy Saver

The Energy Saver program helps you and your Mac in a number of ways. By blacking out the screen after a period of inactivity, it prolongs the life of your monitor. By putting the Mac to sleep after you've stopped using it, Energy Saver cuts down on electricity costs and pollution. On a laptop, Energy Saver extends the length of the battery charge by controlling the activity of the hard drive and screen.

Best of all, this pane offers the option to have your computer turn off each night automatically—and turn on again at a specified time in anticipation of your arrival at the desk.

Sleep Sliders

The Energy Saver controls are different on a laptop Mac and a desktop Mac, but both present a pair of sliders (Figure 15-9).

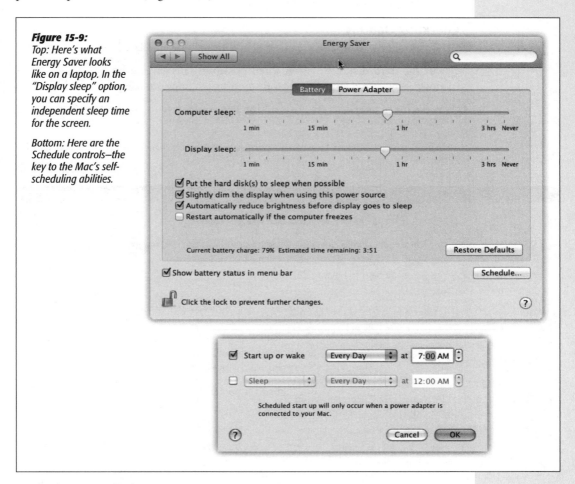

Figure 15-9:
Top: Here's what Energy Saver looks like on a laptop. In the "Display sleep" option, you can specify an independent sleep time for the screen.

Bottom: Here are the Schedule controls—the key to the Mac's self-scheduling abilities.

The top slider controls when the Mac will automatically go to sleep—anywhere from 1 minute after your last activity to Never. (Activity can be mouse movement, keyboard action, or Internet data transfer; Energy Saver won't put your Mac to sleep in the middle of a download.)

At that time, the screen goes dark, the hard drive stops spinning, and your processor chip slows to a crawl. Your Mac is now in *sleep* mode, using only a fraction of its usual electricity consumption. To wake it up when you return to your desk, press any key. Everything you were working on, including open programs and documents, is still onscreen, exactly as it was. (To turn off this automatic sleep feature entirely, drag the slider to Never.)

The second slider controls when the *screen* goes black to save power. Yes, you can make the screen go to sleep independently of the Mac itself, although there's no screamingly obvious reason why you'd want to do that.

Checkbox Options

Below the sliders, you see a selection of additional power-related options:

- **Put the hard disk(s) to sleep when possible.** This saves even more juice—and noise—by letting your drives stop spinning when not in use.

- **Wake for network access.** This option lets you access a sleeping Mac from across the network.

- **Allow power button to put the computer to sleep.** On desktop Macs, it can be handy to sleep the Mac just by tapping its ⏻ button.

GEM IN THE ROUGH

Mysteries of the Battery Menulet

If you've got a laptop, don't miss the checkbox in Energy Saver called "Show battery status in the menu bar." It puts a handy status indicator in the menu bar (⊂⊃) that keeps you informed of your battery's life.

When used as a menu, this menulet lets you choose to display the actual number of minutes left until a battery is depleted, the percentage of battery life that remains, or a visual emptying-battery icon.

If you've opted to view the numeric version, you may notice that sometimes the number, or the percentage, is in parentheses, like this: (1:25). That's your signal that the laptop is plugged in and charging; you're seeing the number of minutes left until the battery is fully recharged (or the percentage of full charge you've achieved so far). Either way, the readout is counting down (or up) to that joyous moment.

If you're seeing only the battery icon (no text) in the menu bar, here's what the readouts mean:

Power cord in the battery. The laptop is plugged in, and the battery is 100 percent charged. Ready to roll, Captain!

Lightning bolt in the battery. The laptop is plugged in, but the battery is still charging.

Superimposed X. The laptop is plugged in, but the battery isn't in right, it's missing, or it isn't getting a charge for some other reason.

Emptying black battery. The laptop is running off of battery power and has at least 25 percent power left. (The width of the bar reveals how much charge is left.)

Emptying red battery. You're running off of battery power, and you have less than 25 percent charge remaining.

A nearly invisible red bar means you have less than 9 minutes left. Save those documents, buddy.

(Bonus tip: If you Option-click the menulet, you see a health report for your battery. It might say, for example, "Condition: Normal." When the condition needs your attention—when it says "Service Battery," "Replace Soon," "Replace Now," or "Check Battery," you don't have to press Option. You'll see that message every time you open the menulet.)

- **Restart automatically if the computer freezes.** This option is handy if you leave your Mac unattended and access it remotely, or if you use it as a network file server or Web server. It ensures that, if your lonely Mac seizes up or crashes, it will start itself right back up again. (On a laptop, it's available only when you're adjusting Power Adapter mode.)

Tip: If you also turn on (or leave on) "Restore windows when quitting and re-opening apps" in System Preferences→General, then your Mac will both restart *and* restore everything you were doing. You may, in fact, never even realize that a crash or freeze occurred while you were away! (The telltale sign: Any Web pages you had to log into, like a banking Web site, will have logged you out.)

- **Slightly dim the display when using this power source.** You see this checkbox only on the Battery tab for a laptop. It means "Don't use full brightness, so I can save power."

Tip: And when your laptop is plugged in, the sudden dimming of the screen becomes a handy signal that you've lost power. Maybe your power cord needs replugging, the power strip went out, or there's a massive blackout in your half of the country.

- **Automatically reduce the brightness of the display before display sleep.** When this option is on, the screen doesn't just go black suddenly after the designated period of inactivity; instead, it goes to half brightness as a sort of drowsy mode that lets you know full sleep is coming soon.
- **Show battery status in the menu bar.** This on/off switch (laptops only) controls the battery menulet described in the box below.

Note: On a laptop, notice the two tabs at the top of the dialog box. They let you create different settings for the two states of life for a laptop: when it's plugged in (Power Adapter) and when it's running on battery power (Battery). That's important, because on a laptop, every drop of battery power counts.

Scheduled Startup and Shutdown

By clicking the Schedule button, you can set up the Mac to shut itself down and turn itself back on automatically (Figure 15-9, bottom).

If you work 9 to 5, for example, you can set the office Mac to turn itself on at 8:45 a.m. and shut itself down at 5:30 p.m.—an arrangement that conserves electricity, saves money, and reduces pollution, but doesn't inconvenience you in the least. In fact, you may come to forget that you've set up the Mac this way, since you'll never actually see it turn itself off.

Note: The Mac doesn't shut down automatically if you've left unsaved documents open onscreen. It will go to sleep, though.

General

This panel is mostly about how things look on the screen: windows, menus, buttons, scroll bars, and fonts. (It used to be called Appearance, but "General" is more like—yes, you guessed it—the iPhone and iPad.) Nothing you find here lets you perform any *radical* surgery on the overall Mac OS X look—but you can tweak certain settings to match your personal style.

Changing Colors

Two pop-up menus let you crank up or tone down Mac OS X's overall colorfulness:

- **Appearance.** Choose between Blue and Graphite. Blue refers to Mac OS X's factory setting—bright, candy-colored progress bars, ￼ menu, and pulsing OK buttons—and those shiny red, yellow, and green buttons in the corner of every window. If you, like some graphics professionals, find all this circus-poster coloring a bit distracting, then choose Graphite, which renders all those interface elements in various shades of gray.

- **Highlight color.** When you drag your cursor across text, its background changes color to indicate that you've selected it. Exactly what color the background becomes is up to you—just choose the shade you want using the pop-up menu. The Highlight color also affects such subtleties as the lines on the inside of a window as you drag an icon into it.

If you choose Other, the Color Picker palette appears, from which you can choose any color your Mac is capable of displaying.

Tweaking the Scroll Bars

These options control the scroll bars of all your windows—including the controversial *removal* of scroll bars in Lion.

- **Show scroll bars.** If you choose "Automatically based on input device," then Mac OS X makes the scroll bars appear or not based on what you have plugged in.

  If you have a multitouch trackpad or a Magic Mouse, for example, Apple assumes that you'll learn to scroll by dragging your fingers—so it figures you won't be needing the scroll bars at the edges of the windows. Therefore, the scroll bars appear only when you're actually scrolling (and then only to show you where you are in the window).

  But if you have no way of using touch gestures—for example, if you have a regular mouse or Apple's own Mighty Mouse—then scrollbars are always visible, so you don't freak out.

- **Click the scroll bar to.** For details on "Jump to the next page" and "Jump to the spot that's clicked," see page 42.

- **Use smooth scrolling.** This option affects only one tiny situation: when you click (or hold the cursor down) inside the empty area of the scroll bar (not on the handle, and not on the arrow buttons). And it makes only one tiny change: Instead of jumping abruptly from screen to screen, the window lurches with slight accelerations and decelerations, so that the paragraph you're eyeing never jumps suddenly out of view.

- **Double-click a window's title bar to minimize.** This option provides another way to minimize a window. In addition to the tiny yellow minimize button at the upper-left corner of the window, you now have a much bigger target—the entire title bar.

Number of Recent Items

Just how many of your recently opened documents and applications do you want the Mac to show using the Recent Items command in the menu? Pick a number from the pop-up menus. For example, you might choose 30 for documents, 20 for programs, and 5 for servers.

Restore Windows when Quitting and Reopening Apps

Here it is: the master on/off switch for the Lion feature responsible for reopening your last-used documents and windows each time you open a window. Usually, this feature saves you time and helps you resume your mental flow—but if you find it disturbing (or you're worried about someone else discovering what you're up to), you can turn it off here.

Use LCD Font Smoothing when Available

The Mac's built-in text-smoothing (*antialiasing*) feature is supposed to produce smoother, more commercial-looking text anywhere it appears on your Mac: in word processing documents, email messages, Web pages, and so on. (See Figure 15-10.) This one has no effect until the next time you open the program in question.

Figure 15-10:
The same 24-point type with text smoothing turned on (top) and off, shown magnified for your inspection pleasure. You don't get a choice of degrees of smoothing—it's just on or off.

Smoothing is turned on.

Smoothing is turned off.

iCloud

This pane is, of course, the master setup page for Apple's free iCloud synchronization service (Chapter 10).

Keyboard

The changes you make on this panel are tiny but can have a cumulatively big impact on your daily typing routine. The options have been organized on two panes: Keyboard and Keyboard Shortcuts.

Keyboard

On this pane, you have these choices:

- **Key Repeat Rate, Delay Until Repeat.** In Lion, holding down letter and number keys no longer makes them repeat, much to the disappointment of people who like to type, for example, "AAAAAARRRRRGGGGHHH!" Instead, holding down a key produces a palette of alternative accented versions of that letter, like é, è, ê, ë, and so on.

  Only the punctuation keys still repeat, so at least you can still type ****** or ????? or !!!!!!!.

  There are sneaky ways to make your regular keys repeat, as they did in days gone by; see page 187. In the meantime, these two sliders govern the repeating behavior of the punctuation keys. On the right: a slider that determines how long you must hold down a key before it starts repeating (to prevent triggering repetitions accidentally). On the left: a slider that governs how fast each key spits out characters once the spitting has begun.

- **Use all F1, F2, etc. keys as standard function keys.** This option appears *only* on laptops and aluminum-keyboard Macs. It's complicated, so read page 157 slowly.

- **Automatically illuminate keyboard in low light.** This setting appears only if your Mac's keyboard does, in fact, light up when you're working in the dark—a showy feature of many Mac laptops. You can specify that you want the internal lighting to shut off after a period of inactivity (to save power when you've wandered away, for example), or you can turn the lighting off altogether. (You can always adjust the keyboard brightness manually, of course, by tapping the ·:· and ·:· keys.)

- **Show Keyboard & Character Viewer in menu bar.** You can read all about these special symbol-generating windows on page 189. For years, the on/off switch for these handy tools has been buried in the International pane of System Preferences; now there's a duplicate on/off switch here, for your convenience.

- **Modifier Keys.** This button lets you turn off, or remap, the functions of the Option, Caps Lock, Control, and ⌘ keys. It's for Unix programmers whose pinkies can't adjust to the Mac's modifier-key layout; for anyone using a PC keyboard on which the Option (Alt) and ⌘ (Windows) keys are in the "wrong" positions relative to each other; and for anyone who keeps hitting Caps Lock by accident during everyday typing.

Keyboard Shortcuts

This pane lets you make up new keystrokes for just about any function on the Mac, like capturing a screenshot, operating the Dock, triggering one of the Services, or operating a menu in *any program* from the keyboard. You can come up with keyboard combinations that, for example, are easier to remember, harder to trigger by accident, or easier to hit with one hand.

Step-by-step instructions for using this pane appear on page 168.

Language & Text

The primary job of this pane is to set up your Mac to work in other languages. If you bought your Mac with a *localized* operating system—a version that already runs in your own language—and you're already using the only language, number format, and keyboard layout you'll ever need, then you can ignore most of this panel. But when it comes to showing off Mac OS X to your friends and loved ones, the "wow" factor on the Mac's polyglot features is huge.

Details appear on page 187.

Mail, Contacts & Calendars

This System Preferences pane is identical to the one in the iPhone and iPad. It's a single, handy, central place to set up your email, calendar, and address-book accounts (Gmail, Yahoo, Exchange, and so on).

To get started entering your account names and passwords, click one of the big-name logos (Gmail, Yahoo, whatever)—or click the **+** button below the list. Lion is smart enough to feed the account information here into the right programs (Mail, iCal, Address Book).

Mission Control

Mission Control, the Lion joint venture of the Exposé, Spaces, and Dashboard window-management features, is described in detail in Chapter 4—and so is this joint-venture control panel.

MobileMe

For details on the old MobileMe service—and the System Preferences pane that governed it—see the free downloadable PDF appendix "MobileMe" from this book's "Missing CD" page at *www.missingmanuals.com*.

Mouse

This pane looks different depending on what kind of mouse (if any) is attached to your Mac.

Tracking Speed, Double-Click Speed

It may surprise you that the cursor on the screen doesn't move 5 inches when you move the mouse 5 inches on the desk. Instead, the cursor moves farther when you move the mouse faster.

How *much* farther depends on how you set the first slider here. The Fast setting is nice if you have an enormous monitor, since you don't need an equally large mouse pad to get from one corner to another. The Slow setting, on the other hand, forces you to pick up and put down the mouse frequently as you scoot across the screen. It offers very little acceleration, but it can be great for highly detailed work like pixel-by-pixel editing in Photoshop.

The Double-Click Speed setting specifies how much time you have to complete a double-click. If you click too slowly—beyond the time you've allotted yourself with this slider—the Mac "hears" two *single* clicks instead.

Note: On a laptop without any mouse attached, the Mouse pane still appears in System Preferences—but its sole function is to help you "pair" your Mac with a wireless Bluetooth mouse. At that point, the Mouse pane looks just as it does on a desktop Mac.

The Mighty Mouse and Magic Mouse

Just by looking, you'd never know that these Apple mice have both a right button and a left button. Once you turn on the two-button feature in System Preferences (Figure 15-11), though, each side clicks independently.

The Magic Mouse is especially useful in Lion. Its unusually flat, broad top surface is also a trackpad. You can drag your finger across its surface to trigger many of Lion's trackpad gestures.

The Mighty Mouse is the white mouse that has come with desktop Macs since 2005.

Figure 15-11:
This enormous photographic display shows up if you have the Magic Mouse, one of Apple's secretly "two-button" mouse. The controls here let you program the right and left buttons.

This is also where you can turn the right-clicking feature on (just choose Secondary Button from the appropriate pop-up menu)—or swap the right- and left-click buttons' functions.

Tip: If you have a real mouse attached, you also see the "Zoom using scroll wheel while holding Control" checkbox at the bottom of this pane. What this means is that you can magnify the *entire* screen, zooming in, by turning the little ball or wheel atop your mouse while you press the Control key. It's great for reading tiny type, examining photos up close, and so on.

Network

See Chapter 14 for the settings you need to plug in for networking.

Parental Controls

These controls are described at length in Chapter 13.

Print & Scan

Chapter 9 describes printing and scanning. This panel offers a centralized list of the printers, scanners, and fax modems you've introduced to the Mac.

Security & Privacy

See Chapter 13 for details on locking up your Mac.

Sharing

Mac OS X is an outstanding, upstanding network citizen, flexible enough to share its contents with other Macs, Windows PCs, people dialing in from the road, and so on. On this panel, you'll find on/off switches for each of these sharing channels.

In this book, many of these features are covered in other chapters. For example, **Screen Sharing** and **File Sharing** are in Chapter 14; **Printer Sharing** and **Scanner Sharing** are Chapter 9; and **Internet Sharing** is in Chapter 10.

Here's a quick rundown on the other items:

- **DVD or CD Sharing.** This feature was added to accommodate Macs that don't have built-in CD/DVD drives, like MacBook Airs and some Mac Minis. When you turn on this option, such driveless computers on the network can "see," and borrow, your Mac's DVD drive for the purposes of installing new software or running Mac disk-repair software. (Your drive shows up under the Remote Disc heading in the driveless Mac's Finder Sidebar.)

- **Remote Management.** Lets someone else control your Mac using Apple Remote Desktop, a popular add-on program for teachers and system administrators.

- **Remote Apple Events.** Lets technical gurus send commands to Macs across the network.

- **Xgrid Sharing.** Xgrid is powerful software that lets you divide up a complex computational task—like computer animation or huge scientific calculations—among a whole bunch of Macs on your network, so that they automatically work on the problem when they're otherwise sitting idle. If you're intrigued—and if you have pretty decent programming chops—visit *http://developer.apple.com/hardware/hpc/xgrid_intro.html*.

- **Bluetooth Sharing.** This pane lets you set up Bluetooth file sharing, a way for other people near you to shoot files over to (or receive files from) your laptop—without muss, fuss, or passwords. Page 199 has the details.

Software Update

If you're used to Windows, then this item should seem familiar: Whenever Apple improves or fixes some piece of Mac OS X or some Apple-branded program, the Software Update program can notify you, download the update, and install it into

Figure 15-12:
When Software Update finds an appropriate software morsel, it presents this dialog box that offers to install it automatically. (If you see a smaller version of this dialog box, with no visible list of the new components, then click the Details button.)

Apple has always created updated and bug-fixing versions of its software components, but they don't do you any good if you don't know about them. Software Update means you no longer have to scour Mac news Web sites to discover that one of these components has been released and then hunt down the software yourself.

your system automatically. These updates may include new versions of programs like iPhoto and iMovie; drivers for newly released printers, scanners, cameras, and such; bug fixes and security patches; and so on. See Figure 15-12.

Sound

Using the panes of the Sound panel, you can configure the sound system of your Mac in any of several ways.

Tip: Here's a quick way to jump directly to the Sound panel of System Preferences–from the keyboard, without ever having to open System Preferences or click Sound. Just press Option as you tap the ◀, ◀), or ◀)) key on the top row of your Apple keyboard.

Sound Effects Tab

"Sound effects" means *error beeps*—the sound you hear when the Mac wants your attention, or when you click someplace you shouldn't.

Just click the sound of your choice to make it your default system beep. Most of the canned choices here are funny and clever, yet subdued enough to be of practical value as alert sounds (Figure 15-13). As for the other controls on the Sound Effects panel, they include these:

Figure 15-13:
You can adjust your overall speaker volume independently from the alert-beep volume, thank goodness.

- **Alert volume.** The *main* volume slider for your Mac is the "Output volume" slider at the bottom of the Sound pane. The "Alert volume" slider is *just* for error beeps; Apple was kind enough to let you adjust the volume of these error beeps independently.

- **Play user interface sound effects.** This option produces a few subtle sound effects during certain Finder operations: when you drag something off the Dock, into the Trash, or into a folder, or when the Finder finishes a file-copying job.

- **Play feedback when volume is changed.** Each time you press one of the volume keys (◀, ◀◦, ◀»)), the Mac beeps (or, rather, pops) to help you gauge the current volume.

  That's all fine when you're working at home. But more than one person has been humiliated in an important meeting when the Mac made a sudden, inappropriately loud sonic outburst—and then amplified that embarrassment by furiously and repeatedly pressing the volume-down key, beeping all the way.

  If you turn off this checkbox, then the Mac won't make any sound at all as you adjust its volume. Instead, you'll see only a visual representation of the steadily decreasing (or increasing) volume level.

Tip: The Shift key reverses the logic. So if you have "Play feedback" turned *on,* holding down Shift as you tap the volume keys makes them silent. If it's turned *off,* you can force the volume-gauging beeps to play by pressing Shift as you tap the volume keys.

- **Use audio port for: Sound Output/Sound Input.** Most Mac laptops have only a single audio jack on the side—a miniplug that can accommodate either an audio *output* device like headphones or speakers, or an *input* device (that is, a microphone). Here you tell your laptop which of these personalities you want that jack to have.

Output Tab

"Output" means speakers or headphones. For most people, this pane offers nothing useful except the Balance slider, with which you can set the balance between your Mac's left and right stereo speakers. The "Select a device" wording seems to imply that you can choose which speakers you want to use for playback. But Internal Speakers is generally the only choice, even if you have external speakers. (The Mac uses your external speakers automatically when they're plugged in.)

A visit to this pane is necessary, however, if you want to use USB speakers or a Bluetooth or USB phone headset. Choose its name from the list.

Note: Mac OS X is nice enough to remember your volume setting for headphones and speakers independently.

Input Tab

This panel lets you specify which sound source you want the Mac to "listen to," if you have more than one connected: external microphone, internal microphone, line input, USB headset, or whatever. It also lets you adjust the sensitivity of that microphone—its *input volume*—by dragging the slider and watching the real-time Input level meter above it change as you speak. Put another way, it's a quick way to see if your microphone is working.

Speech

The Mac is quite talented when it comes to speech. Its abilities fall into two categories: speech recognition and reading text aloud.

Talking to the Mac

The Apple marketing machine may have been working too hard when it called this feature "speech recognition"— Mac OS X doesn't take dictation, typing out what you say. (For that, you need a program like Dragon, *www.nuance.com*.)

Instead, Mac OS X's speech recognition feature is what's known as a *command-and-control* technology. It lets you open programs, trigger AppleScripts, choose menu commands, trigger keystrokes, and click dialog box buttons and tabs—just by speaking their names.

The on/off switch for speech recognition in Mac OS X is the Speech→Speech Recognition pane of System Preferences (Figure 15-14). Where you see "Speakable items," click On.

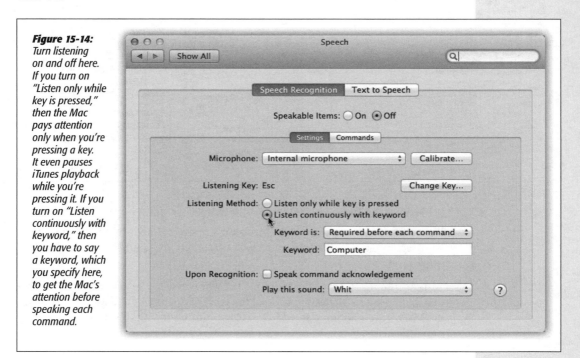

Figure 15-14:
Turn listening on and off here. If you turn on "Listen only while key is pressed," then the Mac pays attention only when you're pressing a key. It even pauses iTunes playback while you're pressing it. If you turn on "Listen continuously with keyword," then you have to say a keyword, which you specify here, to get the Mac's attention before speaking each command.

The Feedback window

Check out your screen: A small, microphone-like floating window now appears (Figure 15-15). The "Esc" in its center indicates the "listen" key—the key you're supposed to hold down when you want the Mac to respond to your voice. (You wouldn't want the Mac listening all the time—especially when you said, for example, "Hey, it's cold in here. *Close the window.*" Therefore, the Mac comes set to listen only when you're pressing that key.)

When you start talking, you'll see the Mac's interpretation of what you said written out in a yellow tooltip just over the Feedback window.

The Speech Commands window

The only commands the Mac understands are listed in the Speech Commands window. (If it's not open, see Figure 15-15.) Keeping your eye on this window is essential, because it offers a complete list of everything your Mac understands. As you can see, some of the commands represent shortcuts that would take several steps if you had to perform them manually.

Figure 15-15:
Left: The Feedback window lacks the standard Close and Minimize buttons. If it's in your way, just double-click it (or say, "Minimize speech feedback window") to shrink it into your Dock. If you choose Speech Preferences from its bottom-edge triangle, you open the Speech Preferences window.

Right: Choosing Open Speech Commands window, of course, opens the list of things you can say.

Here are a few examples of what you'll find in the list at first:

- **Phone for [Madonna].** Displays Madonna's phone number in huge digits across your screen—the fastest way yet to look up somebody's number in your Address Book program.

  You can also say "Chat with Madonna" (or whomever) to begin a new chat session in iChat, "Mail to Madonna" to send the current document as a Mail attachment, or "Meet with Madonna" to add an iCal appointment with this person's information attached.

- **Set alarm for 30 minutes.** (You can say any number of minutes or hours—"Set alarm for 2 hours," or whatever.) The Mac asks you to type a little message, which will serve as the iCal dialog box that appears at the specified time.

Tip: Check out the complete list of iCal and Address Book commands in the Speech Commands window.

- **Close this window.** Closes the frontmost window instantly.

- **Empty the Trash.** Works only when you're in the Finder.

- **Switch to Safari.** Brings Safari to the front. (Actually, you can say, "Switch to" and then the name of *any* running or recently used program.)

- **Log me out.** Saves you the trouble of switching into each program and choosing Quit.

- **Open the Speech Commands window** or **Show me what to say.** Opens the Speech Commands window, of course.

- **What day is it?** Tells you the date.

- **Tell me a joke.** Begins a pathetic/funny knock-knock joke. You've got to play along, providing the "Who's there?" and "So-and-so *who?*" answers.

Mac OS X *updates* the listing in the Speech Commands window in real time, according to the context. When you switch from one program to another, you see a list of the local commands that work in the new program. You'll discover that when you use the "Tell me a joke" command, for example, you don't necessarily have to say, "Who's there?" You can also say, "Stop," "Go away," or "Stop with the jokes!" (It must really be fun to work at Apple.)

Speaking to the Mac

Finish up on the Speech pane of System Preferences. Use the Microphone pop-up menu to specify which microphone you'll be using (if you have a choice). Click Calibrate to adjust its sensitivity.

Now you're ready to begin. While pressing the Esc key (if that's still the one identified in the Feedback window), begin speaking. Speak normally; don't exaggerate or shout. Try one of the commands in the Speech Commands list—perhaps "What time is it?" If your mike is set up properly, the round Feedback window displays animated sound waves when you speak.

Customizing Speech Recognition

You can tailor the speech recognition feature in two ways: by adjusting the way it looks and operates, and by adding new commands to its vocabulary.

Changing when the Mac listens

When you first turn on the speech recognition feature, the Mac expects you to alert it by pressing a key, like Esc, when you speak.

If you'd rather not have to press some key whenever you want the computer's attention, click the other option in this pane, "Listen continuously with keyword." Now to get the computer's attention, you must speak the keyword—which you type into the Keyword box—before each command. For example, you might say, "Computer, open Numbers," or "Hal, what day is it?" The word you specify appears in the middle of the round Feedback window.

Note: This method of getting the computer's attention is less reliable than the push-a-key-to-talk system. Especially if you name the computer "Hal." Although that's hilarious in theory, polysyllabic words work better in practice.

By using the "Keyword is" pop-up menu, meanwhile, you can specify how big your window of opportunity is:

- **Optional before commands.** If you work alone in a quiet room, this is the choice for you. It means you don't have to press a key *or* say the Mac's name when issuing a voice command. *Everything you say* is considered a command.

- **Required before each command.** Nothing you say is interpreted as a command unless you say the computer's keyword first, as in, *"Macintosh,* switch to Microsoft Word."

- **Required 15 seconds after last command, Required 30 seconds after last command.** Sometimes you want to issue several commands in a row and would feel foolish saying, "Computer, close all windows. Computer, empty the Trash. Computer, switch to Calculator." When you turn on this option, you can say the keyword just once; all commands you issue in the next 15 or 30 seconds "belong to" that first salutation. The push-to-talk key and the spoken keyword, in this case, serve as a master on/off switch for the Mac's listening mode.

Triggering menus by voice

On the Speech pane of System Preferences, click the Speech Recognition tab, and then click the Commands minitab. Here you find a list of the command categories that Speakable Items can understand. As you turn each checkbox on or off, watch the Speech Commands window. Giant swaths of commands appear or disappear as you fool with these checkboxes, giving you a good indication as to their function. Here's a rundown:

- **Address Book.** These commands let you look up numbers; add appointments to iCal; set up alarm reminders for yourself; mail things to people; and begin text, audio, or video chats with people whose names are already in your Address Book.

- **Global Speakable Items.** This is the master list of Speakable Items, shown in Figure 15-15.

- **Application-Specific Items.** Certain Mac OS X programs come with preset lists of commands that work only when you're in the relevant program. For example, whenever you're in the Finder, you can say, "Empty the Trash," "Go to my Home directory," "Hide the Dock," "Minimize all windows," "Make a new folder," and so on. When this checkbox is off, the Mac no longer recognizes any of these handy commands.

- **Application Switching.** This is the command category at the bottom half of the Speech Commands list—"Switch to Address Book," "Switch to Firefox," and so on.

- **Menu Bar.** This command lets you open menus (in the menu bar) by speaking their names.

- **Front Window.** In your Speech Commands window, note the appearance of a new category of commands, called Front Window. The idea here is to provide you with quick speech-recognition access to the most prominent buttons, tabs, and icons in whichever window is before you. Figure 15-16 elaborates on the idea.

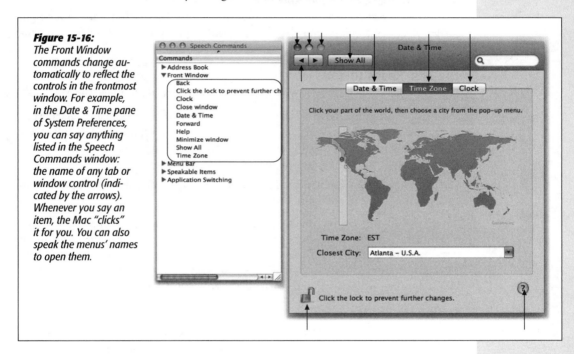

Figure 15-16:
The Front Window commands change automatically to reflect the controls in the frontmost window. For example, in the Date & Time pane of System Preferences, you can say anything listed in the Speech Commands window: the name of any tab or window control (indicated by the arrows). Whenever you say an item, the Mac "clicks" it for you. You can also speak the menus' names to open them.

Once you say its name ("File menu," for example), the menu opens. Now you can say any command in the open menu ("New Playlist," "Save," or whatever). The Menu Bar category of the Speech Commands window changes to remind you of what you can say at any given moment.

The combination of Front Window and Menu Bar commands lets you do quite a bit of work on your Mac without ever needing the mouse or keyboard.

Improving the Mac's vocabulary

By putting an alias of a favorite document, folder, disk, or program into your Home→Library→Speakable Items folder, you can teach the Mac to recognize its name and open it for you on command. You can name these icons anything you want.

Note: The Library folder in your Home folder is generally invisible, but you can jump right to it by pressing Option as you choose Go→Library.

You can also rename the starter set that Apple provides. You'll have the best luck with multiword or polysyllabic names—"Microsoft Word," not just "Word."

Speech tips, tricks, and troubleshooting

When you're creating new commands, click the Helpful Tips button at the lower-right corner of the Commands pane (of the Speech Recognition pane of the Speech pane of System Preferences).

The Mac Reads to You

The conversation doesn't have to be one-way; it's even easier to make the Mac *talk*.

Most Apple programs have a Start Speaking command built right in: Safari, Mail, TextEdit, iChat, Stickies, Pages, and so on. Just right-click inside a window full of text and, from the pop-up menu, choose Speech→Start Speaking. Your Mac can read your email or a Web article to you while you're getting dressed.

You can add a Speak command in FileMaker Pro scripts. Mac OS X's Chess and Calculator programs can talk back, too.

But that's kid stuff. Truth is, the Mac can read almost anything you like: text you pass your cursor over, alert messages, menus, and *any text document in any program.* It can speak in your choice of dozens of synthesizer voices, ages 8 to 50. Most read with a twangy, charmingly Norwegian accent—but some of the newest voices (like Alex, Jill, Samantha, and Tom) sound scarily like a professional human voice-over artist.

Setting Up the Mac's Voice

To configure the way the Mac talks, revisit the Speech pane of System Preferences. Click the Text to Speech tab at the top of the window. As you can see in Figure 15-17, you can control which of the Mac's voices you want your computer to use, as well as how fast it should speak.

As shown in Figure 15-17, though, Lion comes with a huge range of additional voices that you can add to the pop-up menu here.

Here are all the different occasions when the Mac can talk to you.

Announce when alerts are displayed

If you turn on this checkbox, you can make the Mac read aloud error messages and alert messages that may appear on your screen. If you click the Set Alert Options button, you'll find these useful controls:

- **Voice.** Use this pop-up menu to specify the voice you want reading your error messages. (It doesn't have to be the same as the standard Mac default voice that's used for other purposes.)

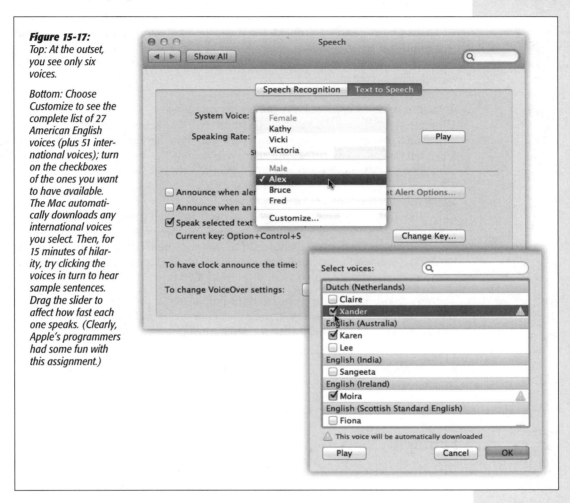

Figure 15-17:
Top: At the outset, you see only six voices.

Bottom: Choose Customize to see the complete list of 27 American English voices (plus 51 international voices); turn on the checkboxes of the ones you want to have available. The Mac automatically downloads any international voices you select. Then, for 15 minutes of hilarity, try clicking the voices in turn to hear sample sentences. Drag the slider to affect how fast each one speaks. (Clearly, Apple's programmers had some fun with this assignment.)

- **Phrase.** Use this pop-up menu to specify which utterance the Mac speaks before the actual error message—for example, "*Excuse me!* The Trash could not be emptied," or "*Attention!* The document could not be printed." Better yet, choose Edit Phrase List to open a dialog box where you can specify your own words of frustration. (Apple Inc. is not liable for any trouble you may get into with people in neighboring cubicles.)

- **Delay.** The ostensible purpose of the Talking Alerts feature is to get your attention if you've wandered away from your Mac—mentally or physically. The chances are slim, but an urgent problem might occur that, if left undetected, could land you in trouble. (A 500-page printout brought to its knees by a paper jam comes to mind.)

In other words, if you're still sitting in front of your Mac, you may not need the Mac to speak to get your attention; you could simply read the onscreen message. That's why you can set this slider to make the Mac wait, after the error message appears, for up to a minute before trying to flag you with its voice. That way it won't harangue you unnecessarily. (Click Play for a sense of how long the Mac will delay before speaking.)

Announce when an application requires your attention

A jumping Dock icon means that the program is trying to get your attention. It might be because your printer is out of paper, or it might be because you've tried to shut down but one program still has open, unsaved documents. In any case, now the Mac can tell you, in so many words, which program needs some loving care.

Speak selected text when the key is pressed

This is the feature that makes the Mac read you any Web page, any email message, any sticky note—a welcome break for sore eyes. Furthermore, if you do any kind of writing at all, you'll discover the value of having your material read back to you out loud; it's a proofreading technique that reveals all kinds of typos and wordos that you wouldn't catch just by reading, even if you read it 50 times.

The very first time you turn on this checkbox, the Mac prompts you to specify a keystroke. (Later, you can always change the keystroke by clicking Set Key.) Choose a keystroke that doesn't conflict with the program you're using, like Control-T.

Now go to the program where you'd like the reading to happen. Highlight some text (or press ⌘-A to select all of it). Then press the keystroke you specified. The Mac begins reading it aloud immediately. To interrupt the playback, press the same keystroke again.

And be glad you were alive to see the day.

Spotlight

Here's how you tell the Mac (a) which categories of files and information you want the Spotlight search feature to search, (b) which folders you *don't* want searched, for privacy reasons, and (c) which key combination you want to use for summoning the Spotlight menu or dialog box. Details are in Chapter 3.

Startup Disk

Use this panel to pick the System Folder your Mac will use the next time it starts up—when you're swapping between Mac OS X and Windows (running with Boot Camp), for example. Check out the details in Chapter 8.

Time Machine

Here's the master on/off switch and options panel for Time Machine, which is described in Chapter 5.

Trackpad

You may love your Mac laptop now, but wait until you find out about these special features. They make your laptop *crazy* better. It's one of Lion's most famous characteristics—that you can point, click, scroll, right-click, rotate things, enlarge things, hide windows, and switch programs, all on the trackpad itself, without a mouse and without ever having to lift your fingers. (You can do most of this on a desktop Mac, too, if it has an Apple Magic Mouse, or an external trackpad like Apple's Magic Trackpad.)

Apple keeps adding new "gestures" with each new laptop, so yours may not offer all these options. And even in Lion, you might see different options and layouts depending on what Mac you have.

On the latest Macs, you see a dialog box composed of three tabs across the top. Each offers on/off switches or pop-up menus that govern how you do pointing, clicking, scrolling, and other mouselike maneuvers. Each time you click one, the right half of the dialog box plays a tidy, looping movie that shows you that technique clearly and visibly.

Here's what's on the three main tabs:

Point & Click

- **Tap to Click.** Usually, you touch your laptop's trackpad only to move the cursor. For clicking and dragging, you're supposed to push down on the clicker (either the button *beneath* the trackpad or, on recent models, the lower half of the actual trackpad surface).

  Many people find, however, that it's more direct to tap and drag directly on the trackpad, using the same finger that's been moving the cursor. That's the purpose of this checkbox. When it's on, you can tap the trackpad surface to register a mouse click at the location of the cursor. Double-tap to double-click.

- **Secondary click.** This means "right-click." As you know, right-clicking is a huge deal; it unleashes useful features just about everywhere.

  On all Mac laptops, you can trigger a right-click by clicking with your thumb while resting your index and middle fingers on the trackpad.

On the latest laptops—the ones without a separate clicker button—this pop-up menu offers you three other options. You can click with two fingers; click once in the lower-right corner of the trackpad; or click once in the lower-left corner. Weird, but wonderful.

- **Look up.** This gesture lets you double-tap the trackpad (*don't* click—just touch the surface without clicking) to bring up a handy dictionary definition for the word you're double-tapping. Details are on page 186.

- **Three-finger drag.** This option lets you move a window around the screen, or change its size and shape, without actually clicking. Instead, you rest three fingers on the trackpad and drag. For example, move a window by pointing to the title bar and then dragging three fingers. Make it wider by pointing to its right or left edge and then dragging three fingers. Change its shape by pointing to the lower-right corner and then dragging three fingers.

- **Tracking speed.** This is a duplicate of the Tracking Speed slider described under "Mouse" earlier in this chapter—but it lets you establish an independent tracking speed for the *trackpad*.

Scroll & Zoom

- **Scroll direction: natural.** And here it is, the heart of Lion's most controversial new feature: scrolling *up* when you drag your fingers (or the scroll wheel, or the scroll bar) *up*. That's exactly opposite of what we've been doing for years.

  If you can't stand this new arrangement, turn it off here. But first read the discussion on page 11.

- **Zoom in or out.** If you've used an iPhone, this one will seem familiar. What it means is, "Put two fingers on the trackpad and spread them apart to *enlarge* what's on the screen. Slide two fingers *together* to shrink it down again." It doesn't work in every program—it affects icons on the desktop, pictures and PDFs in Preview, photos in iPhoto, text in Safari, and so on—but it's great when it does.

- **Smart zoom.** On the iPhone/iPad, you can double-tap a block of text or a graphic on a Web page to enlarge just that block to full-screen size. The "smart" element of this is the way the software senses that block's borders and zooms in exactly right.

  Now you can do that on your Mac, too. Double-tap your trackpad (touch, don't click) with *two* fingers to do it.

- **Rotate.** Place two fingers on the trackpad, and then twist them around an invisible center point, to rotate a photo or a PDF document. This doesn't work in all programs or in all circumstances, but it's great for turning images upright in the Finder, Preview, iPhoto, Image Capture, and so on.

More Gestures

- **Swipe between pages.** Drag two fingers horizontally across the trackpad to skip to the next or previous page or image in a batch. Here again, this feature doesn't work in all programs, but it's great for flipping through images or PDF pages in Preview or iPhoto, or to go back or forward a page in Safari.

  Note that the tiny pop-up menu here lets you *change* the swiping gesture. You can swipe with two fingers, three fingers, or—if you're a fan of variety—two *or* three fingers.

- **Swipe between full-screen apps.** If you've embraced Lion's new full-screen feature, or its Mission Control feature, you'll definitely want to learn this one. Here's the gesture that lets you flip between full-screen apps: either with four fingers on the trackpad or (if you change the setting using the pop-up menu) three.

- **Mission Control.** This gesture lets you enter and exit Mission Control (see Chapter 4) by swiping up or down with four fingers. (You can change the setting to *three* fingers.)

- **App Exposé.** If this checkbox is on, you can trigger App Exposé (page 156) by swiping four fingers downward. (You can change the setting to *three* fingers.)

- **Launchpad.** Launchpad wouldn't be very useful if it took several steps to open. Fortunately, this option lets you fire up Launchpad by pinching on the trackpad with three fingers and your thumb. (You can also exit Launchpad by *spreading* those four fingers.)

- **Show Desktop.** You can spread three fingers and your thumb to trigger Desktop Exposé (page 158). Once there, *pinch* those fingers to return to what you were doing.

Note: Here again, Apple has created *levels* of four-finger pinching. Pinching once opens Launchpad; spread *twice* from there to show the desktop. Likewise, pinching *twice* from Show Desktop takes you straight into Launchpad.

Universal Access

The Universal Access panel is designed for people who type with one hand, find it difficult to use a mouse, or have trouble seeing or hearing. (These features can also be handy when the mouse is broken or missing.)

Accessibility is a huge focus for Apple. In fact, there's a whole Apple Web site dedicated to explaining all these features: *www.apple.com/accessibility.* Here, though, is an overview of the noteworthiest features.

Seeing Tab (Magnifying the Screen)

If you have trouble seeing the screen, then, boy, does Mac OS X have features for you (Figure 15-18).

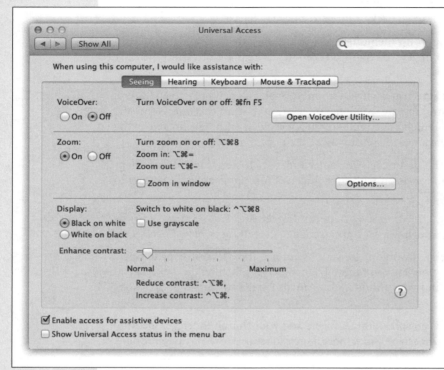

Figure 15-18:
You'll be amazed at just how much you can zoom into the Mac's screen using this Universal Access pane. In fact, there's nothing to stop you from zooming in so far that a single pixel nearly fills the entire monitor. (That may not be especially useful for people with limited vision, but it can be handy for graphic designers learning how to reproduce a certain icon, dot by dot.)

VoiceOver

The Mac has always been able to read stuff on the screen out loud. But Apple has taken this feature light-years further, turning it into a full-blown *screen reader* for the benefit of people who can't see. VoiceOver doesn't just read every scrap of text it finds on the screen—it also lets you control everything on the screen (menus, buttons, and so on) without ever needing the mouse.

On a Mac with a multitouch trackpad, you can interact with what's visible on the screen by using the trackpad itself as a map of the current window or screen area; VoiceOver speaks whatever's under your finger. You can flick in any direction to move to the next thing on the screen. You hear a sound whenever VoiceOver finds blank spaces on the screen, all in the name of helping you "feel" where everything is.

Mac OS X can also read entire Web pages, navigate Web tables, hop from link to link, and so on. You can navigate by pressing arrow keys, using the mouse or the trackpad.

Obviously, learning VoiceOver is a *huge* task that can take days or weeks—but if it's your ticket to being able to use a computer at all, you'll probably be happy to have such a full-fledged monster of a program.

Zoom

This Zoom feature lets you enlarge the area surrounding your cursor in any increment. It's just incredibly useful, incredibly often, especially if you have over-40 eyes.

Tip: If you have a laptop, just holding down the Control key while swiping up the trackpad with two fingers is a far faster and easier way to magnify the screen. It works even when *this* one is turned off.

To make it work, press Option-⌘-8 as you're working. Or, if the Seeing panel is open, click On in the Zoom section. That's the master switch.

No zooming actually takes place, however, until you press Option-⌘-plus (to zoom in) or Option-⌘-minus (to zoom out). With each press, the entire screen image gets larger or smaller, creating a virtual monitor that follows your cursor around the screen.

If you click Options, you're offered an array of customization options. For example, you can substitute the Option or ⌘ key, if Control isn't working out for you. Furthermore, you can specify how you want to scroll around within your zoomed-in screen image. The factory setting, "Continuously with pointer," is actually pretty frustrating; the whole screen shifts around whenever you move the cursor. ("So the pointer is at or near the center of the image" is very similar.) "Only when the pointer reaches an edge" is a lot less annoying and lets you *use* the cursor (to click buttons, for example) without sending the entire screen image darting away from you.

Now then. See "Zoom in window"? It contains the zoomed-in portion within a picture-in-picture rectangle on the screen, as shown in Figure 15-19.

Figure 15-19:
This new inset window makes it easier for you to keep your bearings. It zooms into the screen only within this inset window.

When this option is turned on, the dialog box that appears when you click Options is totally different. It offers these choices:

- **Stationary.** The inset remains parked on the screen. You can't move or resize it—at least not once you've left the Options dialog box.

Tip: You *can* change its size and position for good, though, by clicking the Adjust Size and Location button in the corner of the Options dialog box. You'll be offered the chance to drag the edges of the little inset window. When you like the result, click OK.

- **Follow mouse cursor.** The inset window follows your cursor around.

- **Tiled along edge.** The magnified inset becomes much bigger—in fact, it becomes an enormous rectangular swath at the left side of your screen. The image scrolls as you move your cursor around.

Tip: One of the best options here is "Enable temporary zoom." What that means is that at any time, in any program, you can summon the magnified-inset window at your cursor location by holding down your Control and Option keys together. (It works only if Zoom is turned *on* in Universal Access.) It's a great way to dip into a magnified view of something on your screen, briefly.

Display (inverted colors)

Pressing Control-Option-⌘-8, or clicking the White on Black button, inverts the colors of the screen, so that text appears white on black—an effect that some people find easier to read. (This option also freaks out many Mac fans who turn it on by *mistake*.)

Hearing Tab (Flashing the Screen)

If you have trouble hearing the Mac's sounds, the obvious solution is to increase the volume, which is why this panel offers a direct link to the Sound preferences pane (click Adjust Volume).

GEM IN THE ROUGH

Zooming In, the Shortcut Way

It's been one of the Mac's standout features forever: You can zoom into the screen image, magnifying the whole thing, just by dragging two fingers up or down the trackpad while you're pressing the Control key. You can zoom in so far that the word "zoom" in 12-point type fills the entire monitor. (If you have a mouse, turning the wheel or trackpea while pressing Control does the same thing.)

This feature comes in handy with amazing frequency. It's great for reading Web pages in tiny type, or enlarging Web movies, or studying the dot-by-dot construction of a button or icon that you admire. Just Control-drag upward to zoom in, and Control-drag downward to zoom out again.

This feature works even if Zoom is turned off in System Preferences→Universal Access. What's weird, though, is that the *options* in Universal Access still affect the Control-key zooming—yes, even when Zoom is turned off there. Even the new "Zoom in window" feature still works when you Control-key zoom.

Fortunately, hearing your computer usually isn't critical (except when working in music and audio, of course). The only time audio is especially important is when the Mac tries to get your attention by beeping. For those situations, turn on "Flash the screen when an alert sound occurs" (an effect you can try out by clicking the Flash Screen button). Now you'll see a white flash across the entire monitor whenever the Mac would otherwise beep—not a bad idea on laptops, actually, so that you don't miss beeps when you've got the speakers muted.

(The "Play stereo audio as mono" option is intended for people with hearing loss in one ear. This way, you won't miss any of the musical mix just because you're listening through only one headphone.)

Keyboard Tab (Typing Assistance)

This panel offers two clever features designed to help people who have trouble using the keyboard.

- **Sticky Keys** lets you press multiple-key shortcuts (involving keys like Shift, Option, Control, and ⌘) one at a time instead of all together.

  To make Sticky Keys work, first turn on the master switch at the top of the dialog box. Then go to work on the Mac, triggering keyboard commands as shown in Figure 15-20.

  If you press a modifier key *twice,* meanwhile, you lock it down. (Its onscreen symbol gets brighter to let you know.) When a key is locked, you can use it for several

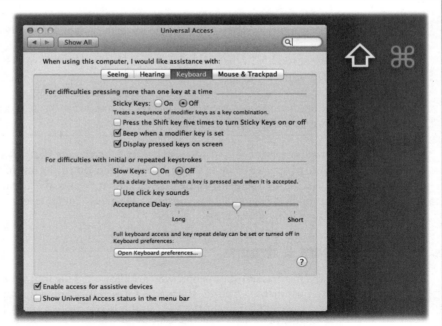

Figure 15-20:
With Sticky Keys turned on, whenever you want to press a multiple-key keystroke like Shift-⌘-D, press them one at a time. You'll see ghost images of these keys superimposed on your screen, as though to show you which keystrokes you've added to your temporary collection. To "unpress" a key you've already pressed, press it again twice.

commands in a row. For example, if a folder icon is highlighted, you could double-press ⌘ to lock it down—and then type O (to open the folder), look around, and then press W (to close the window). Press the ⌘ key a third time to "un-press" it.

Tip: The checkbox called "Press the Shift key five times to turn Sticky Keys on or off" gives you the flexibility of turning Sticky Keys on and off at will, without even taking a trip to System Preferences. Whenever you want to turn on Sticky Keys, press the Shift key five times in succession. You'll hear a special clacking sound effect alerting you that you just turned on Sticky Keys. (Repeat the five presses to turn Sticky Keys off again.)

- **Slow Keys** doesn't register a key press at all until you've held down the key for more than a second or so—a feature designed to screen out accidental key presses.

Mouse & Trackpad Tab (Cursor Control from the Keyboard)

Mouse Keys is designed to help people who can't use the mouse—or who want more precision when working in graphics programs. It lets you click, drag, and otherwise manipulate the cursor by pressing the keys on your numeric keypad. (It's not very useful on keyboards that don't *have* separate numeric keypads, like laptops.)

Note: On a Mac without a trackpad, this tab is just called Mouse.

When Mouse Keys is turned on, the 5 key acts as the clicker—hold it down for a moment to "click the mouse," do that twice to double-click, and so on. Hold down the 0 key to lock down the mouse button, and the period key to unlock it. (The amount of time you have to hold them down depends on how you've set the Initial Delay slider.)

Move the cursor around the screen by pressing the eight keys that surround the 5 key. (For example, hold down the 9 key to move the cursor diagonally up and to the right.) If you hold one of these keys down continuously, the cursor, after a pause, begins to move smoothly in that direction—according to the way you've adjusted the sliders called Initial Delay and Maximum Speed.

Tip: The checkbox called "Press the Option key five times to turn Mouse Keys on or off" saves you the trouble of opening System Preferences.

At the bottom of this window, you'll find the Cursor Size slider. It's a godsend not only to people with failing vision, but also to anyone using one of Apple's large, super-high-resolution screens; as the pixel density increases, the arrow cursor gets smaller and smaller. This slider lets you make the arrow cursor larger—much larger, if you like—making it much easier to see.

Users & Groups

This is the master list of people who are allowed to log into your Mac. It's where you can adjust their passwords, startup pictures, self-opening startup items, permissions to use various features of the Mac, and other security tools. All of this is described in Chapter 13.

The Freebie Programs

Right out of the box, Mac OS X comes with a healthy assortment of about 50 freebies: programs for sending email, writing documents, doing math, even playing games. They're designed not only to show off some of Mac OS X's most dramatic technologies, but also to let you get real work done without having to invest in additional software.

Your Free Mac OS X Programs

A broad assortment of programs sit in the Applications folder in the main hard drive window, and another couple dozen less frequently used apps await in the Applications→Utilities folder.

This chapter guides you through every item in your new software library, one program at a time. (Of course, your Applications list may vary. Apple might have blessed your particular Mac model with some bonus programs, or you may have downloaded or installed some on your own.)

Tip: A reminder: You can jump straight to the Applications folder in the Finder by pressing Shift-⌘-A (the shortcut for Go→Applications), or by clicking the Applications folder icon in the Sidebar. You might consider adding the Application folder's icon to the Dock, too, so you can access it no matter what program you're in. Shift-⌘-U (or Go→Utilities) takes you, of course, to the Utilities folder.

Address Book

The Address Book is a database that stores names, addresses, email addresses, phone numbers, and other contact information. See page 365.

App Store

See the beginning of Chapter 4 for full details on the Mac App Store.

Automator

This software-robot program is described in the free online PDF Appendix to this book. It's on this book's "Missing CD" at *www.missingmanuals.com.*

Calculator

The Calculator is much more than a simple four-function memory calculator. It can also act as a scientific calculator for students and scientists, a conversion calculator for metric and U.S. measures, and even a currency calculator for world travelers.

The little Calculator widget in the Dashboard is quicker to open, but the standalone Calculator program is far more powerful. For example:

- Calculator has three modes: Basic, Advanced, and Programmer (Figure 16-1). Switch among them by choosing from the View menu (or pressing ⌘-1 for Basic, ⌘-2 for Advanced, or ⌘-3 for Programmer).

- You can operate Calculator by clicking the onscreen buttons, but it's much easier to press the corresponding number and symbol keys on your keyboard.

Figure 16-1:
The Calculator program offers a four-function Basic mode, a full-blown scientific calculator mode, and a programmer's calculator (shown here, and capable of hex, octal, decimal, and binary notation). The first two modes offer a "paper tape" feature (Windows→Paper Tape) that lets you correct errors made way back in a calculation. To edit one of the numbers on the paper tape, drag through it, retype, and then click Recalculate Totals. You can also save the tape as a text file by choosing File→Save Tape As, or print it by selecting File→Print Tape.

- As you go, you can make Calculator speak each key you press. The Mac's voice ensures that you don't mistype as you keep your eyes on the receipts in front of you, typing by touch.

    Just choose Speech→Speak Button Pressed to turn this feature on or off. (You choose *which* voice does the talking in the Speech panel of System Preferences.)

- Press the C key to clear the calculator display.

- Once you've calculated a result, you can copy it (using Edit→Copy, or ⌘-C) and paste it directly into another program.

- Calculator even offers Reverse Polish Notation (RPN), a system of entering numbers that's popular with some mathematicians, programmers, and engineers, because it lets them omit parentheses. Choose View→RPN to turn it on and off.

Tip: How cool is this? In most programs, you don't need Calculator or even a Dashboard widget. Remember that the Spotlight menu is a calculator, too. Type or paste an equation into the Spotlight search box; instantly, the answer appears in the results menu.

Conversions

Calculator is more than a calculator; it's also a conversion program. No matter what units you're trying to convert—meters, grams, cubic inches, miles per hour, euros—Calculator is ready.

1. **Clear the calculator (for example, type the letter C on your keyboard). Type in the starting measurement.**

    To convert 48 degrees Celsius to Fahrenheit, for example, type *48.*

2. **From the Convert menu, choose the kind of conversion you want.**

    In this case, choose Temperature. When you're done choosing, a dialog box appears.

3. **Use the pop-up menus to specify which units you want to convert to and from.**

    To convert Celsius to Fahrenheit, choose Celsius from the first pop-up menu, and Fahrenheit from the second.

4. **Click OK.**

    That's it. The Calculator displays the result—in degrees Fahrenheit, in this example.

The next time you want to make this kind of calculation, you can skip steps 2, 3, and 4. Instead, just choose your desired conversion from the Convert→Recent Conversions submenu.

Calculator is especially amazing when it comes to *currency* conversions—from pesos to American dollars, for example—because it actually does its homework. It goes online to download up-to-the-minute currency rates to ensure that the conversion is accurate. (Choose Convert→Update Currency Exchange Rates.)

Tip: If you're working with big numbers, don't forget to turn on View→Show Thousands Separators. Calculator will add commas (like 1,242,939) to help you read your big numbers more easily.

Chess

Mac OS X comes with only one game, but it's a beauty (Figure 16-2). It's a traditional chess game played on a gorgeously rendered board with a set of realistic 3-D pieces.

Note: The program is actually a sophisticated Unix-based chess program, Sjeng, that Apple packaged up in a new wrapper.

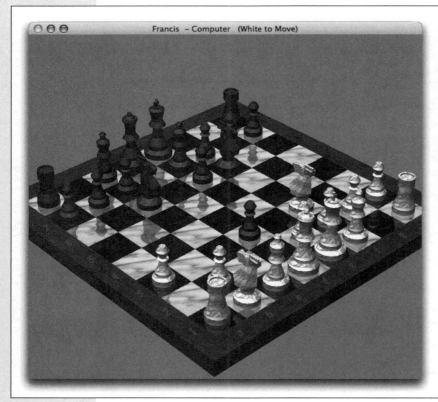

Francis – Computer (White to Move)

Figure 16-2:
You don't have to be terribly exact about grabbing the chess pieces when it's time to make your move. Just click anywhere within a piece's current square to drag it into a new position on the board (shown here in its Marble incarnation). And how did this chessboard get rotated like this? Because you can grab a corner of the board and rotate it in 3-D space. Cool!

Playing a Game of Chess

When you launch Chess, you're presented with a fresh, new game that's set up in Human vs. Computer mode—meaning that you, the Human (light-colored pieces) get to play against the Computer (your Mac, on the dark side). Drag the chess piece of your choice into position on the board, and the game is afoot.

If you choose Game→New Game, however, you're offered a pop-up menu with choices like Human vs. Computer, Human vs. Human, and so on. If you switch the pop-up menu to Computer vs. Human, then you and your Mac trade places; the Mac takes the white side of the board and opens the game with the first move, and you play the black side.

Tip: The same New Game dialog box also offers a pop-up menu called Variant, which offers three other chess-like games: Crazyhouse, Suicide, and Losers. The Chess help screens (choose Help→Chess Help, and then click "Starting a new chess game") explain these variations.

On some night when the video store is closed and you're desperate for entertainment, you might also want to try the Computer vs. Computer option, which pits your Mac against itself. Pour yourself a beer, open a bag of chips, and settle in to watch until someone—either the Mac or the Mac—gains victory.

Chess Prefs

Choose Chess→Preferences to find some useful controls like these:

- **Style.** Apple has gone nuts with the computer-generated materials options in this program. (Is it a coincidence that Steve Jobs was also the CEO of Pixar, the computer-animation company?)

  In any case, you can choose all kinds of wacky materials for the look of your game board (Wood, Metal, Marble, or *Grass*) and for your playing pieces (Wood, Metal, Marble, or *Fur*).

- **Computer Plays.** Use this slider to determine how frustrated you want to get when trying to win at Chess. The farther you drag the slider toward the Stronger side, the more calculations the computer runs before making its next move—and, thus, the harder it gets for you to outthink it. At the Faster setting, Chess won't spend more than 5 seconds ruminating over possible moves. Drag the slider all the way to the right, however, and the program may analyze *each move* for as long as 10 fun-filled hours. This hardest setting, of course, makes it all but impossible to win a game (which may stretch on for a week or more anyway).

  Choosing the Faster setting makes it only mildly impossible.

- **Speech.** The two checkboxes here let you play Chess using the Mac's built-in voice-recognition features, *telling* your chess pieces where to go instead of dragging them, and listening to the Mac tell you which moves it's making.

Studying Your Games

You can choose Game→Save to save any game in progress, so you can resume it later.

To analyze the moves making up a game, use the Window→Game Log command, which displays the history of your game, move by move. A typical move would be recorded as "Nb8 – c6," meaning the knight on the b8 square moved to the c6 square. Equipped with a Chess list document, you could recreate an entire game, move by move.

Tip: If you open this window before you begin a new game, you can see the game log fill in the moves *as they happen*.

Dashboard

Dashboard, described in Chapter 4, is a true-blue, double-clickable application. As a result, you can remove its icon from your Dock, if you like.

Dictionary

For word nerds everywhere, the Dictionary (and thesaurus) is a blessing—a handy way to look up word definitions, pronunciations, and synonyms. To be precise, Mac OS X comes with electronic versions of multiple reference works in one:

- The entire New Oxford American Dictionary. The *third* edition, actually.

- The complete Oxford American Writer's Thesaurus.

- A dictionary of Apple terms, from "A/UX" to "Xsan." (Apparently there aren't any Apple terms that begin with Y or Z.)

- Wikipedia. Of course, this famous open-source, citizen-created encyclopedia isn't actually on your Mac. All Dictionary does is give you an easy way to search the *online* version, and display the results right in the comfy Dictionary window.

- A Japanese dictionary, thesaurus, and Japanese-to-English translation dictionary.

Tip: You don't ordinarily see the Japanese reference books. You have to turn them on in Dictionary→ Preferences.

Mac OS X also comes with about a million ways to look up a word:

- **If you have a trackpad, point to a word in a basic Mac program, and then double-touch the trackpad (don't actually click) with three fingers.** (It doesn't work unless you've turned it on in System Preferences→Trackpad.)

- **Double-click the Dictionary icon.** You get the window shown at top in Figure 16-3. As you type into the Spotlight-y search box, you home in on matching words; click a word, or highlight it and press Return, to view a full, typographically elegant definition, complete with sample sentence and pronunciation guide.

Tip: And if you don't recognize a word in the definition, click *that word* to look up *its* definition. (Each word turns blue and underlined when you point to it, as a reminder.) You can then click again in *that* definition—and on, and on, and on.

(You can then use the ⊙ and ⊙ buttons on the toolbar, or the ⌘-[and ⌘-] keystrokes to go back and forward in your chain of lookups. Hold down the ⊙ for a pop-up menu of recent lookups.)

It's worth exploring the Dictionary→Preferences dialog box, by the way. There you can choose U.S. or British pronunciations and adjust the font size.

- **Press** ①. Yes, the Dictionary is one of the widgets in Dashboard.

Figure 16-3:
When you open the Dictionary, it generally assumes that you want a word's definition (lower left). If you prefer to see the Wikipedia entry (top right) at startup time instead, for example, choose Dictionary→ Preferences—and drag Wikipedia upward so that it precedes New Oxford American Dictionary. That's all there is to it!

- **Right-click a highlighted word.** In modern programs, you get a shortcut menu; choose Look Up [word]. You get a panel that pops out of the highlighted word or the Dictionary program opens to that word.

- **Use the *dict://* prefix in Safari.** This might sound a little odd, but it's actually ultra-convenient, because it puts the dictionary right where you're most likely to need it: on the Web.

  Turns out that you can look up a word (for example, *preposterous)* by typing *dict:// preposterous* into the address bar—the spot where you'd normally type *http://www. whatever.* When you hit Return, Mac OS X opens Dictionary automatically and presents the search results from all of its resources (dictionary, thesaurus, Apple terms, and Wikipedia).

- **Point to a word in a basic Mac program, and then press Control-⌘-D.** That keystroke makes the definition panel sprout right from the word you were pointing to. (The advantage here, of course, is that you don't have to highlight the word first.) "Basic Mac program," in this case, means one of the Apple standards: Mail, Stickies, Safari, TextEdit, iChat, and so on.

The *front matter* of the Oxford American Dictionary (the reference section at the beginning) is here, too. It includes some delicious writers' tools, including guides to spelling, grammar, capitalization, punctuation, chemical elements, and clichés, along with the full text of the Declaration of Independence and the U.S. Constitution. Just choose Go→Front/Back Matter—and marvel that your Mac comes with a built-in college English course.

Tip: Got a big screen or poor eyesight? Then bump up the type size. Dictionary's toolbar has bigger/smaller buttons, and there's a Font Size pop-up menu in the Preferences window.

DVD Player

DVD Player, your Mac's built-in movie projector, is described in Chapter 9.

FaceTime

FaceTime is Apple's video-chat program. It lets you make free video calls to other Macs, or to i-gadgets like iPhones, iPads, and iPod Touches. (This assumes of course, that you and your conversation partner both have high-speed Internet connections. You also both need Macs with Mac OS 10.6.6 or later, and cameras, either built-in or external. And you need an Apple ID; see the box below. If this is your first time, enter your Apple ID and password on the right side of the window, and click Sign In.)

To make a video call, open FaceTime. It starts out looking a little weird—the panel that displays the actual video (you, at first) is tall and skinny, as though you're using—what else?—an iPhone.

UP TO SPEED

The Apple ID

Once you become a member of the Apple cult, the key that unlocks all Apple doors is your Apple ID. The same email address and password gets you into the iTunes Music Store, the Apple Store, the App Store, iChat, MobileMe or iCloud, and, yes, FaceTime.

In the unlikely event that you don't yet have an Apple ID, you can get one by filling out the form at *https://appleid. apple.com*.

You can also create a new account right from within Face-Time. Choose FaceTime→Preferences, click Account, and then click Create New Account.

Place a FaceTime Call

Now you have to choose someone to call. Ironically, this setup step usually begins with a more old-fashioned communication—a phone call or a text message, for example. ("Want to FaceTime now?")

Figure 16-4:
Yes, iChat also offers video calls—but FaceTime doesn't need as fast an Internet connection. You'll often be able to make FaceTime video calls in situations when iChat gives up.

The panel on the right side of the window offers three tab buttons (at the bottom). Click Contacts to see everyone in your Mac OS X address book. If there *is* nobody in your address book, click the **+** button at upper right and enter the FaceTime contact information of your first calling buddy. If you're calling an iPhone, the contact info should be a phone number. For any other machine, it's an email address. Click Done when you've entered the information.

(As in the actual Address Book app, you can put people into groups, like "Work" or "Social Circle." If you plan to use this feature, be sure to click Groups and select the proper one *before* you click **+** to add a new person.)

Tip: If you're smart, you'll pluck out the people you plan to FaceTime with most frequently and put them into your Favorites list (the first tab at the bottom). To do that, click the person's name on the Contacts tab and then click Add to Favorites. (If there's more than one email address or phone number, a subsequent screen lets you click the one you want to use.)

To remove someone from the Favorites list, click the Edit button (on the Favorites tab) and then click the ⊖ button next to the person's name.

All right then. To make the actual call, take one of these steps:

• **Click the person's name** in your Favorites list.

• **Click the Recents tab**, where you'll see a list of FaceTime calls you've recently made or received. Click the person's name.

• **Click Contacts.** Click Groups, if you use the Groups feature, and click the group the person is in. Use the search box, or just scroll, to find the person you want to call. Click the name; if you have multiple email addresses or phone numbers for that person, click the one you want.

In any case, your Mac now attempts to connect to your FaceTime-equipped buddy. After a moment, the video image of *you* is replaced by the video image of your calling buddy (Figure 16-4). If you both have fast Internet connections, and if the other guy has a recent Mac (with a so-called FaceTime HD camera), the video should look pretty amazing—hi-def, actually.

Once You're Connected

Once the FaceTime session has begun, just talk normally. You're on camera!

Here's some of the fun you can have during your call:

• **Resize the window.** Drag any window edge, click the Zoom button (upper left), or choose Window→Zoom to make the window fill the screen.

• **Go full-screen.** Click the ⬚ button (upper right) to make the window fill your entire screen. (Click it again to restore the window.)

Tip: You can also enter or exit full-screen mode by spreading or pinching two fingers on your trackpad.

• **Move the inset.** The little picture-in-picture rectangle shows *you.* You can drag it to a different corner of the video window, if you like.

• **Rotate the screen.** If you're calling an iPad/iPhone/iPod Touch, the shape of the video-image rectangle changes automatically to match. But you can change the orientation of the window yourself, too. Either use the Video menu (choose Use Portrait or Use Landscape), or click the curved arrow in the inset that shows you, or use the Rotate gesture on your trackpad (two fingers, rotate).

- **Mute the mike.** Either choose Video→Mute, or click the 🎤 button at the bottom of the video window. The video continues. This is handy when you have to make ugly throat-clearing sounds or yell at your kid in the background.

- **Pause the call.** You can also pause the audio *and* video, for use when you have to perform small acts of personal grooming. To do that, choose FaceTime→Hide FaceTime, or Control-click the FaceTime icon in the Dock and choose Hide from the shortcut menu.

Tip: The call is also paused whenever you minimize FaceTime.

Receiving Calls

Life is even simpler when somebody calls *you*. You hear the little chirpy incoming-call sound, and a message appears on your screen. (If iTunes is playing music, it pauses automatically. Sweet.)

Click Accept to start the call, or Decline if now is not the time. (In that case, your caller will be told that you're not available.)

FaceTime doesn't have to be running for you to receive a call. That's generally a cool feature—but if you really don't want to be interrupted, you can hang up a digital "Do Not Disturb" sign in any of these ways:

- In FaceTime, choose FaceTime→Turn FaceTime Off.

- In FaceTime, choose FaceTime→Preferences; click the Off switch.

- Sign out of FaceTime. (Choose FaceTime→Preferences, click Account, and then click Sign Out.)

Font Book

For details on this font-management program, see page 272.

GarageBand

GarageBand, Apple's do-it-yourself music construction kit, isn't actually part of Mac OS X. If you have a copy, that's because it's part of the iLife suite that comes on every new Mac (along with iMovie, iPhoto, and iWeb).

iCal

In many ways, iCal is not so different from those "Hunks of the Midwest Police Stations" paper calendars people leave hanging on the walls for months past their natural life span. In fact, in the Lion extreme makeover of iCal, it looks more than ever like a physical calendar.

Tip: iCal's Dock icon displays today's date—even when iCal isn't running.

But iCal offers several advantages over paper calendars. For example:

- It can automate the process of entering repeating events, such as weekly staff meetings or gym workouts.

- iCal can give you a gentle nudge (with a sound, a dialog box, or even an email) when an important appointment is approaching.

- iCal can share information with your Address Book program, with Mail, with your iPod or iPhone, with other Macs, or with "published" calendars on the Internet. Some of these features require one of those iCloud accounts described in Chapter 10. But iCal also works fine on a single Mac, even without an Internet connection.

- iCal can subscribe to other people's calendars. For example, you can subscribe to your spouse's calendar, thereby finding out when you've been committed to after-dinner drinks on the night of the big game on TV. You can also tell iCal to display your online calendars from Google and Yahoo, or even your company's Exchange calendar.

Working with Views

When you open iCal, you see something like Figure 16-5. By clicking one of the View buttons above the calendar, or by pressing ⌘-1, ⌘-2, ⌘-3, or ⌘-4, you can switch among these views:

Figure 16-5:
In iCal, the ◄ and ► buttons at top right take you to the previous or next day, week, month, or year (depending on your current view). In the new Day view, shown here, you can click the tiny numbers on the mini-calendar (top left of page) to change days. Double-click any appointment to open its Info balloon, shown in Figure 16-7.

- **Day** looks exactly like a day-at-a-time desk calendar. On the right-side "page," you see today's schedule on an hour-by-hour chart. On the left "page," you get a simple list of appointments for today and the next few days.

  If you choose iCal→Preferences, you can specify what hours constitute a workday. This is ideal both for those annoying power-life people who get up at 5 a.m. for two hours of calisthenics and for the more reasonable people who sleep until 11 a.m.

Tip: iCal provides three quick ways to get to the current day's date. Click Today (upper-right corner, between the ◀ and ▶), choose View→Go to Today, or press ⌘-T.

- **Week** fills the main display area with seven columns, reflecting the current week. (You can establish a five-day workweek instead in iCal→Preferences.)

Tip: If you double-click the date above the calendar, you open the Day view for that day.

- **Month** shows the entire month that contains today's date. Double-click a date number to open the Day view for that date.

Tip: If a Month-view square is too small to show everything you've got scheduled that day, you'll see a notation at the bottom of the square like, "3 more…" Sometimes, making the window bigger (or full screen) helps make more room, or you can just double-click the date's number to switch to Day view and see everything at once.

Figure 16-6:
Lion's Year view shows the entire year. The colors of the squares are a "heat map" that indicate how hectic your schedule is. If this book were in color, you'd see a range of shades from light yellow (not very busy) to deep red (you're in big trouble). Double-click a date to open the Day view for that date.

To save space, iCal generally doesn't show you the *times* of your appointments in Month view. If you'd like to see them anyway, choose iCal→Preferences, click General, and turn on "Show event times." Now each event's starting time appears in light gray, off to the right.

Tip: If your mouse has a scroll wheel, you can use it to great advantage in iCal. For example, when entering a date, turning the wheel lets you jump forward or backward in time. It also lets you change the priority level of a To Do item you're entering, or even tweak the time zone as you're setting it.

• **Year** view displays a "heat map" of the entire year (Figure 16-6).

In any of the views, *double-click* an appointment to see more about it. The very first time you do that, you get the summary balloon shown at top right in Figure 16-7. If you want to make changes, you can then click the Edit button to open a more detailed view.

Tip: In Week or Day view, iCal sprouts a handy horizontal line that shows where you are in time right now. (Look in the hours-of-the-day "ruler" down the left side of the window to see this line's little red bulb.) A nice touch, and a handy visual aid that can tell you at a glance when you're already late for something.

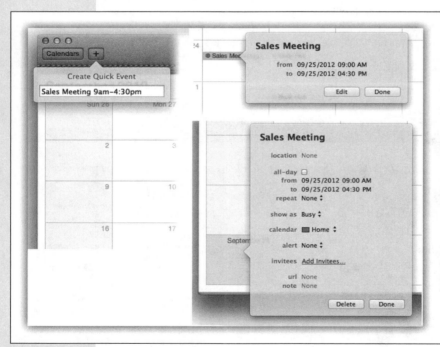

Figure 16-7:
Left: Type the name of the event and a time slot—for example, "Sales meeting 9am-4:30." Press Enter. Marvel as iCal interprets the times you typed and inserts "Sales meeting" into the right time slot. Right: All the details for an appointment sprout right out of the appointment itself in this balloon/box, shown here in both its collapsed (top) and expanded views. Tab your way to an organized life.

Also in any view, you can switch into full-screen view by clicking the ⬈ icon in the upper-right corner of the window. See page 11 for more on full-screen view.

Making an Appointment

The basic iCal calendar is easy to figure out. After all, with the exception of one unfortunate Gregorian incident, we've been using calendars successfully for centuries.

Even so, there are two ways to record a new appointment: using the mouse, or using the new Quick Event box.

The mousy way

You can quickly record an appointment using any of several techniques, listed here in order of decreasing efficiency:

- In Month view, double-click a blank spot on the date you want. Type the name of the event and a time slot—for example, *Sales meeting 9am-4:30*. (See "The Quick Event way," below, for details on how iCal interprets these time notations.)

- In Day or Week view, double-click the starting time to create a one-hour appointment. Or drag vertically through the time slots that represent the appointment's duration. Either way, type the event's name inside the newly created colored box.

- In any view, right-click a date and choose New Event from the shortcut menu. Type the event's name.

  Unless you use the drag-over-hours method, a new event believes itself to be one hour long. But in Day or Week view, you can adjust its duration by dragging the bottom edge vertically. Drag the dark top bar up or down to adjust the start time.

In many cases, that's all there is to it. You've just specified the day, time, and title of the appointment. Now you can get on with your life.

Tip: If the Edit balloon is blocking a part of the calendar you need to see, no biggie: Just drag the balloon out of the way, using any blank spot as a handle.

The Quick Event way

iCal understands notations like "7 pm Friday," and puts your new appointment into the right time slot automatically.

To use this method, press ⌘-N. (Or click the **+** button—top left of the window—or choose File→New Event). The Quick Event box appears. Proceed as shown in Figure 16-7.

Note: iCal proposes adding the new appointment to your *default calendar*—that is, the category you use most often (read on for details on these calendar categories). Supposedly, you've already told it which category is your preferred one by using the iCal→Preferences→General→Default Calendar pop-up menu.

But as you add a new appointment this way, you can override that setting by *holding down* the **+** button. You get a pop-up menu of your calendar categories; only after you click the one you want do you see the Quick Event box shown in Figure 16-7.

Into the Quick Event box, you're supposed to type the name of your appointment and its date and time. For example, you could type *Report deadline Aug 12,* or *"Titanic 2: The Return" Sat 7 pm,* or *Cara date 11-11:15am.*

When you press Return, iCal interprets what you typed, using these rules:

- If you didn't specify an ending time, iCal sets the appointment to 1 hour long.

- If you didn't enter *any* time information, iCal figures you meant an all-day event like a birthday, holiday, or deadline.

- If you typed *breakfast* or *morning,* iCal sets the appointment to start at 9 a.m.; *lunch* or *noon,* it starts at 12 p.m.; *dinner* or *night,* it starts at 8 p.m.

- If you enter a weekday (for example, *Chicago Monday*), iCal assumes you mean the very next occurrence of that day. (If that's not what you want, enter the date, like *Chicago Jul 3.*)

- If you enter a time but not a date or day (for example, *Fishing 3:30 pm*), iCal assumes you mean today.

Alarms, repeats, and other details

No matter which method you use to create the basic event (the mouse way or the Quick Event way), you're now presented with the information balloon shown at lower right in Figure 16-7. Here's where you go to town filling in the details. (This same balloon will appear when you double-click any existing appointment later.)

Tip: After you've already edited an appointment once, the full info balloon is a little more effort to open; double-clicking an event produces only the summary balloon shown in Figure 16-5.

The short way to open the full balloon is to click the appointment and then press ⌘-E (which is short for Edit→Edit Event). The long way is to double-click the appointment to get the summary balloon and then click Edit inside it.

But the *best* solution to this problem is to avail yourself of an option in iCal→Preferences→Advanced. It's the checkbox called "Open events in separate windows." Now when you double-click an appointment in iCal, it opens immediately into a full-size Details window, saving you that intermediate step forever. (You can close the window with a quick ⌘-W.)

For each appointment, you can Tab your way to the following information areas:

- **subject.** That's the name of your appointment. For example, *Fly to Phoenix.*

- **location.** You might type a reminder for yourself like *My place,* a specific address like *212 East 23,* or some other helpful information, like a contact phone number or flight number.

- **all-day.** An "all-day" event, of course, refers to something that has no specific time of day associated with it: a holiday, a birthday, a book deadline. When you turn on this box, you see the name of the appointment jump to the top of the iCal screen, in the area reserved for this kind of thing.

- **from, to.** You can adjust the times shown here by typing, clicking buttons, or both. Press Tab to jump from one setting to another, and from there to the hours and minutes of the starting time.

  For example, start by clicking the hour, and then increase or decrease this number either by pressing ↑ and ↓ or by typing a number. Press Tab to highlight the minutes and repeat the arrow-buttons-or-keys business. Finally, press Tab to highlight the AM/PM indicator, and type either *A* or *P*—or press ↑ or ↓—to change it, if necessary.

Tip: If you specify a different ending date, a *banner* appears across the top of the calendar.

- **time zone.** This option appears only after you choose iCal→Preferences→Advanced and then turn on "Turn on time zone support." And you would do *that* only if you plan to be traveling on the day this appointment comes to pass.

  Once you've done that, a time zone pop-up menu appears. It starts out with "America/New York" (or whatever your Mac's usual time zone is); if you choose Other, a tiny world map appears. Click the time zone that represents where you'll be when this appointment comes due. From the shortcut menu, choose the major city that's in the same zone you'll be in.

Tip: The time zone pop-up menu remembers each new city you select. The next time you travel to a city you've visited before, you won't have to do that clicking-the-world-map business.

Now, when you arrive in the distant city, use the time zone pop-up menu at the top-right corner of the iCal window to tell iCal where you are. You'll see all of iCal's appointments jump, like magic, to their correct new time slots.

- **repeat.** The pop-up menu here contains common options for recurring events: every day, every week, and so on. It starts out saying None.

  Once you've made a selection, you get an *end* pop-up menu that lets you specify when this event should *stop* repeating. If you choose "Never," you're stuck seeing this event repeating on your calendar until the end of time (a good choice for recording, say, your anniversary, especially if your spouse might be consulting the same calendar). You can also turn on "After (a certain number of times)," which is a useful option for car and mortgage payments. And if you choose "On date," you can specify the date when the repetitions come to an end; use this option to indicate the last day of school, for example.

  "Custom" lets you specify repeat schedules like "First Monday of the month" or "Every two weeks."

- **show as (busy/free/tentative/out of office).** This little item shows up only if you've subscribed to a calendar server, like an Internet-based calendar (in geek-speak, a CalDAV server) or your company's Exchange calendar. It communicates to your colleagues when you might be available for meetings.

Note: If your calendar comes from a CalDAV server, then your only options are "busy" and "free." The factory setting for most appointments is "busy," but for all-day events it's "free." Which is logical; just because it's International Gecko Appreciation Day doesn't mean you're not available for meetings (rats!).

You might think: "Well, *duh*—if I've got something on the calendar, then I'm obviously busy!" But not necessarily. Some iCal entries might just be placeholders, reminders to self, TV shows you wanted to watch, appointments you'd be willing to change—not things that would necessarily render you unavailable if a better invitation should come along.

- **calendar.** A *calendar,* in iCal's confusing terminology, is a subset—a category—into which you can place various appointments. You can create one for yourself, another for family-only events, another for book-club appointments, and so on. Later, you'll be able to hide and show these categories at will, adding or removing them from iCal with a single click. Details begin on page 565.

Tip: Use this same pop-up menu to *change* an appointment's category. If you filed something in "Company Memos" that should have been in "Sweet Nothings for Honey-Poo," then open the event's information balloon and reassign it. Quick.

- **alert.** This pop-up menu tells iCal how to notify you when a certain appointment is about to begin. iCal can send any of four kinds of flags to get your attention. It can display a message on the screen (with a sound, if you like), send you an email, run a script (if you're handy with AppleScript), or open a file on your hard drive. (You could use this unusual option to ensure that you don't forget a work deadline by having iCal fling the relevant document open in front of your face at the eleventh hour.)

Once you've specified an alarm mechanism, a new pop-up menu appears to let you specify how much advance notice you want for this particular appointment. If it's a TV show you'd like to watch, you might set up a reminder 5 minutes before airtime. If it's a birthday, you might set up a two-day warning to give yourself enough time to buy a present. In fact, you can set up more than one alarm for the same appointment, each with its own advance-warning interval.

Tip: In iCal→Preferences→Advanced, you can opt to prevent alarms from going off—a good checkbox to inspect before you give a presentation in front of 2,000 people. There's also an option to stifle alarms *except* when iCal is open. In other words, just quitting iCal is enough to ensure that those alarms won't interrupt whatever you're doing.

- **invitees.** If the appointment is a meeting or some other gathering, you can type the participants' names here. If a name is already in your Address Book program, iCal proposes autocompleting the name for you.

If you separate several names with commas, iCal automatically turns each into a shaded oval button. You can click it for a pop-up menu of commands like Remove

Attendee and Send Email. (That last option appears only if the person in Address Book has an email address, or if you typed a name *with* an email address in brackets, like this: *Chris Smith <chris@yahoo.com>.*)

Once you've specified some attendees, a Send button appears in the Info box. If you click it, iCal fires up Mail and prepares ready-to-send messages, each with an *iCal.ics* attachment: a calendar-program invitation file. See the box below.

- **attachments.** This option lets you fasten a file to the appointment. It can be anything: a photo of the person you're meeting, a document to finish by that deadline, the song that was playing the first time you met this person—whatever.

- **url.** A *URL* is a Uniform Resource Locator, better known as a Web address, like *www. apple.com.* If there's a URL relevant to this appointment, by all means type it here. Type more than one, if it'll help you; just be sure to separate them all with commas.

- **note.** Here's your chance to customize your calendar event. You can type, paste, or drag any text you like in the note area—driving directions, contact phone numbers, a call history, or whatever.

Your newly scheduled event now shows up on the calendar, complete with the color coding that corresponds to the calendar category you've assigned.

What to Do with an Appointment

Once you've entrusted your agenda to iCal, you can start putting it to work. iCal is only too pleased to remind you (via pop-up messages) of your events, reschedule them, print them out, and so on. Here are a few of the possibilities.

UP TO SPEED

Inviting Guests

The truth is, this business of automatic invitations to iCal events hasn't really caught on yet. Unless you've hooked up iCal to your company's Exchange server, the invitations system is still fairly complicated, and it requires compatible software on the receiving end.

When you click Send at the bottom of the info balloon, your guests receive your invitation. If they use iCal, the invitation appears in their Notifications panels. (To open the Notifications panel, click the tiny envelope icon in the lower-left corner of the window.) They can click Accept, Decline, or Maybe.

In your Notifications window, you then see the status of each invitee's name: a checkmark for Accepted, an X for Declined, a ? for Maybe, and an arrow for Not Yet Responded.

(Your guests, meanwhile, will be delighted to find that the appointment automatically appears on their calendars once they commit.)

Now, suppose you send an invitation to your sister, who doesn't have a Mac. She just gets an email message that says, "Chris Smith has invited you to the event: Company Hoedown, scheduled for February 02, 2012 at 3:00 PM. To accept or decline this invitation, click the link below." Unfortunately, there generally *is* no link. She just has to know to open the .ics attachment.

If she uses a calendar program that understands this attachment, the appointment appears on her calendar, and her RSVP shows up in your iCal Notification panel.

Editing events

To edit a calendar event's details, you have to open its Info balloon, as shown in Figure 16-5.

If you just want to change an event's name, Option-double-click it in place. And if you want to change only an appointment's category, right-click it and, from the shortcut menu, choose the category you want. In both cases, you bypass the Info balloon.

You don't have to bother with this if all you want to do is reschedule an event, however, as described next.

Rescheduling events

If an event in your life gets rescheduled, you can drag an appointment block vertically in a Day- or Week-view column to make it later or earlier the same day, or horizontally to another date in any view. (If you reschedule a recurring event, iCal asks if you want to change only *this* occurrence, or this *and* all future ones.)

If something is postponed for, say, a month or two, you're in trouble, since you can't drag an appointment beyond its month window. You have no choice but to open the Info balloon and edit the starting and ending dates or times—or just cut and paste the event to a different date.

Lengthening or shortening events

If a scheduled meeting becomes shorter or your lunch hour becomes a lunch hour-and-a-half (in your dreams), changing the length of the representative calendar event is as easy as dragging the bottom border of its block in any column view (see Figure 16-8).

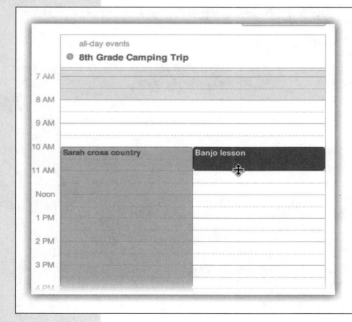

Figure 16-8:
You can resize any iCal calendar event just by dragging its bottom border. As your cursor touches the bottom edge of a calendar event, it turns into a double-headed arrow. You can now drag the event's edge to make it take up more or less time on your calendar.

Tip: In Week view, if you've grabbed the *bottom* edge of an appointment's block so that the cursor changes, you can drag *horizontally* to make an appointment cross the midnight line and extend into a second day.

Printing events

To commit your calendar to paper, choose File→Print, or press ⌘-P. The resulting Print dialog box lets you include only a certain range of dates, only events on certain calendars, with or without To Do lists or mini-month calendars, and so on.

Deleting events

To delete an appointment, just select it and then press the Delete key. If you delete a recurring event (like a weekly meeting), iCal asks whether you want to delete only that particular instance of the event, or the whole series from that point forward.

Searching for Events

You should recognize the oval text box at the top of the iCal screen immediately: It's almost identical to the Spotlight box. This search box is designed to let you hide all appointments except those matching what you type into it. Figure 16-9 has the details.

Figure 16-9:
As you type into the search box (top right), iCal builds a little search-results list at the bottom of the window. Double-click any row of the list to jump to and highlight the corresponding event on the calendar and open up its summary balloon.

The "Calendar" Category Concept

Just as iTunes has *playlists* that let you organize songs into subsets and iPhoto has *albums* that let you organize photos into subsets, iCal has *calendars* that let you organize appointments into subsets. They can be anything you like. One person might have calendars called Home, Work, and TV Reminders. Another might have

Me, Spouse 'n' Me, and Whole Family. A small business could have categories called Deductible Travel, R&D, and R&R.

To create a calendar, choose File→New Calendar. From the pop-up menu, specify *where* you want this category to live: either On My Mac (which means "on your Mac")—or, if you've subscribed to an online calendar or two, the name of the online account, like Google or Exchange. Type a name that defines the category in your mind.

Tip: Click a calendar name *before* you create an appointment. That way, the appointment will already belong to the correct calendar.

To see your list of categories, click the Calendars button (upper left of the window). A pop-up list appears. To change the color-coding of your category, Control-click (right-click) its name in this pop-up list; from the shortcut menu, choose Get Info. The Calendar Info box appears. Here, you can change the name, color, or description of this category—or turn off its alarms.

You assign an appointment to one of these categories using the pop-up menu (on its Info balloon), or by Control-clicking (right-clicking) an event and choosing a calendar name from the shortcut menu. After that, you can hide or show an entire category of appointments at once just by turning on or off the appropriate checkbox in the Calendars pop-up list.

Tip: iCal also has calendar *groups:* calendar containers that consolidate the appointments from several *other* calendars. (For example, you could have a calendar group called Kids, containing the individual calendars for each of your offspring. Super-calendars like this make it easier to manage, hide, show, print, and search subsets of your appointments.

To create a calendar group, choose File→New Calendar Group. Name the resulting item in the Calendar list; for the most part, it behaves like any other calendar. Drag other calendar names onto it to include them. Click the flippy triangle to hide or show the component calendars.

"Publishing" Calendars to the Web

One of iCal's best features is its ability to post your calendar on the Web, so that other people (or you, on a different computer) can subscribe to it, which adds *your* appointments to *their* calendars. Anyone with a Web browser—or only people you designate—can also *view* your calendar, right online.

For example, you might use this feature to post the meeting schedule for a club that you manage, or to share the agenda for a series of upcoming financial meetings that all your coworkers will need to consult.

Publishing

If you don't have iCloud: Begin by clicking the Calendars button; in the list of categories, click the calendar you want to publish. (iCal can publish only one calendar category at a time. If you want to publish more than one calendar, then create a calendar *group*.)

Now choose Calendar→Publish; the dialog box shown at top in Figure 16-10 appears. This is where you customize how your saved calendar is going to look and work. You can even turn on "Publish changes automatically," so whenever you edit the calendar, iCal connects to the Internet and updates the calendar there. (Otherwise, you'll have to choose Calendar→Refresh every time you want to update the Web copy.)

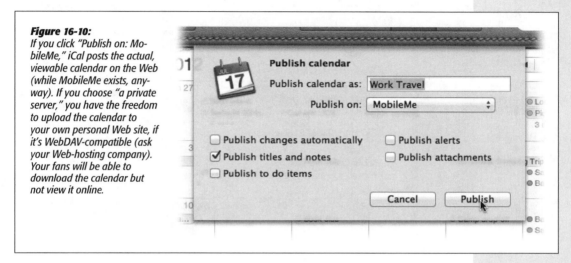

Figure 16-10:
If you click "Publish on: MobileMe," iCal posts the actual, viewable calendar on the Web (while MobileMe exists, anyway). If you choose "a private server," you have the freedom to upload the calendar to your own personal Web site, if it's WebDAV-compatible (ask your Web-hosting company). Your fans will be able to download the calendar but not view it online.

When you click Publish, your Mac connects to the Web and then shows you the Web address (the URL) of the finished page, complete with a Send Mail button that lets you fire the URL off to your colleagues.

Tip: Whenever you want to send someone the subscription information, click the Calendars button; click the calendar category you've published; and choose Calendar→Send Publish Email. iCal will prepare an outgoing email message containing details on subscribing to your calendar.

To stop publishing that calendar, click its name in the Calendars pop-up list and then choose Calendar→Unpublish.

If you have iCloud: Click the Calendars button; in the list of categories, click the calendar you want to publish. It has to be one of the ones in the iCloud ("@me.com") group.

Now choose Calendar→Share Calendar. In the resulting dialog box, specify Everyone (anyone can see, but not edit, the calendar) or "Only the people you invite" (they'll be able to edit the calendar, too—a delightful, two-way collaboration—a terrific way for a couple or family to coordinate their calendars, for example). If you choose the latter, fill in the invitees in the little list that appears. Finally, click Share.

Later, you can modify the settings by choosing Calendar→Share Calendar, or stop sharing by choosing Calendar→Stop Sharing.

Tip: You can also share an iCloud calendar at *www.icloud.com.* Proceed as shown in Figure 16-11.

Figure 16-11:
You can share a calendar with another iCloud member by clicking the .ℕ button. Supply that member's me.com address and press Return. Now, as shown here, you can change the other person's access from "View and Edit" to "View Only," if you so desire. Click Share. (In the next box, indicate whether you want an email note every time the other person makes a change.)

Subscribing

If somebody else has published a calendar, you can subscribe to it by choosing Calendar→Subscribe. In the Subscribe to Calendar dialog box, type in the Internet address you received from the person who published the calendar.

You can also specify how often you want your own copy to be updated (assuming you have a full-time Internet connection) and whether or not you want to be bothered with the publisher's alarms and notes.

When it's all over, you see a new "calendar" category in your left-side list, representing the published appointments.

Tip: Want to try it out right now? Visit *www.icalshare.com*, a worldwide clearinghouse for sets of iCal appointments. You can subscribe to calendars for shuttle launches, Mac trade shows, National Hockey League games, NASCAR races, soccer matches, the *Iron Chef* and *Survivor* TV shows, holidays, and much more. You'll never suffer from empty-calendar syndrome again.

Google and Yahoo Calendars

If you maintain a calendar online—at *www.google.com/calendar* or *http://calendar.yahoo.com,* for example, you may take particular pleasure in discovering how easy it is to bring those appointments into iCal. It's one handy way to keep, for example, a husband's and wife's appointments visible on each other's calendars.

Setting this up is ridiculously easy (see Figure 16-12).

In a minute or so, you'll see all your Google or Yahoo appointments show up in iCal. (Each Web calendar has its own heading in the left-side list.) Better yet: It's a two-way sync; changes you make to these events in iCal show up on the Web, too.

Figure 16-12:
To bring your Yahoo or Google calendar into iCal for free two-way syncing, choose iCal→Preferences→Accounts. Click the + button below the list. Enter your Google or Yahoo address (for example, ned.flanders@gmail.com) and password, as shown here. Click Create.

To Do Lists

iCal's Reminders feature lets you make a To Do list and shepherds you along by giving you gentle reminders, if you so desire (Figure 16-13). What's nice is that Mac OS X maintains a single To Do list, which shows up in both iCal and Mail.

To see the list, choose View→Show Reminders (or press ⌘-Option-T). Add a new task by double-clicking a blank spot in the list that appears, or by choosing File→New Reminder. After the new item appears, you can type to name it.

To change the task's priority, alarm, and so on, double-click it. An Info balloon appears, just as it does for an appointment.

Tip: Actually, there's a faster way to change a To Do item's priority—click the tiny three-line ribbed handle at the right side of the list. Turns out it's a shortcut menu that lets you choose Low, Medium, or High priority (or None).

To sort the list (by priority, for example), use the pop-up menu at the top of the Reminders list. To delete a task, click it and then press the Delete key.

Tip: You have lots of control over what happens to a task listing *after* you check it off. In iCal→Preferences→ Advanced, for example, you can make tasks auto-hide or auto-delete themselves after, say, a week or a month. And if you asked them to auto-hide themselves, you can make them reappear temporarily using the Show All Completed Items command in the pop-up menu at the top of the To Do list.

Also in that pop-up menu: the new Hide Items After Calendar View command. It declutters your Reminders list by omitting all appointments whose due dates fall after the currently displayed day, week, month, or year.

Figure 16-13:
Using the To Do Info balloon, you can give your note a priority, a calendar (category), or a due date. Tasks that come due won't show up on the calendar itself, but a little exclamation point triangle appears in the To Do Items list.

Syncing iCal with Your iPhone, iPad, and Other Computers

Here's the real magic of iCal, iCloud, and the rest of Apple's software archipelago: Your calendar can be auto-synced among all your machines, like your iPhone, iPad, and Macs. Add an appointment on your phone, change an appointment on your iPad, whatever—all your other gadgets are wirelessly and automatically synced to match. See Chapter 10 for details on this amazing setup.

iChat

Details on the iChat instant-messaging program can be found in Chapter 12.

iDVD

iDVD isn't really part of Mac OS X, although you probably have a copy of it: As part of the iLife software suite, iDVD comes free on every new Mac. iDVD lets you turn your digital photos or camcorder movies into DVDs that work on almost any DVD player, complete with menus, slideshow controls, and other navigation features. iDVD handles the technology; you control the style.

Image Capture

This unsung little program was originally designed to download pictures from a camera and then process them automatically (turning them into a Web page, scaling them to emailable size, and so on). Of course, after Image Capture's birth, iPhoto came along, generally blowing its predecessor out of the water.

Even so, Apple includes Image Capture with Mac OS X for these reasons:

- Image Capture is a smaller, faster app for downloading all or only some pictures from your camera (Figure 16-14). iPhoto can do that nowadays, but sometimes that's like using a bulldozer to get out a splinter.

- Image Capture can grab images from scanners, too, not just cameras.

- Image Capture can download your *sounds* (like voice notes) from a digital still camera; iPhoto can't.

You can open Image Capture in either of two ways: You can simply double-click its icon in your Applications folder, or you can set it up to open automatically whenever

Figure 16-14:
In many ways, Image Capture is like a mini iPhoto; use the slider in the lower right to change the thumbnail sizes. Use the "Delete after import" checkbox (lower left) if you want your camera's card erased after you slurp in its photos. You can choose the individual pictures you want to download, rotate selected shots (using the buttons at the top), or delete shots from the camera.

you connect a digital camera and turn it on. To set up that arrangement, open Image Capture manually. Using the "Connecting this camera opens:" pop-up menu, choose Image Capture.

Once Image Capture is open, it looks like Figure 16-14. When you connect your camera, cellphone, or scanner, its name appears in the left-side list. To begin, click it. After a moment, Image Capture displays all the photos on the camera's card, in either list view or icon view (your choice).

Import To:

Use this pop-up menu to specify what happens to the imported pictures. Image Capture proposes putting photos, sounds, and movies from the camera into your Home folder's Pictures folder. But you can specify any folder (choose Other from the pop-up menu).

Furthermore, there are some other very cool options here:

- **iPhoto.** Neat that you can direct photos from your camera *to* iPhoto *via* Image Capture. Might come in handy when you didn't *expect* to want to load photos into your permanent collection, but you change your mind when you actually look them over in Image Capture.

- **Preview** opens the fresh pictures in Preview so you can get a better (and bigger) look at them.

- **Mail** sends the pix directly into the Mac's email program, which can be very handy when the whole point of getting the photos off the camera is to send them off to friends.

- **Build web page** creates an actual Web page of your downloaded shots. Against a dark-gray background, you get thumbnail images of the pictures in a Web page document called *index.html*. Just click one of the small images to view it at full size, exactly as your Web site visitors will be able to do once this page is actually on the Web. (Getting it online is up to you.)

Note: Image Capture puts the Web page files in a Home folder→Pictures→Webpage on [today's date and time] folder. It contains the graphics files incorporated into this HTML document; you can post the whole thing on your Web site, if you like.

Image Capture automatically opens up this page in your Web browser, proud of its work.

- **MakePDF.** What is MakePDF? It's a little app you didn't even know you had.

When you choose this option, you wind up with what looks like a Preview window, showing thumbnails of your photos. If you choose Save right now, you'll get a beautiful, full-color PDF of the selected photos, ready to print out and then, presumably, cut apart with scissors or a paper cutter. But if you use the Layout menu, you can choose different layouts for your photos: 3 × 5, 4 × 6, 8 × 10, and so on.

And what if a photo doesn't precisely fit the proportions you've selected? The Crop commands in the Layout menu (for example, "Crop to 4 × 6") center each photo within the specified shape and then trim the outer borders if necessary. The Fit commands, on the other hand, *shrink* the photo as necessary to fit into the specified dimensions, sometimes leaving blank white margins.

Note: The "crop" commands never touch the actual downloaded photos. The downloaded image files themselves retain their full sizes and resolutions.

• **Other.** The beauty of the Image Capture system is that people can, in theory, write additional processing scripts. Once you've written or downloaded them, drop them into your System→Library→Image Capture→Automatic Tasks folder. Then enjoy their presence in the newly enhanced Import To pop-up menu.

Import Some, Import All

Clicking Import All, of course, begins the process of downloading the photos to the folder you've selected. A progress dialog box appears, showing you thumbnail images of each picture that flies down the wire.

If you prefer to import only *some* photos, select them first. (In list view, you click and Shift-click to select a bunch of *consecutive* photos, and ⌘-click to add *individual* photos to the selection. In icon view, you can both ⌘-click and *Shift*-click to select individual photos.) Then click Import.

Scanning

If you own a scanner, chances are good that you won't be needing whatever special scanning software came with it. Instead, Mac OS X gives you two programs that can operate any standard scanner: Image Capture and Preview. In fact, the available controls are identical in both programs. See page 298.

iMovie, iPhoto

Here's another pair of iLife apps—not really part of Mac OS X, but kicking around on your Mac because iLife comes with all new Macs.

Tip: Masterfully written, in-depth guides to these programs are available in the form of iMovie '11 & iDVD: The Missing Manual and iPhoto '11: The Missing Manual. (Corresponding Missing Manual titles are available for earlier versions of these programs, too.)

---

iTunes

iTunes is Apple's beloved digital music–library program. Chapter 9 tells all.

Launchpad

See Chapter 4 for the full story about Lion's program-opening Home screen.

Mail

See Chapter 11 for the missing Mail manual.

Mission Control

Chapter 4 covers Lion's new window-management tool.

Photo Booth

It may be goofy, it may be pointless, but the Photo Booth program is a bigger time drain than Solitaire, the Web, and *Dancing with the Stars* put together.

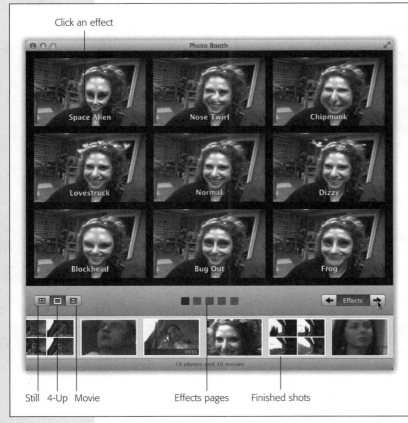

Click an effect

Figure 16-15:
The Photo Booth effects must have been dreamed up one night in the midst of a serious beer party at Apple. They're disturbingly creative. If you decide that you really look best without any help from Apple's warped imagery, click the Normal icon in the center.

Still 4-Up Movie   Effects pages   Finished shots

It's a match made in heaven for Macs that have a tiny video camera above the screen, but you can also use it with a camcorder, iSight, or Webcam. (Photo Booth doesn't even open if your Mac doesn't have *some* kind of camera.)

Open this program and then peer into the camera. Photo Booth acts like a digital mirror, showing whatever the camera sees—that is, you.

But then click the Effects button. You enter a world of special visual effects—and we're talking *very* special. Some make you look like a pinhead, or bulbous, or like a Siamese twin; others simulate Andy Warhol paintings, fisheye lenses, and charcoal sketches (Figure 16-15). In fact, there are five whole pages of effects, nine previews on a page. (The last two pages hold *backdrop* effects, described below.)

To page through them, click the left or right arrow buttons, or press ← or →, or swipe with two fingers on your trackpad (one finger on the Magic Mouse).

Tip: The first page contains eight effects that are new in Lion. Some of them use sophisticated face-recognition smarts to track your face as it moves around the frame. That's how Dizzy and Lovestruck are able to keep the animated birds or hearts circling your head, and how Chipmunk, Nose Twirl, and Bug Out are able to distort your cheeks, nose, and eyeballs even as you move around.

Some of the effects have sliders that govern their intensity; you'll see them appear when you click the preview.

Still Photos

When you find an effect that looks appealing (or unappealing, depending on your goals here), click the camera button, or press ⌘-T. You see and hear a 3-second countdown, and then *snap!*—your screen flashes white to add illumination, and the resulting photo appears on your screen. Its thumbnail joins the collection at the bottom.

Tip: If that countdown is getting on your nerves, *Option*-click the camera button. You can get rid of the screen flash, too, by *Shift*-clicking. Needless to say, if you press Option *and* Shift, you get neither the countdown nor the flash.

4-Up Photos

If you click the 4-Up button identified in Figure 16-15, then when you click the Camera icon (or press ⌘-T), the 3-2-1 countdown begins, and then Photo Booth snaps *four* consecutive photos in 2 seconds. You can exploit the timing just the way you would in a real photo booth—make four different expressions, horse around, whatever.

The result is a single graphic with four panes, kind of like what you get at a shopping-mall photo booth. (In Photo Booth, they appear rakishly assembled at an angle; but when you export the image, they appear straight, like panes of a window.) Its icon plops into the row of thumbnails at the bottom of the window, just like the single still photos.

Movies

Photo Booth can also record *videos*, complete with those wacky distortion effects. Click the third icon below the screen, the Movie icon (Figure 16-15), and then click the camera button (or press ⌘-T). You get the 3-2-1 countdown—but this time, Photo Booth records a video, with sound, until you click the Stop button. (The little digital counter at left reminds you that you're still filming.) When it's over, the movie's icon appears in the row of thumbnails, ready to play or export.

Tip: If you click a movie's thumbnail after recording it, a Trim button appears at the right end of the scroll bar. When you click it, yellow trim handles appear at both ends of the scroll bar (the same ones you'd see when trimming a video on the iPhone or iPad, or in iPhoto). Drag them inward to trim off any dead air at the beginning or end of your video clip. Hit the space bar to check your work. If the trim is OK, click the ◉ button to confirm the trim.

Still and Video Backdrops

Photo Booth and iChat are cousins, and they're closer than ever. One particular feature, in fact, is identical in each: custom backdrops. You can replace the actual, mundane background of your office or den with something far more exciting: a rushing waterfall, for example, or a rider's-eye view of a roller coaster. In fact, you can use any photo or video you want as the background.

It's just like the bluescreen or greenscreen technology that Hollywood uses to put actors someplace they're not—but without the bluescreen or greenscreen.

To replace your background in Photo Booth, click Effects. The fourth page of effects offers eight *canned* backgrounds, prepared by Apple for your enjoyment: various spectacular stills (cloudscape, color dots, the moon) and videos (Eiffel Tower plaza, aquarium, roller coaster, tropical beach, Yosemite waterfall).

The final page offers eight empty preview squares. You're supposed to drag a still or a video from your desktop (or iPhoto) into these empty squares, making them not so empty.

In any case, prepare the backdrop by clicking one of the preview squares. Photo Booth says, "Please step out of the frame." Do it. Photo Booth is going to memorize what its field of view looks like without you in it, so that when you reappear, it can tell *you* apart from your boring office background.

Now, when you record the movie or take the photo, you'll be amazed to discover that Photo Booth has just transplanted you to the far more exotic locale you selected. (Alas, blotches may result if the background includes movement or highly contrasting elements.)

Exporting Shots and Movies

To look at a photo or movie you've captured, click its thumbnail in the scrolling row at the bottom of the screen. (To return to camera mode, click the ⊙ button.)

Fortunately, these masterpieces of goofiness and distortion aren't locked in Photo Booth forever. You can share them with your adoring public in any of these ways:

- Click the photo or movie, and then choose File→Export. You're asked to name and save the exported image or video.

Tip: If you choose File→Export Original instead, the exported photo or video lacks any of the effects that you've applied. You get the original, undistorted, underlying photo—a useful new option in Lion.

- Drag a thumbnail out of the window to your desktop.
- Control-click (or right-click) a thumbnail. From the shortcut menu, choose Reveal in Finder. You're taken to the actual image or movie file on your hard drive, ready for copying, moving, deleting, renaming, or whatever.

Note: These files are stored in a single icon, a package file (page 136), that sits in your Home→Pictures folder. It's called Photo Booth Library. You'll find one JPEG apiece for single shots, four JPEG files for a 4-up, and a MOV file for videos.

- Click Email to send the photo or movie as an outgoing attachment in Mail.
- Click the Add to iPhoto button to import the shot or movie into iPhoto.
- Click User Picture to make this photo represent you on the Login screen.
- Click Buddy Picture to make this photo represent you in iChat (Chapter 12).

And speaking of interesting headshots: If you export a 4-up image and choose it as your Buddy Picture, you'll get an *animated* buddy icon. That is, your tiny icon cycles among the four images, creating a crude sort of animation. It's sort of annoying, actually, but all the kids are doing it.

As you set off on your Photo Booth adventures, a note of caution: Keep it away from children. They won't move from Photo Booth for the next 12 years.

Tip: Photo Booth is one of the certified full-screen apps. Click the ⊠ icon in the upper right to make the app fill your screen, for added graphic juiciness.

Preview

Preview is Mac OS X's scanning software, graphics viewer, fax viewer, and PDF reader. It's always been teeming with features that most Mac owners never even knew were there. It's a flagship Mac program, offering cutting-edge features like Autosave, Versions, and full-screen mode.

Tip: For the first time, Preview can open Microsoft Office documents (Word, PowerPoint, Excel) and iWork documents (Pages, Numbers, Keynote). You can't edit them in Preview, but you can read them, search them, and print them. No longer must you pay homage to Microsoft's bottom line just to have a look at the documents people send you.

Importing Camera Photos

Preview can import pictures directly from a digital camera (or iPhone), meaning that there are now *three* Mac OS X apps that can perform that duty. (iPhoto and Image Capture are the other two.) It's sometimes handy to use Preview for this purpose, though, because it has some great tools for photos: color-correction controls, size/resolution options, format conversion, and so on.

The actual importing process, though, is *exactly* like using Image Capture. Connect your camera, choose File→Import from [your camera's name], and carry on as described on page 572.

Operating Your Scanner

Preview can also operate a scanner, auto-straighten the scanned images, and export them as PDF files, JPEG graphics, and so on.

This, too, is *exactly* like using Image Capture to operate your scanner. Only the first step is different. Open Preview, choose File→Import from Scanner→[your scanner's name], and proceed as described on page 298.

Clearly, Apple saved some time by reusing some code.

Figure 16-16:
The Sidebar can display thumbnails, a table of contents, or annotations, or it can appear as a full-screen array of thumbnail images. Drag the central scroll bar to make the Sidebar bigger; drag the lower-right corner of the Sidebar to make the whole Preview window bigger.

Multiple Pages, Multiple Views

One hallmark of Preview is its effortless handling of *multiples:* multiple fax pages, multiple PDF files, batches of photos, and so on. The key to understanding the possibilities is mastering the Sidebar, shown in Figure 16-16. The idea is that these thumbnails let you navigate pages or graphics without having to open a rat's nest of individual windows.

Tip: You can drag these thumbnails from one Preview window's Sidebar into another. That's a great way to mix and match pages from different PDF documents into a single new one, for example.

To hide or show the Sidebar, chose one of these three commands from the View menu:

- **Thumbnails.** This standard view (Figure 16-16, left) offers a scrolling vertical list of miniature pages or photos. Click one to see it at full size in the main window. Make the thumbnails larger or smaller by dragging the window/Sidebar dividing line.

- **Table of Contents.** If you're looking over photos, this option turns the Sidebar into a scrolling list of their names. If you've opened a group of PDFs all at once, you see a list of them. Or, if you have a PDF that contains chapter headings, you see them listed in the Sidebar as, yes, a table of contents.

- **Contact Sheet.** When you choose this view, the *main* window scrolls away, leaving you with a full screen of thumbnail miniatures. It's like a light table where you can look over all the photos or PDF pages at once. Make them bigger or smaller using the slider in the lower left.

Preview as Graphics Viewer

Preview is surprisingly versatile. It can display and manipulate pictures saved in a wide variety of formats, including common graphics formats like JPEG, TIFF, PICT, and GIF; less commonly used formats like BMP, PNG, SGI, and TGA; and even Photoshop, EPS, and PDF graphics.

Tip: Don't miss the Tools→Show Magnifier command. It gives you a loupe: a magnifying circle (or, in a PDF document, a magnifying rectangle) that lets you inspect part of your graphic or PDF file more closely.

Bunches o' graphics

If you highlight a group of image files in the Finder and open them all at once (for example, by pressing ⌘-O), Preview opens the first one but lists the thumbnails of the whole group in the Sidebar. You can walk through them with the ↑ and ↓ keys, or you can choose View→Slideshow (Shift-⌘-F) to open a full-screen slideshow.

Tip: You can change the order of the photos just by dragging them around in the Sidebar, in any of its views.

Cropping graphics

To crop graphics in Preview, drag across the part of the graphic that you want to keep. To redraw, drag the round handles on the dotted rectangle; or, to proceed with the crop, choose Tools→Crop. (The keyboard shortcut is ⌘-K.)

Since Preview is an Autosave program, you can always return to the original if you change your mind someday.

Tip: You can also rotate an image—even a PDF document—in 90-degree increments and then flip it vertically or horizontally, using the commands in the Tools menu. In fact, if you select several thumbnails in the Sidebar first, you can rotate or flip them all simultaneously.

Fixing up photos

Preview is no Photoshop, but it's getting closer every year. Let us count the ways:

- **Choose Tools→Show Inspector.** A floating palette appears. Click the first tab to see the photo's name, when it was taken, its pixel dimensions, and so on. Click the second one for even more geeky photo details, including camera settings like the lens type, ISO setting, focus mode, whether the flash was on, and so on. The third tab lets you add keywords, so you'll be able to search for this image later using Spotlight. (The fourth is for PDF documents only, not photos; it lets you add

Figure 16-17:
Humble little Preview has grown up into a big, strong mini-Photoshop. You can really fix up a photo if you know what you're doing, using these sliders. Or you can just click the Auto Levels button. It sets all those sliders for you, which generally does an amazing job of making almost any photo look better.

annotations. A fifth tab appears only in PDF documents—for rotating, cropping, and resizing the file.)

- **Choose Tools→Adjust Color.** A translucent, floating color-adjustment palette appears, teeming with sliders for brightness, contrast, exposure, saturation (color intensity), temperature and tint (color cast), sharpness, and more. See Figure 16-17.

- **Choose Tools→Adjust Size.** This command lets you adjust a photo's resolution, which comes in handy a lot. For example, you can scale an unwieldy 10-megapixel, gazillion-by-gazillion-pixel shot down to a nice 640 × 480 JPEG that's small enough to send by email. Or you can shrink a photo down so it fits within a desktop window, for use as a window background (page 53).

There's not much to it. Type in the new print dimensions you want for the photo, in inches or whatever units you choose from the pop-up menu. If you like, you can also change the resolution (the number of pixels per inch) by editing the Resolution box.

Converting file formats

Preview doesn't just open all these file formats—it can also convert among most of them. You can pop open some old Mac PICT files and turn them into BMP files for a Windows user, pry open a TIFF file from a scanner and turn it into a JPEG for use on your Web site, and so on.

POWER USERS' CLINIC

Scaling and Resampling

When you're fooling around with a picture's size and resolution in the Change Size dialog box, you might find that a couple of the options take a little explaining.

If "Scale proportionally" is turned on, Preview changes the Height number when you change the Width number, and vice versa. In other words, it won't let you change the *shape* of the photo; that's why a little padlock icon appears to bracket the Height and Width boxes.

If "Resample image" is turned off, then Preview adjusts the image's size by making the exist-

ing dots bigger or smaller—but never changes the *number* of dots. (That's why a padlock bracket links all three boxes together. For example, you can make the image larger—but you'll lower the number of dots per inch.)

If "Resample image" is turned *on,* then you're giving Preview permission to add or subtract pixels as necessary to scale the photo up or down. Of course, it can't create detail that wasn't there in the original, but if you're scaling the picture *up,* it does a decent job of generating new pixels by averaging the colors of the neighboring ones.

Tip: What's even cooler is you can open raw PostScript files right into Preview, which converts them into PDF files on the spot. You no longer need a PostScript laser printer to print out high-end diagrams and page layouts that come to you as PostScript files. Thanks to Preview, even an inkjet printer can handle them.

All you have to do is open the file you want to convert and choose File→Export. In the dialog box that appears, choose the new format for the image using the Format pop-up menu (JPEG, TIFF, PNG, or Photoshop, for example). Finally, click Save to export the file.

Preview as PDF Reader

Preview is a nearly full-blown equivalent of Adobe Reader, the free program used by millions to read PDF documents. It lets you search PDF documents, copy text out of them, add comments, fill in forms, click live hyperlinks, add highlighting, circle certain passages, type in notes—features that used to be available only in Adobe's Acrobat Reader. And now, in the Lion version, you can even *sign PDF contracts,* slapping your actual signature onto the electronic document.

GEM IN THE ROUGH

A Lion Special: Sign PDF Documents with Your Real Signature

Of Lion's 250 new features, very few are quite as slick or useful as the PDF signature option. It lets your Mac *take a picture* of your actual written signature, which Preview then stores so that you can slap it into the PDF documents that will come through your life.

The first step is to teach Preview what your signature looks like. To do that, sign your name on a piece of plain white paper, using black ink. On the Annotations toolbar, click the Signature pop-up menu ⌄⌄S, and choose Create Signature from Built-in Camera. (You'll see your actual camera name, like iSight Camera or FaceTime HD Camera. And if you don't see the Annotations toolbar, choose View→Show Annotations Bar.)

Now hold up your written signature page in front of your Mac's camera. Make sure it's big enough to fill the box on the left side—never mind that it appears backwards—and position it so that it sits on the blue line, as shown here.

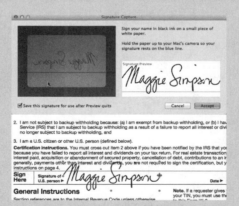

After a moment, your isolated, beautifully photographed signature appears in the Preview box.

When the positioning looks good, click Accept. You've just stored your signature. (You have to do this only once—per signature, anyway.)

When the time comes to sign a document, make the Annotations bar visible. From the ⌄⌄S pop-up menu, choose the signature's name. (Preview can store more than one signature; that's why this step is necessary.)

Now just click the document where you want the signature to appear. If there's a line you're supposed to sign on (such as a "Sign here" line), Preview is smart enough to shrink your scanned signature so that it fits on the line. Nice, huh?

You can delete signatures (and add new ones), if you like, using the Manage Signatures dialog box. Choose Manage Signatures from the ⌄⌄S pop-up menu on the Annotate bar.

Tip: Don't forget that Preview is one of Lion's certified full-screen apps. That is, you can make it fill your screen, border to border, by clicking the ⬚ icon in the upper-right corner. You can also flip through the pages of a PDF using the "next page" gesture: a two-finger swipe on the trackpad.

Here are the basics:

- Zoom in and out using ⌘-plus and ⌘-minus.

- Use the View menu commands to control how the PDF document appears: as two-page spreads; as single scrolling sheets of "paper towel"; with borders that indicate ends of pages; and so on.

- Press the space bar to page through a document (add Shift to page *upward*. The Page Up and Page Down keys do the same thing.)

Tip: Some PDF documents include a table of contents, which you'll see in Preview's Sidebar, complete with flippy triangles that denote major topics or chapter headings (Figure 16-16). You can use the ↑ and ↓ keys alone to walk through these chapter headings, and then expand one that looks good by pressing the → key. Collapse it again with the ← key.

In other words, you expand and collapse flippy triangles in Preview just as you do in a Finder list view. (The View→Sidebar submenu also includes Expand All and Collapse All commands.)

- Bookmark your place by choosing Bookmarks→Add Bookmark (⌘-D); type a clever name. In future, you'll be able to return to that spot by choosing its name from the Bookmarks menu.

- You can type in notes (in a box or a bubble), add clickable links (to Web addresses or other spots in the document), or use circles, arrows, rectangles, strikethrough, underlining, or yellow highlighting to draw your readers' attention to certain sections, as shown in Figure 16-18.

Figure 16-18: Click the button you want, and then drag diagonally to define a rectangle, oval, arrow, link, speech bubble, or thought bubble. You can look over the master list of notes using the Tools→ Show Inspector palette.

Tip: Preview ordinarily stamps each text note with your name and the date. If you'd rather not have that info added, choose Preview→Preferences, click PDF, and then turn off "Add name to annotations."

These remain living, editable entities even after the document is saved and re-opened. These are full-blown Acrobat annotations; they'll show up when your PDF document is opened by Acrobat Reader or even on Windows PCs.

Tip: You can add circles, arrows, rectangles, and text boxes, even on image files like photos.

- **Turn smoothing on or off to improve readability.** To find the on/off switch, choose Preview→Preferences, and click the PDF tab. Turn on "Smooth line art and text." (Though antialiased text generally looks great, it's sometimes easier to read very small type with antialiasing turned off. It's a little jagged, but clearer nonetheless.)

- **To find a word or phrase somewhere in a PDF document,** press ⌘-F (or choose Edit→Find→Find) to open the Find box—or just type into the ⚲ box at the top

Figure 16-19:
Type into the search box. Matches appear in the Sidebar, with page numbers; click one to go there. You can sort the found list either by rank (how likely Preview thinks it is to be what you're looking for) or in page order; click the appropriate phrase about the list to sort.

of the Sidebar, if it's open. Proceed as shown in Figure 16-19.

- **If you want to copy material out of a PDF document**—for pasting into a word processor, for example, where you can edit it—click the Text tool (the letter A on the toolbar) or choose Tools→Text Tool. Now you can drag through some text (and even graphics) and then choose Edit→Copy, just as though the PDF document were a Web page. You can even drag across page boundaries.

Tip: Ordinarily, dragging across text selects the text from one edge of the page to the other, even if the PDF document is laid out in columns. But Preview is a bit smarter. It can tell if you're trying to get the text in only one column and highlights just that part automatically.

• Add keywords to a graphic or PDF (choose Tools→Show Inspector, click the ⚲ tab, click the **+** button). Later, you'll be able to call up these documents with a quick Spotlight search for those details.

The Toolbar

You can have hours of fun with Preview's toolbar. You can customize it (by choosing View→Customize Toolbar), rearrange its icons (by ⌘-dragging them sideways), and remove icons (by ⌘-dragging them downward).

QuickTime Player

QuickTime is Apple's preferred video file format (like WMV files on Windows). Like any movie, it creates the illusion of motion by flashing many individual frames (photos) per second before your eyes, while also playing a synchronized soundtrack.

The cornerstone of Mac OS X's built-in movie-playback software is QuickTime Player, which sits in your Applications folder. Despite the name, QuickTime Player lets you *edit* videos as well. You can chop them up, rearrange the chunks, tack on new movies, and trim the ends. In fact, you can even record *new* video, either using your Mac's built-in camera or by recording screen activity. Finally, when everything looks good, you can post your masterpiece to YouTube, Facebook, Vimeo, or another online site.

You can open a movie file by double-clicking it. When QuickTime Player first opens, you get a very cool, borderless playback window. Just hit the space bar to play the movie.

There's a control toolbar at the bottom of the window (Figure 16-20), but it fades away after a few seconds—or immediately, if you move the cursor out of the frame. The toolbar reappears anytime your mouse moves back into the movie frame. These are the controls:

• **Rotate or flip.** The Edit menu contains commands for Rotate Right, Rotate Left, Flip Horizontal, and Flip Vertical. Those commands can be handy when a movie turns out to be flipped or rotated—or when you *want* to flip or rotate it for creative purposes.

• **Volume slider** (◐…◀⑴). Click in the slider, or drag the dot, to adjust the volume— although it's actually easier to just tap the ↑ or ↓ keys.

Tip: To mute the sound, click the ◀ icon or press Option-↓. Press Option-↑ to make the volume slider jump to full-blast position.

- **Rewind, Fast-forward** (◄◄, ►►). By clicking one of these buttons, you get to speed through your movie at double speed, backward or forward, complete with sound. Click again for 4X speed, again for 8X.

Tip: You don't have to keep your mouse button pressed on these buttons, as in the olden days. Just click once and let QuickTime Player do the work. Click ► or tap the space bar to stop scanning.

Figure 16-20:
QuickTime Player displays this control bar only when you move your mouse into its window, or whenever playback is stopped.

- **Play/Pause** (►/❚❚). Click ► to start playback, ❚❚ to pause/stop. Or just tap the space bar for both functions.

- **Scroll bar.** Drag the little diamond, or just click inside its track, to jump to a different spot in the movie. The counters at the beginning and end of the scroll bar tell you, in "hours:minutes:seconds" format, how far your playhead cursor has moved into the movie, and how far you are from the end. (Click the right-hand readout to see the total movie duration.)

Tip: You can also press the ← and → keys to step through the movie one frame at a time. If you press Option-← or Option-→, you jump to the beginning or end of the movie. That's important to know, since there are no longer dedicated Jump to Start/Jump to End buttons on the control bar.

- **Window edges.** Drag any edge, or the lower-right corner, to make the window bigger or smaller. QuickTime Player always maintains the same *aspect ratio* (relative dimensions) of the original movie, so you won't accidentally squish it.

- **Share button** (✉). Click for a pop-up menu of choices for passing on this video to your adoring fans: iTunes, YouTube, Vimeo, Flickr, Facebook, Mail, or iCloud. The iMovie option lets you shoot the video over to iMovie for more in-depth editing, and the Trim command is here, too. All of these options are described below.

- **Full Screen** (⬛). Click to make the video fill your entire monitor, just as though you'd chosen View→Enter Full Screen. And what if the proportions of the movie don't quite match your screen? If you make the menu bar return by pointing to the top of your screen, you can handle this problem using one of the choices in the View menu, described next.

Fancy Playback Tricks

Nobody knows for sure what Apple was thinking when it created some of these additional features—exactly how often do you want your movie to play backward?—but here they are:

- **Change the screen size.** As noted above, you can drag the window to any size using the edges as handles. But the View menu commands are handy, too.

  Actual size represents the movie on your screen at its real size—no larger. (If it's truly huge, larger than your screen, it may be scaled *smaller* to fit. But that's a rarity.) **Fit to Screen** fills your screen without cropping or distorting; the menu bar and other windows remain visible.

  Fill Screen is especially satisfying, because it turns your entire monitor into a movie playback area. **Panoramic** squishes the outer edges of the video, distorting them slightly, so that nothing gets chopped off *and* the movie fills the screen. (These two options are available only in Full Screen mode.)

Tip: These same options are available via keyboard shortcuts—⌘-3, ⌘-4, and ⌘-5. There's even a little button on the control bar, second from right, that switches back and forth between Fit to Screen and Fill Screen. (This button appears only when you're already in Full Screen mode.)

  Making the window larger may also make the movie coarser, because QuickTime Player simply enlarges every dot that was present in the original. Still, when you want to show a movie to a group of people more than a few feet back from the screen, these larger sizes are perfectly effective.

Tip: You can make the movie window bigger or smaller by pressing ⌘-plus (+) or ⌘-minus (-).

- **Play more than one movie.** You can open several movies at once and run them simultaneously. (Of course, the more movies you try to play at once, the jerkier the playback gets.)

- **Loop the movie.** When you choose View→Loop and then click Play, the movie repeats endlessly until you make it stop.

- **Navigate chapters.** A few movies, like the ones you buy or rent from Apple, come with built-in chapter markers, just like a DVD. They let you jump around in the film at your whim.

Editing movies

QuickTime Player is actually QuickTime Editor. The program still doesn't offer selection handles, so you might think there's no way to select a portion of the middle of a movie (to chop it out, for example). But in fact, the commands for trimming, splitting, and merging video clips let you perform just about any editing trick you can imagine. Read on.

- **Trimming video from the ends.** You can very easily trim dead space off the ends of a video. Figure 16-21 shows how.

Tip: Once you're in Trim mode, the Edit menu sprouts a very cool command: Select All Excluding Silence. It automatically adjusts the yellow trim handles so that they cut out any silent portions of the video (at the beginning or end). That's a handy shortcut if you, like many impromptu videographers, let the camera roll a bit before and after the main event.

Figure 16-21:
Top: To trim a video, choose Edit→Trim, or press ⌘-T. Drag the yellow handles inward to isolate the chunk you want to preserve. (You can click ► or tap the space bar to check your work.) When everything looks good, click Trim or press Return.

Bottom: If you choose View→Show Audio Track, then you can use the soundwaves as a guide to your precision editing.

You don't have to worry about damaging the original video when trimming—you couldn't modify the original if you tried. The instant you use the Trim command, QuickTime Player peels off the shortened version as a new, untitled movie, which you'll have to name and save separately (choose File→Export).

- **Splitting a clip.** The Lion edition of QuickTime Player introduces the new concept of *clips:* sub-sections of a movie. To chop a movie in two, move the playhead to the spot where you want the movie to split, and then choose Edit→Split Clip. As shown in Figure 16-22, a clips map appears at the bottom of the window, showing the two resulting clips.

Figure 16-22:
The new Split Clip command chops the video into two clips—and produces the map shown at bottom. If you click a clip and then press the space bar to play the video, you'll see the red vertical line that represents the playhead. To chop one of your clips up into further sub-clips, move that red line into position, and then use the Split Clip command again.

- **Chopping video out of the middle.** If you want to trim some video from the *middle* of a movie, first open up the clips map. Then split the movie as described above. Once you've split a movie into a couple of clips, you can double-click *one* of the clips to produce trim handles *just for it*. In this way, you can cut unwanted sections from the *middle* of a video.

Or just split the clip into three chunks—and delete the middle one.

- **Rearranging clips.** Once you've chopped up a video into sub-clips using the Split Clip command, you can drag them around within the map. (If you don't see the map, shown in Figure 16-22, then choose View→Show Clips.)

You can use the Cut, Copy, and Paste commands in the Edit menu, too, to move chunks around—even among different movies. (Just remember to first split the target movie at the spot where you want to paste the new clip. The pasted material appears just *after* whatever clip is currently highlighted.)

- **Combining movies.** Combining clips, as described above, is one way to merge videos together. But you can also merge entire movie files that are sitting in the Finder.

Start by opening the first movie. If you want the second movie to appear at the *end* of it, just choose Edit→Add Clip to End.

Tip: If you press Option, the command says Add Clip to Beginning. Sneaky!

The Open dialog box now appears. Find and double-click the clip you want to tack on. Repeat as necessary.

You can also drag movie clips' icons from the desktop right into a movie window. QuickTime Player adds them to the end of the existing movie.

If you want the second movie to appear somewhere in the middle of the first movie, open up the clip map (View→Show Clips). Click the clip that appears right *before* the spot where the new movie will go. Choose Edit→Insert Clip After Selection; in the resulting dialog box, find and double-click the movie file you want to bring in.

Or drag a movie file from the Finder directly into the gap between two sub-clips.

Tip: QuickTime Player automatically shrinks or crops the incoming movies so that they fit the same "screen size" as the original. If they're *not* exactly the same size or proportions, you can then use the Edit→Clip Alignment submenu (Top, Left, Center, and so on) to specify which edge of the movie frame the imported video should hug.

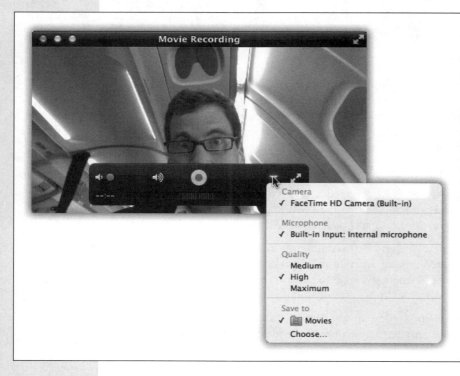

Figure 16-23:
Use the pop-up menu to set up your flick; check the audio level (reflected by the dancing "VU-meter" bars at the bottom of the control bar); choose a folder location for the finished movie; and choose a camera and mike.

Recording movies with QuickTime Player

QuickTime Player does more than *play* movies; it can also *record* them. Yes, your Mac is now a camcorder, and a darned handy one; you can pop out quick video greetings, gross out your former roommates, impress your coworkers with a dress rehearsal of your pitch, and so on.

Laptops and iMacs, of course, have a video camera built right in, above the screen. If you have another model, you can attach a Webcam, an old iSight camera, or even a FireWire camcorder.

Then open QuickTime Player and choose File→New Movie Recording. The preview window appears. Use the pop-up menu shown in Figure 16-23 to specify what mike and camera you want to use (in the unlikely event that you have more than one), what video quality you want, and where you want to store the result.

Then, to record, click the red Record button (or press the space bar). Do your schtick. Press the space bar again to stop recording.

Your new video appears in its own playback window. Check it out, trim it if necessary, and then shoot it off to iTunes, Vimeo, YouTube, or whatever.

Recording screen movies

You can also record movies *of the screen.*

Why is it useful to capture screen activity as a video? Because you can make mini-tutorials to give little lessons to techno-clueless relatives. You can make video podcasts that show how to do things in your software programs. You can preserve Web animations that you used to think you had no way to capture.

There are limitations. Your movies don't include the Mac's own sounds (game soundtracks and so on), so forget about capturing videos playing on YouTube. (It can record from the *mike,* though, so you can narrate what you're doing.)

But who cares? It's fantastically handy. And in Lion, you can now capture only a *portion* of the screen—one particular window, for example—instead of being stuck with the entire monitor's worth.

To make a screen recording, choose File→New Screen Recording. Use the pop-up menu on the resulting Screen Recording panel to turn the microphone on or off, to choose a quality setting, and to indicate where you want the finished movie stored.

Tip: This pop-up menu also contains Show Mouse Clicks in Recording. It helps your viewers understand when and where you actually clicked the mouse during the tutorial—by briefly displaying a little circle around the cursor each time you click. (It appears only in playback—not while you're recording.)

Finally, click the red Record button (or press Return), and then proceed as shown in Figure 16-24.

Press Return, or click Start Recording, to begin the capture. When you finally click the ■ button in the floating Screen Recording window, your finished movie appears in a regular playback window, ready to trim or to send away to your fans.

Figure 16-24:
This message appears when you tap the Record button. If you just click to start recording, you'll capture the entire monitor. But if you drag first, defining a rectangle, you'll capture only that area.

Audio Recording

You can also make audio-only files. Choose File→New Audio Recording. Use the pop-up menu to specify the audio quality and sound source (Figure 16-25). Click the round, red Record button and begin to speak; click the square Stop button to finish up. Now you can use the volume slider and the ▶ button to listen to your masterpiece.

Tip: Don't adjust the tiny volume slider in the Audio Recording window unless you're wearing headphones. This slider lets you monitor the sound—and turning it up while the Mac's speakers are live risks producing the hideous shriek known as feedback.

Figure 16-25:
There's a lot going on in this tiny window. The pop-up menu lets you choose audio quality and audio input. At bottom, as you record, you see a VU meter (audio level) and an indication of the recording's length and file size.

Behind the scenes, the Mac has created a new AAC audio file called *Audio Recording. mov* in your Home→Movies folder. (Additional recordings are called Audio Recording

2, 3, 4, and so on.) You can double-click it to open it right back up into QuickTime Player for trimming (read on). Or, if you think it needs more in-depth editing, you can open it with GarageBand and really go to town.

Eight Ways to Export Your Video

One of QuickTime Player's most important talents is *sharing* a video: posting it directly to YouTube or Flickr; converting it to the right format for an iPod, iPhone, or cellphone; stashing it in iTunes for easy transfer to your iPod/iPhone; handing it off to iMovie for further editing; saving it to the hard drive as a double-clickable movie; and so on.

Let us count the ways.

Send to iTunes

The main reason you'd want to send your video to iTunes is because you have an iPod, iPhone, iPad, or Apple TV. Once it's in iTunes, you can sync your video easily to that other Apple gadget and have it ready to view at all times.

To make this transfer happen, choose Share→iTunes. Or click the 📤 icon on the control bar and choose iTunes from the pop-up menu.

Either way, you see the dialog box in Figure 16-26. Click the appropriate gadget/screen size, and then click Share. When it's all over, your video will appear safely nestled in iTunes, in the Videos category, ready to watch or sync.

Figure 16-26:
This dialog box gives you three size choices for the movie you're exporting, which correspond to the screen sizes of the three Apple gadgets available. (The Computer option is just there in case you like to play videos right in iTunes, right on the screen. It's dimmed if the original movie isn't big enough to fill the screen.)

Post to YouTube, Vimeo, Flickr, Facebook

The Share menu offers one-click commands for posting to YouTube (the world's most popular and famous Web site for short videos), Vimeo (a less well-known, but classier, more high-def video-sharing site), Flickr (mainly a photo-sharing site, but handles videos too), or Facebook (the most visited Web site on earth). Instead of using the Share menu, you can also click the ✉ icon on the control bar and then choose from the pop-up menu.

All of these services require that you first sign up for a free account. (You do that online, not in QuickTime Player.)

Then, with your movie open in QuickTime Player, choose from the Share menu. You're asked for your name and password for the service. If you turn on "Remember this password in my keychain," you won't have to enter it the next time.

Finally, click Sign In. On the next screen, type a title and description for the movie. Enter keywords (search categories like "funny" or "sports") so people on that service will find your video when they search.

Work through the remaining upload screens; click Share. In a few minutes, your video will be live for the whole world to see—no charge.

Send to iMovie

The Share→iMovie command hands off your QuickTime Player video to iMovie, where you can add music, opening credits, crossfades, and other fancy edits. From there, you can post the masterpiece online.

Send to Mail

Most email systems have fairly tight limits on the sizes of file attachments. In other words, sending a movie by email doesn't work unless your movie is pretty small. "Small," in this context, refers to both the size of the movie's "screen" and to the quality of the video.

To email your video, choose Share→Mail. QuickTime Player asks if you want to send the movie as actual size (its original form) or in 480p format, which has limited dimensions and video quality. Make your choice and click Share; QuickTime Player goes to work, scaling the video if necessary, and then hands off the result to a new, outgoing message in Mail.

Even if you choose 480p, though, there's no guarantee that the resulting movie file will be small enough. You'll be allowed to send it just fine, but the recipient's email system may reject it as being too big. You'll get a "bounce back" message, in that case.

Maybe that'll teach you to adopt more concise filming and editing habits.

Saving the finished movie

After you've edited a movie (or not), you can use one of the two Export commands to specify a new name for your masterpiece—and, if you wish, to convert it to a different format, depending on what kind of machine will be playing it.

Here are your options if you choose File→Export:

- **480p.** You're creating a video in H.264 format, with a resolution of 640 × 480 pixels (standard-definition TV size). It requires 3 megabits per second of Internet speed, which means that almost anyone can watch it online.

- **720p.** You're saving a high-definition H.264 video (1280 × 720 pixels). Requires more bandwidth to watch online: 7.5 Mbits per second.

- **1080p.** An even higher-def high-def movie (1920 × 1080). Requires 10 Mbits per second.

- **iPod Touch & iPhone 3GS.** This option makes a 480p copy of the movie, in MPEG format. Perfect size for the iPhone 3GS and iPod touch (third generation or later). Also plays on computers and Apple TV.

- **iPad, iPhone 4 & Apple TV.** Creates a 720p (high-def) copy of the movie. Sized for the higher-resolution screens of the iPod touch (fourth generation), iPhone 4 or 4S, iPad, and Apple TV (second generation).

- **Audio Only.** This option lets you export just the *audio* from a movie. That's handy if you want to listen on your phone or iPod, post an interview online, or use the audio track in another movie.

Tip: Most people think that those are the only options—but there are a few more choices that can handle earlier gadgets. To see them, press Option as you open the Format pop-up menu. Now you also get choices for older iPods and iPhones (and for slower Internet connections—1.5 megabits a second), and first-generation Apple TVs.

There's also the File→Export for Web command. It produces a dialog box with three options: WiFi, Cellular, and Broadband. Turn on as many of them as you like.

An Export Progress dialog box appears, and the Mac chews away at the job of creating differently sized versions of the movie, at different frame and data rates, for the different kinds of visitors your Web site might encounter.

When it's over, the dialog box displays a link to a Web page (an HTML document) that's been saved to your hard drive. Click the link to see user-friendly instructions for embedding this movie on your own Web site (well, as user-friendly as HTML code fragments get). There's even a playable preview, so you can try the finished product before you post it online.

Safari

Apple's Web browser harbors enough tips and tricks lurking inside to last you a lifetime. Details in Chapter 12.

Stickies

Stickies creates virtual Post-it notes that you can stick anywhere on your screen—a triumphant software answer to the thousands of people who stick notes on the edges of their actual monitors. Like the Stickies widget in Dashboard, you can open this program with a keystroke (highlight some text, and then press Shift-⌘-Y)—but the program is a lot more powerful than the widget.

You can use Stickies to type quick notes and to-do items, paste in Web addresses or phone numbers you need to remember, or store any other little scraps and snippets of text you come across. Your electronic Post-it notes show up whenever the Stickies program is running (Figure 16-27).

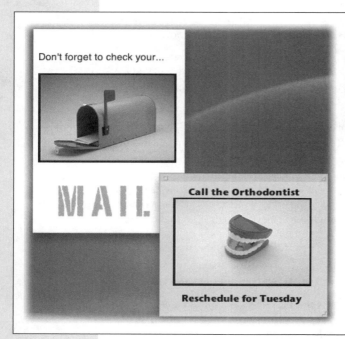

Figure 16-27:
In the old days of the Mac, the notes you created with Stickies were text-only, single-font deals. Today, however, you can use a mix of fonts, text colors, and styles within each note. You can even paste in graphics, sounds, and movies (like PICT, GIF, JPEG, QuickTime, AIFF, whole PDF files, and so on), creating the world's most elaborate reminders and to-do lists.

Creating Sticky Notes

The first time you launch Stickies, a few sample notes appear automatically, describing some of the program's features. You can quickly dispose of each sample by clicking the close button in the upper-left corner of each note or by choosing File→Close (⌘-W). Each time you close a note, a dialog box asks if you want to save it. If you click Don't Save (or press ⌘-D), the note disappears permanently.

To create a new note, choose File→New Note (⌘-N). Then start typing. Or drag highlighted text or graphics into the note from another program, or paste, or choose File→Import and select any plain text file or RTF (Rich Text Format) document to bring it into a note. (You can also drag Web addresses into a note directly from a Web browser's address bar.)

Tip: If one particular note contains your most important information—your to-do list, say—you can force it to remain in front of all other windows, even if Stickies itself gets shunted to the background. Just click the note, and then choose Note→Floating Window.

Have a favorite style for your sticky notes? First create a new note, choosing the color and text style you like and setting it to the size you prefer. Then choose Note→Use as Default. All new notes you create now appear in the size, font, and color you've chosen.

Growing and Shrinking Notes

Stickies includes a few built-in tricks for managing a deskful of notes:

- There's a small resize handle on the lower-right corner of each note. Drag it to make notes larger or smaller onscreen.

- Use the small triangle in the upper-right corner of each note to zoom and shrink note windows with a single click. The first click expands a note nearly to full-screen size. Another click pops the note back down to normal size.

- The best option: Double-click anywhere along the dark strip at the top of each note to collapse it into a compact one-line mininote, as shown in Figure 16-28. You also can collapse a selected note by choosing Window→Collapse (⌘-M).

Tip: The most efficient way to use Stickies is to keep the notes in their collapsed state, as shown in Figure 16-28. When a note is collapsed, the first line of text shows up in tiny type in the collapsed title bar of the note, so you don't have to expand the note to remember what's in it. And since many—if not most—of your notes can probably be summed up in a couple of words ("Pick up dry cleaning," "Call Mom"), it's possible to keep your sticky notes in their collapsed state permanently.

Figure 16-28:
If the first line of text gets truncated, as in the third note shown here, you can tug the right corner of the note and drag it wider without de-miniaturizing it.

Formatting Notes

Stickies has word processor–like commands for creating designer sticky notes, with any combination of fonts, colors, and styles (explore the Font menu). You can also choose from six background colors from the Color menu.

Saving Sticky Notes

The notes you create in Stickies last only as long as you keep them open. If you close a note to get it out of the way (and click Don't Save in the confirmation box), it vanishes permanently.

If you want to preserve the information you've stuffed into your notes in a more permanent form, use File→Export Text to save each note as a standalone TextEdit document. When you use the Export Text command, you have the following options:

- **Plain Text.** This option saves your note as a plain text file, with neither formatting nor pictures.

- **RTF.** RTF stands for Rich Text Format, a special exchange format that preserves most formatting, including font, style, and color choices. You can open the resulting RTF file in just about any word processor with all your formatting still intact.

- **RTFD.** RTFD, a strange and powerful variant of RTF, is a Rich Text Format document *with attachments*. When you export the note as an RTFD file, the result is a TextEdit document that has embedded within it the *entire* program or document you dragged in. The program icon appears just as it did in the sticky note, but if you double-click the icon, the program actually opens.

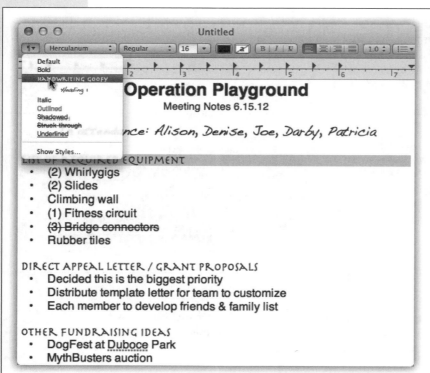

Figure 16-29:
The text ruler gives you control over tab stops, paragraph justification, and so on. Pressing ⌘-R makes it appear and disappear. On the toolbar, the Style pop-up menu lists canned sets of character and paragraph formatting, so you can apply them consistently throughout a document.

If you don't have embedded programs or documents in your notes, then exported RTFD files are exactly the same as their RTF counterparts.

System Preferences

This program opens the door to the nerve center of Mac OS X's various user preferences, settings, and options. Chapter 15 covers every option in detail.

TextEdit

TextEdit is a basic word processor—but it's not nearly as basic as people think it is. You can create real documents with real formatting, using style sheets, colors, automatic numbering and bullets, tables, and customized line spacing. You can even open, edit, and create Microsoft Word documents. If you had to, you could write a children's book in TextEdit, and it would look pretty decent.

Better yet, TextEdit (Figure 16-29) is a showcase for Lion's iPaddish features, like full-screen mode, Autosave, and Versions (see Chapter 4). And TextEdit works with Mac OS X's long list of built-in text-editing features: smart links, smart quotes, smart dashes, smart copy/paste, abbreviation expansion, auto–typo correction, data detectors, and so on. They're all described in Chapter 5.

UP TO SPEED

The Deal with Microsoft Word

Yes, it's true: Humble TextEdit can open and create Microsoft Word documents! Your savings: the $400 price of Microsoft Office!

Well, sort of.

When you open a Microsoft Word document in TextEdit, most of the formatting comes through alive: bold, italic, font choices, colors, line spacing, alignment, and so on. Even very basic tables make it into TextEdit, although with different column widths.

A lot of Word-specific formatting does not survive crossing the chasm, however: borders, style sheets, footnotes, and the like. Bullets and numbered lists don't make it, either, even though TextEdit can create its own versions of these. And TextEdit doesn't recognize the comments and tracked changes your collaborators might use to mark up your manuscript.

Saving a new TextEdit document as a Word document is a better bet, because Word understands the many kinds of formatting that TextEdit can produce—including bullets, numbering, and tables. (You can create a Word file the first time you save it from TextEdit, or you can convert a document into Word format later by choosing File→Duplicate, then File→Save.)

The one disappointment is that Word doesn't recognize any style sheets you've set up in TextEdit. The formatting applied by those style names survives—just not the style names themselves.

Even so, a built-in Word-document editor is a huge, huge step for the Mac OS. It means that in many cases, you can be a first-class citizen on the playing field of American business. Nobody ever needs to know that you're (a) using a Mac, and (b) not using the real Microsoft Word.

TextEdit's Two Personalities

The one confusing aspect of TextEdit is that it's both a *plain text editor* (no formatting; globally compatible) and a true *word processor* (fonts, sizes, styles; compatible with other word processors). Here's the scheme:

- You can change a plain text document to a formatted one by choosing Format→ Make Rich Text. The ruler appears automatically to remind you that a new world of formatting has just become available.

- Conversely, you can change a formatted document (a Word file you've opened, for example) to a plain text document by choosing Format→Make Plain Text. An alert message appears to point out that you're about to lose all formatting.

- If you know what kind of document you *always* want to open, go to the TextEdit→ Preferences dialog box; on the New Document tab, select Rich Text or Plain Text. That's what you'll get each time you choose File→New.

Tip: Here's also where you can turn on smart links, smart quotes, smart dashes, and the other smart text-processing features described in Chapter 5.

Working in TextEdit

As you begin typing, all the usual word processing rules apply, with a few twists:

- Choose bold, italic, and font sizes using the new formatting toolbar. (You can still use the commands in the Format menu.) You can even create subscripts or superscripts, change the color of the text (Format→Font→Show Colors), and so on.

- Common paragraph-alignment options—Align Left, Align Right, Center, Justify— are all available as toolbar buttons and also reside in the Format→Text submenu. Adjust the line spacing (single, double, or any fraction or multiple) using the Spacing pop-up menu in the toolbar.

- The toolbar also offers automatic bulleting and numbering of paragraphs. Just choose the numbering style you prefer from the pop-up menu at the right end of the toolbar.

- You can select several nonadjacent bits of text *simultaneously*. To pull this off, highlight your first piece of text by dragging, and then press ⌘ as you use the mouse to select more text. Bingo: You've highlighted two separate chunks of text.

  When you're done selecting bits of text here and there, you can operate on them en masse. For example, you can make them all bold or italic in one fell swoop. You can even use the Cut, Copy, and Paste commands, as described in the next section. When you cut or copy, the command acts upon all your selections at once.

  You can also drag any *one* of the highlighted portions to a new area, confident that the other chunks will come along for the ride. All the selected areas wind up consolidated in their new location.

Tip: If you *Option*-drag one of the highlighted bits, you *copy* all selected chunks, leaving the originals in place.

- Similarly, you can use the Find command. To do that, choose Edit→Find→Find (or just press ⌘-F). Fill in the search box; the sought-for term appears highlighted everywhere in your document at once. (You can also search and *replace,* using the other commands in the Edit→Find submenu.)

- If you Option-drag vertically, you can freely select an arbitrary column of text (not necessarily the entire page width). This technique is very useful when you want to select the numbers in a list and format them all at once.

Style Sheets

A *style* is a prepackaged collection of formatting attributes that you can apply and reapply with a click of the mouse (bold, 24-point Optima, double-spaced, for instance). You can create chapter headings, sidebar styles, and so on. You end up with a collection of custom-tailored styles for each of the repeating elements of your document.

Once you've created your styles, you can apply them as you need them, safe in the knowledge that they'll be consistent throughout the document. During the editing process, if you notice that you accidentally styled a *headline* using the *Subhead* style, you can fix the problem by simply reapplying the correct style.

- **Creating a named style.** To create a style, format some text so it looks the way you like it, complete with font, color, line spacing, tab settings, and so on.

Figure 16-30:
Top: Highlight the text you want to format. Then, from the ¶ pop-up menu in the toolbar, choose Show Styles. With each click of the ▶ button, you summon a snippet of the next chunk of formatting. When you find one you like, you can either click Apply (to zap the highlighted text into submission) or Add To Favorites (to reuse this canned style later). In the latter case, you can give the new style a name (bottom).

Then, from the ¶ pop-up menu at the left end of the toolbar, choose Show Styles (Figure 16-30, top). Click Add to Favorites, type a name for the style, turn on both checkboxes (Figure 16-30, bottom), and then click Add.

- **Applying a style.** Later, when you want to reuse the formatting you set up, highlight some text and then choose the appropriate name from the ¶ pop-up menu. TextEdit applies the formatting immediately.

Tip: If you simply click inside a paragraph, applying a style affects only paragraph attributes, like line spacing, tab stops, and alignment. If you highlight a random chunk of text instead, applying a style affects only character attributes, like the font and type size. If you highlight an entire paragraph, however, both text and paragraph formatting appear.

- **Deleting a style.** To delete a superfluous style, choose Show Styles from the ¶ pop-up menu on the toolbar. Click the Favorite Styles button, choose the unwanted style's name from the pop-up menu, and then click Remove From Favorites. (Deleting a style doesn't affect any formatting that's already in your document; it just removes the name from the Styles menu.)

- **Replacing all occurrences.** You can highlight every occurrence of a certain style at once—and then change, copy, or delete them all at once.

  To make this work, choose Show Styles from the ¶ pop-up menu. Choose the style you want to work on. (If "Document styles" is selected, click the ▶ button to page through the styles; if "Favorite styles" is selected, choose from the pop-up menu.) Then click Select.

  In the little details sheet that appears, click the options you want, and then click Select. TextEdit highlights every occurrence of that style in the entire document (or selection). At this point, you can use any of the usual text-formatting controls to modify them all simultaneously.

- **Formatting by example.** In TextEdit, you can also use Option-⌘-C and Option-⌘-V (Format→Font→Copy Style and Format→Font→Paste Style) to grab formatting from one place in your document and reuse it elsewhere. (Of course, you can't apply styles in text-only documents.)

Tables

Tables can make life a heck of a lot easier when you want to create a resumé, agenda, program booklet, list, multiple-choice test, Web page, or another document where numbers, words, and phrases must be aligned across the page. In the bad old days, people did it by pressing the Tab key to line up columns—a technique that turned into a nightmare as soon as you tried to add or delete text. But using a word processor's *table* feature is light-years easier and more flexible, because each row of a table expands to contain whatever you put into it. Everything else in its row remains aligned.

Tip: Tables are sometimes used for designing Web pages. Even though you can't see the table outlines, many a Web page is filled with columns of text that are aligned invisibly by tables. And now that TextEdit can save your work as an HTML document, it's suddenly a viable candidate for designing basic Web pages.

Figure 16-31:
Note to Web designers: TextEdit may not be Dreamweaver, but it's great for spinning out quick Web pages, thanks to the table features. Here you can see that a big table forms the underlying structure for this Web page, along with a couple of nested ones and color selections.

- **Create a table** by choosing Format→Table. The floating Table palette appears (Figure 16-31). Use it to specify how many rows and columns you want. The placeholder table in your document adjusts itself in real time.

- **Format the table** using the other controls in the Table palette. The Alignment controls let you specify how the text in the table cells hugs its border. Cell Border controls the thickness of the line around the selected cells' borders (or, if you enter 0, makes the table walls invisible). The color swatch next to Cell Border specifies the color of the solid lines. The Cell Background controls let you color in the table cells with colors of your choice. (Choose Color Fill from the pop-up menu, and then click the color swatch.) This is an especially valuable option for Web designers.

- **Adjust the rows and columns** by dragging the cell borders.

- **Merge two selected cells** by clicking Merge Cells in the Table palette. Once you've done that, you can use the Split Cell button to split them apart again. (Split Cell doesn't work except in cells you've previously merged.)

• **Nest one table inside a cell of another** by clicking in the cell and then clicking Nest Table. Change the numbers in the Rows and Columns boxes to set up its dimensions (Figure 16-31).

TextEdit as Web Designer

The Table palette isn't the only clue that Apple intends TextEdit to be a quick-and-dirty Web page design program. Consider these other tools:

• You can easily add graphics to the page by dragging or pasting them into a document. The program understands TIFF, PICT, JPEG, and GIF formats.

• You can add Web-style hyperlinks by highlighting "Click here" (or whatever the link says), choosing Edit→Add Link, and then entering the Web address in the resulting dialog box. Or just drag a link in from Safari, Mail, or another program. (To edit the link later, Control-click it, and then choose Edit Link.)

Tip: Of course, you can also have TextEdit convert typed links into clickable ones *automatically* as you type them. That's the purpose of the Smart Links option in TextEdit→Preferences.

• To save a brand-new document as an HTML (Web page) file, choose File→Save; from the File Format pop-up menu, choose Web Page. (To save an existing TextEdit document as an HTML file, choose File→Duplicate, and then File→Save; choose Web Page from the pop-up menu.)

• Don't miss the HTML options in TextEdit→Preferences. On the Open and Save tab, you can specify what kind of HTML document you want to produce, what cascading style sheets (CSS) setting you want, and whether or not you want TextEdit to include code to preserve blank areas (white space) in your layout.

Tip: When you open a Web page document—that is, an HTML document—TextEdit is faced with a quandary. Should it open up the page as though it's a Web page, interpreting the HTML code as though it's a browser? Or should it reveal the underlying HTML code itself?

Actually, that's up to you. When you choose File→Open, turn on "Ignore rich text commands" to make the document open up as HTML code. (To make this change permanent, turn on the same checkbox on the Open and Save pane of the TextEdit→Preferences dialog box.)

Time Machine

This marquee feature of Mac OS X is described in Chapter 5.

Utilities: Your Mac OS X Toolbox

The Utilities folder (inside your Applications folder) is home to another batch of freebies: a couple of dozen tools for monitoring, tuning, tweaking, and troubleshooting your Mac.

The truth is, you're likely to use only about six of these utilities. The rest are very specialized gizmos primarily of interest to network administrators or Unix geeks who are obsessed with knowing what kind of computer-code gibberish is going on behind the scenes.

Tip: Even so, Apple obviously noticed that as the sophistication of Mac OS X fans grows, more people open the Utilities folder more often. That's why there's a menu command and a keystroke that can take you there. In the Finder, choose Go→Utilities (Shift-⌘-U).

Activity Monitor

Activity Monitor is designed to let the technologically savvy Mac fan see how much of the Mac's available power is being tapped at any given moment.

The Processes table

Even when you're only running a program or two on your Mac, dozens of computational tasks (*processes*) are going on in the background. The top half of the dialog box, which looks like a table, shows you all the different processes—visible and invisible—that your Mac is handling at the moment.

Check out how many items appear in the Process list, even when you're just staring at the desktop. It's awesome to see just how busy your Mac is! Some are easily recognizable programs (such as Finder), while others are background system-level operations you don't normally see. For each item, you can see the percentage of the CPU being used, who's using it (either your account name, someone else's, or *root*, meaning the Mac itself), whether or not it's been written as a 64-bit app, and how much memory it's using.

Or use the pop-up menu above the list to see views like these:

- **All Processes.** This is the complete list of running processes; you'll notice that the vast majority are little Unix applications you never even knew you had.

- **All Processes, Hierarchically.** In Unix, one process launches another, creating a tree-like hierarchy. The big daddy of them all is the process called *launchd*. Here and there, you'll see some other interesting relationships: For example, the Dock launches DashboardClient.

- **My Processes.** This list shows only the programs that pertain to *your* world, your login. There are still plenty of unfamiliar items, but they're all running to serve *your* account.

- **System Processes.** These are the processes run by *root*—that is, opened by Mac OS X itself.

- **Other User Processes.** Here's a list of all *other* processes—"owned" by neither root nor you. Here you might see the processes being run by another account holder, for example (using Fast User Switching), or people who have connected to this Mac from across a network or the Internet.

- **Active Processes, Inactive Processes.** Active processes are the ones that are actually doing something right now; inactive are the ones that are sitting there, waiting for a signal (like a keypress or a mouse click).

- **Windowed Processes.** Now *this* is probably what you were expecting: a list of actual programs with actual English names, like Activity Monitor, Finder, Safari, and Mail. These are the only ones running in actual windows, the only ones that are *visible*.

The System monitor tabs

At the bottom of Activity Monitor, you're offered five tabs that reveal intimate details about your Mac and its behind-the-scenes efforts (Figure 16-32):

- **CPU.** As you go about your usual Mac business, opening a few programs, playing QuickTime movies, playing a game, and so on, you can see the CPU graphs rise and fall, depending on how busy you're keeping the CPU. You see a different bar

Figure 16-32:
The many faces of Activity Monitor.

Top: It can be a graph of your processor (CPU) activity, your RAM usage at the moment, your disk capacity, and so on. For most people, only the processes listed here with tiny icons beside their names are actual windowed programs—those with icons in the Finder, the ones you actually interact with.

Don't miss the top-left Quit Process button. It's a convenient way to jettison a locked-up program when all else fails.

Bottom: If you double-click a process's name, you get a two- or three-tab dialog box that offers stunningly complete reams of data (mostly of interest only to programmers) about what that program is up to. (The Open Files and Ports tab, for example, shows you how many files that program has opened, often invisibly.)

for each of your Mac's cores (independent sub-chips on your processor), so you can see how efficiently Mac OS X is distributing the work among them.

Tip: You may also want to watch this graph right in your Dock (choose View→Dock Icon→Show CPU Usage) or in a bar at the edge of your screen (choose Window→Floating CPU Window→Horizontally).

Finally, there's the View→Show CPU History command. It makes a resizable, real-time monitor window float on top of all your other programs, so you can't miss it.

- **System Memory.** Here's a colorful graph that reveals the state of your Mac's RAM at the moment.

  The number below the graph shows how much memory is installed in your Mac. If, when your Mac is running a typical complement of programs, the Wired number plus the Active number nearly equals your total RAM amount, it's time to consider buying more memory. You're suffocating your Mac.

- **Disk Activity.** Even when you're not opening or saving a file, your Mac's hard drive is frequently hard at work, shuffling chunks of program code into and out of memory, for example. Here's where the savvy technician can see exactly how frantic the disk is at the moment.

- **Disk Usage.** This little graph offers one of the quickest ways to check out how full your hard drive is. (If you have more than one drive—say, a flash drive, tape-backup drive, or whatever—choose another drive's name from the pop-up menu.)

- **Network.** Keep an eye on how much data is shooting across your office network with this handy EKG-ish graph.

AirPort Utility

You use the AirPort Utility to set up and manage AirPort base stations (Apple's wireless WiFi networking routers).

If you click Continue, it presents a series of screens, posing one question at a time: what you want to name the network, what password you want for it, and so on. Once you've followed the steps and answered the questions, your AirPort hardware will be properly configured and ready to use.

AppleScript Editor

This little is where you can type up your own *AppleScripts,* as described in the free "AppleScript & Automator" PDF Appendix to this book. It's on this book's "Missing CD" at *www.missingmanuals.com.*

Audio MIDI Setup

This program has a split personality; its name is now a literal description of its two halves:

- **Audio.** When you first open Audio MIDI Setup, you see a complete summary of the audio inputs and outputs available on your Mac right now. It's a lot like the

---

Sound pane of System Preferences, but with a lot more geeky detail. Here, for example, you can specify the recording level for your Mac's microphone, or even change the audio quality it records.

For most people, this is all meaningless, because most Macs have only one input (the microphone) and one output (the speakers). But if you're sitting in your darkened music studio, which is humming with high-tech audio gear whose software has been designed to work with this little program, you'll smile when you see this tab.

There's even a Configure Speakers button, for those audiophilic Mac fans who've attached stereo or even surround-sound speaker systems to their Macs.

Tip: Using the ✿ menu at the bottom of the window, you can turn your various audio inputs (that is, microphones, line inputs, and so on) on or off. You can even direct your Mac's system beeps to pour forth from one set of speakers (like the one built into your Mac), and all other sound, like music, through a different set.

- **MIDI.** MIDI stands for Musical Instrument Digital Interface, a standard "language" for inter-synthesizer communication. It's available to music software companies who have written their wares to capitalize on these tools.

  When you choose Window→Show MIDI Window, you get a window that represents your recording-studio configuration. By clicking Add Device, you create a new icon that represents one of your pieces of gear. Double-click the icon to specify its make and model. Finally, by dragging lines from the "in" and "out" arrows, you teach your Mac and its MIDI software how the various components are wired together.

Bluetooth File Exchange

One of the luxuries of using a Mac that has Bluetooth is the ability to shoot files (to colleagues who own similarly clever gadgets) through the air, up to 30 feet away. Bluetooth File Exchange makes it possible, as described on page 199.

Boot Camp Assistant

This program helps you create (or destroy) a partition of your hard drive to hold a copy of Microsoft Windows. Details in Chapter 8.

ColorSync Utility

If you use ColorSync, then you probably know already that this utility is for people in the high-end color printing business. Its tabs include these two:

- **Profile First Aid.** This tab performs a fairly esoteric task: repairing ColorSync profiles that may be "broken" because they don't strictly conform to the *ICC profile* specifications. (ICC [International Color Consortium] profiles are part of Apple's ColorSync color management system.) If a profile for your specific monitor or printer doesn't appear in the Profiles tab of this program when it should, Profile First Aid is the tool you need to fix it.

- **Profiles.** This tab lets you review all the ColorSync profiles installed on your system. The area on the right side of the window displays information about each ColorSync profile you select from the list on the left.

Console

Console is a viewer for all of Mac OS X's logs—the behind-the-scenes, internal Unix record of your Mac's activities.

Opening the Console log is a bit like stepping into an operating room during a complex surgery: You're exposed to stuff the average person just isn't supposed to see. (Typical Console entries: "kCGErrorCannotComplete" or "doGetDisplayTransferBy-Table.") You can adjust the font and word wrapping using Console's Font menu, but the truth is that the phrase "CGXGetWindowType: Invalid window -1" looks ugly in just about *any* font!

Console isn't useless, however. These messages can be of significant value to programmers who are debugging software or troubleshooting a messy problem, or, occasionally, to someone you've called for tech support.

For example, your *crash logs* are detailed technical descriptions of what went wrong when various programs crashed, and what was stored in memory at the time.

Unfortunately, there's not much plain English here to help you understand the crash, or how to avoid it in the future. Most of it runs along the lines of "Exception: EXC_BAD_ACCESS (0x0001); Codes: KERN_INVALID_ADDRESS (0x0001) at 0x2f6b657d." In other words, it's primarily for the benefit of programmers. Still, tech-support staff may occasionally ask to see the information in one of these logs.

DigitalColor Meter

DigitalColor Meter can grab the exact color value of any pixel on your screen, which can be helpful when matching colors in Web page construction or other design work. After launching the DigitalColor Meter, just point anywhere on your screen. A magnified view appears in the meter window, and the RGB (red-green-blue) color value of the pixels appears in the meter window.

Here are some tips for using the DigitalColor Meter to capture color information from your screen:

- To home in on the exact pixel (and color) you want to measure, drag the Aperture Size slider to the smallest size—one pixel.

- Press ⌘-X (View→Lock X) to freeze your cursor at its current horizontal position; you can now move it only horizontally. Or press ⌘-Y (View→Lock Y) to freeze your cursor at its current vertical position. You can also lock the cursor in both directions. (Press the keystroke again to unlock.) The idea is to make it easier for you to snap exactly the pixel you want.

- When the Aperture Size slider is set to view more than one pixel, DigitalColor Meter measures the *average* value of the pixels being examined.

Disk Utility

This important program serves two key functions:

- It serves as Mac OS X's own little Norton Utilities: a powerful hard drive administration tool that lets you repair, erase, format, and partition disks. In everyday life, you'll probably use Disk Utility most often for its *Repair Permissions* feature, which solves an uncanny number of weird little Mac OS X glitches. But it's also worth keeping in mind in case you ever find yourself facing a serious disk problem.

- Disk Utility also creates and manages *disk images,* electronic versions of disks or folders that you can exchange electronically with other people.

The following discussion tackles the program's two personalities one at a time.

Disk Utility, the hard drive repair program

Here are some of the tasks you can perform with this half of Disk Utility:

- Repair folders, files, and programs that don't work because you supposedly don't have sufficient "access privileges." This is by far the most common use of Disk Utility, not to mention the most reliable and satisfying. Using the Repair Disk Permissions button fixes an *astonishing* range of bizarre Mac OS X problems, from programs that won't open to menulets that freeze up the works.

- Get size and type information about any disks attached to your Mac.

- Fix disks that won't appear on your desktop or behave properly.

- Completely erase disks—including rewritable CDs and DVDs (such as CD-RW and DVD-RW discs).

- Partition a disk into multiple *volumes* (that is, subdivide a drive so that its segments appear on the desktop with separate disk icons).

Tip: Disk Utility can even create or enlarge disk partitions without requiring you to erase the entire hard drive. Details below.

- Set up a *RAID array* (a cluster of separate disks that acts as a single volume).

Note: Disk Utility can perform *some* of its magic on the startup disk–the disk that's running Mac OS X at the moment. For example, it can check the disk for damage, fix the permissions of the disk, or even adjust its partitions.

But any other operation, like reformatting, erasing, or actually repairing the disk, still requires the Mac to start up from a different disk (an external hard drive, for example, or Lion's secret recovery partition). Otherwise, it'd be like a surgeon performing an appendectomy on himself–not a great idea.

The left Disk Utility panel lists your hard drive and any other disks in or attached to your Mac at the moment. When you click the name of your hard drive's mechanism, like "500 GB Hitachi iC25N0…" (not the "Macintosh HD" volume label below it), you see a panel with five tabs, one for each of the main Disk Utility functions:

SWITCHING TO THE MAC: THE MISSING MANUAL

- **First Aid.** This is the disk-repair part of Disk Utility, and it does a terrific job at fixing many disk problems. When you're troubleshooting, Disk Utility should always be your first resort.

  To use it, click the icon of a disk and then click either Verify Disk (to get a report on the disk's health) or Repair Disk (which fixes whatever problems the program finds). In other words, First Aid attempts to perform the same healing effects on a sick hard drive as, say, a program like Norton Utilities.

  If Disk First Aid reports that it's unable to fix the problem, *then* it's time to invest in a program like DiskWarrior (*www.alsoft.com*).

  You may wind up using the Verify and Repair Disk *Permissions* buttons even more often. Their function is to straighten out problems with the invisible Unix file permissions that keep you from moving, changing, or deleting files or folders. (The occasional software installer can create problems like this.) You'd be surprised how often running one of these permission checks solves little Mac OS X glitches.

  Chapter 14 has a much more detailed discussion of permissions.

- **Erase.** Select a disk, choose a format—*always* Mac OS Extended (Journaled), unless you're formatting a disk for use on a Windows PC—give it a name, and then click Erase to wipe a disk clean.

POWER USERS' CLINIC

Partition Adjustments on the Fly

You can expand, shrink, or create partitions without having to erase the whole hard drive. If you're into partitioning at all, this is a *huge* convenience.

Expanding a partition. Suppose, for example, that your main hard drive has two partitions: a main one (200 gigs) and a secondary one (50 gigs) that used to hold all your photos and movies. But you've outgrown the second partition and have moved all those photos and movies to their own external hard drive. Wouldn't it be nice to add the newly unoccupied 50 gigs to your main partition?

You can do that without having to erase the whole hard drive. (This process, however, nukes everything on the *second* partition, so make sure you're prepared to lose it all.)

Open Disk Utility. Click the name of the hard drive (for example, "Hitachi HTS541616J9SA00"–*not* "Macintosh HD"). Click Partition. You see a display like the one in Figure 16-33.

Click the second partition (or third, or whatever partition is *just after* the one you want to expand) and then click the **–** button below the list. Poof! It's gone.

Now you can drag the main partition's bottom edge downward (or type a new size into the Size box), expanding it into the free area. Take a deep breath, and then click Apply.

Shrinking a partition. In Figure 16-33, you can see that a portion of the first partition is lightly shaded. (It's blue in real life.) The blue represents data; you can't shrink a partition so much that it crowds out your files. You can, however, shrink the partition to eliminate empty space. Just drag the lower edge of its map chunk upward.

Creating new partitions. Anytime there's leftover space on the drive, you can create *new* partitions from it. To do that, click the **+** button, and then proceed as described in Figure 16-33.

Tip: The Erase tab is the key to using FileVault (page 454) on flash drives and other external drives. In other words, you can encrypt external disks so that nobody can access them without a password. The trick is to erase the drive using "Mac OS Extended (Journaled, Encrypted)" format.

• **Partition.** With the Partition tools, you can erase a hard drive in such a way that you subdivide its surface. Each chunk is represented on your screen by another hard drive icon (Figure 16-33).

Figure 16-33:
Partitioning your drive with Disk Utility no longer involves erasing it completely. Select the drive you want to partition from the list on the left, and then click the Partition tab. Click the + button for each new partition you want.

Now drag the horizontal dividers in the Volumes map to specify the relative sizes of the partitions you want to create. Assign a name and a format for each partition in the Volume Information area, and then click Apply.

There are some very good reasons *not* to partition a drive these days: A partitioned hard drive is more difficult to resurrect after a serious crash, requires more navigation when you want to open a particular file, and offers no speed or safety benefits.

On the other hand, there's one very good reason *to* do it: Partitioning is the only way to use Boot Camp, described in Chapter 8. When you're using Boot Camp, your Mac is a Mac when running off of one partition, and a Windows PC when starting up from another one. (But you don't use Disk Utility in that case; use Boot Camp Assistant.)

• **RAID.** RAID stands for Redundant Array of Independent Disks and refers to a special formatting scheme in which a group of separate disks are configured to work together as one very large, very fast drive. In a RAID array, multiple disks share the job of storing data—a setup that can improve speed and reliability.

Most Mac owners don't use or set up RAID arrays, probably because most Mac owners have only one hard drive (and Disk Utility can't make your startup disk part of a RAID array).

But if you're using multiple hard disks—in a Mac Pro, for example—you can use Apple RAID to merge them into one giant disk. Just drag the icons of the relevant disks (or disk partitions) from the left-side list of disks into the main list (where it says, "Drag disks or volumes here to add to set"). Use the RAID Type pop-up menu to specify the RAID format you want to use. (Stripe is a popular choice for maximizing disk speed; Mirror RAID is extra safe, because it creates a perfect backup clone of your main drive.) Name your new mega-disk, and then click Create. The result is a single "disk" icon on your desktop that actually represents the combined capacity of all the RAID disks.

- **Restore.** This tab lets you make a perfect copy of a disk or a disk image, much like the popular shareware programs Carbon Copy Cloner and SuperDuper. You might find this useful when, for example, you want to make an exact copy of your old Mac's drive on your new one. You can't do that just by copying your old files and folders manually. If you try, you won't get the thousands of *invisible* files that make up Mac OS X. If you use the Restore function, though, they'll come along for the ride.

  Start by dragging the disk or disk image you want to copy *from* into the Source box. Then drag the icon of the disk you want to copy *to* into the Destination box.

Tip: If you want to copy an online disk image onto one of your disks, you don't have to download it first. Just type its Web address into the Source field.

If you turn on Erase Destination, then Disk Utility obliterates all the data on your target disk before copying the data. If you leave this checkbox off, however, Disk Utility simply copies everything onto your destination, preserving all your old data in the process (although it replaces files that have the same names and locations as the ones you're copying).

Finally, click the Restore button. (You might need to type in an administrator password.) Restoring can take a long time for big disks, so go ahead and make yourself a cup of coffee while you're waiting.

Disk Utility, the disk-image program

Disk images are very cool. Each one is a single icon that behaves precisely like an actual disk—a flash drive or hard drive, for example—but can be distributed electronically. For example, a lot of Mac OS X add-on software arrives from your Web download in disk-image form, as shown below.

Disk images are popular for software distribution for a simple reason: Each image file precisely duplicates the original master disk, complete with all the necessary files in all the right places. When a software company sends you a disk image, it ensures that you'll install the software from a disk that *exactly* matches the master disk.

As a handy bonus, you can password-protect a disk image, which is the closest Mac OS X comes to offering the ability to password-protect an individual folder.

It's important to understand the difference between a *disk-image file* and the *mounted disk* (the one that appears when you double-click the disk image). If you flip back to page 131 and consult Figure 4-2, this distinction should be clear.

Tip: After you double-click a disk image, click Skip in the verification box that appears. If something truly got scrambled during the download, you'll know about it right away—your file won't decompress correctly, or it'll display the wrong icon, for example.

In fact, you can make Disk Utility always skip that verification business, which is a relic from the days of floppy disks. To do so, choose Disk Utility→Preferences, and turn off "Check images on locked media."

You can create disk images, too. Doing so can be very handy in situations like these:

- You want to create a backup of an important CD. By turning it into a disk-image file on your hard drive, you'll always have a safety copy, ready to burn back onto a *new* CD. (This is an essential practice for educational CDs that kids will be handling soon after eating peanut butter and jelly.)

- You want to replicate your entire hard drive—complete with all its files, programs, folder setups, and so on—onto a new, bigger hard drive (or a new, better Mac), using the Restore feature described earlier.

- You want to back up your entire hard drive, or maybe just a certain chunk of it, onto an iPod or another disk. (Again, you can later use the Restore function.)

- You want to send somebody else a copy of a disk via the Internet. You simply create a disk image, and then send *that*—preferably in compressed form.

Here's how to make a disk image.

- **To image-ize a disk or partition.** Click the name of the disk in the list, where you see the disks currently in, or attached to, your Mac. (The topmost item is the name of your *drive*, like "484.0 MB MATSHITA DVD-R" for a DVD drive or "74.5 GB Hitachi" for a hard drive. Beneath that entry, you generally see the name of the actual partition, like "Macintosh HD," or the CD's name as it appears on the screen.)

  Then choose File→New→Disk Image from [whatever the disk or partition's name is].

- **To image-ize a folder.** Choose File→New→Disk Image from Folder. In the Open dialog box, click the folder you want, and then click Image.

Tip: Disk Utility can't turn an individual file into a disk image. But you can put a single file into a folder, and then make a disk image of it.

Either way, the next dialog box (Figure 16-34) offers some fascinating options.

• **Image Format.** If you choose "read/write," your disk image file, when double-clicked, turns into a superb imitation of a hard drive. You can drag files and folders onto it, drag them off of it, change icons' names on it, and so on.

If you choose "read-only," however, the result behaves more like a CD. You can copy things off of it but not make any changes to it.

The "compressed" option is best if you intend to send the resulting file by email, post it for Web download, or preserve the disk image on some backup disk for a rainy day. It takes a little longer to create a simulated disk when you double-click the disk image file, but it takes up a lot less disk space than an uncompressed version.

Finally, choose "DVD/CD master" if you're copying a CD or a DVD. The resulting

Figure 16-34:
These two pop-up menus let you specify (a) what kind of disk image you want, and (b) whether or not you want it password-protected. The latter option is great when you want to password-protect one folder, without bothering with your entire Home folder.

file is a perfect mirror of the original disc, ready for copying onto a blank CD or DVD when the time comes.

• **Encryption.** Here's an easy way to lock private files away into a vault that nobody else can open. If you choose one of these two AES encryption options (choose AES-128, if you value your time), you'll be asked to assign a password to your new image file. Nobody can open it without the password—not even you. On the other hand, if you save it into your Keychain (page 460), it's not such a disaster if you forget the password.

• **Save As.** Choose a name and location for your new image file. The name you choose here doesn't need to match the original disk or folder name.

When you click Save (or press Return), if you opted to create an encrypted image, you're asked to make up a password at this point.

Otherwise, Disk Utility now creates the image and then *mounts* it—that is, turns the image file into a simulated, yet fully functional, disk icon on your desktop.

When you're finished working with the disk, eject it as you would any disk (Control-click it and choose Eject, for example). Hang onto the .dmg disk image file itself, however. This is the file you'll need to double-click if you ever want to recreate your "simulated disk."

Turning an image into a CD

One of the other most common disk-image tasks is turning a disk image *back* into a CD or DVD—provided that your Mac has a CD or DVD burner, of course.

All you have to do is drag the .dmg file into the Disk Utility window, select it, and click the Burn icon on the toolbar (or, alternatively, Control-click the .dmg icon and choose Burn from the shortcut menu). Insert a blank CD or DVD, and then click Burn.

Grab

Grab takes pictures of your Mac's screen, for use when you're writing up instructions, illustrating a computer book, or collecting proof of some secret screen you found buried in a game. You can take pictures of the entire screen (press ⌘-Z, which for once in its life does *not* mean Undo) or capture only the contents of a rectangular selection (press Shift-⌘-A). When you're finished, Grab displays your snapshot in a new window, which you can print, close without saving, or save as a TIFF file, ready for emailing or inserting into a manuscript.

Now, as experienced Mac enthusiasts already know, the Mac OS has long had its *own* built-in shortcuts for capturing screenshots: Press Shift-⌘-3 to take a picture of the whole screen, and Shift-⌘-4 to capture a rectangular selection. (See page 242 for all the details.)

Tip: Don't forget that you can choose different, easier-to-remember keyboard shortcuts for these functions, if you like. Just open System Preferences→Keyboard→Keyboard Shortcuts, click Screen Shots, click where it now says Shift-⌘-3 (or whatever), and then press the new key combo.

So why use Grab instead? In many cases, you shouldn't. The Shift-⌘-3 and Shift-⌘-4 shortcuts work like a dream. But there are some cases when it might make more sense to opt for Grab. Here are three:

- Grab can make a *timed* screen capture (choose Capture→Timed Screen, or press Shift-⌘-Z), which lets you enjoy a 10-second delay before the screenshot is actually taken. After you click the Start Timer button, you have an opportunity to activate windows, pull down menus, drag items around, and otherwise set up the shot before Grab shoots the picture.

- With Grab, you have the option of including the cursor in the picture, which is extremely useful when you're showing a menu being pulled down or a button being clicked. (Mac OS X's screenshot keystrokes, by contrast, always eliminate the pointer.) Use the technique described in Figure 16-35 to add the pointer style of your choice to a Grab screenshot.

Tip: Actually, if you're going to write a book or manual about Mac OS X, the program you really need is Snapz Pro X; a trial version is available from this book's "Missing CD" at *www.missingmanuals.com*, among other places. It offers far more flexibility than any of Mac OS X's own screenshot features. For example, you have a choice of file format, you can neatly snip out just one dialog box or window with a single click, and you can even capture movies of screen activity.

Figure 16-35:
Unlike the Shift-⌘-3 or Shift-⌘-4 keystrokes, Grab lets you include the pointer/cursor in the picture—or hide it. Choose Grab→Preferences and pick one of the eight pointer styles, or choose to keep the pointer hidden by activating the blank button in the upper-left corner.

Grapher

This little unsung app is an amazing piece of work. It lets you create 2-D or 3-D graphs of staggering beauty and complexity.

When you first open Grapher, you're asked to choose what kind of virtual "graph paper" you want: two-dimensional (standard, polar, logarithmic) or three-dimensional (cubic, spherical, cylindrical). Click a name to see a preview; when you're happy with the selection, click Open.

Now the main Grapher window appears (Figure 16-36). Do yourself a favor. Spend a few wow-inducing minutes choosing canned equations from the Examples menu, and watching how Grapher whips up gorgeous, colorful, sometimes animated graphs on the fly.

When you're ready to plug in an equation of your own, type it into the text box at the top of the window. If you're not such a math hotshot, or you're not sure of the equation format, work from the canned equations and mathematical building blocks that appear when you choose Equation→New Equation from Template or Window→Show Equation Palette (a floating window containing a huge selection of math symbols and constants).

Tip: If you don't know the keystroke that produces a mathematical symbol like π or θ, you can just type *pi* or *theta*. Grapher replaces it with the correct symbol automatically.

Once the graph is up on the screen, you can tailor it like this:

- **To move a 2-D graph** in the window, choose View→Move Tool and then drag; to move a 3-D graph, ⌘-drag it.

- **To rotate a 3-D graph,** drag in any direction. If you add the Option key, you flip the graph around on one axis.

- **To change the colors, line thicknesses, 3-D "walls," and other graphic elements,** click the ❶ button (or choose Window→Show Inspector) to open the formatting palette. The controls you find here vary by graph type, but rest assured that Grapher can accommodate your every visual whim.

- **To change the fonts and sizes,** choose Grapher→Preferences. On the Equations panel, the four sliders let you specify the relative sizes of the text elements. If you click the sample equation, the Font panel appears (page 277), so you can fiddle with the type.

Figure 16-36:
In general, you type equations into Grapher just as you would on paper (like z=2xy). If in doubt, check the online help, which offers enough hints on functions, constants, differential equations, series, and periodic equations to keep the A Beautiful Mind *guy busy for days.*

- **Add your own captions, arrows, ovals, or rectangles** using the Object menu.

When it's all over, you can preserve your masterpiece using any of these techniques:

- **Export a graphic** by choosing File→Export.

- **Copy an equation to the Clipboard** by Control-clicking it and choosing Copy As→TIFF (or EPS, or whatever) from the shortcut menu. Now you can paste it into another program.

- **Export an animated graph** by choosing Equation→Create Animation. The result-ing dialog box lets you specify how long you want the movie to last (and a lot of other parameters).

Tip: If you Shift-drag the starting or ending images at the bottom, you can change their size.

Finally, click Create Animation. After a moment, the finished movie appears. If you like it the way it is, choose File→Save As to preserve it on your hard drive for future generations.

Java Preferences

Programmers generally use the Java programming language to write apps that can run on any kind of computer (Mac, Windows, Linux). A lot of corporate applica-tions use Java.

To run a Java program, you need a Java runtime (sort of a playback engine)—and Lion doesn't come with one. So the first time you open Java Preferences, or any Java program, the Mac offers to download and install one.

In any case, Java Preferences contains a bunch of advanced settings that geeks can use to modify how Java runs on their Macs.

Keychain Access

Keychain Access memorizes and stores all your secret information—passwords for network access, file servers, FTP sites, Web pages, and other secure items. For instruc-tions on using the Keychain, see page 460.

Migration Assistant

This little cutie automates the transfer of all your stuff your old PC to your Mac: your documents, network settings, programs, and more. This also comes in extremely handy when you buy a newer, better Mac—or when you need Time Machine to recover an entire dead Mac's worth of data. (It can also copy everything over from a second-ary hard drive or partition.) The instructions on the screen guide you through the process (see Chapter 6).

Network Utility

Network Utility gathers information about Web sites and network citizens. It offers a suite of standard Internet tools like Netstat, Ping, Traceroute, DNS Lookup, and Whois—advanced tools, to be sure, but ones that even Mac novices may be asked to fire up when calling a technician for Internet help.

Otherwise, you probably won't need to use Network Utility to get your work done. However, Network Utility can be useful when you're performing Internet detective work.

- **Whois** ("who is") can gather an amazing amount of information about the owners of any particular domain (such as apple.com)—including name and address info, telephone numbers, and administrative contacts.

- Use **Ping** to enter an address (either a Web address like *www.google.com* or an IP address like 192.168.1.110), and then "ping" (send out a "sonar" signal to) the server to see how long it takes for it to respond to your request. Network Utility reports the response time in milliseconds—a useful test when you're trying to see if a remote server (a Web site, for example) is up and running. (The time it takes for the ping to report back to you also tells you how good your connection to it is.)

- **Traceroute** lets you track how many "hops" are required for your Mac to communicate with a certain server (an IP address or Web address). Just type in the network address or URL, and then click Trace. You'll see that your request actually jumps from one *trunk* of the Internet to another, from router to router, as it makes its way to its destination. You'll learn that a message sometimes crisscrosses the entire country before it arrives at its destination. You can also see how long each leg of the journey took, in milliseconds.

Podcast Capture

This program is a front end for Podcast Producer, a professional-league podcast recording and publishing program that's part of Apple's Mac OS X Server software suite. Unless you work in an office where a Mac OS X Server hums away in a back room, you can ignore this program.

RAID Utility

Another program you probably don't need. It's useful only if your Mac has an Apple RAID (multiple-disk system) card installed.

System Information

System Information is a great tool for learning exactly what's installed on your Mac and what's not—in terms of both hardware and software. The people who answer the phones on Apple's tech-support line are particularly fond of System Profiler, since the detailed information it reports can be very useful for troubleshooting nasty problems.

There are three ways to open System Information. Two of them involve a preliminary visit to the dialog box shown in Figure 16-37, which is a consolidated view of the system information you might care most about.

Anyway, here are the three ways:

- **Slow.** Choose →About This Mac. You get a bare-bones info screen that reveals your Mac OS X version, your Mac's memory amount, and what processor it has inside.

Tip: If you click your Mac OS X version number twice in the About box, you get to see your Mac's serial number!

If you then click More Info, you get Lion's new About This Mac details screen, shown in Figure 16-37. If that information isn't all you need, then click System Report to open the actual System Information program.

- **Medium.** Burrow into your Applications→Utilities folder; double-click System Information.

- **Fast.** Hold down the Option key, which makes the →About This Mac command *change* to say System Information. Choose it, and then proceed as shown in Figure 16-37.

Figure 16-37:
This dialog box, new in Lion, gives you a plain-English display of the Mac details you probably care the most about: memory, screen, storage, serial number, Mac OS X version, and so on. (Click the tabs across the top for more details.) To proceed from here to the full System Information program, click System Report.

Figure 16-38:
Does your MacBook's chip run at 2 GHz or 2.6? What percentage of your external hard drive is filled up? What are the version numbers of every program installed on your Mac? Can your DVD burner burn dual-layer discs? And (shown here): Does your laptop have any open slots for extra RAM?

When System Information opens, it reports information about your Mac in a list down the left side (Figure 16-38). The details fall into these categories:

- **Hardware.** Click this word to see precisely which model Mac you have, what kind of chip is inside (and how many), how much memory it has, and its serial number.

  If you expand the flippy triangle, you get to see details about which **Memory** slots are filled and the size of the memory module in each slot; what kind of **Disc Burning** your Mac can do (DVD-R, DVD+R, and so on); what **PCI Cards** are installed in your expansion slots; what **Graphics/Displays** circuitry you have (graphics card and monitor); what's attached to your SATA bus (internal drives, like your hard drive); and much more.

- **Network.** This section reveals what **WiFi** components you have, what Internet connection **Locations** you've established, and so on.

- **Software.** Click this heading to see exactly which version of Mac OS X you have and what your computer's name is, as far as the network is concerned ("Chris's Computer," for example).

  The **Applications** list documents every program on your system, with version information—a quick inventory of what you've installed on your Mac.

  Other categories include self-explanatory lists like **Fonts, Preference Panes,** and **Startup Items.**

  Finally, the **Logs** panel reveals your Mac's secret diary: a record of the traumatic events that it experiences from day to day. (Many of these are the same as those revealed by the Console utility; see page 645.)

Tip: If any of these screens is showing you more technical information than you'd like, use the File→Show Less Information command to pare down the overload to just the human-recognizable items.

Saving a report

To create a handsomely formatted report that you can print or save, choose File→Export as Text, and then choose Rich Text Format from the File Format pop-up menu. Note, however, that the resulting report can be well over 500 pages long. In many cases, you're better off simply making a screenshot of the relevant Profiler screen, as described on page 242, or saving the thing as a PDF file.

Terminal

Terminal opens a terminal window with a *command line interface,* taking you deep into the world of Unix, the operating system on which Mac OS X is based. If you're technically inclined, a free online Appendix called "Terminal Crash Course" awaits you on this book's "Missing CD" at *www.missingmanuals.com.*

VoiceOver Utility

For details on this screen-reader software, see page 445.

6

Part Five:
Appendixes

Installation

If your computer came with Lion already installed on it, you can skip this appendix—for now. But if you're running an earlier version of the Mac OS and want to savor the Lion experience, this appendix describes how to install the new operating system on your Mac.

As you'll soon discover, the process isn't quite like any other operating system you've installed before. You can't buy Lion in a box, or on a DVD; you're supposed to download it from the Mac App Store.

There are some very attractive elements to the download-only system. For example, there's no copy protection and no serial numbers to type in. You don't have to pay extra for multiple copies; your one-time $30 covers as many Macs as you own. (In other words, there's no Family Plan for Lion.)

And there's no disc to hunt down later, when you want to install Lion again (onto a new Mac, for example). And when you do need a copy again, you'll download the latest version—10.7.3 or whatever it is—instead of having to install the updates that have come out since you got your DVD.

(And what if you don't have a fast Internet connection for downloading Lion? The world won't come to an end; read on.)

Hardware Requirements

For starters, you need to make sure you and your Mac have what it takes to handle Mac OS X Lion—specifically:

- **A Mac with a recent Intel processor.** You need a Mac with an Intel Core 2 Duo, i3, i5, i7, or Xeon chip inside; if you have an old Core Solo or Core Duo processor instead, you can't install Lion. (How do you find out? Choose →About This Mac. The resulting dialog box clearly identifies your processor.)

  Basically, most Macs manufactured since late 2006 are eligible.

- **Mac OS X Snow Leopard.** Your Mac has to be running the most recent pre-Lion software version, Mac OS X 10.6 (Snow Leopard). (The main reason: You need the App Store to get Lion, and the App Store debuted in Snow Leopard.) Even if you already have Snow Leopard, run Software Update to make sure you have the *latest* version, 10.6.8.

  If you don't have Snow Leopard, then the cost of Lion just went up. You'll have to buy and install Snow Leopard and then buy and install Lion.

- **Free hard disk space.** You need at least 10 GB free to install Mac OS X 10.7.

- **A lot of memory.** Mac OS X absolutely *loves* memory. For the greatest speed, install 4 gigabytes—more if you can afford it. (And these days, you probably can.)

- **The latest firmware.** *Firmware* describes the low-level, underlying software instructions that control the actual circuitry of your Mac. Every now and then, Apple updates it for certain Mac models, and it's very important that your Mac have the absolute latest. If yours doesn't, a message will appear to let you know during the installation. Quit the installer and grab the latest update from *http://support. apple.com/kb/HT1237.*

- **A full backup.** It's a really, *really* good idea to back up your entire Mac before you begin this, or any, upgrade. Even if things go wrong for only, say, 0.01 percent of Mac owners, that's still thousands of people. If you don't have a second hard drive, this is your excuse to buy one; they're dirt cheap these days. You can use Snow Leopard's version of Time Machine to make a complete, automatic backup of your Mac as it is now.

Psychological Requirements

Upgrading an operating system is always a traumatic experience for a computer—and, too often, for its owner. If you can rein in your excitement long enough to perform just a few extra steps, you'll be glad you did.

- **Check your hard drive.** Open Disk Utility (page 610), click your main hard drive's name and then click Verify Disk. If the program reports that you have problems, you'll have to start up from a different disk (like the Snow Leopard DVD), run Disk Utility again, and use the Repair Disk button this time.

- **Turn off FileVault, if you're using it.** (You'd remember turning on this Home-folder-encryption feature in Snow Leopard.)

- **Make sure your software will run.** Most modern programs run very smoothly on Lion. But some older ones won't run—in particular, programs like AppleWorks and Microsoft Office 2004 that relied on Snow Leopard's now-defunct Rosetta translation technology. Find out for sure by visiting *http://roaringapps.com/apps:table* and looking up the programs you own.

Tip: You can also look up your own programs using the System Profiler program in your Applications→Utilities folder. In the left-side column, click Applications. Click the Kind column heading to sort your programs. The programs listed as *PowerPC* or *Classic* won't run in Lion.

The Standard Installation

To do the actual installation, open the App Store program on your Mac. If you don't see "OS X Lion" advertised right there on the home page, then you can find it by searching for *lion*. Click the $29.99 button, and then click again when it changes to say Install (Figure A-1).

Figure A-1:
Enter your Apple ID and password when you're asked for it, and enjoy a hot mug of your favorite beverage as the download begins. If you have a typical broadband Internet connection, expect to wait about half an hour.

When the download begins, behind the scenes, the App Store puts a 3.8-gigabyte program called Install Mac OS X Lion into your Applications folder.

Tip: If you don't have a fast Internet connection, or if your Internet provider imposes monthly data limits, you might not be thrilled about the prospect of waiting for a 4-gigabyte download. Fortunately, you have two alternatives.

First, you can take your Mac to an Apple Store and use *its* free, fast WiFi to download Lion (or a friend's house, a library, a coffee shop…). Second, you can buy a flash drive with the Lion installer on it for $70 from Apple.

You'll know when the downloading is over, because the actual installer opens up automatically and presents you with the proud animal shown in Figure A-2.

Figure A-2:
Your installation adventure is about to begin. You've never experienced such a simple operating-system installation. You don't even have to restart the computer before you start. You have far fewer options and decisions to make.

The procedure from here:

1. **Click Continue.**

   The installer follows a pattern: Read the instructions, make a couple of choices, and then click Continue to advance to the next screen. As you go, the list on the left side of the screen reveals where you are in the overall procedure.

2. **Click Agree to pass the Software License Agreement screen, and then Agree again.**

   The Software License Agreement requires you to agree with whatever Apple's lawyers say.

3. **Choose the disk or partition where you want to install Mac OS X.**

   The installer proposes the screamingly obvious hard drive: the main one inside your Mac.

   If you have other drives, you can click Show All Disks to see their icons and choose one. Yellow exclamation-mark icons mean, "You can't install here," for one technical reason or another. You can install Lion only onto a blank hard drive, formatted as a Mac drive (technically, Mac OS Extended [Journaled] format), or onto a drive that has Snow Leopard on it.

4. **Click Install. Enter an administrator's account name and password when you're asked for it.**

   Now you're in for a 20- to 30-minute wait as the Installer copies software onto your hard drive. (That's why, if you're using a laptop and it's not plugged in, you'll be encouraged to plug it in.) At one point, it restarts the Mac and carries right on.

Mac OS X 10.7 is now installed on your Mac. Rest assured, it was a far less harrowing experience than previous Mac OS X installations. You're never asked what kind of installation you want, which language translations or printer drivers you want installed, which optional components you want, and so on.

Still, you're not quite ready to use Lion yet. See "The Setup Assistant" on the next page.

POWER USERS' CLINIC

Reinstalling Lion: Tricks of the Trade

You can install Lion on as many Macs as you own, all for the same $30. To install it on a second Mac, for example, open the App Store. Click the Purchases tab at the top. You'll see your previous Lion purchase listed there; just click Install to start installing Lion on *that* Mac.

That's what most people will do, anyway. Unfortunately, that means downloading the 4-gigabyte installer again for each Mac. That takes a lot of time and eats up a lot of your monthly Internet data allotment.

There is, fortunately, a trick that saves you the trouble of redownloading Lion over and over again: Copy the Install Mac OS X Lion installer program from the *first* Mac to all your other Macs (over the network or on a flash drive, for example). There's also a tricky part to this trick: Ordinarily, installing Lion on the first Mac *deletes* that installer program

once it's finished, to save you the disk space.

The trick to this trick, then, is to copy the installer to another Mac or drive (or at least take it out of your Applications folder) *before* you install Lion on the first Mac.

There may also be times when you want to install Lion again on the *same* Mac. But if you visit the App Store, you'll discover that you're not allowed to download it again on that machine; the "$29.99" button becomes an unclickable "Installed" button.

To fool the App Store, Option-click the OS X Lion link in the App Store. Or Option-click the Purchases tab at the top of the screen. Or hold down the Option key as you open the App Store program. One of those three tricks should restore the Buy button for Lion so that you can download it again. (You won't be charged again.)

The Setup Assistant

What you see depends on whether you installed Lion onto a Snow Leopard drive or an empty drive.

After Installing Over Snow Leopard

If you installed onto a Snow Leopard drive that already had stuff on it—accounts, files, settings, and so on—then after the Mac restarts, all you have to do is log in as usual. Enjoy the box that warns you about Lion's upside-down scrolling habit (page 11). Click Start Using Lion, and start using Lion.

Note: It's possible, at this point, that Lion will display a message warning you that it found some incompatible software on your Mac during the installation. You'll discover that this outdated software has been summarily tossed into a folder called Incompatible Software in your startup disk's main window.

After Installing onto a Blank Drive

If you installed Lion onto an empty drive, the Setup Assistant is a little more involved.

Once again, you're in for a click-through-the-screens experience, this time with the aim of setting up your Mac's various options. After answering the questions on each screen, click Continue.

The number and sequence of information screens you encounter may vary, but here are some of the possibilities:

- **Welcome.** Click the name of the country you're in.

- **Select Your Keyboard.** Different countries require different keyboard layouts. For example, if you choose the Canadian layout, pressing the] key on a U.S. keyboard produces the ç symbol. Click Continue.

- **Select a Network Connection.** This is your chance to introduce the Mac to any networks in the vicinity. Click the name of the WiFi hot spot you want to join, for example. If there's no wireless hot spot at all—hey, it could happen—click Different Network Setup to specify, say, a wired or cellular network hookup.

- **Transfer Information to This Mac.** This is one of Apple's slickest tricks. The Setup Assistant can suck all your old programs, files, folders, and settings from the old Mac to the new one—or even from an old *Windows PC* to your new Mac. You're about to meet the Mac OS X Migration Assistant, shown in Figure A-3.

   Your choices here are **From another Mac** (connect your old Mac to this one over a network, even a wireless one); **From a Windows PC** (see page 216); **From Time Machine or other disk** (connect your new Mac to your backup drive); and **Don't Transfer now.**

Tip: If you're in a hurry, you can always perform this rather sluggish task later. Just open the Migration Assistant program, which sits in your Applications→Utilities folder, whenever it's a better time. See page 216 for more on migrating from Windows.

If you choose one of the first options and then click Transfer, the data-copying process begins. It can take a *wicked* long time.

- **Enter Your Apple ID.** Here you're offered the chance to type in an Apple ID (an email address and password for all your Apple dealings), which is more essential in Lion than ever before. If you don't have one, just click Continue; you can get one and fill it in later.

- **Registration Information.** This is your chance to become a grain of sand on the great beach of the Apple database (and to set up your own "card" in Mac OS X's Address Book program).

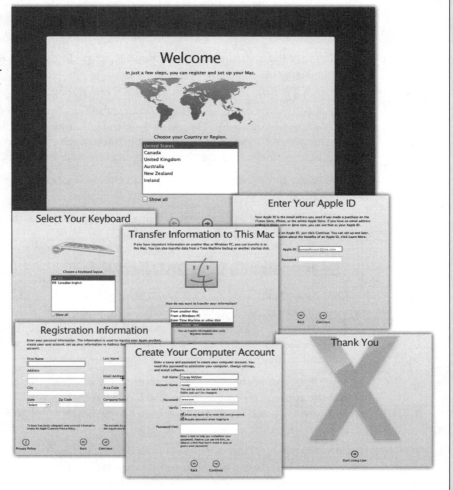

Figure A-3:
The Setup Assistant walks you through the final steps of getting a new Mac (or a clean Lion installation) ready. It includes the newly improved Migration Assistant, which transfers all your files from a backup, an old Mac, or an old Windows PC to your new Mac.

Tip: If you're not interested in providing your personal information to Apple, or if you've already done so during a previous installation, press ⌘-Q. A message offers you Skip, Shut Down, and Cancel buttons. If you click Skip, you jump straight ahead to Create Your Computer Account, below.

- **Create Your Computer Account.** Most of the steps up to this point have been pretty inconsequential, but this is a big moment. You're about to create your *account*—your Administrator account, in fact, as described in Chapter 13.

  All you have to do is make up a name, usually a short variation of your name, and a password. Choose carefully, because you can't easily change your account name later.

  What you come up with here is extremely important, especially if several people use this Mac at different times, or if other people connect to it on a network. See page 459 for details on creating a password and a hint that will help you remember it.

  If you're the only one who uses your Mac, it's perfectly OK to leave the password blank empty.

- **Select a Picture For This Account.** If your Mac has a built-in camera (laptops and iMacs do), you can take a photo of yourself to use as your account icon. Just click "Take a video snapshot." You get a 3-second countdown, and then the Mac snaps your photo. (You can always reshoot it.) Adjust the cropping by dragging inside the photo, and adjust the size by dragging the slider beneath it.

  If you're camera-shy, of course, you can choose "Choose from the picture library" and find an Apple-provided icon instead.

- **Thank You.** When you click Start Using Lion, you wind up at the Mac OS X desktop, just as described in Chapter 2.

The Homemade Lion Installer Disk

Lion's download-only schtick is revolutionary and, in most cases, incredibly convenient. But sometimes, you'll miss having a physical disk with the Lion installer on it. You might wish you had one if, for example, you want to install Lion on a huge array of Macs, like the ones at a school or in a business; downloading that 4-gig installer over and over again would drive you crazy.

You might also wish you had an installation disk when your Mac starts acting up, and the tricks described in Appendix B don't seem to work. And you need such a disk when you want to install Lion over a copy of Mac OS X 10.5 (Leopard) instead of Snow Leopard.

One way to get a Lion installation flash drive is to buy it from Apple for $70. As it turns out, though, you can make one yourself fairly easily. All you need is a hard drive, flash drive, or even a blank DVD. (Hard drives and flash drives are much faster at performing the actual installation.)

Phase 1: Format the Drive

If you're planning to use a flash drive or hard drive, the first step is to format it so that the Mac will be able to start up from it. To do that, connect or insert the drive. (It needs at least 5 gigabytes of free space. These steps assume that there's nothing else on it.)

Now open Disk Utility (it's in your Applications→Utilities folder). In Disk Utility, click the drive's name in the left-side list (not the partition name beneath it). Then click the Partition tab in the main window.

Under Partition Layout, choose 1 Partition. Then click the actual partition—the big rectangle "map" in the middle of the window—and then click Options beneath it. In the resulting dialog box, click GUID Partition Table; click OK.

Tip: Actually, it's fine to create multiple partitions, so you don't wind up wasting a lot of disk space. Just give the installation partition at least 5 gigabytes so it will have room for the Lion installer.

Now, back at the Partition window, you can type a name for your drive. From the Format menu, choose Mac OS X Extended (Journaled). Click Apply. Click Partition in the confirmation window. The process may take a minute or two.

Phase 2: Build Your Installer

Now you'll turn your formatted drive into a Lion installer.

Start by grabbing the *Install Mac OS X Lion.app* program that winds up in your Applications folder when you first buy Lion. (You have to think of this *before* you actually run it, as described in the box on page 629. That box also tells you how you can redownload the Lion installer app if it's too late for that.)

Right-click the installer's icon. From the shortcut menu, choose Show Package Contents.

In the resulting folder, open Contents, and then open Shared Support. Inside is a disk-image file called *InstallESD.dmg*. Your job is to convert this disk image into an actual disk.

To do that, open Disk Utility again. Drag the *InstallESD.dmg* disk image into the list at the left side of Disk Utility's window. Click *InstallESD.dmg* in the list; then click the Restore tab. Insert the flash drive, or connect the hard drive, that you formatted in Phase 1.

Last steps: Drag your drive's icon out of the left-side list into the Destination box (Figure A-4). Click Restore; enter your administrator name and password when you're asked.

Note: If you want to create a Lion DVD (instead of a flash drive or hard drive), here's the only different step. Instead, just click *InstallESD.dmg* in the left-side list, and then click Burn in the toolbar. Insert a blank DVD and then click Burn.

When the "restoring" process is complete, you wind up with an actual Lion flash drive or hard drive that you baked all by yourself.

To use it, turn off the Mac. Connect your homemade installer drive. When you turn on the Mac, hold down the Option key so that a choice of startup disks appears. Click your homemade installer to start up from it.

Figure A-4:
This is what the setup should look like in Disk Utility just before you actually create the installation disk.

Now you can install Lion as usual, or use any of the recovery features described in Appendix B.

Uninstalling Mac OS X 10.7 Lion

There isn't any easy way to remove Lion if you decide you don't like it.

The chief problem is that thousands of its pieces are invisible. Even if you start up the Mac from another disk and then drag all the visible Mac OS X folders to the Trash, you'll leave behind many megabytes of software crumbs that you can't see.

So if you want to retreat to something earlier, back up the data that's worth preserving—mainly, your Home folder and Applications folder—and then erase the hard drive or partition and reinstall the operating system that you prefer.

Troubleshooting

Whether it's a car engine or an operating system, anything with several thousand parts can develop the occasional technical hiccup. Mac OS X is far more resilient than its predecessors, but it's still a complex system with the potential for occasional glitches.

Most freaky little glitches go away if you just try these two steps, one at a time:

- Quit and restart the wayward program.

- Log out and log back in again.

It's the *other* problems that'll drive you batty.

Minor Eccentric Behavior

All kinds of glitches may befall you, occasionally, in Mac OS X. Your desktop picture doesn't change when you change it in System Preferences. A menulet doesn't open when you click it. A program won't open—it just bounces in the Dock a couple of times and then stops.

When a single program is acting up like this, but quitting and restarting it does no good, try the following steps, in the following sequence.

First Resort: Repair Permissions
An amazing number of mysterious glitches arise because the *permissions* of either that item or something in your System folder—that is, the complex mesh of invisible settings that describe the Mac's underlying Unix files—have become muddled.

When something doesn't seem to be working right, therefore, open your Applications→
Utilities folder and open Disk Utility. Proceed as shown in Figure B-1.

This is a really, *really* great trick to know.

Figure B-1:
*Click your hard
drive's name in the
left-side list, click the
First Aid tab, click
Repair Disk Permis-
sions, and then read
an article while the
Mac checks out your
disk. If the program
finds anything
amiss, you'll see
messages like these.
Among the text, you
may recognize some
Unix shorthand for
read, write, and
execute privileges.*

Second Resort: Look for an Update

If a program starts acting up immediately after you've installed it, chances are good
that it has some minor incompatibility. Chances are also good that you'll find an
updated version on the company's Web site.

Third Resort: Toss the Prefs File

A corrupted preference file can bewilder the program that depends on it.

Before you go on a dumpfest, however, take this simple test: Log in using a *different
account* (perhaps a dummy account that you create just for testing purposes). Run the
problem program. Is the problem gone? If so, then the glitch exists only when *you* are
logged in—which means it's a problem with *your* copy of the program's preferences.

Return to your own account. Open your Home→Library→Preferences folder, where
you'll find neatly labeled preference files for all the programs you use. (To open the
hidden Library folder, press the Option key as you open the Go menu; choose Library.)

Each preference file ends with the file name suffix *.plist.* For example, *com.apple.finder.plist* is the Finder's preference file, *com.apple.dock.plist* is the Dock's, and so on.

Put the suspect preference file into the Trash, but don't empty it. The next time you run the recalcitrant program, it will build itself a brand-new preference file that, if you're lucky, lacks whatever corruption was causing your problems.

If not, quit the program. You can reinstate its original .plist file from the Trash, if you find that helpful as you pursue your troubleshooting agenda.

Remember, however, that you actually have *two* Preferences folders. In addition to your own Home folder's stash, there's a second one in the Library folder in the main hard drive window (which administrators are allowed to trash; this one contains system-wide preferences, like your network configuration).

In any case, the next time you open the sick program or log in, the Mac creates fresh, virginal preference files.

Fourth Resort: Restart

Sometimes you can give Mac OS X or its programs a swift kick by restarting the Mac. It's an inconvenient step, but not nearly as time-consuming as what comes next. And it can fix problems that cropped up when you started up the computer.

Last Resort: Trash and Reinstall the Program

Sometimes reinstalling the problem program clears up whatever the glitch was.

First, however, throw away all traces of it. Open the Applications folder and drag the program's icon (or its folder) to the Trash. In most cases, the only remaining pieces to discard are its .plist file (or files) in your Home→Library→Preferences folder, and any scraps bearing the program's name in your Library→Application Support folder. (You can do a quick Spotlight search to round up any other pieces.)

Then reinstall the program from its original disc or installer—after first checking the company's Web site to see if there's an updated version, of course.

Frozen Programs (Force Quitting)

The occasional unresponsive application has become such a part of Mac OS X life that, among the Mac cognoscenti online, the dreaded, endless "please wait" cursor has been given its own acronym: SBOD (Spinning Beachball of Death). When the SBOD strikes, no amount of mouse clicking and keyboard pounding will get you out of the recalcitrant program.

Here are the different ways you can go about *force quitting* a stuck program (the equivalent of pressing Ctrl+Alt+Delete in Windows), in increasing order of desperation:

- **Force quit the usual way.** Choose →Force Quit to terminate the stuck program, or use one of the other force-quit methods described on page 139.

- **Force quit the sneaky way.** Some programs, including the Dock, don't show up at all in the usual Force Quit dialog box. Your next attempt, therefore, should be to open the Activity Monitor program (in Applications→Utilities), which shows *everything* that's running. Double-click a program and then, in the resulting dialog box, click Quit to force quit it.

Tip: If all this seems like a lot to remember, you can always force restart the Mac. On most Macs, you do that by holding down the power button for 5 seconds. If that doesn't work, press Control-⌘-power button.

Recovery Mode: Three Emergency Disks

Lion doesn't come on a DVD. When your Mac won't even start up, there's no DVD to insert as a backup startup disk, as there always was before. That's a scary place to be; if your hard drive is sick, then everything on it may be inaccessible to you. What you need is an emergency drive that can repair the hard drive and get you back in operation.

Apple is way ahead of you on this one. It offers *three* simulated repair disks: three ways to supply disk-repair and system-software repair tools in times of crisis.

The Recovery HD

Here's the sneaky surprise: When you install Lion, it automatically creates an invisible hidden "hard drive" (a partition of your main drive that has its own icon) called Recover HD. It's a 650-megabyte "drive" that's generally invisible to you. It's even invisible to Disk Utility, so even if you erase your hard drive, the Recovery HD is still there to help you.

But if you can't seem to start up your Mac properly, or if your hard drive is acting a little flaky, you'll be glad you had this "separate" startup disk. On it, Apple has provided some emergency tools for fixing drive or software glitches, restoring files, browsing the Web, and even reinstalling Lion.

Note: The Lion installer creates the Recovery HD partition only if your startup drive is an internal hard drive. In certain other situations, it won't create the partition—for example, if the disk you're installing Lion onto is a RAID volume or has a non-standard Boot Camp partition setup.

You can power up your Mac from the Recovery HD in either of two ways:

- **Hold down ⌘-R as the Mac is starting up.** You can let go when you see the Apple logo appear.

- **Hold down the Option key as the Mac is starting up.** When you see the Startup Manager (Figure B-2, top), let go. Click the up-arrow button below the Recovery HD icon.

Either way, you wind up at the Utilities screen shown in Figure B-2, bottom.

Here, Apple has supplied you with four important tools:

- **Restore From Time Machine Backup.** If your Mac is really hosed, this is the option you want. It restores your *entire* software world—programs, data, settings, Mac OS X itself—from the Time Machine backup you carefully set up as you read Chapter 5.

  This option *completely erases* your existing hard drive, so—you know. Be sure.

Figure B-2:
Top: This simple display of disk icons is known as the Startup Manager. It's simply an easy way to specify which disk you want to start up from.

Bottom: Here's the point of the Recovery HD partition: a screen full of emergency utilities that can fix your Mac's regularly scheduled hard drive. If there's a pop-up menu at the bottom, it's for choosing a WiFi hot spot so that you can access the rest of your network. That might be useful when, for example, you want to access your Time Capsule backups.

Once you choose this option, click Continue. You're now asked to choose the Time Machine drive, then the time-stamped backup you want to restore from, and, finally, the drive or partition you want to wipe out. You get one more warning that you're about to wipe out the destination drive. When you click Continue, the restoration begins. When it's all over—usually a couple of hours later—the Mac restarts as though nothing ever happened.

- **Reinstall Mac OS X: Set up and install a new copy of Lion.** You can use this option to install a copy of Lion onto any hard drive—for example, you could reinstall it on your main internal drive.

Note: This option will download the actual copy of Lion from the Internet—all 4 gigabytes of it. In other words, it requires an Internet connection and a *lot* of patience.

- **Get Help Online: Browse the Apple Support Web site to find help for your Mac.** This option opens your Safari Web browser, which presents you with some helpful information about using the Recovery Mode that you've fired up. You're actually online at this point, so you can also visit any other Web site you might find helpful.

Quit Safari when you're finished browsing; you return to the main Mac OS X Utilities window.

- **Disk Utility: Repair or erase a disk using Disk Utility.** Use this option to open Disk Utility, the Mac's hard drive diagnostics-and-repair program. You can use it to check, fix, erase, or partition any of your hard drives.

For example, you can repair the main startup disk, which is often the most useful option.

Those four options are the big-ticket items, but don't miss the menu bar. The commands here let you open advanced technical tools like the Firmware Password Utility, Network Utility, and Terminal.

Lion Internet Recovery

OK, the Recovery HD concept is clever. And most of the time, it's all you need.

But what if your hard drive is *completely* hosed? What then, smart guy? You can't very well boot up from the Recovery HD if it's sitting on the same dead hard drive.

Or what if you've just installed a brand-new, bigger, or faster hard drive? It doesn't have Lion on it. It doesn't have Recovery HD on it. How are you supposed to install Lion?

In those situations, new Mac models—those released after Lion, like the 2011 MacBook Airs and Mac minis—offer an even cleverer option: Lion Internet Recovery. This mode offers the same exact options that the Utilities screen of Recovery HD would have—but you're connecting to that software *online,* over a high-speed Internet connection. You're literally starting up from *Apple's* hard drives, thousands of miles away.

So even if your hard drive is dead as a doornail, you can still repair it, reinstall Lion, and so on.

To fire up Internet Recovery, make sure your computer is in a WiFi hot spot or connected to an Ethernet network. Then hold down ⌘-R as the computer is starting up. You can let go when you see the screen that asks you to choose a WiFi network. Do that, and then enter the password for the network, if necessary.

Now your Mac downloads a disk image containing just enough software to get you to the Utilities screen described in the previous section.

Note: Once you're up and running, you can redownload the copies of iPhoto, iMovie, and GarageBand that came with your Mac. Just open the App Store program, log in with your Apple ID, click Purchases, and click Accept to download those iLife programs. You won't be charged for them.

Physical Recovery Disks

But what if the hard drive is so sick that you can't start up from the Recovery HD—*and* your Mac isn't new enough to offer the Internet Recovery feature? (Or what if it *does* offer that feature, but you'd rather repair your Mac a quicker way?)

One solution is to build yourself a bootable Lion flash drive, DVD, or hard drive, as described in Appendix A. Not only is it capable of starting up or reinstalling Lion, but it also has a complete set of recovery tools on board.

But creating a bootable drive takes a lot of steps, and it requires sacrificing an 8-gigabyte (or bigger) flash drive. If you have any flash drive, even a 2-gigabyte one that somebody handed you at a trade show, you can load it up with just the recovery tools, to use in times of trouble. Creating this kind of emergency flash drive is somewhat easier than creating the kind of full-blown reinstallation flash drive described in Appendix A.

Note: To create an emergency "disk," your Mac must have Lion on it already, including the invisible Recovery HD partition. That's because it *relies* on the data and software on that partition.

Also, you have to format the flash drive correctly, as described on page 633. It's OK if the flash drive is partitioned; just leave at least 2 gigs for the recovery partition.

To get started, download Apple's free Lion Recovery Disk Assistant. (It's available from this book's "Missing CD" page at *www.missingmanuals.com.*)

Insert your flash drive into the Mac. Open the Lion Recovery Disk Assistant; click Agree to get through the legalese screen.

Click the name of the flash drive, and then click Continue. You're warned that this process will *erase* the flash drive (or its partition), and you're asked to authenticate yourself with an administrator name and password.

When you click OK, your Mac begins creating the recovery disk. After a minute or so, a message congratulates you, and the newly created drive's icon appears in the Lion Recovery Disk Assistant program, bearing the name Recovery HD.

To use this emergency disk, hold down the Option key as the Mac starts up. You wind up at the Startup Manager screen shown in Figure B-2, top. From the pop-up menu, choose your WiFi hot spot.

Now click the up-arrow button below the Recovery HD icon. (You may even see *two* Recovery HD icons—one of them is the USB flash drive, and the other is the invisible partition on your hard drive.) Your Mac is starting up from the flash drive! After a moment, you wind up at the Utilities screen described earlier in this appendix.

Note: The recovery flash drive you made will work only on the Mac model you used to make it.

Application Won't Open

If a program won't open (if its icon bounces merrily in the Dock for a few seconds, for instance, but then nothing happens), begin by trashing its preference file, as described on page 636. If that doesn't solve it, reinstalling the program, or installing the Lion-compatible update for it, usually does.

Startup Problems

Not every problem you encounter is related to running applications. Sometimes trouble strikes before you even get that far. The following are examples.

Kernel Panic

When you see the cheerful, multilingual dialog box shown in Figure B-3 you've got yourself a *kernel panic*—a Unix nervous breakdown.

You need to restart your computer. Hold down the Power button for several seconds or press the Restart button.

Veuillez redémarrer votre ordinateur. Maintenez la touche de démarrage enfoncée pendant plusieurs secondes ou bien appuyez sur le bouton de réinitialisation.

Sie müssen Ihren Computer neu starten. Halten Sie dazu die Einschalttaste einige Sekunden gedrückt oder drücken Sie die Neustart-Taste.

コンピュータを再起動する必要があります。パワーボタンを数秒間押し続けるか、リセットボタンを押してください。

Figure B-3:
A kernel panic is almost always related to some piece of add-on hardware. And look at the bright side: At least you get this handsome dialog box. That's a lot better than the Mac OS X 10.0 and 10.1 effect—random text gibberish superimposing itself on your screen.

(In such situations, *user panic* might be the more applicable term, but that's programmers for you.)

If you experience a kernel panic, it's almost always the result of a *hardware* glitch—most often a bad memory (RAM) board, but possibly an accelerator card, graphics card, or USB hub that Mac OS X doesn't like. A poorly seated AirPort card can bring on a kernel panic, too, and so can a bad USB or FireWire cable.

If simply restarting the machine doesn't help, detach every shred of gear that didn't come from Apple. Restore these components to the Mac one at a time until you find out which one was causing Mac OS X's bad hair day. If you're able to pinpoint the culprit, seek its manufacturer (or its Web site) on a quest for updated drivers, or at least try to find out for sure whether the add-on is compatible with Mac OS X.

Tip: This advice goes for your Macintosh itself. Apple periodically updates the Mac's *own* "drivers" in the form of a *firmware update.* You download these updates from the Support area of Apple's Web site (if indeed Mac OS X's own Software Update mechanism doesn't alert you to their existence).

There's one other cause for kernel panics, by the way, and that's moving, renaming, or changing the access permissions for Mac OS X's essential system files and folders—the Applications or System folder, for example. This cause isn't even worth mentioning, of course, because nobody would be that foolish.

Safe Mode (Safe Boot)

In times of troubleshooting, on Windows, you press an F-key to start up in Safe Mode. That's how you turn off all nonessential system-software nubbins in an effort to get a sick machine at least powered up.

Mac OS X offers the same kind of emergency keystroke. It can come in handy when you've just installed some new piece of software and find that you can't even start up the machine, or when one of your fonts is corrupted, or when something you've designated as a login item turns out to be gumming up the works. With this trick, you can at least turn on the computer so that you can uninstall the cranky program.

The trick is to *press the Shift key* as the machine is starting up. Hold it down from the startup chime until you see the words "Safe Boot," in red lettering, on the login screen.

Welcome to Safe Mode.

What have you accomplished?

- **Checked your hard drive.** The Shift-key business makes the startup process seem to take a very long time; as the progress bar suggests, Mac OS X is actually scanning your entire hard drive for problems.

- **Brought up the login screen.** When you do a safe boot, you must click your name and enter your password, even if you normally have Automatic Login turned on.

- **Turned off noncritical kernel extensions (drivers).** All kinds of software nuggets load during the startup process. Some of them you choose yourself, like icons you add to the Login Items list in the System Preferences→Accounts pane. Others are normally hidden, including a large mass of *kernel extensions,* which are chunks of software that add various features to the basic operating system. (Kernel extensions live in your System→Library→Extensions folder.)

  If you're experiencing startup crashes, some non-Apple installer may have given you a kernel extension that doesn't care for Mac OS X 10.7—so in Safe Mode, they're all turned off.

- **Turned off your fonts.** Corrupted fonts are a chronic source of trouble—and because you can't tell by looking, they're darned difficult to diagnose. So just to make sure you can at least get into your computer, Safe Mode turns them all off (except the authorized, Apple-sanctioned ones that it actually needs to run, which are in your System→Library→Fonts folder).

- **Trashed your font cache.** The font cache is a speed trick. Mac OS X stores the visual information for each of your fonts on the hard drive so the system won't have to read every single typeface off your hard drive when you open your Font menus or the Font panel.

  When these files get scrambled, startup crashes can result. That's why a Safe Boot moves all these files into the Trash. (You'll even see them sitting there in the Trash after the startup process is complete, although there's not much you can do with them except walk around holding your nose and pointing.)

- **Turned off your login items.** Safe Mode also prevents any Finder windows from opening *and* prevents your own handpicked startup items from opening—that is, whatever you've asked your Mac to auto-open by adding them to the System Preferences→Accounts→Login Items list.

  This, too, is a troubleshooting tactic. If some login item crashes your Mac every time it opens, you can squelch it just long enough to remove it from your Login Items list.

Tip: If you don't hold down the Shift key until you click the Log In button (after entering your name and password at the login screen), you squelch *only* your login items but *not* the fonts and extensions.

Once you reach the desktop, you'll find a long list of standard features inoperable. You can't use DVD Player, capture video in iMovie, use a wireless network, use certain microphones and speakers, or use your modem. (The next time you restart, all this goodness will be restored, assuming you're no longer clutching the Shift key in a sweaty panic.)

In any case, the beauty of Safe Mode is that it lets you get your Mac going. You have access to your files, so at least the emergency of crashing-on-startup is over. And you can start picking through your fonts and login items to see if you can spot the problem.

Forgotten Password

If you or one of the other people who use your Mac have forgotten the corresponding account password, no worries: Just read the box on page 450.

Fixing the Disk

What happens if something goes wrong with the complex software that operates the hard drive itself?

Fortunately, Mac OS X comes with its own disk-repair program. In the familiar Mac universe of icons and menus, it takes the form of a program in Applications→

Utilities called Disk Utility. In the barren world of Terminal and the command-line interface, there's a utility that works just as well but bears a different name: *fsck* (for file system check).

In any case, running Disk Utility or its alter ego *fsck* is a powerful and useful trouble-shooting tool that can cure all kinds of strange ills, including these problems, among others:

- Your Mac freezes during startup, either before or after the login screen.
- The startup process interrupts itself with the appearance of the text-only command line.
- You get the "applications showing up as folders" problem.

Method 1: Disk Utility

The easiest way to check your disk is to use the Disk Utility program. Use this method if your Mac can, indeed, start up. (See Method 2 if you can't even get that far.)

Disk Utility can't fix the disk it's *on* (except for permissions repairs, described at the beginning of this appendix).That's why you have to restart the Mac into Recovery Mode and run Disk Utility from there. The process goes like this:

1. **Start up the Mac from the Recovery HD, or a recovery flash drive.**

   They're both described earlier in this appendix. You wind up, after some time, at the Utilities screen.

2. **Click "Disk Utility: Repair or erase a disk using Disk Utility."**

   After a moment, the Disk Utility screen appears.

3. **Click the disk or disk partition you want to fix, click the First Aid tab, and then click Repair Disk.**

   The Mac whirls into action, checking a list of very technical disk-formatting parameters.

If you see the message, "The volume 'Macintosh HD' appears to be OK," that's meant to be *good* news. Believe it or not, that cautious statement is as definitive an affirmation as Disk Utility is capable of making about the health of your disk.

Disk Utility may also tell you that the disk is damaged but that it can't help you. In that case, you need a more heavy-duty disk-repair program like DiskWarrior (*www.alsoft.com*).

Method 2: fsck at the Console

Techier folk can also boot into the Mac's raw Unix underlayer to perform some diagnostic (and healing) commands.

Specifically, you can run the Unix program *fsck,* for which Disk Utility is little more than a pretty faceplate.

Note: Even so, Apple recommends that you use Disk Utility if at all possible. Use *fsck* only if all else fails.

To get there in times of startup troubleshooting, press ⌘-S while the Mac is starting up. (If you're stuck at the frozen remnants of a previous startup attempt, you may first have to force restart your Mac; hold down the ⏻ button for 5 seconds.)

Instead of arriving at the usual desktop, you see the Console screen shown in Figure B-4. This technical-looking text scrolling up a black screen is the *command line*. In console mode, you get white type against black, no windows or icons in sight. Abandon the mouse, all ye who enter here; in console mode, you can't do anything but type commands.

The Mac runs its various startup routines. When it finally stops at the *localhost#* prompt, you're ready to type commands. You're now in what's called *single-user mode*, meaning that the Unix multiple-accounts software has yet to load. You won't be asked to log in.

At the *root#* prompt, type *fsck -y* (note the space before the hyphen) and press Return. (The *y* means "yes," as in "yes, I want you to fix any problems automatically.")

```
Found old device 0x0cdea00
IOFireWireDevice,  ROM unchanged 0x0xcdea00
IOFireWireDevice 0x0xcdea00,  ROM generation zero
Got boot device =
IOService:/Core99PE/pc@f20000000/AppleMacRiscPCI/mac-
io@17/KeyLargo/ata-4@1f000/KeyLargoATA/ATADeviceNube0/IOA
TABlockStorageDriver/IOATABlockStorageDevice/IOBlockStorageDr
iver/QUANTUM FIREBALL CX13.6A
Media/IOApplePartitionScheme/Untitled
@9
BSD root: disk0s9, major 14, minor 9
Rereading ROM up to 25 quads
devfs on /dev
USB:    4.947: AppleUSBKeyboard[0xD0E80014::start    USB Generic
Keyboard @ 3 (0x18110000)
Mon Nov 19 23:18:53 EST 2001
Singleuser  boot -- fsck not done
Root device is mounted read-only
If you want to make modifications to files,
run '/sbin/fsck -y' first and then '/sbin/mount -uw/'
localhost#
```

Figure B-4:
In console mode, your entire screen is a command line interface. Unix jockeys can go to town here. Everyone else can timidly type "fsck -y" after the local-host:/root # prompt—see this prompt on the very last line?—and hope for the best.

Now the file system check program takes over, running through five sets of tests. When it's complete, you'll see one of two messages:

- **The volume Macintosh HD appears to be OK.** All is well. Type *exit* and press Return to proceed to the usual login screen and desktop.

- **File system was modified.** A good sign, but just a beginning. You need to run the program again. One *fsck* pass often repairs only one layer of problems, leaving another to be patched in the next pass. Type *fsck -fy* a second time, a third time, and so on, until you finally arrive at a "disk appears to be OK" message.

Type *exit* at the prompt and press Return to get back to the familiar world of icons and windows.

Where to Get Troubleshooting Help

If the basic steps described in this appendix haven't helped, the universe is crawling with additional help sources. In general, this is the part in any Mac book where you're directed to Apple's Support Web site, to various discussion forums, and so on—and, indeed, those help sources are listed below.

But the truth is, the mother of all troubleshooting resources isn't any of those—it's Google. You'll find more answers faster using Google than you ever will using individual help sites. That's because Google *includes* all those help sites in its search!

Suppose, for example, that you've just installed the 10.7.2 software update for Lion, and it's mysteriously turned all your accounts (including your own) into Standard accounts. And without any Administrator account, you can't install new programs, change network settings, add or edit other accounts, and so on.

You could go to one Web site after another, hunting for a fix, repeating your search—or you could just type *lion 10.7.2 standard accounts* into Google. You'll get your answers after just a few more seconds of clicking and exploring the results.

Help Online

These Web sites contain nothing but troubleshooting discussions, tools, and help:

- **Apple Discussion Groups** (*http://discussions.apple.com*). The volume and quality of question-and-answer activity here dwarfs any other free source. If you're polite and concise, you can post questions to the multitudes here and get more replies from them than you'll know what to do with.

- **Apple's help site** (*www.apple.com/support*). Apple's help site includes downloadable manuals, software updates, frequently asked questions, and many other resources.

  It also has a search box. It's your ticket to the Knowledge Base, a collection of 100,000 individual technical articles, organized in a searchable database, that the Apple technicians themselves consult when answering calls for help. You can search it either by typing in keywords or by using pop-up menus of question categories.

- **MacFixIt** (*www.macfixit.com*). The world's one-stop resource for Mac troubleshooting advice; alas, you have to pay to access the good stuff.

Help by Telephone

Finally, consider contacting whoever sold you the component that's making your life miserable: the printer company, scanner company, software company, or whatever.

If it's a Mac OS problem, you can call Apple at 800-275-2273 (that's 800-APL-CARE). For the first 90 days after your purchase of Mac OS X, the technicians will answer your questions for free.

After that, unless you've paid for AppleCare for your Mac (a three-year extended warranty program), Apple will charge you to answer your questions. Fortunately, if the problem turns out to be Apple's fault, they won't charge you.

The "Where'd-It-Go?" Dictionary

I f you're switching to Mac OS X from Windows, this appendix is for you. It's an alphabetical listing of every common Windows function and where to find it in Mac OS X. After all, an operating system is an operating system. The actual functions are pretty much the same—they're just in different places.

About [this program]

To find out the version number of the program you're using, don't look in the Help menu. Instead, look in the *application* menu next to the menu—the one that bears the name of the program you're in. That's where you find the About command for Macintosh programs.

Accessibility Options control panel

The special features that let you operate the computer even with impaired vision, hearing, or motor control are called Universal Access in Mac OS X. They're in System Preferences (see Chapter 15).

Active Desktop

The Mac never displays Web pages directly on the desktop—and knowing Apple, that's probably a point of pride. But Dashboard (Chapter 4) keeps Internet data only a keystroke away.

Add Hardware control panel

The Mac requires no program for installing the driver for a new external gadget. The drivers for most printers, mice, keyboards, cameras, camcorders, and other accessories are preinstalled. If you plug something into the Mac and find that it doesn't work immediately, just install the driver from the included CD (or the manufacturer's Web site).

Add or Remove Programs control panel

Here's another one you just don't need on the Macintosh. Installing a program onto the Mac is described in Chapter 4. Removing a program simply involves dragging its icon to the Trash. (For a clean sweep, inspect your Home→Library→Preferences and Library→Application Support folders to see if any preference files got left behind.)

All Programs

There's no Programs menu built into Mac OS X, like the one on the Windows Start menu. If you'd like one, drag your Applications folder into the end of the Dock. Now its icon is a tidy pop-up menu of every program on your machine.

Alt key

On the Mac, it's the Option key, although the key usually says "Alt" on it, too. (In some countries, it says *only* Alt.) You can substitute Option for Alt in any keystroke in most popular programs. The Option key has a number of secondary features on the Mac, too: It hides the windows of one program when you click into another, and so on.

Automatic Update

The →Software Update command does exactly the same thing.

Backspace key

It's in the same place on the Macintosh keyboard, but it's called the Delete key.

Battery level

The battery-level graph (⬭) for your Mac laptop appears in the menu bar, rather than in the system tray. (If you don't see it, open System Preferences→Energy Saver and turn it on.)

BIOS

You'll never have to update or even think about the ROM of your Macintosh (the approximate equivalent of the BIOS on the PC). It's permanent and unchanging. The very similar *firmware* of your Macintosh does occasionally have to be updated in order to work with a new version of the Mac operating system or some dramatic new feature—once every four years, perhaps. You'll be notified on the screen when the time comes.

Briefcase

The Briefcase is a Windows invention designed to help you keep your files in sync between a laptop and a desktop computer. You can use free services like Dropbox.com and SugarSync.com to achieve exactly the same result with your Mac. Or, if it's your calendar, address book, or mail account that you want to sync, just use iCloud, as described in Chapter 10.

Calculator

The Calculator program in Mac OS X can not only do arithmetic, but it can also perform conversions (temperature, distance, currency, and so on) and features an editable "paper tape." It sits in your Applications folder and is described in Chapter 16. (There's a simpler Calculator in Dashboard, too. And don't forget that you can type quick math equations into the ⌕ Spotlight menu.)

Camera and Scanner Wizard

When you connect a digital camera or scanner to your Mac, iPhoto or Image Capture opens automatically and prepares to download the pictures automatically. Details are in Chapter 9.

CDs

To open the CD/DVD drawer, or, if you have a slot-loading drive, to spit out the disc that's in it, hold down the ⏏ key on your Mac keyboard. If it's an older Mac keyboard without a ⏏ key, you can eject a CD (or any other disc) by Control-clicking (or right-clicking) its desktop icon and then choosing Eject from the shortcut menu. There are various other ways to eject a disc, but the point is that you never do so by pushing the Eject button on the disc drive itself.

Character Map

This Windows program helps you find what keys you need to press to trigger trademark symbols, copyright symbols, and other special characters. The equivalent on the Mac is called the Keyboard Viewer (page 190)—but the Character Viewer (page 189) is even easier to use.

Clean Install

The Lion installer can give you a fresh copy of the operating system, just as the Windows installer can. Instructions are in Appendix A.

Clipboard

The Mac's Clipboard works much like the one in Windows. In the Finder, you can choose Edit→Show Clipboard to see whatever you most recently copied or cut.

Command line

In Mac OS X, the command line is alive and well—but it speaks Unix, not DOS. You get to it by opening Terminal, which is described a free online appendix to this book called "Terminal Crash Course." It awaits you on this book's "Missing CD" at *www.missingmanuals.com*.

Control Panel

The Control Panel in Mac OS X is called System Preferences, and you open it from your menu. As in Windows, you can view these icons either by category or in a simple alphabetical list: Just choose either Organize by Categories or Organize Alphabetically from the View menu.

Copy, Cut, Paste

When you're editing in a word processor or graphics program, the Mac OS X Cut, Copy, and Paste commands work exactly as they do in Windows.

At the desktop, however, there are a few differences. You can indeed copy icons and paste them into a new window using the Copy and Paste commands—but *cutting* them out of a window, as you can in Windows, works slightly differently: After you've copied the icons from the first window, open the destination window. Then press the Option key, open the Edit menu, and choose Move Items Here.

Ctrl key

On the Macintosh, you generally substitute the ⌘ key in keystrokes that would involve the Ctrl key in Windows. In other words, the Save command is now ⌘-S instead of Ctrl+S, Open is ⌘-O instead of Ctrl+O, and so on.

Date and Time

To set your Mac's calendar and clock, open Date & Time in System Preferences.

Delete Key (Forward Delete)

Most desktop Mac keyboards have a forward-delete key (labeled ⌦ or *Del*) exactly like the ones on PCs. On Mac laptops, and on Apple's aluminum keyboards, you trigger the forward-delete function by pressing the Delete key while simultaneously pressing the Fn key.

Desktop

The Macintosh desktop is pretty much the same idea as the Windows desktop, with a few key differences:

- Disk icons show up on the Mac desktop as soon as they are inserted or connected. You don't have to open a window to see their icons.

- You change the desktop picture using the Desktop & Screen Saver panel of System Preferences.

- The Trash is an icon in the Dock, not on the desktop.

Directories

Most people call them *folders* on the Mac.

Disk Defragmenter

There's no such utility included with Mac OS X; the system auto-defragments in the background. (A *defragmenting* program moves around the pieces of files on your hard drive in an effort to optimize their placement and speed of opening.)

Disks

Working with disks is very different on the Mac. Every disk inside, or attached to, a Macintosh can be represented on the screen by an icon. Mac OS X does have something like the Computer or My Computer window (choose Go→Computer), but the icons there reflect only the disks currently inserted in your Mac. You'll never see an icon for an empty drive, as you do on Windows, and there's no such thing as drive letters (because the Mac refers to *disks,* not to *drives*—and calls them by name).

Mac OS X Lion doesn't display icons for disks on the desktop, as earlier Mac OS X versions did—but you can bring them back by choosing Finder→Preferences→General and turning on the checkboxes for different kinds of disks.

Display control panel

The functions of the Windows Display control panel lurk in the Mac OS X System Preferences program—just not all in one place. You set up your desktop picture and screen saver using the Desktop & Screen Saver pane and adjust your monitor settings using the Displays pane. (Mac OS X offers no equivalent to the Appearance tab in Windows, for changing the system-wide look of your computer.)

DLL files

The Macintosh equivalent of DLL files—shared libraries of programming code—are invisible and off limits. As a result, no Macintosh user ever experiences DLL conflicts or out-of-date DLL files.

DOS prompt

There's a command line in Mac OS X, but it's Unix, not DOS. For details, see the online appendix to this book called "Terminal Crash Course" on this book's "Missing CD" at *www.missingmanuals.com.*

Drivers

See "Add or Remove Programs."

End Task dialog box

If some Macintosh program is hung or frozen, you escape it pretty much the same way you would in Windows: by forcing it to quit. To bring up the Force Quit dialog box, you press Option-⌘-Esc or choose →Force Quit.

Exiting programs

You can quit a program either by choosing Quit from the menu bearing its name (next to the menu), or by right-clicking (or Control-clicking) its Dock icon and then choosing Quit from the pop-up menu.

Explorer

The Mac has its own "tree" view of the files and folders on your hard drive: list view. By expanding the "flippy triangles" of your folders, you build a hierarchy that shows you as much or as little detail as you like.

If you prefer the Explorer effect of clicking a folder in *one* pane to see its contents in the next, try column view instead. Both views are described in Chapter 2.

Favorites

In Mac OS X, there isn't one single Favorites menu that lists both favorite Web sites and favorite icons. The Bookmarks menu of Safari, the Web browser, lists only Web sites, and the Sidebar at the desktop (page 39) lists only favorite files, folders, disks, and other icons.

Faxing

Faxing is no longer built into Mac OS X, but you can always buy a non-Apple fax modem and use the software that comes with it.

File Sharing

See Chapter 14 for an in-depth look at the Macintosh networking and file-sharing system.

Floppy disks

Floppy drives on Macs disappeared in about 1998. It's much more efficient to transfer files between machines using an Ethernet cable or improvised wireless network (Chapter 14), a CD or DVD that you burned, or email.

Folder Options

The Folder Options control panel in Windows is a collection of unrelated settings that boil down to this:

- **General tab.** Exactly as in Windows, it's up to you whether or not double-clicking a folder opens up a second window—or just changes what's in the first one. On the Mac, you make these changes using the Finder→Preferences command. There you'll find the option called "Always open folders in a new window."

- **View tab.** Most of the options here don't exist on the Mac. For example, system files are *always* hidden on the Mac; you can't opt to make them visible (at least not with the built-in controls). You can, however, choose whether you want to see the file name extensions in your desktop windows (like .doc and .html). Choose Finder→Preferences→Advanced, and turn "Show all file extensions" on or off.

- **File Types tab.** Just as in Windows, you can reassign certain document types so that double-clicking opens them up in the program of your choice. But on the Mac, you can reassign either a whole class of files at once, as in Windows, *or* one file at a time. To do it, you use the Get Info window, as described on page 103.

- **Offline files.** There's no equivalent feature on the Mac.

Fonts

The Mac and Windows PCs both use TrueType, PostScript, and OpenType fonts. (In fact, your Mac can even use the exact font files you had in Windows.) On the Mac, however, there are actually three different folders that can contain them. A complete discussion is in Chapter 9.

Help and Support

At the desktop, choose Help→Mac Help. In other programs, the Help command is generally at the right end of your menus, exactly as in Windows.

Hibernation

The Mac can't hibernate at all, as modern PCs do, cutting all power but remembering what programs and documents you had open for a faster restart later. Sleep mode is the closest it gets; see "Standby mode."

Internet Explorer

Microsoft has abandoned the Mac version of Internet Explorer. Apple would prefer, of course, that you try Safari, its own Web browser, but many a power user prefers Firefox, which is nearly identical to the Windows version.

Internet Options

On the Mac, you find the options for your Web browser by choosing Safari→ Preferences.

IRQs

They don't exist on the Mac.

Java

This interpreter of tiny Web-page programs is alive and well in Mac OS X. Java programs run fine in all Mac Web browsers.

Keyboard control panel

You can make exactly the same kinds of settings—and more—on the Keyboard & Mouse pane of System Preferences.

Logging in

The multiple-accounts feature of Mac OS X is extremely similar to that of Windows 2000, XP, Vista, and 7. In each case, you can, if you wish, create a requirement to log in with a name and password before using the computer. This arrangement keeps separate the documents, email, and settings of each person who uses the computer. (Chapter 13 tells all.)

Mail control panel

Mac OS X comes with its own email program (described in Chapter 11); all its settings are contained within the program.

Maximize button

On the Mac, clicking the Zoom button (the green button in the upper-left corner of a window) does something like the Maximize button in Windows: It makes your window larger. On the Mac, however, clicking the zoom button never makes the window expand to fill the entire screen. Instead, the window grows—or *shrinks*—precisely enough to enclose its contents.

Of course, if you see the ⊡ button in the upper-right corner of your window, then you can do even better: You can take that program into *full-screen mode,* where every last pixel of screen space is put to work displaying your document.

Menus

On the Macintosh, there's only one menu bar, always at the very top of the screen. The menus change depending on the program and the window you're using, but the point is that the menu bar is no longer inside each window you open.

Tip: Just because you don't see the little underlines in the menus doesn't mean you can't operate all the menus from the keyboard, as in Windows. See page 166 for details.

Minimize button

You can minimize a Mac OS X window to the Dock, just the way you would minimize a Windows window to the taskbar. You do so by double-clicking its title bar, pressing ⌘-M, choosing Window→Minimize Window, or clicking the yellow Minimize button at the top left of a window. (Restore the window by clicking its icon in the Dock.)

Mouse control panel

The equivalent settings can be found in the Mouse panel of System Preferences.

(My) Computer

The Mac's Computer window is very similar (choose Go→Computer), in that it shows the icons of all disks (hard drive, CD, and so on). On the other hand, it shows *only* the disks that are actually inserted or connected. (See "Disks.")

(My) Documents, (My) Pictures, (My) Music

The equivalent buckets for your everyday documents, music files, and pictures are the Documents, Pictures, and Music folders in your Home folder.

(My) Network Places

On the Mac, the "network neighborhood" is almost always on the screen: It's the Sidebar, the panel at the left side of every Finder window. All the Macs and PCs on your network are always listed here, in the Shared category (unless you turned this feature off in Finder→Preferences, of course).

Network Neighborhood

See the previous entry.

Notepad

There's no Mac OS X Notepad program. But give Stickies a try, or use the Mail program's Notes feature (page 364).

Personal Web Server

Your Mac can be a state-of-the-art Web server (Google "Mac OS X Web sharing").

Phone and Modem Options control panel

To find the modem settings for your Mac, see page 308.

Power Options

To control when your Mac goes to sleep and (if it's a laptop) how much power it uses, use the Energy Saver pane of System Preferences (Chapter 15).

Printer Sharing

To share a USB inkjet printer with other Macs on the network, open the Sharing pane of System Preferences on the Mac with the printer. Turn on Printer Sharing.

To use the shared printer from across the network, open the document you want to print, choose File→Print, and choose the name of the shared printer from the first pop-up menu.

Printers and Faxes

For a list of your printers, open the Print & Scan pane of System Preferences (Chapter 15). Faxing is no longer built into Mac OS X.

PrntScrn key

You capture pictures of your Mac screen by pressing Shift-⌘-3 (for a full-screen grab) or Shift-⌘-4 (to grab a selected portion of the screen). There are many options available; see the end of Chapter 14.

Program Files folder

The Applications folder (Go→Applications) is like the Program Files folder in Windows—except that you're not discouraged from opening it and double-clicking things. On the Macintosh, every program bears its true name; Microsoft Word, for example, is called Microsoft Word, not WINWORD.EXE.

Properties dialog box

You can call up something very similar for any *icon* (file, folder, program, disk, printer) by highlighting its icon and then choosing File→Get Info. But objects in Macintosh *programs* generally don't contain Properties dialog boxes.

Recycle Bin

Mac OS X has a Trash icon at the end of the Dock. In general, it works exactly like the Windows Recycle Bin—and why not, since the Macintosh Trash was Microsoft's inspiration?—but there are a couple of differences. The Macintosh never automatically empties it, for example. That job is up to you: The simplest way is to Control-click it, or right-click it, and then choose Empty Trash from the shortcut menu.

The Mac never bothers you with an "Are you sure?" message when you throw something into the Trash, either. The Mac interrupts you for permission only when you choose File→Empty Trash. And you can even turn that confirmation off, if you like (in Finder→Preferences).

To put icons into the Trash, drag them there, or highlight them and then press ⌘-Delete.

Regional and Language Options control panel

The closest equivalent is the International panel of System Preferences.

Registry

There is no registry. Let the celebration begin!

Run command

The Mac's command line is Terminal, which is described in an online appendix to this book, "Terminal Crash Course," on this book's "Missing CD" at *www.missing-manuals.com*.

Safe Mode

You can press the Shift key during startup to suppress the loading of certain software libraries, but Mac OS X's "safe mode" isn't quite as massively stripped down as Windows' Safe Mode.

ScanDisk

Just like Windows, the Mac automatically scans and, if necessary, repairs its hard drive every time your machine starts up. To run such a check on command, open Disk Utility (located in the Applications→Utilities folder), click the name of your hard drive, and then click the First Aid tab.

Scheduled Tasks

To schedule a task to take place unattended, use the *launchd* Unix command in Terminal or one of the scheduling programs listed at *www.versiontracker.com*.

Scrap files

On the Mac, they're called *clipping files*, and they're even more widely compatible. You create them the same way: Drag some highlighted text, or a graphic, out of a program's window and onto the desktop. There it becomes an independent clipping file that you can drag back into either the same window or a different one.

Screen saver

The Mac's screen savers are impressive. Open System Preferences and click the Desktop & Screen Saver icon.

Search

In Mac OS X, you have the ultimate file-searching tool: Spotlight (Chapter 3). Get psyched! To find Web sites, use the Google search box at the top of the Safari browser.

Shortcut menus

They work exactly the same as they do in Windows. You produce a shortcut menu by Control-clicking things like icons, list items, and so on. (If you have a two-button mouse, feel free to right-click instead of using the Control key.)

Shortcuts

On the Mac, they're known as *aliases*. See page 96.

Sounds and Audio Devices

Open System Preferences; click the Sound icon. You may also want to explore the Audio MIDI Setup program in Applications→Utilities.

Speech control panel

The Mac's center for speech recognition and text-to-speech is the Speech panel of System Preferences. As Chapter 15 makes clear, the Mac can read aloud any text in any program, and it lets you operate all menus, buttons, and dialog boxes by voice alone.

Standby mode

On the Mac, it's called Sleep, but it's the same idea. You make a Mac laptop sleep by closing the lid. You make a Mac desktop sleep by choosing →Sleep, or just walking away; the Mac goes to sleep on its own, according to the settings in the Energy Saver pane of System Preferences.

Start menu

There's no Start menu in Mac OS X. Instead, you stash the icons of the programs, documents, and folders you use frequently onto the Dock at the edge of the screen, or into the Places section of the Sidebar at the left edge of every Finder window.

Exactly as with the Start menu, you can rearrange these icons (drag them horizontally) or remove the ones you don't use often (drag them away from the Dock and then release). To add new icons of your own, just drag them into place (applications go to the left of the Dock's divider line, documents and folders to the right).

Startup folder

To make programs launch automatically at startup, include them in the list of Login Items in the System Preferences→Accounts pane.

System control panel

The Mac has no central equivalent of the System window on a Windows PC. But its functions have analogs here:

- **General tab.** To find out your Mac OS X version number and the amount of memory on your Mac, choose →About This Mac.

- **Computer Name tab.** Open System Preferences, click Sharing, and edit your computer's network name here.

- **Hardware tab.** The closest thing the Mac has to the Device Manager is System Profiler (in your Applications→Utilities folder).

- **Advanced tab.** In Mac OS X, you can't easily adjust your virtual memory, processor scheduling, or user profile information.

- **System Restore tab.** Mac OS X's Time Machine feature is like System Restore on steroids; see Chapter 5.

- **Automatic Updates tab.** Choose →Software Updates.

- **Remote tab.** Mac OS X offers remote control in the form of Screen Sharing, described in Chapter 14.

System Tray

The Mac OS X equivalent of the system tray (also called the notification area) is the row of *menulets* at the upper-right corner of your screen.

Taskbar

Mac OS X doesn't have a taskbar, but it does have something very close: the Dock (Chapter 2). Open programs are indicated by a small, shiny dot beneath their icons in the Dock. If you hold down your cursor on one of these icons (or Control-click it, or right-click it), you get a pop-up list of the open windows in that program, exactly as in Windows XP, Vista, and 7.

On the other hand, some conventions never die. Much as in Windows, you cycle through the various open Mac programs by holding down the ⌘ key and pressing Tab repeatedly.

Taskbar and Start Menu control panel

To configure your Dock (the equivalent of the taskbar and the Start menu), choose →Dock→Dock Preferences, or click the Dock icon in System Preferences.

"Three-fingered salute"

Instead of pressing Ctrl+Alt+Delete to jettison a stuck program on the Mac, you press Option-⌘-Esc. A Force Quit dialog box appears. Click the program you want to toss, click Force Quit, confirm your choice, and then relaunch the program to get on with your day.

ToolTips

Small, yellow identifying balloons pop up on the Mac almost as often as they do in Windows. Just point to a toolbar icon or truncated file name without clicking. (There's no way to turn these labels off.)

TweakUI

The closest equivalent for this free, downloadable, but unsupported Microsoft utility for tweaking the look of your PC is TinkerTool for Mac OS X.

User Accounts control panel

Like Windows 2000, XP, Vista, and 7, Mac OS X was designed from Square One to be a multiuser operating system, keeping each person's files, mail, and settings separate. You set up and manage these accounts in System Preferences→Accounts (Chapter 13).

Windows (or WINNT) folder

Mac OS X's operating system resides in a folder simply called System, which sits in your main hard drive window. Exactly as in recent Windows versions, you're forbidden to add, remove, or change anything inside. Also as in Windows, most of it is invisible anyway.

Windows logo key

The Mac has no equivalent for the ⊞ key on most PC keyboards.

Windows Media Player

The Mac comes with individual programs for playing multimedia files:

- **QuickTime Player** (Chapter 16) to play back movies and sounds.
- **iTunes** (Chapter 16) to play CDs, Internet radio, MP3 files, and other audio files. (As a bonus, unlike Windows XP, iTunes can even *create* MP3 files.)
- **DVD Player** (Chapter 9) for playing DVDs. This program is in the Applications folder.

Windows Media Player *is,* however, available in an aging Macintosh version, paradoxical though that may sound. You can download it from *www.microsoft.com/mac.*

Windows Messenger

Mac OS X's instant-messaging, audio- and videoconferencing software is called iChat, and it's described in Chapter 12.

WordPad

The TextEdit program (in the Applications folder) is a word processor along the lines of WordPad. It can even open and save Word files, as WordPad can.

Zip files

Zip files exist on the Mac, too, and you create them almost the same way: Control-click (or right-click) a file or folder and choose Compress from the shortcut menu.

The Master Mac OS X Keystroke List

Here it is, by popular, frustrated demand: the master list of every secret (or not-so-secret) keystroke in Mac OS X Lion, including all the keys you can press during startup. Clip and post to your monitor (unless, of course, you got this book from the library).

Note: For the most part, the following list doesn't include the keystrokes already listed in your menus, like ⌘-P for Print, ⌘-S for Save, and so on.

Startup Keystrokes

Keys to Hold Down	Effect
C	Starts up from a CD or DVD
N	Starts up from a network server
R	Resets the laptop screen
⌘-R	Starts Recovery Mode
T	Puts the Mac into FireWire or Thunderbolt Target Disk mode
Option	Shows icons of all startup disks and partitions, so you can choose one for starting up.
Shift-Option-⌘-Delete	Starts up from external drive (or CD)
Option-⌘-P-R	Zaps the parameter RAM (PRAM). (Hold down until you hear the second chime.)
⌘-V	Shows Unix console messages during startup, logout, and shutdown

⌘-S	Starts up in single-user (Unix command-line) mode
Mouse down	Ejects a stuck CD or DVD
6 and 4 keys	Starts up in 64-bit mode
Shift	Just after powering up: Turns off *kernel extensions*
Shift	Just after logging in: Prevents Finder windows and startup items from opening. (They'll return the next time you start up.)

In the Finder

⌘-space	Highlights Spotlight box
Option-⌘-space	Opens Spotlight window
→, ←	Expands or collapses a selected folder in list view
Option-→	Expands a folder in a list view *and* all folders inside it
Option-←	Collapses a folder *and* all folders inside it
⌘-↑	Opens parent folder
Shift-Option-⌘-↑	Selects the desktop
⌘-↓ (or ⌘-O)	Opens the selected icon
Option-click the flippy triangle	Expands or collapses all folders within that window
Tab	Selects next icon alphabetically
Shift-Tab	Selects previous icon alphabetically
space bar	Opens Quick Look preview of highlighted icon(s)
space bar	During a spring-loaded folder drag, opens the disk or folder under the mouse immediately
Option-click Zoom button	Enlarges the window to full screen
Option-click Close button	Closes all Finder windows
Option-click Minimize button	Minimizes all windows (works in most apps)
⌘-drag an icon	Moves it into, or out of, the System folder (administrator password required)
Option	Changes Quick Look button to Slideshow button
⌘-drag	Rearranges or removes menulets or toolbar icons
⌘-click window title	Opens a pop-up menu showing the folder path

Menu

Option	Changes "About This Mac" to "System Information"
Shift-⌘-Q	Logs out
Shift-Option-⌘-Q	Logs out without confirmation box

Finder Menu

Option	Eliminates the confirmation box from Empty Trash and Secure Empty Trash
Shift-⌘-Delete	Empties the Trash
Shift-⌘-Delete	Puts back a highlighted icon in the Trash
Shift-Option-⌘-Delete	Empties the Trash without confirmation box
Option-Empty Trash	Empties the Trash without confirmation box
⌘-comma	Opens Preferences
⌘-H	Hide this program
Shift-⌘-H	Hide other programs

File Menu

⌘-N	New Finder window
Shift-⌘-N	New folder
Option-⌘-N	New smart folder
⌘-O or ⌘-↓	Open
Control-⌘-O	Open in new window
Option-click File menu	Changes "Open With" to "Always Open With"
⌘-W	Close window
Option-⌘-W	Close All
⌘-I	Get Info
Option-⌘-I	Show Inspector
Control-⌘-I	Summary Info (of selected icons)
⌘-D	Duplicate
⌘-L	Make Alias
⌘-Y	Quick Look
Option-⌘-Y	Slideshow (of selected icons)
⌘-R	Show Original (of alias)
⌘-T	Add to Sidebar
Shift-⌘-T	Add to Favorites
⌘-Delete	Move to Trash
⌘-E	Eject

| ⌘-F | Find |
| Shift-⌘-F | Find by Name |

Edit Menu

⌘-Z	Undo
⌘-C, ⌘-X, ⌘-V	Copy, Cut, Paste
Shift-⌘-V	Move copied icons to this window
⌘-A	Select All
Option-⌘-A	Deselect All

View Menu

⌘-1, -2, -3, -4	Icon, list, column, Cover Flow views
Control-⌘-1, -2, -3, -4, -5, -6	Arrange by Name, Date Modified, Date Created, Size, Kind, Label
Option	Changes "Clean Up Selection" to "Clean Up"
Option	Changes "Arrange By" to "Sort By"
Option-⌘-T	Show/Hide Toolbar
Option-⌘-S	Show/Hide Sidebar
⌘-J	Show/Hide View Options palette

Go Menu

⌘-[, ⌘-]	Back, Forward
⌘-↑	Enclosing folder
Control-⌘-↑	Enclosing folder in new window
Option-⌘-T	Show/Hide Toolbar
Shift-⌘-F	All My Files window
Shift-⌘-O	Documents window
Shift-⌘-D	Desktop window
Option-⌘-L	Downloads window
Shift-⌘-H	Home window
Option	Makes Library command appear
Shift-⌘-C	Computer window
Shift-⌘-R	AirDrop window
Shift-⌘-K	Network window
Shift-⌘-I	Open iDisk (until MobileMe shuts down)
Shift-⌘-A	Applications window
Shift-⌘-G	Go to Folder
⌘-K	Connect to Server

Window Menu

⌘-M   Minimize

Option-⌘-M   Minimize All

Option   Changes Bring All to Front to Arrange in Front

Help Menu

Shift-⌘-?   Opens help search box

Power Keys

Control-⏏   Brings up dialog box for shutdown, sleep, or restart

Option-⌘-⏏   Sleep

Control-Option-⌘-⏏   Shut Down

Control-⌘-power   Restart

The Dock

Option-click a Dock icon   Switches to new program and hides previous one

Option-⌘-D   Hides/shows the Dock

⌘-click a Dock or Stacks icon   Reveals its actual Finder icon

Option-⌘-click a Dock icon   Switches to this program and hides all others

Control-click a Dock icon   Opens a shortcut menu

Hold mouse down on Dock app icon   Triggers Exposé (shows all windows of that app in miniature)

⌘-drag an icon onto a Dock icon   Prevents Dock icons from moving, so you can drop your icon onto one of them

⌘-drag a Dock icon   Drags the actual item

Option-⌘-drag an icon onto the Dock   Forces a Dock program to open the icon you're dropping on it

Managing Programs

Option-click a Dock icon   Switches to new program and hides the previous one

Option-click in a window   Switches to new program and hides the previous one

⌘-H   Hide this program's windows (works in most apps)

Option-⌘-H   Hide all *other* programs' windows (most apps)

Control-←, →   Previous/next Spaces screen

F9   Exposé: Shrinks and tiles all windows in all programs

Shift-F9	Exposé: Shrinks and tiles all windows in slow motion
F10	Exposé: Shrinks and tiles all windows in front-most program
F11	Exposé: Flings all windows in all programs to edges of screen, revealing desktop
F12	Dashboard widgets
⌘-Tab	Press and release: Switches back and forth between current and previous open program
⌘-Tab	Hold down ⌘: Displays floating icons of open programs. Press Tab repeatedly to cycle through them. (Add Shift to cycle *backward* through open programs on the Dock.)
⌘-~	Switches to next open window in this program. (Add Shift to cycle in the opposite direction.)
Option-⌘-Esc	Opens the Force Quit dialog box (to close a stuck program)
Shift-⌘-3	Captures the screen image as a PDF file on your desktop
Shift-⌘-4	Produces a crosshairs; drag to capture a se-lected portion of the screen as a PDF graphics file. (Press space to get the "camera" cursor that snips out just a menu, icon, or window.)
⌘-space	Switches keyboard layout (if more than one is installed). (If you use Spotlight, you must choose a different keystroke for this function.)

Dialog Boxes

⌘-comma	Opens Preferences dialog box (any Apple program)
Esc	"Clicks" the Cancel button in a dialog box
Enter or Return	"Clicks" the OK button (or other blue, high-lighted button) in a dialog box
Option-⌘-F	Moves the insertion point to the search box in most Apple programs
⌘-D, ⌘-R	"Clicks" the Don't Save or Replace button

Trackpad Gestures

You can change many of these gestures, or turn them on and off, in the Trackpad pane of System Preferences. But here are the factory settings:

Two-finger click	Right-click
Two-finger drag up/down	Scroll up/down
Two-finger swipe left-/right	Move among open Web or document pages
Two-finger pinch or spread	Zoom in or out of a picture, PDF, or Web page
Two-finger rotate	Rotate photo or PDF
Two-finger double-tap (not click)	"Smart zoom" into Safari or Preview page
Three-finger swipe up	Mission Control
Three-finger swipe down	Show all windows in this app (Exposé)
Three-finger swipe left/right	Previous/next Spaces screen or full-screen app
Four-finger pinch	Open Launchpad
Four-finger spread	Reveal desktop (Exposé)

Magic Mouse Gestures

A few important gestures also work on the top surface of the Magic Mouse:

One-finger double-tap (not click)	"Smart zoom" into Safari or Preview page
Two-finger double-tap (not click)	Mission Control
One-finger swipe left-/right	Move between open Web or document
Two-finger swipe left/right	Previous/next Spaces screen or full-screen app

SWITCHING TO THE MAC: THE MISSING MANUAL

Index

Index

Colophon

This book was written on a black MacBook laptop that remained attached to David Pogue like an appendage. It was typed in Microsoft Word, with substantial assistance from the typing-shortcut program TypeIt4Me (*www.typeit4me.com*) and the macro program QuicKeys (*www.quickeys.com*).

The screenshots were captured with Snapz Pro X (*www.ambrosiasw.com*), edited in Adobe Photoshop CS4 (*www.adobe.com*), and overlaid with labels, lines, and circles in Macromedia Freehand Mac OS X (*www.adobe.com*).

The author wrote the index, entry by entry, using a highly tweaked FileMaker database (*www.filemaker.com*) and a clever Perl script that converted FileMaker's output into a fully formatted index.

The book was designed and laid out in Adobe InDesign CS4 on a MacBook Pro and Mac Pro. The fonts include Formata (as the sans-serif family) and Minion (as the serif body face). To provide the symbols (, ⌘, ⏏, and so on), Phil Simpson designed two custom fonts using Macromedia Fontographer.

The book was then exported as Adobe Acrobat PDF files for final transmission to the printing plant.

mL   10-12